REBECCA JAY

MARTIN JAY is Sidney Hellman Ehrman Professor of History at the University of California, Berkeley. Among his books are *Refractions of Violence* (2003), *The Dialectical Imagination: A History of the Frankfurt School and the Institute of Social Research, 1923–1950* (second edition, California, 1996), *Downcast Eyes: The Denigration of Vision in Twentieth-Century French Thought* (California, 1993), and *Marxism and Totality: The Adventures of a Concept from Lukács to Habermas* (California, 1984).

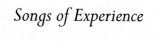

Songs of Experience

OTHER BOOKS BY MARTIN JAY

The Dialectical Imagination: A History of the Frankfurt School and the Institute of Social Research, 1923–1950 (1973 and 1996)

Marxism and Totality: The Adventures of a Concept from Lukács to Habermas (1984)

Adorno (1984)

Permanent Exiles: Essays on the Intellectual Migration from Germany to America (1985)

Fin-de-Siècle Socialism and Other Essays (1988)

Force Fields: Between Intellectual History and Cultural Critique (1993)

Downcast Eyes: The Denigration of Vision in Twentieth-Century French Thought (1993)

Cultural Semantics: Keywords of Our Time (1998)

Refractions of Violence (2003)

La crisis de la experiencia en la era postsubjetiva, ed. Eduardo Sabrovsky (2003)

Songs of Experience

MODERN AMERICAN AND EUROPEAN
VARIATIONS ON A UNIVERSAL THEME

Martin Jay

UNIVERSITY OF CALIFORNIA PRESS

BERKELEY   LOS ANGELES   LONDON

University of California Press
Berkeley and Los Angeles, California

University of California Press, Ltd.
London, England

© 2005 by the Regents of the University of California

Library of Congress Cataloging-in-Publication Data

Jay, Martin, 1944–
    Songs of experience : modern American and
European variations on a universal theme / Martin Jay.
        p.   cm.
    Includes bibliographical references and index.
    ISBN 0-520-24272-6 (alk. paper)
        1. Experience.   2. History—philosophy.
    I. Title.
    B105.E9J39   2004
    128' .4—dc22   2004009708

Manufactured in the United States of America

14   13   12   11   10   09   08   07   06   05
10   9   8   7   6   5   4   3   2   1

The paper used in this publication meets the minimum
requirements of ANSI/NISO Z39.48-1992 (R 1997)
(*Permanence of Paper*).

For Sammy

CONTENTS

ACKNOWLEDGMENTS

Acknowledging the help extended to an author over the life of his book, stretching from its inception to its publication, is both an exhilarating and terrifying experience. The exhilaration comes from the chance to express gratitude in public for the many kindnesses that allow any project to make its way along the perilous journey to completion. The terror follows from the realization that memory at the end of the day will inevitably fail to register all the debts one actually owes. Experience as retrospective cumulative wisdom is never fully congruent with all the immediate experiences that it can only unevenly and selectively preserve. So let me apologize in advance to those whose names may have been omitted inadvertently from the honor roll that follows.

I want to begin by thanking the institutions whose generosity provided me the means to carry out my research and writing, and did so with the added benefit of an intellectual community whose critical responses were invaluable in improving the results: the Stanford Humanities Center in 1997–1998 and the Institute for Advanced Study in Princeton in 2001–2002. The latter supported my residence with a grant from the National Endowment for the Humanities. I also benefited from the support of a University of California President's Research Fellowship in the Humanities, when I first launched this project some time in the far-distant past. And let me not forget the University of California Humanities Research Fellowship and the Sidney Hellman Ehrman Chair, which it has been my honor to share with my distinguished colleague Jan de Vries, since 1997.

Over the years, I have also incurred debts of various kinds, large and small, to many people who have invited me to discuss my research, responded to questions, improved drafts of my writing, and just kept the conversation going: Frank Ankersmit, Keith Baker, John Bender, Jeanne Wolf Bernstein,

Mark Bevir, Warren Breckman, Fred Dallmayr, Susan Buck-Morss, Paul Breines, Eduardo Cadava, Kenneth Cmiel, Paul Crowther, Carolyn Dean, Edward Dimendberg, John Efron, Ales Erjavec, Andrew Feenberg, Jaimey Fisher, Hal Foster, Michael Timo Gilmore, Lohren Green, David Gross, Peter Gordon, Gary Gutting, Malachi Hacohen, Miriam Hanssen, Carla Hesse, Andrew Hewitt, Horace Jeffrey Hodges, David Hollinger, Peter Uwe Hohendahl, Denis Hollier, Axel Honneth, Robert Hullot-Kentor, Craig Ireland, Jonathan Israel, Gerald Izenberg, Anton Kaes, Robert Kaufman, James Kloppenberg, Lawrence Kritzman, Dominick LaCapra, Thomas Laqueur, Pamela Matthews, David McWhirter, Louis Menand, Samuel Moyn, Elliot Neaman, John O'Neill, Mark Poster, Anson Rabinbach, Paul Rabinow, Paul Robinson, David Roberts, John Rundell, Eduardo Sabrovsky, Carl Schorske, Joan W. Scott, Richard Shusterman, Brent Sockness, Jerrold Seigel, Randolph Starn, Paul Thomas, Michael Guy Thompson, James Vernon, Hayden White, Morton White, the late Bernard Williams, Jay Winter, Richard Wolin, and Lewis Wurgaft. Let me also acknowledge the many scholarly audiences in places as different as Tokyo, Jyvaskyla, Taipei, Copenhagen, Berlin, Ljubljana, Frankfurt, and Santiago de Chile, who have brought their own experiences to bear on my attempt to make sense of the word and its history. In particular, I want to thank those who attended the 2002 Gauss Seminars at Princeton, where I delivered versions of three chapters of the book. Excellent research help over the years was provided by David Moshfegh, Vincent Cannon, Andrew Jainchill, Emanuel Rota, Benjamin Lazier, Julian Bourg, and Knox Peden, who also prepared the index. I owe, once again, a debt to the editorial staff at the University of California Press, in particular Sheila Levine, Sue Heinemann, Charles Dibble, and Danette Davis. The Press is also to be commended for choosing two readers, Lloyd Kramer and Wayne Proudfoot, whose careful and extensive responses to the manuscript were models of constructive criticism. Thanks also go to the journals in which parts or variations of chapters have previously appeared: *Constellations, The Yale Journal of Criticism, Filozofski Vestnik,* and *Prismas,* as well as to the presses that included them in anthologies: Éditions Belin, the University of Minnesota Press, SoPhi, Berghahn Books, and the University of Massachusetts Press.

As always, my greatest debts are owed to the people who make everyday life sing with peak experiences, Shana, Ned, Frances and Samuel Lindsay; Rebecca Jay and Max Landes; and my closest reader, most tolerant critic, and unwavering life support system, my wife, Catherine Gallagher.

INTRODUCTION

Calling this book *Songs of Experience* will be understood, I hope, more as an act of homage than as a gesture of hubristic appropriation. William Blake's justly celebrated poem cycle of the same name, counterpoised as it was to his *Songs of Innocence,*[1] provides insights into what he called "the Two Contrary States of the Soul" that a sober scholarly treatise can only hope in vain to emulate. No prose "Tyger" will ever blaze as brightly in the night as did his poetry, no academic worm-eaten "Rose" ever seem as sickly. With their brilliant explorations of the religious, political, moral, and psychological implications of the Fall from grace, Blake's poems set a standard that only the most foolhardy would try to emulate.

What makes the temptation to borrow Blake's title so irresistible is the perfection of its fit with the subject matter of this book, which is less about the elusive reality of what is called experience than the "songs" that have been sung about it. That is, my intention is not to provide yet another account of what "experience" really is or what it might be, but rather to understand why so many thinkers in so many different traditions have felt compelled to do precisely that. Many, if not all, have done so with an urgency and intensity that rarely accompanies the attempt to define and explicate a concept. Theirs have been, I hope to show, as much "songs" of passion as sober analyses. At some times, these songs have been lyrical panegyrics, at others, elegiac laments, at still others, bitter denunciations, but they have almost always been deeply felt. "Experience," it turns out, is a signifier that unleashes remarkable emotion in many who put special emphasis on it in their thought. "Experience, freedom," writes a recent commentator "—these two words are per-

---

1. They were first published together in 1794 with a title page showing the expulsion of Adam and Eve from the Garden of Eden.

haps the most potent slogans in the English language. Anglo-American thought has never ceased to draw on them in order to define its grounds, methods, and goals."[2] Not for nothing have commentators been able to talk of a "cult," "myth," "idolatry," or "mysticism" of experience in other cultural traditions as well, so powerful has its lure often been.[3]

It is, in fact, only because of the normally positive charge on the word that other observers have been able to speak darkly of a crisis in the very possibility of having experiences in the modern world. Walter Benjamin often deplored what he called the "poverty of human experience,"[4] Theodor W. Adorno warned that "the very possibility of experience is in jeopardy,"[5] and Peter Bürger bemoaned "the loss of opportunities for authentic experience."[6] On the basis of such laments, the Italian philosopher Giorgio Agamben could conclude in 1978 that "the question of experience can be approached nowadays only with an acknowledgement that it is no longer accessible to us. For just as modern man has been deprived of his biography, his experience has likewise been expropriated. Indeed, his incapacity to have and communicate experience is perhaps one of the few self-certainties to which he can lay claim."[7]

What, however, is less certain is the precise meaning of the auratic term "experience" itself, which Hans-Georg Gadamer has justly called "one of the most obscure that we have."[8] Indeed, because there is as much a crisis of the word "experience" as there is of what it purports to signify, we must speak of "songs" in the plural. For it will quickly become apparent to anyone seeking a meta-narrative of this idea's history that no such single story can be

2. Peter Fenves, "Foreword: From Empiricism to the Experience of Freedom," in Jean-Luc Nancy, *The Experience of Freedom*, trans. Bridget McDonald (Stanford, Calif., 1993), p. xiii.

3. See, for example, Philip Rahv, "The Cult of Experience in American Writing," *Literature and the Sixth Sense* (New York, 1969); George L. Mosse, *Fallen Soldiers: Reshaping the Memory of the World Wars* (Oxford, 1990), chapter 10 (treating the "Myth of the War Experience"); Max Weber, "Science as Vocation," in *From Max Weber: Essays in Sociology*, ed. H. H. Gerth and C. Wright Mills (New York, 1958), p. 137 (calling "personal experience" an "idol"); and Paul Mendes-Flohr, "Buber's *Erlebnis*-Mysticism," *From Mysticism to Dialogue: Martin Buber's Transformation of German Social Thought* (Detroit, 1989).

4. Walter Benjamin, "Experience and Poverty" (1933), in *Selected Writings*, vol. 2, *1927–1934*, ed. Michael W. Jennings, Howard Eiland, and Gary Smith, trans. Rodney Livingstone and others (Cambridge, Mass., 1999), p. 732.

5. Theodor W. Adorno, "In Memory of Eichendorff," *Notes to Literature*, 2 vols., trans. Shierry Weber Nicholsen (New York, 1991), vol. 1, p. 55.

6. Peter Bürger, *The Decline of Modernism*, trans. Nicholas Walker (University Park, Pa., 1992), p. 17.

7. Giorgio Agamben, *Infancy and History: Essays on the Destruction of Experience*, trans. Liz Heron (London, 1993), p. 13. The original Italian edition appeared in 1978.

8. Hans-Georg Gadamer, *Truth and Method* (New York, 1975), p. 310.

told. Rather than force a totalized account, which assumes a unified point of departure, an etymological *archē* to be recaptured, or a normative telos to be achieved, it will be far more productive to follow disparate threads where they may lead us. Without the burden of seeking to rescue or legislate a single acceptation of the word, we will be free to uncover and explore its multiple, often contradictory meanings and begin to make sense of how and why they function as they often have to produce so powerful an effect.

In so doing, I hasten to add, the goal is not to debunk the word as hopelessly confused nor to characterize those who invoke it as irreparably naive. There was, in fact, a widespread inclination during the last decades of the twentieth century, especially among those who characterized themselves as poststructuralist analysts of discourse and apparatuses of power, to challenge "experience" (or even more so "lived experience") as a simplistic ground of immediacy that fails to register the always already mediated nature of cultural relations and the instability of the subject who is supposedly the bearer of experiences. In the heated debates over "identity politics" in the 1980s and 1990s, black scholars like Joyce A. Joyce and Barbara Christian, who defended the importance of experience, found themselves on the defensive against adepts of theory like Henry Louis Gates Jr. and Houston Baker.[9] Similar battles were waged by feminists, many of whom moved beyond their earlier celebration of the value and uniqueness of women's experience.[10]

In fact, the unlamented "demise of experience" became in some quarters almost conventional wisdom.[11] To take one example, which will be examined later in greater depth, the American historian Joan Wallach Scott warned against the "essentialist" assumption of a unitary subject prior to his or her discursive constitution who can act as the bearer of the experience historians seek to recover.[12] Against the belief that shared experiences serve as an ultimate ground of cultural differences, she claimed that such an approach undermines any attempt to explore the impersonal processes that construct the subject in the first place. And yet, despite her adamant denial of any foundationalist authority to the term, Scott concluded by conceding that "*expe-*

9. See the contributions of Joyce A. Joyce, Henry Louis Gates Jr., and Houston Baker to "A Discussion: The Black Canon: Reconstructing Black American Literary Criticism," *New Literary History* 18, no. 2 (Winter 1987); and Barbara Christian, "The Race for Theory," *Cultural Critique* 6 (Spring 1987).

10. For a recent survey that examines the literature and tries to defend a phenomenological notion of experience, see Sonia Kruks, *Retrieving Experience: Subjectivity and Recognition in Feminist Politics* (Ithaca, N.Y., 2001).

11. Alice A. Jardine, "The Demise of Experience: Fiction as Stranger than Truth?" *Gynesis: Configurations of Woman and Modernity* (Ithaca, N.Y., 1985).

12. Joan Wallach Scott, "The Evidence of Experience," *Critical Inquiry* 17, no. 4 (Summer 1991).

rience is not a word we can do without, although, given its usage to essentialize identity and reify the subject, it is tempting to abandon it altogether.
But *experience* is so much a part of everyday language, so imbricated in our
narratives that it seems futile to argue for its expulsion. . . . Given the ubiquity of the term, it seems to me more useful to work with it, to analyze its
operations and to redefine its meaning."[13]

It is precisely because of the term's ubiquity that no totalizing account can
hope to do justice to its multiple denotations and connotations over time
and in different contexts; some hard choices will have to be made. Not only
is "experience" a term of everyday language, but it has also played a role in
virtually every systematic body of thought, providing a rich vein of philosophical inquiry ever since the Greeks. The principle of selection that will
allow us to avoid being overwhelmed by the magnitude of the problem is as
follows: We will pay closest attention to those thinkers in the modern period
who have put "experience" to greatest work in their thought, while expressing the emotional intensity that allows us to call their work "songs of experience." Our task will be not only to explore their invocations of the term,
but also explain as best we can why it has functioned with such power in
their vocabularies. When and why, we will ask, did it gain the foundationalist authority that makes its recent critics so uneasy? To what is the invocation of "experience" a response? Under what circumstances does that invocation lose its power?

Even within these limits, we are faced with a welter of difficult choices. It
might be tempting to provide a comparative analysis of the way the term has
functioned in the vocabularies of non-Western thinkers. Attention has recently been drawn, for example, to its importance in the work of the great
twentieth-century Japanese philosopher Kitaro Nishida, who explicitly called
"pure experience" the "foundation of my thought."[14] Scholars of Indian

13. Ibid., p. 797. It would be a mistake to assume that the issues raised by legitimating ideas via an
appeal to the experiential privilege of those who espouse them is definitively over. For a recent attack on
the fetish of contextual legitimation, see David Simpson, *Situatedness; or, Why We Keep Saying Where We're
Coming From* (Durham, N.C., 2002), and my review of it in the *London Review of Books,* November 28,
2002.

14. Kitaro Nishida, *An Inquiry into the Good,* trans. Masao Abe and Christopher Ives (New Haven,
1990), p. xxix. This work originally appeared in 1911. For helpful analyses, see Andrew Feenberg and Yoko
Arisaka, "Experiential Ontology: The Origins of the Nishida Philosophy in the Doctrine of Pure Experience," *International Philosophical Quarterly* 30, no. 2 (1995); and Andrew Feenberg, "Experience and
Culture: Nishida's Path 'To the Things Themselves'," *Philosophy East and West* 49, no. 1 (January 1999),
pp. 28–44.

thought have probed its dimensions in their indigenous traditions.[15] But it will demand enough of the author to try to explicate its role in thinkers closer to home, whose languages he can read. Our scope therefore will be confined to British, French, German, and American thinkers from many different disciplines for whom "experience" has been an especially potent term. Although we will inevitably have to prepare the ground by discussing prior invocations by such central figures as Francis Bacon and Michel de Montaigne, our focus will be primarily on thinkers from the past three centuries.

Our main cast of characters will be large and diverse enough to make any sustained attempt to contextualize the origin and development of their individual ideas practically impossible. It is important to acknowledge, moreover, that such attempts generally presuppose a given notion of the experience out of which the ideas are alleged to emerge. But it is, of course, against precisely the self-evidence of such an assumption that this book is aimed. That is, we cannot presume to explain variations on the concept of experience by reference to the experience of those who were doing the varying. In a few cases, to be sure, it will be hard to ignore what previous commentators have seen as the interaction between certain intellectual claims and the lives of those who made them, but we will always do so with an awareness of the circularity of such an approach.

To organize our account, it will be useful to spin out the Blakean metaphor a bit further and think in terms of song cycles, in which adjectival variants of experience have been thematically developed. Beginning with the crucial issue of the status of experience in epistemological discourse, we will move on to its specifically religious, aesthetic, political, and historical modalities. We will then conclude with three chapters that address attempts to overcome such distinctions and produce more or less totalizing notions of experience, whether dialectical, pragmatist, phenomenological, or poststructuralist.

In trying to step back from experience as a lived reality and coolly examine its modal subtypes as cultural constructs, we immediately come across an apparent paradox: the word "experience" has often been used to gesture toward precisely that which exceeds concepts and even language itself. It is frequently employed as a marker for what is so ineffable and individual (or specific to a particular group) that it cannot be rendered in conventionally communicative terms to those who lack it. Although we may try to share or

15. William Halbfass, *India and Europe: An Essay in Philosophical Understanding* (New Delhi, 1990), chap. 21; and Ananta Ch. Sukla, "Aesthetic Experience and Experience of Art and Nature: Arguments from Indian Aesthetics," in Sukla, *Art and Experience* (Westport, Conn., 2003).

represent what we experience, the argument goes, only the subject really knows what he or she has experienced. Vicarious experience is not the real thing, which has to be directly undergone. As the mantras of identity politics make clear—"it's a guy thing, you wouldn't understand," "it's a black thing, you wouldn't understand," and so on—experience is often taken to be a non-fungible commodity. Indeed, it is perhaps because experience can sometimes become an end in itself that it escapes the exchange principle. Who, after all, would want to trade one's own experience of sex for an account of another's? Who would be fully content with ceding to others the right to speak in one's name (to have, for example, male feminists always represent the situation of women or only whites, however well intentioned, speak on behalf of silenced minorities)?

But for those sensitive to the lessons of the so-called linguistic turn that increasingly dominated twentieth-century philosophy, the assumption of absolute experiential self-sufficiency has itself come into question. Since nothing meaningful can appear outside the boundaries of linguistic mediation, they argue, no term can escape the gravitational pull of its semantic context. Once again to quote Joan Scott, the point is "to refuse a separation between 'experience' and language and to insist instead on the productive quality of discourse."[16] Rather than foundational or immediate, "experience" is itself only a function of the counter-concepts that are posed against it in a discursive field, for example, "reflection" or "theory" in epistemological discourse, "dogma" or "theology" in religious discourse, "the art object" in aesthetic discourse, or "innocence" in moral discourse. "The authority of experience," to quote the title of one study of its role in the Enlightenment,[17] is in danger when the very notion of self-sufficient authors able to be its bearer is called into question.

Neither of these alternatives, it seems to me, is fully convincing. It would be more fruitful to remain within the tension created by the paradox. That is, we need to be aware of the ways in which "experience" is both a collective linguistic concept, a signifier that yokes together a class of heterogeneous signifieds located in a diacritical force field, and a reminder that such concepts always leave a remainder that escapes their homogenizing grasp. "Experience," we might say, is at the nodal point of the intersection between public language and private subjectivity, between expressible commonalities

16. Scott, "The Evidence of Experience," p. 793.

17. John C. O'Neal, *The Authority of Experience: Sensationist Theory in the French Enlightenment* (University Park, Pa., 1996).

and the ineffability of the individual interior. Although something that has to be undergone or suffered rather than acquired vicariously, even the most seemingly "authentic" or "genuine" experience may be already inflected by prior cultural models (an insight that novels, if René Girard's celebrated argument about mediated desire is right,[18] have made especially clear). Experience may also be made available for others through a process of post facto recounting, a kind of secondary elaboration in the Freudian sense, which turns it into a meaningful narrative. When shared, such reconstructions and recountings of experience can become the stuff of group identities, as the so-called consciousness-raising exercises of feminists showed. When thwarted, they may lead to the traumatic blockage that has been called unclaimed experience.[19]

The paradox is evident in yet another way. However much we may construe experience as a personal possession—"no one can take my experiences away from me," it is sometimes argued—it is inevitably acquired through an encounter with otherness, whether human or not. That is, an experience, however we define it, cannot simply duplicate the prior reality of the one who undergoes it, leaving him or her precisely as before; something must be altered, something new must happen, to make the term meaningful. Whether a "fall" from innocence or a gain of new wisdom, an enrichment of life or a bitter lesson in its follies, something worthy of the name "experience" cannot leave you where you began. Even writing a book about "experience" is in this sense an experience, for it involves many encounters with the texts of countless others who have pondered the same issues before, and if it finds readers, it will enter into the thoughts of those who come after. As one of the protagonists of our story, who is less often accounted a singer of experience than he should be, once put it, "I aim at having an experience myself—by passing through determinate historical content—an experience of what we are today, of what is not only our past but also our present. And I invite others to share the experience. That is, an experience of our modernity that might permit us to emerge from it transformed."[20] All his books, Michel Fou-

18. René Girard, *Deceit, Desire, and the Novel: Self and Other in Literary Structure*, trans. Yvonne Freccero (Baltimore, 1965). Girard's focus is on the mediation of desire, but his point can easily be extended to experience as dependent on prior models. Even mature sexual experience, as Sigmund Freud demonstrated, draws on urges and gratifications that were felt during the period of purported childhood "innocence."

19. Cathy Caruth, *Unclaimed Experience: Trauma, Narrative, and History* (Baltimore, 1996).

20. Michel Foucault, "How an 'Experience-Book' is Born," in *Remarks on Marx: Conversations with Duccio Trombadori*, trans. R. James Goldstein and James Cascaito (New York, 1991), pp. 33–34.

cault came to understand, were in this sense "experience-books" more than "truth-books" or "demonstration-books." Although I am not as eager to choose between such rigid alternatives, the experience of writing *Songs of Experience* may lead me where I do not expect to go. You, the reader, will soon know how it will end; I, the author, am, at the moment of writing these words, still eager to find out.[21]

21. From the perspective of this footnote, written after the manuscript was completed, this sentence from 1997 may seem disingenuous. I now, of course, do know the outcome. But it is worth retaining for the following reason. The normal convention of scholarly publication is to efface the traces of the process that produces the final result, a bit like covering over the brushstrokes on what came to be called the "licked canvases" of traditional painting. In so doing, however, what is produced is like the "secondary elaboration" Freud posited as one component of the dream work, in which the waking dreamer replaces the disorder of his nocturnal thoughts and feelings with a more coherent narrative. In so doing, he tacitly privileges a certain notion of experience, one that provides retrospective coherence and closure to what was undergone at the time in a much more chaotic way. In fact, scholarly books strive to appear as if their arguments were concocted all at once without any reference to the specificity of time and place of their actual genesis, what can be called their deictic particulars. But in so doing, they work to hide the experimental, uncertain character of their genesis, which is, after all, one of the alternative meanings of experience. In fact, as we will see in the case of Denis Hollier's reading of Georges Bataille's *Inner Experience*, it is precisely the desire to capture this temporal open-endedness and resist post-facto coherence that animates certain attempts to write about experience in heterodox ways. By preserving the tension between the sentence in my text and this footnote, written six years later, I want to provide a very modest performative example of such efforts.

ONE

The Trial of "Experience"

From the Greeks to Montaigne and Bacon

"'EXPERIENCE', OF ALL THE WORDS in the philosophic vocabulary is the most difficult to manage;" warns Michael Oakeshott, "and it must be the ambition of every writer reckless enough to use the word to escape the ambiguities it contains."[1] Such an ambition, however, may be more typical of philosophers anxious to still the play of language and come to firm conclusions about what it purports to represent than of intellectual historians interested in the ambiguities themselves. Typically, the former employ one of two methods to reduce or eliminate polysemic uncertainty: either they legislate a privileged meaning and banish others to the margins (Oakeshott himself follows this model, explicitly stating that "I will begin, then, by indicating what I take it to denote"[2]), or they seek a ground of authenticity in the word's putatively "original" meaning.

Such attempts to "manage" a word, in Oakeshott's telltale metaphor, are especially dangerous when it comes to "experience." For they impose a rigid and atemporal singularity on precisely what should be acknowledged as having had a varied and changing development—on what might provisionally be itself called a semantic experience. While admitting some limits to the infinite flexibility of any term, it would be unwise to decide in advance that certain meanings are proper and others not. The lessons of Ludwig Wittgenstein's stress on meaning as use and deconstruction's tolerance of catachresis suggest that when a word has had as long and complex a history as "experience," no justice can be done to its adventures by premature semantic closure.

---

1. Michael Oakeshott, *Experience and Its Modes* (Cambridge, 1933), p. 9.
2. Ibid.

Etymology, to be sure, need not always be in the service of stilling linguistic ambiguity. As Derek Attridge has noted, even questionable attempts to locate a word's origin—folk etymologies, as they are often called—can make us aware of the richness of a term's denotative and connotative history: "it depends on the way in which words we regularly encounter, and treat as solid, simple wholes (representing solid, simple concepts), can be made to break apart, melt into one another, reveal themselves as divided and lacking in self-identity, with no clear boundaries and no evident center."[3] Without therefore pretending that we can recapture a true point of linguistic origin—Greek, Hebrew, or Latin, the favored ur-languages of much etymological inquiry, were, after all, themselves preceded by still earlier tongues—it will be helpful to cast a glance at the evidence of sedimented meanings that many singers of the "songs of experience" have themselves invoked.[4]

The English word is understood to be derived most directly from the Latin experientia, which denoted "trial, proof, or experiment." The French expérience and Italian esperienza still can signify a scientific experiment (when in the indefinite form). Insofar as "to try" (expereri) contains the same root as periculum, or "danger," there is also a covert association between experience and peril, which suggests that it comes from having survived risks and learned something from the encounter (ex meaning a coming forth from). Perhaps for this reason, it can also connote a worldliness that has left innocence behind by facing and surmounting the dangers and challenges that life may present.

The Greek antecedent to the Latin is empeiria, which also serves as the root for the English word "empirical." One of the Greek schools of medicine, which drew on observation rather than authority or theory, had, in fact, been called the Empiriki and was opposed to the competing factions known as the Dogmatiki and the Methodiki. Here a crucial link between experience and raw, unreflected sensation or unmediated observation (as opposed to reason, theory, or speculation) is already evident. So too is the association between experience as dealing more with specific than general matters, with particulars rather than universals. As such, it contributes to the belief, which

3. Derek Attridge, "Language as History/History as Language: Saussure and the Romance of Etymology," in Derek Attridge, Geoff Bennington, and Robert Young, eds., Post-structuralism and the Question of History (Cambridge, 1987), p. 202.

4. The following is based on the Oxford English Dictionary; the entries for "experience" and "empirical" in Raymond Williams, Keywords, rev. ed (Oxford, 1983); F. E. Peters, Greek Philosophical Terms: A Historical Lexicon (New York, 1967); and the entry "Erfahrung" in the Historisches Wörterbuch der Philosophie.

we will encounter in certain usages, that experiences are personal and incommunicable, rather than collective and exchangeable.

Another Greek word, *pathos,* is sometimes included among the antecedents to the modern concept, even if the etymological link is absent. It basically means "something that happens" in the sense of what one suffers or endures. When experience suggests an experiment, its more active or practical dimensions are activated, but when it is linked to pathos, its passive moment— the acknowledgment that experiences can befall one without being sought or desired—comes to the fore. Here patience can become a virtue, and waiting for an encounter that one cannot force is understood as a source of experience.

In German, the equivalents of "experience" merit special attention and in fact have been widely remarked in the general literature on the subject outside of Germany. *Erlebnis* and *Erfahrung* are both translated by the one English word, but have come to imply very different notions of experience. In the writings of certain theorists keen on exploiting the distinction, such as Wilhelm Dilthey, Martin Buber, and Walter Benjamin, one is often contrasted invidiously with the other (although, as we will see, not always with the same definition or evaluation). *Erlebnis* contains within it the root for life *(Leben)* and is sometimes translated as "lived experience." Although *erleben* is a transitive verb and implies an experience of something, *Erlebnis* is often taken to imply a primitive unity prior to any differentiation or objectification. Normally located in the "everyday world" (the *Lebenswelt*) of commonplace, untheorized practices, it can also suggest an intense and vital rupture in the fabric of quotidian routine. Although *Leben* can suggest the entirety of a life, *Erlebnis* generally connotes a more immediate, pre-reflective, and personal variant of experience than *Erfahrung.*

The latter is sometimes associated with outer, sense impressions or with cognitive judgments about them (especially in the tradition associated with Immanuel Kant). But it also came to mean a more temporally elongated notion of experience based on a learning process, an integration of discrete moments of experience into a narrative whole or an adventure. This latter view, which is sometimes called a dialectical notion of experience, connotes a progressive, if not always smooth, movement over time, which is implied by the *Fahrt* (journey) embedded in *Erfahrung* and the linkage with the German word for danger *(Gefahr).* As such, it activates a link between memory and experience, which subtends the belief that cumulative experience can produce a kind of wisdom that comes only at the end of the day. Although by no means always the case, *Erlebnis* often suggests individual ineffability, whereas *Erfahrung* can have a more public, collective character. But we will see variants of each invoked in the opposite way.

If the etymological evidence suggests anything, it is that "experience" is a term rife with sedimented meanings that can be actualized for a variety of different purposes and juxtaposed to a range of putative antonyms. As the German case shows, two distinct and competing variants of what in English is one term are even possible. It enables both the lamentation, which we encountered in the introduction, that "experience" (in one of the senses of *Erfahrung*) is no longer possible and the apparently contradictory claim that we now live in a veritable "experience society" *(Erlebnisgesellschaft).*[5] It allows us both to "appeal" to experience, as if it were always a thing in the past, and to "hunger" for it, as if it were something that one might enjoy in the future. It permits a distinction between the noun "experience" as something that one can be said to "have" or "to have learned from" and the verb "to experience" or the process of "experiencing," the latter suggesting what one is now "doing" or "feeling."[6] Because it can encompass what is being experienced as well as the subjective process of experiencing it, the word can sometimes function as an umbrella term to overcome the epistemological split between subject and object; the American pragmatists were especially fond of using it in this way. If one adds the possibility of frequently employed adjectival modifiers, such as "lived," "inner," and "genuine," it is easy to understand why the term has had so lively a history and continues to exercise such a hold on our imagination.

That history, it should be immediately emphasized, has not always been one of consistent celebration. In fact, in classical thought, it is frequently argued, what we now recognize as the antecedents of the term played a very modest, at times even negative, role. "In the Greek period," runs a typical account, "the notion did not exist much beyond the bare term *empeiria,* which occurs, for example, in the *Metaphysics* and *Ethics* of Aristotle as a kind of semantic seed for his commentators to develop. Perhaps following this lead, the notion of experience in the Latin period was confined to the action of the sensible thing making itself an object by its own action upon the organ of sense."[7] The neglect or even denigration of experience in classical thought

---

5. Gerhard Schulze, *Die Erlebnisgesellschaft: Kultursoziologie der Gegenwart* (Frankfurt, 1992).

6. For a psychological attempt to distinguish between "experiencing" and "experience," see Eugene T. Gendlin, *Experiencing and the Creation of Meaning: A Philosophical and Psychological Approach to the Subjective* (New York, 1962).

7. John Deely, *New Beginnings: Early Modern Philosophy and Postmodern Thought* (Toronto, 1994), p. 17.

is often connected to the hierarchical bias of the rationalist tradition that elevates ideas, intellect, and purity of form over the messiness and uncertainty of everyday life.

Perhaps the most influential exponent of this characterization was the American philosopher John Dewey, who was anxious to ground his pragmatist alternative to idealist rationalism in a renewed respect for experience.[8] According to Dewey, the classical denigration of experience prevailed until the seventeenth century and was based on contempt for the imperfections of mere opinion, as opposed to the certainties of science. Experience, reliant more on custom and habit than on rational explanations for the causes of things, was distrusted by Plato as an obstacle to true knowledge. He disliked it not because it was "subjective," a charge later leveled by modern defenders of a putatively "objective" science, but because it dealt with matters of chance and contingency. Experience meant for Plato and the tradition he engendered, so Dewey averred, "enslavement to the past, to custom. Experience was almost equivalent to established customs formed not by reason or under intelligent control but by repetition and blind rule of thumb."[9] At the opposite end of the spectrum were the necessary truths of mathematics, which were eternally valid, whether derived from the experience of a fallible subject or not.

Although Aristotle modified his predecessor's hostility to *empeiria* and rejected a faith in intuitive rationality and deductive demonstration, even he saw a progress from mere sense impressions, driven as they were in large measure by appetite, through organized perceptions to a more rational form of cognition based on dispassionate science. The latter had to transcend the contingency of individual events and be true universally.[10] If experience had a location for classical philosophy, as Dewey understood it, it was in the noncontemplative activities that were subsumed under the category of "practice." Whereas theory, as the etymology of the word *theoria* suggests, was understood to rely on a disinterested, spectatorial view of the world, practice was deemed insufficiently distant from the world in which it was immersed to produce reliable knowledge. Summarizing his argument, Dewey specified three flaws of experience for Greek philosophy:

8. For Dewey's discussion of the classical notion of experience, see especially his *Reconstruction in Philosophy* (New York, 1920), chapter 4; and "An Empirical Survey of Empiricisms," in *The Later Works, 1925–1953*, vol. 2, *1935–37*, ed. Jo Ann Boydston (Carbondale, Ill., 1987), first published in 1935. See also his remarks in *Experience and Nature* (La Salle, Ill., 1987), chapter 9, first published in 1925.

9. Dewey, *Reconstruction in Philosophy*, p. 92.

10. Aristotle, *Posterior Analytics*, 1.31: "One necessarily perceives an individual and at a time and at a place, and it is impossible to perceive what is universal and holds in every case."

There is the contrast of empirical knowledge (strictly speaking, of belief and opinion rather than knowledge) with science. There is the restricted and dependent nature of practice in contrast with the free character of rational thought. And there is the metaphysical basis for these two defects of experience: the fact that sense and bodily action are confined to the realm of phenomena while reason in its inherent nature is akin to ultimate reality. The threefold contrast thus implies a metaphysical depreciation of experience, an epistemological one, and, coloring both of the others and giving them their human value, a moral one: the difference in worth between activity that is limited to the body and to physical things, originating in need and serving temporal utilities, and that which soars to ideal and eternal values.[11]

Although conceding that the Greeks were right to suspect the reliability of experience as they knew it—prior, that is, to the advent of experimental methods that could intersubjectively verify what had been experienced—Dewey claimed that the Greeks were wrong to pit reason against it as if the opposition were eternal and unbridgeable. Their fetish of universality, necessity, and abstraction meant that the classical philosophers had failed to understand the value of practical, if fallible, activity in the world, which Dewey set out to rescue.

Whether Dewey's own account of experience was itself fully successful is an issue we will try to address in a later chapter. Whether his characterization of the Greeks was itself valid has been called into question by a variety of commentators. They have raised four major objections: First, it has been demonstrated that Greek science, especially such fields as medicine, optics, and acoustics, was not as a priori and hostile to empirical observation and even calculated experimentation as Dewey assumed.[12] Filtered through later accounts by critics such as the Skeptics and early Christians, Greek science had been mischaracterized as based entirely on dubious thought-experiments, on syllogistic deductions, rather than on the sense-based results of *empeiria*. The same prejudice informed Francis Bacon's influential remarks on the sub-

11. Dewey, "An Empirical Survey of Empiricisms," pp. 74–75.

12. An early argument implicitly against Dewey can be found in John Burnet, "Experiment and Observation in Greek Science," in *Essays and Addresses* (Freeport, N.Y., 1930). Since that time a spirited debate had been conducted over the extent and role of empirical observation in Greek science, which involved, among others, Francis Cornford, Karl Popper, G. S. Kirk, and Gregory Vlastos. For the state of the question today and a summary of the debates, see G. E. R. Lloyd, *Magic, Reason and Experience: Studies in the Origin and Development of Greek Science* (Cambridge, 1979); *The Revolutions of Wisdom: Studies in the Claims and Practice of Ancient Greek Science* (Berkeley, 1987); and *Methods and Problems in Greek Science* (Cambridge, 1991). Lloyd shows that it is necessary to examine specific fields of inquiry and different periods before making grand generalizations about Greek scientific practices.

ject, which were motivated in part by his hostility to the still potent effects of Aristotelian Scholasticism.[13] But more recent research, combined with a dissolution of the rigid distinction between theory and empirical observation, has shown how problematic such sweeping generalizations really are.

Second, it has been noted that literary evidence suggests a considerable popular reservation about the wisdom of purely "theoretical" man.[14] Despite Plato's attempt to banish it from the state, the legacy of the Homeric epic— and has there ever been as vivid a depiction of the perilous *Fahrt* in *Erfahrung* as the *Odyssey?*—was never entirely forgotten. In the plays of Euripides and Aristophanes, the tradition of anti-empirical idealism identified by Dewey with Greek thought *tout court* was subjected to withering satire.[15] Plato's notorious hostility to theatrical representation was earned in part by the resistance, presented on the stage, to his celebration of rational speculation.

Third, it has been argued that however much the mainstream philosophical tradition may have privileged the *vita contemplativa,* in the daily life of the Greek citizen in the democratic *polis,* the *vita activa* was given its due.[16] In direct opposition to Plato's authoritarian republic run by philosopher-kings, the Athens of Pericles was a locus of political practice in which deeds and words rather than pure ideas were paramount. Political life was itself akin to theater in its performative affirmation of heroism in the presence of an appreciative audience, an audience capable of turning deeds into narratives to be shared with future generations. The value of what the Greeks called *phronesis,* or practical wisdom, also meant that pure speculation was not the only valid mode of knowledge. It combined, a recent commentator has noted, "the generality of reflection on principles with the particularity of perception into a given situation. It is distinguished from theoretical knowledge (episteme) in that it is concerned, not with something universal and eternally the same, but with something particular and changeable. It requires experience as well as knowledge."[17]

Finally, the value of experience within Greek philosophy itself has become more widely appreciated since the time of Dewey. In part this has meant ac-

13. Francis Bacon, *Novum Organum,* trans. and ed. Peter Urbach and John Gibson (Chicago, 1994), pp. 80–87.

14. See the discussion in Franz Boll, "Vita Contemplativa," *Sitzungsberichte der Heidelberger Akademie der Wissenschaften* (Heidelberg, 1920).

15. See, for example, Euripides' *Antiope* or Aristophanes' *Clouds.*

16. The most celebrated and influential argument for this claim is Hannah Arendt, *The Human Condition* (Chicago, 1958).

17. David Couzens Hoy, *The Critical Circle: Literature and History in Contemporary Hermeneutics* (Berkeley, 1978), p. 58.

knowledging, as one recent observer has put it, that "philosophically, the notion of experience traces to Greek thought, especially to Aristotle."[18] Although Aristotle's final remarks in book 6 of his *Nicomachean Ethics* do denigrate *phronesis* in favor of *theoria,* elsewhere he notes that "the unproved assertions and opinions of experienced, old, and sagacious people deserve as much attention as those they support by proofs, for they grasp principles through experience."[19] Aristotle's brief, but seminal discussions of the scientific dependency on *empeiria* in the *Metaphysics* and *Posterior Analytics* recognize its links with memory and particularity,[20] even if Aristotle himself was ultimately unable to break entirely with what has been called the "aristocratic" bias for universals and demonstrative logic inherited from Plato.

A less equivocal appreciation of the significance of experience can be discerned among other ancient philosophers, most notably the Cynics and the Sophists. Diogenes' transgressive restitution of the body with all of its squalid needs and irreparable imperfections against the idealist celebration of the rational mind—his basely materialist reversal of the traditional hierarchy of values—implied an openness to what specific sensual experiences might teach.[21] His famous lantern was directed at worldly sights encountered on a voyage of discovery, not at the eternal forms blazing in a Platonic firmament.

So too, the Sophists' insistence on Man rather than Platonic Forms as the focus of philosophical inquiry meant that sense-experience had to be taken seriously as a vehicle of knowledge. According to Protagoras, "man is the master of all experiences, in regard to the 'phenomenality' of what is real and the 'non-phenomenality' of what is not real."[22] Although Gorgias concluded that experience, riven by contradictions, could never be reconciled with reason,

18. John J. McDermott, *The Culture of Experience: Philosophical Essays in the American Grain* (New York, 1976), p. 8.

19. Aristotle, *Ethics,* 1143b, 10–15.

20. In the *Posterior Analytics,* Aristotle wrote, "sense perception gives rise to memory, as we call it; and repeated memories of the same give rise to experience [*empeiria*]; because memories though numerically many, are a single experience. And from experience, that is from the whole universal that has come to rest in the soul, there comes a principle of art [*techne*] or of science [*episteme*]—of art if it concerns producing, of science if it concerns what is" (99b38–100a9). For a discussion of the significance of this passage, see Patrick H. Byrne, *Analysis and Science in Aristotle* (Albany, N.Y., 1997), pp. 173–76. Byrne notes that for Aristotle, experience means a "developed habit in the human soul that makes a person capable of good judgment in an area of familiarity, i.e., where one has sufficiently developed memories" (p. 175). But he then goes on to point out that it was still inferior to the kind of analysis that led to an explanation for the connections observed by experience.

21. For a recent appreciation of Diogenes and what he calls the "kynical" tradition, see Peter Sloterdijk, *Critique of Cynical Reason,* trans. Michael Elred (Minneapolis, 1987).

22. Quoted in Mario Untersteiner, *The Sophists,* trans. Kathleen Freeman (Oxford, 1954), p. 42.

other Sophists such as Antiphon sought to promulgate a more holistic understanding of the term, which would avoid irrationalist skepticism.[23] The Sophists' stress on rhetoric against dialectic, logic, and mathematics meant that they were alert to the importance of oral as opposed to written language, language meant to persuade and influence an audience rather than demonstrate a truth, language for the ear and not the eye.[24] In its performative mode, language was thus tied both to the theatricality decried by the Platonic tradition and to the intersubjectivity that was part of experience understood as an encounter with otherness.

One last consideration must be mentioned, which concerns the reception of Platonism in the history of debates over experience. For ironically, although it has often served as a barrier to the acceptance of experience as an epistemological category, when experience was understood in aesthetic or religious terms, the Platonic notion of intuition could be a positive influence. As Ernst Cassirer has shown, the revival of Platonism in the Renaissance and its spread to England through the Cambridge School (most notably Henry More, Benjamin Whichcote, and Ralph Cudworth) in the seventeenth century helped generate the discourse of aesthetic experience launched by Shaftesbury.[25] Friedrich Schleiermacher, the foremost defender of religious experience, was also deeply indebted to Plato, all but three of whose *Dialogues* he translated into German.[26]

These caveats notwithstanding, it is still hard to deny a certain truth to Dewey's characterization of the relatively modest role played by experience, however defined, in mainstream classical thought. Sophistic rhetoric did not, after all, win its struggle with demonstrative logic, and Cynics like Diogenes remained outsiders with little immediate impact until they were remade into bourgeois heroes in the eighteenth century.[27] The legacy of Plato and Aristotle, with varying coherence and often eclectically combined with elements of non-Greek thought, dominated medieval philosophy. As a result, the ephemeral happenings of everyday life were rendered marginal in the search for universal truths. Although medieval writers were fond of invoking the

23. For a discussion of these debates, see ibid.

24. Eric Havelock was the first to link the Platonic stress on eternal, ideal truths, and the fixity of writing as opposed to the transience of oral performance. See his *Preface to Plato* (Cambridge, Mass., 1963).

25. Ernst Cassirer, *The Platonic Renaissance in England*, trans. James P. Pettegrove (New York, 1970).

26. For a discussion of Schleiermacher's debts to Plato, see Albert L. Blackwell, *Schleiermacher's Early Philosophy of Life: Determinism, Freedom, and Phantasy* (Chico, Calif. 1982), part 2, chapter 2. We will see a similar enthusiasm in the work of Rudolf Otto, discussed in chapter 3.

27. Klaus Herding, "Diogenes als Bürgerheld," in *Im Zeichen der Aufklärung: Studien zur Moderne* (Frankfurt, 1989).

Aristotelian formula "nihil in intellectu quod non prius in sensu" (nothing in the intellect that was not first in the senses),[28] they quickly moved on to the higher truths of divinely inspired reason. Instead of the evidence of the senses or the results of controlled experimentation, church doctrine and the authorities of the Ancients provided the grounds of metaphysical belief and, to a great extent, natural philosophy.[29] Scholasticism was more interested in making rational arguments for the existence of God than in probing the religious experience of the believer. Aristotle's claim that sensation meant the reception of sensible forms was preserved in the belief that objective "species" were the source of perception. Even when the thirteenth-century monk Roger Bacon proposed a *Scientia Experimentalis* to complement the *Sacra Doctrina,* he meant divine illumination as much as sense perception and seems to have included within it occult practices such as alchemy and astrology.[30] In general, little respect was accorded to empirical observation by itself as a valid source of wisdom or reliable knowledge in the sense of *scientia* rigorously differentiated from mere opinion, although medieval students of astronomy, anatomy, and other sciences did rely, at least in part, on observation.[31] Significantly, *experimentum* was often associated with magic and other "low sciences," and the term "Emperick" was used in a derogatory manner, often in medical contexts as a synonym for a quack, well into the seventeenth century.[32]

28. See, for example, John of Salisbury, *The Metalogican,* trans. Daniel D. McGarry (Berkeley, 1962), p. 223. Some have argued that such expressions of faith in the senses meant that medieval science was prevented from using experiments to arrive at counterintuitive knowledge by its reliance on naive experience. See, for example, Anneliese Maier, *Metaphysische Hintergründe der spätscholastischen Philosophie* (Rome, 1955), p. 405. But it is not clear that commonsense experience could triumph over doctrinal authority.

29. Robert Grosseteste, for example, rebuked those who would rely on experiments without a firm foundation in *doctrine.* See the discussion in Bruce S. Eastwood, "Medieval Empiricism: The Case of Grosseteste's Optics," *Speculum* 43 (1968), pp. 306–21.

30. For a discussion of Roger Bacon and experience, see E. J. Dijksterhuis, *The Mechanization of the World Picture,* trans. C. Dikshoorn (London, 1969), pp. 135–41.

31. See Charles B. Schmitt, "Experience and Experiment: A Comparison of Zabarella's View with Galileo's in *De Motu,*" *Studies in the Renaissance* 16 (1969). This excellent essay traces the transition from the still Aristotelian science of Jacopo Zabarella (1533–1589) to that of the young Galileo Galilei (1564–1642). Whereas the former did value something called "experience" and was in this sense a proto-empiricist, he did not yet use *experimenta* to test hypotheses or actively intervene to wrest nature's secrets from her. The latter, however, advocated what he called a *periculum* precisely for that end in his early work *De Motu* (1589–1592), even though he still used the word *experimenta* in its more passive sense of mere observation and privileged mathematics over both. After he moved to Padua, Schmitt argues, Galileo developed a method that was closer to the one championed by Bacon.

32. Williams provides an example from 1621 in *Keywords,* p. 99.

Perhaps the one major exception to this general disdain for experience, at least in one of its varieties, can be found in the work of Augustine, whose confessional ruminations on his own spiritual journey have often been seen as the starting point for later explorations of "inner experience." "It is hardly an exaggeration to say," writes Charles Taylor, "that it was Augustine who introduced the inwardness of radical reflexivity and bequeathed it to the Western tradition of thought."[33] Augustine's reliance on first-person narrative and the role of personal recollection promoted the development of a practice of introspective examination that took experience seriously. According to Hans Blumenberg, "Augustine's *memoria* [memory] specifies for the first time an organ and a content from which something that can be described as 'inner experience' can constitute itself."[34]

Augustinian inner experience was, to be sure, not yet directed at encounters with the profane world—in fact, his abhorrence of the sin of *curiositas* led to the opposite outcome—and memory could be marshaled in the service of a more impersonal Platonic anamnesis. Although there were certainly medieval movements that implicitly valued experience over following rules, such as the communal order of Franciscans who imitated Jesus's life of poverty and humility, they were still relatively isolated occurrences, often losing out in the struggle against dogmatic church authority.[35] It was not really until the dawning of what we now like to call the modern age that the "trial" of experience, like that of the curiosity whose comparable valorization is traced by Blumenberg in *The Legitimacy of the Modern Age*,[36] ended in an acquittal for the defendant, or more precisely, with a hung jury that continues to debate its merits to this day. With the erosion of trust in Scholastic rationalism, the loss of the Catholic Church's corner on spiritual power, and the reversal of the hierarchy of the Ancients and the Moderns, modernity sought a new ground of legitimacy. As Jürgen Habermas has put it, "Modernity can

33. Charles Taylor, *Sources of the Self: The Making of the Modern Identity* (Cambridge, Mass., 1989), p. 131.

34. Hans Blumenberg, *The Legitimacy of the Modern Age*, trans. Robert M. Wallace (Cambridge, Mass., 1983), p. 287.

35. On the Franciscans, see Malcolm D. Lambert, *Franciscan Poverty* (London, 1961). Before this era, the impersonal Lordship of Jesus was generally emphasized over His Sacred Humanity and His own experience as a vulnerable, suffering individual was not yet fully appreciated. For a discussion that compares the early Christian mystics with those of the later Middle Ages according to the relative presence of the suffering Christ in their experiences, see Jess Byron Hollenback, *Mysticism: Experience, Response, and Empowerment* (University Park, Pa., 1996), pp. 86–87.

36. Hans Blumenberg, *The Legitimacy of the Modern Age*, part 3. The link between curiosity and a certain notion of experience is evident in the cult of experience for its own sake, evident in such works as Goethe's *Faust.*

and will no longer borrow the criteria from the models supplied by another epoch; *it has to create its normativity out of itself.*"[37]

In one sense, to be sure, this search meant a tacit disdain for experience when it was identified solely with the accumulated wisdom of the past and thus considered a bulwark of traditional authority. In fact, according to Reinhart Koselleck, modernity (in German, *Neuzeit*) was first conscious of itself as a "new time"—he puts the change in the eighteenth century—when "expectations have distanced themselves from all previous experience."[38] That is, a spatial notion of past and present as simultaneously effective, with no privilege given to what is most recent or potentially to come, was replaced in modernity by a temporal alternative in which a horizon of expectation finds its legitimacy in an imagined future unbeholden to the past. The very historical sense that we associate with modern self-consciousness, in particular its belief in progress, is, Koselleck argues, dependent on the loss of faith in the seamless continuity of past with present and future.

Although, as we will see when examining the politically conservative appeal to something called past "experience" in figures such as Edmund Burke, the rupture was not complete, at least one acceptation of the term—which identifies it entirely with learning from the "lessons" of the past—had now paradoxically acquired the pejorative meaning lingering from the classical period. Even so resolute a twentieth-century champion of *Erfahrung* as Walter Benjamin would have to work his way past that negative connotation in his effort to revive the term for radical purposes.[39] But understood more in terms of a present reality than as a residue of the past and benefiting from the new appreciation of transience and ephemerality, "experience" did emerge at the threshold of modernity as at least a serious contender for the role abdicated by older and now discredited grounds of legitimacy.

The changed attitude was evident in a number of different contexts. In re-

37. Jürgen Habermas, *The Philosophical Discourse of Modernity: Twelve Lectures,* trans. Frederick Lawrence (Cambridge, Mass., 1987), p. 7 (emphasis in original).

38. Reinhart Koselleck, *Futures Past: On the Semantics of Historical Time,* trans. Keith Tribe (Cambridge, Mass., 1985), p. 276.

39. See Benjamin's 1913 essay "Experience," written when he was in the Youth Movement and hostile to the claims made by adults to superior wisdom, in *Selected Writings,* vol. 1, ed. Marcus Bullock and Michael W. Jennings (Cambridge, Mass., 1996). In *Philosophical Discourse of Modernity,* Habermas contrasts the later Benjamin with Koselleck by noting that "Benjamin proposes a *drastic reversal* of horizon of expectation and space of experience. To all past epochs he ascribes a horizon of unfulfilled expectations, to the future-oriented present he assigns the task of experiencing a corresponding past through remembering, in such a way that we can fulfill its expectations with our weak messianic power" (p. 14) (emphasis in original).

ligion, where the unity of the medieval church and its monopoly of doctrinal authority had been shattered, both the Reformation and the Counter-Reformation found in "experience" a possible resource in the struggle for souls. For many Protestants, what has been called the "affirmation of ordinary life"[40] meant a new focus on the details of quotidian existence in the family or pious community rather than on the fidelity to doctrinal teachings or the rituals of the church. "Not scripture alone," Martin Luther insisted, "but experience also. . . . I have the matter itself and experience together with Scripture. . . . Experience alone makes a theologian."[41] The spiritual journey, that "pilgrim's progress" best exemplified in John Bunyan's celebrated parable, involved the perilous encounter with otherness and retrospective narration that were central aspects of the dialectical notion of experience. Although one's natural birth may not have been experienceable, a conversion crisis—being, in the now familiar metaphor, "born again"—certainly was. The immediacy of spiritual life, no longer filtered through the offices of an ecclesiastical hierarchy, produced a constant examination of behavior and motivations, grounded in the belief that, as the Pietist leader Count von Zinzendorf put it in 1732, "religion must be a matter which is able to be grasped through experience alone without any concepts."[42] The powerful tradition of a specifically "religious experience," which we will examine more closely in chapter 3, first emerged in this context.

If among many Protestants, the evocation of "experience" could mean a democratic leveling of access to the holy, for certain figures in the Catholic Counter-Reformation, a very different implication might be drawn. Here the value of a specifically mystical variant of religiosity, which Thomas Aquinas had specifically defined as "cognitio dei experimentalis"[43] (knowledge of God through experience), gained a new hearing. According to Gershom Scholem, the great historian of its Jewish variant, mysticism tends to appear at a stage of religious development when a prior unity between the sacred and the profane, between God and His world, is felt with particular keenness as a lost but potentially recapturable condition.[44] Operating within

40. Taylor, *Sources of the Self,* p. 14.

41. These remarks from Luther's *Table Talk* are quoted in B. A. Gerrish, *Continuing the Reformation: Essays on Modern Religious Thought* (Chicago, 1993), p. 186. Gerrish contends that "by focusing theological interest on what it means to live by faith, Luther created a theology of experience that foreshadowed the modern view of theology as an anthropocentric study of a theocentric phenomenon" (p. 56).

42. Nikolaus Ludwig von Zinzendorf, *Der Deutsche Socrates* (Leipzig, 1732), p. 289, reprinted in *Pietists: Selected Writings,* ed. Peter C. Erb (New York, 1983), p. 291.

43. Thomas Aquinas, *Summa Theologica,* quoted in Gershom G. Scholem, *Major Trends in Jewish Mysticism* (New York, 1974), p. 4.

44. Scholem, *Major Trends in Jewish Mysticism,* p. 8.

traditional religions, rather than constituting radical attempts to create new ones, mysticism seeks to repair the rupture that it sees between the divine and the mundane.

Although certainly antedating the Reformation—indeed, one might argue that the mystical quest for unity begins with the monotheistic separation of a transcendent God from His creation—it seems to have been given a new impetus by the crisis of medieval Christianity, as well as by social and political upheavals.[45] Unlike the everyday vigilance against sin promoted by Protestant preachers as a practice for all to follow, mystical experience was reserved only for religious virtuosi, those with a special gift for ecstatic self-immolation or the discipline to focus intently the mind and emotions on only one goal, which has been called recollection.[46] As the seventeenth-century French mystic Jean-Joseph Surin explained in his *Science expérimentale,* whereas "faith" is the commonplace path to salvation for the many, genuine mystical "experience" is only for "the few."[47] By the time of William Blake, however, the elitist implications of mysticism could be challenged and the hope expressed that all men might sing "songs of experience."[48] But whatever the possibilities for the realization of such a program, "experience" had gained a new connotation, as an especially intense and deep phenomenon that can even become an end in itself once its religious function is left behind.

In the more humanist environment that produced the Renaissance, a comparable valorization of the exceptional individual, that self-fashioning *uomo singolare* or *uomo unico* whose importance has been recognized ever since Jakob Burckhardt,[49] can be discerned. But here too a somewhat more egalitarian implication might ultimately be drawn from the new fascination with the singular subject. Perhaps the great exemplar of this new sensibility was Michel de Montaigne (1533–1592), who, despite his occasional placement within the Baroque era or even within a putative counter-Renaissance,

45. According to Michel de Certeau, "during the sixteenth and seventeenth centuries the mystics were for the most part from regions or social categories which were in socio-economic recession, disadvantaged by change, marginalized by progress, or destroyed by war." *Heterologies: Discourse on the Other,* trans. Brian Massumi (Minneapolis, 1986), p. 84. Mysticism was, however, perhaps at its height during the fourteenth century, a period of considerable turmoil within the church. According to Evelyn Underhill, mysticism usually flourishes directly after a period of intellectual and aesthetic creativity, such as the era of High Gothic or the Renaissance. See her *Mysticism* (New York, 1961), p. 453.

46. Hollenbeck, *Mysticism,* chapter 5.

47. Quoted from a manuscript in the Bibliothèque Nationale in de Certeau, *Heterologies,* p. 93.

48. On Blake's place in the mystical tradition and his attempt to democratize it, see Underhill, *Mysticism,* p. 235.

49. Jacob Burckhardt, *The Civilization of the Renaissance in Italy,* trans. S. G. C. Middlemore and Irene Gordon (New York, 1960), p. 121.

typifies the Renaissance fascination with experience, now extended to commonplace people and mundane events. Insofar as his remarkable contribution to the discourse on experience has become a standard against which many others have been compared and often found wanting, it will be necessary to linger for a while in Montaigne's presence (a temptation to which it is easy to succumb because of the undiminished power of his remarkable oeuvre).

MONTAIGNE AND HUMANIST EXPERIENCE

Montaigne's celebrated *Essays* significantly culminate with a long meditation written in 1587–88, when he was fifty-six, entitled "Of Experience." Having himself been an active participant in the affairs of his day—an aristocrat by birth, he served as magistrate for the Bordeaux parlement from 1557 to 1570—Montaigne had retired to his chateau in the Périgord for the last two decades of his life to ruminate on the humbling lessons he had learned.[50] As he pointedly remarked, "on the loftiest throne in the world we are still sitting only on our own rump."[51] Although returning to public service for periods in the 1580s, he had the leisure to produce the most elaborate record of introspection—a kind of extended auto-interview, as one commentator has called it[52]—in the more than a millennium between Augustine's *Confessions* and those of Jean-Jacques Rousseau.

Montaigne's *Essays*—their very title suggesting exploratory, tentative experiments rather than settled dogma—document his journey of self-discovery, as well as his extraordinarily keen observations about the human condition. Colloquial, idiosyncratic, accessible in style, they struggle to allow the personal voice of the author to emerge amid the alienated writing on his page. That voice is clearly in search of a sympathetic ear, such as the one Montaigne had lost with the death of his beloved friend Étienne de la Boètie in 1563.[53] Confession in the traditional Christian sense of speaking through a

50. For helpful introductions, see Peter Burke, *Montaigne* (Oxford, 1981); and Arne Melberg, *Versuch über Montaigne,* trans. Lothar Schneider (Egginen, 2003).

51. Montaigne, "Of Experience," in *The Complete Essays of Montaigne,* trans. Donald Frame (Stanford, 1965), p. 857.

52. Mavì de Fillipis, "L'esperienza secondo Montaigne," *La Cultura* 18, no. 1 (1980), p. 106.

53. For an analysis of Montaigne's texts as an attempt to speak once again to his late friend Étienne de la Boétie, see de Certeau, "Montaigne's 'Of Cannibals'," *Heterologies.* For the larger context in which the *Essays* were written, see Natalie Zemon Davis, "Boundaries and the Sense of Self in Sixteenth-Century France," in Thomas C. Heller, Morton Sosna, and David E. Wellbury, eds., *Reconstructing Individualism: Autonomy, Individuality, and the Self in Western Thought* (Stanford, 1986).

priest to God will no longer suffice; Montaigne's imagined dialogue is with a worldly audience, which will recognize itself in his reflections. Here experiences are to be shared, not hoarded.

But Montaigne also seems to have understood the limits to vicarious identification and the uniqueness of his particular life history. Schooled in classical learning but reluctant to accept the priority of the ancients, he defiantly exclaimed, "I would rather be an authority on myself than on Cicero."[54] Revealing a fondness for cheeky irreverence that recalls Diogenes of Sinope, Montaigne preferred the debunking materialist to the Platonic idealist, whose faith in universal rationality he could not share. Noting that a philosopher had once implored Diogenes to read more books, he approvingly cited the Cynic's reply: "You are jesting. . . . you choose real and natural figs, not painted ones, why don't you also choose real and natural exercises, not written ones?"[55]

Reversing the traditional hierarchical privileging of timeless verities over transient appearances and tacitly rejecting the mystical quest for unity with the divine, Montaigne boldly asserted, "I do not portray being: I portray passing."[56] Time, he understood, should not be measured against a putative eternal plenitude and found wanting; living in the moment was not inferior to living for eternity. Nor could imperfect memory serve to totalize the entire story into a fully meaningful narrative at the end of the day, however much it might be worth probing for shards of the past.[57] As a result, Montaigne could be interpreted by some observers as typifying the heightened sensitivity to the transitory, fleeting, and ephemeral that characterized the Baroque, with its embrace of the manifold contradictions of experience.[58]

Significantly, in the remarkable essay that bears that name, Montaigne never

54. Montaigne, "Of Experience," *Complete Essays,* p. 882.

55. Montaigne, "Of the Education of Children," *Complete Essays,* p. 124.

56. Montaigne, "Of Repentence," *Complete Essays,* p. 611.

57. See Richard Regosin, "The Text of Memory: Experience as Narration in Montaigne's *Essais,*" in John D. Lyons and Nancy J. Vickers, eds., *The Dialectic of Discovery* (Lexington, Ky., 1984), for a discussion of the role of imperfect, weak memory in Montaigne. Memory's imperfection serves to free us from obedience to the authorities of the past, but it is not so faulty as to prevent it from contributing to a sense of narrative coherence over time for the self, especially when its active, reconstructive moment is foregrounded. The very writing of the *Essays* functions in this way for Montaigne himself: "On a personal level, the essays allow his experience to be more than a mere succession of discrete instants in a never-ending present. If the writer appears to exercise his judgment in the moments of actuality, his experience is also that of a life lived over time" (p. 147).

58. See, for example, F. J. Warnke, *Versions of the Baroque* (New Haven, 1972); and José Antonio Maravall, *Culture of the Baroque: Analysis of a Historical Structure,* trans. Terry Cochran (Minneapolis, 1986), chapter 7.

attempted to define (or in Oakeshott's sense, "manage") the word "experience," allowing its meaning—or multiple meanings—to be revealed piecemeal in the process of reading itself.[59] The essay's lessons come in part from comparing successive examples in a way that subtly acknowledges both their similarities and their differences.[60] More like an unruly life than a logical demonstration, "Of Experience" meanders digressively, combining anecdotes and *aperçus* with arguments and quotations, reprising themes and coming at them from different angles. Its own temporality, rhythmically uneven and irreducible to a unified narrative, duplicates the unsystematic ruminations on time itself to be found in Montaigne's work as a whole.[61] What Goethe indignantly said when asked whether his greatest play could be reduced to an idea—"the life I portray in *Faust* is rich and many-colored and very various, and a fine thing it would have been, I must say, if I had attempted to thread that on to the thin string of a single pervading idea!"[62]—could just as easily have served as Montaigne's defense for the seemingly undisciplined structure of "Of Experience," which performatively instantiates what it substantively argues.

To define unequivocally or reason deductively, Montaigne implied, was to short-circuit the unpredictable learning process that made experience so valuable. Spurning the comparable attempt to achieve justice by legislating binding and univocal laws under which cases could effortlessly be subsumed, Montaigne drew instead on his own years as a magistrate to make a brief for individual judges to interpret and apply abstract rules in specific cases on the basis of feeling as well as intellect.[63] Efforts by Protestants to still debate by appealing to the literal word of Holy Scripture, he likewise argued, were based on an equally fruitless premise, "as if there were less animosity and bitterness in commenting than in inventing!"[64]

59. For an attempt to sort out the multiple meanings on the basis of a comparative analysis of usages in early modern France, see W. G. Moore, "Montaigne's Notion of Experience," in Will Moore, Rhoda Sutherland, and Enid Starkie, eds., *The French Mind: Essays in Honor of Gustave Rudler* (Oxford, 1952). Moore concludes that Montaigne uses the word more frequently in the sense of direct, personal knowledge opposed to speculation or imagination than in the sense of cumulative retrospective know-how or wisdom.

60. On the issue of exemplarity in Montaigne, see John D. Lyons, "Circe's Drink and Sorbonnic Wine: Montaigne's Paradox of Experience," in Alexander Gelley, ed., *Unruly Examples: On the Rhetoricity of Exemplarity* (Stanford, 1995).

61. For a discussion of this theme, see F. Joukovsky, *Montaigne et le problème du temps* (Paris, 1972).

62. Goethe, conversation with Johann Peter Eckermann on May 6, 1827, quoted in *Conversations and Encounters*, trans. and ed. David Luke and Robert Pick (Chicago, 1966), p. 160.

63. The similarity to Kant's argument for "reflective" (as opposed to "determinant") judgments of aesthetic objects in the Third Critique, which we will examine in chapter 4, is hard to miss. For other parallels, see Ernst Cassirer, *Kant's Life and Thought*, trans. James Haden (New Haven, 1981), p. 86.

64. Montaigne, "Of Experience," *Complete Essays*, p. 815.

Montaigne's distrust of any attempt to achieve absolute truth evinces the debt he owed to the revival of skepticism that came with the recovery of the Pyrrhonist writings of Sextus Empiricus in the 1560s and renewed interest in the "Academic" skepticism of Cicero.[65] Although never explicitly rejecting Catholicism, Montaigne clearly had absorbed many of the criticisms leveled against its dogmatic theology during the Reformation, refusing to believe in miracles or witchcraft and resisting arguments for natural sinfulness. His friendship with the French king Henri IV has often been accounted of significance in the promulgation of the Edict of Nantes in 1598, which authorized tolerance of the Huguenots. Resolutely worldly, attuned to the pleasures and pains of the flesh, Montaigne delighted in the creaturely sensuality that the church so often had repudiated. He thus focused his attention not on salvation, but on living the good life, a lesson that would endear him to the freethinkers of the eighteenth-century Enlightenment.[66]

But what "experience" had taught him was that no life was free of its paradoxes, ironies, and disappointments. Whether or not one accepts the traditional periodization of his career into stoical, skeptical, and then epicurean phases, it is clear that Montaigne was keenly aware throughout of the limits of the human condition, including the uncertain reliability of the senses.[67] Even Protagoras's celebrated claim, so dear to humanist self-affirmation, that Man was the measure of all things did not escape his suspicion.[68] As a result, a reading of his legacy in fideistic terms was possible, as shown by the Christian Pyrrhonism of the Counter-Reformation theologians Pierre Charon and Jean-Pierre Camus, which owed so much to his example.[69]

Montaigne, in fact, never allowed his doubts to turn into outright misanthropy or a disillusioned retreat from the world of his fellow men. When he chose as his motto the skeptical question "Que sais-je?" (what do I know?), he seems to have meant it as a tribute to the figure of Socrates, who was wise to the extent that he knew the limits of his knowledge, which meant the in-

---

65. For an account of the importance of the latter, which was less absolute than Pyrrhonism, see José R. Maia Neto, "Academic Skepticism in Early Modern Philosophy," *Journal of History of Ideas* 58, no. 2 (April 1997).

66. On Montaigne's importance for the Enlightenment, see Peter Gay, *The Enlightenment: An Interpretation*, 2 vols., 1: *The Rise of Modern Paganism* (New York, 1968), pp. 287–90; and Ira O. Wade, *The Intellectual Origins of the French Enlightenment* (Princeton, 1971), pp. 84–107.

67. In "Apology for Raymond Sebond," Montaigne acknowledged that all we know comes through the senses, but in them "lies the greatest foundation and proof of our ignorance." *Complete Essays*, p. 443.

68. Ibid., p. 418.

69. For an account, see Richard H. Popkin, *The History of Skepticism from Erasmus to Descartes* (New York, 1964), chapter 3.

ability to refute as well as confirm many of our beliefs.[70] The lesson he derived from Socrates, as Montaigne's great admirer Ralph Waldo Emerson put it, was that "knowledge is the knowing that we can not know."[71] Socrates, moreover, did not pit the mind against the senses, thus avoiding a problematic dualism: "He prizes bodily pleasure as he should," Montaigne approvingly noted, "but he prefers that of the mind, as having more power, constancy, ease, variety, and dignity. The latter by no means goes alone, according to him—he is not so fanciful—but only comes first. For him temperance is the moderator, not the adversary, of pleasures."[72] Montaigne's attitude toward the body was that of someone who inhabited it fully as a lived reality, not that of an observer who could examine it from afar as an object in the world. Self-understanding, he demonstrated, should not be the same as an autopsy performed on a corpse, a sentiment that has earned him comparison with such twentieth-century phenomenologists as Maurice Merleau-Ponty.[73]

Montaigne's own remarkable serenity and balance, his capacity to live with uncertainty and doubt and find solace in a world of contradictions and ambiguities, was perhaps best expressed in his acceptance, even affirmation, of the frailty of the human condition and the inevitability of the one threshold that could not really be experienced: that of death. "To philosophize," he agreed with Cicero (and anticipated Martin Heidegger), "is nothing else but to prepare for death. . . . Let us rid it of its strangeness, come to know it, get used to it. Let us have nothing on our minds as often as death."[74] But unlike other challenges, it was impossible, he admitted, to learn about death through actual experience: "for dying, which is the greatest task we have to perform, practice cannot help us. A man can, by habit and experience, fortify himself against pain, shame, indigence, and such other accidents; but as for death, we can try it only once: we are all apprentices when we come to it."[75] The closest we can approximate it is by swooning into unconsciousness, thus momentarily losing our grip on selfhood. Our experience of sleep

70. As Stephen Toulmin notes, "Humanist skeptics . . . no more wished to *deny* general philosophical theses than to *assert* them. Like the two classical philosophers to whom Montaigne compares himself, Pyrrho and Sextus, the humanists saw philosophical *questions* as reaching beyond the scope of experience in an indefensibile way." *Cosmopolis: The Hidden Agenda of Modernity* (Chicago, 1990), p. 29.

71. Ralph Waldo Emerson, "Montaigne; or, The Skeptic," *Selections from Ralph Waldo Emerson,* ed. Stephen E. Whicher (Boston, 1960), p. 296.

72. Montaigne, "Of Experience," *Complete Essays,* p. 855.

73. Daniel Aris and François Joukovsky, "Une philosophie de l'expérience," *Bulletin de la société des amis de Montaigne* 21–22 (July–December 1990), p. 87.

74. Montaigne, "That to Philosophize Is to Learn to Die," *Complete Essays,* pp. 56–60.

75. Montaigne, "Of Practice," *Complete Essays,* p. 267.

provides another suggestive analogue, but one that is mediated at best. Montaigne, Giorgio Agamben writes, "can formulate the ultimate goal of experience as a nearing to death—that is, man's advance to maturity through an anticipation of death as the extreme limit of experience. But for Montaigne this limit remains something that cannot be experienced, which can only be approached."[76] In this exploration of what more recent thinkers would call a "limit-experience," Montaigne revealed an awareness of the unresolvable paradoxes within even the most authentic and fulfilled experience. In this sense, as Richard Regosin has remarked, "paradoxically, death becomes an emblematic experience"[77] for Montaigne because it signifies the limits of all experience. Whereas the later adepts of limit-experiences were to evince a restless desire to push the boundaries as far out as possible, Montaigne seems to have been cheerfully resigned to what life as he knew it might provide.

BACON AND EXPERIENCE AS SCIENTIFIC EXPERIMENT

In fact, it was this reserve about the desirability of turning experience into a potentially perilous experiment that made Montaigne, for all his attractions, an inadequate model for modern man at his most restless and ambitious. "Montaigne, the skeptic, is conservative," Blumenberg observes, "because he sees man's imagination as constrained by the limits of his experience; and for him, the realm of that experience is still a constant magnitude. He cannot know that any progress whatever would be possible here."[78] But modern thinkers who were keen on "progressing" beyond a state of relativist tolerance for ambiguity and the endurance of life's misfortunes could not rest content with Montaigne's credo, "I study myself more than any other subject. That is my metaphysics, that is my physics."[79] They wanted to move out into the world and scrutinize it instead in the hope of finding new and reliable knowledge, knowledge that would help master what had hitherto been outside of human control. Montaigne's skepticism about sense experience led them not to introspective resignation, but to a search for a new means of

76. Giorgio Agamben, *Infancy and History: Essays on the Destruction of Experience,* trans. Liz Heron (New York, 1993), p. 19.
77. Regosin, "The Text of Memory," p. 157.
78. Hans Blumenberg, *The Genesis of the Copernican World,* trans. Robert M. Wallace (Cambridge, Mass., 1987), p. 629.
79. Montaigne, "Of Experience," *Complete Essays,* p. 821.

compensating for its failings and for instruments that would overcome the untrustworthy effects of raw sensation.

"Experience," the great experimental chemist Robert Boyle insisted, "is but an assistant to reason, since it doth indeed supply information to the understanding, but the understanding still remains the judge, and has the power or right to examine and make use of the testimonies that are presented to it."[80] But the understanding is itself in the service of a more practical outcome. Modern science had what Amos Funkenstein has called an ergetic, as opposed to a contemplative, model of knowledge, one based on doing more than on mere reasoning.[81] Francis Bacon in particular sought to tie truth to utility and integrate science and technology.[82] But it was a doing whose end was not experience for its own sake, but rather the knowledge of the external world that it might provide.

Thus, at virtually the same time as the trial of "experience" seemed to leave it victorious over an antiquated scholastic rationalism or religious dogmatism, providing a holistic integration of soul and body, individual and culture, knowledge and faith, new critics emerged to call its value—or at least self-sufficiency—into question. In the towering figures of Francis Bacon (1561–1626) and René Descartes (1596–1650), a more specifically modern distrust of the claims of at least one variant of experience—that defended by Montaigne's *Essays*—was first made explicit.[83] Rejecting the serenity of Montaigne's chateau in the Périgord, Bacon and Descartes set out to pass through the pillars of Hercules—as had Odysseus depicted on the frontispiece of Bacon's 1620 *Instauratio magna (Great Renewal)*[84]—and explore the unknown world. Whereas he was content to remain on the level of particularity and idiosyn-

80. Robert Boyle, *The Works of the Honourable Robert Boyle,* ed. Thomas Birch, 6 vols. (London, 1672), vol. 5, p. 539, quoted in E. A. Burtt, *The Metaphysical Foundations of Modern Science* (Garden City, N.Y., 1954), p. 171.

81. Funkenstein, *Theology and the Scientific Imagination* (Princeton, 1986), p. 298. Descartes' commitment to actual experimentation was somewhat less firm than Bacon's. For a discussion, see Bernard Williams, *Descartes: The Project of Pure Enquiry* (New York, 1978), chapter 9.

82. On this issue, see Paolo Rossi, "Truth and Utility in the Science of Francis Bacon," trans. Salvator Attanasio, in Benjamin Nelson, ed., *Philosophy, Technology and the Arts in the Early Modern Era* (New York, 1970). For a critique of the claim that Bacon was a proto-utilitarian in the strong sense, see Perez Zagorin, *Francis Bacon* (Princeton, 1998), p. 88.

83. For a comparison of the legacy of Montaigne with that of Bacon and Descartes, which bemoans the victory of the latter over the former, see Toulmin, *Cosmopolis.* For an earlier discussion of the relation between Bacon and Montaigne, see Pierre Villey, *Montaigne et Francis Bacon* (Paris, 1913).

84. The accompanying motto read "Multi pertransibunt et augibetur scientia" (many will pass through and knowledge will be increased).

crasy, mulling over the lessons of common sense, they sought systematic and universal knowledge—Bacon still talked of "forms" in nature[85]—that would transcend the prejudices of hoi polloi. Whereas he acknowledged the often messy conflation of logic and rhetoric, they generally sought to privilege the former over the latter.[86] Whereas he remained satisfied with opinion, ephemerality, and probability, they desired scientific truth and absolute certainty based on designed, rather than random, encounters with the external world and rule-governed explanations of those encounters.[87] Whereas his approach was totalizing and dialectical, theirs was atomistic and reductive, seeking truth beneath the level of visible surfaces. Whether we see the ambitions of Bacon and Descartes as a bold new departure or, as Stephen Toulmin has suggested,[88] a frightened response to the increased political, religious, and economic turmoil of the seventeenth century, the result was a loss of faith in the possibility of that integrated, balanced, holistic, but always open-ended and provisional experience celebrated in Montaigne's *Essays*.

Perhaps nothing demonstrates the change more clearly than the difference in their attitudes toward the greatest challenge to everyday, commonsensical experience produced by the new science: the Copernican revolution in astronomy. In his "Apology for Raymond Sebond," Montaigne notes Copernicus's new theory, which he says contradicts traditional wisdom, and then asks: "What are we to get out of that, unless that we should not bother which of the two is so? And who knows whether a third opinion, a thousand years from now, will not overthrow the preceding? . . . Thus when some new doctrine is offered to us, we have great occasion to distrust it, and to consider

85. For a discussion, see Antonio Pérez-Ramos, "Bacon's Forms and the Maker's Knowledge Tradition," in Markku Peltonen, ed., *The Cambridge Companion to Bacon* (Cambridge, 1996).

86. See, for example, Bacon's disparaging remarks on rhetorical method in *Novum Organum*, p. 96. For a discussion of the resistance of Bacon and Descartes to rhetoric, see Thomas M. Conley, *Rhetoric in the European Tradition* (Chicago, 1990), chapter 6. Bacon, to be sure, did not put demonstrative logic above induction as a source of new knowledge, as had previous critics of rhetoric. See the discussion in Lia Formigari, *Language and Experience in 17th-Century British Philosophy* (Amsterdam, 1988), chapter 1. For a recent attempt to argue that rhetoric was not always subordinated to dialectic in Bacon, see Brian Vickers, "Bacon and Rhetoric," in Peltonen, *The Cambridge Companion to Bacon*. But even Vickers concludes that Bacon hoped science would ultimately place us directly in connection with things without the intermediary of treacherous words. Bacon, to be sure, was critical of the self-enclosed Aristotelian logic of the Scholastics as a flawed tool of discovery about the world. For a discussion, see Zagorin, *Francis Bacon*, chapter 2.

87. On the struggle between notions of probability and certainty, see Paula R. Backscheider, ed., *Probability, Time, and Space in Eighteenth-Century Literature* (New York, 1979); and Barbara J. Shapiro, *Probability and Certainty in Seventeenth-Century England* (Princeton, 1983).

88. Toulmin, *Cosmopolis*, chapter 1.

that before it was produced its opposite was in vogue; and, as it was overthrown by this one, there may arise in the future a third invention that will likewise smash the second."[89] For Bacon and Descartes, in contrast, the Ptolemaic universe had been definitively disproven, and the geocentric, commonplace "experience" that had made it plausible was discarded in favor of a truer understanding of the cosmos, one that eagerly moved beyond the finite perspective of the contingent human subject.[90]

The "quest for certainty" Dewey famously called the tradition that descended from Bacon and Descartes, a desire for a knowledge that can transcend the framework out of which it emerges and earn from all rational men a justified confidence in its veracity.[91] If Montaigne's experience seemed to provide only perspectivalist, fallible knowledge and a return to the discredited rationalism of the Scholastics was impossible, it was necessary to begin anew, providing what Bacon called a "great instauration"[92] and trust only in what could be verified by rigorous rules of inquiry. "Experience" in its traditional sense, Bacon complained, "is blind and silly, so that while men roam and wander along without any definitive course, merely taking counsel of such things as happen to come before them, they range widely, yet move little further forward."[93] But there was an alternative: "the right order for experience is to kindle a light, then with that light to show the way, beginning with experience ordered and arranged, not irregular and erratic, and from that deriving axioms, and from the axioms thus established deriving again new experiments, just as the word of God operated in an orderly way on the unformed matter of creation."[94] What Bacon called *experientia literata*—informed or learned experiences that have been "taught how to read and write"—was the first step to essential knowledge.[95] The result would

89. Montaigne, *Complete Essays*, p. 429.

90. On the implications of the new astronomy for the depreciation of commonplace experience, see Blumenberg, *The Genesis of the Copernican World*, p. 62. Interestingly, Bacon himself expressed certain reservations about the telescope, although not about the Copernican revolution. In *Novum Organum*, he said he was disappointed that it had led to so few discoveries (p. 226).

91. Dewey, *The Quest for Certainty* (New York, 1960).

92. *Instauratio*, the Latin noun from which the word was taken, means restoration as well as renewal, but Bacon stressed the latter sense. See the discussion in Zagorin, *Francis Bacon*, p. 76.

93. *Novum Organum*, pp. 78–79.

94. Ibid., pp. 91–92.

95. See Lisa Jardine, "*Experientia literata* or *Novum Organum?* The Dilemma of Bacon's Scientific Method," in William A. Sessions, ed., *Francis Bacon's Legacy of Texts* (New York, 1990). Jardine notes the tension in Bacon's work between the more modest *experientia literata* model, which is closer to empiricism in the sense of Gassendi and Hume, and the *novum organum* model, which seeks firmer knowledge of essential forms.

be those privileged cognitive units that modern science would deem verifiable "facts."[96]

The belief that the proper procedure might be found that could provide such a God-like verification began well before the scientific revolution—Walter Ong traced its origins back to the Greek *methodus,* a pursuit of knowledge developed in particular by the second-century Hellenic rhetorician Hermogenes, and discerned its revival in the dialectical logic of the sixteenth-century Frenchman Peter Ramus[97]—but it is only with the scientific revolution that what might be called a fetish of method can be said to have begun.[98] As one commentator has put it, "'Method' served an analogous function to that of the Holy Spirit in the Catholic tradition because it identified the hidden source of a tradition's legitimacy."[99] Although the result was never a wholesale repudiation of the testimony of unaided sense experience—Descartes, after all, had said we are sometimes deceived, not always[100]—the growing prestige of mathematics and the increased tempo of technological innovation combined to diminish its authority.

Descartes' more deductive and geometric rationalism, based on a belief in innate ideas,[101] was ultimately less successful among scientists than the in-

96. For recent discussions of the growth of the concept of "fact" and its relationship to experience, see Mary Poovey, *A History of the Modern Fact: Problems of Knowledge in the Sciences of Wealth and Society* (Chicago, 1998); and Barbara J. Shapiro, *A Culture of Fact, 1550–1720* (Ithaca, N.Y., 2000).

97. Walter J. Ong, *Ramus, Method, and the Decay of Dialogue* (Cambridge, Mass., 1983), chapter 11. See also Neal W. Gilbert, *Renaissance Concepts of Method* (New York, 1960); and Peter Dear, "Method in the Study of Nature," in Michael Ayers and Daniel Garger, eds., *The Cambridge History of Seventeenth-Century Philosophy* (Cambridge, 1998).

98. Erich Auerbach provocatively argued that Montaigne himself should be included in this generalization: "Montaigne's apparently fanciful method, which obeys no preconceived plan, is basically a strictly experimental method, the only method which conforms to such a subject. . . . It is this strict and, even in the modern sense, scientific method which Montaigne endeavors to maintain." *Mimesis: The Representation of Reality in Western Literature,* trans. Willard R. Trask (Princeton, 1953), p. 256. But whereas Montaigne's approach may have been suitable to the study of flux and ephemerality, that of the new science sought structural regularity and essential truth.

99. Peter Dear, *Discipline and Experience: The Mathematical Way in the Scientific Revolution* (Chicago, 1995), p. 121. Dear demonstrates the importance of the new respect for mathematics, especially among seventeenth-century Jesuit philosophers, in fostering a modern notion of experimental science.

100. D. M. Clarke has identified six distinct uses of *expérience* in Descartes: introspection, untutored test, sense of observation, objective phenomena, ordinary experience, and scientific experiment. See his *Descartes' Philosophy of Science* (Manchester, 1982), pp. 17–24. Cartesian doubt, it should also be noted, was not indiscriminately directed at all of our beliefs and habits. For example, those that provided religious experience were excluded. See the discussion in Nicholas Wolterstorff, *John Locke and the Ethics of Belief* (Cambridge, 1996), chapter 3.

101. It might be argued that Descartes thought innate ideas were themselves a variety of inner experience. In fact, in his 1628 *Rules for the Direction of the Mind,* Descartes identified experience with "what

ductive alternative preached by Bacon, who stressed the importance of an organized and continuous program of research carried out by a community of scientists.[102] Montaigne had cautioned in his "Of Experience" that "the inference that we try to draw from the resemblance of events is uncertain, because they are always dissimilar; there is no quality so universal in this aspect of things as diversity and variety."[103] But such qualms were brushed aside in the wake of the discoveries produced by the scientific revolution. The enormously influential Isaac Newton was taken to be on Bacon's side rather than Montaigne's or, for that matter, Descartes'. Gone was the assumption of earlier figures such as Paracelsus that sympathetic insight into and identification with the hidden workings of nature, like the Protestant's inner illumination, could be a source of valid knowledge.[104] Gone too was the prejudice against anomalous cases, those "monsters" presumed to be irrelevant to an understanding of the ordinary workings of God's nature; now they could be taken as privileged instances of still deeper regularities.[105] Soon the ideal of generalization from replicable experiences, which then sought to explain what had been observed according to the workings of natural laws, became enthroned as the "scientific method" *tout court,* however often it may have been violated in actual scientific practice and whatever the problems it may have posed for certain sciences such as evolutionary biology.

Among the consequences of the fetish of method for the fortunes of "experience," four can be singled out for special attention. First, the new identification of reliable and certain experience with verifiable experimentation meant a belief in the repeatability and public quality of experience, at

we perceive in sense, what we hear from the lips of others, and generally whatever reaches our understanding either from external sources or from that contemplation which our mind directs backwards on itself." *The Philosophical Works of Descartes,* trans. Elizabeth Haldane and G. R. T. Ross (Cambridge, 1968), pp. 43–44. But in most contexts, he reserved the word for what came through the senses. For an account of the relations between Bacon and the Cartesians, see Antonio Pérez-Ramos, "Bacon's Legacy," in Peltonen, *The Cambridge Companion to Bacon,* pp. 312–14.

102. Induction for Bacon did not mean simply gathering examples and generalizing from them, as is sometimes assumed; he understood the importance of hypotheses and the process of excluding unsatisfactory explanations. For a discussion, see Zagorin, *Francis Bacon,* pp. 91–103.

103. Montaigne, "Of Experience," in *Complete Essays,* p. 815.

104. Walter Pagel, *Paracelsus* (Basel, 1982), p. 50. The Paracelsian tradition did not retreat immediately. In fact, in England it enjoyed a revival in mid-century, at the time of the Puritan revolution. As Evelyn Fox Keller has noted, "the emphasis on illumination derived from direct experience (available to anyone who pursues the art) accorded well with the political and religious ambitions of the times." *Reflections on Gender and Science* (New Haven, 1985), pp. 45–46. By the 1670s, however, the Baconians had triumphed.

105. On the changed attitude toward anomalies, see Dear, *Discipline and Experience,* pp. 20–21.

least when it was invoked to provide a source of valid knowledge. Although as a first move Descartes may have emulated Montaigne's retreat into the skeptical self that had only its doubt as an indisputable truth, he quickly returned to the reality of the world that was present—courtesy of a non-deceiving God—in clear and distinct ideas in the consciousness of that indubitable self. He had, to be sure, restricted certain knowledge to aspects of reality, notably the extension and movement of bodies, while acknowledging that others, such as color or sound, were dependent on the untrustworthy sensorium of the subject.[106] But Descartes was confident that at least what philosophers were soon to call "primary" as opposed to "secondary" characteristics could be known by all.

With Bacon, the uniqueness and ineffability of "inner experience" was replaced by the intersubjectively confirmable data of the controlled experiment. Because the right method could be learned by others, experience must be communicable, not merely intelligible. It must, in fact, be potentially available to anyone willing to follow the prescribed procedures, which, unlike the secret devices of magicians (or the special exercises of religious virtuosi) were to be fully accessible.[107] Scientists were not to be like Montaigne's judges, relying on the uncertainties of the hermeneutic arts, but should be governed instead by the right rules of inquiry and proof. "Solomon's House," which Bacon described in *The New Atlantis* of 1627, became the model for the proliferation of scientific academies that began with the Royal Society in 1662. The project of a great encyclopedia of all known knowledge, whose implementation had to await Diderot and the *philosophes,* was already there in Bacon's call for an inventory of scientific knowledge open to all eyes.[108] Although it is true, as Timothy J. Reiss has argued, that those with access to this knowledge were still for Bacon a tacit elite possessing a kind of "experimental literacy," in principle the method was learnable by everyone.[109] A new

106. See the discussion in his *Meteorology* (1637), in *Discourse on Method, Optics, Geometry, and Meteorology,* trans. Paul J. Olscamp (Indianapolis, 1965), p. 338.

107. Bacon, to be sure, did owe certain debts to earlier magical and occult attempts to master nature and penetrate its hidden secrets. See William Leiss, *The Domination of Nature* (New York, 1972). But the model of an open scientific society was not one of them.

108. For a comparison of Bacon and the *philosophes* on this and other points, see Wade, *The Intellectual Origins of the French Revolution,* pp. 118–26.

109. Timothy J. Reiss, *The Discourse of Modernism* (Ithaca, N.Y., 1982), chapter 6. Drawing on Foucault's argument about power and knowledge, Reiss detects a political dialectic at work in Bacon's method. "The concept of a general experience—universal and reasonable, as the grammarians will have it—is one that permits the elaboration and practice of the liberal state, founded upon a contract between equal individuals, each possessed of a similar will. Like Descartes, Bacon will have a powerful share in the creation of the 'discursive space' making possible such an idea of knowledge and social

confidence in verifiable and trustworthy reports of specific experiments—what has been called "virtual witnessing"[110] extrapolated from gentlemanly codes of honorable conduct and civility—allowed the rapid dissemination of new findings. Paradoxically, this democratization of the subject of experience also meant its implicit reduction to a single universal model, which was the disembodied, spectatorial Cartesian *cogito,* assumed to be normative for all humans. Although Montaigne's subject was able to share with others his unique experiences, he did not assume that these experiences were perfectly fungible with those of his interlocutors. With the Cartesian and Baconian subject, in contrast, qualitative difference was subsumed under quantitative commensurability and a tacit metasubject of cognition, enjoying a "view from nowhere," was born. The psychological subject with all its personal history and idiosyncratic appetites was split off from its epistemological double, with the latter now assumed to be species-wide in scope. As Taylor puts it, "what Descartes calls on us to do is to stop living 'in' or 'through' the experience, to treat it itself as an object, or what is the same thing, as an experience which could just as well have been someone else's."[111] Not surprisingly, later critics of the Eurocentric and androcentric underpinnings of modern subjectivity would find Descartes' *cogito* and Bacon's collective domination of nature inviting targets and seek to bring back a more culturally mediated and corporeally situated notion of incommensurable experiences.[112]

A second significant implication followed from this distinction between the psychological and epistemological subject. The transcendentalization and depersonalization of the latter meant the extension of its lifespan beyond that of the individual human being. The project of exploring nature was a cumulative one, with no terminal point except perfect knowledge.[113] As a result, that profound confrontation with our inevitable finitude so much a part

---

practice" (p. 206). But what is occulted from this model, he claims, is the fact that it is based on a discourse that refuses to reveal itself as such, a discourse which reflects power relations allowing only some people the right to be experimentally "literate."

110. Steven Shapin, "Pump and Circumstance: Robert Boyle's Literary Technology," *Social Studies of Science* 14 (1984), pp. 481–520; see also Steven Shapin and Simon Schaffer, *Leviathan and the Air-Pump: Hobbes, Boyle, and the Experimental Life* (Princeton, 1985); and Steven Shapin, *A Social History of Truth: Civility and Science in Seventeenth-Century England* (Chicago, 1994).

111. Taylor, *Sources of the Self,* p. 162.

112. See, for example, Susan R. Bordo, *The Flight to Objectivity: Essays on Cartesianism and Culture* (Albany, N.Y., 1987); and Keller, *Reflections on Gender and Science.* For an attempted defense, see Zagorin, *Francis Bacon,* p. 122.

113. According to Blumenberg, Descartes and Bacon held out hope for a final state of perfect knowledge. Infinite striving for it becomes a theme only with Pascal. See *The Legitimacy of the Modern Age,* pp. 83–84.

of Montaigne's notion of experience was now banished. He had said that "there is no end to our researches; our end is in the other world;"[114] Bacon, Descartes, and their followers replied that the subject of scientific experience, the ongoing community of disinterested inquirers, was immortal. The limit-experience that was death no longer interrupted its interminable quest for knowledge.

Third, whereas for Montaigne (and the more dialectical notion of experience) the memory of past trials and failures remains part of the experience itself, for the scientific method that memory is deliberately obliterated as no longer relevant. For the scientific method, as Hans-Georg Gadamer notes, "experience is valid only if it is confirmed; hence its dignity depends on its fundamental repeatability. But this means that experience, by its very nature, abolishes history."[115] Descartes' well-known gesture of sweeping away the past as doubtful authority was matched by Bacon's unmasking of the false ideas, or *idola* (of the Tribe, the Cave, the Marketplace, and the Theater), whose mystifying charms had produced only confusion in previous thinkers. The foundationalist quest so often attributed to modern philosophy as a whole was thus intimately tied to that growing gap between past experience and the horizon of expectation noted by Koselleck as an identifying mark of the *Neuzeit*. Montaigne's cautious respect for the ancients, as well as his fascination with the proverbs and maxims handed down by folk tradition, was now seen as outmoded. A new respect for unique historical experiences, the *experimentum crucis* that could be narrated as having happened at a specific time and place, may have defined the new scientific mentality, as Peter Dear has persuasively shown,[116] but the history of past missteps and false assumptions nonetheless lost credibility.

Fourth and finally, the bodily learning based on the senses that Montaigne had championed as the fallible yet necessary ground of experience was now increasingly replaced by "objective" instruments whose registering of stimuli from the external world were purportedly more accurate and disinterested. What has been called "the testimony of nonhumans"[117] now replaced that

114. Montaigne, "Of Experience," *Complete Essays*, p. 817.

115. Gadamer, *Truth and Method* (New York, 1986), p. 311.

116. Dear, *Discipline and Experience*, where he locates the change occurring in the 1670s with the work of Newton and Boyle. In contrast, the older notion of experience, based on Aristotelian and Scholastic rationalist universalism, understood it as "a statement of *how things happen* in nature, rather than a statement of *how something had happened* on a particular occasion" (p. 4 [emphasis in original]).

117. Bruno Latour, *We Have Never Been Modern*, trans. Catherine Porter (Cambridge, Mass. 1991), p. 22.

of flesh-and-blood witnesses, whose mortality was irrelevant, in the laboratories of modern science. These instruments did not, to be sure, automatically bring the certainty they were designed to provide. "The view through Galileo's telescope," Agamben has gone so far as to claim, "produced not certainty and faith in experience but Descartes's doubt, and his famous hypothesis of a demon whose only occupation is to deceive our senses." But paradoxically, the antidote was then assumed to be ever more precise and impartial prosthetic devices. "The scientific verification of experience which is enacted in the experiment . . . responds to this loss of certainty by displacing experience as far as possible outside the individual: on to instruments and numbers."[118] The introspective reflexivity that defined Montaigne's version of experience was now repressed or bracketed. The objects of scientific inquiry—whether "revealed" by new technical means or "constructed" by new theories—grew ever more distant from the familiar world of everyday life.

Insofar as the most innovative instruments of the era—the telescope and the microscope—extended the range and acuity of one sense in particular, scientific experience tended to privilege the visual, with its capacity to produce knowledge at a distance, over the other senses.[119] Even when Bacon castigated normal vision for staying on the surface of things and failing to pay attention to the invisible world beneath, he hoped that ultimately its secrets would be "brought to light."[120] Paracelsus's metaphor of "overhearing" nature's secrets was laid to rest.[121] Abetted by innovations in the perspectivalist depiction of space on Renaissance canvases, which seemed to be in tune with the rationalized universe assumed by the new science, the hegemony of

118. Agamben, *Infancy and History,* p. 17. Bacon, to be sure, was not as keen on mathematicizing and geometrizing the world as Descartes, Galileo, and Newton, which has allowed some historians of science, such as Alexandre Koyré, to discount his importance for the scientific revolution. For an attempt to pluralize that revolution and allow Bacon a place in it by contextualizing him within the tradition of craftsmen who experimented with nature, see Thomas Kuhn, "Mathematical versus Experimental Traditions in the Development of the Physical Sciences," in *The Essential Tension: Selected Studies in Scientific Tradition and Change* (Chicago, 1977).

119. I have tried to explore some of the ramifications of the ocularcentric bias of modernity in "Scopic Regimes of Modernity," in *Force Fields: Between Intellectual History and Cultural Critique* (New York, 1993); and *Downcast Eyes: The Denigration of Vision in Twentieth-Century French Thought* (Berkeley, 1993). For a recent caution against overestimating the importance of optical instruments for Bacon, see Catherine Wilson, *The Invisible World: Early Modern Philosophy and the Invention of the Microscope* (Princeton, 1995), p. 50.

120. Bacon, *Novum Organum,* p. 60. On Bacon's use of light as an image of truth and knowledge, see Zagorin, *Francis Bacon,* p. 88.

121. Pagel, *Paracelsus,* p. 50.

the eye meant not only the denigration of the other senses, but also the detextualization of experience in general. A few unheralded figures aside—the Portuguese philosopher John Poinsot (1589–1644) has been recently raised from obscurity to play the role of rule-proving exception[122]—modern thinkers tended to suppress the semiotic and cultural mediation of experience and seek to ground it firmly in pure, primarily visual, observation and controlled experimentation.

It has often been remarked since at least the time of Max Weber that modernity has meant a differentiation of increasingly specialized value spheres. Cognitive, moral, and aesthetic institutions and discourses have gained relative autonomy and generated their own immanent logic of development. Indeed, within them, specialization produced a welter of distinct sub-spheres and isolated disciplines without easy commensurability. The whole, however it may be defined, ceased to hang together in a coherent way. No longer understood in terms of a great chain of being, a multiplicity of resonating similitudes, or a cosmopolis in which the cosmos and the polis are in tune with each other, the modern world struggled to come to terms with what Friedrich von Schiller, in the phrase made famous by Weber, called its "disenchantment." What Bruno Latour has identified as the modern disaggregation of hybrids into their component parts—subject and object, culture (or society) and nature, mind and matter—has meant a penchant for purification and boundary creation.[123] Even if one avoids nostalgia for a supposed era before the fall into "diremption," "alienation," or "fragmentation," it does seem clear that modernity was accompanied by an increasing specialization of function and the loss of a more integrated sense of life.

A comparable process can be discerned in the explicit differentiation of the holistic experience Montaigne sought to unify into several discrete subvariants. The scientific version, based on a transcendental, disembodied, immortal species subject located more in impartial instruments than fallible bodies, activated the etymological link we have seen between experience and experiment, while suppressing the value of accumulated wisdom from the past. But rather than quelling doubts, it only created new ones for students of epistemology, the investigation of the subject and conditions of knowledge that emerged in the wake of rational metaphysics' decline in the eighteenth century. What has been recently been called "Descartes' Problem" had

122. Deely, *New Beginnings*.
123. Latour, *We Have Never Been Modern*.

two dimensions.[124] The first entailed the split or at least unexplained link between everyday sense experience and the mechanical and mathematical workings of the world that were now assumed to produce that experience. What was the relationship, philosophers and scientists increasingly wondered, between hidden depths of reality (called the "occult" by the Scholastics) and its observed surface phenomena?[125] The second dimension of the problem involved the relationship between sense experiences and the propositional thoughts or linguistic representations that were fashioned from them.

In the next chapter, we will trace the central debates that arose among theorists who sought to explicate the role of something called "experience" in cognition, beginning with John Locke, David Hume, and Immanuel Kant. In chapter 3 we will focus attention on the ways in which experience was explored in the moral realm, or more precisely, in that of religion, where, as we have already noted, the valorization of everyday life and mysticism had staked their claims during an earlier era. We will pass on, in chapter 4, to the specific claims of experience in the newly developed discourse about art, which came into its own only in the eighteenth century. The possibility of something called "aesthetic experience" as separate from works of art per se and from other types of experience, cognitive or moral, will be at issue. Chapter 5 will explore the appeal to experience in political terms, noting its capacity to be mobilized by champions of both conservative and radical thought. Chapter 6 will deal with the attempts made by historians and philosophers of history to understand the role of experience as an object of historical inquiry and as something produced by that inquiry in the present. Then in the second half of our narrative, we will turn to the attempts made by a wide range of thinkers in the last century to heal what they lamented as the ruptures of experience and generate or recover a more holistic alternative, restoring—at least to a certain extent—the views of Montaigne. Showing how that alternative was premised on a radical critique of the Cartesian subject of modernity, producing a seemingly paradoxical "experience without a subject," will be the task of our final chapters.

124. John T. Kearns, *Reconsidering Experience: A Solution to the Problem Inherited from Descartes* (Albany, N.Y., 1996).

125. See Keith Hutchison, "What Happened to Occult Qualities in the Scientific Revolution?" *Isis* 73 (1982), pp. 233–53. Ironically, these qualities became less occult as science seemed progressively to reveal nature's secrets, but returned when skeptics like Hume questioned the reliability of the results.

TWO

Experience and Epistemology

The Contest between Empiricism and Idealism

MICHEL DE MONTAIGNE's precariously affirmative skepticism—his tolerance for the fallibility of the senses and the weaknesses of the body—did not easily survive the impatience of early modern thinkers anxious to achieve certain knowledge about the world being laid bare by science.[1] Nor did his attentiveness to the lessons of folk wisdom and the teachings of the ancients, which he honored despite his refusal to follow them blindly. With René Descartes came a desire to start fresh, avoid the errors of the past, and look confidently toward the future. The new prestige of science also meant jettisoning Montaigne's preoccupation with introspection and self-discovery; to be worth taking seriously, experience had to be public, replicable, and verified by objective instruments.[2] Accordingly, Montaigne's stress on coming to terms with our individual mortality as the essential task of living seemed irrelevant to a mentality that identified the subject with the deathless community of scientific researchers.[3] The scientific quest was understood as fundamentally

1. Montaigne did, to be sure, continue to have some defenders. See, for example, Matthew Prior's delightfully witty "A Dialogue between Mr. John Lock [sic] and Seigneur de Montaigne" of 1721, reprinted in *The Literary Works of Matthew Prior,* ed. H. Bunker Wright and Monroe K. Spears, vol. 1 (Oxford, 1959). Prior makes a case for Montaigne's use of rhetoric, disdain for method, and situatedness in the social world, as opposed to Locke's claim to focus entirely on the generic Human Understanding. He has Montaigne say that "All the while you wrote you were only thinking that You thought; You, and Your understanding are the *Personae Dramatis,* and the whole amounts to no more than a dialogue between John and Lock" (p. 620).

2. Descartes' initial move, relying on the certainty of his *cogito* as a source of his being, did, of course, involve an introspective look inward, but his successors soon abandoned this step in the argument about the reality of the external world.

3. This is not to say that early modern men and women were oblivious to the great question of how to confront mortality. For an account of religious and secular approaches, see John McManners, *Death*

different from that of the pilgrim progressing to redemption or the humanist maturing into a stoic able to look death in the face; it was an infinite search for knowledge whose telos was mastery, not reconciliation. The insatiably curious species subject was thus uncoupled from the contingent subject of individual happiness or salvation.[4]

But the doubts that Descartes and Francis Bacon tried so vigorously to still were not slow in returning, as their solutions to the conundrum of experience lost much of their allure. Descartes' faith in deductive reason and innate ideas and Bacon's confidence in inductive experimentation were exposed as what they were: faiths that could not provide the foundation of certainty they had sought. "Pyrrhonism," as Richard Popkin argues at the conclusion of his classic study of modern skepticism, "was to remain a specter haunting European philosophy while philosophers struggled to find a way either to overcome theoretical doubt, or to discover how to accept it without destroying all human certitude."[5] Although scientists, especially those whose fields were grounded in mathematics (such as mechanics and astronomy), continued to be optimistic about the project of attaining certain knowledge, many philosophers began to waver in their confidence, even as they struggled to avoid outright skepticism. Descartes' precarious reconciliation of reason and the senses—his belief that a mechanical understanding of essential reality could ultimately be reconciled with the everyday encounter with its appearances—came undone.

The result, at least among those unable to follow Benedict Spinoza or Nicholas Malebranche in championing a pure, rationalist metaphysics, was a new respect for the realm of the probable as opposed to the certain, and a willingness to countenance its role even in scientific inquiry. Renaissance rhetoricians like Rudolf Agricola had combined dialectic with probability; now similar inclinations were to surface among thinkers whose disdain for the rhetorical tradition remained strong.[6] Despite the frequent characterization of modernity as the victory of the imperious Cartesian quest for cer-

---

and the Enlightenment: Changing Attitudes to Death in Eighteenth-Century France (Oxford, 1985). But when personal experience was subordinated to the transcendental experience of the subject of science, death was turned into a problem to be solved rather than a limit-experience to be explored. According to McManners, "since the rise of modern science, the seventeenth century had seized on the idea that Nature might be manipulated and controlled—leading to speculations on the possibility of breaking the barrier on the human life span; Descartes and Bacon touch on the idea in their vision of a scientific future" (p. 116).

4. See Hans Blumenberg, *The Legitimacy of the Modern Age,* trans. Robert M. Wallace (Cambridge, Mass. 1983), chapter 10.

5. Richard H. Popkin, *The History of Skepticism from Erasmus to Descartes* (New York, 1964), p. 217.

6. On Agricola, see Thomas M. Conley, *Rhetoric in the European Tradition* (Chicago, 1990), pp. 125–28.

tainty over Montaigne's tentative alternative,[7] many Enlightenment thinkers were willing to settle for something less than clear and distinct innate ideas or inductively generated eternal truths (or perhaps were hopeful of gaining something more, even if that "more" were less apodictically true). As a result, the exile of "experience" into supposedly objective instruments and the timeless world of impersonal numbers gradually ended. But when unmediated experience returned to center stage, it was a somewhat withered and diminished figure. No longer the robust facilitator of wisdom, teaching, as Montaigne had put it, that "greatness of soul is not so much pressing upward and forward as knowing how to set oneself in order and circumscribe oneself,"[8] experience was reduced to a modest, problematic, yet indispensable means of knowing or, better put, "understanding" the external world. In addition, what for Montaigne had been an awareness of the limits *within* an essentially holistic notion of experience became a stress on limits or boundaries *between* variants of experience. The entire lived body as a locus of experience was, moreover, replaced by the five senses, in particular that of sight, as the medium of a quest for "reliable" (but not certain) knowledge.

Although Descartes' hopes for a new foundation for absolute truth may have been dashed, his disdain for the "experience" of past authorities nonetheless remained potent in the tradition of modern epistemology. A fully dialectical notion of experience (as opposed to a scientific one), generously including past trials and errors rather than moving beyond them, would have to wait until Georg Wilhelm Friedrich Hegel to be revived, although only with mixed success. When "experience" as learning from the past was allowed back in by earlier thinkers (as we will see was the case with David Hume), it functioned on a psychological level to explain mere belief rather than to ground secure knowledge; to many this seemed a capitulation to skepticism. Although certain French Enlightenment thinkers such as the marquis de Condorcet and Étienne de Condillac acknowledged the importance of the method of "errancy" or conjectural wandering and accepted the risk of error in the process of discovery, modestly acknowledging the ways in which human cognition would always fall short of perfection, they did not incorporate error itself into a higher dialectical notion of truth, as did Hegel.[9]

It is not surprising that various late nineteenth- and twentieth-century

7. See, for example, Stephen Toulmin, *Cosmopolis: The Hidden Agenda of Modernity* (Chicago, 1990).

8. Michel de Montaigne, "Of Experience," *The Complete Essays of Montaigne*, trans. Donald M. Frame (Stanford, 1965), p. 852.

9. On the positive role of error in Enlightenment epistemology, see David Bates, *Enlightenment Aberrations: Error and Revolution in France* (Ithaca, N.Y., 2002).

efforts to recapture a more integrated and robust notion of experience would find fault with its reduction to epistemological questions, exaggerated dependence on visual observation, and preoccupation with natural science, an attitude best captured in Wilhelm Dilthey's often-cited complaint that "there is no real blood flowing in the veins of the knowing subject fabricated by Locke, Hume, and Kant, but only the diluted lymph of reason as mere intellectual activity."[10] Whether it was reason or something else that flooded through those veins can be disputed, but Dilthey expressed a widespread assumption about the wan and restricted quality of the experience examined by the figures he mentioned.

They, of course, belonged to what is normally understood to be the two distinct philosophical traditions that have come to be called empiricism (sometimes sensationalism or associationism) and idealism (or more precisely transcendental idealism). They were, however, united in their refusal to privilege deductive reason, dogmatic revelation, or textual authority as the foundation of knowledge, putting experience in their place. In addition, they shared a common responsibility for the reduction of experience itself to an essentially epistemological question, bracketing its other dimensions. In this chapter, we will attempt to sketch in broad strokes the main lineaments of their struggle to come up with a viable understanding of the role of experience in constituting a knowledge that was more or less foundational, even if no longer pretending to absolute certainty about ontological truths. John Locke and David Hume will take their accustomed places as defenders of an essentially passive notion of experience, while Immanuel Kant will appear in his traditional guise as the instigator of a more activist moment in the epistemological tradition, one grounded in a transcendental rather than merely psychological understanding of the active mind. But we will also attend to the ways in which these conventional portraits are complicated by other tendencies in their writings, which call the simple active/passive dichotomy into question.

Because of the impossibility of presenting all of the intricate arguments and counter-arguments that have been and continue to be made by philosophers and historians of philosophy working in the field of epistemology, only the most central will attract our attention before we pass on to competing variants of the discourse of experience, those that in fact are more deserving of the metaphor of songs we have borrowed from William Blake. What fol-

---

10. Wilhelm Dilthey, *Introduction to the Human Sciences: An Attempt to Lay a Foundation for the Study of Society and History*, trans. Ramon J. Betanzos (Detroit, 1988), p. 73.

lows is thus more in the nature of an ideal type or rational reconstruction than an attempt to do justice to the complexities of the figures whose work has been and continues to be the source of endless commentary. Its justification is not merely the dauntingly large body of material that under the best of circumstances would require some distillation, but also the fact that many of the critics of the epistemological tradition themselves worked with an essentialized, and often reductive, understanding of its legacy.

LOCKE AND THE EXPERIENCE OF THE SENSES

Although never entirely shedding the pejorative connotation clinging to it since the days of Greek medicine and medieval and Renaissance occult practices or losing its linkage to the skeptical tradition launched by Sextus Empiricus, the word "empirical" began to gain a new respect in the seventeenth century, especially in Britain.[11] Isaac Newton's "philosophical modesty," as Voltaire called it, began to win out over Descartes' comparative arrogance, especially when the latter was seen to produce questionable scientific results (the Cartesian claim, for example, that light was transmitted instantaneously was refuted by the Danish astronomer Ole Roemer's observations of the moons of Jupiter in 1676). Increased contact with non-European lands, where previously unknown peoples, flora, and fauna defied incorporation into the neat categories of received thought, bestowed a new respect for the fruits of observation, which had also been given added prestige by the Copernican revolution in astronomy abetted by the telescope. In fields such as medicine, the effects of nondogmatic flexibility and a willingness to experiment, so long associated with quackery, began to produce salutary benefits by the 1750s.[12]

Contrasted with deductive reason, theoretical speculation, and intuitive understanding, empiricism came to be loosely associated with the inductive scientific method whose power had been trumpeted since the time of Francis Bacon. Bacon was himself called the father of empiricism by no less a commentator than Hegel.[13] In the *Novum Organum*, he had, however, dis-

11. See the entry for "Empirical" in Raymond Williams, *Keywords* (New York, 1983).

12. According to Peter Gay, "it was not until mid-century, when the philosophes were at the height of their influence, and partly as a result of their propaganda, that pluralistic empiricism changed the course of medical research." *The Enlightenment: An Interpretation*, vol. 2: *The Science of Freedom* (New York, 1969), p. 22.

13. G. W. F. Hegel, *Vorlesungen über die Geschichte der Philosophie 3, Werke*, ed. E. Moldenhauer and K. M. Michel, vol. 20 (Frankfurt, 1971), pp. 76ff.

paragingly compared empiricists to ants, who "merely collect things and use them,"[14] and sought a method of forcing nature to reveal her secrets more trustworthy than unaided observation. In the hands of the most prominent British empiricists, John Locke, George Berkeley, and David Hume,[15] a significant shift of emphasis occurred. Not only was Bacon's confidence in revealing the mysteries of nature, her universal "forms," through inductive experimentation qualified, so too was his faith in the absolute reliability of the procedures and instruments that were used to wrest those secrets from her. The aggressive and dominating impulse in Baconian science was subtly modified as the more passive and patient moment in "experience" once again came to the fore, a shift signaled by the new concern for what became known as the "givens" of sense data.[16] By the time of Hume, induction itself was questioned as an epistemic tool.[17]

The backdrop against which this change occurred has been dubbed the "emergence of probability" by Ian Hacking.[18] Initially associated with the realm of mere opinion as opposed to true knowledge and identified with the "approbation" of ideas promulgated by learned authorities, probability had been further tarnished by its linkage with the casuistry of the Jesuits in the sixteenth century. The dubious method of "probabilism," as their appeal to testimony and expediency came to be called, had to be overcome before a modern science of probability could be launched. Historians concur that the crucial turning point came around 1660 with the brilliant group of Jansenist theologians/logicians/mathematicians at Port-Royal, most notably Antoine Arnauld, Pierre Nicole, and Blaise Pascal.

14. Francis Bacon, *Novum Organum,* trans. and ed. Peter Urbach and John Gibson (Chicago, 1994), p. 105. Whether Bacon could be called the father of empiricism, as he was approvingly by Robert Hooke and disapprovingly by Hegel, is a matter of much dispute.

15. For a useful overview of their lives and work, see John Dunn, *Locke;* J. O. Urmson, *Berkeley;* and A. J. Ayer, *Hume,* collected as *The British Empiricists* (New York, 1992).

16. The passivity of empiricism was a favorite target of later critics, both in the idealist and pragmatist camps. But as with much else in the reception of empiricism, even the relative importance of passivity in its epistemology has been contested. H. H. Price claims it is "historically false that the empiricists thought the human mind passive. It would be more just to criticize them for making it more active than it can possibly be." *Thinking and Experience* (Cambridge, Mass., 1962), p. 199. Although this may be true in the sense that the empiricists included many unconscious and unintended activities in the understanding, they did not foreground the aggressively active intervention in the world that characterized Baconian science. Moreover, those activities were understood to be temporally subsequent to the givens that came from without.

17. Even recent attempts to salvage some notion of induction acknowledge the power of Hume's critique. See, for example, Max Black, "Induction and Experience," in Lawrence Foster and J. W. Swanson, eds., *Experience and Theory* (Amherst, Mass., 1970).

18. Ian Hacking, *The Emergence of Probability* (Cambridge, 1975).

Hacking notes the dual face of the new theory. Probability meant not only what we have seen it to be in Montaigne, that is, an epistemological tolerance for ambiguity and uncertainty on the part of the knower, which Bacon and Descartes had scorned as unworthy of true science, however it might serve rhetoricians like Agricola. It also meant, and this was the great innovation, a theory of likely frequencies in large numbers of events, such as the throwing of dice or the growth of a population. This latter acceptation, which Hacking calls aleatory as opposed to epistemological, is based on the assumption that beneath the surface of seemingly random events, there can be found regular and stable patterns capable of being revealed through what became known as statistical calculations. Although the mathematical rigor brought to bear on determining those patterns by Pascal and later contributors to probability theory such as Jacob Bernoulli and Pierre-Simon Laplace was far more sophisticated than anything that went before, the premise of their enterprise was surprisingly premodern. The "low sciences" such as alchemy and astrology, condemned by Bacon and Descartes, had been based on the assumption that nature was a legible text. Paracelsus's "doctrine of signatures" meant that the world worked by similitudes and affinities, which could be deciphered.[19] Probability theory also looked to signs of deeper patterns in the seemingly random surface of events, but it did so by applying a mathematical calculus of likely outcomes.

The relationship between the two faces of probability theory, the epistemological and the aleatory (or what might also be called the subjective and objective) was as follows: although humans can have only an imperfect and uncertain understanding of the workings of nature or of society, opinion never being entirely replaceable by fully accurate knowledge, it was wrong to retreat into a debilitating skepticism. For beneath the surface, patterns did indeed exist, patterns that governed the behavior of large numbers of events, if not each individual one. Although even the latter might ultimately be determined rather than random, humans, fallible as they are, will have to be satisfied with the grosser, approximate patterns that a calculus of probabilities revealed to them and should give up the hope for God-like omniscience. But what they need not fear is the chaos that skepticism taken to an extreme might engender. Although ultimate causes might remain hidden, at least the regular patterns that ensued in nature—and perhaps society as well—could

19. As we will see, it was precisely the revival of this approach that characterized Walter Benjamin's attempt in the early twentieth century to restore a robust notion of experience that would reverse its reduction to scientific and epistemological methods. But he did so without any recourse to probability theory.

be discerned. And, so might those that extend into the future, as more optimistic students of probability, like the eighteenth-century *philosophe* Condorcet, would come to believe.[20]

Thus, the revival of a non-Baconian notion of experience, one that relaxed a bit Bacon's stringent standards of knowing the ultimate truth and modified his faith in impersonal instruments of knowledge, could follow in the wake of probability's emergence. Although one might still talk of a lingering cultural crisis during the heyday of British empiricism—and indeed, the memory of the mid-seventeenth-century wars of religion was still fresh enough to produce some anxiety about the residual force of "enthusiasm"[21]—by and large its founders were no longer as exercised by the traumas of post-Reformation Europe as the generations that preceded them. Expecting less of knowledge than Descartes or Bacon, operating in a climate in which tolerance of different religions was gaining acceptance, they were more content with the imperfections of human experience, understood largely in epistemological terms. Although by no means entirely exorcized, the bugaboo of skepticism was no longer quite as frightening.[22] What soon came to be called "common sense" philosophy returned the focus of attention to the everyday world of the common man, and away from the rarified procedures of the religious or scientific virtuoso.[23]

Although Pierre Gassendi's dual critique of Cartesianism and Pyrrhonism was an important prelude to the British empiricist tradition,[24] we must

20. See Keith Michael Baker, *Condorcet: From Natural Philosophy to Social Mathematics* (Chicago, 1976), chapter 3. Baker shows that Condorcet's residual Cartesian hope for a universal science was based on a calculus of probabilities.

21. For an account of Locke that sees his work as a response to the dual threats of skepticism and religious fanaticism, see Nicholas Wolterstorff, *John Locke and the Ethics of Belief* (Cambridge, 1996). Enthusiasm was the bugaboo of Anglican theologians like Henry More (1614–87), whose distaste for emotionally charged rhetoric has been linked by Conley (*Rhetoric in the European Tradition*, p. 168) to the preference for Baconian "plain style" in the newly created Royal Society.

22. See Richard H. Popkin, "Scepticism with regard to Reason in the 17th and 18th Centuries," and G. A. J. Rogers, "Locke and the Skeptical Challenge," in G. A. J. Rogers and Sylvana Tomaselli, eds., *The Philosophical Canon in the 17th and 18th Centuries: Essays in Honor of John W. Yolton* (Rochester, N.Y., 1996).

23. Sometimes "common sense" was marshaled against the empiricists' more paradoxical arguments, the textbook instance being Dr. Johnson's kicking a stone to refute Berkeley's anti-materialism. The Scottish School of Common Sense, led by Thomas Reid and Sir William Hamilton, often sought to respond to the skeptical implications they detected in empiricism. But in many respects Locke, Berkeley, and Hume were themselves appealing to what they construed as the shared perceptions and meanings of the ordinary man.

24. For a good short account, see Ira O. Wade, *The Intellectual Origins of the French Enlightenment* (Princeton, 1971), pp. 207–30. Some of those troubled by the rationalist moments in Locke consider

begin with John Locke (1632–1704), whose contribution to the history of "experience" was as seminal as that of any figure in our story, but whose progeny were an unruly and contentious brood. The responsibility for that outcome belongs largely to Locke himself, who, writing at the dawn of modern philosophy, had not yet acquired the habit of rigorous and consistent usage of a technical vocabulary, so that, as one exasperated commentator has put it, "on almost every topic, there is disagreement over what Locke meant."[25]

The fault also lies with what seems to be a certain number of conceptual confusions and self-contradictions that no amount of philological attentiveness to intentionality can put aright. "Locke," we might say, will forever remain the sum of his texts rather than signify the unified, coherent consciousness behind them (an argument that can be made about virtually every prolific and inventive writer). His main contribution to the tradition of epistemology, his *Essay Concerning Human Understanding*, was, after all, the fruit of nineteen years of sporadic labor before its publication in 1690 and shows the effects of what its author admitted was the stringing together of "incoherent parcels."[26] Written and rewritten during periods of exile and intense political involvement, competing for attention with his great tract on toleration and two treatises on government, it bears the scars of its troubled composition. And finally, the ambiguity of Locke's legacy can be explained by the tension, at times conflict, between what Locke purported to say and the way— rhetorical, figurative, metaphorical, narrative, tropological—that he said it.[27]

Thomas Hobbes the true father of British empiricism, but historically it is Locke who was usually given that honor. In the first chapter of *Leviathan*, Hobbes had claimed that "the original of . . . all [the thoughts of man] is that which we call *sense*, for there is no conception in a man's mind which hath not at first, totally or in parts been begotten upon the organs of sense." *Leviathan; or The Matter, Forme and Power of a Commonwealth Ecclesiasticall and Civil*, ed. Michael Oakeshott (New York, 1962), p. 21. Hobbes's definition of experience was more restricted: "much memory, or memory of many things" (p. 24).

25. I. C. Tipton, "Introduction," *Locke on Human Understanding: Selected Essays* (Oxford, 1977), p. 2. Locke, to be sure, was fully aware of the need to clarify terms in philosophical discourse. See *An Essay Concerning Human Understanding*, ed. John Yolton (London, 1995), p. 280. How successful he was in accomplishing this aim is an open question.

26. Locke, *An Essay Concerning Human Understanding*, p. 4.

27. The importance of Locke's tropological mode of argumentation was noted as early as 1704 in Leibniz's *New Essays Concerning Human Understanding*. It was perhaps not until Paul de Man's "The Epistemology of Metaphor," in *Critical Inquiry* 5, no. 1 (Autumn 1978) that it returned to the foreground. Four recent books by literary critics read Locke rhetorically, although with different conclusions: John Richetti, *Philosophical Writing: Locke, Berkeley, Hume* (Cambridge, Mass., 1983); Cathy Caruth, *Empirical Truths and Critical Fictions: Locke, Wordsworth, Kant, Freud* (Baltimore, 1991); Jules David Law, *The Rhetoric of Empiricism: Language and Perception from Locke to I. A. Richards* (Ithaca, N.Y., 1993); and William Walker,

A moderate tolerance for uncertainty is, to be sure, one of the earmarks of the tradition launched by Locke, so it need not be a source of despair that we have so much trouble knowing exactly what he meant to say, or indeed if what he meant was fully coherent, let alone entirely plausible. His great work, like that of Montaigne before him, was presented, after all, in the form of a tentative essay, not a finished treatise. Our experience of reading and interpreting Locke might itself be called a lesson in the value of probability. It is also an exercise in which the trials and errors of previous interpreters need to be taken seriously rather than dismissed as simple misreadings to be overcome, for they often made powerful contributions to the history of "experience" as it unfolded.

One place to begin is with the question of Locke's relation to the tradition we have identified with Bacon and Descartes, which accompanied the rise of modern science as a model of improved and corrected "raw" experience. Locke was himself trained in physiology and chemistry and studied natural philosophy. He was friendly with such eminent men of science as "the skeptical chymist" Robert Boyle, whose materialist, corpuscular physics he took seriously and from whom he learned the crucial distinction between primary and secondary qualities.[28] Locke also knew and respected the achievements of Newton.[29] It is therefore questionable, as was once the fashion, to claim that Locke was largely disdainful of science because of its untenable use of hypothetical reasoning.[30]

It seems, in fact, that Locke's specific medical training, which resulted in an important paper that was discovered only in the nineteenth century en-

Locke, Literary Criticism, and Philosophy (Cambridge, 1994). Whereas Richetti stresses the drive toward literalizing metaphors in Locke, de Man sees endless figurality. Law argues for a tension between these two tendencies. Caruth continues de Man's analysis, while Walker subjects it to critical scrutiny. For a response, see Adam Potkay, "Writing About Experience: Recent Books on Locke and Classical Empiricism," *Eighteenth-Century Life* 19 (1995).

28. Peter Alexander, "Boyle and Locke on Primary and Secondary Characteristics," in Tipton, *Locke on Human Understanding,* and "Locke's Philosophy of Body," in Vere Chappell, ed., *The Cambridge Companion to Locke* (Cambridge, 1994), p. 60. *The Skeptical Chymist* was the title of a book by Boyle published in 1661. The corpuscular theory was a revival of the atomism espoused by the Greek philosophers Democritus and Epicurus, which had been made popular again by Gassendi.

29. See James L. Axtell, "Locke, Newton, and the Two Cultures," in John Yolton, ed., *John Locke: Problems and Perspectives: A Collection of New Essays* (Cambridge, 1969).

30. See, for example, R. M. Yost Jr., "Locke's Rejection of Hypotheses about Sub-Microscopic Events," *Journal of the History of Ideas* 12, no. 1 (1951); for a critique, see Laurens Laudan, "The Nature and Sources of Locke's Views on Hypotheses," in Tipton, *Locke on Human Understanding*. See also Margaret J. Olser, "John Locke and the Changing Ideal of Scientific Knowledge," *Journal of the History of Ideas* 31, no. 1 (1970).

titled "De Arte Medica," disabused him of the notion that hypotheses without experiential verification were worth anything.[31] As in the case of the Greek Empiriki, he was willing to suspend judgment about ultimate causes and operate on the level of what seemed to be effective in treating an illness. It was necessary, he argued, to work back from effects to possible causes, insofar as the latter might ever be determined. Locke extrapolated this attitude to a general defense of the value of everyday knowledge as opposed to that sought by scientific investigation of ultimate truths ordered systematically. In the *Essay*, he invoked the goodness of God to explain the priority of the former over the latter:

> The infinite wise Contriver of us and all things about us hath fitted our senses, faculties, and organs to the convenience of life and the business we have to do here. We are able, by our senses, to know and distinguish things, and to examine them so far as to apply them to our uses, and several ways to accommodate the exigencies of life. . . . But it appears not that God intended we should have a perfect, clear, and adequate knowledge of them: that perhaps is not in the comprehension of any finite being.[32]

Playing on a celebrated metaphor that had intrigued Boyle and was to play a major role in the Deist argument for God's existence from design, Locke illustrated his point by claiming that it was less important to know the internal workings of a clock than to be able to read its face to tell the time.[33] Implicitly making a teleological argument that reveals his ultimate reliance on religion, however "reasonable," he suggested that the limits of our understanding were introduced for a purpose, the pragmatic one of making our way in the everyday world.

Although Locke, like Descartes before him, called on a benign God at a crucial point in his argument, he differed from his predecessor in two fundamental ways: he never doubted as thoroughly the untrustworthy world of

31. Locke was a colleague of the celebrated physician Thomas Sydenham, who may have been the author of "De Arte Medica." See the discussion in J. R. Milton, "Locke's Life and Times," in Chappell, *The Cambridge Companion to Locke*, p. 9. For discussions of the importance of his medical training, see Patrick Romanell, "Some Medico-Philosophical Excerpts from the Mellon Collection of Locke's Papers," *Journal of the History of Ideas* 25, no. 1 (1964); and Douglas Odegard, "Locke's Epistemology and the Value of Experience," *Journal of the History of Ideas* 26, no. 3 (1965).

32. Locke, *An Essay Concerning Human Understanding*, p. 154.

33. Ibid., p. 155. For a discussion of the metaphor, see Laurens Laudan, "The Clock Metaphor and Probablism," *Annales of Science* 22 (1966).

common sense and opinion, and he never sought to remedy it by recourse to the clear and distinct, innate ideas placed in the mind by the Creator. Descartes, it will be recalled, had included "whatever reaches our understanding either from external sources or from that contemplation which our mind directs backwards on itself"[34] in his definition of experience. Locke, in contrast, followed Pierre Gassendi in tilting the balance—although not entirely, as he still held on to moral intuitions—in favor of external sources. The doctrine of innate ideas was too easily marshaled by those who wanted to defend habitual prejudices as if they were timeless, and Locke, as shown by his celebrated argument for an original social contract, was impatient with claims for traditional legitimacy in epistemology as well as politics. As the celebrated passage in the *Essay* puts it:

> Let us then suppose the mind to be, as we say, white paper void of all characters, without any *ideas*. How comes it to be furnished? Whence comes it by that vast store which the busy and boundless fancy of man has painted on it with an almost endless variety? Whence has it all the materials of reason and knowledge? To this I answer, in one word, experience; in that all our knowledge is founded, and from that it ultimately derives itself.[35]

Lacking innate knowledge imprinted by God, then, the mind was, in the famous phrase (which Locke in fact used only sparingly[36]), a *tabula rasa* whose "ideas" were caused entirely by "experience." By "idea" he meant immediate entities or objects "in the mind," which includes everything called "*phantasm, notion, species,* or whatever it is which the mind can be employed about in thinking."[37] Vaguely formulated and extended beyond the more traditional acceptation of ideas as visual images (from the Greek *eidos*),[38] Locke's "ideas" have sometimes been understood as indirect representations of external ob-

---

34. Descartes, *Rules for the Direction of the Mind,* in *The Philosophical Works of Descartes,* trans. Elizabeth Haldane and G. R. T. Ross (Cambridge, 1968), p. 44.

35. Locke, *An Essay Concerning Human Understanding,* p. 45.

36. The term appears only in the 1671 draft of the *Essay,* not in the final published version. For a discussion, see Walker, *Locke, Literary Criticism, and Philosophy,* pp. 31–32.

37. Locke, *An Essay Concerning Human Understanding,* p. 17.

38. The primacy of vision in Locke's work has been much debated. For an excellent discussion of the entanglement of the visual and the verbal in his "grammar of reflection," see Law, *The Rhetoric of Empiricism,* chapter 2. Catherine Wilson has argued that the rationalists were actually more sensitive to the paradoxes of visual experience than was Locke. See her "Discourses of Vision in Seventeenth-Century Metaphysics," in David Michael Levin, ed., *Sites of Vision: The Discursive Construction of Sight in the History of Philosophy* (Cambridge, Mass., 1997), p. 118.

jects and sometimes as more direct and thus more reliable manifestations of the real objects themselves.[39] The former suggests a phenomenalist empiricism, registering only the play of surface qualities, the latter a realist alternative, positing access to the individual objects that possessed those qualities.[40] "Ideas" have also been seen to include both discrete objects of knowledge and the effects of the ratiocination about them, which are normally called concepts.

However they were understood—and there is warrant in Locke's texts for several different interpretations—ideas were put in the mind by the action of external objects on the senses, that action being produced by material "corpuscles" or atoms traveling from one to the other.[41] In this sense, Locke was a firm realist about the existence of material objects outside of subjective consciousness. The effects of the impingement of those objects appeared on the first level of conscious awareness as "perceptions." "In bare naked *perceptions,*" wrote Locke, "the mind is, for the most part, only passive; and what it perceives, it cannot avoid perceiving."[42] Because of this description of perception as inherently involuntary, John Dewey could claim that "what characterizes sensation and observation, and hence experience, is, in Locke's thought, their coerciveness."[43] Perceptions were, however, for Locke only the building blocks of understanding, for they often have to be aided and improved by what he called judgment. Thus, for example, the eye may see only a flat circle in its visual field but then understand it because of other clues, such as tactile solidity or prior acquaintance with it, as actually a three-dimensional globe.

39. This is not the place to try to resolve the thorny problem of what Locke might have meant by "an idea." For important contributions to the debate, see Maurice Mandelbaum, "Locke's Realism," in *Philosophy, Science, and Sense Perception* (Baltimore, 1964); John W. Yolton, *Locke and the Compass of Human Reason* (Cambridge, 1970) and *Perceptual Acquaintance* (Oxford, 1984); Douglas Greenlee, "Locke's Idea of 'Idea'," in Tipton, *Locke on Human Understanding;* Vere Chappell, "Locke's Theory of Ideas," in Chappell, *The Cambridge Companion to Locke.*

40. For a discussion of the distinction, see Lorenz Krüger, "The Grounding of Knowledge on Experience: A Critical Consideration of John Locke," *Contemporary German Philosophy* 2 (1983), p. 29.

41. Locke, *An Essay Concerning Human Understanding,* p. 310. For an account of Locke's debt to corpuscularism, see Edwin McCann, "Locke's Philosophy of Body," in Chappell, *The Cambridge Companion to Locke.*

42. Locke, *An Essay Concerning Human Understanding,* p. 78.

43. John Dewey, "An Empirical Survey of Empiricisms," *The Later Works, 1925–1953,* vol. 2, *1935–37,* ed. Jo Ann Boydston (Carbondale, Ill., 1987), p. 77. For a critique of the claim that Locke saw the mind as entirely passive, see John W. Yolton, "The Concept of Experience in Locke and Hume," *Journal of the History of Philosophy* 1, no. 1 (1963).

Thus, rather than settling the question of the origin of understanding, Locke's formulations only complicated it. For he acknowledged that "our observation, employed either about *external sensible objects, or about the internal operations of our minds perceived and reflected on by ourselves, is that which supplies our understandings with all the materials of thinking.*"[44] That is, in addition to the perceptions caused by external objects somehow striking our senses, experience also might involve "internal operations" of the mind, such as judgment. What precisely were these operations and processes, since they were not innate ideas, and what role did they play in relation to the stimuli from without? Locke, despite his metaphor of a *tabula rasa*, did admit that something—albeit not ideas—existed in the mind prior to its being written on by external stimuli: "nature, I confess, has put into man a desire of happiness and aversion to misery: these indeed are innate practical principles which (as practical principles ought) do continue constantly to operate and influence all our actions without ceasing; these may be observed in all persons and all ages, steady and universal."[45] However, precisely what the substance of such desires and aversions actually was, Locke insisted, could not be derived universally, as demonstrated by the proliferation of different personal preferences and moral imperatives around the world.

What was shared by all minds, however, was the capacity for what Locke called reflection. It was through such reflective operations as judging, doubting, willing, reasoning, remembering, and believing that the data of the senses, the involuntary input leading to the awareness that Locke called perceptions, were transformed into genuine understanding. Reflection is employed on "simple ideas," which were the immediate effects of the senses, in the way that pleasure and pain could be the immediate effect of sense impressions. Reflection on simple ideas then turns them into "complex ideas" through combinations, abstractions, or comparisons (all of which were more than mere associations).[46] Our understanding of modes, relations, and substances involved complex ideas, which were produced by reflections on the input from the senses. To a certain extent, the passivity of perception had to be supplemented by the labor of a mental agency, which returned to experience a modicum of the active energy that the *tabula rasa* metaphor seemed to deny it.

44. Locke, *An Essay Concerning Human Understanding*, p. 44 (emphasis in original).
45. Ibid., p. 31.
46. Locke, in fact, links mere association with madness in chapter 33 of book 2 of the *Essay*, which shows how far he was from the "associationism" of a David Hartley. For a discussion that sees the irrationality of associationism haunting Locke's account of empirical experience, see Caruth, *Empirical Truths and Critical Fictions*, pp. 20–33.

Locke says that complex ideas can always be traced back to simple ones, of which they are combinations, and the mind does this combining. As a result, some commentators have claimed that Locke's empiricism was always balanced by a residual rationalism, insofar as concepts are made by the mind rather than inductively generated—for example the concept of a centaur.[47] Locke himself conceded as much to his critic Edward Stillingfleet, bishop of Worcester:

> I never said that the general idea of substance comes in by sensation and reflection; or that it is a simple idea of sensation or reflection, though it be ultimately founded in them: for it is a complex idea, made up the general idea of something, or being, with the relation of a support to accidents. For general ideas come not into the mind by sensation or reflection, but are the creatures or inventions of the understanding.[48]

But however much reflection was needed to supplement the information provided by perception, it could not produce the ultimate knowledge of truths that traditional *scientia* had sought. The only essences that might be known, Locke followed Boyle in concluding,[49] were "nominal" rather than "real."

In so arguing, Locke acknowledged the importance of the linguistic mediation of the understanding produced by experience. Book 3 of the *Essay* was, in fact, devoted entirely to the question "Of Words." Although not much remarked in his time and marginalized in the subsequent history of empiricism, Locke's animadversions on language allow him to be called one of the fathers of modern semiotics, as Charles Sanders Peirce came to appreciate.[50] His critique of innatism, it has been more recently argued by Hans Aarsleff,[51]

---

47. See, for example, Elliot D. Cohen, "Reason and Experience in Locke's Epistemology," *Philosophy and Phenomenological Research* 45, no. 1 (September, 1984). In chapter 17 of the *Essay's* fourth book, Locke admits that "sense and intuition reach but a very little way. The greatest part of our knowledge depends upon deductions and intermediate *ideas*" (*An Essay Concerning Human Understanding*, p. 395).

48. Locke to Stillingfleet, *The Works of John Locke*, 10 vols., vol. 4 (London, 1823), p. 19.

49. In his *Origin and Forms of Qualities* of 1666, Boyle had already warned against substantialist, essentialist forms, as had Gassendi before him in his *Syntagma philosophicum* of 1658.

50. In the *Essay*, Locke calls semiotics or "the doctrine of signs" the third branch of knowledge, after natural philosophy and ethics (p. 415). For discussions of Locke's contribution to semiotics, his appreciation by Peirce and the relation of his work to that of his contemporaries and predecessors, see Lia Formigari, *Language and Experience in 17th-Century British Philosophy* (Amsterdam, 1988), chapter 3; John Deely, *New Beginnings: Early Modern Philosophy and Postmodern Thought* (Toronto, 1994), chapter 5; and Norman Kretzmann, "The Main Thesis of Locke's Semantic Theory," in Tipton, *Locke on Human Understanding*.

51. Aarsleff, *From Locke to Saussure: Essays on the Study of Language and Intellectual History* (Minneapolis, 1982).

may well have been aimed as much against an "Adamic" view of language, one in which original names were perfectly at one with their referents, as at Cartesian ideas. Thus, an implicit line can be drawn from Locke via Condillac and Wilhelm von Humboldt up to the linguistic conventionalism of Ferdinand de Saussure, a line which suggests that any purely sensationalist notion of experience for Locke, such as that operative in much of the nineteenth century's criticism of him, was mistaken.[52] As one recent commentator puts it, "at every turn, the tension between rhetorical and expository discourse shapes empiricism's most basic claims concerning what can and cannot be *experienced.*"[53]

Locke, to be sure, had not yet taken a complete "linguistic turn." In comparison with the dominant trends of empiricism in our own day, his was still more concerned with objects and ideas than propositions or other linguistic expressions.[54] Nor had he arrived at the Wittgensteinian conclusion that the context of use rather than the word and its object is the source of meaning.[55] He called articulate sounds "*signs of internal conceptions . . .* marks for the *ideas* within [the speaker's] own mind," and argued that "if we could trace them to their sources, we should find in all languages the names, which stand for things that fall not under our senses, to have had their first rise from sensible *ideas.*"[56] But when it came to anything more complex, Locke was a staunch nominalist, who railed against the confusion of abstract concepts with real objects in the world. As a result, it is difficult to sustain the view that he was in every respect a naive referentialist, either about objects in the world or a mental discourse prior to its linguistic expression.[57]

For all of these reasons, Locke's empiricism was modest about its capacity to know that level of reality sought by *scientia,* whether Aristotelian or Baconian. "The *way* of getting and *improving our knowledge in substances only by experience* and history, which is all that the weakness of our faculties in

52. In his essay on "Locke's Reputation in Nineteenth-Century England," Aarsleff notes one major exception: Henry Rogers, who in an 1854 review of Locke's works criticized the reduction of his notion of experience to unmediated sensation. *From Locke to Saussure,* p. 138.

53. Law, *The Rhetoric of Empiricism,* p. 13 (emphasis in original).

54. Twentieth-century analytic philosophy, to be sure, did not always put language in the place of perception. W. V. O. Quine, for example, maintained that "truth in general depends on both language and extralinguistic fact" ("Two Dogmas of Empiricism," in *From a Logical Point of View* [New York, 1963], p. 36).

55. See the discussion in Jonathan Bennett, *Locke, Berkeley, Hume: Central Themes* (Oxford, 1971), p. 148.

56. Locke, *An Essay Concerning Human Understanding,* pp. 225, 226 (emphasis in original).

57. Ian Hacking's claim that "Locke did not have a theory of meaning. He did not have a theory of public discourse. He had a theory of ideas. That is a theory of mental discourse" *(Why Does Language Matter to Philosophy?* [Cambridge, 1975], p. 52) may thus go a bit too far.

this state of *mediocrity* which we are in this world can attain to," he conceded, "makes me suspect that natural philosophy is not capable of being made a science."[58] Such an attitude seemed to many a perfect accompaniment to the proto-liberal defense of tolerating diverse opinions that Locke provided in political and religious terms. But it left a welter of unanswered questions that his followers in the empiricist tradition and their critics among later idealists struggled to answer, as they sought to find a more coherent and defensible epistemological notion of experience. As one of his most distinguished modern interpreters, John Yolton, has put it:

> If Locke restricts experience to sensation and introspection, then he has not shown how all ideas are derived from experience. But if we allow the extension of this concept of experience to cover any act of the mind, then clearly any mental content will be experiential. Such a position may have been sufficient for Locke, with innatism as the enemy, but it would hardly seem satisfactory for empiricism.[59]

In short, if both everything *in* the mind is experience and everything in the mind *arises* from experience, then experience is just another word for the contents of the mind and fails to explain very much of anything.

HUME BETWEEN SKEPTICISM AND NATURALISM

In the canonical history of British empiricism, Locke's legacy is next developed by George Berkeley (1685–1753), who rose in the Anglican Church in Ireland to become bishop of Cloyne. His major opus, *A Treatise Concerning the Principles of Human Knowledge,* was published in 1710, a year after his important *Essay towards a New Theory of Vision.* Sharing Locke's suspicion of innate ideas as well as his belief that sense impressions were the foundation of experience, Berkeley radicalized his predecessor's empiricism in several crucial ways. Whereas Locke had subscribed to a materialist realism based on corpuscular atoms as the building blocks of the world of objects, Berkeley reasoned that since experience itself gives us no direct acquaintance with

58. Locke, *An Essay Concerning Human Understanding,* p. 380 (emphasis in original).
59. Yolton, "The Concept of Experience in Locke and Hume," *Journal of the History of Philosophy* 1, no. 1 (1963), p. 60. It might be argued in Locke's favor, however, that he never meant to equate absolutely everything in the mind with experience, for example, the desires that seem hard-wired, so this equation is an exaggeration. Still, the ambiguities in his writing could lead to this conclusion.

such substances in themselves, there was no warrant for believing in their existence. "Esse," he liked to insist, "est percipi." Further applying Occam's razor, he dismissed the distinction between primary and secondary characteristics on the same grounds; who, after all, had ever experienced one without the other? Insensible, solid objects absent colored surfaces were verbal abstractions, not actual entities. Although he admired much in Newton's work and welcomed the advances in understanding produced by the systematic inquiries of science, Berkeley decried the claim that empirical evidence could lead to any deeper knowledge of absolute time, space, or motion. Much of his philosophy was thus aimed at subverting improper inferences, often caused by the imperfections of our language.[60]

One need only divide the world, Berkeley argued, into a perceiving spirit and that which was perceived, those ideas in the mind that Locke had assumed were somehow produced by external reality. Ideas included thoughts as well as sensations and perceptions. Berkeley's radical immaterialism, which seemed to many like a refutation of common sense, was based on the belief that we do not actually experience material objects. Their apparent coherence and reliability could be explained instead by the intervention of a benign God who planted the impressions—Berkeley's favored metaphor is "imprint"—on our perceptual apparatus. Our world is not a phantasm of our imagination or no more than a dream, but is as real as we take it to be. We cannot will it into existence, nor can we escape its vivacity and regularity, which set it apart from the figments of our nocturnal imagination. Berkeley, as Popkin has emphasized,[61] was thus not an advocate of skepticism, despite the ways in which he was often read. In fact, because he believed it makes no sense to distinguish at all between ideas and the objects that they represent and resisted a phenomenalist agnosticism about essences, from one angle he can be considered an ontological realist rather than a believer that all we can know are mere surfaces. For mental objects were no less real than material ones. And *pace* Dr. Johnson, he could thus also be understood as reinforcing the belief in the world shared by common sense.

Or at least, Berkeley hoped he was doing so. The results were very different. As Jules David Law has recently put it:

60. As in the case of Locke, much attention has recently been paid to the importance of language in Berkeley. See, for example, Richetti, *Philosophical Writing;* Law, *The Rhetoric of Experience;* and Colin M. Turbayne, *The Myth of Metaphor* (Columbia, S.C., 1970).
61. Richard Popkin, "Berkeley and Pyrrhonism," *Review of Metaphysics* 3 (1951).

the central paradox of Berkeley's philosophical career lies in the fact that every-thing he could say or do to make the world appear more real, more accessible, more certain, served only to make it appear more chimerical, fantastical, and theatrical. No philosopher has ever produced more counter-intuitive-sounding claims from more thoroughly empirical observations or from more common-sensical axioms.[62]

Perhaps the most vulnerable dimension of Berkeley's argument was its re-liance on a benevolent God to insure the reality of the perceptions that con-stituted experience. No less than Descartes and perhaps more than Locke, Berkeley fell back on the assumption of an interventionist deity, who served as the cause of the perceptions/ideas in the human mind, guaranteed the ex-istence of objects, even when they were not perceived, and generally accounted for the regularity and order in the experienced universe. There was a divine language, he claimed, that allowed us as well to translate the data of one sense into that of another.[63]

But what if such a *deus ex machina* were denied? How could a thorough-going skepticism be kept at bay? The answer can be seen in the radicaliza-tion of the empiricist tradition by David Hume, whose "pagan"[64] distrust of any explanation based on the providential intervention of God both under-mined earlier notions of experience and helped establish new ones. His provocative reconceptualization of the role of experience provided not only a model for later empiricists, but also a challenge to those in the idealist tra-dition, such as Kant, who found his solutions untenable. And as an ancillary effect, it also helped launch the career of experience as a political touchstone, whose trajectory from conservatives like Edmund Burke to Marxists like Ray-mond Williams and E. P. Thompson we will trace in chapter 5.

62. Law, *The Rhetoric of Empiricism*, p. 94.

63. For a discussion of this claim, see Geneviève Brykman, "Common Sensibles and Common Sense in Locke and Berkeley," in Rogers and Tomaselli, *The Philosophical Canon in the 17th and 18th Centuries.*

64. In *The Enlightenment: An Interpretation*, 1: *The Rise of Modern Paganism* (New York, 1968), Peter Gay calls Hume "the modern pagan" (p. 67) and situates his work in a general Enlightenment appropri-ation of classical thought. Hume lost his own religious belief when he read Locke and Clarke in his early twenties, wrote against miracles, clerical hypocrisy, enthusiasm, and superstition, and published a de-bunking *Natural History of Religion* in 1757. For discussions, see James Noxon, "Hume's Concern with Religion," in Kenneth R. Merrill and Robert W. Shahan, eds., *David Hume: Many-sided Genius* (Norman, Okla., 1976); and J. C. A. Gaskin, "Hume on Religion," in David Fate Norton, ed., *The Cambridge Com-panion to Hume* (Cambridge, 1993). Although Hume attacked rational arguments for the existence of God, such as the proof from design, his skeptic's reservation about disproving anything categorically, and his belief that there may be, despite everything, some sort of Supreme Being prevented him from being an unequivocal atheist.

Hume shared Locke's suspicion of innate ideas and the abuse of deductive reason, agreeing that Newton's "experimental method" could be applied to the moral, as well as natural, sciences. He ridiculed as absurd Malebranche's claim that Adam came into the world with all of his rational powers intact.[65] But Hume took seriously Berkeley's argument against Locke's ontological realism and distinction between primary and secondary qualities. There was, he agreed, no warrant for a belief in material objects beyond objects of our conscious experience; double-existence is one too many.[66] He rejected as well Berkeley's idealist alternative, discerning instead in his work "the best lessons of skepticism, which are to be found either among ancient or modern philosophers."[67] Moreover, although approving Locke's abandonment of the quest for certainty (indeed, extending it to the moral realm as well), he doubted that probability would permit the degree of confidence in the underlying regularity of the world that Locke had assumed it did; in no sense, he warned, could it be construed as a variant of rational understanding.[68] In his major epistemological works, *A Treatise of Human Nature* of 1739 and *Enquiry Concerning Human Understanding* of 1748, Hume radically reduced the remnant of rationality that remained in his empiricist predecessors, leaving only the mathematical truths that were purely in the realm of ideas.

Along with the reduction of rationality went a radical diminution of the subject whose reason was assumed to be congruent with that of the world outside. Locke and Berkeley had maintained a traditional Cartesian sense of the existence of the conscious subject—a thinking, rather than extended substance—who had experiences, even if they deprived it of innate ideas. Their "tabula" was thus never completely "rasa," as shown by the mind's reflective capacities to turn simple impressions into complex ideas. With Hume, on the other hand, the coherent and enduring identity of the self prior to the sense experiences "it" had was far from self-evident. Rejecting Locke and Berkeley's belief in the immortality of the soul, he sought to ground think-

65. Hume, *An Abstract of a Book Lately Published, entitled, A Treatise on Human Nature etc.* (Cambridge, 1938), pp. 13–14.

66. For a discussion of this theme, see Yolton, *Perceptual Acquaintance*, chap. 8.

67. David Hume, *An Enquiry Concerning Human Understanding* (La Salle, Ill., 1966), p. 173.

68. See David Owen, "Hume's Doubts about Probable Reasoning: Was Locke the Target?" in M. A. Stewart and John P. Wright, eds., *Hume and Hume's Connexions* (Edinburgh, 1994). For a more positive assessment of Hume's belief in the ability of probability to provide a modicum of valid knowledge, which draws on Norman Kemp Smith's interpretation of Hume as a naturalist, see Baker, *Condorcet*, chapter 3. See also the discussion in Paul K. Alkon, "The Odds against Friday: Defoe, Bayle, and Inverse Probability," in Paula Backscheider, ed., *Probability, Time, and Space in Eighteenth-Century Literature* (New York, 1979), pp. 39–40.

ing in the matter of the body, on which impressions were imprinted.[69] In certain places in his writings, the subject is equated simply with the succession of sensations that follow each other, the heap or bundle of impressions that are experience itself. Personal identity, he anticipated Friedrich Nietzsche in arguing, is a verbal artifact, a function of grammar, not reality.[70] It is as if the dissolution of the object world exterior to sense experience is mirrored by the comparable dissolution of the subject that has it; what is left is only the fleeting, impermanent reality of sense experience itself. This is normally taken to be a variant of the extreme phenomenalist reading of empiricism applied inwardly as well as outwardly, an interpretation that turns Hume into a precursor of later philosophers like Ernst Mach.[71]

Hume, however, was by no means entirely consistent in his description of the subject of experience, with the result that his commentators have struggled for centuries trying to reconcile his radically skeptical outbursts with the contrary arguments that suggest a more naturalist philosophy of commonsensical belief in some sort of enduring self, which was not entirely a function of its accumulated external impressions.[72] What Hume had argued in the section "Of Personal Identity" in the *Treatise* was itself qualified in the appendix to the book, where he admitted that "all my hopes vanish, when I come to explain the principles, that united our successive perceptions in our thought or consciousness. I cannot discover any theory, which gives me satisfaction on this head."[73] Hume's struggle is also shown by the fact that

69. Hume, "Of the Immortality of the Soul," in *Essays: Moral, Political and Literary,* ed. Eugene F. Miller (Indianapolis, 1987). See also John P. Wright, "Hume, Descartes, and the Materiality of the Soul," in Rogers and Tomaselli, *The Philosophical Canon in the 17th and 18th Centuries.*

70. Hume, *Treatise of Human Nature,* p. 262. Compare with Nietzsche's claim that we will not get rid of the biggest subject of them all, God, unless we abolish grammar.

71. As early as Thomas Reid's *Inquiry into the Human Mind* of 1764, Hume has been read as a thoroughgoing phenomenalist. For dissenting interpretations which deny that phenomenalism is Hume's final position, see Livingston, *Hume's Philosophy of Common Life,* chapter 1; and Charles H. Hendel, *Studies in the Philosophy of David Hume* (Indianapolis, 1963), appendix 4. For an argument that "as a philosopher Hume was a phenomenalist, but it was only as a philosopher that he accepted phenomenalism: in his other capacities or moods he did not," see Mandelbaum, *Philosophy, Science, and Sense Perception,* p. 122.

72. The classical defense of Hume's naturalism can be found in Norman Kemp Smith, *The Philosophy of a David Hume* (London, 1941); see also Barry Stroud, *Hume* (London, 1977), and R. A. Mall, *Naturalism and Criticism* (The Hague, 1975). For a response reasserting his skepticism, see Robert J. Fogelin, *Hume's Skepticism in the Treatise of Human Nature* (London, 1985). For a defense of him as a "post-Pyrrhonian," see Donald W. Livingston, *Hume's Philosophy of Common Life* (Chicago, 1984). For a pro-skeptical rebuttal, see Wayne Waxman, *Hume's Theory of Consciousness* (Cambridge, 1994). Most recently, Claudia M. Schmidt has read Hume as a historical rather than naturalist thinker, who escapes skepticism by locating reason in history. See her *David Hume: Reason in History* (University Park, Pa., 2003).

73. Hume, *Treatise of Human Nature,* p. 636.

at times he resorted to the visual metaphor of the theater as a way to describe the mind, which suggests a spectatorial self external to its impressions, but then hastened to warn that "the comparison with the theater must not mislead us. They are the successive perceptions only, that constitute the mind."[74]

One possible way out of the dilemma is to argue that Hume rejected a strong a priori, epistemic notion of the mind, such as that which Kant would later call transcendental, but he did allow for something gradually to emerge as the product of discrete encounters with the world over time, which left some sort of permanent residue. That is, for Hume, experience once again gained its temporal dimension as accumulated learning, an acceptation that was clearly in operation when he discussed the value of experience in political matters, where abstract reason was a misleading guide, and defended the importance of studying history.[75] Memory, which was a marginal issue for earlier empiricists, here regained the central role in experience that we have seen it enjoy in Montaigne. Hume thus emphasized the importance of temporality and even narrative as a fundamental dimension of experience.[76]

In the epistemological sense—or rather more precisely, the psychological—the self was the function of the repetition of discrete experiences over time. Whereas Locke disdained the association of ideas through repetition as an inferior form of knowledge, Hume fell back on it as the primary source—but not logical justification—of those inductive judgments that he denied were based in even a probabilistic knowledge of the real world external to the self.[77] His famous critique of the relation that we assert between an effect and its apparent cause was based on the argument that we tend to attribute causality to what habitually precedes something else, but there is no rational

74. Ibid., p. 253.

75. For example, Hume claimed in his essay "On the Independence of Parliament" that if "separate interest be not checked, and be not directed to the public, we ought to look for nothing but faction, disorder and tyranny from such a government. In this opinion I am justified by experience. . . ." *Essays: Moral, Political and Literary,* p. 43. He praised the study of history, to which he devoted much of his energies, in the following terms: "we should be forever children, were it not for this invention, which extends our experience to all past ages, and to the most distant nations. . . ." "Of the Study of History," in *Essays: Moral, Political and Literary,* p. 566.

76. For accounts of the importance of temporality and narrative for Hume, which undercut the assumption that he saw experience in atomistic and mechanistic terms, see Livingston, *Hume's Philosophy of Common Life,* chapter 5; and Schmidt, *David Hume.*

77. In so doing, Hume was anticipated by defenders of rhetoric such as Chesneau DuMarsais (1676–1756), whose *Des Tropes* of 1730 is discussed in Conley, *Rhetoric in the European Tradition,* pp. 197–98. In general, Hume was far friendlier to rhetoric than Locke. See his lament about the decline of classical eloquence in "Of Eloquence," *Essays: Moral, Political and Literary.*

inference to be drawn about the necessity of this link.[78] In matters of fact (as distinct from pure "relations of ideas," or what Kant would later call analytical truths),[79] constant conjunction, contiguity in space and time, leads us to expect a continuation of what has happened in the past, but we have no logical guarantee that it will happen again. Indeed, the very claim that the future will replicate the past is based on a circular assumption that supposes precisely the resemblance or identity between the two that it needs to (and cannot) demonstrate.[80]

Custom, habit, and repetition were all part of experience in the broad sense of the term, which provided the grounds of plausible *belief* about the likely course of the future as well as the past, but not firm *knowledge*. Epistemology is here reduced largely to the psychology of credibility and cultural conditioning based on convention. Hume himself, it should be noted, did not claim anything more for his own philosophy, which could not pretend to scientific rigor based on deductive demonstration or inductive proof.[81] Although he vigorously argued that external impressions and observation were the sources of all understanding,[82] his own practice, grounded as it was on tacit

78. Hume, it should be noted, did not deny causality per se, only the ability to justify it inferentially. "I never asserted so absurd a proposition as that anything might arise without a cause," he wrote to a friend, "I only maintained that our certainty of the Falsehood of that proposition proceeded neither from Induction nor Demonstration, but from another source." Quoted in Mall, *Naturalism and Criticism*, p. 6.

79. Hume acknowledged that mathematical truths were based on "relations of ideas" that were different from "matters of fact." See *An Enquiry Concerning Human Understanding*, p. 25. This distinction was operative in one of the most famous passages in his work: "If we take in our hand any volume, of divinity or school metaphysics, for instance, let us ask, *Does it contain any abstract reasoning concerning quantity or number?* No. *Does it contain any experimental reasoning concerning matter of fact and experience?* No. Commit it then to the flames: for it can contain nothing but sophistry and illusion." *An Enquiry Concerning Human Understanding*, p. 184. For a discussion of his use of the distinction, see Alexander Rosenberg, "Hume and the Philosophy of Science," in Norton, *The Cambridge Companion to Hume*. It was thus incorrect of John Dewey to argue (in *The Quest for Certainty: A Study of the Relation between Knowledge and Action* [New York, 1929], p. 156) that "the failure of empiricism to account for mathematical ideas is due to its failure to connect them with acts performed. In accord with its sensationalist character, traditional empiricism sought their origin in sensory impressions, or at most in supposed abstractions from properties antecedently characterizing physical things." Whether all of Hume's "relations of ideas" were precisely the same as Kant's analytic truths, based on tautological identity, and his "matters of fact" equivalent to Kant's synthetic judgments has been contested by Robert E. Butts, "Hume's Skepticism," *Journal of the History of Ideas* 20, no. 3 (June–September, 1959).

80. Hume, *An Enquiry Concerning Human Understanding*, p. 39.

81. For a discussion of this premise, see Yolton, "The Concept of Experience in Locke and Hume," pp. 63–65.

82. In the introduction to the *Treatise*, Hume wrote of all explanations of ultimate truths in the sciences and the arts, "none of them can go beyond experience, or establish any principles which are not founded on that authority" (p. xviii).

premises that were never simply derived from passive encounters with reality, performatively indicated otherwise.

When pressed to explain why unsupported beliefs were so powerful—beliefs that subtended the assumption of both subjective and objective identity beyond the discrete impressions of ephemeral qualities—Hume turned to a characteristic of the mind that had played a marginal role in his empiricist predecessors: the imagination.[83] "Experience is a principle, which instructs me in the several conjunctions of objects for the past," he wrote. "Habit is another principle, which determines me to expect the same for the future; and both of them conspiring to operate upon the imagination, make me form certain ideas in a more intense and lively manner, than others, which are not attended with the same advantages."[84] Although it was the vivacity of immediate sense data that allowed us to know that impressions were prior to ideas, the imagination, along with memory (which was at least assumed to be based on past encounters with the real world), provides us with the connecting tissue that results in commonsensical ideas of objects and subjects enduring over time and able to cause effects in each other. It adds strength to the propensity to believe, allowing us to anticipate the future as a continuation of the past, even if it cannot support certain or even probable knowledge that it will. The imagination also plays a critical role in the development and intensity of the human passions, which was one of Hume's great themes.[85] To this extent, despite his apparent emphasis on passivity in our reception of impressions from without, which led many to think of him as a defender of an entirely a posteriori empiricism based on "immediate" sense perception, Hume allowed some place for a modicum of constitutive activity in the mind. But what was crucial is that the imagination was a non-reflective faculty that could not supply demonstrative and indicative arguments based on evidence for its conclusions. Like raw perception itself, imagination was unsystematic, prior to judgment, and unbeholden to its critical strictures. As P. F. Strawson puts it, imagination is for Hume, "a concealed art of the soul, a magical faculty, something we shall never fully understand."[86]

83. For accounts of its importance in his thought, see Mall, *Naturalism and Criticism,* chapter 2; Yolton, *Perceptual Acquaintance,* chapter 9; and Waxman, *Hume's Theory of Consciousness,* chapter 2.

84. Hume, *Treatise of Human Nature,* p. 265.

85. Ibid., pp. 424–27. Book 2 of the *Treatise* is devoted to the passions, whose importance is evident in one of Hume's most widely quoted remarks: "Reason is, and ought only to be the slave of the passions, and can never pretend to any other office than to serve and obey them" (p. 415). For a discussion of this issue, see Fogelin, *Hume's Skepticism in the Treatise of Human Nature,* chapter 9.

86. P. F. Strawson, "Imagination and Perception," in Foster and Swanson, *Experience and Theory,* p. 34.

Placing imagination above reason could, of course, open the door to a philosophy that had no way to distinguish between figments (or even hallucinations) and legitimate perceptions. Although he distrusted deductive rationality, Hume was not seeking to overturn "reasonable" belief. The critical check on fancy producing total fabrications and counterfeit beliefs, which Hume was anxious to distinguish from warranted ones, was the frequent repetition of the latter in the experience of all men. "I must distinguish in the imagination," Hume explained, "betwixt the principles which are permanent, irresistible, and universal; such as the customary transition from causes to effects, and from effects to causes; And the principles, which are changeable, weak, and irregular."[87] Oddly, the imagination was thus given a powerful role by Hume only when it confirms what is already part of prior experience, only when it is in harmony with custom and habit and reinforces our sense of the world's reality. We are not yet on the threshold of the Romantic age, when imagination would be given a much more constitutive and transfigurative role (and contrasted with wild and unproductive "fancy"). Hume's corrosive skepticism was thus kept in check by his conservative reliance on the irresistible power of customary belief.[88] If this were a naturalism, it was one based on a view of human nature that complacently saw in what had existed for a long time a reflection of eternal human qualities.[89] As one recent commentator put it, "natural in the Humean sense is all that is easy and genuine. Natural is opposite to unusual, miraculous and artificial."[90]

Whether skeptical or naturalist, Hume's radicalization of the empiricist account of experience left it with many unanswered questions. How, for example, could one isolate the sense impressions that were purportedly prior to the beliefs we have of the objects they appear to signify? If our experience is always already structured by beliefs based on memory, habit, custom, and imagination, how could Hume claim that it was immediate observation or perception that was the basis of his anti-realist phenomenalism? Why assume that such immediate encounters with the external world could

87. Hume, *Treatise of Human Nature*, p. 225. Later, he will define the understanding as "the general and more establish'd properties of the imagination" (p. 267).

88. Hume's epistemology was thus of a piece with his avowed politics, which have allowed him to be called the "first conservative philosopher." Livingston, *Hume's Philosophy of Common Life*, p. 122.

89. In his *Treatise* (pp. 280–81), Hume explicitly argued for the universality and unalterability of human nature. It was not difficult for later critics to show that he had generalized too quickly from the well-bred gentlemen of his day, whose trustworthiness had been a premise of the scientific revolution as well, according to Steven Shapin, *A Social History of Truth: Civility and Science in Seventeenth-Century England* (Chicago, 1994).

90. Mall, *Naturalism and Criticism*, p. 38.

be broken down into simple components—the pure redness, say, of a red dress—rather than being intrinsically complex, multi-layered, and irreducible to its supposed elemental components (what might be called, following A. J. Ayer, sense-fields)?[91] Why assume that those discrete components were what recurred in different experiences, allowing memory and imagination to support belief, rather than variations and shadings, which the mind—or perhaps the categorizing power of language—yoked together into a single, identical quality? What Wilfrid Sellars, writing from a Hegelian/Wittgensteinian position, would later denounce as the "Myth of the Given"[92] involved positing a temporal order—basic perceptions first, followed by reflection, memory, imagination, etc.—that had little plausible warrant in our normal way of being in the world.

No less problematic was Hume's account of the self, which oscillated between a passive receptor of stimuli from without, possessing no genuine identity over time, and an imaginative generator of the unjustified but necessary beliefs that allowed us to function in daily life. Never fully explaining what faculties of the mind beyond the vaguely defined "imagination" allowed us to remember, compare, and then associate discrete impressions in ways that produced belief, or demonstrating how conventional pressures could account for purportedly universal experiences, Hume's psychologistic vaporization of the enduring epistemic self thus left as many questions open as it resolved. If Hume's inconclusive account of the subject was difficult to accept for very long, so too was his dissolution of the object into nothing but a succession of its discrete experienced qualities. How, after all, could empiricism sustain its claim that the foundation of probable knowledge or reasonable belief was in everyday observation when the objects of scientific knowledge grew more and more theoretical and counterintuitive? As the gap between even inferential observations and the theoretically or mathematically generated objects of science widened, it became increasingly difficult to fall back on sense impressions as the basis of truth claims. What John T. Kearns calls Descartes' Problem, the disparity between commonsensical and scientific versions of reality, could not be sidestepped forever. As he notes, "once objects that can't be observed came to be a scientific commonplace, Hume's principles were undermined. . . . we can't point to experiences which confer intelligibility on concepts of things unobservable."[93] In short, as John Yolton has concluded, Hume's

91. A. J. Ayer, *Hume*, in *The British Empiricists*, p. 229.
92. Wilfrid Sellars, *Empiricism and the Philosophy of Mind* (Cambridge, Mass., 1967).
93. John T. Kearns, *Reconceiving Experience: A Solution to a Problem Inherited from Descartes* (Albany, N.Y., 1996), p. 104.

"science of human nature" was an attempt at a kind of introspective enterprise, but it is really a metaphysic of experience, asserting conclusions which could not—and which are not—established through observation and experiment. In fact, most of his conclusions—those supposed to be typically "Humean"— can be deduced from two principles: that perceptions are all that are present to the mind and that ideas are always preceded by and copies of impressions. In short, Hume used the method of reasoning rather than his own announced method of experiment and observation.[94]

If the empiricist attempt to generate a plausible account of experience in epistemology thus foundered, the return to innate ideas and deductive rationality had nonetheless been successfully blocked. A new initiative would have to be launched in order to provide a more defensible concept of the term, one that would try to address the unanswered questions left by the skeptical implications of phenomenalism and the conservative conventionalism of its naturalist, associationist, psychologistic alternative. The task was taken up, as every schoolboy historian of philosophy knows, by Immanuel Kant, to whose reconceptualization of experience—always *Erfahrung*, with the connotation of a journey over time, never *Erlebnis*, suggesting pre-reflective, holistic immediacy[95]—we now turn.

KANT AND THE TRANSCENDENTALIZATION OF COGNITIVE EXPERIENCE

Hume was first translated into German in 1755, with Johann Georg Sulzer's edition of *An Enquiry Concerning Human Understanding*. Its appearance shortly after the death of the last giant of rationalist metaphysics, Christian Wolff, signaled a new turn in German philosophy. Paradoxically, the way had been prepared by a religious thinker, the Pietist philosopher and theologian Christian August Crusius, who stressed the limitations of human knowledge and the need for fideistic rather than logical or metaphysical arguments for God's existence.[96] Although it took a while for Kant to absorb the full im-

94. Yolton, "The Concept of Experience in Locke and Hume," p. 69.

95. The "setting out on a journey" in Kant's *Erfahrung* has been recently stressed by Charles P. Bigger in *Kant's Methodology: An Essay in Philosophical Archeology* (Athens, Ohio, 1996), p. 1. Drawing on phenomenological arguments, he claims as well that "method" connotes "being on the way."

96. On the importance of Crusius, see Giorgio Tonelli, "Crusius, Christian August," *Encyclopedia of Philosophy*, I, p. 270. Crusius was part of the school of Christian Thomasius, which was more pragmatic and experientially inclined than the rival school of Christian Wolff, which was more purely rationalist.

pact of Hume's work—not all of which was immediately available in a language he could read—he was deeply affected by what he took, rightly or wrongly, to be Hume's devastating exercises in radical skepticism.[97] Their profound impact on his abandonment of the deductive rationalism that had characterized the German philosophy of his day—helping him awaken, as he famously put it, from his "dogmatic slumber"—meant that for a dozen years Kant struggled to find an answer to what he read as the corrosive and irrationalist implications of Hume's thought.[98] Kant was especially anxious to find a new foundation for knowledge that would go beyond the associationist conventionalism that he took to be Hume's final resting place. Hume, he worried, had reduced the mind to its psychological functioning and substituted the fragile consensus of common sense and habitual repetition for the stronger certainties of logical inference and universal reason. As a result, he could provide no bulwark against the twin dangers of religious fanaticism and irrationalist emotivism, which Kant, a staunch defender of the *Aufklärung* and critic of the rule-breaking poets of the *Sturm und Drang*, was so determined to resist. Relying on the lesser certainties of probability theory or sacrificing philosophical rigor to rhetorical argumentation was, he feared, insufficient as an answer to the threat of radical doubt, which no amount of naturalist common sense could set to rest.[99] And even imagination, which in its more sober form had come to the rescue for Hume, could not supply

97. There have been many attempts to spell out precisely when and in what sense Kant was affected by Hume, as well as to assess the validity of his grasp of what he read (which apparently did not include all of the *Treatise*). See, for example, Arthur Lovejoy, "On Kant's Reply to Hume," *Archiv für die Geschichte der Philosophie* 19 (1906); E. W. Schipper, "Kant's Answer to Hume's Problem," *Kant-Studien*, 53 (1961); M. E. Williams, "Kant's Reply to Hume," *Kant-Studien*, 55 (1965); Mall, *Naturalism and Criticism;* Lewis White Beck, *Essays on Kant and Hume* (New Haven, 1978), and his "A Prussian Hume and a Scottish Kant," in Beryl Logan, ed., *Immanuel Kant's Prolegomena to Any Future Metaphysics: in Focus* (London, 1996); and Manfred Kuehn, "Kant's Conception of 'Hume's Problem'," also in Logan. Kuehn provides a detailed description of the waves of Hume's reception in eighteenth-century Germany.

98. For a close reading of the years between Kant's first encounter with Hume and the publication of the *Critique of Pure Reason,* which draws on unpublished material, see Paul Guyer, *Kant and the Claims of Knowledge* (Cambridge, 1987).

99. In the preface to the first edition of the *Critique of Pure Reason,* Kant wrote: "As regards *certainty,* I have bound myself by my own verdict: that holding *opinions* is in no way permissible in this kind of study; and that whatever in it so much as resembles a hypothesis is contraband, which is not to be offered for sale at even the lowest price but must be confiscated as soon as it is discovered." *Critique of Pure Reason,* unified edition, trans. Werner S. Pluhar (Indianapolis, 1996), p. 10. I will refer to the pages in this edition rather than the older convention of giving both "A" and "B" pages according to which original edition (1781 or 1787) is cited; they are given in the margins of this edition for those who want to verify their provenance. For a discussion of Kant's hostility to rhetoric, see Conley, *Rhetoric in the European Tradition,* p. 244.

enough of the ballast to hold down the flights of fancy that Kant had so disliked in the *Schwärmerei* of visionaries like Emanuel Swedenborg.[100] Although he did accord it an essential role in perceiving identities over time and subsuming different objects under the same concept, Kant could not follow Hume in assigning imagination the purely associative task of producing unsubstantiated beliefs in continuity.[101]

This is clearly not the place to hazard yet another extended rehearsal, let alone serious critique, of Kant's complex response to Hume's challenge, which seemed to some a capitulation to skepticism, to others the hopeful prolegomenon, as Kant himself put it, to a future metaphysics.[102] We only have time to make a few central points about the role of experience, as he conceptualized it, in that response. Although Kant could not return to the discredited deductive rationalism of earlier metaphysicians, with their systematic claim to know the whole of reality, he found at least some inspiration in one aspect of their legacy, which had been particularly developed by Gottfried Wilhelm Leibniz: the active, self-legislating quality of the human mind. He agreed with his German predecessor that the mind was not, as Descartes

100. The importance of Kant's abhorrence of Swedenborg is stressed in Hartmut Böhme and Gernot Böhme, "The Battle of Reason with the Imagination," in James Schmidt, ed., *What Is Enlightenment? Eighteenth-Century Answers and Twentieth-Century Questions* (Berkeley, 1996).

101. In the literature on Kant, there has been vigorous debate over how far his suspicion of the imagination extended. For a recent discussion of it, focusing on Heidegger's critique and Dieter Henrich's response, see Jane Kneller, "The Failure of Kant's Imagination," in Schmidt, *What Is Enlightenment?* See also Jonathan Bennett, *Kant's Analytic* (Cambridge, 1966); and Eva Schaper, *Studies in Kant's Aesthetics* (Edinburgh, 1979), which stress his disdain, and Strawson, "Imagination and Perception," which argues for a more generous reading. See also John H. Zammito, *The Genesis of Kant's Critique of Judgment* (Chicago, 1992), which shows that in Kant's later work on aesthetics, imagination came to play a still more positive role. For a suggestive attempt to read the entirety of Kant's work that sees the role of productive imagination as crucially significant in all of the Critiques, see Sarah L. Gibbons, *Kant's Theory of Imagination: Bridging Gaps in Judgement and Experience* (Oxford, 1994). The issue is complicated by the possibility that the term did not have the identical meaning for the two thinkers, which has led one commentator to claim that Hume's imagination is "simply the Kantian understanding in disguise." See W. H. Walsh, "Hume's Concept of Truth," in *Reason and Reality,* Royal Institute of Philosophy Lectures, vol. 5 (London, 1970–71), p. 116. A similar argument is made by Mall, in *Naturalism and Criticism,* who claims that the "a priori imagination" in Hume provided "principles" that were loose versions of the "categories" supplied by Kant's "understanding."

102. For an account of the immediate reception of Kant's work, see Frederick C. Beiser, *The Fate of Reason: German Philosophy from Kant to Fichte* (Cambridge, Mass., 1987). Beiser shows that there were Lockeans in Germany, who regarded it as a return to scholastic rationalism, as well as those, like Moses Mendelssohn, who feared the skeptical implications of his "all-destroying" philosophy. Kant's own characterization of his work in terms of the ground-clearing for a more viable, non-dogmatic metaphysics is captured in the title of his 1783 work *Prolegomena to Any Future Metaphysics* (where the phrase "dogmatic slumber" is introduced). It is usefully available with commentaries in Logan, *Immanuel Kant's Prolegomena to Any Future Metaphysics.*

and Spinoza had maintained, a substance, but an activity (an assumption that was to be crucial for his celebrated defense of human freedom and moral autonomy). The British empiricists, to be sure, were themselves never supporters of a fully passive notion of the mind, as we have had ample opportunity to note. But from the point of view of Kant, they had relied too much on the external generation of ideas through the senses to provide a coherent epistemology that would fulfill the requirements of true *scientia* (or in German, *Wissenschaft*).

Kant's famous "Copernican revolution"[103] in philosophy boldly sought an answer by focusing less on the object of knowledge than the subject, a constitutive subject that was far more than the succession of its perceptions or site of habitual repetition.[104] As a result, his notion of experience has sometimes been linked to that active interventionism in the world characterizing Baconian scientific method, which itself has been situated in a tradition dubbed "maker's knowledge" that included figures as disparate as Nicolaus of Cusa and Giambattista Vico.[105] What perhaps set Kant apart from others in that tradition was his restriction, at least in the *Critique of Pure Reason*, to objects formed solely by knowledge, which he carefully distinguished from actual objects in the world as well as from objects of pure thought. Against Berkeley's reduction of those objects to nothing but ideas in the mind put there by God, illusions to the extent that they were taken for independent, external realities, Kant upheld the independent existence of such

103. The validity of this metaphor for his work (a metaphor that was never in fact used by Kant himself), has been challenged by Robert Hahn in *Kant's Newtonian Revolution in Philosophy* (Carbondale, Ill., 1988). Hahn argues that Kant was far closer to Newton's hypothetico-deductive method than anything in Copernicus. Most commentators still hold to it because it suggests two fundamental aspects of Kant's philosophy: its challenge to commonsensical notions of knowledge based on the apparent evidence of the senses (the sun, as Copernicus showed, does not go around the earth, as our senses tell us it does), and its shifting of the center of gravity from the object of inquiry to the subject (roughly equivalent in effect to the move from a geocentric to a heliocentric cosmos, although the latter would seem to be less anthropocentric in implication than the former).

104. For a suggestive alternative to this reading, see Guyer, *Kant and the Claims of Knowledge*. Guyer argues that Kant never successfully overcame his early ambivalence about whether to emphasize the concept of an "object of experience" itself, which somehow brings its own necessary and universal rules with it, or the constitutive, transcendental subject who imposes those rules.

105. Antonio Pérez-Ramos, *Francis Bacon's Idea of Science and the Maker's Knowledge Tradition* (Oxford, 1988), p. 60. Vico's celebrated *verum/factum* principle, which maintained that making and knowing were convertible, was confined to the historical world, which could be said to be made by humans. In the First Critique, Kant was interested in nature rather than history, although in such later works as "Idea for a Universal History with a Cosmopolitan Intent" (1784), he did address its implications. His account was primarily based on a providential interpretation of history's trajectory, but it entailed a growing role for human intervention in the working out of that plan.

things in themselves.[106] His idealism, he insisted, should thus be called "formal, or better still . . . critical" to distinguish it from the "dogmatic idealism" of Berkeley.[107] Entities in the world do exist, even if unperceived; they are real objects that might possibly be experienced. It would be left to later German idealists and their Marxist successors to extend the active making to historical and even ontological constitution (without, to be sure, falling back on Berkeley's dissolution of matter into a mere idea of God). Kant's reconstruction of the concept of experience involved the setting of limits, which many of his successors—and arguably Kant himself in his later works— would attempt to overcome.

In many respects, Kant's reconstruction of epistemology in the wake of Hume's devastating critique of traditional metaphysics with its vulnerable inflation of the power of reason depended on the positing of those limits. Experience, as he developed it in the First Critique, involved questions of reliable knowledge, not the entire range of human encounters with the world that had been included in, say, Montaigne's expansive use of the term.[108] Personal happiness was subordinated to cognitive judgment or moral/spiritual development. As a result, Kant has been a tempting target for later critics, who would accuse him, unlike Hume, of excluding the body, emotions, desires, historical memory, and the like from his concern.[109] Nor did Kant's

106. Not all commentators have been convinced by Kant's distinction, which he made in reaction to an early review of the First Critique conflating the two positions. See, for example, Colin Turbayne, "Kant's Relation to Berkeley," in Lewis White Beck, ed., *Kant Studies Today* (LaSalle, Ill., 1969). For powerful rebuttals, see Gordon Nagel, *The Structure of Experience: Kant's System of Principles* (Chicago, 1983), chapter 1; and Arthur Collins, *Possible Experience: Understanding Kant's Critique of Pure Reason* (Berkeley, 1999). See also Guyer, *Kant and the Claims of Knowledge,* part 4, and the essays in Ralph Walker, *The Real and the Ideal* (New York, 1989).

107. Kant, *Prolegomena to Any Future Metaphysics,* p. 131. Kant also distinguished his position from what he called Descartes' "skeptical idealism."

108. As one of his current champions, Gordon Nagel, puts it: "Kant's theory of experience is the basis of all his other theories—of science, of mathematics, of religion, ethics, aesthetics, and education. . . . Kant's theory of experience plays a somewhat different foundational role in the case of each of the offshoot theories, but to each it is in some way fundamental. Science takes its topic matter from the empirical content of experience. Mathematics relies on, and explores, some of the formal aspects of experience. Because religion and ethics transcend experience, the theory of experience defines boundaries beyond which they may operate and sets conditions to which they are subject. Kant's theories of aesthetics and education rely on discoveries that he makes about the nature of the mind in the course of his investigation of experience." *The Structure of Experience,* p. 30.

109. See, for example, Mikel Dufrenne, *The Notion of the A Priori,* trans. Edward S. Casey (Evanston, Ill., 1966), which draws on Husserlian phenomenology to extend Kant's idea of a priori structures to history, art, society, and the body, where feeling as well as the understanding is crucial. See also Robin May Schott, *Cognition and Eros: A Critique of the Kantian Paradigm* (Boston, 1988), which attacks Kant from a Marxist-feminist perspective for ascetically reducing sensibility to a neutral recording of reified objects

celebrated decision to "limit reason to make room for faith" satisfy even some of his contemporaries, such as F. H. Jacobi, who thought that faith must itself be grounded in immediate religious experience and not merely in abstract moral law.[110] In his later *Critique of Judgment,* Kant contributed to the development of a specific notion of aesthetic experience, which was not the same as its cognitive counterpart, and one of his final works, *Anthropology from a Pragmatic Point of View* of 1798, investigated practical questions in the spirit of Christian Thomasius's prudential theory of court philosophy *(Klugheitslehre).*[111] But the more immediately influential First Critique defined a far more restricted notion of what could be called genuine experience.

Kant's development of that notion involved internal limits within knowledge itself. Contrasting deductive, dialectical reason *(Vernunft),* whose speculative dangers he came to appreciate when Hume interrupted his dogmatic slumber, with the more modest, but reliable understanding (*Verstand,* sometimes translated as "intellect") based on concrete encounters with the real world, Kant accepted the empiricists' critique of innate ideas and demolition of deductive proofs about the existence of God or the soul. Knowledge— and he was insistent that such a thing could be distinguished from mere opinion or belief, as well as from deductive reason—came through something called experience. As he put it in the often-cited opening sentences of the introduction to the second edition of *Critique of Pure Reason,* "there can be no doubt that all our cognition begins with experience. For what else might rouse our cognitive power to its operation if objects stirring our senses did not do so?"[112] It was in fact his fundamental principle, what he called in the *Prolegomena* the "*résumé* of the whole [First] *Critique,*"[113] that reason cannot teach us anything more about the objects of possible experience. Kant thus shared with Hume a deep suspicion of a priori ideas that came before experience or went beyond it. These he dubbed "pure" because they were

---

and calls instead for an epistemology based on "lived experience" (p. 196). These types of complaints were made as early as Johann Gottfried von Herder's holistic attack on Kant's division of human faculties in the late 1770s. See the discussion in Zammito, *The Genesis of Kant's Critique of Judgment,* p. 43, and the more extensive account in his *Kant, Herder, and the Birth of Anthropology* (Chicago, 2002). For a recent consideration of these issues that comes to more forgiving conclusions, see Susan Meld Shell, *The Embodiment of Reason: Kant on Spirit, Generation, and Community* (Chicago, 1996).

110. See F. H. Jacobi, *David Hume on Belief; or, Idealism and Realism* (1787).

111. For a discussion, see Holly L. Wilson, "Kant's Experiential Enlightenment and Court Philosophy in the 18th Century," *History of Philosophy Quarterly* 18, no. 2 (April 2001).

112. Kant, *Critique of Pure Reason,* p. 43.

113. Kant, *Prolegomena to Any Future Metaphysics,* p. 119.

purged of the messiness of everyday reality and the apparent imperfections of sense data. He sought to write a critique of them insofar as they were believed to be absolutely prior to all experience. "Experience," he wrote, "is an empirical cognition, i.e., a cognition that determines an object through perceptions."[114]

Where Kant differed from Hume, however, was in his further claim, which was the basis of his response to associationist conventionalism, that such a priori principles *underlay* experience. As he put it in one of the most often quoted passages from the First Critique:

> But even though all our cognition starts *with* experience, that does not mean that all of it arises *from* experience. For it might well be that even our experiential cognition is composite, consisting of what we receive through impressions and what our own cognitive power supplies from itself (sense impressions merely prompting it to do so).[115]

To ferret out the part of cognition that does not arise entirely from experience (understood in the sense of external stimuli alone, the "givens" of the empiricist tradition), Kant introduced perhaps his greatest philosophical innovation: the transcendental method.[116] He carefully distinguished "transcendental" from "transcendent," which meant going beyond experience in an unwarranted way to seek knowledge of pure Ideas, which could only be *thought*, but not *known*. He employed the former term instead to designate the universal and necessary conditions that underlay all possible experience. Deductive reasoning could extract those moments in experience that could not be explained by inputs of data from without, or mere habitual repetition. In particular, transcendental deduction was aimed at uncovering the *formal* aspects of knowledge, which infused every perception of and judgment about the world, however inchoate and ephemeral.[117] This was the realm

---

114. Kant, *Critique of Pure Reason*, p. 247. As Cathy Caruth argues, however, there is a crucial distinction between "experience" and "empirical observation" in Kant: "'Experience' is not a concept derived from empirical observation but a figure generated by discursive arguments to supplement their own self-representation. 'Experience' thus functions as the linguistic example that always accompanies the empirical example." *Empirical Truths and Critical Fictions*, pp. 84–85.

115. *Critique of Pure Reason*, p. 45.

116. Its intricacies have been the source of formidable scholarly literature. For two contrasting accounts, see Henry S. Allison, *Kant's Transcendental Idealism: An Interpretation and Defense* (New Haven, 1983); and Guyer, *Kant and the Claims of Knowledge*.

117. At times, Kant allowed that perceptions and intuitions were prior to judgments, which has suggested to some commentators a delay between the initial registering of data from without and their organization into meaningful experiences. But insofar as space and time were fundamental transcendental

of the understanding, which Kant distinguished both from pure a priori reason and no less pure a posteriori sensibility. Whereas the British empiricists, relying on the latter, had confined their inquiries solely to discrete material objects in the world (whether or not they ultimately accepted their materiality or dissolved them into fleeting sense impressions or divine ideas), Kant expanded his to include the relational, structural aspects of cognition. Although it may be possible to think of forms without content, which is what pure reason sought to do, it was impossible, he argued, to think of content lacking entirely in form, as the empiricists seemed to believe. From the beginning, experience involves the ability to discern near-isomorphisms— although not perfect identities as in logical proofs—in sense data that allow us to make out regularities and order in what would otherwise be a random confusion of overlapping, conflicting, and meaningless stimuli, an incoherent, kaleidoscopic stream of consciousness.

This ability is what the active mind provided, which went beyond the mere imagination of Hume because of the regular, universal, and necessary nature of such fundamental aspects of experience as time, space, and causality.[118] Against the dissolution of the mind into a succession of random and heterogeneous impressions, Kant posited a unified mind that was in fact shared by all humans, which he called the "transcendental unity of apperception." The "I" was the substratum of all experience, and was the locus, as he later argued in the *Critique of Practical Reason,* of moral autonomy. But as such, it could not be reduced to an object of cognitive experience, which was the source of psychologistic fallacies.[119] Strictly speaking, the self—understood in epistemological rather than psychological terms— transcended the phenomenal world and was situated in the realm of

---

contributions to all knowledge and no immediate perception could somehow be outside of a spatio-temporal framework, it is hard to grasp the nature of the delay except as a reflective subsumption of the perception under a rule, such as causality. Only when he talks of specifically aesthetic experience in the Third Critique does the distinction become significant. See the discussion in Zammito, *The Genesis of Kant's Critique of Judgment,* p. 104.

118. Where the imagination did play a role for Kant was in the transition from conceptual rules to individual cases, either through subsumption or, as the Third Critique in particular argued, through analogical and paradigmatic reflection. Analogies, it should be noted, also played a crucial part in the First Critique, where Kant explored three "analogies of experience": the "principle of the permanence of substance," the "principle of temporal succession according to the law of causality," and the "principle of simultaneity according to the law of interaction or community"(pp. 247–82). For an analysis and critique of their significance, see Guyer, *Kant and the Claims of Knowledge,* pp. 61–70. Kant's account of that transition has, in fact, been the source of endless debate, especially over the question of how rule-bound, universal, and necessary the imagination, as opposed to the understanding, can be.

119. For a useful discussion of this issue, see Allison, *Kant's Transcendental Idealism,* chapter 12.

noumena, or unknowable things-in-themselves, an argument that fit well with his contention that the immortal human soul could never be known, even if it could be thought.

Against the assumption that something called inner experience was prior to that of the knowing subject engaged with the world, an implication that could be drawn—with some license—from Hume's psychologistic skepticism by such adepts of spiritualism as the French philosopher Maine de Biran,[120] Kant claimed that

> the presentation *I am,* which expresses the consciousness that can accompany all thinking is what directly includes the existence of a subject; but it is not yet a *cognition* of that subject, and hence is also no empirical cognition—i.e., experience—of it. For such experience involves, besides the thought of something existent, also intuition, and here specifically inner intuition, in regard to which—viz., time—the subject must be determined; and this determination definitely requires external objects. Thus, consequently, inner experience is itself only indirect and is possible only through outer experience.[121]

But that "outer experience" was not entirely produced by those objects. It involved subjective constitution, which moreover was involuntary and coercive; there was no way, Kant averred, to see an elephant that was not in time and space, although it may be possible to *think* of one that might be—and which, for all we know, might actually be said to exist outside of human ken. Our judgments of the world of experienced objects were at once a priori and synthetic in the sense of producing new knowledge that went beyond analytic tautologies. Experience by its very nature thus entailed temporal duration—*Erfahrung* as a journey—as well as spatial location, which was inherently relational.

Kant's attempt to restore the possibility of certain scientific knowledge against the more modest claims of opinion, belief, and probability relied, it can be argued, on the tacit abandonment of a traditional correspondence notion of truth in favor of a coherence model instead. Although an ontologi-

120. For a discussion of the tradition of French spiritualists, which included Félix Ravaisson, Jules Lachelier, and Charles Renouvier as well as Biran, see Philip P. Hallie, "Hume, Biran and the *Méditatifs Intérieurs," Journal of the History of Ideas* 18, no. 3 (June 1957). I do not want to suggest that Kant was reacting specifically to Biran, who was a generation younger, but rather that he was resisting the notion of "inner experience," which Biran, among others, was to propagate. For discussions of that resistance, see Candace Vogler, "Sex and Talk," *Critical Inquiry* 24, no. 2 (Winter 1998); and Collins, *Possible Experience,* chapter 12.

121. Kant, *Critique of Pure Reason,* p. 291.

cal realist rather than phenomenalist,[122] resisting the priority of fleeting sense impressions over the enduring objects that produced them, he denied the possibility of our ever knowing the world as it actually existed; "things-in-themselves" were beyond experience, even as they were necessary to it. What he believed allowed him to escape the skeptical implications of that denial was his claim that referential knowledge was apodictic (from the Greek *apódeixis,* or demonstration) to the extent that it involved the categories and schemas of the understanding, which were necessary, unavoidable, and universal elements of cognitive experience of any kind. Species subjectivism, we might say, was Kant's answer to the individual or cultural subjectivism of the Pyrrhonist tradition.

Kant also provided a suggestive answer to "Descartes' Problem," the apparent disparity between commonplace sense experience and the explanations of natural science.[123] For if both were conceptualized in terms of synthetic a priori judgments, then there was no difference in kind between purportedly naive sense impressions and the theoretical entities of the sciences. Ordinary experience was thus not simply an illusion, and natural science was not based entirely on bypassing its false lessons; both dealt with "objects of experience," not things-in-themselves. Moreover, as he argued in the "third analogy of experience" in the *Critique of Pure Reason,* which explained apparent simultaneity by situating it in a temporal and spatial context of interaction and community (in the sense of communication), the levels of surface appearance and deep structure—what Locke had called primary and secondary characteristics—must themselves be relativized in a dynamic way. At the most profound level, they are part of nature understood at least in a regulative sense as a holistic system.[124]

Whether or not the precise mechanisms that Kant posited as operative in the structuring of all cognition are convincing (most commentators have had their doubts[125]), his audacious attempt to recast the epistemological question of experience on new grounds that would go beyond the fallacies of de-

---

122. For more comprehensive realists such as those in the tradition of the commonsense philosophers William Hamilton and Thomas Reid, Kant never really escaped phenomenalism. See, for example, D. J. B. Hawkins, *The Criticism of Experience* (London, 1947). For convincing analyses of the reasons why he might be said to have done so, see Allison, *Kant's Transcendental Idealism,* pp. 30–34, and Collins, *Possible Experience,* chapter 15.

123. In *Reconceiving Experience,* Kearns calls his own solution a derivation of Kant's within a linguistic framework (p. 109).

124. For a detailed analysis of the importance of the third analogy, see Guyer, *Kant and the Claims of Knowledge,* chapter 11.

125. For an exception, see Nagel, *The Structure of Experience.*

ductive reason and inductive or associationist empiricism, while resisting the psychologization of the active mind, launched a rich and productive debate, which shows few signs of losing its momentum (save for the occasional attempt of neo-pragmatists like Richard Rorty to junk it entirely).

Humean empiricism, understood as more or less phenomenalist, also enjoyed a certain revival in the twentieth century in the work of philosophers like Ernst Mach and Rudolf Carnap, who in different ways sought to dissolve Kant's transcendental subject and his objective thing-in-itself into an undifferentiated realm of sense experience. Analytic philosophy continues to suggest answers to what one of its practitioners calls "the puzzle of experience,"[126] often breaking down the barrier between epistemological and psychological questions that Kant so assiduously constructed (for example, in the work of W.V.O. Quine). Indeed, as we have seen in this chapter, experience as a ground of cognition was from the beginning a contested site, in which issues of passivity and activity, subjective construction and objective imposition, and the competing role of the individual and collective knower, were never laid to rest.

Rather than trace further variations on the "song of experience" played out under the rubric of epistemology, which would entangle us in the coils of even more complex philosophical arguments than those we have already encountered, it is time to turn to other discourses in other contexts. For it is clear that however "experience" was understood in cognitive terms, it could also serve other, very different purposes. It was, in fact, in response to what was perceived as the cramped and limited reduction of experience to nothing but an epistemological function that those alternatives emerged.

Broadly speaking, they assumed two guises. The first was the development and elevation of alternative modalities of experience, such as aesthetic, religious, or political, to a position of superiority over the purportedly dry and desiccated variant identified with modern science. The second and more ambitious led to a search for a new integrated notion that would somehow restore a holistic experience prior to the alienating fissures of modernity, seeking to heal the rupture left behind by what John Dewey disdainfully called Kant's "method of partition."[127] In the chapters that follow, we will trace the ways in which "experience" fragmented into specialized discursive modes, and then examine a number of attempts made in the twentieth century to reto-

126. J. J. Valberg, *The Puzzle of Experience* (Oxford, 1992). See also such collections as Foster and Swanson, *Experience and Theory;* and Tim Crane, ed., *The Contents of Experience: Essays on Perception* (Cambridge, 1992).

127. John Dewey, *The Quest for Certainty* (New York, 1929), p. 61.

talize what had been torn asunder. The place to begin is with the challenge to Kant's cognitive reduction of experience, along with its austere moral supplement, presented by a group of thinkers who contended that neither could do justice to a more fundamental form of experience, which he had woefully neglected. That alternative was the religious experience that gave the pious believer immediate evidence of the divine presence, an alternative first defended in detail by Kant's great critic, Friedrich Schleiermacher, in the twilight of the eighteenth-century *Aufklärung*.

THREE

The Appeal of Religious Experience

Schleiermacher, James, Otto, and Buber

THE REDUCTION OF EXPERIENCE to a question of cognition, whether pursued in empiricist or idealist terms, not only produced the epistemological conundrums that continue to bedevil philosophy in the present century, but also left a gnawing sense that something important in human life had been sacrificed. Contrasting Michel de Montaigne's more robust notion with that emanating from René Descartes, Giorgio Agamben alerts us to what was lost:

> Inasmuch as its goal was to advance the individual to maturity—that is, an anticipation of death as the idea of an achieved totality of experience—[experience] was something complete in itself, something it was possible to have, not only to undergo. But once experience was referred instead to the subject of science, which cannot reach maturity but can only increase its own knowledge, it becomes something incomplete, an "asymptotic" concept, as Kant will say, something it is possible only to *undergo,* never to *have:* nothing other, therefore, than the infinite process of knowledge.[1]

Such a reduction of experience to its scientific variant based on an imagined collective subject, at once impersonal and immortal, opened a space for competing options. If "an achieved totality of experience" in Montaigne's sense no longer seemed possible, what can be called the "modalization" of experience might favor partial alternatives that could provide what the epistemological variant lacked. Two in particular emerged from the shadow of experience as a cognitive tool in the eighteenth century. The first of these

---

1. Giorgio Agamben, *Infancy and History: Essays on the Destruction of Experience,* trans. Liz Heron (London, 1993), p. 23.

modalities was called religious experience; the second, aesthetic. Whereas the spirit may have been hegemonic in the former, while the flesh was paramount in the latter, a volatile mixture of the two distinguished each from the impersonality of the collective scientific subject. For both attempted to restore what was at stake for the suffering, creaturely, embodied individual, whose fleshly pleasures, spiritual yearnings, and finite lifespan meant that experience could not be understood as merely a question of reliable or unreliable knowledge. As a result, both warrant the metaphor of "songs of experience" more than the epistemological alternative because of the often rhapsodic and lyrical ways in which they were presented. In this chapter, we will explore the emergence and development of that modality of experience that understood itself in religious terms; in the next, we will focus on its aesthetic counterpart.

Although the nature of religious experience proved far from easy to define, it is fair to say that all variants opposed the reduction of experience to a purely cognitive category based on the five conventional senses. All saw experiences, in Agamben's terms, as something one has rather than merely undergoes. All, accordingly, foregrounded the importance of inner faculties such as will, belief, or pious awe, rather than the passive reception of stimuli from without. And all were anxious to restore the irreducible personal moment in experience, which had been lost with the alienation of it into scientific instruments or collective communities of inquiry, even if those approaching mysticism often then sought to go beyond it.

The epistemological tradition, to be sure, did not always conform to the caricature of it so often promulgated by its critics; as we have seen, both its idealist and empiricist variants allowed some space for the constitutive activity of the subject, however it was defined. In fact, the contrast between scientific and moral/religious experience, suspending for a moment the task of defining and differentiating the latter, ought not to be rigidly absolutized. It has, in fact, long been a staple of early modern history that certain aspects of Reformation theology and the scientific method shared a number of premises and inclinations, as well as a common target in Aristotelian scholasticism and debt to its nominalist critics. As Charles Taylor has noted,

There was a profound analogy in the way the proponents of both Baconian science and Puritan theology saw themselves in relation to experience and tradition. Both saw themselves as rebelling against a traditional authority which was merely feeding on its own errors and as returning to the neglected sources: the Scriptures on the one hand, experimental reality on the other. Both appealed to what they saw as living experience against dead received doctrine—the experience of personal conversion and commitment, or that of direct observation of nature's workings.[2]

In fact, during colonial America's "Great Awakening," Jonathan Edwards (1703–1748) could imaginatively fashion out of John Locke's anti-rationalist sensationalism a doctrine of a "new sense" of the heart, which offered experiential confirmation—most vividly expressed in born-again conversion—of what mere dogmatic adherence to church doctrine or scripture could never provide.[3] A similar exploitation of David Hume's skepticism for fideistic purposes can be seen in the radical critique of Enlightenment rationalism and Spinozist "nihilism" launched later in the century by the German philosopher F. H. Jacobi.[4]

And yet, despite their shared enemies, what religious thinkers like Edwards or Jacobi meant by experience was not equivalent to that posited by either its empiricist or transcendental idealist defenders. Exploring some of the meanings of what a recent commentator has rightly called this "extremely wide, not to say vague term"[5] will be the task of this chapter. We will try to understand the shift from faith identified primarily with adherence to belief, either rational or willed, in certain propositions about God and His creation to faith understood phenomenologically as devotional or pious behavior derived from something akin to an emotionally charged, perceptual experience of divinity or the holy.[6] Our focus will be on thinkers who resisted reducing

2. Charles Taylor, *Sources of the Self: The Making of the Modern Identity* (Cambridge, Mass., 1989), p. 230. Within Protestantism in general, however, there was a potential tension between literal fidelity to those scriptures and the inspiration of the Holy Spirit, which could lead in antinomian directions.

3. For discussions of Edwards's relation to Locke, see David Laurence, "Jonathan Edwards, John Locke, and the Canon of Experience," *Early American Literature* 15, no. 2 (Fall 1980); Norman Fiering, *Jonathan Edwards's Moral Thought in Its British Context* (Chapel Hill, 1981); and James Hoopes, "Jonathan Edwards's Religious Psychology," *The Journal of American History* 69, no. 4 (1983). His most influential book was *The Religious Affections* of 1746. Edwards did go beyond Locke in believing that we can have direct experience in our souls of the Holy Ghost. For an analysis of the continuities between Edwards and later students of religious experience, see Wayne Proudfoot, "From Theology to a Science of Religions: Jonathan Edwards and William James on Religious Affections," *Harvard Theological Review* 82 (1989).

4. For a good discussion of Jacobi's role in the Pantheism Controversy of the 1780s, in which he developed a personalist and experiential notion of God against his rationalist opponents, see Warren Breckman, *Marx, the Young Hegelians, and the Origins of Radical Social Theory* (Cambridge, 1999), chapter 1.

5. Anthony O'Hear, *Experience, Explanation and Faith: An Introduction to the Philosophy of Religion* (London, 1984), p. 26.

6. For an elaboration of the distinction between belief and behavior, see John Hick, "Religious Faith as Experiencing-As," in *Talk of God*, Royal Institute of Philosophy Lectures, vol. 2, 1967–68 (London, 1969). Hick uses Wittgenstein's contrast between "seeing" and "seeing-as" and Gestalt psychology to

that experience to non-religious sources or subsuming it under more secular explanatory systems. We will look as well at disputes about the status of the "object" or dialogic interlocutor of that experience, which seemed to some its cause and to others its effect. Here we will encounter anxiety about reversing the priority between God and humankind that echoed similar fears in aesthetic, epistemological, and other discourses when experience seemed to mean the hypertrophy of subjectivity.

Our main witnesses will be Protestant theologians in Germany, in particular the influential figures of Friedrich Schleiermacher and Rudolf Otto.[7] William James's classic study *The Varieties of Religious Experience* will also be one of our touchstones. We will conclude by glancing fleetingly at the discourse of religious experience as it emerged in the early work of the twentieth-century Jewish thinker Martin Buber. Buber's cult of that variant of experience known as *Erlebnis,* which owed so much to Schleiermacher, became an inviting target for those like Walter Benjamin and Gershom Scholem who preferred the alternative they identified with *Erfahrung* for reasons that will be explored in a later chapter.

KANT AND RELIGION AS MORAL EXPERIENCE

It is certainly possible to locate appeals to the experiential ground of religion in earlier periods, as we noted in our passing references to Augustine and the traditions of mysticism in chapter 1. Anselm's assertion that "he who has not experienced will not understand" did, in fact, serve as part of the epigraph

---

argue that there is an interpretative element in religious cognition that is not all that different from the interpretative moment in other modes of knowledge.

7. Although British and American theology had its innovators—for example, Samuel Taylor Coleridge, F. D. Maurice, Nathaniel William Taylor, Horace Bushnell, and William Ellery Channing—the main developments in Protestant thought occurred in the German-speaking lands of Central Europe. Theological faculties were more numerous in Germany and doctrinal freedom more extensive there than elsewhere. See Hugh Ross Mackintosh, *Types of Modern Theology: Schleiermacher to Barth* (London, 1945), pp. 3–4.

It should be noted that at times Catholic theology has also had to come to terms with the question of experiential legitimation. See, for example, Michel de Certeau, "L'expérience religieuse: 'Connaissance vécue' dans l'Église," in Luce Giard, ed., *Le voyage mystique de Michel de Certeau* (Paris, 1988). For a recent assessment of the question by a Jesuit theologian, see George P. Schner, "The Appeal to Experience," *Theological Studies* 53 (1992). It has, however, been argued by Robert Orsi that "the deepest roots in the United States of this way of thinking about religion [the primacy and autonomy of religious experience] lie in this culture's endemic anti-Catholicism." See his "Between Theology and Culture: Culture Studies in 'Religion'," *Intellectual History Newsletter* 18 (1996), p. 49.

for Schleiermacher's great treatise *The Christian Faith*.[8] The Reformation had insisted that inward possession of God's truth was more important than outward adherence to ecclesiastical authority. Calvin's *Institutes* put *pietas* ahead of *fides* as the basis of "true religion." Luther's reliance on scripture alone— *sola scriptura*—was premised on the claim, as B. A. Gerrish puts it, that "we must feel the words of Scripture in the heart. Experience is necessary for understanding the Word, which must be lived and felt."[9] Adopting the Stoic doctrine of *katalepsis,* which trusted in the power of clear and unerring impressions of the world on our sense organs, Luther sought to answer Erasmus's skeptical probabilism by appealing to the overpowering compulsion of self-evident experience.[10]

Although Lutheranism itself soon developed its own doctrinal rigidities, inviting the charge of a new Protestant scholasticism leveled against theologians like Johann Gerhardt (1582–1637), the appeal of subjective experience was still active in such schools as seventeenth-century Cambridge Platonism with its support for a religion of the heart based on innate truths.[11] Popular revivalist movements, such as Pietism, Methodism, Quietism, and Hasidism, produced waves of irrationalist "enthusiasm" that periodically challenged the orthodox religious authorities.[12] For all of these anticipations, however, it was not really until the secularizing, anti-clerical, "pagan" Enlightenment's multifaceted assault on religion undermined many of the traditional legitimations of belief that a full-fledged, self-conscious reliance on experience

8. The full quotation (credited to Anselm of Canterbury, Prosol[ogion]. 1.a de fide trin. 2β) reads: "Neque enim quaero intelligere ut credam, sed credo ut intelligam,—Nam qui non crediderit, non experietur, et qui expertus non fuerit, non intelliget." It appears on the title page of Friedrich Schleiermacher, *Der Christliche Glaube: Nach den Grundsätzen der Evangelischen Kirche im Zusammenhange Dargestellt,* 2nd ed., vol. 1 (Berlin, 1930). The quotation does not appear in the English translation.

9. B. A. Gerrish, *The Old Protestantism and the New: Essays on the Reformation Heritage* (Chicago, 1982), p. 57. For extensive references to Luther's appeal to experience, see Gerrish's note 40 on p. 296.

10. For a discussion of the importance of *katalepsis* for Luther, see Marjorie O'Rourke Boyle, *Rhetoric and Reform: Erasmus' Civil Dispute with Luther* (Cambridge, Mass., 1983), chapter 2.

11. Protestant Scholasticism revived interest during the seventeenth century in the Aristotelianism so despised by Luther. See Mackintosh, *Types of Modern Theology,* pp. 8ff. For a discussion of the role of experience in Cambridge Platonism, see Ernst Cassirer, *The Platonic Renaissance in England,* trans. J. P. Pettegrove (Edinburgh, 1953), pp. 30–34. Although the Platonic tradition was, as we have seen, suspicious of sense experience and the unreliability of the body, its stress on intuitive understanding could be translated into a religious notion of non-empirical experience.

12. The term "enthusiasm" was a pejorative hurled at those who seemed to transgress the bounds of religious orthodoxy by trusting in dreams, voices, visions, fits, trances, and other putatively delusional expressions of revelation. Those who were its targets, such as John Wesley, rejected the label. See the discussion in Ann Taves, *Fits, Trances, and Visions: Experiencing Religion and Explaining Religion from Wesley to James* (Princeton, 1999), pp. 16–17.

could emerge as the most potent weapon in the struggle to defend and renew Christianity.

Earlier holding actions, such as the impersonal Deism of the seventeenth-century British theologians Matthew Tindal and John Toland, the anti-revelationist "reasonableness" of the German *Neologen,* or the Spinozist pantheism that inspired certain German thinkers to equate God and nature, had ceded too much to the skeptical debunkers.[13] The great speculative systems of Gottfried Wilhelm Leibniz and Christian Wolff, overly optimistic about reconciling rational philosophy and religion, although having their day during the reign of Frederick the Great, ultimately fared no better.[14] The historical researches of critics like H. G. Reimarus (1694–1768) had cast doubt on the veracity of many of the biblical stories on which faith had been based, providing where possible purely naturalist explanations for purported miracles. Down this road lay the more radical demythologizing of such nineteenth-century biographers of Jesus as David Friedrich Strauss and Ernest Renan. Attempts to fashion a universal "natural theology" common to all men, culminating in William Paley's celebrated tract of 1802 with that title, unconvincingly relied on the argument from design that Hume had effectively demolished a generation earlier.

Hoping to limit reason and knowledge in order to make room for faith, Immanuel Kant continued the demolition, while at the same time seeking to build a new and more secure foundation for its replacement. That foundation was set in the ground of what might properly be called moral, more than religious, experience. As a result, it presented a formidable challenge to the rise of a pure version of the latter, which Schleiermacher understood had to be met before he could move ahead with his own case. Before making sense of how he did so, however, we have to pause for a short while with Kant's powerful defense of the priority of practical reason.

Kant began by persuasively demonstrating that the great Scholastic arguments for believing in God—the so-called ontological, cosmological, and teleological proofs—were untenable deductions and should be discarded as

---

13. For a helpful overview of this period, see Claude Welch, *Protestant Thought in the Nineteenth Century,* vol. 1, *1799–1870* (New Haven, 1972), chapter 2.

14. For a discussion of the links between Prussian absolutism and rational theology in Frederick's reign, see Günter Birtsch, "The Christian as Subject: The World Mind of the Prussian Protestant Theologians in the Late Enlightenment Period," in *The Transformation of Political Culture: England and Germany in the Late Eighteenth Century,* ed. Eckhart Hellmuth (Oxford, 1990). For a comparative analysis of similar trends in Judaism and Catholicism during the Enlightenment, see David Sorkin, *The Berlin Haskalah and German Religious Thought: Orphans of Knowledge* (London, 2000).

useless exercises in "pure speculative reason."[15] It was no less vain, he then argued, to seek credible evidence to decide ultimate questions such as the immortality of the soul or the existence of God through synthetic a priori judgments about the world, dependent as they were on phenomenal sense experience. Strictly speaking, we finite beings can have ideas but no knowledge of such supersensible matters, which are part of that noumenal realm of things-in-themselves inaccessible to human understanding *(Verstand)*. Having fought a ferocious battle with the "enthusiasts" and "spirit-seers" such as Emanuel Swedenborg, Kant was not, however, tempted by mystical and irrationalist alternatives, or willing to tolerate the absurdities and paradoxes that had intoxicated Blaise Pascal and would have the same effect on Søren Kierkegaard.

Instead, Kant turned to the power of what he called practical reason, the categorical imperatives of morality, to provide what he hoped would be a more viable ground of religion.[16] In the *Critique of Practical Reason* (1787) and *Religion within the Limits of Reason Alone* (1793), he offered a defense that would preserve the anti-dogmatic virtues of the Enlightenment, but go beyond the comfortable and often flaccid "reasonableness" of some of its more urbane adherents. Moral experience—our struggle to conform to the obligations placed on us by our inbred sense of duty—is the foundation, Kant argued, on which religion should be based, not vice versa. Such experience is on a different plane from that provided by our encounters through the senses with the natural world. We may be compelled to act as if there were a God legislating moral commands, but we cannot *know* for certain that He exists, as natural theology mistakenly assumed could be demonstrated from His works. God, like human freedom and the immortality of the soul, is simply a postulate of moral reason, not a theoretical dogma. We worship Him because He is good and rational, not because He is ineffable, willful, or capricious. Practice, in the sense of heeding or resisting moral imperatives, is thus prior to theory and cognition, a conclusion that also implied the superiority

15. Theologians, to be sure, continue to debate the conclusiveness of Kant's demolition of these proofs. For a recent attempt to combine aspects of the proofs with a reliance on religious experience, see John E. Smith, *Experience and God* (New York, 1995), chapter 5.

16. Immanuel Kant, *Religion within the Limits of Reason*, trans. T. M Greene and H. H. Hudson (New York, 1960). For discussions, see Allen W. Wood, *Kant's Moral Religion* (Ithaca, N.Y., 1970); Michel Despland, *Kant on History and Religion* (Montreal, 1973); and Gordon E. Michaelson Jr., *The Historical Dimension of a Rational Faith: The Role of History in Kant's Religious Thought* (Washington, D.C., 1979). Wood attempts a defense of Kant's critical approach against Schleiermacher and Otto (pp. 201–7) by stressing the importance of universal communicability in rational judgments, which is absent in inner feelings, religious or otherwise.

of experience—albeit of the obligations more than directly of their divine source—over mere assent to dogma or blind faith.

There is in our experience of feeling obliged by duty, Kant noted, an inevitable tension between our animal instincts, needs, desires, and interests, all grounded in our being part of the natural world, and the demands of the moral law, which appeal to our noumenal selves. In the latter guise, we are inherently free to transgress as well as obey moral imperatives, even if they come to us in the form of categorical and universal laws rather than hypothetical and particular maxims. Natural laws like gravity cannot be broken, but moral ones can. For were we fully holy beings, living in a state of prelapsarian grace, we would paradoxically lose our freedom, which is a result of our very ability to chose. What Kant postulated as humankind's transcendental freedom was therefore predicated on our creaturely faculty of desire, which allows us to intend something (higher, if the intended is the moral good, lower if it is the satisfaction of mere creaturely need). Although we have an inbred "respect" or "esteem" *(Acht)* for the moral law, which derives from our rootedness in the noumenal realm, as denizens of the natural world, we have desires that can sorely tempt us to betray it.

For Kant, Jesus was thus best understood as an exemplary moral guide, the archetype of ethical perfection, articulating in the Sermon on the Mount what was always already immanent in human consciousness. He was not, however, a merciful mediator, whose historical descent into the world was the premise of our redemption. For such dependence on an external figure—at once human and divine in whom "the Word became flesh"—would introduce a measure of heteronomy into the moral world, which Kant sought to keep fully autonomous. Relying on the intercession of a forgiving God who had died for our sins, we would lose our accountability as moral agents and be reduced to little more than the equivalent of animals causally determined by the laws of nature. Although God may be assumed to be the ultimate source of the obligations we feel, the decision to honor them or not is ours alone. Heteronomy, whether the "other" *(heter)* is natural or divine, is an affront to human dignity.

The church, accordingly, should be understood as more of an ideal ethical commonwealth founded by Jesus than a sacred institution fostering salvation or an adumbration of the Kingdom of God on earth. It is, to be sure, a moral community, not a political one, in the sense that it follows the laws of virtue promulgated by God and then freely chosen by humans rather than those set entirely by us. We mere mortals, however, can only hope to approximate perfection, at least on earth. As spelled out in his account of historical progress in his 1784 essay "Idea for a Universal History with a Cosmopolitan Intent,"

Kant thought that the human race could only asymptotically approach complete moral excellence, which functioned therefore as a regulative ideal. The "highest good," which includes happiness as well as virtue, is something we strive to realize, but our finite reason cannot fully grasp it.[17] Thus, there is a radical split in the human subject, whose freedom is bought at the price of the irresolvable conflict between desire and practical reason, inclination and duty, self-interest and disinterested obligation. Although we have a powerful feeling of respect for moral laws and the divinity assumed to have commanded them, although we fervently hope that we might live up to them, there is a nagging sense in Kant of the gap between moral imperatives and human happiness, understood in terms of our finite, creaturely nature. "One cannot fashion something absolutely straight," he ruefully remarked, "from wood which is as crooked as that of which man is made."[18] In fact, radical evil must remain a possibility for the autonomy of the moral will to be meaningful.

Kant's elevation of moral obligation over other possible forms of religious experience had a sustained impact on Protestant theological developments in Germany throughout the nineteenth century, finding an echo, for example, in Albrecht Ritschl's liberal theology of moral values during the Wilhelmian era.[19] Jewish neo-Kantians such as Hermann Cohen were also clearly in its debt.[20] Kant's attentiveness to the experiential dimension of morality anticipated many later thinkers, even if some, such as John Dewey, interpreted it in situational rather than categorical terms.[21]

17. The precise relationship between happiness and virtue in Kant's notion of the "highest good" has been a perennial source of debate among scholars of his work. For an attempt to reconcile them, see Wood, *Kant's Moral Religion*, chapters 2 and 3.

18. Kant, "Idea for a Universal History with a Cosmopolitan Intent," in Carl J. Friedrich, ed., *The Philosophy of Kant: Immanuel Kant's Moral and Political Writings* (New York, 1993), p. 135.

19. For a discussion, see Mackintosh, *Types of Modern Theology*, chap. 5. There were, to be sure, many non-Kantian moments in Ritschl's thought as well, and some of his disciples, such as Wilhelm Hermann, sought to reconcile aspects of Schleiermacher with his neo-Kantianism. See Brent W. Sockness, "The Ideal and the Historical in the Christology of Wilhelm Hermann: The Promise and the Perils of Revisionary Christology," *Journal of Religion* 72, no. 3 (July 1992).

20. Cohen's posthumously published *Die Religion der Vernunft aus den Quellen des Judentums* (Berlin, 1921) did reveal a late departure from his typical neo-Kantian stress on ethics, which allowed him to become an inspiration to figures like Franz Rosenzweig. For a discussion, see Amos Funkenstein, *Perceptions of Jewish History* (Berkeley, 1993), chapter 8. Funkenstein concludes, however, that the fact "that Cohen now, in his latest work, refused to reduce religion into rational ethics does not at all mean that he succumbed to the then fashionable trends of irrationalism; his thought still differs *toto caelo* from the thought of either Buber or Rosenzweig, who owe so much to him. . . . Religion was not to be grounded on the shaky foundations of a *je ne sais quoi* such as Otto's 'numinous'" (p. 282).

21. For a discussion of Dewey's situational ethics, see Gregory F. Pappas, "Dewey's Ethics: Morality as Experience," in Larry A. Hickman, ed., *Reading Dewey: Interpretations for a Postmodern Generation* (Bloomington, 1998).

But Kant's attempt to keep religion "within the limits of reason alone," even if that reason was understood as practical rather than speculative or critical, also soon met with heated opposition.[22] Kant himself was forced to submit to censorship in the wake of the changes wrought after 1788 when a new Prussian monarch, Friedrich Wilhelm II, turned to Johann Christoph Wöllner to enforce a reactionary orthodoxy in which any traces of the *Aufklärung* were banished. The second book of Kant's 1793 treatise was forbidden, and he was denied the right to publish again on religious issues, which he honored until the king's death in 1797.

A far more substantial intellectual challenge to Kant's subsumption of religious experience under the rubric of practical reason was launched a few years later by a wide variety of philosophers and theologians, most notably Johann Georg Hamann (1730–1788), Friedrich Heinrich Jacobi (1743–1819), Jakob Friedrich Fries (1773–1843), and with greatest effect, Friedrich Daniel Ernst Schleiermacher (1768–1834).[23] Impatient with Kant's division of reason into theoretical and practical domains, indeed often suspicious of his privileging of reason in any of its guises, they posited a specifically religious variant of experience that would no longer be subservient to its moral counterpart. Hoping to heal the wound that they saw gaping in Kant's system with its distinction between duty and inclination, they sought a more holistic, organic model of human subjectivity that brought them into the orbit of the nascent Romantic movement. With the Romantics, they came to recognize the role of feeling *(Gefühl)* and self-cultivation *(Bildung)* in the development of the self. Such notions as *Ahndung,* an untranslatable word chosen by Fries to suggest a conceptually unintelligible conviction or inkling, derived from feelings, of the supersensible realm, expressed their quest to overcome the divisions legislated by Kant.[24] Such a desire remained powerful in later considerations of the same issues, as shown by William James's discussion of "the divided self" in his *Varieties of Religious Experience* of 1902.[25] It would be

---

22. For an excellent overview of the critical response to Kant's "ethicotheology," see Walter Jaeschke, *Reason in Religion: The Foundations of Hegel's Philosophy of Religion,* trans. J. Michael Stewart and Peter C. Hodgson (Berkeley, 1990).

23. For an overview of post-Kantian debates about experience, see Frederick C. Beiser, *The Fate of Reason: German Philosophy from Kant to Fichte* (Cambridge, Mass., 1987). He sees Hamann's 1759 text *Sokratischen Denkwürdigkeiten* as one of the first to claim that religious faith was, like a sensation *(Empfindung),* an unmediated experience that produced its own kind of valid knowledge.

24. For a discussion of its role, see Rudolf Otto, *The Philosophy of Religion Based on Kant and Fries,* trans. E. B. Dicker (New York, 1931), chapter 10. In contemporary German, *Ahndung* has become *Ahnung.*

25. William James, *The Varieties of Religious Experience,* ed. Martin A. Marty (New York, 1987), chapter 8.

more precise, however, to say that they sought to overcome the divisions in a separate and irreducible realm of specifically religious experience, whose dignity and value they hoped to restore (the more grandiose attempt to reconcile that realm with philosophy, science, art and every other aspect of existence would have to wait for Hegel).

Their efforts played out against the backdrop of the contagious movement of popular evangelicalism, sometimes culminating in pentecostal *glossolalia*, that so powerfully affected Protestantism on both sides of the Atlantic in the late eighteenth and early nineteenth centuries. Radicalizing the Calvinist or Lutheran notion of the "calling" by freeing it of its "proper" ecclesiastical identification with accredited ministers, its adepts stressed the unmediated nature of their experiential access to the divine. Such access often came through the "spiritual senses," which were able to hear the sounds and see the sights of a world unperceived by secular ears and eyes.[26] Despite the constant threat of being misled by satanic impostures, or duped by the ventriloquism and phantasmagoria of cynical charlatans, the pious believer persisted in trusting the immediacy of his or her personal, first-hand encounter with the divine. But it meant the defense of authentic religious experience had to be waged on two fronts: against both the hollow "formalism" of orthodox doctrine and the excessive "enthusiasm" of delusional, false belief.[27]

SCHLEIERMACHER AND THE RELIGION OF THE HEART

The most sustained and compelling theoretical brief for religious experience was offered by Friedrich Schleiermacher, arguably the most important Protestant theologian since Calvin, whose shadow fell across the entire nineteenth century and well into the twentieth.[28] To do justice to his legacy, which has come down to us in some thirty-one volumes of books, sermons, and un-

26. For a vivid account of the mobilization of the senses, hearing in particular, by the evangelical counter-Enlightenment in America, see Leigh Eric Schmidt, *Hearing Things: Religion, Illusion and the American Enlightenment* (Cambridge, Mass., 2000). Schmidt traces the battle that raged between Enlightenment scientific accounts of the senses, which often debunked the oracular and visionary claims of religion, and their religious opponents, who by the time of Swedenborg were combining scientific with spiritual arguments to defend their position.

27. See Taves, *Fits, Trances, and Visions*, p. 16. Taves points out that these terms were already in use by the Puritans of the seventeenth century.

28. Schleiermacher's relation to Calvin is itself a much-disputed issue. See Gerrish, *The Old Protestantism and the New*, chapter 12; and Gerrish, *Continuing the Reformation: Essays on Modern Religious Thought* (Chicago, 1993), chapter 8.

published papers, as well as thousands of letters,[29] is beyond our scope now, and not only because of the complexity of his ideas and the intricacies of his intellectual development. It is also impossible because, as Wilhelm Dilthey noted in the opening remarks in his classic biography, whereas "the philosophy of Kant can be fully understood without more intimate occupation with his character and his life—Schleiermacher's significance, his worldview, and his works require a biographical presentation to be fundamentally understood."[30] Although this comparison may be somewhat unfair to Kant, whose work can also surely be illuminated by historical and biographical contextualization, it expresses one of the fundamental lessons taught and exemplified by Schleiermacher himself: that life and work, experiences and the ideas they in some way enable, are so intimately intertwined that one cannot be understood without the other. What can be called an expressivist view of intellectual genesis, which grounds it in the personal or social context of its production, has one of its most potent origins here. The so-called hermeneutic method pioneered by Schleiermacher, in which part illuminates whole and vice versa, authorial intention is essential to understanding the meaning of a text, and psychological interpretation supplements philological, cries out to be applied to its own progenitor, as Dilthey was the first to realize.

In the case of Schleiermacher, if we focus only on his early years, such an effort would have to address his birth into a family of pious Reformed Calvinists and his schooling at the seminaries of Moravian Brethren at Niesky and Barby, which ended when he had a crisis of faith in January 1787, shortly after his mother's death. It would discuss his training at the University of Halle, where he came into contact with Kant's critical writings and was convinced by many of their arguments against traditional proofs for the existence of God and the immortality of the soul. It would attempt to explain his early sympathy (lasting as late as 1797) for the French Revolution. It would treat his decision to follow his father's career in the ministry and his first position in Drossen, where he prepared for his theological examinations and formu-

---

29. For a full list, see Terence N. Tice, *Schleiermacher Bibliography* (Princeton, 1966).

30. Wilhelm Dilthey, *Leben Schleiermachers, Gesammelte Schriften* (Göttingen, 1958–90), 13.1, p. xxxiii. The second volume was never completely finished. The other standard biography is Martin Redeker's *Schleiermacher: Life and Thought*, trans. John Wallhausser (Philadelphia, 1973). See also Albert L. Blackwell, *Schleiermacher's Early Philosophy of Life: Determinism, Freedom, and Phantasy* (Chico, Calif., 1982); and Schleiermacher's own *The Life of Schleiermacher as Unfolded in His Autobiography and Letters*, trans. Federica Maclean Rowan, 2 vols. (London, 1860). Dilthey's distinction between Kant and Schleiermacher, one needing no biographical detail to illuminate his thought, the other requiring it, became a standard trope. See, for example, Mackintosh, *Types of Modern Theology*, pp. 31–32, where he rehearses the distinction without mentioning Dilthey.

lated his initial reservations about Kant's privileging of moral experience over its religious counterpart. It would follow him to Schlobitten, Berlin, Landsberg, and back to Berlin, where he arrived in 1796 to take on the position of chaplain at the Charité Hospital.

Perhaps most of it all, it would be obliged to explore his involvement in the Prussian capital with the heady world of young German Romantic poets and philosophers, which he entered through his former student, Count Alexander Dohna, who introduced him to the Jewish salon hostess Henriette Herz and her husband, Markus.[31] For here he not only entered into a series of complicated emotional attachments, often with unattainable married women, but also met and grew close to the great poet and critic Friedrich Schlegel, with whom he shared lodgings for two years and whose transgressive novel *Lucinde* he boldly defended. It was in fact Schlegel and their circle of not very religious friends who prompted Schleiermacher to write the brilliant tract that would launch his career, *On Religion: Speeches to Its Cultured Despisers*, which appeared anonymously in the final year of the eighteenth century.[32]

Any more sustained attempt to explore the entanglement of his life and work would have to probe Schleiermacher's multiple careers as theologian, philosopher, classicist, philologist, educator, social and ecclesiastical reformer, and political activist (including perhaps his brief role as spy in the Prussian resistance to Napoleonic rule). And finally, it would also have to follow his tumultuous love life and many intense friendships, his frequent quarrels with church and state authorities as well as with philosophers like Hegel (his colleague in Berlin from 1818 to 1831), and his contribution to nascent German nationalism. To attempt all of this would be folly, but we have already introduced a sufficient number of elements of his biography to help us bring into better focus our main concern, the concept of religious experience de-

---

31. For treatments of Schleiermacher and Romanticism, see Jack Forstman, *A Romantic Triangle: Schleiermacher and Early German Romanticism* (Missoula, Mont., 1977); and Gerald N. Izenberg, *Impossible Individuality: Romanticism, Revolution, and the Origins of Modern Selfhood, 1787–1802* (Princeton, 1992), chapter 1, in which Schleiermacher's contradictory notion of individuality—at once self-aggrandizing and self-annihilating—is seen as emblematic of Romanticism as a whole.

32. Friedrich Schleiermacher, *On Religion: Speeches to Its Cultured Despisers,* trans. Richard Crouter (Cambridge, 1994). This is a translation of the first edition. The text went through revisions in 1806, 1821, and 1831; the third of these appearing in an English translation by John Oman (New York, 1958). In his excellent introduction, Crouter discusses the variations among the editions. The anonymous publication was a precautionary device to avoid the condemnation of the Prussian censor, who turned out to be Schleiermacher's immediate church superior, F. S. G. Sack. For Sack's complicated response, see Blackwell, *Schleiermacher's Early Philosophy of Life,* pp. 115–18.

veloped in the book that has been justly called "the revolutionary manifesto from which the birth of the new era in theology is commonly dated,"[33] *On Religion.*

The first context to stress in explaining its origin is that of the Pietistic tradition to which Schleiermacher's father had converted from rationalism and which provided the matrix of the son's early religious training at Niesky and Barby. Although his spiritual crisis of 1787 meant a temporary estrangement from the Moravian Brethren (also known as Herrnhuters) and from his deeply disappointed father, Schleiermacher could later recall on a visit in 1802 to the community he had left fifteen years before: "Here it was for the first time I awoke to the consciousness of the relations of man to a higher world. . . . Here it was that mystic tendency developed itself, which has been of so much importance to me, and has supported and carried me through all the storms of skepticism. . . . And I may say, that after all I have passed through, I have become a Herrnhuter again, only of a higher order."[34]

Pietism was an enormously varied and widely dispersed movement of religious renewal, whose history would include chapters on English Puritanism and Wesleyan Methodism, as well as on offshoots in Holland, Scandinavia, and North America.[35] Traditionally its origins are traced to the preface written in 1675 by the Frankfurt pastor Philipp Jakob Spener (1635–1705) to a work of the devotional author Johann Arndt (1555–1621), which was published independently a year later as *Pia desideria (Pious Desires).*[36] The movement swiftly spread through Spener's disciples, August Hermann Francke (1663–1717), Gottfried Arnold (1666–1714), Johann Bengel (1687–1752), Friedrich Christoph Oetinger (1702–1782), and Nicolas Ludwig, Count von Zinzendorf (1700–1782). It was Zinzendorf who gave refuge to the Moravian Brethren community that founded the village of Herrnhut on his estate in Saxony in 1722, the community to which the Schleiermacher family owed its spiritual awakening. Halle, the university where the young Friedrich studied, was, moreover, heavily influenced by Francke's teachings.

Although there were many sectarian quarrels among the separate Pietist communities—Arnold's Radical Pietism, favoring mystical union with God,

---

33. B. A. Gerrish, *A Prince of the Church: Schleiermacher and the Beginnings of Modern Theology* (Philadelphia, 1984), p. 44.

34. Cited in Gerrish, *A Prince of the Church,* pp. 26–27.

35. The most extensive recent treatment can be found in Martin Brecht and Klaus Deppermann, eds., *Geschichte des Pietismus,* 2 vols. (Göttingen, 1993). For a selection of texts in translation, see Peter C. Erb, ed., *Pietists: Selected Writings* (New York, 1983).

36. Philipp Jakob Spener, *Pia desideria,* trans. and ed., Theodore G. Tappert (Philadelphia, 1964).

challenged the church Pietists who remained within the Lutheran establishment; Bengel railed against Zinzendorf's ecumenism and exaltation of sex in marriage—the movement shared certain fundamental premises. All adherents considered the attitude and behavior of piety called *Frömmigkeit* (the German translation in the Zurich Bible of the Latin *justificatus*) more fundamental than *Glaube* (the German for *fides*), faith as mere intellectual assent. Hoping to revitalize pious spiritual life, Pietism emphasized the importance of biblical preaching, the necessity of repentance and rebirth, the value of frequent devotional exercises, and the duty to spread the Word evangelically. Stressing the priesthood of all believers, Spener and his followers challenged the role of theological authorities and put in their place small groups or "conventicles" of believers *(collegia pietatis)*, communities of the converted who would practice their religion, not argue about it through learned, but sterile, disputation. In addition to constant introspection, such practice would often include acts of charity and good deeds, an inclination toward rigorous moral activism that would leave its mark on Kant, whose debt to this aspect of Pietism has frequently been acknowledged.[37]

But what Pietism also emphasized, which had far more influence on Schleiermacher and the tradition he launched than on Kant, was the emotional intensity of religious experience, the heart instead of the head, inner conviction more than external obedience. The key emotion was less respect (Kant's *Acht* for the categorical imperative) than love, figured in Zinzendorf's writings along the lines of conjugal and familial affection. Rather than focusing on God's objective act of redemption through the Incarnation or on the impersonality of the moral law, Spener and his followers looked to the subjective response to and appropriation of that act through the believer's personal relation to Jesus. As Oetinger put it in his *Biblical and Emblematic Dictionary* of 1776, "experience is what one is inwardly when the life spirits are established according to their part. . . . one must not cast experience aside, for without it there is no true knowledge. To know is to have a heightened experience by means of speech; without this one helps oneself with definitions which one does not learn by oneself but borrows."[38] Zinzendorf would

37. See Ernst Cassirer, *Kant's Life and Thought,* trans. James Haden (New Haven, 1981), pp. 16–18, for a discussion of his parents' Pietist beliefs and his education at the Collegium Fredericianum, which he later came to deplore for its fetish of agonized introspection. For a vigorous argument against the idea of Kant's debt to Protestantism in other respects, see Wood, *Kant's Moral Religion,* pp. 197–98. In *Religion within the Limits of Reason Alone,* Kant had in fact attacked "piety" as a passive attitude to God that undermines human autonomy (p. 173).

38. Erb, *Pietists: Selected Writings,* p. 284.

likewise warn in his *Thoughts for the Learned and Yet Good-Willed Students of Truth* of 1732 that "reason weakens experience" and "religion cannot be grasped by reason as long as it opposes experience."[39] It was for this reason that preaching based on personal testimonials of conversion experiences was more important than reasoned arguments or the will to believe (exemplified in the calculated decision of Pascal's wager on God's existence).[40] This was a priority fully endorsed by Schleiermacher.[41]

Such emotionalism could, of course, degenerate into obscurantist anti-intellectualism, as critics of Pietism such as Ritschl often pointed out; even the mature Schleiermacher would protest in the 1820s against a new wave of authoritarian super-piety based on ignorance, superstition, and narrow intolerance for the views of others.[42] Once again, the threat of "enthusiasm" had to be kept at bay. Nonetheless the strong sense of individual, subjective sinfulness and reliance on the personal mediation of Christ to redeem the sinner remained a powerful influence on the arguments of *On Religion* and the renewal they brought to German Protestantism. Twentieth-century champions of that renewal like Rudolf Otto could praise Pietists like Zinzendorf for discovering the "sensus numinis" that was the essence of religious experience.[43] Critics of it like Karl Barth could blame Zinzendorf and his followers for the "intolerable humanizing of Christ that triumphed under the aegis of Schleiermacher in the 19th century."[44] But all had to agree that without Pietism, the experiential turn in theology that so marked Protestantism in the modern era could not easily have occurred.

In the case of Schleiermacher's *Speeches,* however, a second context has to

---

39. Ibid., p. 292.

40. For an account of the confessional literature that was produced in the early Enlightenment by Pietist writers, see Dorothea von Mücke, "Experience, Impartiality, and Authenticity in Confessional Discourse," *New German Critique* 79 (Winter 2000). Mücke shows that these writings were not yet fully sentimental or psychological, providing an impartial rather than empathetic record of conversions that could be compared with other like stories in a virtual community of pious souls. By the time of Schleiermacher, however, they were imbued with a more emotional pathos.

41. Schleiermacher, *The Christian Faith,* p. 69: "Preaching must always take the form of testimony; testimony as to one's own experience, which shall arouse in others the desire to have the same experience."

42. Albrecht Ritschl, *Geschichte des Pietismus,* 3 vols. (Berlin, 1966). Schleiermacher's hostility to the fundamentalist and authoritarian pietism of the 1820s is discussed by John Toews in *Hegelianism: The Path Toward Dialectical Humanism, 1805–1841* (Cambridge, 1980), pp. 245–46. Toews emphasizes the aristocratic roots of the new pietism as opposed to the populist origins of its predecessor.

43. Rudolf Otto, "Zinzendorf Discovered the *Sensus Numinis,*" (1932), reprinted in *Autobiographical and Social Essays* (Berlin, 1996).

44. Karl Barth, *The Theology of Schleiermacher,* ed., Dietrich Ritschl, trans. Geoffrey W. Bromiley (Grand Rapids, Mich., 1982), p. 106.

be brought to the fore as well: the nascent Romantic movement, of which he was so much a part.[45] The "cultured despisers" *(die Gebildeten unter ihren Verächtern)* to whom his work was addressed were, in fact, the group around Schlegel as much, if not more than they were the skeptics or rationalists of the *Aufklärung,* let alone the English or French *philosophes* with their "lamentable empiricism."[46] To convince his friends, Schleiermacher had to show them that the principles of Romanticism, as they were then in the process of being formulated, were fully compatible with religious faith. They in fact were closer to religion than their authors had realized. In rhetorical terms, Schleiermacher made his case by exploiting many of the same devices that marked Romantic prose and poetry: a wealth of metaphorical allusion rather than dry literalism, a rhapsodic intensity of expression, reliance on concrete examples rather than abstract principles, and organic images of dynamic oppositions being overcome by higher mediations. Even the formal regularities of his argumentation, following the geometric patterns favored by the Romantics (circular or elliptical) rather than systematic deduction from first principles, reveal his adherence to their modes of thought.[47]

Unlike the Pietists, whose moralistic disdain for aesthetic pleasure showed their roots in Calvinist asceticism, Schleiermacher, the scholar of Hellenic thought and translator of classical texts, could respond to the lure of the aesthetic, which he believed could be reconciled with religion (although not entirely equated with it). Religious feelings, he liked to argue, are like sacred music accompanying an active life.[48] So too, he shared with the Romantics a high valuation of imagination or fantasy, the free association of ideas and emotions, which Kantian rationalism could not fully appreciate.[49] Their "diversitarian" valorization of multiplicity over simple unity was likewise apparent in his—not very Pietist—celebration of the variety of religious manifestations in history, all expressing a primary human experience of piety, but

45. For an account of the debate over the extent to which Schleiermacher was imbued with Romantic ideals and values, see Crouter's introduction to *On Religion,* pp. 33–34. Christian interpreters of Schleiermacher's work have tended to find his links with Schlegel and their circle an embarrassment, echoing the advice given him by his church superior Sack to break with his dubious friends (whose ties to Jewish salon hostesses and uninhibited love life were added causes for concern).

46. Schleiermacher, *On Religion,* p. 85. Although Schiller and Goethe were unconvinced, Schelling, Fichte, and Novalis were touched in different ways by the work. See the essay by Rudolf Otto introducing John Oman's translation, p. x.

47. Marshall Brown, *The Shape of German Romanticism* (Ithaca, N.Y., 1979).

48. Schleiermacher's devotion to music is shown in such works as his 1805 essay "The Celebration of Christmas: A Conversation," whose importance is discussed in Gerrish, *A Prince of the Church,* pp. 27–31.

49. For a thorough discussion of Schleiermacher's appreciation of fantasy, see Blackwell, *Schleiermacher's Early Philosophy of Life,* part 3.

irreducible to an abstract "natural religion."[50] Schlegel's exaltation of romantic love as more than mere sensual happiness or moral virtue—in *Lucinde,* he even gushes about a "religion of love"—also bears comparison with Schleiermacher's stress on the reciprocal power of the believer's devotion (*Heilandsliebe,* or love of the Savior) and God's love, quintessentially expressed in Christ's martyrdom for humankind's sins.[51] Feeling, the immediate, embodied self-consciousness that subtends the faculties of willing and thinking and indeed is prior to their very differentiation, is at the center of Schleiermacher's psychological ruminations, as it was for most Romantics.[52]

But perhaps of most significance for our purposes, Schleiermacher and the Romantics both stressed the importance of something called *Leben,* or "life," against the mortifying implications of excessive rationation, impersonal legalism, and mechanical causality. Arguing against the sterile literalism of the letter, which he saw in such allegedly "dead religions"[53] as Judaism, he passionately defended the living spirit. It was precisely the embodiment of that spirit in the flesh of a living God that could arouse such passions. It was to this attitude that a primary source of "experience" as *Erlebnis* rather than *Erfahrung* can be traced. Schleiermacher must thus be accounted one of the founding fathers of what became known as *Lebensphilosophie* later in the century. Although as Hans-Georg Gadamer has pointed out, the term *Erlebnis* itself was not yet in common use until the 1870s and Dilthey's biography of Schleiermacher, there are many synonymous locutions in *On Religion* and

50. Precisely how far Schleiermacher's ecumenical tolerance reached was, however, debated from the beginning. As Gerrish has noted, "The cultured despisers were disappointed to find, in the final address, that it was the *Christian* religion they were supposed to embrace. And yet Schleiermacher's fellow churchmen and churchwomen had already decided, by the time they had finished the second address, that what he commended was not Christianity at all." *Continuing the Reformation,* pp. 158–59.

51. In *On Religion,* Schleiermacher would call religious activity "as modest and as delicate as a maiden's kiss, as holy and fruitful as a nuptial embrace; indeed, not *like* these, but *is itself* all of these" (p. 113). Even in the less rhapsodic *Christian Faith,* Schleiermacher would continue to ponder the implications of divine love (pp. 727–32). For a discussion of Schleiermacher's idealization of women, marital love, and the family, see Gerrish, *A Prince of the Church,* p. 29.

52. For an extensive account of the relationship between feeling, life, and embodiment in Schleiermacher, which draws on his often neglected *Dialektik* (the posthumously published lectures he gave between 1811 and 1831), see Thandeka, *The Embodied Self: Friedrich Schleiermacher's Solution to Kant's Problem of the Empirical Self* (Albany, N.Y., 1995).

53. Schleiermacher, *On Religion,* p. 211. This equation of Judaism with dead, legalistic literalism was made by the Berlin *Aufklärung,* including some of its Jewish members. It continued to be a staple of nineteenth-century German thought, returning for example in Nietzsche's critique of Judaism as a "slave-religion" of anti-vitalist resentment. See Nathan Rotenstreich, *Jews and German Philosophy: The Polemics of Emancipation* (New York, 1984); and Michael Mack, *German Idealism and the Jew: The Inner Anti-Semitism of Philosophy and German Jewish Responses* (Chicago, 2003).

elsewhere in his work.[54] *Lebendig* is an adjective, Blackwell has also noted, that can be found throughout the addresses, whose second edition often replaced the verb *bewegen* (to move) with *beleben* (to enliven or animate).[55] Like the Romantics, Schleiermacher believed that a living "intuition of the universe"[56] involved a preference for organic wholeness over analytical dissection. *Erlebnis* would thus suggest prereflective immediacy, intuitive holism, and intensity of feeling, invidiously compared with the prosaic epistemological notions of experience, empiricist or Kantian, we examined in the previous chapter.

On one crucial question, however, Schleiermacher put some distance between his position and that of the Romantics: their understanding of freedom. Although the Romantics' attitude toward freedom was extraordinarily complicated, at least in certain of their moods (when they were not tempted by self-annihilation), they followed the *Sturm und Drang* poets of the previous generation in asserting the human capacity to defy laws, norms, and taboos and create anew. Carried beyond the mere transgression of classical aesthetic rules, this attitude could lead to the aggressive self-assertion manifested in such claims as Schlegel's that "the human is free, when he brings forth deity."[57] Here the artist was a surrogate for God, implying a Promethean self-aggrandizement that any religious thinker would have to question. In philosophical terms, a similar hubris was manifested in Fichte's subjective idealist exaltation of the constitutive ego based on the primacy of practical reason, which Schleiermacher also strenuously resisted.

Schleiermacher in fact formed his attitude toward the question of freedom almost a decade before his encounter with the Romantics. In 1791–92, when he was at Halle, he composed a long, unpublished essay entitled "On Human Freedom," which was a sustained response to Kant's defense of moral autonomy.[58] Kant's dualism, it will be recalled, was premised on the absolute, transcendental possession of freedom in our capacity as moral beings. Practical reason meant that we were utterly unconstrained in our choices to fol-

---

54. Hans-Georg Gadamer, *Truth and Method* (New York, 1986), p. 57. Gadamer lists many synonyms in note 117 on p. 505. Ironically, the first recorded use that he has found appears in a letter by Hegel describing a journey (the *Fahrt* that is normally heard in the older German word, *Erfahrung*). See note 108 on p. 505.

55. Blackwell, *Schleiermacher's Early Philosophy of Life*, p. 133.

56. Schleiermacher, *On Religion*, p. 104.

57. Quoted in Crouter's introduction to Schleiermacher, *On Religion*, p. 35.

58. Schleiermacher, "Über die Freiheit des Menschen," abridged in Dilthey, *Leben Schleiermacher*, 1st ed. For an extensive discussion, see Blackwell, *Schleiermacher's Early Philosophy of Life*, part 1.

low or transgress the imperatives that came to us from our sense of duty, even if as phenomenal beings we were caught in the web of natural causality. For Schleiermacher, as for many other post-Kantians such as Jacobi and Fries, the rigid distinction between noumenal and phenomenal realms was untenable.[59] To reintegrate the intelligible and the sensible and thus unify the personality was one of the goals of his thought. But what must be understood is that he did so largely by reabsorbing the noumenal into the phenomenal and thus recontextualizing the absolute, ungrounded freedom of the putatively autonomous moral subject in the causally determined world of his natural twin. Kant was wrong to banish psychological motives from his analysis of the supposedly rational moral will. Human freedom, Schleiermacher contended, must be empirically situated, conditioned by the finite realities of existence, more an a posteriori result than an a priori given. What in methodological terms he would make famous as the hermeneutic circle, eschewing absolute points of departure or transcendental foundations prior to immersion in the context of meaning, manifested itself in experiential terms in the always already embedded quality of the subject in the world. Such embeddedness mirrored in a way the Incarnation in which the infinite descended into the finite, giving the lie to the view of God, held by Deists and others, as entirely extramundane.

Not surprisingly, there was a certain convergence with Benedict Spinoza's immanentist philosophy in all of this, which subjected Schleiermacher to endless accusations of a monistic pantheism that he was at pains to deny.[60] Spinoza was, in fact, not easy to reconcile with Pietist values; in *The Varieties of Religious Experience,* James would describe him as a "healthy-minded" Rationalist with no use for the dialectic of sin and repentance undergone by the

59. In other ways as well, Schleiermacher might be compared with post-Kantian idealists. Citing Emil Fackenheim's observation that for Schelling, "The true religious experience and the true God are identical," Warren Breckman adds: "Each of the major post-Kantian Idealists advanced a version of this fundamental claim. Hence, for example, Schleiermacher's enormously influential concept of piety centered upon the individual believer's conscious 'feeling' that she or he is 'utterly dependent' or, which is to say the same thing, [is] in relation to God." *Marx, The Young Hegelians, and the Origins of Radical Social Theory,* p. 29.

60. The accusations began as early as Sack's critique of the first edition of *On Religion,* which had already contained a denial (p. 199). How much of Spinoza Schleiermacher actually knew when he wrote that work is a matter of debate, as much of it was filtered through Jacobi's critique. For thorough considerations of this question, see Blackwell, *Schleiermacher's Early Philosophy of Life,* pp. 125–27; and Redeker, *Schleiermacher: Life and Thought,* pp. 43–45. The general fascination for Spinoza among German intellectuals, especially the Romantics (e.g., Schlegel), even after the Pantheism controversy ended, is discussed in Gerrish, *Continuing the Reformation,* chapter 5.

"sick souls" who had to experience a radical conversion in order to achieve salvation.[61] But Schleiermacher did, in fact, ask the readers of *On Religion* to "respectfully offer up with me a lock of hair to the manes of the holy rejected Spinoza . . . [who] was full of religion, full of holy spirit."[62] Although he had absorbed Kant's critique of speculative rationalism and thus could not accept the metaphysical presuppositions of Spinoza's system, such as the equation of God with natural substance, Schleiermacher clearly shared the deterministic implications of that system and the belief that moral will must be situated within the causal nexus of spatial and temporal relations. For Spinoza, God alone was perfectly unconstrained, whereas human freedom was always conditioned. Schleiermacher translated this contention into the claim that freedom entails the realization of the potentials that are instilled in the self by the world, an expressivist notion of subjectivity that was shared by many of his contemporaries.[63] Here freedom meant cultivating and appropriating what had been given, not the absolute, unmotivated autopoiesis or transcendental freedom of the noumenal self, who acts practically in the world. It involved accepting our unavoidable dependence upon the whole into which we had been born, an acceptance with deep religious implications. Such a religion, he claimed, "longs to be grasped and filled by the universe's immediate influences in childlike passivity."[64] For, as he came to put it in the celebrated formula of *The Christian Faith,* the essence of spiritual experience is "the feeling of absolute dependence [*schlechthin abhängig*] or, which is the same thing, of being in relation with God."[65]

61. James, *The Varieties of Religious Experience,* pp. 127–28. One of the charges laid against Schleiermacher by later critics was, in fact, his pollyannish lack of appreciation for the reality of Radical Evil.

62. Schleiermacher, *On Religion,* p. 104.

63. Izenberg, *Impossible Individuality,* pp. 18–27. See also Blackwell's excellent account of Schleiermacher's complex notion of freedom in *Schleiermacher's Early Philosophy of Life,* part 2. For a general analysis of the expressivist notion of subjectivity during this period, see Charles Taylor, *Hegel* (Cambridge, 1975), chapter 1.

64. Schleiermacher, *On Religion,* p. 102.

65. Schleiermacher, *The Christian Faith,* p. 12. *Schlechthin,* traditionally translated as "absolute," also means "without counterpart." Schleiermacher was sufficiently dialectical to note that the feeling of absolute dependence was predicated on the contrary feeling of freedom that we have in relative terms in non-religious, temporal matters. Still, his formula was often taken as an affront to human freedom, perhaps most famously by Hegel, who, preferring absolute knowledge to absolute dependence, mockingly remarked that if Schleiermacher were right, his dog would be the most religious creature alive. See his "Vorrede zu Hinrichs Religionsphilosophie" (1822), in Hegel, *Werke,* ed. E. Moldenhauer and K. M. Michel, 20 vols. (Frankfurt, 1969–72), vol. 11, pp. 42–67. On their tense relationship as colleagues in Berlin, see Richard Crouter, "Hegel and Schleiermacher at Berlin: A Many-Sided Debate," *Journal of the American Academy of Religion* 48 (1980) and Toews, *Hegelianism,* p. 56–67. For a general account of

The distinction between his position and Kant's—and the difference between religious and moral experience—is perhaps nowhere as clearly stated as in the following passage from the second address in *On Religion:*

> Morality proceeds from the consciousness of freedom; it wishes to extend freedom's realm to infinity and to make everything subservient to it. Religion breathes there where freedom itself has once more become nature; it apprehends man beyond the play of his particular powers and his personality, and views him from the vantage point where he must be what he is, whether he likes it or not.[66]

Getting beyond the particular personality, the moral individual yearning to be free, is precisely what religion demands, according to Schleiermacher. Thus the often involuntary nature of religious experience—the feeling of being overwhelmed by something one cannot control—was a mark of its authenticity, rather than being an affront to human dignity.

Although Kantian morality may mistakenly seek to extend the realm of freedom to infinity, Schleiermacher—like most of the Romantics—was himself fascinated by the lure of the infinite, which the immanentist impulse in his worldview led him to locate within the finite, not beyond it. Although one of his most celebrated definitions of religion was "the sensibility and taste for the infinite,"[67] based on an intuition of the universe, he understood that we mere creatures can experience it only on the level of impure, finite particularities. For this reason, despite the mystical nuances of Schleiermacher's appeal to an intuitive grasp of the universe—"truly religious minds," he wrote, "have distinguished themselves through the ages by a mystical tinge"[68]—he resisted the temptation to surrender entirely the individual self in the hope of uniting it with the divine. As Rudolf Otto was to recognize, for all his closeness to Romanticism, Schleiermacher's position "should be characterized as a mysticism of the spirit that on occasion fights against the ecstatic nature-mysticism of his friends."[69] Religious experience may express a mystical yearning, but Schleiermacher understood that a feeling of absolute dependence could only follow from at least some distinction between God and humankind.

Hegel on religion, see Emil L. Fackenheim, *The Religious Dimension in Hegel's Thought* (Boston, 1967). Fackenheim emphasizes the comprehensive realism of Hegel's position, in which all experience is given redemptive resonance.

66. Schleiermacher, *On Religion,* p. 102.

67. Ibid., p. 103.

68. Ibid., p. 152.

69. Rudolf Otto, *West-östliche Mystik* (Gotha, 1929), p. 325.

Nonetheless, that distinction was not to be rigidly absolutized. God's becoming flesh in history Schleiermacher boldly analogized to mean that the infinite had appeared in a variety of different concrete, institutional forms: "the positive religions are these determinate forms in which infinite religion manifests itself in the finite."[70] Unlike the profoundly disaffected and melancholic Kierkegaard, who was to carry anti-institutional subjectivism to an extreme, he did not pit the individual sinner against the historical church or ethical community. Schleiermacher, the fervent believer in Christ's divinity, did, of course, elevate his own faith over all others, writing his second great work in the form of a Christological dogmatics *(Glaubenslehre)* to make his case. But the radical implication of his argument was that primal religious experience was anterior to any one specific doctrinal or ecclesiastical order and subtended each of them. Although it was impossible to distill any generic "natural religion" from all of the concrete manifestations, one could infer an experiential core that they all shared as expressions of *homo religiosus.* The Christian Incarnation may have been the most successful means of awakening that experience, at least for Jesus's followers, but it existed in less developed forms elsewhere. Not only did a theology of pious, lived experience follow from this argument, so too did an emphasis on the realization of the divine in history, a conclusion that was vital for such later historicist theologians as Ernst Troeltsch (1865–1923).[71] Although Schleiermacher was no relativist, a charge often leveled against Troeltsch, his attempt to recover the primal experiential basis of all religions led to a comparativist approach that seemed to some to imply that outcome.

Whatever the truth of this reproach, it was often accompanied by another in the reception of Schleiermacher's ideas: the charge of anthropomorphic psychologism engendered by his allegedly "subjectivist" exaggeration of the importance of experience.[72] When the so-called theology of crisis or dialectical theology developed by the neo-orthodox "Swiss School" of theologians led by Karl Barth (1886–1968) and Emil Brunner (1889–1966) emerged af-

70. Schleiermacher, *On Religion,* p. 195.

71. For discussions of Troeltsch's relationship to Schleiermacher, see Mackintosh, *Types of Modern Theology,* pp. 189–90; and Gerrish, *Continuing the Reformation,* chapter 12. A similar impact can be discerned on the so-called empirical theology of the American theologian Douglas Clyde Macintosh. See his *Theology as an Empirical Science* (New York, 1919). How genuinely historical Schleiermacher actually was, however, is in dispute. For an argument that it was not really until Hegel that religious philosophy took seriously its historical manifestations, see Fackenheim, *The Religious Dimension in Hegel's Thought,* p. 230.

72. See typically, Emil Brunner, *Die Mystik und das Wort* (Tübingen, 1924). For an attempt to rescue Schleiermacher from this charge in relation to his hermeneutics, see Andrew Bowie, *From Romanticism to Critical Theory: The Philosophy of German Literary Theory* (London, 1997), chapter 5.

ter the First World War, Schleiermacher's experiential apology for religion was its main target.[73] Barth, it is said, kept a bust of Schleiermacher always before him as a reminder of the opponent against whom he was struggling.[74] Significantly, in the light of the frequent evocation of *Erlebnis* on the part of those supporting the German war effort—which we will see in the cases of Martin Buber and Ernst Jünger—it was Barth's disdain for theologians and philosophers who defended the war that helped lead him in a very different direction. Although he acknowledged that Schleiermacher himself would likely have refrained from signing the notorious manifesto of ninety-three intellectuals who defended the patriotic "ideas of 1914," he noted with chagrin that "the entire theology which had unmasked itself in that manifesto and everything which followed after it (even in the *Christliche Welt*), was grounded, determined, and influenced decisively by him."[75]

That is, a theology that was too much caught up with the finite, the creaturely, the emotional, the historical—in short, the subjective experience of absolute dependence—could lose its bearings and fail to heed the actual Word of God in the Bible. Instead, it was little more than that illusory human projection atheists like Ludwig Feuerbach and Karl Marx had wrongly condemned as religion *tout court*.[76] For Barth, Schleiermacher had forgotten that "in a meaningful statement about God, God can only be thought of as the *subject* and not the predicate."[77] In his haste to attack speculative theology as a "dead letter," Schleiermacher had imputed life more to the pious believer than to God Himself. His reliance on experience made a mockery of God's promise of eternal life, which, after all, could not be derived from anything

73. Barth, *The Theology of Schleiermacher;* Emil Brunner, *The Christian Doctrine of Faith and Knowledge,* trans. Olive Wyon (Philadelphia, 1946). Throughout the nineteenth century, critiques of Schleiermacher had been made by a number of figures, including Hegel and Ritschl, but it was not until the onslaught of the postwar years, which was foreshadowed by the publication of Barth's commentary on Paul's Epistle to the Romans, *Der Römerbrief,* in 1917, that his influence on German Protestantism was seriously challenged.

74. Forstman, *A Romantic Triangle,* p. 104.

75. Barth, *The Theology of Schleiermacher,* p. 264. *Die christliche Welt* was a liberal Protestant weekly edited by Martin Rade. For a discussion of Barth's antiwar feeling and socialist sympathies, see James Bentley, *Between Marx and Christ: The Dialogue in German-Speaking Europe, 1870–1970* (London, 1982), chapter 4.

76. In fact, Feuerbach had explicitly defended Schleiermacher against Hegel for having realized that subjective feeling was the source of religion, censuring him "only because theological prejudice prevented him from drawing the necessary conclusions from his standpoint, for not having the courage to see and to admit that objectively God is himself nothing but the essence of feeling, if, subjectively, feeling is the central aspect of religion." Ludwig Feuerbach, *Sämtliche Werke,* ed. Wilhelm Bolin and Friedrich Jodl (Stuttgart, 1960), vol. 7, p. 266.

77. Barth, *The Theology of Schleiermacher,* p. 253.

already undergone by even the most pious believer. Trying to find a common denominator subtending all religious experience, Schleiermacher and other liberal theologians had obscured the fundamental Christian premise that there was only one true account of the one true God.[78] In short, the object of devotion had been obliterated as a result of the exaggerated fascination with the subject's mode of experiencing it.

JAMES AND THE PSYCHOLOGY OF RELIGIOUS EXPERIENCE

The anxiety about sliding down a slippery slope into psychologism, which was a common epithet in many contexts during this period,[79] was not groundless, as a flourishing branch of theology had emerged that attempted to use recent developments in psychology to interpret religious experience. In the Germany of Barth's day, it was perhaps Georg Wobbermin of Göttingen who best represented this trend,[80] but its most eminent and still influential manifestation appeared in the Gifford Lectures given in Edinburgh in 1901 and 1902 by the American philosopher, psychologist, and social theorist William James (1842–1910), which became *The Varieties of Religious Experience.*[81]

78. As Brunner would put it, "The Divine Holiness is inseparably connected with that character of absolute intolerance which distinguishes the Biblical idea of God, and differentiates it from all other ideas of God." *Dogmatics,* vol. 1, *The Christian Doctrine of God,* trans. Olive Wyon (Philadelphia, 1950), p. 160.

79. Martin Kusch, *Psychologism: A Case Study in the Sociology of Knowledge* (London, 1995). I have tried to tease out the implications of the critique of psychologism for modernist aesthetics in "Modernism and the Specter of Psychologism," *Cultural Semantics: Keywords of Our Time* (Amherst, Mass., 1998).

80. Georg Wobbermin, *Systematischer Theologie nach religionspsychologischer Methode,* 2 vols. (Leipzig, 1921). Wobbermin translated *The Varieties of Religious Experience* into German in 1907. His own work came too late for James to cite, although he does draw on other prominent contemporary psychologists of religion, such as Edward D. Starbuck and James H. Leuba. For an account of their work, see David Hay, "Psychologists Interpreting Conversion: Two American Forerunners of the Hermeneutics of Suspicion," *History of the Human Sciences* 12, no. 1 (February 1999). For a general history of the psychology of religion, see David M. Wulff, *Psychology of Religion: Classic and Contemporary Approaches* (New York, 1997).

81. James's explorations of religious experience have generated a wide secondary literature. See, for example, Julius Seelye Bixler, *Religion in the Philosophy of William James* (Boston, 1926); Henry Samuel Levinson, *The Religious Investigations of William James* (Chapel Hill, N.C., 1981); Eugene Fontinell, *Self, God, and Immortality: A Jamesian Investigation* (Philadelphia, 1986); Bennett Ramsey, *Submitting to Freedom: The Religious Vision of William James* (Oxford, 1993); and Ellen Kappy Suckiel, *Heaven's Champion: William James's Philosophy of Religion* (Notre Dame, Ind., 1996).

Perhaps James's most radical innovation was to uncouple the concept of religious experience from any one tradition, a process started but not completed by Schleiermacher the devout Christian, and make it a capacious category that embraced all the multifarious phenomena grouped under the rubric. As Ann Taves has noted, "with the publication of *The Varieties,* William James theoretically constituted 'religious experience' as an object of study, defining it as a generic 'something' that informed 'religion-in-general' apart from any tradition in particular."[82] But how broad that something may have been remained a problem. Significantly, James's discussion of devoutness in *The Varieties of Religious Experience* immediately turned into a caution against its "unbalanced" form, which he called fanaticism, a synonym for the "enthusiasm" that often seemed the dark twin of authentic religious experience.[83] But in comparison to the upholders of the one true faith, James's version of that experience was radically ecumenical.

Although a fuller discussion of the place of experience in James's "radical empiricism" in particular and American pragmatism in general must await a later chapter, a few points are warranted here about what James himself called the twin goals of his work:

> *first,* to defend (against all the prejudices of my class) "experience" against "philosophy" as being the real backbone of the world's religious life—I mean prayer, guidance, and all that sort of thing immediately and privately felt, as against high and noble general views of our destiny and the world's meaning; and *second,* to make the hearer or reader believe, what I myself invincibly do believe, that, although all the manifestations of religion may have been absurd (I mean the creeds and theories), yet the life of it as a whole is mankind's most important function.[84]

---

82. Taves. *Fits, Trances, and Visions,* p. 351.

83. James, *The Varieties of Religious Experience,* pp. 340–48.

84. *The Letters of William James,* ed. Henry James, 2 vols. (Boston, 1920), vol. 2, p. 127. The other leading pragmatists had differing responses to religious experience, Charles Sanders Peirce finding it of little interest, John Dewey sharing James's enthusiasm. Peirce's attitude is classically expressed in his 1877 essay "The Fixation of Belief," in David Hollinger and Charles Capper, eds., *The American Intellectual Tradition,* vol. 2 (Oxford, 1997). For an overview of Dewey's attitudes, see Steven C. Rockefeller, *John Dewey: Religious Faith and Democratic Humanism* (New York, 1991), and "Dewey's Philosophy of Religious Experience," in Hickman, *Reading Dewey.* In the latter, Rockefeller observes that "Dewey is careful to point out that his notion of the religious quality of experience does not refer to a special kind of experience that is marked off from aesthetic, scientific, moral, or political experience or from experience as companionship and friendship. The religious quality of experience is not the result of interaction with some distinct religious object like a supernatural deity or the numinous" (p. 138). In the first sentence, he suggests that Dewey was not really following Schleiermacher; in the second, he shows how far he was from both Barth and Otto.

As in his powerful and controversial 1896 essay "The Will to Believe,"[85] James wanted to strike a blow against the claim of critical reason to put all of our unexamined convictions on trial, and he did so by showing that experience was a category that could extend well beyond the limits of scientific or commonsensical epistemology. Schleiermacher himself is not mentioned in *The Varieties of Religious Experience*, although James does obliquely refer to him—or rather projects his arguments onto two different anonymous figures—in a passage in which he disparages authors who vainly try to define the essence of religion: "One man allies it to the feeling of dependence; one makes it a derivative of fear; others connect it with sexual life; others identify it with the feeling of the infinite; and so on."[86] Nor did James evoke the personal experience of piety that Schleiermacher had enjoyed from his Moravian background; indeed he expressed considerable ambivalence throughout his life about his own religious commitments.[87] Although one of his students remembered him as "a profoundly religious man," he would ultimately come to advocate a pluralistic humanism in which God was only a hypothesis.[88] James had no use for dogmatic theology or an organized church, which were mere excrescences on the religion that he identified entirely with "*the feelings, acts, and experiences of individual men in their solitude, so far as they apprehend themselves to stand in relation to whatever they may consider the divine.*"[89]

Yet it is clear that James's own attempt to explore in a friendly fashion the underlying human inclinations, needs, and states of mind that produce a healthy diversity of religious expression was a working out of one of the main

---

85. William James, *The Will to Believe and Other Essays in Popular Philosophy* (Cambridge, Mass., 1979). Its main target was the English mathematician W. K. Clifford, whose positivist skepticism James sought to challenge. For a recent defense of Clifford against James's hasty reading of him, see David Hollinger, "James, Clifford, and the Scientific Conscience," in Ruth Anna Putnam, ed., *The Cambridge Companion to William James* (New York, 1997). For general considerations of James's argument, see Robert J. O'Connell, *William James and the Courage to Believe* (New York, 1984); and James C. S. Wernham, *James's Will-to-Believe Doctrine: A Heretical View* (Kingston, Ontario, 1987). In certain respects, James's position anticipates the defense of prejudice against critical reason made by Hans-Georg Gadamer in his debate with Jürgen Habermas in the 1960s and 1970s.

86. James, *The Varieties of Religious Experience*, p. 27.

87. For a sample of James's ambivalent attitudes toward religious belief, see Suckiel, *Heaven's Champion*, pp. 4–5. For a discussion of the religious milieu in which he grew up, including the "idiosyncratic fusion of Calvinism and republicanism" (p. 11) of his father, Henry James Sr., who was fascinated by Swedenborg and transcendentalism, see Levinson, *The Religious Investigations of William James*, chapter 1.

88. George Angier Gordon, "A Profoundly Religious Man," in Linda Simon, ed., *William James Remembered* (Lincoln, Neb., 1996), p. 46. In 1905, James wrote an essay entitled "The Essence of Humanism," which is included in *Essays in Radical Empiricism* (Lincoln, Neb., 1996).

89. James, *The Varieties of Religious Experience*, p. 31 (emphasis in original).

implications of Schleiermacher's theological revolution, which had had its most profound American parallel in Wesleyan Methodism.[90] Like Schleiermacher, James was hostile to the Kantian claim that religion was founded on morality. Indeed, according to one commentator, he followed his father, Henry James Sr., in believing that "morality and religion are actually bitter enemies because morality depends upon a person's self efforts, whereas religion is rooted in self surrender."[91] Although James and the other pragmatists may well have imbibed their fascination with lived experience from nonreligious sources as well—Dilthey and the French social theorist Alfred Fouillée are often-cited examples[92]—he was clearly drawn to those who had themselves felt the greatest intensities of religious feeling.

For all his allegiance to the scientific method as he understood it, and James was an avid reader of such earlier "scientists of religion" as Max Müller, Emile Burnouf, and E. B. Tylor, he was almost as anxious as Schleiermacher had been before him to differentiate realms of experience, preventing the reduction of one to the other.[93] Underlying this claim was James's belief that *all* experiences were irreducibly *sui generis,* even if tentative typologies might be

90. According to Levinson, in the period preceding the Civil War when James came of age, "the laxity on creedal issues and the emphasis on experience that followed the triumph of Methodism was doubleedged, depending on how one construed 'experience.' Where revivalists emphasized their postmillennialism, salvation and social responsibility went hand in hand both in the North and the South (laying the context for the later belligerence). Where they focused on experience as inward and identified conversion as *the* religious experience, salvation and social responsibility were separated." *The Religious Investigations of William James,* p. 5. Henry James Sr. was one of the northerners concerned with combining the two, a legacy inherited by his son.

91. G. William Barnard, *Exploring Unseen Worlds: William James and the Philosophy of Mysticism* (Albany, N.Y., 1997), p. 244.

92. For a discussion of the importance of these thinkers for American pragmatism, see James T. Kloppenberg, *Uncertain Victory: Social Democracy and Progressivism in European and American Thought, 1870–1920* (New York, 1986), chapters 2 and 3.

93. At one point in *The Varieties of Religious Experience,* James does claim that religious experiences of, say, melancholy, joy, or trancelike illumination, are "each and all of them special cases of kinds of human experiences of much wider scope" (p. 24). Wayne Proudfoot, in *Religious Experience* (Berkeley, 1985), p. 157, notes a contrast with Schleiermacher here. But on the issue of how one is to explain and judge such experiences, both sought to protect religious experience from submission to the same criteria that were appropriate for other variants.

However, as James E. Dittes has pointed out, "the *sui generis* argument is often accompanied by or confused with, but is logically quite distinguishable from the more extreme phenomenological argument: Religious phenomena are inadequately understood if they are understood with categories different from those used by the subjects experiencing the phenomena. The *sui generis* argument is often accompanied by or confused with, but is logically quite distinguishable from the more general, antiscientism argument: The validity of religious experience many not be challenged by any psychological analysis, of whatever variety." "Beyond William James," in Charles Y. Glock and Phillip E. Hammond. ed., *Beyond the Classics? Essays in the Scientific Study of Religion* (New York, 1973), p. 311.

introduced to discern similarities. The audience to which his lectures were delivered was composed less of the Romantic "cultured despisers" addressed by *On Religion* than of the learned philosophers and scientists of his day, likely to be struggling with the positivist challenge to their faith. James was himself a dedicated follower of Darwinian ideas, which had put the last nail in the coffin of the argument from design.[94] But his aim, like Schleiermacher's, was to convince the skeptical of the legitimacy of experiencing religious feelings on their own terms. Although he had no interest in establishing the supernatural or metaphysical legitimacy of such experiences, he was a man of his time in his openness to spiritual phenomena.[95] As one of the founding members of the Society for Psychical Research in America in 1884, two years after its British debut, James took a lively interest in the scientific study of trances, possessions, clairvoyance, and other spiritual phenomena. Mobilizing the vitalist rhetoric of *Lebensphilosophie,* he warned against employing the abstract, conceptual mind to analyze concrete emotion: "Compared with this world of living individualized feelings, the world of generalized objects which the intellect contemplates is without solidity or life."[96] Arguing against the "medical materialism" that sought to reduce mystical visions or conversion experiences to hysteria, lesions on the brain, or dyspepsia, James claimed that the value of religious opinions "can only be ascertained by spiritual judgments directly passed on them, judgments based on our own immediate feeling primarily; and secondarily on what we can ascertain of their experiential relations to our moral needs and to the rest of what we hold as true."[97] As Charles Darwin had shown, origins were far less important than present function in the struggle to survive.[98]

Any psychological approach, if it is to serve as the basis for what he called a "critical Science of Religions," must depend, James insisted, "for its original material on facts of personal experience, and would have to square itself

94. Levinson nonetheless notes the Romantic residue in James's embrace of diversitarian pluralism and opposition to sectarian exclusiveness, which accorded well with the republican ideology of his father, as well as his bias for religious enthusiasm and emotionality. See *The Religious Investigations of William James*, pp. 18–21.

95. For a discussion of James in the context of the respect for spiritualism among late nineteenth-century psychologists, see Judith Ryan, *The Vanishing Subject: Early Psychology and Literary Modernism* (Chicago, 1991), chapter 1; and Taves, *Fits, Trances, and Vision,* chapter 6.

96. James, *The Varieties of Religious Experience,* p. 502.

97. Ibid., p. 18. James did himself situate feelings in the body, not the soul, but it was a vital, irreducible body in which the psychological and physiological levels were inextricably intertwined.

98. For a discussion of James's use of Darwin against medical materialism, see Taves, *Fits, Trances, and Visions,* p. 278.

with personal experience through all its critical reconstructions."[99] A genuinely empirical science must credit such personal experiences, which, following J. H. Leuba, he called faith-states, if it is to do justice to the ubiquity of religious feeling. Personal narratives should not be immediately discounted by reductive explanations. Accordingly, *The Varieties of Religious Experience* provided in rich and vivid detail the accounts of saints, mystics, born-again converts, and other virtuosi (or "religious geniuses," as James called them) from a wide spectrum of religions testifying to their individual encounter with the divine, or more precisely, their sense of the presence of an unseen reality.[100]

That sense, James hastened to add, was not necessarily continuous with the bodily senses normally credited by empiricists with providing knowledge of reality. In the case of mysticism, which he tended to see as the quintessential religious experience, "the records show that even though the five senses be in abeyance in them, they are absolutely sensational in their epistemological quality . . . they are face to face presentations of what seems immediately to exist. The mystic is, in short, *invulnerable*, and must be left, whether we relish it or not, in undisturbed enjoyment of his creed."[101] Although skeptics like Max Nordau, the author of *Degeneration*, may be right to see a continuity with pathological states such as paranoia, which James went so far as to call "a *diabolical* mysticism, a sort of religious mysticism turned upside down,"[102] the feelings that gave rise to positive mystical experiences had to be respected as testimonies of a deeper truth.

James, however, did not rest content with the conclusion that such feelings were always fully conscious. He distinguished between two sides of experience, objective and subjective: "the objective part is the sum total of whatsoever at any given time we may be thinking of, the subjective part is the inner 'state' in which the thinking comes to pass."[103] Availing himself of the recently developed concept of the "subliminal, transmarginal or subconscious self," he concluded that "we have in *the fact that the conscious person is continuous with a wider self through which saving experiences come,* a positive con-

---

99. James, *The Varieties of Religious Experience*, p. 456.

100. There were, to be sure, limits to James's knowledge of and sympathy for different religions. As Levinson points out in *The Religious Investigations of William James* (p. 23), he was cold toward Catholicism, indifferent to Judaism and Buddhism, and dismissive of "pagan" cults. James felt most warmly toward the religions he saw as experimental, non-dogmatic, open-minded, and spiritually alive.

101. James, *The Varieties of Religious Experience*, p. 424 (emphasis in original). For an extensive discussion of James's sympathies toward mysticism, see Barnard, *Exploring Unseen Worlds*.

102. James, *The Varieties of Religious Experience*, p. 427.

103. Ibid., pp. 498–99.

tent of religious experiences which, it seems to me, *is literally and objectively true as far as it goes.*[104] This very tentative conclusion was based on the hypothesis, and James admitted it was only that, that the subconscious self was somehow the "hither" side of what religion had always pointed to as the "farther" side of human existence. Its ultimate cause or explanation, James contended, was not amenable to human understanding; what was important was to provide a phenomenology of religious experience, not an explanation or ontology of it.[105]

Such a conclusion, however, was not very successful in pacifying those, like Barth, who were anxious to restore a non-anthropocentric, non-relativist relationship to the true subject, God. Even later American pragmatist theologians, who stressed the importance of experience, such as John E. Smith, found James's formulations gave away too much to subjectivist psychologism.[106] That James himself may have drawn the same conclusion is shown by his development, after *The Varieties of Religious Experience,* of a concept of "pure experience," which was prior to the split between subject and object and which opened the door for the pluralist pantheism of his last reflections on religion.[107] But such a solution, worried his critics, opened it just as widely to polytheism as it did to the monotheism of the great religions.

There were other problems with the argument of *The Varieties of Religious*

104. Ibid., p. 515 (emphasis in original). James explains his reasons for preferring "subconscious" to "unconscious" on p. 207. The discovery of the realm of the "subliminal" by Frederic Myers in 1886 James calls "the most important step forward in psychology since I have been a student of that science" (p. 233). For a thorough account of the career of the concept of the subconscious, see Taves, *Fits, Trances, and Visions,* chapter 7.

105. James has, in fact, been approvingly called "the *first* to attempt a phenomenology of religious experience in an experiential sense" by James M. Edie, *William James and Phenomenology* (Bloomington, Ind., 1987), p. 52.

106. See John E. Smith, *Experience and God* (New York, 1995), pp. 46–47. See also Vincent M. Coalpietro, ed., *Reason, Experience and Dialogue: John E. Smith in Dialogue* (New York, 1997). James did claim in *The Varieties of Religious Experience* that the fact of personal experience included "a conscious field *plus* its object as felt or thought *plus* an attitude toward the object *plus* the sense of self to whom the attitude belongs" (p. 499). But the object as such is still absent in this formulation. For a different assessment that finds a field concept of experience, not a subjective one in James, see Fontinell, *Self, God, and Immortality,* which makes use of the later works on pure experience.

107. James, *Essays in Radical Empiricism.* These essays, which began to be written in 1904, were first collected by Ralph Barton Perry in 1912. The doctrine of "pure experience" will be examined when we look at other efforts to develop a concept of experience without a subject in the twentieth century. James's last thoughts on religion can be found in *A Pluralistic Universe* (Cambridge, Mass., 1977), first published in 1909. James's lifelong struggle with the relationship between the one and the many ended inconclusively with a position that could just as easily imply polytheism or panentheism (God is within the universe, but not reduced to it) as pantheism.

Experience as well. The typical pragmatist extrapolation from Darwin's survival-of-the-fittest hypothesis that truth was a function of what works effectively, which suggested that the ultimate justification for religious belief was the value it had for curing what James called the believer's sick soul, seemed to many to undercut the very cognitive, noetic pay-off that he had attributed to feelings.[108] James himself may have personally profited from that cure following a severe bout of depression that he had suffered between 1868 and 1872, which found its way into his book disguised as someone else's story,[109] but not everyone could accept such anecdotal evidence as a persuasive argument. Not everyone could agree, in other words, that "the real core of the religious problem," is, as he put it in one of his most direct and revealing formulations, "Help! Help!"[110] For surely this was to add precisely the extrinsic functionality to religious experience—its usefulness in giving our confused lives ultimate meaning—that James's injunction to treat the experiences on their own terms had sought to deny. The humble believer, after all, doesn't selfishly choose to praise God and honor His moral commandments only because it heals his divided self.

Questions were also raised very early in the reception of *The Varieties of Religious Experience* about the plausibility of appealing to a purportedly pure experience, prior to conceptual mediation through theological categories or interpretative frameworks, questions that have not been stilled to this day.[111] James's analogizing from immediate, direct sense experiences, moreover, left unconvinced those who recalled the inadequacy of the naive empiricist "myth of the given" in the epistemological discourse that we examined in the pre-

---

108. This critique was typically made by analytic philosophers like Bertrand Russell and A. J. Ayer, although it reappears in Proudfoot's *Religious Experience* as well (p. 167, where he challenges James's claim that Jonathan Edwards was interested only in the fruits, not roots, of belief). For an account of their position and an attempt to refute it by calling into question the objectivist referentialism it assumed and arguing that James did try to distinguish between truth and mere utility for life, see Suckiel, *Heaven's Champion*, chapter 5. How successfully James made that distinction (which he advances in *The Varieties of Religious Experience*, p. 509), is not, however, clear. Suckiel herself concludes that he was never a consistent realist, despite his rhetoric in the conclusion to *The Varieties*.

109. James, *The Varieties of Religious Experience*, pp. 160–61. This episode of morbid melancholia and the transcendence of it through prayer found a later echo in James's 1895 lecture on suicide to the Harvard YMCA entitled "Is Life Worth Living?," published in *The Will to Believe and Other Essays*. Here James criticizes religious pantheism or natural supernaturalism in favor of belief in an invisible, supernatural reality, which makes life worth living.

110. James, *The Varieties of Religious Experience*, p. 162.

111. A number of the early critics, such as George Coe and James H. Leuba, are discussed in Bixler, *Religion in the Philosophy of William James*, p. 203. A comparable complaint is voiced by Proudfoot, *Religious Experience*, p. 13 and extended back to Schleiermacher as well. For a recent defense of James, see Barnard, *Unseen Worlds*, chapter 2.

vious chapter.[112] Why should the sixth sense that purportedly provides mystical experience be granted exemption from the critique of that naiveté? Even more troubling was the inability to appeal to one of the other senses to confirm what that sixth sense had provided, an appeal that could allow some of the uncertainty of, say, visual evidence to be checked by touch. Equally problematic, complained critics like George Santayana, was James's apologetic assumption that the extreme manifestations of "religious disease" could be taken as emblematic of normal religious experience.[113] And once the vague notion of the "subliminal, transmarginal or subconscious self" had been supplanted by either Freud's unconscious or a more directly physiological explanation of abnormal behavior, such as that posited by Hugo Munsterberg and his followers, his delicate balancing act between the twin dangers of intransigently supernaturalist and secularizing naturalist explanations was harder to sustain. Although such theologians as Ernst Troeltsch, Reinhold Niebuhr, and Martin E. Marty continued to find him an inspiration, as did sociologists like Max Weber, those who tried to develop a genuine science of religion ritually cited James as an honored forebear, but rarely followed him in any meaningful way.[114]

OTTO AND THE EXPERIENCE OF THE NUMINOUS

The project of elaborating a defensible notion of religious experience did not, however, end with James's psychological empiricism. Nor could it be entirely derailed by the stern rebukes of the theologians of crisis with their disdain for anything smacking of anthropological subjectivism. In the work of Rudolf Otto (1869–1937) and Joachim Wach (1898–1955) in particular, it remained a powerful current of thought in postwar Germany (and the America to which Wach emigrated during the Nazi era). Although American prag-

112. See, for example, O'Hear, *Experience, Explanation and Faith,* chapter 2.

113. George Santayana, "William James," in Simon, ed., *William James Remembered,* pp. 98–99.

114. For an account of his poor reception among scientists, see Dittes, "Beyond William James." See also Wilhelm Hennis, "The Spiritualist Foundation of Max Weber's 'Interpretive Sociology': Ernst Troeltsch, Max Weber and William James' *Varieties of Religious Experience,*" *History of the Human Sciences* 11, no. 2 (May 1998), for a discussion of his importance for German sociology. Hennis quotes a text written around 1905 in which Weber argues that "religious experience is as such of course irrational, like *every* experience. In its highest, mystic form it is precisely the experience *kat exochēn [par excellence]*— and as James had very nicely elaborated—distinguished by its absolute incommunicability: it has a *specific* character and appears as *cognition* which cannot be adequately reproduced with our linguistic and conceptual apparata" (p. 90).

matism in general did not fare well in the anti-utilitarian, anti-positivist (and during the war, anti-American) climate of German thought, James's study of religious experience did not go unacknowledged in their work.[115] Otto's contribution will be our focus in what follows, as Wach essentially continued the comparative science of religious experience that we have noted in James and which was modified by Otto, but with only modest theoretical innovations of his own.[116]

Otto's main modifications were two: first, he attempted to restore the transcendental foundation of religious experience, which James's empiricism had lost, a restoration that drew him back to Kant or rather to certain post-Kantian ideas as developed by Jakob Friedrich Fries. Unlike James, he did not rest content with a phenomenological survey based on testimonial evidence alone, although he invoked it when useful in his larger argument. Second, he sought to reestablish the integrity of the Other of experience, the God whose existence the theologians of crisis had claimed was compromised by Schleiermacher and his descendents.

Otto, to be sure, was clearly in that latter category himself, acknowledging as he did in an admiring introduction to his 1899 edition of *On Religion,* that Schleiermacher's masterpiece was "the main gateway to the intellectual world of the later renovators of Protestant theology."[117] He had been introduced to the work by his teacher at the University of Erlangen, where he studied in 1889–90, Franz Reinhold von Frank (1827–1894), who helped wean him from the conservative Lutheranism of his childhood.[118] Schleiermacher, he acknowledged, had rediscovered what Otto, in one of his most famous innovations, was to call the "sensus numinis" underlying all religious experience, which had been first brought to the fore by Zinzendorf.[119] Schleiermacher was also to be commended for understanding that alongside the cog-

115. For a discussion of the skeptical and misleading German response to pragmatism, see Hans Joas, *Pragmatism and Social Theory,* trans. Jeremy Gaines, Raymond Meyer, and Steven Minner (Chicago, 1993), chapter 4.

116. Joachim Wach, *Types of Religious Experience: Christian and Non-Christian* (Chicago, 1951). For an appreciation of Wach's entire career, which began in Leipzig and concluded in exile in America after 1933, when he taught at Brown and the University of Chicago, see Rainer Flasche, *Die Religionswissenschaft Joachim Wachs* (Berlin, 1978). His differences with Otto are outlined in Gregory D. Alles's introduction to his edition of Rudolf Otto, *Autobiographical and Social Essays* (Berlin, 1996), pp. 22–23.

117. It appears in English as the introduction to John Oman's translation of *On Religion,* p. xii. Otto was especially drawn to the first edition of the book, which still had the effusive energies that its more controlled successors lacked.

118. For accounts of Otto's life, see Otto, *Autobiographical and Social Essays,* and Philip C. Almond, *Rudolf Otto: An Introduction to His Philosophical Theology* (Chapel Hill, N.C., 1984).

119. Otto, "How Schleiermacher Rediscovered the *Sensus Numinis,*" *Religious Essays* (London, 1931).

nitive and practical moments in religion—indeed underlying both of them—was the experiential, affective dimension, which had an irreducibly non-rational element. He was also praiseworthy, Otto contended, for his departure from the exclusivist hostility to other religions that marked Protestantism at its most intolerant, and which had been challenged by more historicist theologians like Troeltsch and psychologists of religion like James. Otto's own personal encounters with non-Christian religions, which began with an illuminating episode in a Moroccan synagogue during the long trip he took to Spain, North Africa, India, China, Japan, and Siberia in 1911–12,[120] confirmed for him the wisdom of Schleiermacher's insight. And finally, against James's denigration of Schleiermacher's formula of "absolute dependence," Otto contended that without such a feeling the objective reality of the divine would be lost;[121] contrary to the frequent accusations made against him by Barth and others, Schleiermacher had deliberately sought to avoid absolute subjective anthropocentrism.

Indeed, even after he lost his unqualified enthusiasm for Schleiermacher, Otto revealed his lifelong debt in subtle ways—for example, in the gloss he gave of the German word *Erlebnis* in an essay on guilt he composed for an English audience in 1931:

It is a kind of profound experience. *Er-lebnis* [*sic*] really means to acquire as a component and moment of one's own *Leben* 'life', that is, to acquire as a component and moment of what is immediate and as close as possible to ourselves, of what is certain first and above all. At the same time, *Erlebnis* is not acquired by the weak powers of our analytical understanding and our subsequent explication. It is not what is acquired by the superficial evidence of the senses or through the mediation of "conceptualization." It is what is certain and known in itself, to the extent that we are identical with it. . . . What is called *Selbsterlebnis* in German is the experience in which we ourselves "realize" ourselves according to our very essence in unmediated form, in the very first utterance, and in the closest possible proximity.[122]

Otto's appreciation of Schleiermacher began to erode somewhat as he developed his mature theological position, culminating in *The Idea of the Holy (Das Heilige)*, which appeared in 1917. In fact, as early as 1909 and the pub-

120. See his letters from North Africa (1911) in Otto, *Autobiographical and Social Essays*. Otto returned to the Near East and India in 1925 and 1927.

121. Otto, *The Idea of the Holy*, trans. John W. Harvey (London, 1958), p. 11.

122. Otto, "On Feeling Guilty," in *Autobiographical and Social Essays*, p. 266. Elsewhere in his work he used the term *Erfahrung* as well.

lication of *The Philosophy of Religion Based on Kant and Fries,* he had come to the conclusion that Schleiermacher, for all his virtues, was inferior to Fries as a ground for a viable notion of religious experience.[123] At this time in Germany, a revival of interest in this neglected figure was underway, led by the philosopher and political activist Leonard Nelson (1882–1927), whom Otto met in 1904 in Göttingen.[124] Like Schleiermacher, Fries had been educated by the Moravian Brothers at Herrnhut, but he was more in the tradition of the *Aufklärung* than Romanticism, closer to Kant than to Schlegel. However, unlike Kant, Fries wanted to go beyond the claim that the moral obligations of practical reason provided the essence of religion. Instead, he followed the lead of the *Critique of Judgment* and sought a way to transcend the limits Kant had set in his earlier work to knowledge of things-in-themselves. The key term he introduced to indicate that possibility was *Ahndung,* the inkling or presentiment of some coming ultimate meaning, which was similar to but in some ways more effective than Schleiermacher's "contemplation and sense of the universe." Otto would compare the two in the following manner:

> The source of Fries' doctrine of "Ahndung"—so far as it is not just the positive experience of the man himself—is the Kantian Criticism [*sic*] of Judgment. . . . As a result, the "Ahndung" theory as treated by Fries emerges in solid philosophical form; whereas in Schleiermacher it is primarily a kind of inspired guesswork, which has in it something of the method of "happy thoughts," which the Romantic school used to follow. . . . when in Schleiermacher's later development the original idea is struggling towards clearer expression, nothing is left of the earlier wealth and exuberance but the "feeling of absolute dependence," a very one-sided and inadequate description of religious feeling, which in Fries has found a much more varied and precise development.[125]

123. Rudolf Otto, *The Philosophy of Religion Based on Kant and Fries,* trans. E. B. Dicker (New York, 1931). Otto specifically states on p. 15 that he had reversed his earlier opinion in his 1904 *Naturalism and Religion* of the respective value of each thinker. In the nineteenth century, Fries had enjoyed a modest influence in German theology through such figures as de Wette and Apelt, but it is indicative of his waning importance that he does not merit even a mention in the first volume of Welch's *Protestant Thought in the Nineteenth Century.*

124. Otto shared with Nelson a liberal position in university politics before the war and actually served as a National Liberal member of the Prussian Landtag. For documents of his political involvements, see his *Autobiographical and Social Essays,* pp. 102–61. For a discussion of Nelson's political career, especially during the Weimar Republic, when he led the elitist Internationaler Jugendbund, see Walter Struve, *Elites Against Democracy: Leadership Ideals in Bourgeois Political Thought in Germany, 1890–1933* (Princeton, 1973), chapter 6.

125. Otto, *The Philosophy of Religion Based on Kant and Fries,* p. 23.

Perhaps the major difference between the two, Otto contended, concerned the question of how feeling and knowledge were related. Whereas Schleiermacher sought to keep them apart, Fries had understood that "religious conviction must be *true* and must be able to prove its truth; i.e., it must lay claim to Knowledge."[126]

Such a claim, Otto implied, need not be made in the pragmatist terms introduced by James, which gave too much weight to mere functional efficacy. Not only had Fries already taken seriously the realm of the subconscious introduced by James in *The Varieties of Religious Experience*,[127] but he also understood that it could be explored using the philosophical tools James would wrongly banish as inappropriate. "James," Otto later lamented, "is debarred by his empiricist and pragmatist standpoint from coming to a recognition of faculties of knowledge and potentialities of thought in the spirit itself, and he is therefore obliged to have recourse to somewhat singular and mysterious hypotheses to explain this fact [a feeling of objective presence]."[128] Fries, in contrast, had taken seriously those faculties, which he divided into *Wissen* (scientific cognition), *Glaube* (rational faith), and *Ahndung* (the nonconceptual prevision of the supersensible), which had both a religious and an aesthetic dimension. The first two correspond to the faculties explored in Kant's First and Second Critiques, the third, derived as we have noted from Fries's reading of the *Critique of Judgment*, suggested that feeling can be the vehicle of a deeper knowledge than Kant had granted. It takes the human outside of the restrictive categories of time and space, so important to *Wissen*, and gives us an inkling of the divine. Such a faculty of intuitive divination, Fries had understood, was not the same as the old doctrine of innate ideas, which was a residue of discredited metaphysics. Instead, it entailed an a priori capacity for piety and reverence that was activated by experience, at least in those fortunate enough to be open to it.[129]

Analogizing from aesthetic experience, Otto sought to express the inexpressible insight he thought Fries had achieved, invoking, as did Schleiermacher, Plato's name:

126. Ibid., p. 24. Otto may have been exaggerating the opposition between faith and knowledge in Schleiermacher to make his point.

127. Ibid., p. 26.

128. Otto, *The Idea of the Holy*, p. 11.

129. For a sympathetic account of Otto's argument about a priori foundations, see Ansgar Paus, *Religiöser Erkenntnisgrund: Herkunft und Wesen der Aprioritheorie Rudolf Ottos* (Leiden, 1966). Paus notes that Ernst Friedrich Apelt and Ernst Troeltsch had already introduced the idea of a religious a priori, but with less effect.

In our experience of the sublime and the beautiful we dimly see the eternal and true world of Spirit and Freedom, in nature's life as well, the world of the highest good, the power and the wisdom of the highest good. It is in the truest sense a Platonic *anamnesis* of the Idea, and through it alone is conceivable the unspeakable profundity, the mighty rapture, the spell of mystery that plays around this experience. Only thus is it conceivable that the soul in such experience sometimes almost steps beyond her confines, and on her lips hovers the unspoken word which would reveal the secret of all Being. Here 'mystery in religion' comes into play. Religion itself is an experience of mystery.[130]

Although mysterious, religion is nonetheless not exclusively irrational; indeed, the whole point of employing categories like the a priori was to link it with the transcendental capacities of the mind that had underpinned the Kantian defense of critical reason. It was thus wrong to consider mysticism, as James did, the essence of religious experience, however important it may be.[131] Precisely how the rational and the non-rational were intermingled in religion was the question with which Otto wrestled for the remainder of his career. In his subsequent work, although explicit references to Fries were rare,[132] Otto would return again and again to what he had seen as the special variant of the a priori permitting religious experience. "In Kantian terms," he would typically write in 1932, "we would express it this way. The *sensus numinis* is a vague notion or the possibility of a notion a priori. It cannot be given through sense perception, but sense perception can touch it off and arouse it. It can then lead to a specific conceptualization *(Sinn-deutung)* of the object which set it in motion."[133]

It was, of course, in his most celebrated work, *The Idea of the Holy,* that Otto would most thoroughly explore that sixth sense, which he claimed was at the root of all religious experience, Christian or otherwise. In the year of its publication, 1917, he replaced Wilhelm Herrmann in the chair of theology at the University of Marburg, where he finished his distinguished ca-

130. Otto, *The Philosophy of Religion Based on Kant and Fries,* p. 93. As in the case of Schleiermacher, Otto found in Plato an ally in the struggle for a religious concept of experience. See also his admiring contrast of Plato with Aristotle in *The Idea of the Holy,* p. 94.

131. Otto, *The Idea of the Holy,* p. 22. It is sometimes argued that Otto differentiated radically between numinous and mystical experience, e.g., by Ninian Smart in *Reasons and Faiths* (London, 1958). For a refutation of this view, see Almond, *Rudolf Otto,* p. 127.

132. There were, in fact, certain subtle differences between *The Philosophy of Religion Based on Kant and Fries* and *The Idea of the Holy,* which may explain the relative paucity of references. For a discussion of the differences, especially the latter's insistence on the uniqueness of the religious a priori, see Almond, *Rudolf Otto,* p. 91.

133. Otto, "Zinzendorf Discovered the *Sensus Numinis,*" p. 183.

reer and lived until 1937.[134] Written just as the wave of anti-subjectivist dialectical theology was about to wash over German Protestantism (represented in Marburg after 1921 by Otto's great rival, the New Testament scholar Rudolf Bultmann [1884–1976][135]), the book was nonetheless rapidly acknowledged as a classic of its kind. Even Barth, who worried about its "theological spectator attitude," could write a friend that he had read it "with considerable delight. The subject has a psychological orientation, but points clearly across the border into the beyond with its moments of the 'numinous' which is not to be rationally conceived since it is 'wholly other,' the divine, in God."[136]

Otto had not been the first German thinker to foreground the idea of "the holy." Attention had been paid to it by Wilhelm Windelband (1848–1915), the leading neo-Kantian philosopher of the Baden School, and Wilhelm Wundt (1832–1920), the founder of "folk psychology," as well as by the Swedish theologian Nathan Söderblom (1866–1931).[137] But Otto was the first to argue that it was both a rational and non-rational object, which could be apprehended by the believer, an object that served as the ultimate ground for all other manifestations of religion, ranging from ethical commands and mystical rapture to ritual sacrifice and demonic possession. Understood as the power of a real object, he argued, the holy can produce religious experience, not vice versa.

Although Otto was careful to stress the rational moment in the holy, calling the current fad of the irrational a "favorite theme of all who are too lazy to think or too ready to evade the arduous duty of clarifying their ideas and grounding their convictions on a basis of coherent thought,"[138] his stress was on a quality that went beyond critical reason, as it is normally understood. It would be mistaken, he insisted, to equate "*Geist*," as Hegel had falsely done in his gloss on St. John's "God is a Spirit," with a totalizing notion of "absolute reason." Religious rationalization and moralization are themselves de-

134. For speculations about Otto's possible suicide attempt in October 1936 and death from the complications five months later, see Almond, *Rudolf Otto*, pp. 24–25. Otto appears to have had several severe depressive episodes during his life.

135. Bultmann's project of demythologizing the New Testament was not precisely the same as Barth's, but the two were allies in the criticism of experiential notions of religion.

136. Quoted in Almond, *Rudolf Otto*, p. 1. Later, Barth and his school would be less generous. See the various remarks cited in Gregory Alles's introduction to Otto, *Autobiographical and Social Essays*, pp. 7–9.

137. Their essays are collected in Carsen Colpe, ed., *Die Diskussion um das "Heilige"* (Darmstadt, 1977). For a discussion, see Almond, *Rudolf Otto*, pp. 58–65.

138. Otto, foreword to the first English edition of *The Idea of the Holy*, p. xix.

pendent on something antecedent to their development, which they then "schematize."[139] Deriving a new concept from the Latin word for divinity, *numen,* he dubbed it the "numinous," a coinage that soon enjoyed extraordinary success. Although Otto did not explicitly make the connection, it could not fail to evoke the Kantian notion of the *noumenal,*[140] the realm of the supposedly unknowable "thing-in-itself," which Fries thought *Ahndung* could reach. Both the rational and numinous dimensions of the holy were a priori capacities in the human mind, predispositions in the species to worship the "wholly other."

Struggling to distinguish his position from Schleiermacher's, Otto argued that the numinous was more than a feeling of absolute dependence, which suggested too much of a continuity with the merely relative dependence humans feel on processes of the natural and social world. Such a feeling was thus based on an inferential rather than direct encounter with God. Moreover, it implied the existence of the self prior to the power that is supreme over it, which is precisely what the numinous calls into question. The latter is best understood as a "creature-consciousness" or "creature-feeling," which "is the emotion of a creature, submerged and overwhelmed by its own nothingness in contrast to that which is supreme above all creatures."[141] The "prodigious paradox" of the Christian doctrine of the Incarnation, he insisted, is that "the interval between the creature and Him is not diminished, but made absolute; the unworthiness of the profane in contrast to Him is not extenuated but enhanced."[142] In a phrase that suggested how much he sought to go beyond psychologistic anthropomorphism, Otto concluded that "the numinous is thus felt as objective and outside the self."[143] More precisely, it is felt as a response to a *"mysterium tremendum"* (awful mystery), first present in the dread and awe of primitive men who see their world ruled by "daemons." The shudder at the uncanny, weird, and awful presence of something majestic beyond nature is retained in even the most advanced religious systems, which also preserve a sense of the overwhelming energetic power that is experienced initially as both ineffable divine wrath and the source of infinite fascination.

139. Otto, *The Idea of the Holy,* pp. 45–49. For a critical reading of the schematization doctrine, see Almond, *Rudolf Otto,* pp. 97–102.

140. The etymology of the two words, however, is not the same. Noumenal is derived from the Greek *noumenos,* the past participle of *noein* (to know or think), which comes from *nous,* or mind.

141. Otto, *The Idea of the Holy,* p. 10.

142. Ibid., p. 56.

143. Ibid., p. 11.

To characterize the uncharacterizable object that produces this response, Otto borrowed the phrase *"das ganze Andere"* from Fries, a term that had also been used by Kierkegaard and favored by Barth (and unexpectedly would later find its way into Max Horkheimer's late, religiously inflected version of Frankfurt School Critical Theory).[144] The most extreme example of the presence of the "wholly other" as the opposite of everyday life, Otto claimed, was in mystical experience, but it also appeared in more mundane religious practices. Although it may ultimately find its expression in connection with moral obligations, Otto, anxious to distinguish himself from Kant's overemphasis on practical reason and the neo-Kantian obsession with value theory, contended that it need not. While never positing the ethical and the religious as radically at odds, as Kierkegaard did in the discussion of the "teleological suspension of the ethical" in *Fear and Trembling*, Otto resisted seeing the latter as always entailing the former. In fact, the numinous appears to us mere creatures not as positive commandments, but indirectly in such negative manifestations as the void, darkness, or silence. "Not even music," Otto contended, "which else can give manifold expression to all the feelings of the mind, has any positive way to express 'the holy'."[145]

Much of *The Idea of the Holy* is nonetheless given over to vivid descriptions of how the holy appeared, albeit in indirect, negative form, in the daemons of pagan cults (and Goethe's neo-paganism), the Hebrew Bible, the New Testament, and Lutheran Pietism. In the aesthetic realm, Otto contended, it can be glimpsed in a wide range of examples from the Bhagavad-Gita to the poetry of Blake. Even in religion's cruder phases, he argued, it was fully in evidence, for *"religion is itself present at its commencement:* religion, nothing else, is at work in the early stages of mythic and daemonic experience."[146] Rather than the varieties of religious experience in James's pluralist terms, there was actually a unifying *ur*-experience underlying all of them. All institutionalized religions, he argued, are derived from the capacities of prophets or holy men to gain access to that experience, which their followers then try to emulate. Religion is not the recovery of innate ideas, but the realization of the a priori capacity for awe in all of us, a Platonic anamnesis or recollection of a possibility. The superiority of one religion over

144. Almond, *Rudolf Otto*, p. 154. Horkheimer's invocation of *"ein ganz Anderes"* appears, among other places, in his introduction to Martin Jay, *The Dialectical Imagination: A History of the Frankfurt School and the Institute of Social Research, 1923–1950*, 2nd ed. (Berkeley, 1996), p. xxvi.

145. Otto, *The Idea of the Holy*, p. 70.

146. Ibid., p. 132.

another—and for all his ecumenical tolerance, Otto never doubted that his version of Christianity was preeminent—could be measured in terms of comparative actualization.[147]

In fact, one might say that the premise of Otto's entire work was his having had personal, concrete religious experiences of a certain kind. One of the opening gambits of *The Idea of the Holy* was an invitation to the reader to reflect on his own comparable experiences, which will allow him to understand what follows. "Whoever cannot do this, whoever knows no such moments in his experience," Otto then conceded, "is requested to read no farther, for it is not easy to discuss questions of religious psychology with one who can recollect the emotions of his adolescence, the discomforts of indigestion, or, say, social feelings, but cannot recall any intrinsically religious feelings."[148] In other words, the uniqueness of religious experience is such that unless you have experienced it yourself, it cannot really be conveyed in a meaningful sense. There is a fundamental difference between the believer who experiences the body of Christ in the Host and the skeptic who only sees a thin wafer of bread, even though the same sense data impinges on the sensorium of each of them. What a later discourse would call an incommensurable language game or a "differend" appears here on the level of experience.[149]

It was precisely this limitation of the possibility of communication that frustrated those of Otto's critics who still held onto a Kantian model of judgment as based on universal communicability via rational argumentation.[150] For them, the cost of the irreducibility argument characteristic of virtually all defenses of religious experience—the claim that it must be understood only in its own terms and only by people who actually experience it—is the short-circuiting of any serious attempt to analyze it critically. Even a hermeneutic approach that eschewed the Kantian standpoint of universalizing critical rationality was troubled by the implications of premising claims about religious experience on the specific experience of one type of faith. As Gadamer was to put it in *Truth and Method,*

147. Otto's major comparative works were *India's Religion of Grace and Christianity Compared and Contrasted,* trans. Frank Hugh Foster (New York, 1930), and *Mysticism East and West: A Comparative Analysis of the Nature of Mysticism,* trans. Bertha L. Bracey and Richenda C. Payne (New York, 1932). For a critique of the limits of the latter, which extends as well to James's remarks on mysticism, see Jess Byron Hollenback, *Mysticism: Experience, Response, and Empowerment* (University Park, Pa., 1996), introduction.

148. Otto, *The Idea of the Holy,* p. 8.

149. Jean-François Lyotard, *The Differend: Phrases in Dispute,* trans. Georges Van Den Abbeele (Minneapolis, 1988).

150. See, for example, Wood, *Kant's Moral Religion,* pp. 201–4.

Does there exist in every man a previous connection with the truth of divine revelation because man as such is concerned with the question of God? Or must we say that it is first from God, i.e. from faith, that human life experiences itself as being affected by the question of God? But then the sense of the presupposition that is contained in the concept of fore-understanding becomes questionable. For then the presupposition would be valid not universally but solely from the viewpoint of true faith.[151]

A concomitant worry was expressed by those unconvinced by the ability of *Ahndung* to produce genuine knowledge about objects, divine or otherwise. As early as the first major critique of Otto by Joseph Geyser in 1921, the cognitive, noetic dimension of Otto's neo-Friesian defense of the religious a priori was faulted for confusing feeling with knowledge and failing to provide a criterion to distinguish true from false inklings of noumenal reality.[152] Still other critics were unconvinced by Otto's attempt to find a middle ground between the anthropocentric subjectivism always lurking in any appeal to experience and the desire to honor the integrity of a God who was "wholly other." Many were skeptical that, despite everything, he really had done any better than Schleiermacher or James in avoiding psychologism.[153] Even those who acknowledged the seriousness of his efforts to do so raised fundamental questions. Perhaps Friedrich Karl Feigel put the dilemma most pungently in 1929:

> Either God is in some absolute sense "wholly other," and we cannot experience or say anything about Him, *including that He is wholly other,* or we experience something of God, which means God's essence cannot be determined as "numinous." *The numinous as category*—whether "category" is understood in a transcendental-logical or with Otto a psychological sense—is *a contradictio in adiecto.*[154]

Finally, there were those who were left cold by the very attempt made by defenders of a generic religious experience to escape context and find a unique

151. Gadamer, *Truth and Method,* p. 296.

152. Joseph Geyer, *Intellekt oder Gemüt? Ein philosophische Studie über Rudolf Ottos Buch "Das Heilige"* (Freiburg, 1921). For an excellent discussion of this book and the entire reception of Otto's work, see Alles's introduction to Otto, *Autobiographical and Social Essays.*

153. See for example, Walter Baetke, "Das Phänomen des Heiligen," and the response by Werner Schilling, "Das Phänome des Heiligen: Zu Baetkes Kritik an Rudolf Otto," both in Colpe, *Die Diskussion um das "Heilige."*

154. Friedrich Karl Feigel, "Das Heilige," in Colpe, *Das Diskussion um das "Heilige,"* p. 405.

and universally true essential core, call it the holy or not. What, they wondered, of those pantheistic religions that worshipped an entirely immanent God? How could they be said to have numinous experiences of a "wholly other"? Was it indeed ever possible to identify an *ur*-experience prior to mediation by specific concepts in specific languages, themselves situated in turn in specific practices in specific cultures? What, after all, was the generic notion of "religion," if not an abstraction from a wide variety of often very different beliefs, practices, traditions, and institutions? Wasn't it an abstraction, moreover, that was doing covert explanatory rather than merely descriptive work, tacitly shunting aside other more naturalistic explanations as "reductive"?[155]

For these and other reasons, the appeal to experience in religious terms has lost at least some of its luster in contemporary discourse.[156] Although periodically reappearing even in such unlikely places as post-Hegelian Anglican idealism—for example in the work of C. C. J. Webb[157]—it has had difficulty playing the foundational role that many of its earlier adherents had assigned it. Those who continue the quest for comparative religious truths came to seek uniformities on the level of symbols or myths rather than experiences, as Mircea Eliade was to do in his influential appropriation of the work of Carl Jung.[158] In non-theological circles, functionalist or structuralist accounts of religion, drawing on Emile Durkheim, Sigmund Freud, Bronislaw Malinowski, or Claude Lévi-Strauss, tended to give short shrift to experience on its own terms, seeking to provide explanations that go well beyond a sense of the infinite, a feeling of absolute dependence, or a numinous awe before the "wholly other."

155. See Proudfoot, *Religious Experience,* for an elaboration of this point, which is also made by Steven Katz in *Mysticism and Philosophical Analysis* (New York, 1978).

156. It would be wrong, however, to say it has entirely died. See, for example, the nuanced discussion of it in Schner, "The Appeal to Experience," and Jonathan Shear, "Mystical Experience, Hermeneutics, and Rationality," *International Quarterly* 30, no. 120 (December, 1990). Perhaps the most recent rigorous defense has been mounted by Keith E. Yandell in *The Epistemology of Religious Experience* (Cambridge, 1993). He joins a long-standing debate that has pitted skeptics such as C. B. Martin and George Mavrodes against defenders such as C. D. Broad and David Conway. See Yandell's bibliography for the relevant literature.

157. C. C. J. Webb, *God and Personality* (London, 1918). For a general account of the role of religious experience in his work and that of other British idealists, see Alan P. F. Sell, *Philosophical Idealism and Christian Belief* (New York, 1995).

158. See, for example, Mircea Eliade, *The Sacred and the Profane: The Nature of Religion,* trans. Willard Trask (New York, 1959). Although occasionally echoing Otto (in *The Quest* [Chicago, 1969], p. 25, he writes that religion is "first of all, an experience *sui generis,* incited by man's encounter with the sacred"), Eliade devoted his energies to a hermeneutics of myth and symbols.

And yet, the reverberations of the discourse we have been examining in this chapter cannot be easily ignored. For not only was it a powerful current in liberal Protestant theology from Schleiermacher to Otto, but it also had an impact on other religions, as well as on secular attitudes toward experience. Although there is no need to attempt an exhaustive account of all the ways in which the appeal has functioned outside of the tradition we have been following, a glance at its role in twentieth-century Jewish thought will help us understand its breadth and power. Here our main witness is once again German, although his influence transcended national and religious boundaries: Martin Buber (1878–1965).[159]

At first glance, it may seem paradoxical that the appeal to experience would find an echo in Jewish thought. Judaism, we have seen, was disparaged by Schleiermacher as a moribund religion with no function left in the modern world. In his vividly cruel metaphor, "it has long persevered, as a single fruit, after all the life force has vanished from the branch, often remains hanging until the bleakest season on a withered stem and dries up on it."[160] James was not as explicitly dismissive, but according to one of his commentators, "during a period when the American Jewish population quadrupled, [he] failed to interact with Judaism at all."[161] Otto was a somewhat more sympathetic and interested observer. Although he studied comparative Semitic grammar with the notorious anti-Semite Paul Lagarde in Göttingen in 1891 and never saw fit to denounce Fries for his vicious hatred of the Jews, there is no evidence that he absorbed any of their prejudice; indeed, one of his closest friends, Hermann Jacobsohn, was Jewish (not always an ironic statement!).[162] His first personal contact with the numinous, as we have seen, was

---

159. According to Gershom Scholem, that influence was ironically greater among gentiles than Jews. See his "Martin Buber's Conception of Judaism," in Scholem, *On Jews and Judaism in Crisis*, ed. Werner J. Dannhauser (New York, 1978), p. 128. Elsewhere, however, Scholem confessed that as a schoolboy, he was himself deeply influenced by Buber's early work: "Buber's first books on Hasidism and the 'Three Speeches' raised a tremendous echo in our ears." Quoted in Maurice Friedman, *Martin Buber's Life and Work: The Early Years, 1878–1923* (Detroit, 1988), p. 145, from an essay (in Hebrew) written by Scholem to commemorate Buber's seventy-fifth birthday.

160. Schleiermacher, *On Religion*, p. 213.

161. Levinson, *The Religious Investigations of William James*, p. 23.

162. Almond, *Rudolf Otto*, p. 25, where Jacobsohn's suicide in 1933, caused by his fear of being put into a concentration camp, is discussed as a source of Otto's depression and own probable suicide attempt. On Fries's anti-Semitism, see Shlomo Avineri, *Hegel's Theory of the Modern State* (Cambridge, 1972), pp. 119–21. In addition to writing a pamphlet in 1816 calling for the expulsion of the Jews, mandatory badges for those who remained, and the suppression of Jewish education and marital rights, Fries

in a Sephardic synagogue in Morocco in 1911, and *The Idea of the Holy* pays tribute to the "special nobility" of a religion that rationalized and moralized the numinous, preparing the way for the Holy in its full form in Christianity.[163] Yet he seems to have had little interest in exploring the experiential dimension of early twentieth-century European Jewish life.

Ironically, Buber's turn toward experience must be understood against a comparable assessment of the lamentable state of modern Judaism, at least in Western Europe. Born in Vienna, he was raised, after his mother's abandonment of their family, in the Austrian Galician home of his grandfather, Solomon Buber, a prosperous landowner in Lvov.[164] When he was fourteen, he returned to the estate of his father, Carl, where the ethos was that of instrumental reason and assimilation to modernity. Although enormously dedicated to his grandfather, an eminent scholar of the Jewish Enlightenment *(Haskalah),* and impressed by his father's personal solicitude for peasants and workers on his land, the young Buber grew increasingly restless with what he saw as the legalistic and lifeless formalism of contemporary Jewish life and thought. Determined to end the external exile of the Jewish people, he embraced Zionism, albeit more of the cultural variety espoused by Ahad Ha'am than the political variant championed by Theodor Herzl. No less keen on ending its internal exile, which he identified with the external constraints of sacred law *(Halakhah),* he sought a way back to the spiritual vitality that had been driven from both orthodox and liberal versions of Judaism, disparaged by scholars in the *Wissenschaft des Judentums (Science of Jewry)* tradition, and considered an embarrassment to assimilated Jews in the West.

Like Schleiermacher a century before, Buber found his answer in the piety of lived experience, in his case the non-assimilated *Hasidism (Hasid* is the Hebrew for "pious") of the *shetls* (little towns) of Eastern Europe.[165] Although he had been exposed to Hasidic communities as a child, it was only at the age of twenty-six that he realized their potential as a vehicle of religious renewal. Here he was not alone, as a reversal of the contempt for "pre-modern

---

endorsed the nationalist enthusiasm of the *Burschenschaften* and spoke at the Wartburg Festival in 1819. As a result, he earned Hegel's denunciation in the preface to his *Philosophy of Right.*

163. Otto, *The Idea of the Holy,* p. 75, where he singles out Isaiah in the Hebrew Bible as the most brilliant example of this mixture. Otto also includes Jewish liturgy in his instances of numinous hymns.

164. For discussions of Buber's early life and work, see Maurice Friedman, *Martin Buber's Life and Work: The Early Years, 1878–1923* (Detroit, 1988); Paul Mendes-Flohr, *From Mysticism to Dialogue: Martin Buber's Transformation of German Social Thought* (Detroit, 1989); and Gilya Gerda Schmidt, *Martin Buber's Formative Years: From German Culture to Jewish Renewal, 1897–1909* (Tuscaloosa, Ala., 1995).

165. For his own account, see Martin Buber, "My Way to Hasidism" in *Hasidism and Modern Man,* ed. and trans. Maurice Friedman (New York, 1958).

and obscurantist" *Ostjuden* felt by most rationalist, assimilated Jews was already underway among a number of other intellectuals, such as Micha Yosef Berdichevsky, Simon Dubnow, and Y. L. Peretz.[166] Only with Buber's lyrical translations of the stories and legends of the Hasidism, *The Tales of Rabbi Nachman* and *The Legend of the Baal-Shem,* however, did a full-fledged appreciation begin.[167] Although his scholarly credentials have been subsequently impugned—most famously by Gershom Scholem[168]—Buber's celebration of Hasidic vitality laid the groundwork for what has been called a veritable "cult of the *Ostjuden*" in the next decade.

Before he entered the world of the Hasidim, however, Buber had studied at the secular universities of Leipzig, Vienna, Zurich, and Berlin. Among his professors in Berlin, where he wrote his doctorate in 1904 (entitled "The History of the Problem of Individuation: Nicholas of Cusa and Jacob Böhme") were two of the leading representatives of *Lebensphilosophie,* Wilhelm Dilthey and Georg Simmel.[169] Swept up in the general enthusiasm for Nietzsche as well, an enthusiasm that was shared by many in the very religious movements that the atheist Nietzsche had scorned, Buber came to his Hasidic infatuation already imbued with a passion for *Erlebnis.*[170] Thus, although he rarely cited Schleiermacher directly and eschewed his emphasis on absolute dependence,[171] many of the same impulses we have encountered in nineteenth-century Protestant theology surged through Buber's work, mediated by Ludwig Feuerbach and the secular Philosophers of Life.[172]

While in Berlin from 1899 to 1901, Buber joined the student fraternity *Die*

166. Steven Aschheim, *Brothers and Strangers: The East European Jew in German and German Jewish Consciousness, 1800–1923* (Madison, Wis., 1982), chapter 6.

167. Originally published in 1906 and 1908, they are available in translations by Maurice Friedman.

168. Gershom Scholem, "Martin Buber's Interpretation of Hasidism," *The Messianic Idea in Judaism and Other Essays in Jewish Spirituality* (New York, 1971), which contains Scholem's response to Buber's defense of the earlier version of the critique. Scholem chastises Buber for imposing his own brand of religious anarchism and proto-existentialist pathos on the Hasidic tradition, falsely equating the Kabbalah with Hasidic thought, and wrongly privileging the legends and tales of the tradition over its theoretical texts.

169. For an excellent discussion, see Mendes-Flohr, *From Mysticism to Dialogue,* chapter 1.

170. On Buber's interest in Nietzsche in the context of the general reception of his thought among German Jews, see Steven Aschheim, *The Nietzsche Legacy in Germany, 1890–1990* (Berkeley, 1992), pp. 93–112. He shows that the second generation of Zionists was imbued with Nietzschean ideals via Buber's mediation.

171. Buber did, however, credit Schleiermacher with achieving the most harmonious expression of metaphysical individualism. See the discussion in Schmidt, *Martin Buber's Formative Years,* pp. 44–45.

172. In *Between Man and Man,* trans. Roger Gregor Smith (New York, 1966), Buber wrote: "Unlike Kant, Feuerbach wishes to make the whole being, not human cognition, the beginning of philosophizing. . . . I myself in my youth was given a decisive impetus by Feuerbach" (pp. 146–48).

neue Gemeinschaft, founded by Heinrich and Julius Hart, whose neo-Romantic yearning for an antidote to the alienation of modern life he ardently endorsed. It was here that he met the communitarian anarchist Gustav Landauer (1870– 1919), six years his elder, who was to become a close friend.[173] The two shared an antinomian enthusiasm for mysticism, initially that of the Christian Meister Eckhart, which was specifically tied to the renewal of genuine communal experience. Paul Mendes-Flohr, who has foregrounded the importance of this moment in Buber's development, stresses the religious dimension of their ideology: "The Neue Gemeinschaft also affirmed *Erlebnis* as a *sensus numinis: Erlebnis* provides one with access to a transcendent, sacred reality. Each *Erlebnis,* which varies in content with the flux of becoming, is unique; thus, if the individual responds to each *Erlebnis* with the uniqueness of his or her person, both the *Erlebnis* (residing in the 'I' of the individual) and the corresponding moment of the eternal flux are realized as one."[174]

In his influential *Three Addresses on Judaism* of 1911 and *Daniel: Dialogues on Realization* of 1913,[175] Buber sought to reinvigorate German Jewry. Rehearsing the dichotomy made famous by the sociologist Ferdinand Tönnies between *Gemeinschaft* (community) and *Gesellschaft* (society), Buber deprecated the social realm of abstract individuation (Schopenhauer's *principium individuationis*), which corresponded to the shallow type of epistemological *Erfahrung* favored by empiricists and Kant. Their gaze was fixed on mere surface phenomena, his on noumenal essences, which could not be understood as objective data in the world of appearances. Their starting point was the isolated subjective consciousness; his was the ecstatic experience of primal unity between subject and object based on affect, not cognition. Searching for the deeper level of inner experience that was somehow at one with the divine, Buber borrowed the ominous rhetoric of *volkisch* anti-modernism, including the language of "blood," that would prove such an embarrassment in the light of later historical developments.[176]

---

173. See Eugene Lunn, *Prophet of Community: The Romantic Socialism of Gustav Landauer* (Berkeley, 1973), chapter 3. For the larger context of neo-Romantic thought and its impact on Jewish intellectuals of this era, see Michael Löwy, *Redemption and Utopia: Jewish Libertarian Thought in Central Europe,* trans. Hope Heaney (Stanford, 1992).

174. Mendes-Flohr, *From Mysticism to Dialogue,* p. 50.

175. Martin Buber, *On Judaism,* trans. Nahum N. Glatzer (New York, 1967), and *Daniel: Dialogues on Realization,* trans. Maurice Friedman (New York, 1965). Mendes-Flohr warns against the misleading conflation of the two German words for experience in the latter translation; see his remarks in *From Mysticism to Dialogue,* p. 161.

176. For a critique of the *völkisch* elements in Buber's thought and that of other German Zionists in the prewar era, see George L. Mosse, *Germans and Jews: The Right, the Left, and the Search for a "Third*

It was, in fact, in this spirit that Buber came to endorse the German war effort in 1914, which he defended in terms of its ability to realize the promise of communal experience. Although the intensity of Buber's chauvinism has been disputed,[177] it is clear that his *Erlebnismystik* found a concrete manifestation, at least for a while. Judging from the writings of other German Jews of this period, such as the young Siegfried Kracauer, Buber was not alone in defending the war in experiential terms.[178] Nonetheless, despite his extraordinary prestige among young Jewish intellectuals of this era, his transformation into what even his good friend Landauer mockingly called *Kriegsbuber*[179] soon led to virulent criticism. Significantly, it often focused on this enthusiasm for *Erlebnis,* a salient example being the young Walter Benjamin, whose own brief for a very different version of experience we will encounter later. According to Scholem,

> Benjamin was especially harsh in his rejection of the cult of "experience" [*Erlebnis*], which was glorified in Buber's writings of the time (particularly from 1910 to 1917). He said derisively that if Buber had his way, first of all one would have to ask every Jew, "Have you experienced Jewishness yet?" Benjamin tried to induce me to work into my article a definite rejection of experience and Buber's "experiencing" attitude. I actually did so in a later essay, as Benjamin had greatly impressed me in this matter.[180]

The article in question, "Martin Buber's Conception of Judaism," was not published until 1967,[181] by which time Buber himself had long since left behind the chauvinism of the First World War, as well as the *Erlebnismystik* that helped justify it. A frank exchange of letters with Landauer in May 1916 seems to have weaned Buber from both his war fever and his faith in its experien-

---

Force" in Pre-Nazi Germany (New York, 1970), chapter 4. Later in German Jews Beyond Judaism (Bloomington, Ind., 1985), Mosse's evaluation of the völkisch dimension of Buber's thought is more generous (p. 36).

177. Buber's position is discussed critically in Mendes-Flohr, From Mysticism to Dialogue, chapter 5. For a moderate defense, see Friedman, Martin Buber's Life and Work, chapter 9.

178. Siegfried Kracauer, "Vom Erleben des Kriegs," Schriften 5.1 (Frankfurt, 1990); originally published in Preussische Jahrbücher in 1915.

179. Landauer to Buber, May 12, 1916, in The Letters of Martin Buber, ed. Nahum N. Glatzer and Paul Mendes-Flohr, trans. Richard and Clara Winston and Harry Zohn (New York, 1991), p. 185.

180. Gershom Scholem, Walter Benjamin: The Story of a Friendship, trans. Harry Zohn (New York, 1981), p. 29.

181. It appears in English in Scholem, On Jews and Judaism in Crisis, ed. Werner Dannhauser (New York, 1976).

tial foundation.[182] Buber's new intellectual orientation away from *Erlebnis-mystik* led him toward the dialogical philosophy of I and Thou for which he was ultimately famous. His "radical self-correction," as he later came to call it,[183] involved the same reproach of psychologism that we have seen leveled at Schleiermacher, James, and even Otto. Buber now preferred the relational sphere between men and between them and their God to the interiority of the pious believer. As he put it in the foreword to the 1923 edition of his *Three Addresses,* "An *Erlebnis* is of concern to me only insofar as it is an event *(Ereignis)* or in other words, insofar as it pertains to the real God."[184] Such a God manifests Himself in the dialogical interaction between men, in *Leben* understood as more than the subjectivity of individual *Erlebnis* (but also never reducible to the objectivism of epistemological experience, the realm of I-It relations). Schleiermacher had claimed in *On Religion* that for modern Judaism, "the conversation of Jehovah with his people was viewed as ended."[185] Buber insisted instead that it could and must be reopened.

An attempt such as that of William James to provide empirical accounts of subjective religious experiences, Buber would thus come to argue, "falsifies religious reality by turning it into a psychological content—an experience that a person *has;* it also leads to the pragmatic inversion that causes James and Huxley to encourage others to cultivate these experiences so that they too may know these 'real effects.' The great mystics did not *have* experiences, they *were had* by them."[186] Anyone who deliberately seeks experience, even religious experience, for its own sake, Buber charged, reveals that "he does not 'experience' with his whole being, but only with that part of him which registers the effects, while the other part of him, the one that seeks the experience, remains perforce the detached observer separated from his experience by his very knowledge that he is having it."[187]

182. For an extensive discussion of Landauer's role, see Mendes-Flohr, *From Mysticism to Dialogue,* chapter 5. See also Friedman, *Martin Buber's Life and Work,* chapter 16. Buber's position and change of heart were typical of many German Jews. As George L. Mosse points out in his Leo Baeck Memorial Lecture, "The Jews and the German War Experience, 1914–1918" (New York, 1977), "most German Jews succumbed to the almost irresistible temptation to share to the full the German war experience. But after the war many had a rude awakening and recaptured the liberal and Enlightenment tradition" (p. 25).

183. Martin Buber, "Replies to My Critics," in Paul A. Schlipp and Maurice Friedman, eds., *The Philosophy of Martin Buber* (LaSalle, Ill., 1967), p. 711.

184. Martin Buber, "Preface to 1923 Edition," *On Judaism,* p. 7.

185. Schleiermacher, *On Religion,* p. 213.

186. Martin Buber, *The Knowledge of Man: Selected Essays,* ed. Maurice Friedman (New York, 1965), p. 44.

187. Ibid.

Buber's retreat from his *Erlebnismystik* paralleled the critique made by Karl Barth of the Schleiermacherian tradition in Protestant theology at around the same time, a critique that we have seen was also connected to disillusionment with German hyper-nationalism. But there was one main difference. Whereas Barth's God was unapproachably distant, a figure so ineffable that man could not hope to have any meaningful dialogue with him, Buber's remained proximate and available for human interaction. As he wrote in *I and Thou*, "of course, God is 'the wholly other,' but he is also the wholly same: the wholly present. Of course, he is the *mysterium tremendum* that appears and overwhelms, but he is also the mystery of the obvious that is closer to me than my own I."[188] Buber was, in fact, praised by his gentile friend Florens Christian Rang when *I and Thou* was published precisely for retaining a sense of the presence of God in the world. "You are absolutely right," Rang wrote him, "in opposing the particular theology that shows God as merely the Other of a *mysterium tremendum,* though *fascinum,* and you have vigorously proclaimed the simplicity of daily life in this world as equally an area of holiness."[189] A later observer would even go so far as claiming that *I and Thou* "can be considered a polemic against Otto's *Das Heilige*. Otto's conception of God as the wholly 'Other' *(das Andere)* seems to preclude all divine-human communication, while Buber's dialogic philosophy tries to overcome the abyss between God and man."[190] As such, it sought what might be called a Jewish surrogate for the Christian personal redeemer, an engaged interlocutor who was far more present than the distant law-giver of the Mosaic tradition.

Although Buber ostensibly left behind the cult of subjective *Erlebnis* that marked his prewar thought, he never lost his conviction that dogma, law, and rationalist proofs of God's existence were insufficient to ground religion. His God was always that of Abraham, not that of the philosophers, who reduced Him to an idea rather than the experience of love.[191] Nor did he jettison his belief that dialogic experience might take place without the intermediary of language, at least according to the still skeptical Scholem.[192] In

188. Buber, *I and Thou,* trans. Walter Kaufmann (New York, 1970), p. 127.

189. Christian Florens Rang to Martin Buber, September 19, 1922, in Glatzer and Mendes-Flohr, *The Letters of Martin Buber,* p. 276. This praise is, to be sure, set in the context of a reservation about the overly optimistic nature of Buber's belief in the possibility of an encounter with God.

190. David Biale, *Gershom Scholem: Kabbalah and Counter-History* (Cambridge, Mass., 1979), p. 246.

191. See, for example, his praise for the later work of Hermann Cohen in these terms in "The God of Love and the Idea of the Deity," in *Israel and the World: Essays in a Time of Crisis* (New York, 1963).

192. For a discussion of Scholem's suspicion of the residues of *Erlebnismystik* even in the Buber of the 1920s, see Biale, *Gershom Scholem: Kabbalah and Counter-History,* chapter 4. The issue of language was

fact, Scholem would go so far as to complain that "the immediate evidence for, and validity of, words like 'direct relation,' 'eternal Thou,' the 'interhuman' *(Zwischenmenschliche)* and their like, on which Buber builds, are in no way clear. They continue to terminate in the hypostatization of the old concept of *Erlebnis* unto the ontological realm."[193]

Whether or not Scholem's charge was entirely on the mark, it is significant to note that Buber's great collaborator of the 1920s at the Frankfurt Lehrhaus and co-translator of the first volumes of his rendition of the Hebrew Bible into German, Franz Rosenzweig, himself developed a complicated defense of a certain notion of experience.[194] His "New Thinking," however, renounced subjectivist *Erlebnis* in favor of a reworked concept of *Erfahrung* in ways that bear comparison with Heidegger and Benjamin, both of whom attempted to develop what can be called a paradoxical notion of "experience without a subject." In so doing, they sought to reintegrate religious with other forms of experience, reversing the modalization that began in the eighteenth century.

The difficulty of developing a viable concept of religious experience, one that would avoid the charge of psychologistic anthropomorphism, expressed a fundamental and still unresolved tension in the Judeo-Christian tradition. Variously figured as theology vs. Christology, the *Deus absconditus* vs. a personal savior, the profane world as fallen and corrupt vs. the world as charged with the grandeur of God, and the God of law vs. the God of love, it betrayed a deep uncertainty about the proper relationship between divine and human, creator and creature, that continues to challenge religious thinkers today. As early as 1866, Ludwig Feuerbach had noted with wicked glee that Count Zinzendorf, the founder of Moravian Pietism, was really a "Christian atheist" because of his overemphasis on the human role of piety.[195] Per-

---

particularly important in the wake of Buber's translation of the Bible, initially done in collaboration with Franz Rosenzweig. For an account of the controversy that it spawned, which pitted Benjamin, Scholem, and Siegfried Kracauer against the translators, see Martin Jay, "Politics of Translation: Siegfried Kracauer and Walter Benjamin on the Buber-Rosenzweig Bible," in *Permanent Exiles: Essays on the Intellectual Migration from Germany to America* (New York, 1985).

193. Scholem, "Martin Buber's Conception of Judaism," p. 151.

194. For discussions, see Reiner Wiehl, "Experience in Rosenzweig's New Thinking," and Bernard Casper, "Responsibility Rescued," in Paul Mendes-Flohr, *The Philosophy of Franz Rosenzweig* (Hanover, 1988). See also Leora Batnitzky, "On the Truth of History or the History of Truth: Rethinking Rosenzweig via Strauss," in *Jewish Social Studies Quarterly* 7, no. 3 (2000). Batnitzky shows that Rosenzweig's attempt to find in history expressions of revelatory truth was countered by Leo Strauss's denial that history could be its locus, a denial whose assumptions merit comparison with those underlying the antihistoricism of Barth's critique of Schleiermacher.

195. Feuerbach, "Zinzendorf und die Herrnhüter," *Sämtliche Werke*, ed. Bolin and Jodl, vol. 10, pp. 80–85.

haps all attempts to privilege religious experience were in danger of sliding into an atheistic worship of the believer instead of his God, however valiant the efforts made by the figures we have been examining in this chapter to prevent that outcome.

Ultimately, the attempt to rope off religious experience from other forms of experience also began to run aground, as the desire for a holistic, reintegrated version of the concept grew in ways we will explore in our final chapters. The difficulties were, however, already foreshadowed in the discourse we have been examining above. For although it might have seemed relatively easy to posit a boundary between epistemological notions of experience, either empiricist or transcendental, and religious (albeit less so in the case of post-Kantian idealism), when it came to another variety, aesthetic, the difficulties were much greater. The Romanticism that nurtured Schleiermacher's challenge to the "cultured despisers" of religion was, after all, preeminently an aesthetic movement.[196] As we have also noted in the case of Otto's appropriation of Fries, it was Kant's *Critique of Judgment* that provided him an inspiration for the effort to overcome the boundaries of critical reason and get in touch with a deeper truth. In *The Philosophy of Religion Based on Kant and Fries,* Otto explicitly concluded that *Ahndung* "is not a scientific principle to be used for explanation; it is an 'aesthetic' principle which serves for the religious interpretation of historical development."[197] In *The Idea of the Holy,* he would likewise analogize from art to religion and argue that Schleiermacher's religious faculty of judgment *(Urteilsvermögen)* belonged with the *Urteilskraft* discussed in Kant's Third Critique.[198]

What did experience mean when it was preceded by the adjective "aesthetic"? When did it emerge as one of the main modalities of the modern differentiation of experience? What was its relation to the other modalities we have already encountered? How did it handle the challenge we have seen bedeviling the attempt to defend faith on experiential grounds: the threat of a psychologistic or subjectivist obliteration of the object of that experience? These and other questions will occupy us as we turn in the next chapter to the "song" of experience that perhaps best warrants that metaphor: the experience that is generated by the human response not to a "wholly other" God, but to a very this-worldly "art."

196. For nuanced considerations of the aesthetic component in Schleiermacher's position, see Redeker, *Schleiermacher: Life and Thought,* pp. 45–48; and Jaeschke, *Reason in Religion,* pp. 113–16.

197. Otto, *The Philosophy of Religion Based on Kant and Fries,* p. 144.

198. Otto, *The Idea of the Holy,* p. 148.

FOUR

Returning to the Body through Aesthetic Experience

From Kant to Dewey

WHENEVER EXPERIENCE HAS BEEN in bad odor, distrusted for undermining the certain truths of deductive reason, or attacked as unreliably subjective and incommunicable, its ground in the creaturely human body is often implicitly to blame. Platonism's suspicion of the base needs of the corruptible body and the irrationalism of the emotions was a major source of its hostility to experience per se. Although the epistemological tradition, especially in its empiricist guise, sought to reinstate the evidence of the sensorium, it did so in the hope of somehow avoiding, or at least containing, the relativist implications of relying on sense data. The religious alternatives examined in the previous chapter also sought to ground experience in more than the pleasures and pains of the sentient body, producing, as we have seen, a divided self. Although the Spirit could manifest itself in corporeal symptoms, pious desires were strictly separated from their fleshly counterparts.

In the eighteenth century, however, a new modality of experience emerged as an object of discursive exploration, which sought to moderate—if not entirely to relinquish—this distrust of corporeality. Although there had been some awareness in previous centuries of the perceptual needs of the subjective beholder, the long-standing assumption was that beauty was an objective quality of objects in a world endowed by its creator with intelligible forms and proportional correspondences.[1] Once that belief lost its plausibility, as

1. See Umberto Eco, *Art and Beauty in the Middle Ages,* trans. Hugh Bredin (New Haven, 1986). Eco points to the practical recognition of subjective needs in the distortions of sculptures placed above eye

it did with the disenchantment of the world abetted by philosophical nominalism and the scientific revolution, the door was open for the relocation of
aesthetic value in the bodily responses—and judgments of taste—of those
who experienced the work of art.[2]

Why that threshold was passed in the mid-eighteenth century has been a
source of considerable speculation. Perhaps the ascetic constraint associated
with rationalism and the scientific method, on the one hand, and with moral
rigorism and religious self-denial, on the other, was no longer necessary to
keep the modern subject in line.[3] Possibly, the reassessment of the vice of
luxury, which could be defended as an expression of refinement rather than
the idle indulgence of appetite (and serve the public good as a spur to consumer capitalism), meant a new willingness to countenance certain forms of
bodily enjoyment.[4] Perhaps the growing differentiation of an increasingly
complex and fractured modernity, in which bourgeois specialization and the
division of labor replaced feudal integration, allowed the crystallization of a
specific sub-sphere of art apparently freed from external determination and
frankly appealing to sensual pleasure, a sub-sphere that required theoretical
legitimation.[5] The rise of commercial literature in the nascent capitalist marketplace may have produced a reaction from alarmed defenders of "high art,"
who needed to justify its superiority through appeals to non-instrumental
autonomy.[6] Or perhaps the growing primacy of art criticism and the con-

---

level in cathedrals and acknowledges the rising interest in visual perception in the thirteenth century, but
he concludes that "in the Thomistic view, pleasure is caused by the potentiality in things which is fully
objective" (p. 71).

2. No simple before-and-after story can be told, however, as neo-Platonic aesthetics enjoyed a revival
during the Renaissance and reappeared in later figures like Shaftesbury. In the nineteenth century, writers like John Ruskin still held on to an objectivist view of beauty, a cause championed in the twentieth
by anti-Romantic critics like T. E. Hulme.

3. See Terry Eagleton, *The Ideology of the Aesthetic* (Cambridge, Mass. 1990), chapter 1.

4. An indication of the shift can be seen in David Hume's essay "Of Refinement in the Arts," in *Essays Moral, Political and Literary,* ed. Eugene F. Miller (Indianapolis, 1987). On the general debate over
the concept, see C. J. Berry, *The Idea of Luxury: A Conceptual and Historical Investigation* (Cambridge,
1994). According to Preben Mortensen, the concept of art had to be liberated from the negative aura surrounding luxury and grafted onto the uplifting moral values that had been previously associated with religion. See his *Art and the Social Order: The Making of the Modern Conception of Art* (Albany, N.Y., 1997),
pp. 122–28.

5. See Peter Bürger, *Theory of the Avant-Garde,* trans. Michael Shaw (Minneapolis, 1984), chapter 3.
In his foreword to the book, Jochen Schulte-Sasse assesses the importance of the concept of experience
in Bürger's work, a concept indebted to Walter Benjamin and Theodor Adorno's lament about the withering away of authentic experience (p. xiii–xvii).

6. See Martha Woodmansee, *The Author, Art, and the Market: Rereading the History of Aesthetics* (New
York, 1994).

comitant anxiety over standards of taste in an age when contact with new cultures raised the specter of relativism led to a desire to ground judgments in more philosophical reasoning.[7] Whatever the cause (or multiple causes), the result was a full-blown discourse dubbed aesthetics by the German philosopher Alexander Baumgarten, which had among its central concerns an attempt to articulate and defend a new modality of experience.[8]

Although something called art had been examined by philosophers since at least the time of the Greeks and a faint awareness of its experiential dimension has been discerned as early as Pythagoras, it was only in the Enlightenment that aesthetics as a discrete discourse really came into its own.[9] The separate Muses could now be grouped under one generic concept, whose putative essence could be explored.[10] It was at this time, broadly speaking, that objects that had once functioned as ornaments of social and political power or were revered as sacred implements of religious worship were redescribed and newly legitimated in terms of artistic merit alone. As Hegel sardonically noted in his lectures on aesthetics, the corpses of dead cults could now be revivified in the guise of aesthetic objects. "Fine artists" began to be differentiated from mere

7. According to Ernst Cassirer, in the "age of criticism," "the union of philosophy and literary and aesthetic criticism is evident in all the eminent minds of the century." *The Philosophy of the Enlightenment*, trans. Fritz C. A. Koelln and James P. Pettegrove (Boston, 1951), p. 275.

8. Alexander Baumgarten, *Aesthetica* (1750 and 1758), ed. and trans. Hans Rudolf Schweitzer as *Theoretische Aesthetik* (Hamburg, 1983). There is as yet no complete English translation. Baumgarten had actually first coined the term in his 1735 dissertation. For a contextualization of his work in the Leibnizian tradition, see Jeffrey Barnouw, "The Beginnings of 'Aesthetics' and the Leibnizian Conception of Sensation," in Paul Mattick Jr., ed., *Eighteenth-Century Aesthetics and the Reconstruction of Art* (Cambridge, 1993). The precise term "aesthetische Erfahrung" does not appear in Baumgarten; indeed, it seems to have been first used by Gustav Fechner in his *Vorschule der Ästhetik* of 1876. See the discussion in Wolfgang Welsch, "Rettung durch Halbierung? Zu Richard Shusterman's Rehabilitierung ästhetischer Erfahrung," *Deutsche Zeitschrift für Philosophie* 41, no. 1 (1999), p. 112. Still, many of its components antedate the actual coinage.

9. See Władysław Tatarkiewicz, "Aesthetic Experience: The Early History of the Concept," *Dialectics and Humanism* 1 (1973), and "Aesthetic Experience: The Last Stages in the History of a Concept," *Dialectics and Humanism* 1 (1974). In the first of these essays, Tatarkiewicz notes that Pythagoras spoke of a spectatorial attitude towards life, which he equates with an incipient notion of aesthetic experience (p. 19). We cannot do justice to the national differences in Enlightenment aesthetics, which would repay serious investigation.

10. For a recent consideration of the problematic implications of this generic subsumption, see Jean-Luc Nancy, *The Muses*, trans. Peggy Kamuf (Stanford, 1996). Nancy attributes the change to the Romantics (p. 4), but it is possible to see it at work as early as Charles Batteux's 1746 treatise *Les beaux-arts réduits à un même principe*. It is, of course, possible to continue to explore the specific experiential dimensions of individual artistic genres. See, for example, the essays on pictorial, musical, literary, film, photographic, and dance experience in Ananta Ch. Sukla, ed., *Art and Experience* (Westport, Conn., 2003).

artisanal craftsmen possessing technical skill, a distinction nicely captured in the refusal to include engravers when the Royal Academy of the Arts was established in London in 1768.[11] A growing willingness to value the objects such artists created for their intrinsic, relational qualities rather than as imitations of an ideal or natural world, illustrations of divine narratives, or re-creations of historical events seeded the ground for the modernist credo that art's essence was what Clive Bell and Roger Fry were to call "significant form."[12]

This tendency was abetted by the recontextualization of visual objects in the new quasi-sacred spaces of the *salon,* the public exhibitions that began in 1677 under the auspices of the French Academy of Art, and the museum, in which they were juxtaposed with other such works in a synchronic order of eternal beauty.[13] The transformation of the palace of the Louvre during the French Revolution into a public repository for the nation's cultural patrimony signaled an increasing (although still far from total) democratization of access, as well as an overcoming of the iconoclastic inclinations of some of the revolutionaries. Along with the public exhibition of works went the acceleration of a private collector's market for objects that had previously been owned by religious or secular authorities, as cultural capital and economic capital proved in many instances remarkably fungible.[14] The role of the virtuoso or connoisseur, able to judge both the artistic merit and the economic value of an art object, emerged as a possible guise for the gentleman, whose manners and taste were an indication of his social worth.[15]

In music, a similar process occurred as court and church domination of production and performance eroded with the rise of commercial concert halls,

11. The term "polite arts" had immediately preceded "fine arts," for example in the work of Shaftesbury. This usage shows perhaps more clearly the entanglement of aesthetic refinement and social elitism, as Mortensen has argued in *Art in the Social Order,* p. 136. For a discussion of the still-functionalist interpretation of the *Beaux-Arts* in Diderot's *Encyclopédie,* see Peter Bürger, "Problems in the Functional Transformation of Art and Literature during the Transition from Feudal to Bourgeois Society," in Peter Bürger and Christa Bürger, *The Institutions of Art,* trans. Loren Kruger (Lincoln, Neb., 1992). Bürger sees a full-fledged defense of the absolute autonomy of art emerging with Goethe's friend Karl Philipp Moritz in the 1780s. For an extensive discussion of Moritz's contribution in the context of the political debates of the *Aufklärung,* see Jonathan M. Hess, *Reconstituting the Body Politic: Enlightenment, Public Culture and the Invention of Aesthetic Autonomy* (Detroit, 1999).

12. Clive Bell, *Art* (London, 1927); and Roger Fry, *Vision and Design* (London, 1929).

13. On the effects of these changes, see Thomas E. Crow, *Painters and Public Life in Eighteenth-Century Paris* (New Haven, 1985).

14. Art markets emerged first in Italy, Holland, and Britain, where auctions began in earnest during the Restoration. See Michael North and David Ormod, eds., *Art Markets in Europe, 1400–1800* (Aldershot, 1998).

15. Among the earliest tracts designed to promote this role was Jonathan Richardson, *The Connoisseur: An Essay on the whole Art of Criticism as it relates to Painting* (London, 1719).

originating in private *collegia musica* that were then open to at least middle-class listeners. "Occasional music" written on commission to accompany religious rituals or aristocratic celebrations gave way to compositions that were their own justification, anticipating what nineteenth-century critics such as Eduard Hanslick would call "absolute music."[16] A growing market for works written by a new type of composer who, like Beethoven, could assume the role of creative genius rather than court functionary was generated by listeners trained to focus their attention on the performance before them. The concert hall could thus serve as another locus, alongside the newly legitimated theater, of that nascent bourgeois public sphere of which Jürgen Habermas has made us all so aware.[17]

These transformations have been frequently noticed. But what is often less fully appreciated is the fact that at virtually the same moment that newly defined works of art were being liberated from their entanglement in religious, political, or utilitarian contexts, free to circulate in new networks of value, cultural and economic, and housed or performed in secular temples of culture open to the people, they were paradoxically losing their integrity as self-sufficient entities in the world, definable in intrinsic terms as objective exemplars of universal beauty.[18] In the vocabulary later made famous by Walter Benjamin, the cultic aura surrounding them, an aura predicated on the presence of a unique object at an unbridgeable distance from the beholder, was undergoing a subtle, if not immediately apprehended, loss of strength.

Although some of the numinous atmosphere clinging to sacred objects was undeniably transferred to certain fetishized works of elite art, whose cultural and often economic capital was accordingly high, the philosophical legitimation of that transfer tacitly abandoned the claim that such objects possessed an aesthetic version of the religious notion of "real presence,"[19] an incarnation of ultimate value that was prior to the beholder's response to it.

16. See Lydia Goehr, *The Imaginary Museum of Musical Works: An Essay on the Philosophy of Music* (Oxford, 1992).

17. Jürgen Habermas, *The Structural Transformation of the Public Sphere: An Inquiry into a Category of Bourgeois Society*, trans. Thomas Burger (Cambridge, Mass. 1989), p. 38–40. The precise relationship between the rise of philosophical aesthetics, the doctrine of the autonomy of art, and the public sphere has been subjected to a subtle analysis by Hess in *Reconstituting the Body Politic*. Although drawing to some extent on Habermas's model, he has telling criticisms of several of its elements.

18. This is not to deny that considerable energy was and still is devoted to defining such works and setting their boundaries. For a very insightful recent attempt to sort out the consequences of such efforts, see Gérard Genette, *The Work of Art: Immanence and Transcendence*, trans. G. M. Gosharian (Ithaca, N.Y., 1997).

19. For a recent attempt to restore some of that metaphysical aura to works of art, see George Steiner, *Real Presences* (Chicago, 1989).

No longer able to understand beauty as a function of the intelligibility of an order created by a beneficent—and very artistically talented—divinity, modern aesthetics had to rely instead on the subjective or intersubjective judgment of its human beneficiaries, whose sensual responses were intrinsic to the process. Increasingly, eighteenth-century aesthetic theory shifted attention to the beholder/listener/reader or the communities they formed and away from objective criteria of value. In fact, as we noted in the case of religious experience, the pendulum could swing so far in the new direction that some critics began to worry about the wholesale obliteration of the art object with consequences we will address later in this chapter.

A salient reason for the erosion of certainty about the objective qualities of art objects based on immutable criteria of eternal beauty was the increasing awareness of and appetite for cultural variation, which paralleled the uneven but widening toleration of religious pluralism. This effect not only followed from exposure to non-European cultures, widely reported in the travel accounts and fictions that circulated in the wake of actual explorations, but it also reflected the loss of the aristocracy's monopoly on cultural production and reception.[20] In the early eighteenth century, critics like the abbé Jean-Baptiste Dubos began to question the classical standards promulgated by Nicolas Boileau, the cultural arbiter of Louis XIV's reign, who had claimed the warrant of universal nature for his ideals of harmony, balance, and order.[21] Instead, the variability of natural conditions, recognized at the same time in the relativist sociology of culture and politics developed by Montesquieu, was acknowledged as a source of divergent aesthetic norms. No longer could the ancients be held up as the sole models to be imitated in all circumstances; new genres such as the bourgeois domestic tragedy, genre painting, and the nascent novel began to assert their importance. Nor could the French neoclassicists fend off the claims of national alternatives in Britain and Germany, which abetted the reevaluation of disparaged artists such as Homer and Shakespeare over Virgil and Racine.

Although it has sometimes been argued that a distinct aesthetic discourse

20. For a brief account of the importance of travel fiction, see Ira O. Wade, *The Intellectual Origins of the French Enlightenment* (Princeton, 1971), chapter 9.

21. Jean-Baptiste Dubos, *Réflections critiques sur la poésie, la peinture et la musique* (Paris, 1719). For a discussion, see Cassirer, *The Philosophy of the Enlightenment*, chapter 7. See also Francis X. J. Coleman, *The Aesthetic Thought of the French Enlightenment* (Pittsburgh, 1971); and John C. O'Neal, *The Authority of Experience: Sensationist Theory in the French Enlightenment* (University Park, Pa., 1996). O'Neal shows the importance of French sensationist thought derived from Étienne de Condillac and Charles Bonnet for the aesthetics of the period.

emerged in reaction to the exaggerated prominence of science during the Enlightenment, which robbed the world of its enchantment, often that discourse took seriously the advances in the psychology of subjectivity that were being achieved at the time.[22] The "sentimentalism" of Dubos focused on those who responded to works rather than on the works themselves. The empiricist version of this new credo was best exemplified, once again, by David Hume, who argued in his 1757 essay "Of the Standard of Taste," "beauty is no quality in the things themselves: It exists merely in the mind which contemplates them, and each mind perceives a different beauty."[23] The foundation of rules of aesthetic composition, he insisted, is "the same with that of all the practical sciences, experience; nor are they any things but general observations, concerning what has been universally found to please in all countries and in all ages."[24] Although he did allow that there may be certain qualities in nature that help produce aesthetic experiences, they were often so small or mixed with so many others, that only a man whose sensibility was educated could truly appreciate them. Thus, experience was a foundational term for aesthetics with the same two meanings that we have discerned in Hume's epistemology: a sense-based alternative to innate ideas and the accumulated wisdom produced by habitual learning over time. With these premises, the center of gravity of aesthetic discourse was now firmly located in the subject and his experience or judgment rather than the object. For even if Hume is read as more of a naturalist than a skeptical relativist, which is suggested by his reassuring claim that "the difficulty of finding, even in particulars, the standard of taste, is not so great as it has been represented,"[25]

22. For a skeptical consideration of the argument that aesthetics was a compensatory reaction to the privileging of science, see Mortensen, *Art in the Social Order*, chapter 6. For a discussion of the later nineteenth-century attempts by scientists such as Gustav Fechner and Wilhelm Wundt to study aesthetic experience experimentally, see Tatarkiewicz, "Aesthetic Experience: The Last Stages in the History of the Concept." Such investigations were often decried in turn as "psychologistic" by philosophers such as Edmund Husserl. For a discussion of his critique, see Peter J. McCormick, *Modernity, Aesthetics and the Bounds of Art* (Ithaca, N.Y., 1990), chapter 8.

23. David Hume, "Of the Standard of Taste," in *Essays: Moral, Political, and Literary*, p. 230. For a useful account of Hume's general thoughts on aesthetics, see Peter Jones, "Hume's Literary and Aesthetic Theory," in David Fate Norton, ed., *The Cambridge Companion to Hume* (Cambridge, 1993). For a defense of Hume's position against Kant's, see George Dickie, *The Century of Taste: The Philosophical Odyssey of Taste in the Eighteenth Century* (Oxford, 1996).

24. "Of the Standard of Taste," p. 231.

25. Ibid., p. 242. Underlying Hume's confidence was an assumption that the educated gentlemen of his day could be taken to represent humankind in general. For a critique of this bias, see Richard Shusterman, "Of the Scandal of Taste: Social Privilege as Nature in the Aesthetic Theories of Hume and Kant," in Mattick, *Eighteenth-Century Aesthetics*.

he acknowledged that such a standard was a human construct, not an objective reality.

Significantly, the Greek *aiesthesis,* the origin of the Latin word *aesthetica* used by Baumgarten as the title for his two-volume work of 1750 and 1758, implied gratifying corporeal sensation, the subjective sensual response to objects rather than objects themselves.[26] One of its antithetical terms was *noesis,* which signified pure conceptual thought separated from the senses. Another was *poiesis,* the active making of objects, artistic or otherwise.[27] Some of that activism may have been retained in the ancillary notion of taste, with its latent connotation of tactile intervention in the world,[28] implying experience as experimentation. But even here the emphasis remained on the emotional, even irrational, reception of art epitomized by the *"je ne sais quoi"* attitude of ineffable felicity and mysterious grace that became emblematic of the retreat from conceptualization and production.[29] It stressed what has been called the "mutism" of the initial encounter with art, the "sense of running out of words or of not knowing how or where to begin speaking in the face of the artwork."[30] Along with the loss of words went a certain willingness to be overwhelmed by the encounter. As John Dewey was later to note

26. The term took some time to be universally accepted, after such alternatives as Sir William Hamilton's neologism "apolaustics" were rejected. See the discussion in Reginald Snell's introduction to his translation of Friedrich Schiller, *On the Aesthetic Education of Man in a Series of Letters* (New York, 1965), p. 5. From the beginning it contained an ambiguous emphasis, which has been pointed out by Wolfgang Welsch, on both "sensation" and "perception." The former, which Welsch calls its "hedonistic semantic element," foregrounds pleasure and emotional response in the subject; the latter, which he calls its "theoreticistic semantic element," stresses cognitive values of form and proportion and thus draws attention back to the object. But even the latter, he concedes, "is not interested in the immediate being of things as it is, and it even enjoys the objects peculiar to it at [a] distance—precisely in the manner of contemplation." See his *Undoing Aesthetics,* trans. Andrew Inkpin (London, 1997), p. 12.

27. For a discussion of the *aiesthesis/poiesis* distinction, see Hans Robert Jauss, *Aesthetic Experience and Literary Hermeneutics,* trans. Michael Shaw (Minneapolis, 1982), p. 34.

28. For a discussion of the origins of taste in these terms, see Howard Caygill, *Art of Judgment* (Oxford, 1989), chapter 2, where he points out that the etymology of the word is from the Old French *tast* and Italian *tasto,* which include *touching* in their meanings. The larger implications of the metaphor and its literal sensual origins are discussed in Carolyn Korsmeyer, *Making Sense of Taste: Food and Philosophy* (Ithaca, N.Y., 1999). Korsmeyer points out that the privileging of vision and hearing in aesthetic theory meant that the literal sense of taste, along with the other proximate senses, was denigrated, even as the metaphor of taste as ineffable discrimination emerged into prominence.

29. For a history of this concept, which was popularized by Antoine Gombaud (the chevalier de Méré), see Erich Köhler, *"Je ne sais quoi:* Ein Kapital aus der Begriffsgeschichte des Unbegreiflichen," *Romantisches Jahrbuch* 6 (1953–54). It was assumed that works created by geniuses had such a mysterious quality, which could be appreciated, but not fully understood.

30. Peter de Bolla, *Art Matters* (Cambridge, Mass., 2003), p. 4.

with chagrin, the very concept of the "aesthetic," when set apart from the overlapping but not equivalent term "artistic," tended to render experience as "appreciative, perceiving and enjoying,"[31] rather than productive or creative. As we will see, his alternative was designed to redress precisely this balance.

KANT AND AESTHETIC EXPERIENCE AS CONTEMPLATIVE, REFLECTIVE JUDGMENT

The discourse concerning aesthetic judgment that culminated in Kant's Third Critique did, to be sure, go beyond the passive and culture-bound subjectivism of taste represented by Humean empiricism and sought more universal and communicable criteria to overcome the mutism of the individual beholder. Although refusing to rely on the transcendental deduction of cognitive categories developed in the First Critique, Kant hoped to transcend mere contingent convention and individual whim. But like Hume, he too focused on the response rather than the object per se, on judging rather than producing art. Even if Kant did provide an account of the genius who imitated God and created without criteria—a productive correlate of the beholder, who, as we will see, judges without them as well—the main emphasis of his aesthetics was on judgment and thus on experience in a contemplative and receptive rather than creative mode.[32]

There is not enough space to detail in full the complex ways in which such Enlightenment theorists as Baumgarten, Dubos, Shaftesbury, Hume, and Moritz anticipated Kant's account of aesthetic experience, or to untangle the web of meanings surrounding the crucial term "taste." Instead, only a few central points can be made.[33] First, whether the ground of aesthetic experi-

---

31. John Dewey, *Art as Experience* (New York, 1934), p. 47.

32. It is true that what Kant called "productive imagination" plays a role in aesthetic appreciation, as it does in normal cognition, albeit under the guidance of the understanding. But what was produced was a mental synthesis, not an active intervention in the world. For a discussion of its importance, see Michael R. Neville, "Kant's Characterization of Aesthetic Experience," *Journal of Aesthetics and Art Criticism* 33, no. 2 (Winter 1974), p. 197.

33. For useful accounts, see Dabney Townsend, "From Shaftesbury to Kant: The Development of the Concept of Aesthetic Experience," *Journal of the History of Ideas* 48, no. 2 (April–June 1987), pp. 287–305; and Jauss, *Aesthetic Experience and Literary Hermeneutics*. For more general histories, foregrounding the questionable political implications of aesthetic discourse, see Eagleton, *The Ideology of the Aesthetic*, and Hess, *Reconstituting the Body Politic*.

ence was assumed to be an innate capacity, an unmediated, non-rule-bound sense of what was beautiful comparable to an inbred moral sentiment, as it was for the neo-Platonist Shaftesbury,[34] or understood instead to derive from purely empirical encounters with the world, as the more skeptical Hume believed, it was irreducible to a mere recording of what was intrinsically there in objects deemed beautiful or artistic. The same conclusion was shared by those who saw the source of the aesthetic sense in personal psychology, communal, intersubjective consensus, or the more philosophically grounded "reflective judgment" that Kant had posited as a way to get beyond the apparent antinomy of taste, at once personal and universal. In all of these cases, the stress was on the one or ones who did the experiencing rather than on the intrinsic qualities of the object that was experienced. "The beautiful," as Kant would argue, appeared only as the predicate of a judgment, not as a quality of an object. In some ways reminiscent of the epistemological limits on knowing objects in themselves, whether couched in the empiricist vocabulary of lacking access to primary (as opposed to secondary) qualities or the transcendental idealist vocabulary of unknowable noumena, the object as such was less important than its aesthetic appreciation or enjoyment. Here too, a kind of "Copernican revolution,"[35] to quote the famous metaphor identified with Kant's First Critique, took place, in which ontological or axiological questions were subordinated to those concerning the epistemological or, in this case, aesthetic subject. Objects were admired not for what they were in themselves, but for what they could do to or for us. The telos of this Copernican reversal was an increasing indifference to the inherent qualities of the object as such, perhaps extending even to its very existence.

Before that conclusion was reached—and this is the second point worth emphasizing—the sensual pleasure produced by the object in aesthetic experience had to be distinguished from that enjoyed in other relations between

34. For a discussion of Shaftesbury's debts to the Cambridge Platonists of the seventeenth century and through them to the Florentine neo-Platonism of Marsilio Ficino, see Ernst Cassirer, *The Platonic Renaissance in England*, trans. James P. Pettegrove (New York, 1970), chapter 6. Although we have noted the general Platonist distrust of actual bodily experience, the role of intuition in the Platonic tradition coupled with its stress on transcendent truths meant that it must be credited with a role in preparing the way for the doctrine of disinterested, sublimated aesthetic pleasure. Noting that Hume and the psychological school could only provide a doctrine of reception rather than artistic creation, Cassirer goes so far as to argue that "aesthetics is not a product of the general trend of English empiricism, but of English Platonism" (p. 197).

35. Whether the metaphor, which in this precise form did not appear in Kant, adequately describes the innovations of the *Critique of Pure Reason* need not concern us now. For a skeptical account of its applicability, see Robert Hahn, *Kant's Newtonian Revolution in Philosophy* (Carbondale, Ill., 1988).

self and world. As early as Johannes Scotus Erigena's ninth-century *De divisione naturae*, the spectatorial, non-instrumental nature of the aesthetic attitude had attracted attention.[36] Although one might also covet the same objects for what a later age would call their commodity or exchange value, they were appreciated *qua* objects of art only from a loftier point of view. Rejecting the egocentric anthropology of a Hobbes, whose stress on self-preservation against passion he derided as vulgar, Shaftesbury stressed the fallacy of reducing everything to the question of private interest, appetite, or need.[37] Instead—and this was related to his belief that aesthetic experience was inextricably intertwined with civic virtue and moral sentiment—"disinterested" benevolence was its defining characteristic.[38]

It was in Kant's aesthetic theory that the crucial concept of disinterestedness was fully and most influentially articulated. In the *Critique of Judgment*, Kant claimed that our ability to experience pleasure took three forms.[39] The first, which he called the "agreeable" or "the pleasant" *(das Angenehme)*, is caused directly by sensual stimulation. It involved a purely private and subjective response of attraction and aversion, without any meaningful cognitive or intersubjective dimension. Here the individual body with all its appetites and antipathies is the arbiter, not a cultural or universal norm. Personal gratification or lack thereof is all that matters. The second variety connects pleasure to the question of the "good." That is, we can derive "delight in the good" *(das Wohlgefallen am Guten)* through working for and achieving a beneficent goal, which is set by ideas and principles external to sensual gratification. In this case there is always a functional or utilitarian di-

---

36. See the discussion in Tatarkiewicz, "Aesthetic Experience: The Early History of the Concept," p. 23. Jauss points to other examples of medieval anticipations of aesthetic experience, which produce anxiety because they are linked with idle curiosity about the world rather than immersion in the word of God. See *Aesthetic Experience and Literary Hermeneutics*, p. 4. Cassirer claims the distinction between the pleasurable and the beautiful, the latter based on aesthetic contemplation, can be seen as early as Plato's *Philebus*. See *The Platonic Renaissance in England*, p. 186.

37. The elevation of interests over passions in early capitalism is analyzed in Albert O. Hirschman, *The Passions and the Interests: Political Arguments for Capitalism before Its Triumph* (Princeton, 1977). For a discussion of Shaftesbury's critique of Hobbes, see Mortensen, *Art in the Social Order,* chapter 10.

38. For a history of the concept, see Jerome Stolnitz, "On the Origins of 'Aesthetic Disinterestedness'," *Journal of Aesthetics and Art Criticism* 20, no. 2 (Winter 1961). See also his "The Actualities of Non-Aesthetic Experience," in Michael H. Mitias, ed., *Possibility of the Aesthetic Experience* (Amsterdam, 1986), for a discussion of other types of disinterestedness. For earlier anticipations of the doctrine, see David Summers, *The Judgment of Sense: Renaissance Naturalism and the Rise of Aesthetics* (Cambridge, 1987). It should be noted that an alternative to disinterestedness was presented by those defenders of empathy or what the German Romantics called *Einfühlung,* such as Herder, who stressed the emotional investment involved in aesthetic experience.

39. Immanuel Kant, *Critique of Judgment,* trans. J. H. Bernard (New York, 1951), pp. 37–45.

mension to our pleasure, which is not an end in itself. The real end is the good that is realized, not the pleasure we have in realizing it, although that pleasure may be a subsidiary part of our motivation as well.

The third form of pleasure *(das Wohlgefallen am Schönen)*, Kant argued, is what we can properly call aesthetic. As in the case of the "agreeable," the senses play a role and the body is involved, but with a crucial difference. Whereas in the former the object that produces the pleasure must actually exist—we cannot find a meal pleasant unless there is real food on the table—in the latter, it may not. Or more precisely, our sensation of the aesthetic object and its intrinsic properties or qualities need not coincide, as they must with an agreeable meal (food may look appetizing, but it must taste good to bring us genuine pleasure). Because of this distinction, we have no direct interest in the object, only in its representation or semblance. To be still more precise, because the media of representations can themselves be understood as objects (a gold statue is, after all, made of a substance whose value we find difficult to forget), what is important is a certain kind of experience of the object. Our pleasure in beauty, in short, is disinterested because we are indifferent to the actual object, which is not itself an object of direct sensual desire. Our pleasure comes from enjoying the free play of our faculties. We are no longer immersed in being—*inter-esse,* as the etymology of the word "interest" suggests—but rather somehow outside it. We enjoy an aesthetic meal, as it were, without having to taste and swallow the food, as in the case of certain variants of nouvelle cuisine in which visual more than gustatory pleasure, let alone actual nutrition, seems the main purpose of what is on the plate. It is the same disinterestedness that permits the transformation of the lust-arousing naked human form into the idealized, marmoreal nude and allows us to distinguish between pornography and high art (both of which may be representations of real objects, but are differentiated according to our interest or disinterest in their referents as objects of desire).

As Angelika Rauch's psychoanalytic reading of the ultimately "maternal ground" of Kant's theory of the aesthetic suggests, disinterestedness "implies an uncathected object, something that suggests a self-cathexis in aesthetic experience."[40] That is, the ultimate desire for the body of the mother to overcome the loss of an original unity, which may be one way to understand the yearning for aesthetic pleasure, is repressed because it is impossible to attain, leading to the displacement of it onto the subject's own senses. "If the exte-

---

40. Angelika Rauch, *The Hieroglyph of Tradition: Freud, Benjamin, Gadamer, Novalis, Kant* (Madison, N.J., 2000), p. 81.

rior (beautiful) object is abandoned for the subject as the object of reflection, then the 'object' must be the subject's body as it 'suffers' the affects. Reflecting on the affective experience, as the body's 'sufferings' may not trace a genealogy of affect so much as it masters a *pathology* of past experiences that have not been worked through or consciously put to rest in the subject's memory."[41] This mastery, Rauch claims, is repressed by Kant, who too quickly left behind the material basis of aesthetic experience through his stress on disinterestedness.

Whether or not one accepts the psychoanalytic premises of this argument, Rauch is right to stress the flight from the desiring body in Kant's argument. For aesthetic experience as Kant understands it is indeed also akin to the second form of pleasure in going beyond pre-conceptual sensual gratification or remaining on the level of what he dismissively called the mere "egoism of taste." Aesthetic experience mobilizes cognitive powers; synthesizing transformations of pure sensation evolve into truth or at least value claims, which are then assumed to have universal validity. But it does so without subsuming specific cases under discursive rules, a priori categories, or general principles, as is the case with the determinant judgments of the understanding. The latter seem to come from above, as if through the coercive dictates of a ruler. In contrast, aesthetic judgments, singular rather than categorical, are allowed a kind of nonhierarchical, free play in which each of us can make universal claims of beauty on the basis of analogical and paradigmatic, rather than subsumptive or deductive, reasoning. We move from particular to particular rather than from universal to particular, as was the case with the synthetic a priori judgments of cognition discussed in the First Critique. The concepts involved are thus "indeterminate" because they cannot be expressed in schematic form, as can the cognitive concepts of the understanding. They appeal to a virtual *sensus communis,* an intersubjective community that is to be made, not simply found, as innatist neo-Platonists like Shaftesbury had thought possible.[42] A crucial aspect of disinterestedness for Kant—although not, as we will see, for the devotees of *l'art pour l'art*—was precisely this assumption that aesthetic judgments evoked enjoyment and appreciation that are not just one's own but can be shared by all. To the extent that judgment was an inherent dimension of aesthetic experience, and not something added

---

41. Ibid., p. 79.

42. For an excellent analysis of the multiple layers of meaning in Kant's evocation of common sense in aesthetic judgment, see David Summers, "Why Did Kant Call Taste a 'Common Sense'?" in Mattick, *Eighteenth-Century Aesthetics and the Reconstruction of Art.*

to it after the initial response of the senses, disinterestedness had this crucial communicative implication, which was lacking in personal expressions of idiosyncratic taste.

What also distinguishes aesthetic experience, Kant argued, from the delight in the good, where practical outcomes are sought, is the intrinsic nature of the purposes involved, which are akin to the immanent telos of play rather than work, whose end is a transformation of the world. Kant's celebrated definition of art as "purposiveness without purpose" was designed precisely to set it apart from those activities in which extrinsic purposes dominate and real objects are there to be produced, consumed, possessed, or exchanged. Although aesthetic judgments are normally made by means of a rhetoric of objectivity—"*Mona Lisa is* a beautiful painting," not "*I think* it is a beautiful painting"—Kant stresses that it is the subject who is really the source of the judgment. Objectivity, as one of Kant's recent interpreters, Eva Schaper, has pointed out, is merely an "as-if" concept in his understanding of aesthetics.[43] That is, such judgments act as if they were directed at objects, but those objects are never analyzable for Kant entirely in intrinsic terms, and they become important solely for what they produce in their beholder. Or as another student of the *Critique of Judgment,* John Zammito, puts it: "While Kant stresses the degree to which the subject is affected *(afficiert)* in the experience, nevertheless it is striking how not merely the object but even the representation of the object shifts far into the background. Its form serves as the occasion, becomes at most a catalyst, for a complex subjective response."[44]

It is often argued, as we have seen, that the nature of that response is inherently contemplative, passive, and spectatorial, distancing the self from the world and our appetite to possess or consume it. Although this primarily visual characterization may seem an odd way to describe ways in which some art can seize us and invade our interiority—an experience we undergo perhaps most obviously in aural terms when we listen to music—even here the subject may not always be actively and productively engaged in intervening in the world. Attentive listening, as James Johnson has shown,[45] was an acquired skill in the eighteenth century based on the suppression of the kinesthetic body and the concentration of faculties on a single sensory input. The

---

43. Eva Schaper, *Studies in Kant's Aesthetics* (Edinburgh, 1979), chapter 6. The concept of "as-if" is taken from Hans Vaihinger, but Schaper wants to restrict it to aesthetic judgments, not to the cognitive ones discussed in Kant's First Critique.

44. John H. Zammito, *The Genesis of Kant's Critique of Judgment* (Chicago, 1992), p. 113.

45. James H. Johnson, *Listening in Paris: A Cultural History* (Berkeley, 1995).

experience of passive listening was carefully segregated from that of dancing or communal singing as the ear was educated to have contemplative aesthetic experiences. The public concert hall, as we have noted, worked like the museum to deracinate works that had their origins in the church or aristocratic chamber and turn them into stimuli for pure aesthetic experiences. In literature as well, the habit of looking for actual personal references in concocted narratives had to be lost and what Catherine Gallagher has called "nobody's story," the realization of acknowledged fictionality, put in its place before the novel could come into its own.[46]

There is, in short, no practical or possessive intention realized in the act of listening, reading, or beholding *qua* aesthetic experience. We may, to be sure, also want to own the object for its value in the marketplace or because of our passion to collect, but this is not the same as a purely aesthetic response. The possibility of that experience may be situated in an institutional context or cultural field, as philosophers such as George Dickie and sociologists such as Pierre Bourdieu have argued,[47] but the experience itself could not be reduced to a mere reflex of that enabling context. For it entails precisely the distance from extrinsic functionality that such reductionism wishes to impose on it from without. It is for this reason that Habermas can claim that "the problem of grounding modernity out of itself first comes into consciousness in the realm of aesthetic criticism."[48]

FROM THE AUTONOMY TO THE SOVEREIGNTY OF AESTHETIC EXPERIENCE

What makes any history of the subsequent discourse of aesthetic experience particularly complex is the difficulty it had in maintaining its boundaries as

46. Catherine Gallagher, *Nobody's Story: The Vanishing Acts of Woman Writers in the Marketplace, 1670–1820* (Berkeley, 1994).

47. George Dickie, *Aesthetics* (Indianapolis, 1971); and Pierre Bourdieu, *The Field of Cultural Production: Essays on Art and Literature,* ed. Randal Johnson (New York, 1993). For a critique of Dickie, see Richard Shusterman, *Pragmatist Aesthetics: Living Beauty, Rethinking Art* (Cambridge, Mass, 1999), pp. 38–41. For a critique of Bourdieu, see Paul Crowther, "Sociological Imperialism and the Field of Cultural Production: The Case of Bourdieu," *Theory, Culture and Society* 11, no. 1 (1994).

48. Jürgen Habermas, *The Philosophical Discourse of Modernity,* trans. Frederick Lawrence (Cambridge, Mass., 1987), p. 10. Whether there are heteronomous elements lurking beneath the surface of the new discourse of aesthetic autonomy is a question posed by Hess (in *Reconstituting the Body Politic*), who sees it functioning as a tacit justification for the authoritarian state, even as it pretends to provide a free space alongside of it.

an entirely autonomous subsphere of the social/cultural totality. For not only could it extend beyond reception and contemplation to include creation, but it could also function as a model for lived experience as a whole. That is, for some of its advocates, the point was not to cultivate the ability to appreciate and judge works of art or even to see the world through the lens of an aesthetic sensibility, but rather to live all of life as if it were itself a work of art. As in the case of the rapture experienced by religious mystics, the putative object of this quest could be tacitly reduced to a means to produce an effect in the subject (or more precisely, subject and object could be assumed to be one). Such a desideratum was, to be sure, not always itself fully convincing, especially to those who pondered its moral costs, but it frequently appeared as a potential outcome of the secular religion of art.

In fact, even during the Enlightenment's struggle to establish the relative autonomy of the aesthetic, the boundaries were not always construed as impermeable. Shaftesbury, as we have noted, was intent on refuting Hobbesian notions of self-interest by combining moral intuition and aesthetic appreciation. Recent scholarship has also stressed how in the *Critique of Judgment* Kant struggled to find a way to bridge the gap between cognitive and moral judgments and their aesthetic counterpart.[49] The larger project of the Third Critique was, after all, to explore the ways in which nature could be understood teleologically rather than mechanistically, thus going beyond the rigid limitations on knowledge set by the First Critique. The purposiveness in art could thus be found in nature as well, which suggested a possible reunification of the varieties of reason. "Beauty," Kant also went on to claim, could be understood as "the symbol of morality"[50] because of its emphasis on purposiveness without extrinsic purposes, which was parallel to the moral ideal of treating every person as an end in him/herself implied by the categorical imperative. Although the link between art and ethics could not be established discursively, by drawing on rational arguments, it could be suggested symbolically and analogically. In both cases, the self-reflective subject had to achieve a certain distance to allow judgment to occur.

Even more decisively, that dimension of aesthetic experience Kant followed Longinus and Edmund Burke in calling "the sublime" provided a link with the noumenal origins of practical reason, because it gets us in touch with su-

49. See in particular Zammito *The Genesis of Kant's Critique of Judgment,* in which he discusses what he calls the "cognitive and ethical turn" in the Third Critique.

50. Kant, *Critique of Judgment,* pp. 196–200.

persensible realities that could not be grasped by synthetic a priori judgments, helping produce a feeling of respect for the moral law that was also beyond cognitive understanding.[51] Here the objective correlate to our feelings is even more remote than it is in the case of the beautiful, as the paradoxical attempt to represent the unrepresentable is the essence of the sublime, which registers both the grandeur and the futility of the quest. Kant, in short, was never really satisfied with the radical disentanglement of aesthetic experience from its cognitive and moral counterparts. Although grounded in a renewed respect for the corporeal dimension of experience, its aesthetic variant, at least in the Enlightenment tradition, always contained no less of an acknowledgment of its sublimating and ennobling potential, following what Wolfgang Welsch has called its "elevatory imperative."[52]

How successful Kant's *Critique of Judgment* actually was in reintegrating what his earlier work had seemed so powerfully to split asunder is, of course, a matter of some dispute. In fact, the entire subsequent history of German idealism suggests that at least his immediate successors thought it was a failure and the alienation of art still a wound to be healed.[53] Beginning as early as Friedrich Schiller's *Letters on Aesthetic Education* of 1793, they sought to reunite art with the other spheres in the hope of re-enchanting life and healing the wounds of modernity. The search for an aesthetic state was one version of this quest, which extended well into the twentieth century.[54] What has been called the sovereignty of art (as opposed to its mere autonomy) meant the hope that art might serve as the way to overcome the plural rationalities of a differentiated modernity, indeed to surpass the limits of reason itself.[55] Understood as a model for human development at its highest,

51. It is not hard to see residues of displaced religious awe and selfless love in this position. For a discussion, see M. H. Abrams, "Kant and the Theology of Art," *Notre Dame English Journal* 13 (1981). As we noted in the previous chapter, despite the attempt to separate religious from aesthetic experience, there were many crossover relations between them.

52. Welsch, *Undoing Aesthetics*, pp. 64–68.

53. For an overview of subsequent attempts to overcome the alienation of art, see J. M. Bernstein, *The Fate of Art: Aesthetic Alienation from Kant to Derrida and Adorno* (University Park, Pa., 1992).

54. Schiller hoped that aesthetic play would cultivate "the whole of our sensuous and intellectual powers in the fullest possible harmony." *On the Aesthetic Education*, p. 99. For a general overview of this project from Johann Joachim Winckelmann to Herbert Marcuse and Walter Spies, see Josef Chytry, *The Aesthetic State: A Quest in Modern German Thought* (Berkeley, 1989). From the beginning, it was difficult to imagine the practical ways in which aesthetic redemption might occur. Even in the case of Schiller, the initial political goal of transforming the world was soon replaced by a more purely interior notion of aesthetic freedom. See the discussion in Woodmansee, *The Author, Art, and the Market*.

55. For an exploration of this theme, which attempts to overcome the dichotomy of autonomy and sovereignty through a concept of aesthetic negativity drawn in part from Adorno and Derrida, see

aesthetic experience could be hailed as the totalizer of man's various capacities, or in Schiller's famous formulation as the sublation of the sense impulse, which is "life," and the form impulse, which is "shape," into the play impulse. Schiller, to be sure, acknowledged that "experience affords us no example of any such complete interaction" and conceded that "we might perhaps find it, like the pure Church, or the pure Republic, only in a few select circles."[56] But at least some of his successors hoped to democratize and realize his utopian goal.

Kant's distinction between direct sensual pleasure and the more contemplative detachment he identified with aesthetic disinterestedness also troubled those who saw art as a genuine "promise of happiness," to quote the phrase of Stendhal made famous by Friedrich Nietzsche and Herbert Marcuse.[57] As early as the Romantic criticism of Friedrich Schelling and Friedrich Schlegel, the very term "aesthetics" had been criticized for emphasizing only passive sensation.[58] In the psychoanalytic terms employed by Rauch, they "emphasized the remembrance of the relationship with the mother and an awareness of one's own body,"[59] although they were sensitive to the pain produced by the original separation and the difficulty of healing the breach. In its more activist and optimistic moments, however, the aesthetic redemption of life went beyond Baumgarten's *aisthesis* and extrapolated from the productivist model that derived from the Greek idea of *poiesis,* in which art involved spontaneous making without slavishly following traditional rules.[60] As a result, the already vague definitional boundaries of aesthetic experience

---

Christoph Menke, *The Sovereignty of Art: Aesthetic Negativity in Adorno and Derrida,* trans. Neil Solomon (Cambridge, Mass., 1999).

56. Schiller, *On the Aesthetic Education,* pp. 82 and 140.

57. For Nietzsche's celebrated critique of Kant's notion of disinterestedness, whose pernicious effects he saw in Arthur Schopenhauer as well, see *The Genealogy of Morals,* trans. Walter Kaufmann and R. J. Hollingdale (New York, 1967), pp. 103–4. Nietzsche invokes the "genuine 'spectator' and artist" Stendhal as an antidote to the ascetic "country parson" Kant. Marcuse cites "une promesse de bonheur" in "The Affirmative Character of Culture," *Negations: Essays in Critical Theory,* trans. Jeremy J. Shapiro (Boston, 1968), p. 115. For a recent critique of Kant's aesthetics that continues this complaint, see Robin May Schott, *Cognition and Eros: A Critique of the Kantian Paradigm* (Boston, 1988).

58. For a discussion, see Phillipe Lacoue-Labarthe and Jean-Luc Nancy, *The Literary Absolute: The Theory of Literature in German Romanticism,* trans. Philip Barnard and Cheryl Lester (Albany, N.Y., 1988), p. 103. They show that the German Romantics substituted a notion of "eidaesthetics" in which the subjective production of the Idea is paramount.

59. Rauch, *The Hieroglyph of Tradition,* p. 85.

60. Such an emphasis was already evident in Moritz, Gotthold Lessing, and even the early Baumgarten, who understood mimesis not as passively reflecting the world, but rather representing the creative energy of its author. See the discussion in Hess, *Reconstituting the Body Politic,* p. 164.

were further eroded, as it expanded beyond a mode of responding to the world (understood as either artificial or natural objects and events) to one of helping to transform and perhaps even redeem it.

The figure of the inspired genius, spawned in the Renaissance, developed by the *Sturm und Drang*, and fully realized by the Romantics, was the individual expression of this impulse.[61] If he—and the gender of genius was rarely in doubt—imitated anything, it was not prior types or natural laws, but rather the fecundity of the divine Creator.[62] Possessing more than mere "talent," he created organically, rather than mechanically and used his "imagination" (related to Reason) rather than "fancy" (akin to the Understanding).[63] Debate raged over how irrational, unconstrained, even mad the antinomian genius might be, driven as he was by the old neo-Platonic notion of *furor poeticus*.[64] But in addition to acknowledging his special gift for going beyond conventional rules, there was general agreement that the genius possessed a heightened capacity for authentic experience, which put him above the common herd of men. Here the object of aesthetic creativity was not a freestanding thing in the world, but the artist's own life, which was fashioned as if it were a work of art. As Peter Bürger has noted,

The concept of genius serves to specify an all-embracing and intensive way of experiencing reality which is radically distinguished from the limited kind of experience characteristic of most human beings. Thus the concept also indicates the existence of a limited form of experience in the everyday life of the majority and attempts to respond to this phenomenon. The specific character

61. For helpful surveys of the history of this concept, see the entries by Giorgio Tonelli, Rudolf Wittkower, and Edward E. Lowinsky in the *Dictionary of the History of Ideas: Studies of Selected Pivotal Ideas,* ed. Philip P. Wiener (New York, 1973), vol. 2. On its origins in the Renaissance, see Stephen Greenblatt, *Renaissance Self-Fashioning: From More to Shakespeare* (Chicago, 1980).

62. It would be wrong, of course, to assimilate Romanticism entirely to a model of male productivism. For a discussion of Goethe's "tender empiricism" and resistance to the domination of nature, which sees it as inherently feminine, see Lisbet Koerner, "Goethe's Botany: Lessons of a Feminine Science," *Isis* 84 (1993). Koerner points out that "Goethe grounded knowledge, whether literary or scientific, in what he called *Lebensereignisse* and what Hegel and Dilthey, following Goethe's lead, re-termed *Erlebnis:* the privileged moment of experience. Unlike many later Germans, however, Goethe did not make a cult of experience for its own sake. Rather, he saw *Lebensereignisse* as the irreducible medium through which we grasp literature, the arts and the sciences" (p. 485).

63. These distinctions were most extensively developed by Samuel Taylor Coleridge. See the discussion in M. H. Abrams, *The Mirror and the Lamp: Romantic Theory and the Critical Tradition* (Oxford, 1971), p. 176.

64. In *On the Aesthetic Education,* Schiller said of genius, "we know [it] to border very closely upon savagery" (p. 58).

of the response consists in the fact that instead of asking why experience in general is generally limited the way it is it begins by projecting the possibility of an unlimited form of experience in the figure of the genius.[65]

William Blake, for one, came to understand that both Innocence and Experience, "the two contrary states of the human soul," as he called them in the dual edition of the *Songs* published in 1794, were necessarily intertwined.[66] The child and the father, the virgin and the harlot, the lamb and the "tyger," are all part of a larger plan, for "to be an Error & to be Cast out is a part of God's design." Blake's early Swedenborgian celebration of prelapsarian bliss gave way during the decade after the French Revolution to a dialectical appreciation of the need to pass through the fallen world, indeed to change it radically.[67] No Rousseauist recovery of noble savagery could substitute for the experience of acting—and making mistakes—in the real world. In the prophetic figure of Blake, one might say that the religious and aesthetic notions of experience were fused with "a politics of experience,"[68] a volatile and precarious combination that could not, however, last for very long once the Revolution turned sour.

But surrogates for actual political transformation could still be sought at the level of aesthetic transfiguration, through what has been called a "politics of vision."[69] For the elitist cult of the genius, who was able to experience life to the fullest, often accompanied a faith that his poetic imagination might infuse the seemingly banal world with transcendent aesthetic value (a world that therefore no longer needed actual political or social transformation).

65. Peter Bürger, "Some Reflections upon the Historico-Sociological Explanation of the Aesthetics of Genius in the Eighteenth Century," *The Decline of Modernism*, trans. Nicholas Walker (University Park, Pa., 1992), p. 60.

66. For suggestive analyses of Blake's poetic ruminations on the imbrication of innocence and experience, see Morton D. Paley, ed., *Twentieth-Century Interpretations of Songs of Innocence and Songs of Experience* (Englewood, N.J., 1969); Stewart Crehan, *Blake in Context* (Atlantic Highlands, N.J., 1984); Harold Bloom, ed., *William Blake's Songs of Innocence and Experience* (New York, 1987); E. P. Thompson, *Witness against the Beast: William Blake and the Moral Law* (New York, 1993).

67. M. H. Abrams includes Blake among the dialectical thinkers who follow the pattern of secularizing the "fortunate fall" in religion, comparing him to Schiller and Hegel. See *Natural Supernaturalism: Tradition and Revolution in Romantic Literature* (New York, 1971), p. 262.

68. This is the title of the fourth chapter of Crehan's *Blake in Context*. See also Ronald Paulson, *Representations of Revolution (1789–1820)* (New Haven, 1983), chapter 4. For a more recent consideration of Blake's politics as one of aestheticized enthusiasm and agitation, close to Kant's spectatorial observer of the sublime, which survived the failure of the actual Revolution, see Steven Goldsmith, "Blake's Agitation," *South Atlantic Quarterly* 95, no. 3 (Summer 1996).

69. Abrams, *Natural Supernaturalism*, pp. 356–72.

Somehow that order of intelligible meaning in the cosmos given by God, which had lost its hold on the imagination after the scientific revolution, would be restored by the fiat of the creative artist. Romanticism, of course, has often been seen as a secular version of the religious quest for the sacred—"spilt religion" in T. E. Hulme's famous dismissive epithet[70]—and in many ways the two intertwined in what Thomas Carlyle was to call (in *Sartor Resartus*) "natural supernaturalism."[71] The natural world could be more than the source of the stimuli to the senses probed by the sober epistemologists; it could also be charged with numinous meaning by what has been called the "transfiguration of the commonplace,"[72] the sublimation of the humble into the elevated through aesthetic imagination, the material immanentization of the divinely spiritual.

Aesthetic experience, in this version of its claim to sovereignty, was a means to re-enchant rather than radically transform the existing world, producing the kind of pantheistic redemption that more traditional theists like Kant had distrusted, but which could find its echo, as we have seen, in Friedrich Schleiermacher's celebration of religious experience.[73] In England, critics like Archibald Alison, painters like John Constable, and poets like William Wordsworth were able to validate an "art of the commonplace," which disparaged the notion of an elite art object in favor of the subjective response of the artist or the sensitive beholder to virtually anything, no matter how trivial or mundane.[74] The expansion of the human capacity to appreciate aesthetically hitherto denigrated functional or ritual objects from so-called primitive cultures, which gained in momentum during the early years of twentieth-century modernism,[75] was one benign outcome of this expansion.

But a less positive alternative was also possible, as the extension of aesthetic experience to encompass all relations with the world and other people could lead to problematic results. A widely remarked example is that "aestheti-

70. T. E. Hulme, *Speculations: Essays on Humanism and the Philosophy of Art*, ed. Herbert Read (London, 1924), p. 118.

71. For the now classic account of its significance, see Abrams, *Natural Supernaturalism*.

72. Arthur Danto, *The Transfiguration of the Commonplace: A Philosophy of Art* (Cambridge, Mass., 1981). See also George J. Leonard, *Into the Light of Things: The Art of the Commonplace from Wordsworth to John Cage* (Chicago, 1994).

73. In the "Pantheism Controversy," which followed F. H. Jacobi's 1785 attack on Lessing's supposed embrace of Spinozan pantheism, Kant was a fervent critic of the conflation of the world and God. He resisted what he saw as the determinist implications of this position, which undermined the possibility of human freedom and made practical reason's exercise of will meaningless. See the discussion in Zammito, *The Genesis of the Third Critique*, chapters 11 and 12.

74. For an account of this tradition, see Leonard, *Into the Light of Things*.

75. Robert Goldwater, *Primitivism in Modern Art* (Cambridge, Mass., 1968).

cization of politics" with its weakness for "beautiful gestures" of real violence, against which Walter Benjamin warned during the Fascist era.[76] Another was the relentless narcissism of those virtuosi of aesthetic experience, who tried to live their lives as if they were works of art.

Already in Goethe's *Faust*, the ambiguous implications of trying to experience everything to the full, no matter the cost, was subjected to careful scrutiny. Although the reckless, insatiably striving figure who could say "only restless activity proves a man"[77] is saved at the end of the tragedy despite his breaking his vow with the devil, he is scarcely a positive exemplar of the fulfillment that the quest was designed to provide. In a conversation he had had with F. A. Wolf in 1809, Goethe confessed that "with me the main thing has always been to make use of experience; it was never my way to invent out of the air. I have always regarded the world as a greater genius than myself."[78] Faustian narcissistic self-fashioning and aggressive self-assertion were thus inferior to a more humble stance of waiting for experiences to happen rather than impatiently lusting after novelty and variety for their own sakes. The "tender empiricism" of his scientific work, resisting the masculinist domination of nature, found its parallel in Goethe's distancing himself from the self-indulgent cult of aesthetic experience for its own sake.

Similarly, the libertine figure of Don Giovanni, aesthetically realized as a "sensuous erotic genius" in Mozart's opera, gave way to the "reflective seducer" Johannes in Kierkegaard's *Either/Or* (1843), whose cerebral imagination moves him further and further away from the actual realization of his desires.[79] Trying to live life aesthetically, playing with the emotions of others as in a theatrical production, Kierkegaard warned, leads to dissipation, melancholy, and spiritless malaise, which is the opposite of any robust notion of totalized or cumulative experience.

The frenzied search for immediate sensuous pleasure and an endless variety of stimulation produces indifference to all other values. Ultimately, it turns

76. Walter Benjamin, "The Work of Art in the Era of Mechanical Reproduction," *Illuminations*, ed. Hannah Arendt, trans. Harry Zohn (New York, 1968). For a discussion of the implications of this analysis, see Martin Jay, "'The Aesthetic Ideology' as Ideology; or, What Does It Mean to Aestheticize Politics?" *Force Fields: Between Intellectual History and Cultural Critique* (New York, 1993). See also the analysis of the more general aestheticization of reality in Welsch, *Undoing Aesthetics*, chapter 1.

77. Goethe, *Faust*, trans. Walter Kaufmann (Garden City, N.J., 1961), pp. 186-87.

78. Goethe, *Conversations and Encounters*, ed. and trans. David Luke and Robert Pick (Chicago, 1966), p. 81.

79. Søren Kierkegaard, *Either/Or*, trans. David F. Swenson and Lillian Marvin, 2 vols. (Princeton, N.J., 1959).

into a recipe for anaesthetized boredom, into what Hegel would call the "bad infinity" of the "unhappy consciousness." Or to put it in terms with which we have become familiar, living one's life aesthetically produces only isolated *Erlebnisse,* piling on one another to create a meaningless aggregate, not enriched *Erfahrungen* or totalized, holistically integrated narratives. Entirely stripped of its "elevatory imperative," to borrow once again Welsch's term, aesthetic experience could, in fact, come perilously close to the first type of pleasure described in *The Critique of Judgment:* a hedonistic self-indulgence lacking any residue of contemplative disinterest or negative reflexivity. Indeed, it is possible to interpret the libertine excesses of eighteenth-century writers like Choderlos de Laclos and the Marquis de Sade as already revealing an awareness of the potential for perversion and debasement in the epistemological reliance on sense experience and valorization of hedonistic pleasure in the French Enlightenment.[80]

By the time of Charles Baudelaire, the dark side of seeking experience for its own sake was painfully clear to acute observers. In his autobiographical *My Heart Laid Bare,* the poet may have defiantly identified with the vagabond, self-indulgent life that was Bohemianism, "the cult of multiplied sensation,"[81] but the degraded and self-lacerating implications of that choice could not be easily ignored. It was not by chance that the body, whose centrality to aesthetic experience we have noted, now figured synecdochically for Baudelaire in the organ of the spleen, whose links to melancholy and disease suggested a "horror of life,"[82] not its re-enchantment. The observing, ironic *flâneur,* the man of the crowd, the self-contained, emotionally controlled dandy, rather than the Romantic man of passion, achieves whatever heroism may be left to life in Baudelaire's modern age.[83]

As a result, the belief that the rule-breaking genius who sought to experi-

80. For an argument of this kind, see O'Neal, *The Authority of Experience,* chapter 6.

81. Charles Baudelaire, *Mon coeur mis à nu,* ed. Beatrice Dedier (Paris, 1972), p. 127.

82. See Roger L. Williams, *The Horror of Life* (Chicago, 1980), which explores the importance of illness and hypochondria in Baudelaire, Gustave Flaubert, Jules de Goncourt, Guy de Maupassant, and Alphonse Daudet. Baudelaire's "acceptance of the Bohemian need to live for the multiplication of sensation, with all its attendant sordidness and degradation" has, however, also been seen by Jerrold Seigel as an avatar of "the modernist avant-garde's later discovery that the boundary between art and life could no longer be maintained." See his *Bohemian Paris: Culture, Politics, and the Boundaries of Bourgeois Life, 1830–1930* (New York, 1986), p. 124. If so, it was a troubled and unhappy passage across that boundary.

83. The classic essay on this theme is Baudelaire's "The Painter of Modern Life," in *The Painter of Modern Life and Other Essays,* trans. and ed. Jonathan Mayne (London, 1965). For recent discussions of the *flâneur,* see Keith Tester, ed., *The Flâneur* (London, 1994).

ence everything and fashion his life into a work of art, or even more ambitiously, legislate for the world, in Percy Bysshe Shelley's famous phrase, lost some of its allure (if remaining, to be sure, a model for sporadic revival in the future). Even figures such as Nietzsche, who railed against the life-denying qualities of Kantian disinterest and urged turning one's life into a work of literature, knew that in their own lives this goal was unattainable.[84] Aesthetic self-fashioning, in fact, became the target of parodic accounts such as Joris-Karl Huysmans's "decadent" classic *Against the Grain,* in which devitalized exhaustion and intensified malaise are the inevitable result of trying to live one's life as if it were a work of art. Schiller's "aesthetic education" becomes bitterly "sentimental" in the ironic sense expressed in the title of Gustave Flaubert's great novel of disillusionment.

There was, however, another alternative, which eschewed the ambitious program of aesthetic sovereignty and accepted the differentiation of value spheres. Understood in the more modest terms of a contemplative and passive *aiesthesis* rather than Promethean, self-fashioning *poiesis,* the cult of aesthetic experience could continue to find new devotees. But now the hope we have seen among eighteenth-century theorists, such as Shaftesbury and Kant, that ennobling moral sensibility and exquisite aesthetic taste went together, was tacitly abandoned, as was the politically redemptive mission attributed to the play drive by Schiller. For when their ideas were vulgarized in the nineteenth century, as they were by certain French philosophers like Victor Cousin, they could easily be taken to countenance the opposite conclusion, the extreme aesthetic separatism that became the mark of the *l'art pour l'art* movement.[85] In the *Critique of Judgment,* Kant had carefully exempted the human body from the category of pure or free beauty *(pulchritudo vaga),* seeing it instead as an instance of dependent or adherent beauty *(pulchritudo adhaerens).*[86] This meant, among other things, that humans should be understood to possess inherent moral purposes and therefore to be irreducible to mere objects

---

84. For Nietzsche's diatribe against *l'art pour l'art* and the doctrine of purposelessness in art, see aphorism 24 in *The Twilight of the Idols,* in Walter Kaufmann, ed., *The Portable Nietzsche* (New York, 1968), p. 529. For an account of Nietzsche's plea for living life as if it were a work of literature, see Alexander Nehamas, *Nietzsche: Life as Literature* (Cambridge, Mass., 1985).

85. See John Wilcox, "The Beginnings of *l'art pour l'art,*" *Journal of Aesthetics and Art Criticism* 11, no. 2 (June 1953); Albert L. Guérard, *Art for Art's Sake* (New York, 1963); and Gene H. Bell-Villada, *Art for Art's Sake and Literary Life: How Politics and Markets Helped Shape the Ideology and Culture of Aestheticism, 1790–1990* (Lincoln, Neb., 1996). It was in one of Cousin's lectures that the celebrated formulation "Il faut de la religion pour la religion, de la morale pour la morale, comme de l'art pour l'art" appeared.

86. Kant, *Critique of Judgment,* p. 65.

of pure aesthetic contemplation, praiseworthy in solely formal terms. This qualification was lost with the radicalization of aesthetic autonomy.

As has often been noted, the truculent assertion of the absolute autonomy of the aesthetic, perhaps most classically expressed in Théophile Gautier's infamous preface to his novel *Mademoiselle de Maupin,* came mostly from artists unable to accommodate to the demands of the new publishing and journalistic marketplace. After 1830, proponents of *poésie pure* were caught in the crossfire between utilitarian bourgeois materialists and advocates of a revived religious culture, who were no less contemptuous of their "pagan" aestheticism. But they managed to survive the onslaught and inspire a tradition of increasingly devoted worshipers at the altar of art, whose attachment to other aspects of life grew ever more attenuated. Setting out to burn with a gem-like flame could lead to a vicarious life led, as one wit put it with reference to Walter Pater, in a "womb with a view."[87] Although Symbolists such as Stéphane Mallarmé sought to reinvent poetic language to break through the crust of convention and renew immediate experience, their esoteric efforts rarely produced the desired effect.[88] Edmund Wilson epitomized the anti-vitalist endpoint of aestheticism in *Axel's Castle,* which drew its title from Villiers de l'Isle Adam's play *Axel* of 1890.[89] "Live! Our servants will do that for us," the world-weary protagonists of the drama sigh before they commit suicide. Here paradoxically the fetish of aesthetic experience turns out to discredit experience of any other kind, tacitly reversing that emphasis on bodily pleasure that we have noted was the source of the discourse of aesthetics in the eighteenth century. "Experience," cynically remarks a world-weary character in Oscar Wilde's *Lady Windemere's Fan,* "is the name everyone gives to their mistakes."[90]

A similar development can be seen in certain post-Kantian philosophical considerations of aesthetic experience. With Schopenhauer's 1818 *World as Will and Representation,* aesthetic experience was reduced to the attitude of

87. Graham Hough, *The Last Romantics* (London, 1947), p. 167.

88. For a discussion of such efforts, see Richard Cándida Smith, *Mallarmé's Children: Symbolism and the Renewal of Experience* (Berkeley, 1999). Smith situates Symbolism in the context of William James's attempts to restore a more vital kind of experience.

89. Edmund Wilson, *Axel's Castle: A Study in the Imaginative Literature of 1870–1930* (London, 1959). Wilson makes the now familiar point that "whereas it was characteristic of the Romantics to seek experience for its own sake—love, travel, politics—to try the possibilities of life; the Symbolists . . . carry on their experiments in the field of literature alone; and although they, too, are essentially explorers, explore only the possibilities of imagination and thought" (p. 211).

90. Richard Aldington and Stanley Weintraub, eds., *The Portable Oscar Wilde* (New York, 1981), p. 733.

non-practical, amoral contemplation, a way to fend off, at least temporarily, the meaninglessness of life and the pain of unceasing desire.[91] Here indifference to the object extended even beyond that posited by Kant insofar as the latter still imputed non-instrumental purposiveness to the artwork as an emblem of moral autonomy.[92] Schopenhauer also diminished the importance of the body in aesthetic contemplation insofar as it was the source of the unrealizable longings that art briefly allows us to escape. Lost as well was any hope that aesthetic experience might become a model for a renewed political life or even intersubjective sociability. But interestingly, Schopenhauer did not put in its place a strong notion of the isolated subject whose aesthetic experiences were able to provide temporary respite from the insatiable will. Instead, his celebrated critique of individuation as a mark of illusory egoism anticipated what we will later remark in many twentieth-century contributions to the question: the paradoxical positing of experience without a subject. To his contemporaries, however, and to many artists, such as Richard Wagner and Gustav Mahler, who found inspiration in his work, what was most significant was Schopenhauer's rigorous separation of aesthetic from other forms of experience.

A major source of the retreat from trying to integrate art and life was the fundamental difficulty of reconciling the disinterestedness of aesthetic experience—especially when robbed of the public, communicative moment Kant had attributed to it[93]—with the interested qualities of both its cognitive and moral counterparts. In the case of the former, it was impossible to suspend for very long our interested involvement with the world, which gratified or frustrated our corporeal needs and desires. In the case of the latter, real objects or at least other human beings were necessary to test our will to act morally and be involved in the world of practical consequences. As Paul Crowther has noted, "for Kant the burden of emphasis in moral existence falls on obstacles and responsibilities in relation to the expression of freedom. In aesthetic experience it does not. . . . Hence, whilst the pure aesthetic judgment might figure in a moral image of the world, it could just as

<hr>

91. For an account of the debates concerning the reduction of experience to attitude initiated by Schopenhauer, see Bohdan Dziemidok, "Controversy about Aesthetic Attitude: Does Aesthetic Attitude Condition Aesthetic Experience?" in Mitias, *Possibility of Aesthetic Experience.*

92. For a comparison of Kant and Schopenhauer on this issue, see Eagleton, *The Ideology of the Aesthetic,* p. 169.

93. According to Jauss, "as the new ideal of aesthetic pleasure, self-enjoying subjectivity abandoned the *sensus communis* as the expression of a sociable sympathy at the same moment the aesthetics of genius finally replaced the aesthetics of rhetoric." *Aesthetic Experience and Literary Hermeneutics,* p. 26.

easily, if not more so, incline us to a life of self-indulgent or indolent contemplation, wherein the demands of moral duty were the least of our preoccupations."[94]

There was, to adduce a more social explanation, also a certain tension between the aristocratic leisurely premises of aesthetic disinterestedness—the ability to see a beautiful landscape where peasants toiling in the fields could see only recalcitrant soil—and the moral imperative to treat everyone as an end in him- or herself. Although the class origins of the aesthetic attitude may have become occluded with the emergence of bohemian poverty as a culturally validated alternative, producing a challenge to bourgeois values from a new angle, the elitist implications of contemplative indifference to utilitarian and materialist concerns remained. In fact, with the popular embrace of the Byronic *homme fatale* and Baudelairean *poète maudit,* a distinctly amoral or even immoral artist/aesthete type had emerged, who had license to defy conventional ethical standards. Even when the model of living as if one were a self-fashioning aesthetic genius, like a Faust or a Don Giovanni, lost some of its allure, the contemplative aesthete could also seem indifferent to moral questions in his pursuit of aesthetic experience.

The tension between the self-indulgent, amoral, tacitly aristocratic version of aesthetic experience and its more democratic and moralizing twin was never fully resolved. It can be seen to reemerge in Victorian England, where Shaftesbury's legacy could be given a more egalitarian reading by figures like John Ruskin and William Morris, while the elitist art-for-art's sake impulse reappeared in Walter Pater, James Abbott McNeill Whistler and, in certain of his moods, Oscar Wilde.[95] Variations on it were played out in the "dionysian art and populist politics" of fin-de-siècle Vienna, and in the politicization of bohemianism and the narcissistic "cult of the self" in the France of the same era.[96] It reappeared as well in the distinction between an esoteric modernism that was content to remain within the confines of the institution of art with its own unique kind of experiences, and an avant-garde that attempted to heal the fractured world of modernity and infuse everyday experience with

94. Paul Crowther, "The Significance of Kant's Pure Aesthetic Judgment," *British Journal of Aesthetics* 36, no. 2 (April 1996), p. 118.

95. For an account of the struggle between them, see Linda Dowling, *The Vulgarization of Art: The Victorians and Aesthetic Democracy* (Charlottesville, Va., 1996).

96. William J. McGrath, *Dionysian Art and Populist Politics in Austria* (New Haven, 1974). See also Carl E. Schorske, *Fin-de-Siècle Vienna: Politics and Culture* (New York, 1980); and Jacques Le Rider, *Modernity and Crises of Identity: Culture and Society in Fin-de-Siècle Vienna,* trans. Rosemary Morris (New York, 1993). On the ambiguous political implications of Bohemianism, see Seigel, *Bohemian Paris,* chapter 10.

the redemptive power of art.[97] And it continues in our own day in some of the conflicts between modernist and postmodernist art, the former often defended in terms that continue to stress the autonomy of art and the latter in terms that embrace its heteronomous embeddedness in contexts of power and signification.

DEFENSES OF THE ARTWORK
AGAINST ITS OBLITERATION

Despite the differences between the ideal of art as autonomous and art as sovereign, between retreating from the world into aesthetic experience and transforming it according to the tenets of that experience, a common problem remained. For in virtually all of its manifestations, aesthetic experience meant a privileging of the subject, whether contemplative, productive, or self-fashioning, over the art object. As we have seen, with the decline of an objective standard of beauty, despite rearguard attempts by philosophers like Hegel to revive it,[98] the emphasis fell on the beholding or creating subject (or in the case of judgment, the intersubjective community of taste). Even when the subject's perceptual and corporeal experience was suppressed in the name of a more conceptual and institutional definition of artistic practice, as it was beginning with Marcel Duchamp's revolutionary "readymades," the object was less important than the role of the subject in defining or designating it as somehow aesthetic (or being able to appreciate such designations imposed by those with the institutional legitimacy to make them). Although Duchamp's disdain for what he called "retinal art" implied an assault on the pleasure traditionally produced by aesthetic experience, his even greater hostility to the idea of intrinsic merit in the found objects he designated as "art"

97. The classic, if much debated, account of this struggle remains Bürger, *Theory of the Avant-Garde*. Even the modernists indifferent to the avant-garde project of reuniting life and art could conceptualize their work in terms of the recovery and presentation of immediate, intense, and authentic experience. See the discussion in Sanford Schwartz, *The Matrix of Modernism: Pound, Eliot, and Early 20th-Century Thought* (Princeton, 1985). Schwartz notes that "Pound and Eliot, like Hulme, regard poetry as the presentation of immediate experience. But neither of them seems to possess a consistent view of experience. They seem unable to decide whether it is subjective or objective, or whether the artist's rendering of experience is a form of personal expression or impersonal observation" (pp. 62–63). The former he attributes to the influence of Henri Bergson, the latter to that of Edmund Husserl. The anti-psychologistic impulse in modernism, shown, for example, in Hulme's debt to Husserl, can be seen as a reaction against an overly subjectivist interpretation of aesthetic production. See Martin Jay, "Modernism and the Specter of Psychologism," in *Cultural Semantics: Keywords of Our Time* (Amherst, Mass., 1998).

98. See the introduction to his *Aesthetics*, in Henry Paolucci, ed., *Hegel: On the Arts* (New York, 1979).

meant a further tipping of the balance toward the subject begun with the Enlightenment's privileging of disinterestedness.

As in the case of the opponents of the religious tradition we have traced back to Schleiermacher, voices were raised against the loss. What we have already noted in the case of Karl Barth's critique of the hypertrophy of religious experience, which he faulted for reducing God to nothing but a stimulus to the pious believer's interior state of mind, was paralleled here in the fear that the work of art was being reduced to an equally insignificant role. In both cases, belief in a "real presence"—or its secular equivalent—had been lost in favor of subjective response, the rapture of the pious or aesthetic soul. Martin Heidegger, to take a salient example, would protest that "experience is the source that is standard and not only for art appreciation and enjoyment, but also for artistic creation. Everything is an experience. Yet perhaps experience is the element in which art dies. The dying occurs so slowly that it takes a few centuries."[99] And in "The Origin of the Work of Art," he would add that "even the much-vaunted aesthetic experience cannot get around the thingly aspect of the art work."[100]

From a different perspective, Walter Benjamin, as we will see in chapter 8, would attempt to defend a notion of experience, as much anthropological as aesthetic, that could recapture the lost world of correspondences and similitudes that had withered with the onset of modern disenchantment. Although championing *Erfahrung,* he reinterpreted it in a way that left Kant's notion of disinterested, contemplative judgment far behind. Eschewing the narcissism of those who wanted to turn their lives into works of art and hostile to the aesthetic colonization of the rest of the world, Benjamin sought to restore a frankly metaphysical and absolute notion of experience that paradoxically diminished the importance of the judging subject and restored the importance of the artwork.[101]

99. Martin Heidegger, *Poetry, Language, Truth,* trans. Albert Hofstadter (New York, 1990), p. 79.
100. Martin Heidegger, "The Origin of the Work of Art," in *Basic Writings,* ed. David Ferrell Krell (New York, 1977), p. 151. For an attempt to defend Heidegger's own notion of aesthetic experience by identifying it with the incursion of a non-theorizable "event" or *Ereignis* into the smooth course of history, a protest against the reduction of experience in the modern period to technological calculation, see Krzysztof Ziarek, *The Historicity of Experience: Modernity, the Avant-Garde, and the Event* (Evanston, Ill., 2001). The resulting concept of experience is not only hostile to subjectivism, however; it is also critical of the notion of the art object that results from the positing of the constitutive subject. For in Heidegger's vocabulary, "thingly" is distinguished from being an "object," which involves the positing of a "subject." The result is to dissolve experience into an existential field that is prior to those distinctions and seems indistinguishable from the unveiling of Being that Heidegger sought elsewhere as well.
101. This effort was evident as early as Benjamin's dissertation on "The Concept of Criticism in German Romanticism," which is characterized by Beatrice Hanssen and Andrew Benjamin as "a crucial stage

A similar concern marked the practical criticism of commentators distressed by new ways in which subjective experience seemed to threaten to obliterate the integrity of the work. By the time of the advent of self-consciously conceptual and minimalist works of art in the 1960s, art critics such as Michael Fried were bemoaning the "theatrical" dissolution of timeless works of art into mere occasions for the beholder's temporal reception of them, based on the assumption that "the experience alone is what matters."[102] Well into the 1980s, literary critics such as Murray Krieger were likewise lamenting the leveling down of the arts, producing "the obliteration of the realm of art, its objects, its museums . . . everything immersed within the indivisible flood of experience."[103] Cultural critics of the aesthetic embellishment of modern life, such as Wolfgang Welsch, would argue in the 1990s that "the experiences, however, are indeed not experiences. Rather they are stale and dreary. That is why people quickly seek the next experience and hence rush from one disappointment to the next."[104]

Such objections did not, however, carry the day, at least in much of the art produced during the latter decades of the twentieth century, often influenced by Duchamp's disdain for the object and suspicious of any timeless canon. In a great deal of that art—performative rather objectivizing, ephemeral rather than atemporal, site-specific rather than decontextualized—the "thingly aspect" of art was deliberately jettisoned. Although disinterestedness was often abandoned and contemplation was replaced by kinaesthetic involvement, the subject still dominated the object. The stimulation of ever more intense experiences in subjects who reacted with their entire sensorium

in his attempt to overcome the *Erlebnis* ideology of the early twentieth century, expressed, for example, in the worship of the poet-hero that marked Stefan George's circle and Friedrich Gundolf's criticism, or in the subjectivism that underpinned Wilhelm Dilthey's *Das Erlebnis und die Dichtung (Experience and Poetry).*" "Walter Benjamin's Critical Romanticism: An Introduction," in Hanssen and Benjamin, eds., *Walter Benjamin and Romanticism* (New York, 2002), p. 2.

102. Michael Fried, "Art and Objecthood" (1967), reprinted in *Art and Objecthood: Essays and Reviews* (Chicago, 1998), p. 158. Fried's famous example comes from a car ride taken by Tony Smith down the New Jersey Turnpike in which the artist realizes that traditional art is dead.

103. Murray Krieger, *Arts on the Level: The Fall of the Elite Object* (Knoxville, Tenn., 1981), p. 56. More than two decades later, Peter de Bolla would still feel it necessary to stress the importance of the work for aesthetic experience: "What distinguishes affective or *aesthetic* experience from others is the fact that they are occasioned by encounters with artworks. This proposes a mutual definition, so that what elicits *aesthetic* experience is an artwork and an artwork is defined as an object that produces *aesthetic* experience. This mutuality is sometimes taken to be damaging for an argument—so-called circular reasoning—but it need not be. Many arguments depend on feedback in order to gain greater clarity with respect to their initial premises." *Art Matters*, p. 9.

104. Welsch, *Undoing Aesthetics*, p. 136.

rather than with the contemplative eye or dispassionate ear became, in fact, the goal of much contemporary art, which grew increasingly conflated with the entertainment industry against which it had once pitted itself.[105]

In short, the discourse about aesthetic experience and the production of work that is created to solicit it remains in flux with many questions still unanswered. Should that experience imply disinterested contemplation of objects made by others or artistic self-fashioning in which one experiences the world as raw material for creative play? Should it exclude moral and cognitive considerations entirely or involve an attempt to incorporate them in a totalized notion of human experience at its most robust and fulfilling? Should it imply working on the world as if it could be transfigured through aestheticization or a desperate retreat from a fallen world into the heterocosmic enclave of art for its own sake? Should it privilege the senses and the body or because of its stress on sublimation actually give priority to spiritual and elevatory dimensions that take us beyond our mere creaturely desires? And finally, how can it respect the integrity of the artwork, even if it acknowledges the impossibility of restoring "real presence" to objects in a world bereft of inherent meaning?

RESTORING THE BALANCE: DEWEY AND ART AS EXPERIENCE

If the Enlightenment tradition, culminating in Kant's Third Critique, can be still taken as the major stimulus to thinking about these questions, there has been another important alternative, which has recently attracted renewed attention in our own day. Let us end with a few remarks on its implications. That alternative is identified with the pragmatism of John Dewey, which has enjoyed a revival of interest in the past decade or so. As in the case of William James and religious experience, no account of the aesthetic "song of experience" can afford to neglect the contribution of American pragmatism to its development. Although we will have to wait until chapter 7 to try to do justice to the full import of the pragmatists' celebration of experience, it will be useful to pause at the end of this one with John Dewey's ruminations on the specific nature of its aesthetic variant.[106] In particular, we will have to look at his 1931 William James Lectures at Harvard, published three years later as

---

105. For an attempt to explore these trends, see Martin Jay, "Diving into the Wreck: Aesthetic Spectatorship at the Fin-de-siècle," *Refractions of Violence* (New York, 2003).

106. The most thorough account of Dewey on experience in general remains Gérard Deledalle, *L'idée d'expérience dans la philosophie de John Dewey* (Paris, 1967).

Art as Experience, which has been justly called by Hans Robert Jauss "a pioneering achievement in the field of aesthetic experience."[107] Dedicated to Albert Barnes, the wealthy connoisseur and collector of impressionist art with whom Dewey had formed a fast friendship, the book went beyond James's agnostic, fellow-traveling exploration of the psychology of religious experience to provide a normative model of engaged advocacy.[108] Written in the philosopher's seventh decade, it surprised those who had equated pragmatism with an instrumentalist and utilitarian scientism.[109] It confused others like Stephen Pepper and Benedetto Croce, who saw it as a reversion to Hegelian idealism. Dewey, to be sure, had been trained by the neo-Hegelian George Sylvester Morris at Johns Hopkins in the 1880s,[110] but had cast off what he saw as the metaphysical and rationalist implications of the Hegelian Absolute by the turn of the century. Nor did he not see philosophy superseding art, as Hegel had.

Still, there were strong Hegelian residues in Dewey's impatience with the categorical distinctions of Kant, and, more broadly, his desire to heal the wounds of modern life, or at least move toward overcoming them in an open-ended process of cumulative realization. That process involved what Dewey called "having *an* experience," which meant the achievement of a holistic, organic unity that "carries with it its own individualizing quality and self-sufficiency."[111] Although he insisted on the qualitative immediacy of intense aesthetic experiences, as opposed to the fetish of abstract relations typical of reflective philosophy, Dewey did not ignore the moment of reflexivity in those experiences, nor their cumulative integration over time. In the vocabulary of experience that was not his own, aesthetic experience was thus closer to a di-

---

107. Jauss, *Aesthetic Experience and Literary Hermeneutics,* p. 112.

108. On Dewey's friendship with Barnes and the genesis of the book, see Robert B. Westbrook, *John Dewey and American Democracy* (Ithaca, N.Y., 1991), chapter 11. For a recent appreciation of *Art as Experience*'s place in Dewey's oeuvre, see Thomas M. Alexander, "The Art of Life: Dewey's Aesthetics," in *Reading Dewey: Interpretations for a Postmodern Generation,* ed. Larry A. Hickman (Bloomington, Ind., 1998). See also Thomas Alexander, *John Dewey's Theory of Art, Experience and Nature: The Horizons of Feeling* (Albany, N.Y., 1987); and Ulrich Engler, *Kritik der Erfahrung: Die Bedeutung der ästhetischen Erfahrung in der Philosophie John Deweys* (Würzburg, 1992).

109. For example, Lewis Mumford, *The Golden Day,* 3rd ed. (New York, 1968). Coming to the opposite conclusion, Richard Rorty has argued that "Dewey wants the distinctions between art, science, and philosophy to be rubbed out, and replaced with a vague and uncontroversial notion of intelligence trying to solve problems and provide meaning." *Consequences of Pragmatism: Essays (1972–1990)* (Minneapolis, 1982), p. 51. For a critique of this claim, see David Fott, *John Dewey: America's Philosopher of Democracy* (Lanham, Md., 1998), p. 106.

110. See the discussion in Westbrook, *John Dewey and American Democracy,* chapter 1.

111. Dewey, *Art as Experience,* p. 35.

alectical, historically maturing *Erfahrung* than to an unmediated, instantaneous *Erlebnis.*[112]

Dewey, as we have noted, was deeply troubled by the contemplative and spectatorial impulse behind Kantian notions of aesthetic disinterestedness, which denigrated the more active, engaged attempt to live life on the model of a work of art.[113] Even vision, he argued against the dominant understanding of its cool, distantiating function, "arouses emotion in the form of interest—curiosity solicits further examination, but it attracts."[114] Dewey also wanted to overcome the gap between producer and consumer in modern life, of which the split between artistic creation and aesthetic appreciation was one symptom. But unlike the defenders of the elitist genius, whose narcissistic experiments in aesthetic self-fashioning could end in destructive self-indulgence, he sought to reconcile it with the values of democratic self-realization. Like Ruskin and Morris, he hoped to transcend the distinction between the useful and the ornamental in order to transfigure everyday life. The segregation of "fine" or "high" art in museums and galleries, abetted by the rise of capitalism, Dewey thus saw as largely pernicious: "Objects that were in the past valid and significant because of their place in the life of a community now function in isolation from the conditions of their origin. By that fact they are also set apart from common experience, and serve as insignia of taste and certificates of special culture."[115]

Dewey no less passionately resisted the differentiation of the social totality into distinct subspheres, with the aesthetic set apart from the cognitive and the moral and confined to its own watertight "institution." Like the avant-garde, he hoped to infuse the lifeworld with the redemptive power of art. In fact, all cognitive experiences, he insisted, already have an aesthetic moment in their unifying and concluding character, which is ignored by atomist epistemologies like Locke's and Hume's. Likewise, moral rigorists like Kant had

112. Shusterman claims instead that "the Deweyan distinction between mere experience and '*an* experience' clearly parallels the Diltheyan distinction between *Erfahrung* and *Erlebnis* common in continental hermeneutic theory, though Dewey does not refer to Dilthey in *Art as Experience*." *Pragmatist Aesthetics*, p. 267. Although we will see that Dilthey's conceptualization of the dichotomy is not the same as that of Benjamin's, I think the latter's interpretation of the distinction best captures what Dewey was after.

113. In *Art as Experience*, Dewey faults Kant for being a "past-master in first drawing distinctions and then erecting them into compartmental divisions" and speculated that his "theoretic emphasis" may have reflected the artistic tendencies of the eighteenth century in which reason dominated over passion (pp. 252–53). Dewey's opposition between "artistic" and "aesthetic" can be seen as early as his 1894 *The Study of Ethics: A Syllabus*, in *The Early Works of John Dewey* (Carbondale, Ill., 1971), p. 301.

114. Dewey, *Art as Experience*, p. 237.

115. Ibid., p. 9.

failed to appreciate the aesthetic underpinnings of ethical life: "one great defect in what passes as morality is its anaesthetic quality. Instead of exemplifying wholehearted action, it takes the form of grudging piecemeal concessions to the demands of duty. . . . any practical activity will, provided that it is integrated and moves by its own urge to fulfillment, have aesthetic quality."[116] But unlike some of the more imperialist defenders of the sovereignty of art, Dewey, whose respect for science never waned, wanted a balance among the various types of experience, not a hostile takeover of the others by one.

Even the radical difference between nature and art (or artifice), which was so much a staple of art-for-art's sake aestheticism, he firmly rejected. Dewey's "somatic naturalism" (the term is Richard Shusterman's) meant that he emphasized the continuity between normal physiological processes of humans in their natural environment with the more intense and robust variant of those processes that has come to be called art.[117] Against any notion of disinterestedness, Dewey stressed the origin of aesthetic experiences in an "impulsion," a "movement outward and forward of the whole organism," which proceeds from need.[118] In *Experience and Nature,* published in 1925, he had designated art, which he defined as "the mode of activity that is charged with meanings capable of immediately enjoying possession," as nothing less than "the complete culmination of nature," adding that "science" was "properly a handmaiden that conducts natural events to this happy issue."[119]

Understood in these grandiose terms as the antidote to humdrum routine and the abstraction of life, aesthetic experience was in fact for Dewey the teleological goal of authentic experience *tout court,* in which it attains its "consummatory" character. Here means and ends come together in one organic unity. Or as he put it in *Art as Experience,* "experience in the degree in which it *is* experience is heightened vitality. . . . Because experience is the fulfillment of an organism in its struggles and achievements in a world of things, it is art in germ. Even in its rudimentary forms, it contains the promise of that delightful perception which is aesthetic experience."[120]

116. Ibid., p. 39.
117. Shusterman, *Pragmatist Aesthetics,* p. 6.
118. Dewey, *Art as Experience,* p. 59.
119. Dewey, *Experience and Nature* (La Salle, Ill., 1987), p. 290.
120. Dewey, *Art as Experience,* p. 19. Much art of a later period, our own, has explicitly rejected the notion of organic consummation, preferring to remain in the shards of a broken culture and working with rather than against the disruption of bodily integrity. For an analysis of its implications for Dewey, see Martin Jay, "Somaesthetics and Democracy: John Dewey and Contemporary Body Art," in *Refractions of Violence.*

That delightful perception, Dewey hastened to add, was of a world irreducible to the projection of the aesthetic subject, even as it was intertwined with it. Because of his hostility to idealism, he resisted the dissolution of the aesthetic object, which we have seen was always a threat in the Kantian version of aesthetic experience:

> Extreme instances of the results of separation of organism and the world are not infrequent in aesthetic philosophy. Such a separation lies behind the idea that aesthetic quality does not belong to objects as objects but is projected onto them by mind. It is the source of the definition of beauty as "objectified pleasure" instead of as pleasure in the object, so much *in* it that the object and pleasure are one and undivided in the experience.[121]

Thus, however important the expressive, non-mimetic character of art, it would be wrong to understand aesthetic experience in purely psychologistic terms, entirely as a function of the creative subject or the sensibility of the judging beholder. Even intersubjective communities of taste needed actual objects on which to exercise their judgment, although it would be equally mistaken to fetishize objects as timeless entities indifferent to their effect on their beholders.

At times, to be sure, Dewey could embrace the idea that virtually any object might be aestheticized, thus tacitly following the logic of the "natural supernatural" aesthetic redemption of the world. "Aesthetic experience," he maintained, "is always more than aesthetic. In it a body of matters and meanings, not in themselves aesthetic, *become* aesthetic as they enter into an ordered rhythmic movement towards consummation. The material itself is widely human."[122] It was this argument that disturbed certain friendly critics like Hans Robert Jauss, who worried that Dewey engaged in a circular argument, projecting onto the world what he then claimed he found there as the source of everyday aesthetic experience.[123]

---

121. Dewey, *Art as Experience*, p. 248.

122. Ibid., p. 326.

123. Jauss, *Aesthetic Experience and Literary Hermeneutics*, p. 113. Jauss suggested instead that Dewey should not "maintain the illusion of the objectively beautiful without tracing the aesthetic quality of the objects and phenomena of the everyday world back to the attitude of the observer." In so arguing, he was moving back to the subjectivism (or intersubjectivsm) that pragmatism sought to overcome. Shusterman, another friendly critic, also admits that "one problem is that aesthetic experience seems too slippery to have much explanatory power. Though it undeniably exists, it does not exist as something that we can clearly isolate and define; hence in defining art as aesthetic experience, we are defining the comparatively clear and definite by something obscurely elusive and undefinable." *Pragmatist Aesthetics*, p. 55.

Dewey did, however, concede that his radically democratized notion of aesthetic experience, in which all objects were capable of eliciting such a response, came up against the limits of the modern world, in which "zeal for doing, lust for action, leaves many a person, especially in this hurried and impatient human environment in which we live, with experience of an almost incredible paucity, all on the surface. No one experience has a chance to complete itself because something else is entered upon so speedily. What is called experience is so dispersed and miscellaneous as hardly to deserve the name."[124] Indeed, it was the impoverished nature of everyday experience that allowed the elite notion of art to flourish in compensation.

Such analyses of the difficulty of achieving genuine aesthetic experiences under current conditions were sufficiently cautious for Dewey to win the unexpected praise of a theorist whose own ruminations on the "crisis" of experience, aesthetic and otherwise, we will examine in chapter 8. In *Aesthetic Theory*, Theodor Adorno pitted the "unique and truly free John Dewey" against Hegel, whose overly "scientific" aesthetics he found too securely systematic and naively optimistic. "That aesthetics, in its desire to be more than chatter, wants to find its way out into the open, entirely exposed, imposes on it the sacrifice of each and every security that it has borrowed from the sciences;" Adorno wrote, "no one expressed this necessity with greater candor than the pragmatist John Dewey."[125]

How consistently non-foundational Dewey's concept of experience may have been remains an issue that is much discussed in the literature on him.[126] Suffice it to say for now that when it came to its aesthetic variant, Dewey posited it as a normative goal, a desideratum rather than a given of the human condition. Although he talked of consummation and integration as the essence of the aesthetic, when it came to life lived aesthetically rather than the discrete experience of a work of art, he meant it more as a regulative ideal than a realized state of affairs. He could thus approvingly quote Tennyson to make his point about the moving horizon that forever recedes before us:

124. Dewey, *Art as Experience*, p. 45.

125. Theodor W. Adorno, *Aesthetic Theory*, trans. Robert Hullot-Kentor (Minneapolis, 1997), pp. 335 and 354. On the place of aesthetic experience in Adorno's own work, see Shierry Weber Nicholsen, *Exact Imagination, Late Works: On Adorno's Aesthetics* (Cambridge, Mass., 1997), chapter 1.

126. See, for example, Richard Rorty, "Dewey's Metaphysics," *Consequences of Pragmatism* (Minneapolis, 1982); and Richard Shusterman, *Practicing Philosophy: Pragmatism and the Philosophical Life* (New York, 1997).

Experience is an arch wherethro'
Gleams that untravell'd world, whose margin fades
Forever and forever when I move.[127]

But setting off on the journey was still very much worth the effort.

Art as Experience was a plea to do just that, a plea, in fact, with explicit political implications. As Robert Westbrook has remarked, the book "was not incidental to the radical politics that absorbed Dewey in the 1930's. Indeed, it was one of the most powerful statements of that politics, for it clearly indicated that his was not a radicalism directed solely to the material well-being of the American people but directed as well to the provision of consummatory experience that could be found only outside the circulation of commodities."[128] Another recent commentator, David Fott, adds that for Dewey, as opposed to Richard Rorty with his strict separation between public and private, "we can consider aesthetic experience the goal of our attempts to solve our political problems, which arise when disorder is felt to occur."[129]

Was such experience, however, a displacement of "real" politics, a way to gesture towards redemption without a means to realize it through what normally passes for political practice? Indeed, from its origins in the eighteenth century, the discourse of aesthetic experience has been dogged by the gnawing doubt that it might be more a compensatory simulacrum of political activism than a stimulus to it.[130] Moving too quickly from the sublimated bodily pleasure provided by art to those of a metaphorical body politic might lead to the aestheticization of politics against which Benjamin had warned. Was there a more direct and less displaced way in which experience and politics could be intertwined? And if so, did the results favor any one ideological inclination, or was experience available for mobilization by conservatives, liberals, and radicals alike? It is to these and other vexed questions posed by the "politics of experience" that our next chapter will turn.

Before doing so, let me try to summarize the complicated trajectory we

---

127. Quoted without reference in Dewey, *Art as Experience,* p. 193.

128. Westbrook, *John Dewey and American Democracy,* pp. 401–2.

129. Fott, *Dewey: America's Philosopher of Democracy,* p. 109. Fott faults Dewey, however, for neglecting the role of enthusiasm in politics, which parallels his indifference to the importance of the sublime in aesthetics.

130. See Hess, *Reconstituting the Body Politic,* for an acute analysis of this question in the German context in particular.

have followed in this one. The discourse of a specifically aesthetic variant of experience was enabled by two major developments in European cultural life: the loss of faith in an intelligible world of inherently beautiful objects and the differentiation of art from its religious, political, moral, and economic functions. These changes allowed a new focus on the corporeal, sensual response of the beholder of art, as well as on his capacity to exercise the judgment of taste. The subject who emerged from this discourse was not, however, permitted to follow his fleshly desires and interests, but was instead understood in the tradition that culminated in Kant's *Critique of Judgment* as inherently spectatorial, contemplative, and disinterested.

Virtually all these premises were challenged by later interpreters of aesthetic experience. Some argued that it was wrong to suppress the interest in any genuinely corporeal relationship to the world, no matter how sublimated it might appear. For others, belief in the autonomy of the aesthetic sphere as a realm apart from its moral or cognitive counterparts was replaced by the claim that art was a sovereign enterprise with the right to colonize other cultural subsystems and heal the wounds of modernity on its terms. For the more ambitious of these advocates, this task involved an actual transformation of society into a work of art; for others, it meant the aesthetic transfiguration of what already existed. For the former, the passivity of aesthetic experience had to be enriched by the activity of artistic creation, which could either be elitist or democratic in scope. For the latter, it meant a kind of aesthetic theodicy in which commonplace objects and practices—some perhaps even violent and immoral—could be given an aesthetic justification.

These responses produced in their turn ones of their own. Some critics of the imperialism of aesthetic sovereignty sought a more even-handed balance between different modes of experience. Others were worried by the promiscuous aestheticization of the world in ways that allowed evil to be justified inappropriately. Still others demanded the restoration of the balance between subjective experience and art object or work, which was in danger of being lost in the one-sided stress on enjoyment, judgment, and taste.

To date, no consensus has been reached about what aesthetic experience really is or should be, what and how permeable its boundaries with other modes of experience are, and whether it should rest content with its autonomous status or strive to assert its sovereignty over other types of experience. And what makes any consensus in the future not likely to be reached is the fact that all the while philosophers and aestheticians have been struggling to master the essence of aesthetic experience, practicing artists have been inventing new and unforeseen varieties of the art that seeks to provoke those experiences. To the extent that experience involves a passive waiting for something from the outside to interrupt our expectations, an encounter with an other not yet fully mastered, it might be said that the experience of writing about aesthetic experience is enabled precisely by this happy fact. It too gazes through the arch in Tennyson's poem quoted by Dewey at a horizon it never can reach.

FIVE

Politics and Experience

Burke, Oakeshott, and the English Marxists

"A POLITICS OF EXPERIENCE," warns an eminent feminist critic, "is inevitably a conservative politics."[1] Rather than a check against ideology, adds a prominent Marxist theorist, experience is "ideology's homeland."[2] "Experience," observes a third commentator, was routinely elevated above "analysis" by defenders of "reactionary modernism" in Germany.[3] Such claims, often made by defenders of theory or the linguistic turn in cultural studies, can be taken in one of two ways: either only those normally labeled rightist routinely legitimate their positions by drawing on the lessons of experience, or even those who claim to be politically progressive inadvertently produce conservative outcomes when they defend their position by relying on those same lessons. This second charge, as we will see, was debated with special intensity in what were, to borrow the title of Perry Anderson's contribution to them, the "arguments within English Marxism" of the 1970s.[4]

Understood in the first sense, the claim is easy to debunk empirically, for there are many examples of political thinkers and activists belonging to the party of movement rather than that of order who have found in one version or another of experience an invaluable ally. Not only has the link we have noted between experience and experiment been a boon to those who want to tinker with the established order, so too have the egalitarian implications of relying on experience rather than the authority of texts or the power of

1. Jane Gallop, "Quand nos lèvres s'écrivent: Irigaray's Body Politics," *Romanic Review* 74 (1983), p. 83.

2. Terry Eagleton, *Criticism and Ideology: A Study in Marxist Literary Theory* (London, 1976), p. 15.

3. Jeffrey Herf, *Reactionary Modernism: Technology, Culture and Politics in the Third Reich* (New York, 1990), p. 226.

4. Perry Anderson, *Arguments within English Marxism* (London, 1980).

those allegedly higher in a foreordained great chain of being. In the case of colonial America, to take one salient example, writers like John Smith, William Wood, John Winthrop, Benjamin Tompson, and William Hubbard relied on the new rhetorical power of experience to legitimate their status as equal to that of the British who remained home.[5] Often drawing on Locke's critique of the patriarchal body politic metaphor, they also absorbed some of his stress on the formation of actual bodies through discrete sense experiences. Against rank or social privilege, they pitted the benefits of living in the forbidding climate and untamed environment of New England, which produced a new communal, proto-national identity. Although not intending to be subversive, these authors ended by providing a powerful rationale for separating the colonies from Britain. "After these texts," the historian Jim Egan notes, "experience could not sacralize colonial sacrifices to God or king. In this New World, experience made it sacred for colonials to sacrifice their bodies and lives to colony, to New England, and as now, to the nation."[6]

Historians of the American Revolution have also had little trouble marshaling evidence to show the vital importance of the rhetoric of experience in the discourse of the founding fathers. Patrick Henry proudly asserted that "I have but one lamp by which my feet are guided, and that is the lamp of experience. I know no way of judging the future but by the past."[7] During the Constitutional Convention in Philadelphia twelve years later, John Dickinson urged learning from the long history of British constitutional law by baldly stating that "experience must be our only guide. Reason may mislead us," a sentiment that was shared, albeit with varying degrees of enthusiasm, by Benjamin Franklin, James Madison, George Mason, Alexander Hamilton, and other framers of the document that launched the new experiment in government on these shores.[8] For them, not only the accumulated historical experience of previous polities, but also what they themselves had ac-

5. Jim Egan, *Authorizing Experience: Refigurations of the Body Politic in Seventeenth-Century New England Writing* (Princeton, 1999).

6. Ibid., p. 119.

7. Quoted as an epigraph in H. Trevor Colbourn, *The Lamp of Experience: Whig History and the Intellectual Origins of the American Revolution* (Chapel Hill, N.C., 1965).

8. Quoted and discussed in Douglass G. Adair, "Experience Must Be Our Only Guide: History, Democratic Theory, and the American Constitution," in Jack P. Greene, ed., *The Reinterpretation of the American Revolution, 1763–1789* (New York, 1968), pp. 399–400; and in Jack P. Greene, "'An Instructive Monitor': Experience and the Fabrication of the Federal Constitution," in *Imperatives, Behaviors and Identities: Essays in Early American Cultural History* (Charlottesville, Va., 1992). As Morton White has shown in "Philosophy, *The Federalist*, and the Progressive Era," *Rutgers Law Review* 41, no. 2 (Winter 1989), there was also a fair amount of rationalism in the thinking of James Madison and Alexander Hamilton.

quired in the eleven years since the independent republic was founded—not all of it positive—needed to be taken into account.[9]

In other contexts as well, theorists even more self-consciously belonging to what became known as the Left have relied on a rhetoric of experience to legitimate their positions. As we noted at the end of the previous chapter, John Dewey based his support for radical democracy on the normative goal of aesthetic experience as a model of the good life. Reformist socialists in Europe such as Jean Jaurès and Eduard Bernstein also routinely invoked experience in their critiques of metaphysical materialism.[10] Within twentieth-century Marxism, experience served the Frankfurt School in complicated ways that will be addressed in chapter 8. It also surfaced as an honorific term in the vocabulary of the *Socialisme ou Barbarie* group led by Claude Lefort and Cornelius Castoriadis in the 1950s, as it did twenty years later for the German theorists Oskar Negt and Alexander Kluge in their search for a "proletarian public sphere."[11]

During the 1960s in Britain, the radical psychiatrist R. D. Laing defended the transgressive potential revealed in schizophrenia—beyond the confining dichotomies of subject and object and overturning the repressions of the bourgeois family—and dubbed it "the politics of experience."[12] Attempting to recover what had been lost, he fostered an experiment in communal living at Kingsley Hall, which sought—ultimately with disastrous results—to unleash the intense and authentic experiences denied by modern life. A far more sober expression of the British Left's romance of experience in the 1960s and 1970s can be found in the influential Marxist humanism of the historian E. P. Thompson, the cultural critic and novelist John Berger, the cultural critic Richard Hoggart, and the literary critic and novelist Raymond Williams, whose insistence on its importance generated the "arguments" mentioned

9. To be more precise, as Greene points out in "'An Instructive Monitor'" (p. 324), the anti-Federalists drew on the decentralizing lessons of the pre-1776 era, while the Federalists were more taken with the lessons of the republican experiment after independence. As was so often the case in the appeal to experience, its precise implications could be easily contested.

10. For an account of their efforts, see James Kloppenberg, *Uncertain Victory: Social Democracy and Progressivism in European and American Thought, 1870–1920* (New York, 1986), pp. 224–26.

11. See Claude Lefort, "L'expérience prolétarienne," *Socialisme ou Barbarie* 11 (November–December 1952); and Oskar Negt and Alexander Kluge, *Public Sphere and Experience: Toward an Analysis of the Bourgeois and Proletarian Public Sphere*, trans. Peter Labanyi, Jamie Owen Daniel, and Assenka Oksiloff (Minneapolis, 1993). The foreword, by Miriam Hansen, to this English translation of the 1972 book has astute things to say about the central role of *Erfahrung* in their analysis.

12. R. D. Laing, *The Politics of Experience* (New York, 1967); for an account of Laing's career, see Daniel Burston, *The Wing of Madness: The Life and Work of R. D. Laing* (Cambridge, Mass., 1996).

above with critics who had absorbed the French structuralist disdain for "lived experience." Of this, more anon. But for the moment, I hope the point has been made: many non-conservatives, even proud Marxists in the major European traditions, found in the concept of experience—or just as often, in its putative impoverishment—a valuable tool in their critiques of modern society. Indeed, one observer could plausibly call the radical 1970s a decade ruled by "the hunger for experience."[13]

If then, it would be mistaken to say that only *soi-disant* conservatives consider experience a god-term, what of the more complex claim that even those on the left who use it inadvertently draw conservative consequences? To answer this question will require some initial exploration of the ways in which conservatives themselves have relied on the rhetoric of experience to buttress their positions, which can then be compared with the uses made by their leftist counterparts. If, as we have had ample opportunity to note, the word "experience" can be used to denote many different, even at times contradictory, ideas, it will be necessary to unpack the various meanings in the lexicon of politics before coming to any conclusions about putative continuities. To pursue this task, we will begin with a discussion of the eighteenth-century fathers of conservatism—a term, to be sure, that came into use only after their deaths—David Hume and Edmund Burke.[14] Then we will move to the twentieth century and compare the work of the conservative political theorist Michael Oakeshott with that of the British Marxists Thompson and Williams to see how much of the legacy of Hume and Burke still inspires the politics of experience across the spectrum. For it was on the British Left that the battle over this question was most fervently waged, with the concept of experience playing an analogous role to that played by "praxis" on the continent as the antonym to—or more precisely, dialectical antithesis of—"theory."

---

13. Michael Rutschy, *Erfahrungshunger: Ein Essay über die siebziger Jahre* (Frankfurt, 1982).

14. Perhaps the first use of the term came with the journal *Le Conservateur*, founded by François-René Chateaubriand in 1818. Hume, it might be noted, is occasionally considered a proto-liberal, by, for example, Stephen Holmes in *The Anatomy of Antiliberalism* (Cambridge, Mass., 1993). For a recent account that situates him squarely in the conservative camp, see Donald W. Livingston, *Philosophical Melancholy and Delirium: Hume's Pathology of Philosophy* (Chicago, 1998). A selection of Hume's work appropriately begins *Conservatism: An Anthology of Social and Political Thought from David Hume to the Present*, ed. Jerry Z. Muller (Princeton, 1997). Still, it should be acknowledged that Hume was often an inspiration to the American revolutionaries. See the discussion in Adair, "Experience Must Be Our Only Guide," pp. 401–2. Hume, in fact, was an early advocate of independence for the colonies. See Livingston, *Philosophical Melancholy and Delirium*, chap. 11.

But before pursuing this agenda, a brief excursus will be necessary to make one critical distinction. In the cases of its religious and aesthetic modalities, we have noted that experience has often served as an end in itself, so much so that the objects of that experience—God as "the wholly other" or beautiful things in the world—have tended to recede into the background. What we saw as the aesthete's yearning to live life as if it were a work of art is emblematic of this temptation, which conflates the subject and object of experience. Certain mystical variants of religious experience have followed a similar path. In the case of epistemological debates about the value of experience, in contrast, the goal has almost always been to verify knowledge about the external world, not celebrate the process of knowing as a self-sufficient good. Although there are certainly rewards to be gained from satisfying curiosity and learning more about the world, by and large the cognitive quest has steadily remained focused on the objects of inquiry rather than the immanent pleasures of the process.

What can be said about experience and politics? There have indeed been arguments for (or at least tacit attractions to) the intrinsic satisfactions of the political life in itself. In certain versions of radical politics on both ends of the political spectrum, it has often seemed as if the intoxicating experience of "engaged" or "committed" involvement in a dynamic "movement" was more important than the actual realization of its goals.[15] Indeed sometimes, as in the case with certain nihilistic or anarchistic politics of sheer destruction, the goals seem so far from being realizable through the means employed, it is clear that fantasmatic metapolitics had become a kind of surrogate for anything remotely resembling its normal counterpart. In some cases—say, that of the Russian anarchist Mikhail Bakunin—such a commitment to political experience allowed it to swallow up virtually everything else in their lives. Whether understood as performative self-indulgence, existentialist self-fashioning, or a quest for heroic realization, the lure of intense political experience often motivated entry into the agonistic public realm.

For example, the vitalist *moraliste* Georges Sorel, who oscillated between radical Right and Left, extolled the importance of struggle and sacrifice in themselves, while remaining pessimistic about the permanent effects of the

15. For representative examples of this phenomenon, see David L. Schalk, *The Spectrum of Political Engagement: Mounier, Benda, Nizan, Brasillach, Sartre* (Princeton, 1979); and M. Adereth, *Commitment in Modern French Literature: Politics and Society in Péguy, Aragon and Sartre* (New York, 1968).

general strike he so fervently advocated. Its function, he understood, was that of a myth capable of rousing the masses out of their experiential torpor. Fascism, for which Sorel is sometimes held partly responsible, has often been seen as a variant of sacralized, aestheticized politics in which the mythicized, violent, ritualized surface spectacle, the intoxicating experience of communal self-immolation, was just as important, if not more so, than the functions that it served.[16]

The post–World War I writings of the German novelist and war hero Ernst Jünger, in particular his 1920 *In Stahlgewittern (The Storm of Steel)* and 1922 *Der Kampf als inneres Erlebnis (Struggle as Inner Experience)*, anticipated this outcome by combining a romanticized version of the *Fronterlebnis* with a Sorelian justification of violence's power to regenerate bourgeois man.[17] The result was a coldly ecstatic, self-annihilating consecration of the means rather than the ends of struggle, which translated after the armistice into a sinister meta-politics of nihilistic activism. It expressed itself with brutal directness in the defiant response of the Freikorps leader Ernst von Salomon to the question "what do you believe in?" "Nothing besides action," he answered. "Nothing besides the possibility of action. Nothing besides the feasibility of action. . . . We were a band of fighters drunk with all the passions of the world; full of lust, exultant in action. What we wanted, we did not know. And what we knew, we did not want! War and adventure, excitement and destruction."[18]

What the historian George Mosse dubbed the Myth of the War Experience emerged in the Weimar Republic from this sacralization of violence as a means of justifying the horrible loss of life and preparing the way for another sacrificial slaughter to avenge the defeat of the last.[19] Substituting the logic of generational allegiance—or more precisely, the male bonding that took place in the trenches—for class solidarity based on common economic destinies, the myth was an effective weapon in the Right's campaign against the Left to win over the evaporating middle in the Republic.[20] Even in England, where revulsion from the war and its aftermath left many staunchly

---

16. See, for example, Simonetta Falasca-Zamponi, *Fascist Spectacle: The Aesthetics of Power in Mussolini's Italy* (Berkeley, 1997).

17. Jünger's debts to Sorel are discussed in Elliot Y. Neaman, *A Dubious Past: Ernst Jünger and the Politics of Literature after Nazism* (Berkeley, 1999), p. 29.

18. Ernst von Salomon, *Die Geächteten* (Berlin, 1930), quoted in Robert G. L. Waite, *Vanguard of Nazism: The Free Corps Movement in Postwar Germany 1918–1923* (New York, 1952), p. 269.

19. George L. Mosse, *Fallen Soldiers: Reshaping the Memory of the World Wars* (New York, 1990), p. 7. Mosse traces its origins to the wars of the French Revolution and the German Wars of Liberation against Napoleon, and sees its decline setting in after the Second World War.

20. See Robert Wohl, *The Generation of 1914* (Cambridge, Mass., 1979), p. 54.

opposed to fighting another, disillusioned veterans like Oswald Mosley could derive similar lessons.[21] Whether this kind of contentless politics could be justified as "authentic" expressions of collective effervescence or damned instead as misguided attempts to restore the communal identity and intensity of participatory involvement that had been lost in the modern world is, of course, another question. Sober-minded observers from at least the time of Max Weber and Julien Benda have certainly found much to disturb them in the politics of experience understood in these terms.[22]

Perhaps the most elaborate and thoughtful theoretical defense of the intrinsic value of political experience—sharply distinguished, to be sure, from the exaltation of violence in Sorel, Jünger, and Salomon—was mounted by a refugee from the Fascism to which they contributed, Hannah Arendt. Her work is often taken to be a celebration of freedom in the public sphere, a freedom produced by active political engagement and a concomitant indifference toward the social or economic results of that engagement. As a result, she has sometimes been criticized for aestheticizing politics and minimizing its functional purposes: to improve the lives of the people affected by it—for, in other words, championing a kind of *politique pour la politique* reminiscent of *l'art pour l'art*.[23] Arendt, it must be conceded, did not explicitly privilege the concept of experience, preferring instead to talk of action, but at times she did permit herself to lament the withering of experience *qua* political participation. In *The Human Condition,* for example, she claimed that "if we compare the modern world with that of the past, the loss of human experience involved in this development is extraordinarily striking."[24] And in an interview conducted a few years before her death in 1975, she answered the question, "What is the subject of our thought?" by exclaiming: "Experience! Nothing else! And if we lose the ground of experience then we get into all kinds of theories. When the political theorist begins to build his systems

21. On the importance of the war for Mosley and his later embrace of Fascism, see Robert Skidelsky, *Oswald Mosley* (London, 1975), chapter 3, entitled "A Special Kind of Experience."

22. Max Weber, "Science as Vocation," in Hans Gerth and C. Wright Mills, ed. and trans., *From Max Weber* (New York, 1958), p. 149; Julien Benda, *The Treason of the Intellectuals,* trans. Richard Adlington (New York, 1969), pp. 168 and 173.

23. For my own consideration of these issues, see "'The Aesthetic Ideology' as Ideology: Or, What Does It Mean to Aestheticize Politics?," in *Force Fields: Between Intellectual History and Cultural Critique* (New York, 1993).

24. Hannah Arendt, *The Human Condition* (Garden City, N.Y., 1958), p. 294. Arendt was, of course, close to Walter Benjamin and wrote the introduction to the first English-language edition of his writings, *Illuminations,* which included several important statements of his ideas about experience.

he is also usually dealing with abstraction."[25] Arendt's work shows that even without the dangerous conflation of politics and actual violent struggle, a privileging of the agonistic moment in the public sphere can produce a politics of experience for its own sake, which ignores the instrumental purpose of action.

What Arendt did not do, it should be conceded, was to extend the reach of political experience beyond the public sphere in which she placed it. As a result, she was not tempted by the conflation of public and private that was to be a feature of the later feminist movement, which identified the personal with the political, a claim that had many positive repercussions but also opened the door to an indiscriminate inclusion of everything as potentially political. As in the case of the aesthetic "transfiguration of the commonplace," the danger was a leveling effect that privileged subjective experience over its objects. In the case of politics, this could mean encouraging the belief that acting entirely in the private sphere—say, to reorganize child-rearing responsibilities—was as political an act as running for office, defending a public policy, or even overthrowing a regime. At its most problematic, this assumption could work to substitute the former entirely for the latter, thus providing an unintended apology for abstention from the public realm. A similar substitution sometimes followed from the identity-politics belief that shared group experiences led inexorably to a political position. This was an outcome very much at odds with Arendt's understanding of the self-fashioning nature of political experience in the public realm.

BURKE AND THE WISDOM OF PAST EXPERIENCE

Neither the exhortation to mythical violence in Sorel, Jünger, and Salomon nor Arendt's brief for the value of political participation as an experience in itself was typical of the conservative evocation of experience as legitimating principle.[26] In fact, one criterion that separates the upholders of tradition from their more radical right-wing brethren—and from many on the other end of the spectrum as well—is a lack of faith in the redemptive or cleans-

---

25. Hannah Arendt, "On Hannah Arendt," in Melvin A. Hill, ed., *Hannah Arendt: The Recovery of the Public World* (New York, 1979), p. 308.

26. For general considerations of the conservative tradition and representative texts, see the bibliography in Muller, *Conservatism*. Still indispensable is Karl Mannheim's classic essay, "Conservative Thought," in Kurt H. Wolff, ed., *From Karl Mannheim* (New York, 1971).

ing power of political experience. By and large, conservatives, if one can generalize about a variegated tradition that distrusts abstractions, have had too bleak a view of human nature and its imperfections to hold out any hope for a robust form of participation that would somehow be sufficient unto itself. Instead of celebrating experience for its own sake, they tend to invoke it for the prudential lessons it imparts about the limits of political activism, in particular in the face of misguided attempts to ground politics in speculative reason or abstract theory.

Here they also typically distinguished themselves from liberals who might speak of indisputable human rights and claim with Kant that "experience cannot provide knowledge of what is right."[27] Instead, conservatives at least since the time of Hume were fond of calling on the cautionary lessons of the past to buttress their present beliefs and warn against the positing of abstract theories of rights based on an ahistorical assumption of a normative state of nature.[28] They thus often employed such typical locutions, found in Hume's essays on politics, as "in this opinion I am justified by experience, as well as by the authority of all philosophers and politicians both ancient and modern" and "we have not as yet had experience of three thousand years; so that not only the art of reasoning is still imperfect in this science [politics], as in all others, but we even want sufficient materials upon which we can reason."[29] Here experience combined with other terms, such as "authority," "tradition," "wisdom," "custom," "prejudice," "life," "history," "common sense," and "habit," to form a rhetorical defense against what was seen as the overweening arrogance of rationalist political theory and the dangerous fantasizing of a priori metaphysicians, as well as against the depredations of modernizing rationalization in the world outside.

This discursive constellation was perhaps most extensively developed in Great Britain, where the tradition of common law and an unwritten constitution combined with uneasy memories of the Puritan revolution and religious fanaticism to defeat renewed attempts at radical solutions. The British sensationalist tradition derived from Lockean empiricism could, moreover,

27. Kant, "On the Common Saying: 'This May Be True in Theory, but It Does not Apply in Practice'," *Political Writings*, ed. Hans Reiss, trans. H. B. Nisbet (Cambridge, 1971), p. 86.

28. It would, however, be erroneous to make too radical a dichotomy between history and nature in characterizing the conservative tradition. At least some conservatives sought to combine appeals from both. For a reading of Burke that argues for this combination, see Peter J. Stanlis, *Edmund Burke and the Natural Law* (Ann Arbor, Mich., 1958).

29. David Hume, "Of the Independency of Parliament," and "Of Civil Liberty," in *Essays Moral, Political and Literary*, ed. Eugene F. Miller (Indianapolis, 1987), pp. 43 and 87.

buttress not only protoliberal politics, as in the American colonies, but also its conservative counterpart, even among those like Burke who "revolted against the 18th century."[30] For Hume's stress on the power of belief, sentiment, imagination, sympathy, and analogy, combined with his associationist epistemology, helped turn the tradition away from critical analysis to cautious solidarity with the status quo.

The residues of skepticism toward speculative, systematizing rationalism, found in earlier British writers like Hume, John Dryden, Jonathan Swift, and Samuel Johnson, were then given added political weight when unchecked theoretical reason could be made the culprit for the excesses of the French Revolution. As Burke contemptuously remarked in his *Reflections on the Revolution in France* with reference to the Third Estate delegates to the French National Assembly: "Among them, indeed, I saw some of known rank; some of shining talents; but of any practical experience in the state, not one man was to be found. The best were only men of theory."[31] Thus began a now venerable tradition of disparaging critical intellectuals as utopian enthusiasts, whose lack of practical training led to disastrous attempts to remake the world out of whole cloth, an accusation often illustrated by the example of the Terror, against whose coming Burke had presciently warned.[32]

Another component of the conservative legitimation by experience concerned what might be called its tacit utilitarianism or consequentialism. That is, it often contended that if an institution or practice had survived, it did so because it was doing something right. Origins therefore might be seen as less important than outcomes, which meant that it was foolish to seek some moment of founding, such as an original contract, to legitimate later practices and institutions. Although Burke did appeal to ancient customs, the fact that their beginnings were purportedly "immemorial"—no longer preserved in

30. For a classic discussion of Burke's mixed debt to Locke, see Alfred Cobban, *Edmund Burke and the Revolt against the Eighteenth Century* (London, 1929), chapter 2. On his more profound link with Hume, see Paul Lucas, "On Edmund Burke's Doctrine of Prescription; or, An Appeal from the New to the Old Lawyers," *Historical Journal* 40, no. 1 (1968), pp. 60–61.

31. Edmund Burke, *Reflections on the Revolution in France,* ed. J. G. A. Pocock (Indianapolis, 1987) p. 35.

32. Another classic expression of this claim appears in Alexis de Tocqueville's *The Old Regime and the French Revolution,* trans. Stuart Gilbert (Garden City, N.Y., 1955), where Tocqueville says of the *philosophes* that "their very way of living led these writers to indulge in abstract theories and generalizations regarding the nature of government, and to place blind confidence in these. For living as they did, quite out of touch with practical politics, they lacked the experience which might have tempered their enthusiasms" (p. 140). For a refutation of the charge that the *philosophes* were all as unpracticed in the arts of politics as Burke and Tocqueville asserted, see Peter Gay, *Voltaire's Politics: The Poet as Realist* (New York, 1959).

memory—meant that it was vain to attempt to ground them in some explicit *ur*-act of legitimation, which his opponents (among them, Thomas Paine) had thought was necessary in order to avoid honoring past crimes of usurpation.[33] Indeed, Burke explicitly contended that even if their origins were tainted, "the time of prescription . . . through long usage, mellows into legality governments that were violent in their commencement."[34] A similar argument could be used to justify property rights as well without bothering to worry about the initial act of appropriation—or expropriation.

Longevity could therefore function as a prudential warning against the urge to tinker or innovate in a radical way, although piecemeal, incremental reform might be healthy. Burke's celebrated defense of liberties (in the plural) as an entailed inheritance, a trust passed down to posterity by the past, was predicated on the assumption that experience and experiment were antonyms rather than synonyms.[35] Expediency, to use a word Burke favored, sometimes had to trump abstract principle.[36] The threat, he argued, came not only from rationalizing "enlightened despots" and their revolutionary opponents, both of whom wanted to sweep away the messy but still functioning residues of the past, but also from the new commercial spirit, which led to the instability of a credit economy and the erosion of the old landed aristocracy.[37] Instead, he extolled the virtues of the common law tradition, whose origins

33. On the tangled debate between Burke and Paine over the issue of origins, see Steven Blackmore, *Burke and the Fall of Language: The French Revolution as Linguistic Event* (Hanover, 1988), chapter 2.

34. Burke, *Reflections on the Revolution in France*, p. 145.

35. See, for example, Burke's dismissal of the French revolutionaries in whom "there is nothing of the tender, parental solicitude which fears to cut up the infant for the sake of an experiment." Ibid., p. 146.

36. Whether Burke was a consistent utilitarian has long been debated, at least since the time of John Morley and Leslie Stephens in the late nineteenth century. For a defense of the utilitarian moment in his thought, see Gerald W. Chapman, *Edmund Burke: The Practical Imagination* (Cambridge, Mass., 1967), pp. 156–59. See Stanlis, *Edmund Burke and Natural Law*, and his *Edmund Burke: The Enlightenment and the Revolution* (New Brunswick, N.J., 1991) for the contrary case, made from a Straussian perspective, that natural law appeals were more important to Burke than ones based on utility. For answers to Stanlis that stresses the bourgeois content that Burke puts into traditional Christian natural law, see C. B. McPherson, *Burke* (New York, 1980); Isaac Kramnick, *The Rage of Edmund Burke: Portrait of an Ambivalent Conservative* (New York, 1977), pp. 45–48; and John R. Dinwiddy, "James Mill on Burke's Doctrine of Prescription," *Studies in Burke and His Times* 18 (1977), which occasioned a debate with Stanlis in the next issue of the journal. See also Frank O'Gorman, *Edmund Burke: His Political Philosophy* (Bloomington, Ind., 1973), pp. 12–15; and Conor Cruise O'Brien, *The Great Melody: A Thematic Biography and Commented Anthology of Edmund Burke* (Chicago, 1992), introduction. These critics do not, however, attempt to turn him back into a simple proto-Benthamite. All seem to agree that Burke distinguished between the manifestation of natural law in the concrete realities of history, which he applauded, and its expression in abstract, ahistorical natural rights, which he deplored.

37. For the importance of Burke's critique of the new commercial spirit, see J. G. A. Pocock's introduction to *Reflections on the Revolution in France*.

were lost in the mists of time in what had come to be called the "ancient constitution."[38] Prescription—the right conferred by long use and sustained possession—rather than ostensibly fundamental first principles or the exercise of will, was the basis of political legitimacy. As the American jurist Rufus Choate put it in 1845,

> By the aid of time,—time which changes and tries all things; tries them, and works them pure,—we subject the law, after it is given, to the tests of old experience, to the reason and justice of successive ages and generations, to the best thoughts of the wisest and safest of reformers. And then and thus we pronounce it good. . . . There is a deep presumption in favor of that which has endured so long.[39]

A third dimension of the typical conservative appeal to experience was its collective nature, based on the assumption that social and political entities were organic unities or corporate bodies irreducible to their component parts by corrosive analysis. The inadequacies of isolated individual experience and monologic rationality could be overcome by the accumulated learning of the group, albeit often a tacit learning that might never reach the level of self-conscious reflexivity. Experience in this usage was thus less a matter of interiority than an intersubjective and discursive product, mediated by culture and language and filtered through collective memory. Indeed, Burke's own masterful command of rhetoric, both spoken and written, on behalf of the Rockingham Whig cause in Parliament bore eloquent witness to the entanglement of words and deeds in his own politics of experience, whose links to his seminal writings on aesthetics have often been remarked.[40]

We have already seen that experience can be given a collective inflection through scientific transcendentalization, in which the subject who does the experiencing is assumed to be a universal and immortal cognitive experimentalist, outliving the finite lifespan of individual scientists. In aesthetic terms, the Kantian tradition sought to overcome the idiosyncrasies of indi-

38. For the importance of this idea in Burke, see J. G. A. Pocock, "Burke and the Ancient Constitution: A Problem in the History of Ideas," in *Politics, Language and Time: Essays on Political Thought and History* (New York, 1973). For a subtle and learned response to this essay, which shows that Burke's notion of prescription went considerably beyond what the British common law tradition had granted it, see Lucas, "On Edmund Burke's Doctrine of Prescription."

39. Rufus Choate, "The Position and Functions of the American Bar, as an Element of Conservatism in the State," in Muller, *Conservatism*, pp. 163–64.

40. See, for example, James T. Boulton, *The Language of Politics in the Age of Wilkes and Burke* (London, 1963); and Terry Eagleton, *The Ideology of the Aesthetic* (Oxford, 1990), chapter 2.

vidual taste by positing an intersubjective judgment available, at least potentially, to all beholders of beauty. Religious experience could also take communal forms in which ecstatic or mystical suppressions of the boundaries
between self and other were dissolved; Martin Buber's early *Erlebnis* mysticism, it will be recalled, was grounded in a desire for a new *Gemeinschaft*.
The generational argument we have just encountered in the postwar Weimar
era maintained that the common trauma of trench warfare had forged a common identity separating those who fought and those who stayed at home
(most notably women and aging male politicians).

The conservative notion of collective experience was somewhat different
from all these models. It often assumed that the wisdom of a particular culture was more important than the general lessons learned by the species as a
whole, even if at times it resorted to grandiose claims about all of human experience. Rather than looking to the future, as was the case with the scientific
fiction of an immortal subject of experience, it sought its legitimation in the
past, whose potency was still effective in the present.[41] As a result, it charac-
teristically valued age over youth and championed the authority of parents
over children. Although accepting the role of concrete judgments in politics,
which it counterposed to the subsumptive application of abstract principles
or algorithmic rules, it tended to restrict the critical or subversive potential
of judging, preferring instead to stress judgment's dependency on exemplars
from the past. In the place of the communal ecstasy of evangelical religious
experience, with all its enthusiastic intensity and potential for disruptive an-
tinomianism, it put its trust in more stable institutions and ritual practices,
which contained the congealed experience of past worshipers in their interaction with the divine. And rather than laud the youthful generational identities that could be directed against the "tired old men" in power, it remained
convinced that fathers knew best.

Often, to be sure, left unresolved was the thorny problem of deciding which
long-standing institutions, prejudices, or traditions "worked" for which
groups in society, a problem that came to the fore when institutions such as
primogeniture, indentured servitude, and patriarchy were challenged by those
who were disadvantaged by them. Moreover, as critics of conservatism never
tired of noting, the organic model of society covered over the possibility that
purported functional complementarity might well be a rationale for radical

41. Mannheim argues that "the conservative experiences the past as being one with the present; hence
his concept of history tends to be spatial rather than temporal; it stresses co-existence rather than succession." "On Conservative Thought," p. 170.

disparities in power and rewards. What might seem a "living" tradition for some was the dead weight of the past for others. Claims to avoid a priori reasoning also came up against the charge that prejudices could be understood as expressing hidden assumptions, which derived less from a wise distillation of the full spectrum of past experiences than a biased elevation of one or a few of them to a universal principle. And indeed, for all their championing of cultural specificity and political pluralism, the defenders of these values were often no less eager than their liberal opponents to hold up their own institutions and experiences as models for emulation elsewhere (especially in those countries lucky enough to be colonized by them).

OAKESHOTT AND THE NEO-HEGELIAN CRITIQUE
OF POLITICAL RATIONALISM

Such considerations did not, however, lessen the attraction of legitimation on the grounds of experience for conservatives. This conclusion becomes abundantly clear if we fast-forward to the twentieth century and examine the arguments of Britain's most prominent successor to Hume and Burke: the Cambridge University and London School of Economics political theorist Michael Oakeshott (1901–1990).[42] For we will find in his writings a reprise of virtually all the arguments in the conservative paean to experience begun by his eighteenth-century forebears as an antidote to the evils engendered by "rationalism in politics." Or rather, we will find them filtered through a neo-Hegelianism that paradoxically gave his anti-theoretical argument the trace of a subterranean rationalist pedigree.[43] Oakeshott was schooled in the neo-idealist tradition at Oxford by J. M. E. McTaggart and F. H. Bradley, and wrote his most exhaustive treatment of the theme, *Experience and Its Modes,* in 1933 directly under their influence.[44] Although less explicitly identified as

42. For discussions of his legacy, see W. H. Greenleaf, *Oakeshott's Philosophical Politics* (London, 1966); Paul Franco, *The Political Philosophy of Michael Oakeshott* (New Haven, 1990); Robert Grant, *Oakeshott* (London, 1990); the symposium dedicated to Oakeshott in *Political Theory* 4, no. 3 (August 1976); and the festschrift for his retirement entitled *Politics and Experience*, ed. Preston King and B. C. Parekh (Cambridge, 1968).

43. David Spitz goes so far as to title his essay in the *Political Theory* symposium "A Rationalist *Malgré Lui:* The Perplexities of Being Michael Oakeshott."

44. Michael Oakeshott, *Experience and Its Modes* (Cambridge, 1978), where he notes that "the works from which I am conscious I have learnt the most are Hegel's *Phänomenologie des Geistes* and Bradley's *Appearance and Reality*" (p. 6). For a discussion of Bradley on this issue, see Robert D. Mack, *The Appeal to Immediate Experience: Philosophic Method in Bradley, Whitehead and Dewey* (New York, 1945).

idealist in his later work, a clear distrust of sensationalist atomism and a stress on the concrete interconnectedness of experienced reality mark his brand of conservative political philosophy throughout.[45]

The paradox resolves itself, at least to some degree, if we pause for a moment with Hegel's contribution to the discourse of experience, which left its mark on the young Oakeshott. It would, to be sure, take another book to do justice to that contribution—there are, in fact, already extensive commentaries on it by Martin Heidegger, Hans-Georg Gadamer, and Theodor Adorno[46]—but with reference to its impact on Oakeshott, only certain features need to be emphasized.

It is in the *Phenomenology of Spirit* that Hegel argued for the dialectical interpenetration of knowledge and its objects, contending that "*inasmuch as the new true object issues from it,* this *dialectical* movement which consciousness exercises on itself which effects both its knowledge and its object is precisely what is called *experience (Erfahrung)."*[47] Experience, in other words, does not proceed by a passive subject's encounters with new and unexpected objects from without; rather it is the mutual process that changes both as it unfolds. Consciousness is itself transformed by what it encounters, and so is the object that is encountered. "The new object," Hegel writes, "shows itself to have come about through a *reversal of consciousness itself.* This way of looking at the matter is something contributed by *us,* by means of which the succession of experiences through which consciousness passes is raised into a scientific progression."[48] This progression involves the inclusion of the mistakes and obstacles that are part of the dialectical process; indeed "the way to Science is itself already *Science,* and hence, in virtue of its content, is the Science of the *experience of consciousness."*[49] That is, rather than counterposing true knowledge to all the false leads that prevented its attainment, as did the scientific method from the time of Bacon, or con-

45. For a suggestive recent attempt to discern a quiet shift in Oakeshott's position after *Experience and Its Modes* from idealism to skepticism, a shift signaled by his embrace of Hobbes's political philosophy, see Steven Anthony Gerencser, *The Skeptic's Oakeshott* (New York, 2000). Gerencser admits, however, that Oakeshott read Hobbes not as the materialist and empirical nominalist he is normally understood to have been.

46. Martin Heidegger, *Hegel's Concept of Experience* (New York, 1970); Hans-Georg Gadamer, *Truth and Method* (New York, 1986), pp. 317ff; and Theodor W. Adorno, "The Experiential Content of Hegel's Philosophy," in *Hegel: Three Studies,* trans. Shierry Weber Nicholsen (Cambridge, Mass., 1993).

47. G. W. F. Hegel, *Phenomenology of Spirit,* trans. A. V. Miller (Oxford, 1977), p. 55 (emphasis in original).

48. Ibid. (emphasis in original).

49. Ibid., p. 56 (emphasis in original).

sidering unassimilated objects as alien to consciousness, Hegel included error in truth in a grand synthesis. "The experience of itself which consciousness goes through can, in accordance with its Notion, comprehend nothing less than the entire system of consciousness, or the entire realm of the truth of Spirit."[50] Or to put it differently, theory and experience are not antithetical terms, but at the deepest level synonyms. Nor is there something beyond experience—no world of abstract Platonic essences or Kantian noumena—that is the target of true *Wissenschaft;* instead, that science must remain a phenomenology, attentive to the manifestations of truth, the immanent logic, in the apparent chaos of historical happenings. To try to distill something eternal from the flux is to abstract false generalities from the particular richness of experience in all its motley variety. Abstraction is precisely the failure to acknowledge the concrete mediations that form the relational totality of the absolute, a meaningful whole that comes into consciousness through philosophical reflection.

Although Oakeshott would grow restless with the absolutist claims of philosophy and come to damn rationality of a certain kind as a dangerous imposition on the living reality of the experienced world, in *Experience and Its Modes* he was a loyal follower—one of a dwindling number—of Bradley's neo-Hegelian Idealism.[51] Steering between empirical and rationalist extremes, he upheld the Hegelian sublation of antinomies—subject and object, thought and being, concept and thing, entity and context—in a complexly mediated concrete universal. Defining philosophical experience as "experience without presupposition, reservation, arrest or modification," Oakeshott argued that "philosophical knowledge is knowledge which carries with it the evidence of its own completion."[52] If his book had any single idea, he suggested, it was the "notion of philosophy as experience without reservation or arrest, experience which is critical throughout, unhindered and

---

50. Ibid.

51. Indeed, as late as his last major work, *On Human Conduct* (Oxford, 1975), which is often seen as his most libertarian and least historicist book, Oakeshott could still praise Hegel's understanding of the varieties of human association grounded in the idea of an ethical community or *Sittlichkeit* (pp. 257–63). For a discussion of his debts to Hegel's *Philosophy of Right* and certain departures from Hegel in this text, see Franco, *The Political Philosophy of Michael Oakeshott,* pp. 206–10. It is worth noting that at the time Oakeshott came under their influence, the British neo-Idealists had been almost entirely eclipsed by the analytic philosophy of Bertrand Russell and G. E. Moore, the anti-German feeling unleashed by the First World War, and the decline of religious belief during the interwar era among intellectuals. It is not surprising that *Experience and Its Modes* sold very poorly and was indifferently reviewed, with certain exceptions such as R. G. Collingwood.

52. Oakeshott, *Experience and Its Modes,* p. 2.

undistracted by what is subsidiary, partial or abstract."[53] Acknowledging that the term was "the most difficult to manage" in the entire lexicon of philosophy, Oakeshott followed Hegel in defining "experience" as "the concrete whole which analysis divides into 'experiencing' and 'what is experienced.' Experiencing and what is experienced are, taken separately, meaningless abstractions; they cannot, in fact, be separated. . . . experience is a single whole, within which modifications may be distinguished, but which admits of no final or absolute division; and . . . experience everywhere, not merely is inseparable from thought, but is itself a form of thought."[54] Contrary to the assumption of empiricists, sensation inherently involves judgment, and thus the idea of immediate "raw" experience is a contradiction in terms. Sensation is merely a stage on the road to genuine experience.

Moreover, "no experience can escape the despotism of significance,"[55] and truth is "correlative to experience. It is the world of experience itself in so far as that world is satisfactory to itself."[56] By the tricky word "satisfactory," Oakeshott meant a coherent condition of holistic unity and absolute completion, in which every element is indispensable and necessary, not one of correspondence to an external reality. Indeed, "what is absolute means here that which is absolved or emancipated from the necessity of finding its significance in relations with what is outside itself. It means that which is self-complete, whole, individual, and removed from change."[57] There is thus no need for a Kantian distinction between objects of experience and objects in themselves, nor must one separate ideas and reality, for reality is "a world of ideas; it is experience and nothing save experience."[58] Hegel was right in claiming that reality is "what we are obliged to think; and since to think is to experience, and to experience is to experience meaning, the real is always what has meaning, or is rational."[59]

Although experience is one and unified, it is possible to arrest its flow and abstract out more limited modes, which are nonetheless not truly separate from the whole, but only the whole seen from a partial vantage point. Such modes were "homogeneous but abstract worlds of ideas." Oakeshott singled out Historical (experience understood *sub specie praeteritorum*), Scientific (ex-

53. Ibid., p. 3.
54. Ibid., pp. 9–10.
55. Ibid., p. 26.
56. Ibid., p. 28.
57. Ibid., p. 47.
58. Ibid., p. 57.
59. Ibid., p. 58.

perience understood *sub specie quantitatus*), and Practical (experience understood *sub specie voluntatis*) for detailed exploration in the book, and mentioned others such as Ethical. Aesthetic and Religious he saw merely as variants of Practical. However understood, all the isolated modes "must be avoided or overcome if experience is to realize its purpose."[60]

This is not the place to provide a detailed account of the ways in which Oakeshott characterized the distinct modes of experience or betrayed a certain nostalgia for the time before they were differentiated, but it is worth noting that he had no expectation of restoring a lost wholeness by practical action.[61] Although there are surprising similarities between his lament and that of leftists like Benjamin and Adorno about the fragmentation and atrophy of experience, he held out no real hope for a meaningful alternative. Indeed, by radically distinguishing practical experience from the larger category of the philosophical, Oakeshott resisted the Marxist refunctioning of the Hegelian legacy, classically expressed in the famous Eleventh Thesis on Feuerbach, as well as the pragmatist activism of a Dewey. Arguing against the possibility of moving from the *vita contemplativa* to the *vita activa,* he cautioned:

To turn philosophy into a way of life is at once to have abandoned life and philosophy. Philosophy is not the enhancement of life, it is the denial of life. We must conclude, then, that all attempts whatever to find some practical justification for philosophical thought and the pursuit of philosophical truth, all attempts to replace life with philosophy by subjecting life to the criticism of philosophy, must be set on one side as misguided.[62]

There is thus none of the celebration of robust "life," characteristic of the *Lebensphilosophie* reading of experience, in Oakeshott. He even went so far as to wonder whether there might be something "decadent, something even depraved, in an attempt to achieve a completely coherent world of experience," which is "so difficult and dubious an undertaking, leading us so far aside from the ways of ordinary thought, that those may be pardoned who prefer the embraces of abstraction."[63]

Experience and Its Modes is an oddly assertive book, inviting the charge of

60. Ibid., p. 85.

61. "My intention," he writes, "is not merely to discredit them, much less to attempt to abolish them, but to consider them from the standpoint of philosophy." Ibid., p. 84. In so arguing, however, Oakeshott moved away from Hegel, who would have seen the modes as dialectical moments in a process leading to the full complexity of the realized whole.

62. Ibid., p. 355.

63. Ibid., p. 356.

one early reviewer that Oakeshott's "primary affirmations are left undeveloped. The inseparability of reality from experience needs to be safeguarded *argumentatively* from solipsism."[64] Nor does it provide much guidance for a politics, conservative or otherwise. Although there were intimations of his position on political questions in the 1930s, it was perhaps not until after the Second World War and the victory of the activist Labour Party had introduced the welfare state to Britain that Oakeshott emerged as a vigorous critic of what in his most celebrated essay, published in 1947, he called "rationalism in politics."[65] Despite the title, the residues of his earlier neo-Hegelian defense of experience are still palpable. For Oakeshott's target was not reason per se, but an impoverished version of it, which he identified entirely with its calculating, technical dimension, producing what he damned as "the assimilation of politics to engineering."[66] Attacking Bacon and Descartes for instigating a pernicious faith in the "sovereignty of technique,"[67] he expressed a lament about the domination of the world by instrumental reason that reproduced many of the arguments being made at precisely the same time from the opposite end of the political spectrum by Max Horkheimer and Adorno in *Dialectic of Enlightenment* and *Eclipse of Reason,* and later rehearsed by Alexander Kluge and Oskar Negt.[68] Like the neo-Hegelians of the Left, he hoped to rescue a viable notion of authentic experience, which would not be the abjected "other" of reason, but an integral expression of it. The (instrumental) rationalist in politics, Oakeshott argued, is a gnostic who does not neglect experience but often appears to do so because he insists

> always upon it being his own experience (wanting to begin everything *de novo*), and because of the rapidity with which he reduces the tangle and variety of experience to a set of principles which he will then attack or defend only on ra-

64. T. E. Jessop, review of *Experience and Its Modes,* in *Philosophy* 9 (1934), p. 358.

65. Oakeshott, "Rationalism and Politics," in *Rationalism in Politics and Other Essays* (London, 1962). As early as "The New Bentham" published in the inaugural issue of *Scrutiny* 1 (1932–33), Oakeshott attacked what he called *philosophisme,* the imposition of intellectual solutions on political problems.

66. Oakeshott, "Rationalism in Politics," p. 5.

67. Ibid., p. 16. The tradition they created, Oakeshott claimed, included the American colonists who had rebelled against the English crown. Unaware of what the later research cited above has shown, he contended that "long before the Revolution, then, the disposition of mind of the American colonists, the prevailing intellectual character and habit of politics, were rationalistic" (p. 27). The looseness of Oakeshott's definition of rationalism is shown by his further inclusion of the Nazis in the rationalist camp (p. 32).

68. What the critics of the Left added, of course, was a critique of the impoverishment of experience produced by capitalist commodification, which went beyond instrumental rationality and abstract theory.

tional grounds. He has no sense of the cumulation of experience, only of the readiness of experience when it has been converted into a formula: the past is significant to him only as an encumbrance. He has none of that *negative capability* (which Keats attributed to Shakespeare), the power of accepting the mysteries and uncertainties of experience without any irritable search for order and distinctness, only the capability of subjugating experience.[69]

Oakeshott's version of an expanded notion of reason, unlike that of the neo-Hegelians of the Left, underplayed the element of critique in favor of passive acceptance of what had already transpired. The instrumental rationalist's intellectual ambition, he charged, was "not so much to share the experience of the race as to be demonstrably a self-made man. And this gives to his intellectual and practical activities an almost preternatural deliberateness and self-consciousness, depriving them of any element of passivity, removing from them all sense of rhythm and continuity and dissolving them into a succession of climacterics, each to be surmounted by a *tour de raison.*"[70] Against this calculative, abstractive rationality, based on an a priori standard of value, Oakeshott posited a non-instrumental alternative that has earned a comparison with the ancient Greek concept of *phronesis,* Gilbert Ryle's notion of "knowing how," and Michael Polanyi's "tacit knowledge."[71] In his 1950 essay "Rational Conduct," Oakeshott stressed its inherence in what he called an "idiom of activity," or "the knowledge of how to behave appropriately in the circumstances."[72] More a dialogic conversation than a monologic exercise in logical deduction, reason involves a give-and-take among members of a community. Whether it be science or politics, the rationality involved must be grounded in *"faithfulness to the knowledge we have of how to conduct the specific activity we are engaged in."*[73] Reason, therefore, is less critical than affirmative; it expresses harmony with the social context in which the activity is embedded. Unlike a Kantian "ought," straining to follow a moral law that it can never hope to obey completely, it emerges from a concrete community with unreflectively embodied ethical norms (Hegel's *Sittlichkeit*).[74] Rationality, Oakeshott thus concluded, "is the certificate we give

69. Oakeshott, "Rationalism in Politics," p. 2.
70. Ibid., pp. 2–3.
71. Franco, *The Political Philosophy of Michael Oakeshott,* p. 110.
72. Oakeshott, "Rational Conduct," in *Rationalism in Politics,* p. 101.
73. Ibid., pp. 101–2 (emphasis in original).
74. In his 1948 essay "The Tower of Babel," in *Rationalism in Politics,* Oakeshott attacks the predominance of moral idealism in the present, arguing for a return to a greater emphasis on moral habit (although he does not entirely advocate moving from one extreme to the other).

to any conduct which can maintain a place in the flow of sympathy, the coherence of activity, which composes a way of life."[75]

But how to restore this condition Oakeshott could not say, for the triumph of technological rationality was ultimately the outcome of the irreversible democratization of the political sphere. In one of his most unabashedly elitist statements, Oakeshott asserted that "the politics of Rationalism are the politics of the politically inexperienced, and . . . the outstanding characteristic of European politics in the last four centuries is that they have suffered the incursion of at least three types of political inexperience—that of the new ruler, of the new ruling class, and of the new political society—to say nothing of the incursion of a new sex, lately provided for by Mr. Shaw."[76]

RAYMOND WILLIAMS AND THE MARXIST HUMANIST VERSION OF EXPERIENCE

And yet, despite such blatantly reactionary outbursts, many of Oakeshott's positions could be given a more progressive twist. Experience and reason imbricated together in a coherent and meaningful way of life, an ethical community rather than abstract moral idealism, subjects and objects no longer dualistically opposed, scientism rejected in the name of a more humanist alternative—we hear in all this clear anticipations of the idiom of the British Marxist humanists who were so eager to valorize the concept of experience in their own work in the 1960s and 1970s. It is not surprising therefore to find a positive review of *Rationalism in Politics* in *New Left Review*, where Oakeshott's stress on concrete historical tradition is praised as "in fact very close to the foundation of any serious socialist thinking."[77] And in 1982, Fred Inglis, the admiring historian of the "radical earnestness" of English social theory, could claim that "there has been no really impressive social theorizing by English conservatives since Michael Oakeshott's best work in *Experience and its Modes* and *Rationalism in Politics*."[78] Although it would be imprudent to claim any direct influence of Oakeshott on British Marxist humanism on the question of experience or any other, it is nonetheless telling that several of his earliest efforts appeared in the critical journal, published from 1932 to 1953, that has been widely acknowledged as a powerful stimu-

75. Oakeshott, "Rational Conduct," p. 109.
76. Ibid., p. 23.
77. Colin Falck, "Romanticism in Politics," *New Left Review* 18 (January–February 1963), p. 68.
78. Fred Inglis, *Radical Earnestness: English Social Theory, 1880–1980* (Oxford 1982), p. 175.

lus to the leftist appropriation of themes traditionally developed in the conservative camp: F. R. Leavis's *Scrutiny*.[79] In any account of that appropriation, the dominating school of critical theory that emerged around Leavis and his journal would play a key role. Leavis was himself fond of reading literature as the record of "concrete human experience" and could typically claim that "what we diagnose in expression, as inadequacy in the use of words, goes back to an inadequacy behind the words, an inadequacy of experience."[80] One expression of that inadequacy was the isolation of modes of experience, which we have seen also deplored by Oakeshott. In particular, Leavis bemoaned the differentiation of aesthetic experience from morality, characteristic of the new dandyism he saw around him in 1920s Britain.[81] Eschewing abstract systems, celebrating the plenitudinous diversity of "life," evoking organic metaphors of humanist wholeness, and championing vernacular as opposed to classicist or scientific language, Leavis produced a criticism that Francis Mulhern describes as rooted in "recognition and, where appropriate, affirmation of what was immanent in the concrete literary word. This criticism was, therefore, a form of intuitionism: specifically, it consisted in *the intuition of moral values in literary experience*."[82] It was the critic's role, which Leavis assigned to a small elite of like-minded souls, to preserve that precious legacy, for "upon this minority depends our power of profiting by the finest human experience of the past; they keep alive the subtlest and most perishable parts of tradition."[83]

Although D. H. Lawrence rather than Marx was Leavis's touchstone, his influence on such British Marxists as Raymond Williams, his successor in the Cambridge literature faculty, has been widely remarked.[84] For despite

79. For a history published with the imprimatur of the *New Left Review*, see Francis Mulhern, *The Moment of 'Scrutiny'* (London, 1979). It should be noted that Oakeshott was never an intimate member of the Leavis circle at Cambridge; indeed, he claimed never to have actually met Leavis. Grant, *Oakeshott*, p. 14. Still, there are many convergences in their worldviews. Although he rarely wrote on literature, see Oakeshott's 1962 essay "The Voice of Poetry in the Conversation of Mankind" in *Radicalism in Politics*. Other conservatives, such as Martin Turnell, found a home in *Scrutiny*, although the journal's politics were generally to the Left.

80. F. R. Leavis, *The Common Pursuit* (Harmondsworth, 1976), p. 194; "The Literary Mind," *Scrutiny* I, no. I (May 1932), p. 22.

81. For an account of the new dandyism and reaction to it, see Martin Green, *Children of the Sun: A Narrative of "Decadence" in England after 1918* (New York, 1976).

82. Mulhern, *The Moment of 'Scrutiny*,' p. 171 (emphasis in original).

83. F. R Leavis, *Civilization and Minority Culture* (Cambridge, 1930), p. 4.

84. For example, in Fred Inglis, *Raymond Williams* (London, 1995), chapter 8; and Dennis Dworkin, *Cultural Marxism in Postwar Britain* (Durham, N.C., 1997). According to the latter, Leavis was important as well for Richard Hoggart, whose *Uses of Literacy* of 1957 "extended *Scrutiny*'s critical approach. He

Leavis's anti-materialism, cultural pessimism, nostalgia for rural communities, and distrust of the redemptive mission of the working class, he provided these critics an appreciation, more felt than rigorously defended, of the centrality of something called "lived experience" as a vital category in the struggle against the depredations of the modern world. He also gave them a way to refocus their efforts in the wake of the disillusionment many felt with orthodox dialectical materialism and the Communist Party after the events of 1956 in Eastern Europe, which revealed the cost of imposing abstract theoretical categories on the real world. And by alerting them to the importance of the category of concrete experience—along with "culture," "tradition," "education," "community," and "communication"—Leavis allowed them to reconnect with native traditions of popular resistance to political oppression and the tyranny of the market that needed no inspiration from foreign theory, as well as with their intellectual forerunners on both ends of the political spectrum.

The leftist appropriation of a politics of experience, akin to that we have been describing on the right, was most explicit in two of the founding texts of British Marxist humanism, Williams's *Culture and Society* of 1958 and Thompson's *The Making of the English Working Class* of 1963.[85] The former has been called, with reference to Leavis's celebrated history of the novel, "in many ways a socialist *Great Tradition.*"[86] In it, Williams sought to salvage

---

used literary-critical methods to understand the meaning of cultural experience, reading lived experience as if it were a text" (p. 85). For Williams's own account of his debt to Leavis, see the interviews in Williams, *Politics and Letters: Interviews with New Left Review* (London, 1979); and his "Seeing a Man Running," in Denys Thompson, ed., *The Leavises: Recollections and Impressions* (Cambridge, 1984). For an overview of the lasting impact of Leavis, see Geoffrey H. Hartman, *Minor Prophecies: The Literary Essay in the Culture Wars* (Cambridge, Mass., 1991), chapter 5. One major difference between Leavis and Williams, as Francis Mulhern points out in *Culture/Metaculture* (London, 2000), is that for Leavis "authoritative experience was an exclusive universal. Williams could not, in elementary logic, appeal to 'experience' in this sense. His analysis of creativity was radically anti-essentialist, postulating experience as a historical formation of subjectivity, variable between and within societies, not a perceptual constant" (p. 90).

85. For a general appraisal of their use of the term, see Michael Pickering, *History, Experience and Cultural Studies* (New York, 1997), chapter 6. For general accounts of their careers and legacy, see Bryan D. Palmer, *The Making of E. P. Thompson: Marxism, Humanism, and History* (Toronto, 1981); Jan Gorak, *The Alien Mind of Raymond Williams* (Columbia, Mo., 1988); Alan O'Connor, *Raymond Williams: Writing, Culture, Politics* (Oxford, 1989); Terry Eagleton, ed., *Raymond Williams: Critical Perspectives* (Oxford, 1989); Harvey J. Kaye and Keith McClelland, eds., *E. P. Thompson: Critical Perspectives* (Cambridge, 1990); Nick Stevenson, *Culture, Ideology and Socialism: Raymond Williams and E. P. Thompson* (Aldershot, 1995); Christopher Prendergast, ed., *Cultural Materialism: Essays on Raymond Williams* (Minneapolis, 1995); Jeff Wallace, Rod Jones, and Sophie Nield, eds., *Raymond Williams Now* (New York, 1997); and John Higgins, *Raymond Williams: Literature, Marxism and Cultural Materialism* (London, 1999).

86. Ioan Davies, *Cultural Studies and Beyond: Fragments of Empire* (London, 1995), p. 8.

for the Left a hitherto underappreciated mode of thinking about culture that extended, *inter alia,* from Edmund Burke, William Cobbett, and Samuel Taylor Coleridge through the Romantics, John Stuart Mill, Matthew Arnold, Thomas Carlyle, and Cardinal Newman up to twentieth-century figures like T. S. Eliot, Lawrence, and Leavis. Significantly, one of Williams's opening gambits was to gloss Arnold's celebrated praise of Burke, "Almost alone in England, he brings thought to bear upon politics, he saturates politics with thought," in the following way:

> It is not "thought" in the common opposition to "feeling"; it is rather a special immediacy of experience, which works itself out, in depth, to a particular embodiment of ideas that become, in themselves, the whole man. The correctness of these ideas is not at first in question; and their truth is not, at first to be assessed by their usefulness in historical understanding or in political insight. Burke's writing is an articulated experience, and as such it has a validity which can survive even the demolition of its general conclusions. It is not that the eloquence survives where the cause has failed; the eloquence, if it were merely the veneer of a cause, would now be worthless. What survives is an experience, a particular kind of learning; the writing is important only to the extent that it communicates this. It is, finally, a personal experience become a landmark.[87]

What was the personal experience that was so transformed? For Williams, Burke's "doctrines rest on an experience of stability, containing imperfections, but not essentially threatened. As the current of change swelled, the affirmation became a desperate defense."[88] Burke's plea for the preservation of an organic society against the corrosive power of capitalist industrialism and laissez-faire individualism, Williams noted, was soon reduced by the Romantics and later by John Ruskin and Walter Pater to a defense of the special value of art. "The obstruction of a certain kind of experience," he lamented,

> was simplified to the obstruction of poetry, which was then identified with it and even made to stand for it as a whole. Under pressure, art became a symbolic abstraction for a whole range of human experience: a valuable abstraction, because indeed great art has this ultimate power; yet an abstraction nonetheless, because a general social activity was forced into the status of department or province, and actual works of art were in part converted into a self-pleading ideology.[89]

87. Raymond Williams, *Culture and Society, 1780–1950* (New York, 1958), p. 5.
88. Ibid, pp. 10–11.
89. Ibid., p. 47.

Here hostility to the abstraction of aesthetic experience from a more robust alternative that expresses culture as a whole way of life, a hostility worthy of Oakeshott, is readily apparent. Against the elite notion of high culture, Williams sought to mobilize its broader anthropological meaning in a way that matched Oakeshott's neo-Hegelian embrace of *Sittlichkeit*. No less anathema to both thinkers was the isolation of theoretical speculation from lived experience. John Stuart Mill, Williams complained, "is apt to divorce opinions and valuations both from experience and from social reality" and Charles Dickens's *Hard Times* is "an analysis of Industrialism, rather than experience of it."[90] T. E. Hulme's speculations on an essential human nature, he further complained, are "the replacement of one rationalization by another . . . [T]he acceptance of actual experience, commitment to a real situation from which by no effort of abstraction we can escape, is harder than Hulme supposed."[91]

In the twentieth century, however, the differentiation of art from the other spheres of lived experience was beginning to be challenged: "The isolation of aesthetic experience, which had been evident in England between Pater and Clive Bell, and which by the 'twenties had become a kind of orthodoxy, was attacked along several different lines. From Eliot came the re-emphasis of tradition and faith; from Leavis a rediscovery of the breadth of general emphasis which Arnold had given to culture; from the Marxists the application of a new total interpretation of society."[92] Except for the last, however, the idea of culture and the renewal of experience still had the elitist implications of Coleridge's "clerisy" and Arnold's "remnant." Leavis had been wrong, Williams charged, in restricting his hopes to a small minority of sensitive critics, for "in the work of continuity and change, and just because of the elements of disintegration, we cannot make literary experience the sole test, or even the central test. We cannot even, I would argue, put the important stress on the 'minority', for the idea of the conscious minority is itself no more than a defensive symptom, against the general dangers."[93] What is needed to counter it could perhaps be found in George Orwell's work, which Williams praised for vividly recording "the experience of a victim."[94]

90. Ibid., pp. 52 and 93.
91. Ibid., p. 193.
92. Ibid., p. 244.
93. Ibid., p. 261.
94. Ibid., p. 292. Williams's later judgment of Orwell would be less forgiving. See his Modern Masters study *George Orwell* (New York, 1971), and his critical remarks in *Politics and Letters,* pp. 384–92. For a general consideration of his attitude toward Orwell, see David Lloyd and Paul Thomas, *Culture and the State* (New York, 1998), epilogue.

The intimate relationship between "experience" of any kind and "culture" in Williams's account—he argued, for example, that Newman's idea of culture could be derived from a "convinced experience of the divine order"[95]—may have led to a problematic conflation of the two, which seemed to some readers a loss of critical leverage.[96] But his intention was clearly to rescue both terms for the vocabulary of the contemporary Left.

Culture and Society concluded with a call for the rejuvenation of a common culture that would suture the wounds of industrial modernization and restore the possibility of genuine communication based on "an effective community of experience."[97] Although his account paid no sustained attention to the working-class culture whose achievements had been explored and validated by Hoggart in *The Uses of Literacy*, Williams's instincts were democratic, inclusive, and cautiously optimistic. Less individualist than collective, working-class culture, he argued, is "a very remarkable creative achievement."[98] Tacitly drawing on his personal experience as an outsider from Wales, a scholarship boy at the elite institutions of Britain, and a champion of adult education, he urged, in his next major work, "the long revolution," in which the experience of the "masses" would come to be acknowledged as the foundation of a new egalitarian culture.[99] The record of that experience, he contended, was evident in a "structure of feeling," murkily defined as "the particular living result of all the elements in the general organization" of that culture, which can be accessed retrospectively through its arts.[100] It was the task of the radical critic to rescue the vital experience of the past, with all its contradictions and unrealized yearnings, in order to make it avail-

95. Ibid., p. 127.
96. See, for example, Gorak, *The Alien Mind of Raymond Williams*, p. 54. As Catherine Gallagher also points out in "Raymond Williams and Cultural Studies," in Prendergast, *Cultural Materialism,* there is a tension between Williams's hostility to abstraction and his celebration of culture, insofar as the latter inevitably involves essentializing tendencies through its processes of signification. For an earlier critique of the culture concept that makes a similar point, which Williams seems not to have known, see Theodor W. Adorno, "Cultural Criticism and Society," *Prisms,* trans. Samuel and Shierry Weber (London, 1967).
97. Williams, *Culture and Society,* p. 317.
98. Ibid., p. 327.
99. Raymond Williams, *The Long Revolution* (London, 1961). According to Inglis, "his subject was always the connection between social experience, especially his own, and imaginative grasp" (*Raymond Williams,* p. 248). The thinly fictionalized accounts of his life in such novels as *Border Country* (1960) and *Second Generation* (1964) were one place in which Williams approached it. For discussions, see Dennis L. Dworkin and Leslie G. Roman, eds., *Views Beyond the Border Country: Raymond Williams and Cultural Politics* (New York, 1993); and Tony Pickney, *Raymond Williams* (Bridgend, Mid Glamorgan, 1991). The latter argues that he is best understood as a postmodernist novelist.
100. Williams, *The Long Revolution,* p. 48.

able for contemporary emancipatory purposes. However repressed and muffled, however resistant to direct articulation, such experiences could be the stuff of a potential counter-history to the dominant narrative of bour-, geois triumphalism.[101]

E. P. THOMPSON AND HISTORY FROM BELOW

E. P. Thompson, writing from a longer-standing and more forthright commitment to Marxism, responded to Williams in a major review in 1961 with sharp criticism of his concept of culture as a "whole way of life." Instead, he advocated a "whole way of struggle," which registered the exploitation and power inequalities elided by the inherently conservative tradition of cultural holism. He also lamented Williams's indifference to Marx (as opposed to second-rate English Marxists like Christopher Caudwell), as well as his scant account of actual working-class life and ideas. Where, he wondered, was the confrontational, even violent, dimension of revolution in "the long revolution"? Despite these qualms, Thompson had no hesitation in validating the central role that experience played in Williams's account.[102]

Thompson's own project to recover the lost experience of those forgotten by history, of what would come to be called "history from below," was most powerfully expressed two years later in his monumental *The Making of the English Working Class*.[103] In the stirring, often-quoted words from its preface,

I am seeking to rescue the poor stockinger, the Luddite cropper, the "obsolete" hand-loom weaver, the "utopian" artisan, and even the deluded follower of

---

101. For a discussion of Williams's contribution to the idea of counter-history, which animated the New Historicist movement in literary criticism, see Catherine Gallagher and Stephen Greenblatt, *Practicing New Historicism* (Chicago, 2000), pp. 60–66. Gallagher and Greenblatt distinguish his work from Thompson's because of his greater sensitivity to the occluded, hidden, and repressed quality of experience.

102. E. P. Thompson, "The Long Revolution," *New Left Review* 9 (May–June 1961); and "The Long Revolution II," *New Left Review* 10 (July–August 1961). For Thompson's later recollection of this review and his deep disagreements with Williams's "culturalism," see "The Politics of Theory," in Raphael Samuel, ed., *People's History and Socialist Theory* (London, 1981), pp. 397–98.

103. E. P. Thompson, *The Making of the English Working Class* (New York, 1966). The most important locus for work on "history from below" and everyday life was the Ruskin College, Oxford, History Workshop, founded in 1967, which produced the journal *History Workshop*. Composed of worker-historians and socialist scholars, the workshop drew on Thompson, as well as on a vigorous tradition of Marxist historiography in Britain that included Christopher Hill, Rodney Hilton, and Maurice Dobb. See the discussion in Dworkin, *Cultural Marxism in Postwar Britain,* chap. 5; and Raphael Samuel, "On the Methods of History Workshop: A Reply," *History Workshop* 9 (Spring 1980).

Joanna Southcott from the enormous condescension of posterity. Their crafts and traditions may have been dying. Their hostility to the new industrialism may have been backward-looking. Their communitarian ideals may have been foolhardy. But they lived through these times of acute social disturbance, and we did not. Their aspirations were valid in terms of their own experience; and, if they were casualties of history, they remain, condemned in their own lives, as casualties.[104]

Against a sterile Marxism that reduced class to a rigid structure or thing and class-consciousness to its automatic reflection, Thompson saw it as a dynamic, historical relationship that was always embodied in living, struggling people. "The class experience," he insisted, "is largely determined by the productive relationship into which men are born—or enter involuntarily. Class-consciousness is the way in which these experiences are handled in cultural terms: embodied in traditions, value-systems, ideas and institutional forms. If the experience appears as determined, class-consciousness does not."[105] The latter, rather than just happening, has to be made, a making that expressed the agency of those whose consciousness is raised as a result. Although Thompson acknowledged the loss of an earlier way of life, which he called the "moral economy" of pre-industrial England, and recognized the "terrible defeats of 1834–1835" ending the heroic phase of that self-fashioning, his narrative was a paean to the legacy of those who had achieved the class consciousness that their collective experience of oppression and struggle had so painfully nurtured.

The British Marxist elevation of "experience" to a normative standard, both as a riposte to abstract theory and a fund of valuable lessons from the past, would not, however, survive intact in the tumultuous decade after *The Making of the English Working Class*. Although one can find continued appeals to it in, say, the novels and essays of John Berger, who explored its role in peasant villages, its self-evident status came under increased critical scrutiny.[106] As the leading role of the labor movement in radical politics began to be challenged by new groups—students, women, ethnic, and sexual minorities— who complicated any notion of a unified "whole way of life," so too the humanist assumptions of Williams, Thompson, and their peers came under pressure from the incorporation of theoretical currents from across the

104. Thompson, *The Making of the English Working Class*, pp. 12–13.
105. Ibid., p. 10.
106. For a discussion of its continued role in Berger's work, see Bruce Robbins, "Feeling Global: John Berger and Experience," *Boundary 2*, 11, nos. 1 and 2 (Fall/Winter 1982/83).

waters.[107] Neatly encapsulated in the bitter leadership struggle within the editorial board of *New Left Review*, which saw Perry Anderson and his colleagues Tom Nairn and Robin Blackburn succeed the older generation around Thompson and John Saville in 1963, the transformation opened the way for the reception of what Maurice Merleau-Ponty had dubbed "Western Marxism."[108]

Although Antonio Gramsci, Georg Lukács, Jean-Paul Sartre, Ernst Bloch, Lucien Goldmann, Galvano Della Volpe, and the members of the Frankfurt School played a role in that reception, it was the writings of Louis Althusser and what became known as "structuralist Marxism" that had the most impact on the British Marxist debate over experience. Duly acknowledged was Althusser's debt to the anti-empiricist tradition of the French philosophy of science associated with Gaston Bachelard and Georges Canguilhem, with its "rectification of the philosophical category of *experience* by a correct appreciation of the function of *instruments* in the production of scientific concepts."[109] So too was his anti-humanist hostility to the ideology of wholeness, which subtended any belief in the integral subject of experience, a position that he derived in part from Lacanian psychoanalysis.[110] But it was perhaps Althusser's insistence that experience could not be set apart from the invasive mediations of the more fundamental structures of the capitalist mode of production that had the greatest impact. In his 1966 "A Letter on Art," Althusser had specifically cautioned that

> when we speak of ideology we should know that ideology slides into all human activity, that it is identical with the "lived" experience of human existence

107. It should not be forgotten, however, that questions were already being raised within the British Left by figures such as Stuart Hall, who contended that capitalist commodification had invaded the working-class experience extolled by Hoggart. For a discussion of the replacement of Hoggart by Hall as the leading figure of the Centre for Contemporary Cultural Studies in the early 1960s, see Mulhern, *Culture/Metaculture*, pp. 93–131.

108. For my own attempt to trace its history, see *Marxism and Totality: The Adventures of a Concept from Lukács to Habermas* (Berkeley, 1984). For a discussion of the battle over the direction of the *New Left Review* from Thompson's perspective, see his 1973 "An Open Letter to Leszek Kolakowski" in *The Poverty of Theory and Other Essays* (New York, 1978). For Anderson's version, see *Arguments within English Marxism*, chapter 5.

109. Dominique Lecourt, *Marxism and Epistemology: Bachelard, Canguilhem and Foucault*, trans. Ben Brewster (London, 1975), p. 137 (emphasis in original). This translation was published in the New Left Editions series.

110. Althusser's relationship with Lacan was not always a smooth one, but the translation of his 1964 essay "Freud and Lacan" in the *New Left Review* in 1969 had a strong impact on the British reception of his ideas. Lacan's own, by no means entirely hostile thoughts on experience (the French *expérience* also means "experiment") have been discussed by François Regnault, "Lacan and Experience," in Alexandre Leupin, ed., *Lacan and the Human Sciences* (Lincoln, Neb., 1991).

itself: that is why the form in which we are "made to see" ideology in great novels has as its content the "lived" experience of individuals. This "lived" experience is not a *given,* given by a pure "reality," but the spontaneous "lived experience" of ideology in its peculiar relationship to the real . . . the "lived experience" is also an object of science.[111]

Genuine knowledge required a radical rupture with the language of experiential immediacy. Although directed against existentialist Marxists in France like Sartre, these were words that could easily be turned against Left Leavisites and Marxist humanists in Britain as well, and they soon were.

THE QUARREL OVER EXPERIENCE IN BRITISH MARXISM

"Experience," in fact, became a central bone of contention between Williams, Thompson, and their generation, on the one hand, and the new, theoretically ambitious, politically militant—mostly Trotskyist—editorial board of *New Left Review,* on the other. The opening salvo came in 1976 from Williams's former student Terry Eagleton, in an essay that served as the basis for a chapter in his widely read *Criticism and Ideology.*[112] With a fervor that seemed to many patricidal in origin, Eagleton mercilessly blasted the romantic populism, gradualist reformism, and sentimental humanism that led his teacher to an uncritical embrace of Leavis's fetish of literary culture, indeed of the problematic concept of culture itself. *Scrutiny,* Eagleton insisted, had been little more than a petit-bourgeois ideological formation, whose "naive sensuous empiricism, epitomized in the act of 'practical criticism,' was a 'progressive' testing of aesthetic categories against the immediacies of lived experience. . . . To combat 'ideology,' *Scrutiny* pointed to 'experience'—as though that, precisely, were not ideology's homeland."[113] The Left-Leavisism of *Culture and Society* meant that it was still beholden more to Lawrence than Marx, closer to the anti-scientism of Lukács and the Frankfurt School than to genuine historical materialism. Ultimately, Eagleton concluded, behind it all was a conservative pedigree: "Unless reasoning springs organically from

111. Louis Althusser, *Lenin and Philosophy and Other Essays,* trans. Ben Brewster (London, 1971), p. 223. For a discussion of Althusser's understanding of experience, see Ted Benton, *The Rise and Fall of Structural Marxism: Althusser and His Influence* (London, 1984), pp. 203–9.

112. Terry Eagleton, "Raymond Williams—An Appraisal," *New Left Review* 95 (January–February 1976). For an account of the turmoil caused by this essay, see Inglis, *Raymond Williams,* pp. 249–51.

113. Eagleton, *Criticism and Ideology,* p. 15.

lived experience, it is likely to be suspect: this vein of commonplace English empiricism runs throughout all of Williams' work, inherited from *Scrutiny*, and accounting among other things for his admiration for David Hume."[114] The latter accusation stemmed from a laudatory essay of 1964 in which Williams had praised Hume's grounding of reason on experience, affirmative rather than cynical skepticism, social utilitarianism, and organic understanding of the link between morality and the social process.[115]

Even when Williams struggled to accommodate Western Marxist ideas, as in his subsequent adoption of Gramsci's notion of hegemony, his fetish of experience kept getting in the way. "It is symptomatic of Williams' own method," Eagleton charged, "that he should point to the *experiential* force of hegemony as an index of its structural primacy. Hegemony is deeply, pervasively lived, and so cannot be superstructural since the superstructural is the 'secondary': i.e. the 'weakly experienced'. It goes logically with this confusion that his concept of hegemony is itself a structurally undifferentiated one."[116]

These accusations were based on Eagleton's attempt to produce a "science of the text," which expressed a moment of Marxist theoretical hubris that he himself ultimately came to regret.[117] He was so hostile to any concept of experience that even when he wrote an account of Walter Benjamin's legacy a few years later, he chose to minimize the importance of the concept in the German critic's work.[118] But for a decade or so his animus was typical of the British Althusserian assault on Marxist humanism. Thus even when a nuanced attempt to defend Williams against Eagleton's assault was made in *New Left Review* by Anthony Barnett in 1976, on the question of experience he conceded as much as he defended. Barnett began by claiming that unlike Leavis, Williams understood experience not as "unalterable or metaphysical value—a single paradigmatic criterion of subjective judgment. It

---

114. Ibid., p. 32.

115. Raymond Williams, "David Hume: Reasoning and Experience," in Hugh Sykes Davies and George Watson, eds., *The English Mind: Studies in the English Moralists Presented to Basil Willey* (Cambridge, 1964). "His whole enterprise," Williams concluded, "can be seen as an attempt to restore the identity of social and personal virtues, at a time when the tensions of change had forced and were forcing them apart. That he failed was inevitable; he could only succeed, in his own clear sight, by an unconscious limitation of what was relevant social experience. Yet the enterprise, like Burke's enterprise in the emphasis on community, passed into the stream of thought, beyond its local failure" (p. 144).

116. Eagleton, *Criticism and Ideology*, p. 42.

117. For Eagleton's second thoughts on the legacy of Althusserianism, whose alternatives to Marxist humanism, he admitted, "turned out to be gravely and sometimes equally at fault," see his *Against the Grain: Essays 1975–1985* (London, 1986), p. 3. An apology for the "acerbic and ungenerous" tone of his attack on Williams was made in Eagleton's introduction to *Raymond Williams: Critical Perspectives*, pp. 10–11.

118. Terry Eagleton, *Walter Benjamin; or, Towards a Revolutionary Criticism* (London, 1981), p. 35.

too is subject to history—he refers to the 'sense of an experience and ways of *changing* it' (my emphasis). Williams' development of the concept 'structure of feeling' is designed exactly to restore the category of experience to the world, as a part of its mutable and various social history."[119] But then in a lengthy footnote, Barnett allowed that despite his intention to be historical and materialist,

> Williams mistakenly gave "experience" a privileged role as the determining organizer of knowledge. His insistence on the "living" obstructs Williams's efforts to construct an overall social theory, simply because he has regarded experience as *the* repository of truth. Obviously experience *can be* a vital instrument of discovery, especially the active experience of practice. But however much experience may be a valid check on theory, the laws of motion of capitalism as a global system obviously can only be uncovered by arguments of the abstract kind. The consequences of these laws of motion will be experienced, but the reality of the process behind such efforts cannot be uncovered by experience.[120]

Barnett then joined with two other *New Left Review* editors, Perry Anderson and Francis Mulhern, in a series of wide-ranging and searching interviews with Williams conducted in 1977 and 1978, in which the issue of experience was once again a central focus.[121] In the interim, Williams had published *Marxism and Literature,* in which he made a valiant but not fully successful effort to incorporate the lessons of Western Marxist literary theory.[122] Although he sought to explicate some of his less self-evident concepts, such as "structure of feeling," Williams did not put much pressure on the concept of experience, which was tellingly absent from the first edition of his lexicon *Keywords,* published in 1976.[123] His *New Left Review* interlocutors were not eager, however, to let him off the hook.

119. Anthony Barnett, "Raymond Williams and Marxism: A Rejoinder to Terry Eagleton," *New Left Review* 99 (September–October 1976), p. 62.

120. Ibid.

121. Williams, *Politics and Letters.* For an account of their composition, see Inglis, *Raymond Williams,* chapter 11.

122. Raymond Williams, *Marxism and Literature* (Oxford, 1977). It should be noted that as early as his 1971 memorial essay on Lucien Goldmann, reprinted in *Problems in Materialism and Culture* (London, 1980), Williams was beginning to explore continental Marxist theory. For a consideration of his response to it as a whole, see Michael Moriarty, "'The Longest Cultural Journey': Raymond Williams and French Theory," in Prendergast, *Cultural Materialism.*

123. Raymond Williams, *Keywords: A Vocabulary of Culture and Society* (London, 1976); the lacuna was filled in the 1984 second edition.

In the very first interview, which dealt with Williams's boyhood, he was asked to describe his own experience growing up in rural Wales. When he acknowledged that he had had little direct contact with the exploitation underpinning class relations, the conflict between mental and manual labor, or even the deep split between country and city, his interviewers triumphantly responded, "your early experience appears to have been exempt from a whole series of typical conflicts and tensions which most people of your generation would have felt at some point."[124] If Williams's own experience was therefore not a reliable explanation for his mature politics, then what of the concept in general?

To hammer the point home, Anderson, Barnett, and Mulhern pressed Williams on his overly generous reading of figures like Burke and Coleridge in *Culture and Society,* based on the dubious contrast between the truth of ideas and "a deeper and more durable experience that does not necessarily correspond to any kind of ordinary discursive truth." Williams conceded their point by admitting he was the victim of his training as a literary critic, which taught him that "the first duty of the reader was to respond to the articulated experience or instance that the poem represented, which was much more important than the ideas or beliefs that were found in it . . . the hard-learnt procedure of literary judgment was a kind of suspension before experience."[125] Was the idea of a "structure of feeling," they probed, merely a way of continuing Leavis's problematic stress on experience, even if in more objective form? "Yes," Williams admitted, "'experience' was a term I took over from *Scrutiny.*" But he would now want to distinguish between structures of feeling that articulate felt experiences, often encapsulated in a great work of literature, and those that do not. When there is an ideological blockage preventing the oppressed from understanding their situation, "it is very dangerous to presume that an articulate structure of feeling is necessarily equivalent to inarticulate experience."[126]

Although his interviewers granted that such a distinction was valuable, they still faulted his claim in *The Long Revolution* that experience was epistemologically privileged. One major difficulty of this assumption was its tacit nationalist bias, its implication that local knowledge was superior to its comparative counterpart. Williams conceded that an international perspective might be valuable, especially when conventions transgressed national bor-

124. Williams, *Politics and Letters,* p. 35.
125. Ibid., pp. 120–21.
126. Ibid., p. 165.

ders. Unassuaged, his interviewers doggedly returned to what they called the "perplexing" problem of experience:

In writing it is a subjectivist notion of value—of "life." Despite the fact that you have transformed its *Scrutiny* usage, the term does continue to carry something of its intellectual heritage. For your most recent discussion of a structure of feeling defines it as the field of contradiction between a consciously held ideology and emergent experience. The idea of an emergent experience beyond ideology seems to presuppose a kind of pristine contact between the subject and the reality in which this subject is immersed. Doesn't that leave the door sufficiently ajar for a Leavisian notion of "life" or "experience" to return?[127]

No, Williams protested with some exasperation, that's not what he meant at all. "The peculiar location of a structure of feeling is the endless comparison that must occur in the process of consciousness between the articulated and the lived. The lived is only another word, if you like, for experience: but we have to find a word for that level."[128] His interviewers remained unmollified. Identifying Williams's use of the term with Sartre's tainted notion of *l'expérience vécu* in his study of Flaubert, they insisted that a better alternative existed: "In Althusser's work, experience is simply a synonym for illusion. It is ideology in its pure state—the opposite of science, or truth. That is a position he has taken over, more or less unmodified, from Spinoza. . . . In your work up to this point the impression is conveyed that experience on the contrary is the domain of direct truth. . . . This emphasis obviously has a long history: it can be traced back, in fact to Locke. Philosophically, it represents the classical position of European empiricism."[129] Although admitting that Althusser went too far in giving pride of place to concepts alone, they spurned the claim that experience had any epistemological privilege, as shown in the case of a psychological disorder whose experiential surface hid depths of meaning unknown to the subject of the experience. Despite Williams's reformulations of the question, there remained the danger of positing experience as somehow in excess of the concepts that articulate it.

Battered by his interlocutors' relentless critique, Williams conceded that historically they were right: "From the industrial revolution onwards, qualitatively altering a permanent problem, there has developed a type of society which is less and less interpretable from experience—meaning by expe-

127. Ibid., p. 167.
128. Ibid., p. 168.
129. Ibid.

rience a lived contact with the available articulations, including their comparison." But just because of the power of this insidious process, it was necessary to avoid complicity with it: "it is an ideological crisis of just this society, that this inevitable awareness has also led to a privileged dominance of the techniques of rational penetration and a corresponding undervaluation of areas where there is some everyday commerce between the available articulations and the general process that has been termed 'experience.' Experience becomes a forbidden word, whereas what we ought to say about it is that it is a limited word, for there are many kinds of knowledge it will never give us, in any of its ordinary senses."[130]

Finally placated, the *New Left Review* interviewers accepted this balanced answer, even adding one positive use of the term in the socialist tradition of their own, which they associated with Lenin. When one calls a working-class militant "experienced," they acknowledged, it means he has learned from his organizational struggles in the past and therefore is likely to be more effective than a neophyte. However, here too, one needed to be cautious, for "it is also true that fetishization of experience within an organization can become a form of conservatism: experience won today does not necessarily dictate the tactics or strategy of tomorrow—partly because the enemy itself learns from experience."[131]

Williams, for his part, never seems to have lost what his biographer Fred Inglis called "an absolute trust in the truths of his own experience."[132] His final attempt to sort it out conceptually came in the second edition of *Keywords* in 1983, which showed the effects of his dialogue with the *New Left Review*. The entry for "Experience" begins by noting that the older link with experiment has become virtually obsolete in the two main contemporary usages. The first he identified with the conservative appeal to "knowledge gathered from past events, whether by conscious observation or by consideration and reflection,"[133] which he illustrated with a quotation from Burke. This notion of "experience past," based on "lessons" to be learned and experiments to be avoided, Williams then contrasted with "experience present," which he defined as "a particular kind of consciousness, which can in some contexts be distinguished from 'reason' and 'knowledge'."[134] Noting that this version was paramount in religious and aesthetic usages and illustrating it with an

130. Ibid., pp. 171–72.
131. Ibid., p. 172.
132. Inglis, *Raymond Williams*, p. 299.
133. Raymond Williams, *Keywords: A Vocabulary of Culture and Society* (New York, 1984), p. 126.
134. Ibid.

example from T. S. Eliot, Williams noted that it "involves an appeal to the whole consciousness, the whole being, as against reliance on more specialized or more limited states of faculties."[135] Recalling his earlier argument, he then linked it closely with the holistic concept of culture, which meant that experience was more than merely subjective and individual, but now acknowledged that "the stress on wholeness can become a form of exclusion of other nominated partialities."[136] This exclusion was especially likely when religious adepts (for example, the Methodists) turned it into the ground of the most authentic truths. But the exaggerations in this claim, Williams pointed out in tacit response to his Althusserian critics, have led in turn to the opposite argument, no less overdrawn, that experience is merely the effect of social conditions or beliefs.

Still hopeful of avoiding these two extremes, Williams concluded his account by noting that "experience past" includes "those processes of consideration, reflection and analysis which the most extreme use of experience present—an unquestioned authenticity and immediacy—excludes. Similarly, the reduction of experience to material always produced from elsewhere depends on an exclusion of kinds of consideration, reflection and analysis which are not of a consciously separated systematic type. It is then not that such kinds should not be tested, but that in the deepest sense of experience all kinds of evidence and its considerations should be tried."[137]

Williams's growing willingness to explore the limits of experience was not yet apparent in the spirited defense of its importance that exploded on the British scene in 1978: E. P. Thompson's biting and unforgiving polemic against the baleful effects of Althusserianism, "The Poverty of Theory; or, An Orrery of Errors." Thompson's considerable mastery of invective and no less profound capacity for moral indignation were all on display in his attack on "the Aristotle of the new Marxist idealism,"[138] whose political effect would be the restoration of the Stalinism Thompson had been fighting since 1956. Prefaced by epigraphs from two of England's most celebrated defenders of experience, Francis Bacon and William Blake—the latter of whom was to be the admired subject of Thompson's last work—he set out to slay the dragon of structuralist Marxism. Among the very first charges he leveled concerned the issue that, as we have seen, was at the center of the debate: because of Althusser's isolated, academic rather then real-life existence, "he has no category (or way of han-

135. Ibid., p. 127.
136. Ibid., p. 128.
137. Ibid., pp. 128–29.
138. Thompson, *The Poverty of Theory,* p. 4.

dling) 'experience' (or social being's impingement upon social consciousness); hence he falsifies the 'dialogue' with empirical evidence inherent in knowledge-production, and in Marx's own practice, and thereby falls continually into modes of thought designated in the Marxist tradition as 'idealist'."[139] Experience, Thompson insisted, was on the side of a genuine materialism, which knows the resistance of the world to mere ideological mystification. Without recognizing the ways in which evidence interacts with categories and events in history to challenge preconceived formulae, Marxist historiography is doomed to scholasticism. Moreover, it will be unable to take into account the ways in which social consciousness can be altered by those events, for "above all, they continually give rise to *experience*—a category which, however imperfect it may be, is indispensable to the historian, since it comprises the mental and emotional response, whether of an individual or of a social group, to many interrelated events or to many repetitions of the same kind of event."[140]

Challenging the belief that experience is merely a low-level form of knowledge, little better than common sense and always in need of "scientific" explanation, Thompson described such a claim as "a very characteristic delusion of intellectuals, who suppose that ordinary mortals are stupid." Although admitting that the knowledge it produces might only be partial—a farmer may know about the seasons and a sailor the seas, but not the intricacies of royal power or cosmological speculation—it is nonetheless valid and effective within certain limits. But the major point Thompson wanted to hammer home was that experience and intellect were not opposites; "experience arises spontaneously within social being, but it does not arise without thought; it arises because men and women (and not only philosophers) are rational, and they think about what is happening to themselves and their world. . . . experience is *determining* in the sense that it exerts pressure upon existent social consciousness, proposes new questions, and affords much of the material which the more elaborated intellectual exercises are about."[141]

Ironically, Thompson argued, the rigid Althusserian distinction between history and science reveals an unexpected congruence with Oakeshott's claim in *Experience and Its Modes* that the two were entirely different variants of experience and would only produce monsters if joined together.[142] The di-

---

139. Ibid.
140. Ibid., p. 7 (emphasis in original).
141. Ibid., p. 8 (emphasis in original).
142. Ibid., p. 194. Thompson cited p. 168 of Oakeshott's book to make his claim, but ignored the larger argument of *Experience and Its Modes* that at the highest level, philosophical experience included both its historical and scientific modes.

alogue between consciousness and social being is lost in Althusser's rarified account of the production of theoretical knowledge with its contemptuous dismissal of all versions of empiricism. Today it is necessary to attend to this dialogue, because "'Experience'—the experience of Fascism, Stalinism, racism, and of the contradictory phenomenon of working-class 'affluence' within sectors of capitalist economies—is breaking in and demanding that we reconstruct our categories."[143] That reconstruction, to be sure, cannot be solely an intellectual enterprise, "for people do not only experience their own experience as ideas, within thought and its procedures, or (as some theoretical practitioners suppose) as proletarian instinct, etc. They also experience their own experience as *feeling*, and they handle their feelings within their culture, as norms, familial and kinship obligations and reciprocities, as values or (through more elaborated forms) within art or religious beliefs."[144] In short, it is only through experience that "structure is transmuted into process, and the subject re-enters history."[145]

Thompson's brief for the recovery of experience as the fundamental task of the historian, whatever his or her political inclinations, will be more carefully examined in the next chapter. Suffice it to say now that it helped ignite a vigorous debate among practitioners of "history from below" in the pages of *History Workshop,* and occasioned a book-length response by Perry Anderson in 1980.[146] In *Arguments within English Marxism,* Anderson provided a critical appreciation of Thompson's major historical work, not only *The Making of the English Working Class* but also his *William Morris—Romantic to Revolutionary* and *Whigs and Hunters,* as well as an answer to his tirade against Althusserianism. Agreeing that Althusser was wrong to deny that certain kinds of sense perception might well yield valuable knowledge in no need of "scientific" explanation, Anderson nonetheless detected a waffling in Thompson's use of the notion of experience. At times, Thompson located it within subjective consciousness; at others, he saw experience as something between being and consciousness. Citing Oakeshott's reminder that the word

<hr>

143. Ibid., p. 25.
144. Ibid., p. 171.
145. Ibid., p. 170.
146. The most important contributions to the *History Workshop* debate included Richard Johnson, "Edward Thompson, Eugene Genovese, and Socialist-Humanist History," 6 (Autumn 1978); Keith McClelland, "Some Comments on Richard Johnson, 'Edward Thompson, Eugene Genovese, and Socialist-Humanist History'," and Gavin Williams, "In Defense of History," 7 (Spring 1979); Simon Clarke, "Socialist Humanism and the Critique of Economism," and Gregor McClennan, "Richard Johnson and His Critics: Towards a Constructive Debate," 8 (Autumn 1979); and David Selbourne, "On the Methods of the History Workshop," and Raphael Samuel, "History Workshop Methods," 9 (Spring 1980).

was notoriously ambiguous and chiding Thompson—as well as Oakeshott himself—for not heeding this warning to attend to its multiple meanings, Anderson distinguished between two basic acceptations, one neutral ("an occurrence or episode as it is lived by the participants, the subjective texture of objective actions") and the other positive ("a subsequent process of learning from such occurrences, a subjective alteration capable of modifying ensuing objective actions").[147] Thompson, Anderson charged, unconsciously imbued the first of these meanings with all the virtues of the second. Challenging Thompson's examples of farmers and sailors, whose experientially gained knowledge warranted recognition, Anderson asked,

> if we substitute, say, for Thompson's pair the "parishioner" knows his "prayers," the "priest" his "'flock," what conclusion would we arrive at? Is religious experience valid and effective within determined limits?' Obviously not. . . . religious experience, while subjectively *very intense and real,* while enormously *effective* in moving great masses of men and women down the ages to routine duties and exceptional enterprises alike, is not "valid" as knowledge, and never was.[148]

Thompson, Anderson added, also believes that the lessons taught by experience will inevitably be the right ones, whereas there is no historical evidence to bolster this assumption. "Experience as such is a concept *tous azimuts,* which can point in any direction. The self-same events can be lived through by agents who draw diametrically opposite conclusions from them."[149]

Not even when Thompson's second definition—experience as in part an objective dimension of social being—is operative does he really avoid an overly voluntarist account of the working-class's self-fashioning. For in all the nine hundred pages of the book, Anderson charged, there is no serious consideration of the objective, structural conditions that allowed the making to take place. Thompson compounds the problem by generalizing from his account of the English proletariat to those elsewhere, which he assumes will be equally self-made. In sum, what Thompson does is simply to invert Althusser's scientist hostility to experience, going too far in the other direction:

147. Anderson, *Arguments within English Marxism,* p. 26.

148. Ibid., pp. 27–28. It is significant that Anderson's own allegiance to the purely epistemological version of experience is obvious here. The only important issue is whether it provides more valid knowledge than theoretical analysis.

149. Ibid., pp. 28–29.

For Althusser immediate experience is the universe of illusion—Spinoza's *vaga experientia,* which induces only error. Science alone, founded on a work of conceptual transformation, yields knowledge. The incompatibility of this view with any materialist account of physical sensation or practice, as eliminable bases of the natural sciences, is plain. For Thompson, on the other hand, experience is the privileged medium in which consciousness of reality awakens and creative response to it stirs. Index of authenticity and spontaneity, it links being to thought, and checks the flights of theory towards artificiality and unreason. This account, in turn, is irreconcilable with the blinkering from reality and the depth of the disaster which such salient experiences as religious faith or national loyalty have brought upon those in their grasp.[150]

To avoid the extremes represented by each position, Anderson concluded, what is needed "is *conceptual* clarification of the very different senses and forms of 'experience,' and *empirical* study of the respective historical variations encompassed by each."[151]

Thompson's final word on the issue came in a talk he delivered to a tense and tumultuous History Workshop conference in 1979. Responding to his critics—Stuart Hall and Richard Johnson in person, and Anderson in absentia—he grudgingly conceded that his use of "experience" may have led to some confusion. Defining it anew as "exactly what makes the junction between culture and not-culture, lying half within social being, half within social consciousness,"[152] Thompson protested the charge that he was a "culturalist" Marxist, a tendency he had already criticized in his early review of Williams's *Culture and Society.* To clarify his position, he proposed a distinction between what he called "experience I," which he identified with "lived experience" and "experience II," which was "perceived experience." It was the latter, he argued, which preoccupied many contemporary epistemologists and sociologists, who were then able to show that it was already permeated by ideological mediations.

But, he concluded, "historians within the Marxist tradition—as well as many without—have for so long been using the term 'experience' in a different way that I had come to assume this usage so deeply myself that in *The Poverty of Theory* I did not adequately explain it."[153] This more basic prereflective experience was what he had meant when he said that "experience

150. Ibid., p. 57.
151. Ibid., p. 58.
152. E. P. Thompson, "The Politics of Theory," in Raphael Samuel, ed., *People's History and Socialist Theory* (London, 1981), p. 405.
153. Ibid., p. 406.

walks in without knocking at the door, and announces deaths, crises of subsistence, trench warfare, unemployment, inflation, genocide."[154] Experience in this sense "cannot be indefinitely diverted, postponed, falsified or suppressed by ideology. . . . Experience I is in eternal friction with imposed consciousness, and, as it breaks through, we, who fight in all the intricate vocabularies and disciplines of experience II, are given moments of openness and opportunity before the mould of ideology is imposed once again."[155] Without knowing it, Thompson thus ironically ended by elevating *Erlebnis* over *Erfahrung* as the object of the historical imagination, thus recapitulating the argument of Wilhelm Dilthey, to which we will turn in our next chapter.

Once the dust settled from the increasingly acrimonious "arguments within English Marxism," it was clear that both sides had lost. Raphael Samuel's despondent description of the effect of Thompson's truculent response to his critics at the History Workshop conference captures the frustration felt by many in the movement: "The result was that subsequent discussion was almost impossible. The aftermath of the Saturday night's fusillade hung like a pall of smoke over the rest of the conference."[156] With the victory of Margaret Thatcher and the increasing isolation of the left wing of the Labour Party, both the confidence in "scientific" theory on the part of the British Althusserians— their counterparts in France already in terminal disarray—and the trust in the working class's experiential wisdom of the Marxist humanists were shaken. The long revolution, it seemed, was going to be longer than expected. Although in 1990 a collection of "critical perspectives" on Thompson once again addressed his use of "experience," the verdict was not a positive one.[157]

Although Thompson would no longer debate the meaning and value of experience, he did, however, continue to evoke it in his final political struggle, the campaign to end the Cold War and bring about nuclear disarmament. As Michael Bess, the historian of that effort has noted, "other speakers might be just as sincere or morally committed as Thompson, but he possessed a rare talent for showing his ideas as they emerged from the full complexity of a struggling, groping, and also deeply *personal* experience."[158]

154. Ibid., cited from *The Poverty of Theory*, p. 9.
155. Ibid.
156. Samuel, *People's History and Socialist Theory,* p. 378.
157. Harvey J. Kaye and Keith McClelland, eds., *E. P. Thompson: Critical Perspectives* (Oxford, 1990). See in particular William H. Sewell Jr., "How Classes are Made: Critical Reflections on E. P. Thompson's Theory of Working-Class Formation," Robert Gray, "History, Marxism and Theory," and Kate Soper, "Socialist Humanism."
158. Michael Bess, *Realism, Utopia, and the Mushroom Cloud: Four Activists and Their Strategies for Peace, 1945–1989* (Chicago, 1993), p. 128 (emphasis in original).

The debate over experience on the left was not, however, over, but rather moved to a new terrain, that of the nascent cultural-studies movement in academia, which accompanied the emergence of so-called identity politics in the larger world outside. The assumption of a unified working class whose making Thompson had so vividly portrayed came under fire from feminists who challenged his marginalization of women and emphasis on productive labor.[159] Williams's belief in culture as a "whole way of life" did not easily survive the arrival of ethnic multiculturalism, in which hybridity, fragmentation, and diasporic deterritorialization were the new markers of distinction. The importance of the submerged imperial dimension in the national narrative, exploding its pretension to self-enclosed immanence, could also no longer be ignored.[160]

Ironically, as Craig Ireland has recently noted, in some respects Thompson's belief in the identity-building function of experience in a vertical struggle with a class enemy could migrate into an identity politics that pitted one group against one another in a horizontal war of recognition.[161] In both cases, experience could become a tool in the defense of an exclusive claim to political legitimacy. But there was also an anti-essentializing version of the argument, which sought to undercut the tribal implications of this displacement. For although the Althusserian version of structuralist Marxism went into eclipse, new poststructuralist proponents of the discursive construction of culture continued its distrust of empiricism and the immediacy of lived experience. How the concept of experience weathered these changes is a story to be told at the end of our narrative.

A CONCLUDING BALANCE SHEET

What can be said in summation of the debate over the politics of experience? Can we now provide a definitive answer to the question of its putative conservative bias, even when employed by thinkers on the left? There are obvious points of convergence. Burke's hostility to metaphysical rationalism re-

---

159. See, for example, Joan Scott, "Women in *The Making of the English Working Class*," in *Gender and the Politics of History* (New York, 1988); and Morag Shiach, "A Gendered History of Cultural Categories," in Prendergast, *Cultural Materialism*.

160. See, for example, Gauri Viswanathan, "Raymond Williams and British Colonialism," in Prendergast, *Cultural Materialism*.

161. Craig Ireland, "The Appeal to Experience and Its Consequences: Variations on a Persistent Thomp-

verberates through Thompson's diatribe against Althusserian scholasticism, as does his accusation that those who propound it are unworldly intellectuals with no concrete experience of politics. Often both identify abstract theory with the threatening incursion of foreign ideas—usually emanating from Paris—without roots in the particular experience of the British people.[162] So too, Oakeshott's critique of instrumental rationality and "political science" finds its echo in the distrust of the Marxist humanists for the scientistic pretensions of the Althusserians. Both camps also resist the reduction of experience to its purely cognitive function, stressing instead its emotional, rhetorical, and even corporeal dimensions. The knowledge that does flow from experience involves practical "know-how" rather than a priori blueprints. In addition, both camps claim that genuine experience combines moral and aesthetic dimensions with those that produce knowledge, and they lament its differentiation into distinct modes in the modern world.

They share as well an emphasis on the collective and intersubjective, as opposed to individual, nature of experience, which they see as more than an inner phenomenon of the isolated psyche. The holistic and communitarian inclinations of conservative organicism are also evident in Williams's insistence on culture as a whole way of life and Thompson's stress on the self-fashioning class subject of history, although the latter is understood to constitute itself through struggle with its enemies. And both camps remain suspicious of abstract notions of natural rights, typical of liberal political theory, that hover above the world of historical experience.[163]

Although not as explicitly idealist as the Oakeshott of *Experience and Its Modes,* Williams and Thompson steadfastly resist the reduction of experience to a matter of sense perception in the crude empiricist sense, defying the Althusserian claim that all talk of experience simply means empiricism. Constantly struggling to get their formulations under control, they seek a notion of experience that would somehow mediate between subjects and objects, agents and institutions, processes and structures, and in so doing approach Oakeshott's neo-Hegelian version of a totalized experience. No less

---

sonian Theme," *Cultural Critique* 52 (Fall 2002), p. 95. See also Ireland's *The Subaltern Appeal to Experience: Self-Identity, Late Modernity, and the Politics of Immediacy* (Montreal, 2004).

162. For a consideration of this issue, see Bill Readings, "Why Is Theory Foreign?," in Martin Kreiswirth and Mark A. Cheethem, eds., *Theory between the Disciplines* (Ann Arbor, Mich., 1990). Readings contrasts theory with the ideal of a native style of "reading" that matches the interiority of the reader with that of the text, an ideal he traces to Leavis.

163. There have been, as we have seen, attempts to make Burke a believer in natural law, but they have not been fully persuasive. See above, note 36.

characteristic of both camps is the belief that the record of past experience, whether understood as coherent "tradition" or merely the messiness of "history," preserves valuable lessons for the present and future. Although the utilitarian argument at work in certain conservative defenses of prescription is scorned by their leftist counterparts, who ask hard questions about whose interests are served by the preservation of which institutions, they tacitly share the assumption that much of value can be retrieved from the successes of those who struggled against oppression (as well as learned from their defeats and hopes). When Thompson protests against the simple equation of experience and ideology, arguing that the common man possesses the reason to make sense of his experience, he reveals some of the same optimism about the imbrication of reason and experience that fueled Oakeshott's neo-Hegelianism. Williams in his *Keywords* entry also evinces respect for the "processes of consideration, reflection, and analysis" that he sees in the conservative ideal of "experience past." And finally, both camps worry, with varying degrees of nostalgia, about the gap between the potential for authentic lived experience and the structural abstractions that govern modern life, abstractions that are institutional rather than merely conceptual.

There is, therefore, considerable warrant for the argument that the Left's evocations of experience carry with them strong residues of its use in the rhetoric of the Right. But before too quick and easy an identity is assumed, three important distinctions have to be made. First, the recognition that robust, immediate, and authentic experience is denied us today meant—especially for Williams in his later ruminations—that some theoretical conceptualization of the larger structures of the social world, structures that may be only indirectly present in lived experience, was warranted. Experience alone would not suffice to help dispel the effects of ideological mystification however much it might resist being entirely submerged by them, a conclusion that was especially true at the present time. Unlike the conservatives, even the most "workerist" of Marxists retains some faith in the liberating function of historical materialism as a theoretical optic through which to understand the world. In fact, Thompson invited criticism precisely for his tacit and unexamined assumption of a Marxist philosophy of history underlying his conceptualization of the working class's self-fashioning, an assumption that belied his principled hostility to theoretical impositions on the world.[164]

164. See Sewell, "How Classes are Made," p. 63, where Sewell writes that because of his overly general notion of experience, "Thompson hides from himself the extent to which his narrative tacitly assumes not

Second, unlike the conservative celebration of experience, which admired the prudent lessons it taught but was wary of it as a goal in itself, some of that positive aura surrounding experience for its own sake we noted above in theorists like Sorel, Jünger, and Arendt can be detected in the writings of Williams, Thompson, and their supporters. Whereas the Althusserians focused entirely on the cognitive flaws of experience, which they opposed to a Marxist science purportedly free from ideological taint, the humanists saw experience itself, emotional as well as cognitive, gained in struggle with the forces of oppression, producing class solidarity over time, situated in a holistic and communal way of life, as worthy of approbation in its own right. Thus Williams could still lament in 1984 that "there are major features in the social structure which are barring intense experiences. They lie very deep within the whole cast of civilization which is, for its own deepest reasons and often while denying that it is doing so, repressing intensely realized experiences of any kind."[165] There was, in short, a certain utopian inflection to the humanists' celebration of experience, which shows its pedigree in the aesthetic and religious usages explored in previous chapters. Thompson's last work, his paean to Blake, in fact, explicitly celebrated the very antinomian religious "enthusiasm"—which he traced, in the case of the poet, to the Muggletonians of the 1640s—that conservatives had found so unsettling.[166]

Finally, there was in Williams, Thompson, and their followers none of that hostility to its practical mode we have seen Oakeshott express in *Experience and Its Modes*. Although the dialectic of theory and praxis so powerfully present in continental Marxism seemed submerged in the debate over theory and experience, the activist spirit of Marxism was never lost in their attempt to harness intellectual work for radical change in the real world. Subjective agency was always a vital moment in their concept of experience, which distinguished it from the more passive modes derived from empiricism at its most sensationalist or conservative neo-Hegelianism at its most fatalistic. While their refusal to distinguish among various "practices" in the Althusserian manner courted the reproach that they lacked analytic rigor, stressing the holistic implications of experience helped them avoid the sterile com-

---

only a determination in the last instance by the base of productive relations, but also an over-determination by a whole series of relatively autonomous cultural, institutional and political systems. In this respect, his tacit model of the architectonics of society is actually very close to Althusser's."

165. Raymond Williams, *Writing in Society* (London, 1984), pp. 162–63.

166. E. P. Thompson, *Witness against the Beast: William Blake and the Moral Law* (New York, 1993).

partmentalization of roles that allowed structuralist Marxism to function as an elite ideology of theoretical practitioners.[167]

As we will see again when examining the idea of *Erfahrung* in Benjamin and Adorno, the politics of experience could creatively combine the two senses that Williams had registered in *Keywords,* the prudential lessons of the past and "the fullest, most open, most active kind of consciousness" in the present. And it could do so by asking hard questions about the ways in which the residues of past experience were active (or could be activated) in the present and the ways in which present experiences—however impoverished, contradictory and permeated by ideology—inflected our efforts to rescue the past. As such, "experience" revealed itself to be an unstable amalgam, a signifier capable of floating in several different directions, which defies all attempts to categorize it as inherently conservative or progressive. It is telling, we might note in conclusion, that Edmund Burke himself could pointedly invoke it against the tyranny of established authority, represented by Lord North's highhanded imperial domination, when he protested in 1775: "we have no sort of *experience* in favor of force as an instrument in the rule of our colonies."[168] Even the revered father of conservatism, it turns out, understood the critical potential in a politics of experience.

167. For a critique of Williams's stress on the indissolubility of practices as lived and experienced, see Stuart Hall, "Politics and Letters" in Eagleton, *Raymond Williams: Critical Perspectives,* p. 62. One might also note from an Arendtian point of view that the stress on "making" in Thompson privileged one mode of the *vita activa,* that associated with man as *homo faber,* and marginalized others, such as those associated with the household and reproductive rather than productive labor. His feminist critics were quick to foreground this limitation in Thompson's notion of experience.

168. Edmund Burke, "Speech on Conciliation with America, March 22, 1775," *The Works of Edmund Burke* (16 vols., 1815–27), vol. 3, p. 48 (emphasis in original).

SIX

History and Experience

Dilthey, Collingwood, Scott, and Ankersmit

MINCING NO WORDS, Michael Oakeshott scornfully derided the historical mode of experience in *Experience and Its Modes* as merely "an arrest in experience. History is a world of abstractions. It is a backwater, and, from the standpoint of experience, a mistake. It leads nowhere; and in experience, if we have been unable to avoid it, we can regain the path to what will afford satisfaction only by superseding it and destroying it."[1] Judged from the lofty, neo-idealist vantage point of the absolute notion of Experience as the holistic unity prior to any modalization, historical experience, he continued, is "a mutilation of present experience . . . experience deformed and restricted by being thrown in to the mould of the historical past, by being conceived under the category of the past."[2] Echoing without acknowledgment Friedrich Nietzsche's celebrated excoriation of historicism as inimical to robust living in "On the Uses and Disadvantages of History for Life" of 1874, Oakeshott warned against fetishizing the past for its own sake, living solely in that dead past, and organizing experience *sub specie praeteritorum*.[3]

---

1. Michael Oakeshott, *Experience and Its Modes* (Cambridge, 1933), p. 148. Oakeshott returned in 1955 to the issue of history in "The Activity of Being an Historian," *Rationalism in Politics and Other Essays* (London, 1962), and *On History and Other Essays* (Oxford, 1983), but did not substantially change his position. For considerations of his argument, see William H. Dray, "Michael Oakeshott's Theory of History," in Preston King and B. C. Parekh, eds., *Politics and Experience* (Cambridge, 1968); David Boucher, "The Creation of the Past: British Idealism and Michael Oakeshott's Philosophy of History," *History and Theory* 23 (1984); Christopher Parker, *The English Idea of History from Coleridge to Collingwood* (Aldershot, 2000), chapter 8; and Luke O'Sullivan, *Oakeshott on History* (Exeter, 2003).

2. Oakeshott, *Experience and Its Modes*, p. 152.

3. For a helpful overview of Nietzsche's critique of history, see David D. Roberts, *Nothing but History: Reconstruction and Extremity after Metaphysics* (Berkeley, 1995), chapter 4. For an attempt to discern

Oddly, in the light of the typical conservative appeal to the past as a ground of prescriptive legitimation and an antidote to excessive rationalism, Oake-shott displayed no less disdain for the attempt to harness the purported lessons of the past for practical ends in the present, a mistake he traced back to Edmund Burke. "No guidance for practical life can be expected from the organization of experience *sub specie praeteritorum*. The world of history has no data to offer of which practical experience can make use; and to conceive it as offering such data is to misconceive its character."[4]

What was that character in Oakeshott's eyes, and what was it for other commentators, less idiosyncratically bilious than he about its value, who have tried to make sense of a specifically historical notion of experience? What has the appeal to experience meant to practicing historians who are reflective about their craft? How does experience in the discourse of history differ from its counterparts in science, aesthetics, religion, and politics? Does an experience in the present justify being called historical if it responds to the undigested residues of the past, resisting turning them into moments in an overly coherent narrative? Or is it precisely the recognition that we ourselves are embedded in such a narrative that makes current experience truly historical?

In this chapter, we will focus on two figures in particular, the German philosopher and historian Wilhelm Dilthey (1833–1911) and the English philosopher and historian R. G. Collingwood (1889–1943), and then explore some of the ways in which these questions have exercised later historians self-conscious about their craft. Here our main focus will be on the influential poststructuralist critique made by the American feminist historian Joan Wallach Scott, and the defense of a postmodernist alternative offered by the Dutch philosopher of history Frank R. Ankersmit. But let us stay for a while with Oakeshott, who, despite his evident disdain for the inadequacies of historical experience, nonetheless devoted a substantial chapter of his book to its explication, and in so doing produced what Collingwood could extol as "a new and valuable achievement for English thought."[5]

---

a distinction between Oakeshott and Nietzsche on the utility of the past, see Parker, *The English Idea of History*, p. 142.

4. Oakeshott, *Experience and Its Modes*, p. 158. The Latin phrase means "from the point of view of what precedes." In his essay on history in *Rationalism in Politics*, Oakeshott continued to make the same claim, arguing that "the practical man reads the past backwards. He is interested in and recognizes only those past events which he can relate to present activities. . . . But in the specifically 'historical' attitude . . . , the past is *not* viewed in relation to the present, and it is *not* treated as if it were the present" (pp. 153–54). For a critical appraisal of the distinction, see W. H. Walsh, "The Practical and the Historical Past," in King and Parekh, *Politics and Experience*.

5. R. G. Collingwood, *The Idea of History* (New York, 1956), pp. 155–56.

Experience, it might well seem, enters the universe of historical discourse at two points: the experience either of those whose history is being recounted or of those who are doing the recounting. That is, the task of the historian can be construed as somehow getting access to and representing what was "experienced" by men and women in the past; or it can be understood as something that happens to us now when we think historically about those residues of the past that are manifest to us—or that we construe as manifested—in the present. For even though there can be no question of having an empirical "eyewitness" acquaintance with the past, which is no longer here to be experienced by the senses, it may be possible to speak of experience in connection with historical knowledge nonetheless. Assuming that these two poles are maintained (and that there is a consensus on the meaning of experience itself), the most vexed methodological question faced by historians is the passage from one to the other. What, in other words, is the relationship between the writing, reading, and judging of historical accounts in the present and what was experienced by those who are assumed to be the protagonists of those accounts? How does the subject producing historical writing relate to the object of that writing, who is understood to have been an experiencing subject as well?

What immediately strikes the reader of Oakeshott's ruminations on the subject is that they explicitly challenge this very polarity. Extrapolating a fundamental premise of his holistic account of absolute experience to one of its modes, Oakeshott insisted that "the distinction between history as it happened (the course of events) and history as it is thought, the distinction between history itself and merely experienced history, must go; it is not merely false, it is meaningless. The historian's business is not to discover, to recapture, or even to interpret; it is to create and to construct. . . . History is experience, the historian's world of experience; it is a world of ideas, the historian's world of ideas."[6] The only possible distinction between the raw material of history and history itself is that the latter may display a bit more coherence and intelligibility. But those traits come from the historian himself, for "history is the historian's experience. It is 'made' by nobody save the historian; to write history is the only way of making it. It is a world, and a world of ideas."[7]

6. Oakeshott, *Experience and Its Modes*, p. 93.
7. Ibid., p. 99.

Echoing Benedetto Croce and anticipating Hayden White, Oakeshott vigorously contested the positivist notion of bracketing present interpretive mediations to record the past "as it actually was" through an inductive distillation of the evidence.[8] To embrace this illusion was to subsume historical experience under another of experience's modalities, that of science, which understands the world *sub specie quantitatis* and seeks general laws. Both, to be sure, abstract from experience in the absolute sense. But when the historian abstracts through his or her "making" of the past, he or she does so, Oakeshott insisted, by exclusively focusing on the pastness of the past, thus severing it from the total realm that is absolute experience. Historical abstraction does not therefore mean deriving universal generalizations from a welter of incommensurable concrete cases, which is the form of abstraction practiced by science and thus inappropriately imposed on historical explanation. The latter is contained entirely in the narrative itself, which is always about concrete and individual happenings. But even non-pseudoscientific history is still an abstraction, still divorced from the larger truth, because "the only absolute individual is the universal as a whole."[9]

Although constructed by the historian, historical experience, Oakeshott continued, must not be confused with the remembered past of the individual historian, whose memory is personal (Oakeshott had no interest in purported collective memory). Nor is it entirely the historian's fantasy of a past that never existed, for the ideas that make up historical experience do exist prior to the making, even if the latter is necessary to bring them to a higher coherence. While the belief in an "objective" recording of the past free from the experience of the historian is absurd, that experience is not completely "subjective" either. It is thus irreducible to the political prejudices of the present historian, whose role is not to judge the past, but rather simply to create it through historical imagination. Or rather, judgments and creation are so intimately intertwined in the experience of the historian that no distinction can be drawn between them. For "there is no fact in history which

8. Oakeshott even repeats (without citation) on p. 109 Croce's celebrated formula that "all history is contemporary history," which was made in the Italian philosopher's *History: Its Theory and Practice*, trans. Douglas Ainslee (New York, 1921). For a comparison of the two, see Jack W. Meiland, *Scepticism and Historical Knowledge* (New York, 1965). Meiland argues that there were significant differences between them: Croce stressed the interested intervention of the historian in the present, which Oakeshott denied, and Croce believed in the existence of distinctly past events, which Oakeshott claimed could neither be experienced nor judged. White, for his part, seems not to have relied on Oakeshott to come to similar conclusions, and never, to my knowledge, cites him.

9. Oakeshott, *Experience and Its Modes*, p. 151.

is not a judgment, no event which is not an inference. There is nothing whatsoever outside the historian's experience."[10]

And yet, there is an inherent paradox in historical experience, which is a main source of its ultimate failure in Oakeshott's eyes: it lies entirely in the present, generated by the "making" of the historian today, but it is concerned entirely with the dead past, which it hopes to understand for its own sake. It is thus "the continuous assertion of a past which is not past and of a present which is not present."[11] Reading the present backwards into the past and turning it into a mere prelude to our current situation produces a politically presentist "Whig history," which violates the past for its own sake, and yet it is only the present that makes historical experience.

Having ruled out the unification of practical and historical experience as an impossible amalgam, Oakeshott was left with the odd conclusion that although thoroughly constructed in the present, historical experience was made only by historians who could somehow bracket and suspend all of their current interests or needs. Groping to come up with a way to express this paradox, Oakeshott revealed the limits of his own historical moment (or at least his personal gender biases) by claiming that practical experience "deals with the past as with a man, expecting it to talk sense and have something to say apposite to its plebian 'causes' and engagements. But for the 'historian' for whom the past is dead and irreproachable, the past is feminine. He loves it as a mistress of whom he never tires and whom he never expects to talk sense."[12]

The past as a mindless (and perhaps even lifeless) sex object constructed by an assumed male historian, who loves it only for its ability to arouse lust without end and not what it can teach us in the present—it is no wonder that Oakeshott's animadversions on historical experience were ultimately of little inspiration to historians who did not share his neo-Hegelian idealist premises.[13] For once the holistic belief in absolute experience was jettisoned

---

10. Ibid., p. 100.
11. Ibid., p. 111.
12. Oakeshott, "The Activity of Being an Historian," p. 166.
13. Even conservative historians like Gertrude Himmelfarb, who would be hard pressed to be considered a feminist, found it offensive. See her "Does History Talk Sense?" *The New History and the Old: Critical Essays and Reappraisals* (Cambridge, Mass., 1987), p. 175. She concludes that "the most striking thing about Oakeshott's theory is how little hope it holds out, either for the future of English historiography or for the past. There is no future in it because it is more a prescription for the nonwriting of history than for the writing of it. And there is no past because it illegitimizes almost the entire corpus of historical writing. . . . Oakeshott may be guilty of the fallacy of rationalism that he himself has so brilliantly diagnosed" (p. 181).

as the higher standard of experiential truth and historical experience was no longer seen as a mere "arrest" in that larger totality, the vexed question of how experience in the present relates to experience in the past was once again squarely on the agenda. Oakeshott may have damaged his case by figuring the current historian as a randy male and the past as a dim-witted female love object, produced by some sort of heterosexual masturbatory fantasy. But even if he had been less a prisoner of his sexist assumptions, his account of the unity of historical experience provides little guidance in working with—let alone getting beyond—the paradox it had suggestively identified as central to historical experience.

For history—the very word in English ambiguously denoting both what happened and what has been written about what happened—necessarily involves a complex negotiation between past and present, not a wholesale takeover by one of the other. Even when languages distinguish, as German does, between "Geschichte" and "Historie," they too register the irreducible interaction between them.[14] However much Oakeshott thought he could cut the Gordian knot by proclaiming that historical experience was one and indissoluble (if, to be sure, still an abstraction in comparison with the higher standard of absolute experience), the distinction between experience past and experience present stubbornly remained. For as we have seen in the cases of cognitive, religious, aesthetic, and political experience, unless some sort of tension is preserved between the subject of experience and the object—whether it be nature, God, things of beauty, or political goals—there is a danger of losing precisely the very encounter with otherness and the moment of passivity that are so deeply embedded in the concept of experience in most of its guises. Moreover, as Hans-Georg Gadamer has noted, Hegelian notions of experience that equate it with self-knowledge without remainder fail to register the inevitable finitude of historical experience, which never comes to a final resting place and never achieves the perfection of closure.[15] This limitation is true both of historical experience in the past and the historian's attempt to write about it in the present, an attempt that is always surpassed by later interpretations and narratives. History, we might say, *pace* Hegel and Oakeshott, is not a totality, but a "bad infinity" that may not be so bad after all.

When Oakeshott's problematic neo-Hegelian constructivism is set aside, the real question faced by historians and those that philosophize about what

14. Reinhart Koselleck, "Transformation of Experience and Methodological Change," in *The Practice of Conceptual History: Timing History, Spacing Concepts*, trans. Todd Samuel Presner and others (Stanford, 2002).

15. Hans-Georg Gadamer, *Truth and Method* (New York, 1986), p. 319.

they are doing resurfaces: how do present constructs emerge from, duplicate, give shape to, modify, and/or betray the past, that "foreign country" whose very strangeness is a major reason for choosing to journey to it in the first place? With particular reference to our own concerns, it entails a consideration of the relation between what was experienced in the past and the historian's account—or re-experiencing/re-enacting—of it. Beyond that question, it involves as well a judgment about how much of that past can plausibly be understood under the category of experience and how much—whether conceptualized as facts, events, structures, trends, institutions, or discourses— eludes it. And finally, it forces us to consider the possibility that "experience" itself may have a history, which means that it is not a question of recovering it in "the past," but rather acknowledging that it may have had many different pasts, which defy easy homogenization. It may therefore raise the further question, as we will see it did for Walter Benjamin and Theodor Adorno: has the very capacity for experience, at least in one of its guises, changed over time?

DILTHEY AND THE RE-EXPERIENCING OF PAST *ERLEBNIS*

Many of these fundamental questions, still vexing philosophers of history and working historians to this day, were initially pondered in all of their seriousness in the nineteenth century by the German historian and philosopher Wilhelm Dilthey.[16] We have already encountered Dilthey as the first biographer of Friedrich Schleiermacher, who understood that one could write an account of the theologian's ideas only by situating them in his life history. Like Schleiermacher, he rejected dogmatic rationalism in theology in favor of an experiential notion of Protestantism.[17] Dilthey was also instrumental in popularizing the German word *Erlebnis* as an alternative to *Erfahrung* in such works as *Das Erlebnis und die Dichtung* (Poetry and Experience) of 1905,

16. It would also be possible to focus entirely on a British idealist tradition that goes back to Samuel Taylor Coleridge, included figures like Bernard Bosanquet and F. H. Bradley, and culminated in Oakeshott and Collingwood. This tradition challenged the skeptical implications of Hume's empiricism and sought a firmer ground for historical knowledge. See Parker, *The English Idea of History from Coleridge to Collingwood.* But Dilthey explored the issue of experience with greater complexity than any of his nineteenth-century British counterparts.

17. For evidence of Dilthey's youthful interest in theology and sympathy for Friedrich Schleiermacher's version of religious experience, see *Der junge Dilthey: Ein Lebensbild in Briefen und Tagebüchern, 1852–1870,* ed. Clara Misch née Dilthey (Göttingen, 1960).

although it had been introduced as early as Wolfgang von Goethe's reception of Jean-Jacques Rousseau.[18] Often grouped with the "philosophers of life" of the late nineteenth century—Henri Bergson, Friedrich Nietzsche, Georg Simmel—Dilthey nonetheless valued what went beyond the merely biological standard suggested by that term, without, however, being tempted by metaphysical vitalism.

But it was perhaps in his role as an advocate of the special status of historical reason, whose critique he hoped to add to those written by Immanuel Kant a century earlier, that he made his greatest mark. Over a long and distinguished career, Dilthey struggled to defend the autonomy of historical from scientific cognition, striving to resist the imperialism of a positivist methodology that threatened to swamp all its rivals, and yet avoid the alternative of relativist subjectivism.[19] The now familiar dichotomy between the so-called cultural or human sciences *(Geisteswissenschaften)* and natural sciences *(Naturwissenschaften)* was enabled in large measure because of his labors (and those of neo-Kantians like Heinrich Rickert and Wilhelm Windelband).[20] So too was the expansion of interest in the interpretative methods, pioneered by Schleiermacher, that

18. Dilthey, *Poetry and Experience, Selected Works,* ed. Rudolf A. Makkreel and Frithjof Rodi (Princeton, 1985); and Gadamer, *Truth and Method,* p. 56. See also René Wellek, "Genre Theory, the Lyric, and 'Erlebnis'," in Herbert Singer and Benno von Wiese, eds., *Festschrift für Richard Alweyn* (Cologne, 1967).

19. Only fragments of Dilthey's *Gesammelte Schriften,* 20 vols. (Göttingen, 1958–90), have been published in English. See H. P. Rickman, ed., *Pattern and Meaning in History: Thoughts on History and Society* (New York, 1962); H. P. Rickman, ed., *Wilhelm Dilthey: Selected Writings* (Cambridge, 1976); and Rudolf Makkreel and Frithjof Rodi, ed., *Wilhelm Dilthey: Selected Works,* 6 vols. (Princeton, 1985–). Among the extensive secondary literature, the following accounts stand out: H. A. Hodges, *The Philosophy of Wilhelm Dilthey* (London, 1952); Otto Friedrich Bollnow, *Dilthey: Eine Einführung in seine Philosophie* (Stuttgart, 1955); William Kluback, *Wilhelm Dilthey's Philosophy of History* (New York, 1956); Rudolf A. Makkreel, *Dilthey: Philosopher of the Human Sciences* (Princeton, 1975); Michael Ermarth, *Wilhelm Dilthey: The Critique of Historical Reason* (Chicago, 1978); H. P. Rickman, *Wilhelm Dilthey: Pioneer of the Human Mind* (Berkeley, 1979); Ilse Bulhof, *Wilhelm Dilthey: A Hermeneutic Approach to the Study of History and Culture* (The Hague, 1980); Theodore Plantinga, *Historical Understanding in the Thought of Wilhelm Dilthey* (Toronto, 1982); and Jacob Owensby, *Dilthey and the Narrative of History* (Ithaca, N.Y., 1994).

20. For a still useful overview of the critique of positivism shared by Dilthey and the neo-Kantians, see H. Stuart Hughes, *Consciousness and Society: The Reorientation of Social Thought, 1880–1930* (New York, 1958). For more recent accounts of Dilthey's relation to the neo-Kantians, see Klaus Christian Köhnke, *The Rise of Neo-Kantianism: German Academic Philosophy between Idealism and Positivism,* trans. R. J. Hollingdale (Cambridge, 1991); and Charles R. Bambach, *Heidegger, Dilthey, and the Crisis of Historicism* (Ithaca, N.Y., 1995). *Geisteswissenschaften* is sometimes translated as "human studies," but the empirical moment in Dilthey's understanding of his practice suggests that "science" may be closer to his intentions. *Wissenschaft,* as is often noted, always means more than just the natural sciences.

came to be called hermeneutics.[21] And in many respects, Dilthey's emphasis on the lifeworld of practices, habits, and worldviews prior to critical reflection can be understood to anticipate the work of the phenomenologists Edmund Husserl and Martin Heidegger, as well as the American pragmatists.[22]

In all these contexts, the issue of how to construe and get retrospective access to something called experience (normally denoted by *Erlebnis* and often translated as "lived experience"[23]) was crucial. There is a rich and detailed literature devoted to all of the twists and turns, as well as stops and starts, of Dilthey's lengthy attempt to do so, but we have space only to highlight its most characteristic features.[24] The first point to make with reference to experience is Dilthey's explicit repudiation of what he saw as its reductively empiricist acceptation. Responding to English thinkers like John Stuart Mill, whose attempt to defend a notion of the moral, as opposed to natural, sciences he found suggestive but ultimately wanting, Dilthey wrote: "Empiricism has been just as abstract as speculative thought. The human being that influential empiricist schools have constructed from sensations and representations, as though from atoms, contradicts the inner experience from whose elements the idea of human being is, after all, derived."[25] Whatever *Erlebnis* may have meant for Dilthey, it clearly was distinct from, albeit not absolutely opposed to, the observable exterior behavior that empiricists had posited as the object of epistemological inquiry.[26] In fact, he cautioned against

21. Dilthey's role in the history of hermeneutics is discussed, *inter alia*, in Richard E. Palmer, *Hermeneutics: Interpretation Theory in Schleiermacher, Dilthey, Heidegger, and Gadamer* (Evanston, Ill., 1969); Roy J. Howard, *Three Faces of Hermeneutics: An Introduction to Current Theories of Understanding* (Berkeley, 1982); and David Couzens Hoy, *The Critical Circle: Literature and History in Contemporary Hermeneutics* (Berkeley, 1978).

22. See Rudolf A. Makkreel and John Scanlon, eds., *Dilthey and Phenomenology* (Washington, D.C., 1987). For a discussion of the differences between Dilthey and Heidegger, see Bambach, *Heidegger, Dilthey, and the Crisis of Historicism*. For an attempt to stress similarities, at least between Dilthey and the early Heidegger, see Robert C. Scharff, "Heidegger's 'Appropriation' of Dilthey before *Being and Time*," *Journal of the History of Philosophy* 25, no. 1 (January 1997). For a comparison of Dilthey and the Pragmatists, see James Kloppenberg, *Uncertain Victory: Social Democracy and Progressivism in European and American Thought, 1870–1920* (New York, 1986), chapter 2.

23. The qualifier "normally" has to be added because Dilthey was not always consistent in his contrasting use of the two German words for "experience." In his earlier works in particular, he could employ *Erlebnis* and *Erfahrung* interchangeably.

24. In addition to the works cited above, see Karol Sauerland, *Diltheys Erlebnisbegriff: Entstehung, Glanzzeit und Verkümmerung eines literaturhistorisches Begriffs* (Berlin, 1972).

25. Dilthey, *Introduction to the Human Sciences: An Attempt to Lay a Foundation for the Study of Society and History*, trans. Ramon J. Betanzos (Detroit, 1988), p. 173.

26. For a discussion of the relative, rather than absolute, distinction between inner and outer experience, see Ermarth, *Wilhelm Dilthey*, p. 104. Dilthey liked to distinguish between the *Empirismus* he

all spectatorial relations to experience, theoretical as well as empirical, which he dubbed "ocularism."[27] Even introspection, understood as a distanced relationship to one's inner life as if it were an object to be observed from afar, was inadequate.[28] Such an approach might work for natural science, but other modes of recapturing experience would be required of the historian.

These were not, however, to be understood in terms of the model of a priori structuring of sense impressions posited by Kant, which Dilthey identified with *Erfahrungen*. In a frequently quoted passage from his preface to his *Introduction to the Human Sciences* of 1883, Dilthey chided both those who reduce experience to a matter of passive sensation and those who reduce it to active thought:

> There is no real blood flowing in the veins of the knowing subject fabricated by Locke, Hume, and Kant, but only the diluted juice of reason as mere intellectual activity. But dealing with the whole man in history and psychology led me to take the whole man—in the multiplicity of his powers: this willing—feeling—perceiving being—as the basis for explaining knowledge and its concepts (such as outer world, time, substance, cause), even though, to be sure, knowledge appears to weave these concepts solely out of raw material it gets from perceiving, imagining, and thinking.[29]

Whereas *Erfahrungen* remained on the level of perception or intellect, *Erlebnisse* involved a deeper level of interiority involving volition, emotion, and creaturely suffering, a level that suggested a more subjective or psychological truth, which was irreducible to the rational workings of the mind. Qualitatively distinct, it was a truth that defied reduction to quantitative generalization, revealing individuals rather than general types or patterns. These individuals were themselves meaningful wholes, whose lives could not be further atomized into discrete and unrelated moments. "A lived experience," Dilthey wrote in 1907/8, "is a distinctive and characteristic mode in which reality is there-for-me. A lived experience does not confront me as something perceived or represented; it is not given to me, but the reality of lived experience is there-

identified with positivism and his own notion of *unbefangene Empirie*, an "*unbiased* empiricism" that included both external and internal experience. See his *Gesammelte Schriften*, vol. 1, p. 81.

27. For a discussion of his hostility to the privileging of the eye, see Ermarth, *Wilhelm Dilthey*, pp. 118–19. Here, of course, he was not alone, as I have tried to show in *Downcast Eyes: The Denigration of Vision in 20th-Century French Thought* (Berkeley, 1993).

28. Dilthey also argued against Nietzsche's non-spectatorial valorization of introspection because of its indifference to historicity. See his remarks in *Pattern and Meaning in History*, p. 92.

29. Dilthey, *Introduction to the Human Sciences*, p. 73.

for-me because I have a reflexive awareness of it, because I possess it immediately as belonging to me in some sense."[30] Rather, therefore, than knowing,
willing, or feeling *Erlebnisse,* one knows, wills, and feels through them.

But an *Erlebnis,* however intimate, came to mean for Dilthey more than
just solipsistic subjectivity understood in isolation from its links with cultural and spiritual realities outside of the individual psyche.[31] Experience entailed being in the world, not retreating from it. Throughout his career, to
be sure, Dilthey courted the charge of psychologism, even though his "descriptive and analytical psychology" sought to avoid reduction to the typically scientistic or associationist versions of his day.[32] Dilthey, however, resisted the implication that *Erlebnis* meant the loss of any trans-subjective
epistemological validity beyond the particular context of its origin. In this
sense, he was a consistent opponent of Romanticism, at least in its subjectivist, particularizing, emotionalist guise. Gadamer has noted that in Dilthey's
biography of Schleiermacher, he had seen religious experience as connected
with the infinite; each of the theologian's *Erlebnisse,* Dilthey wrote, "is a separate picture of the universe taken out of the explanatory context."[33] The
pantheistic moment that we have observed in Schleiermacher's critique of
Kantian critical philosophy thus left a trace in Dilthey's usage of *Erlebnis,*
which one commentator could go so far as to define as "an event of spiritual
vividness."[34] But he nonetheless never went entirely in the direction of fully
realized pantheism, resisting a Hegelian or Spinozan reconciliation that reduced difference to an emanation of monistic sameness, as well as mystical
religious notions of complete fusion. He likewise rejected the radical apri-
orism of Hermann Cohen's rewriting of Kant's notion of experience, which
did away entirely with the independence of things-in-themselves in the name
of a radical constructivism.[35] Such a view, he worried, would turn historical
experience into a mere projection of the constituting subject.

30. Dilthey, "Fragments for a Poetics," *Selected Works,* vol. 5, p. 223.

31. On the broader implications of "inner experience" in Dilthey, see Owensby, *Dilthey and the Narrative of History,* p. 28.

32. Dilthey, *Descriptive Psychology and Historical Understanding,* trans. Richard M. Zaner and Kenneth L. Heiges (The Hague, 1977). For a good discussion of Dilthey and psychologism, see Makkreel,
Dilthey: Philosopher of the Human Sciences, pp. 9ff, and his introduction to *Descriptive Psychology and Historical Understanding.* For a general account of the battle over that vexed concept, see Martin Kusch, *Psychologism: A Case Study of the Sociology of Philosophical Knowledge* (New York, 1995).

33. Dilthey, *Leben Schleiermachers,* 2nd ed. (Berlin, 1922), p. 341, quoted in Gadamer, *Truth and Method,*
p. 58.

34. Kluback, *Wilhelm Dilthey's Philosophy of History,* p. 76.

35. See Köhnke, *The Rise of Neo-Kantianism,* pp. 178–89, for an account of Cohen's apriorist reinterpretation of Kant's notion of experience.

Experience for Dilthey was instead a relational concept, which entailed something beyond absolute immanence and immediacy. Even if at times he seemed to be endorsing the view that immediate, inner knowing was prior to its objectified reflection, he always insisted that experience meant an encounter with something beyond the interiority of the self. Another way in which the relationality of experience was clearly evident—and this is why Dilthey was so central a figure in the history of hermeneutics—was in the role of meaning in experience. "Experience in its concrete reality," he wrote, "is made coherent by the category of meaning. This is the unity that, through memory, joins together what has been experienced either directly or through re-experiencing. Its meaning does not lie in something outside the experiences which give them unity but is contained in them and constitutes the connections between them."[36] This unity was situated in the larger context of a life, whose totality needed to be taken into account; indeed, only at the hour of death might the final meaning become clear.

The neo-Kantian attempt to separate facts from values Dilthey also forcefully rejected. The verb *erleben* suggested "living through" rather than a static moment, however intense. For this reason, *Erlebnis* was not the succession of discrete, raw stimuli produced by a transient, impersonal flux, but rather a temporal structure or pattern of intensity, value, and coherence—a distinction that anticipated what other observers like John Dewey would call "having *an* experience" as opposed to "mere experience."[37] Having such a meaningful experience, moreover, required judgment as well as perception, judgment that was akin to the reflective rather than determinant variety discussed in Kant's *Critique of Judgment*. "Experience *(empeiria, experientia)* is knowledge on the basis of perception," Dilthey insisted. "Perception as such is not yet experience; rather, the latter consists of judgments and involves an extension of the knowledge of facts."[38]

If having "an experience" involved reflective judgments in Kant's sense of the term, it is not surprising that Dilthey has sometimes been interpreted as privileging aesthetic experiences as the most vital of *Erlebnisse*.[39] For such judgments were aimed precisely at making sense out of and evaluating individual instances of intelligibility, which included sensual as well as spiritual

36. Dilthey, *Pattern and Meaning in History,* p. 74 (translation slightly emended).
37. John Dewey, *Art as Experience* (New York, 1958), chapter 3. *Erlebnis,* understood in this way, ironically came close to what later commentators like Gadamer and Benjamin would call *Erfahrung,* once that term was freed from its scientific or empiricist denotation.
38. Dilthey, *Selected Works,* vol. 1, p. 270.
39. See in particular, Makkreel, *Dilthey: Philosopher of the Human Sciences.*

or mental *(geistige)* dimensions. They sought truth, not merely the appreciation of beauty for its own sake.[40] Art, moreover, suggested the objectification and externalization of inner experience, making it available for the judgments of others. "The human world exists for the poet," Dilthey wrote of Goethe, "insofar as he experiences human existence in himself and tries to understand it as it confronts him from the outside. . . . in understanding he projects all his inner experience into other human beings, and yet at the same time the unfathomable alien depths of another great being or a powerful destiny lead him beyond the limits of his own; he understands and gives shape to what he would never be able to experience personally."[41] Autobiography, the most complete act of aesthetic self-narrativizing, was in a way the *ne plus ultra* of this process, "the highest and most instructive form in which the understanding of life confronts us."[42] Biography of another figure extends the process by taking into account the historical context and posthumous effects of a life.

Although Dilthey never reduced historical experience simply to poetic production, the qualities of making meaningful objects associated with the latter informed his understanding of the former. Especially in his later work *Aufbau der geschichtlichen Welt in den Geisteswissenschaften (The Constitution of the Historical World in the Human Sciences* [1910]), written in the shadow of Husserl's critique of psychologism,[43] Dilthey strove to find a way to locate meaning not in the interiority of the subject, but rather in the "objective spirit" left behind by individual endeavors. These delimited and fixed objectifications contained a residue of the teleological intentions of their authors, and as such were what Dilthey called an *Ausdruck*—normally translated as "expression," but sometimes as "objectification"—of their *Erlebnis*. "Lived experience," he wrote, "generates its own expressions."[44] Included among them are linguistic utterances, actions, and nonverbal signs such as gestures or body language. All can be more than the embodiment of authorial emotions, containing instead the whole gamut of lived experiences.[45] They are mediated by worldviews *(Weltanschauungen)*, which

---

40. For a discussion of Dilthey's search for truth in art, see Palmer, *Hermeneutics*, p. 122.

41. Dilthey, *Poetry and Experience*, p. 278.

42. Dilthey, *Pattern and Meaning in History*, p. 85.

43. See Makkreel, *Dilthey: Philosopher of the Human Sciences*, chapter 7, for a discussion of Dilthey's reponse to, and dialogue with, Husserl.

44. Dilthey, "Fragments for a Poetics," *Selected Works*, vol. 5, p. 229.

45. For a discussion of the distinction between expressivist theories of art based on emotions and feelings and Dilthey's use of *Ausdruck*, see Palmer, *Hermeneutics*, pp. 111–12.

Dilthey thought could be typologically categorized.[46] Such expressions, as Hegel and Johann Gustav Droysen had pointed out before Dilthey, gained a certain autonomy from that experience, which meant that they needed to be hermeneutically deciphered to yield their meaning. The skills developed by earlier interpreters of contested sacred texts could be applied to all expressions of human creativity.

Here the critical role of what Dilthey called "understanding" *(Verstehen)* in the process of recovering the past was paramount.[47] Deeper than a mere cognitive grasp of exterior realities or rational subsumption under categories, more than mere "explanation" *(Erklärung)* of causes and effects implied by Kant's *Verstand* (translated as often by "intellect" as "understanding"), it involves the prereflective grasp of the inner meaning of an "expression" of the *Erlebnis* of those—or at least some of those—who went before us.[48] Here life, the meaningful life of the historian, allows access to the meaningful lives of those he or she studies. Following Giambattista Vico's celebrated *verum-factum* principle, which said that those who make something can know it better than those who have not, Dilthey claimed that we can know what has been made in the past by human intentionality, because we partake of the same activity.[49] The range of the *Geisteswissenschaften,* he argued, "is determined by the objectification of life in the external world. The mind can only understand what it has created. Nature, the subject matter of the natural sci-

46. Dilthey, *Dilthey's Philosophy of Existence: Introduction to Weltanschauungslehre,* trans. William Kluback and Martin Weinbaum (Westport, Conn., 1978). The types he privileged were "materialism or naturalism," "objective idealism," and "subjective idealism or idealism of freedom."

47. As with virtually all of Dilthey's terms, *Verstehen* has been shown to have a variety of overlapping meanings. For a useful attempt to sort them out, see Owensby, *Dilthey and the Narrative of History,* chapter 5. One major ambiguity concerned the distinction between understanding the objective meaning of, say, a geometric proof, and the motives or reasons of those who generated it or came to be persuaded by it. The former involves understanding the logic of an argument, the latter its conditions of emergence and dissemination. Without distinguishing between the two, what has come to be called the genetic fallacy follows. Reliving the experience of those who are persuaded by an argument is not the same as coming to understand its ahistorical logical force.

48. The qualifier "some of those" is necessary because Dilthey came increasingly to recognize the difficulty of reducing all cultural expressions to the biographies of their creators. See footnote 30 in chapter 3 (p. 89).

49. For comparisons of the two, see H. P. Rickman, "Vico and Dilthey's Methodology of the Human Studies," and H. A. Hodges, "Vico and Dilthey," in Giorgio Tagliacozzo and Hayden White, eds., *Giambattista Vico: An International Symposium* (Baltimore, 1969); and H. N. Tuttle, "The Epistemological Status of the Cultural World in Vico and Dilthey," in Giorgio Tagliacozzo and Donald P. Verene, eds., *Giambattista Vico's Science of Humanity* (Baltimore, 1976). See also David D. Roberts, *Nothing but History,* chapter 2.

ences, embraces the reality which has arisen independently of the activity of the mind."[50] And elsewhere, he contended that "the first condition for the possibility of historical science lies in the fact that I myself am a historical being: that he who investigates history is the same as he who makes history."[51]

The process by which the present historian enters into the experience of actors in the past is what Dilthey called "re-experiencing" *(Nacherleben)* or less frequently "re-creation"*(Nachbilden)*, which goes beyond mere emotional empathy *(Einfühlung)*.[52] "A thorough understanding of historical development is first achieved," Dilthey wrote, "when the course of events is re-experienced in imagination at the deepest points where the movement forward takes place."[53] Comparable to the active understanding that occurs when we enter into a fictional narrative (say, in a play or novel) that draws on our own experiences, our own pre-understandings, to make sense of those presented to us, re-experiencing is able to interpret the expressions of past experience in meaningful ways. As Jacob Owensby puts it,

> *Nacherleben* is the revitalization by the interpreter of life-relations embodied in the expressions used in data. It is to bring together again, using the individual as a focal point, a dynamic nexus of life-relations. Insofar as we transform the lives of historical figures into narratives, we are capable of understanding both their expressions in terms of the unfolding of their lives as well as the unfolding of their lives as embodiments of the development and interaction of more encompassing sociohistorical systems.[54]

Although it can thus be likened to an act of poetic imagination, "re-experiencing" is never as exclusively a figural imposition on the past as later commentators like Hayden White claimed it was; Dilthey stubbornly remained a realist, not a metahistorian, when it came to historical knowledge.[55]

50. Dilthey, *Pattern and Meaning in History,* p. 125.

51. Dilthey, "Plan der Fortsetzung zum Aufbau der geschichtlichen Welt in den Geisteswissenschaften," *Gesammelte Schriften,* vol. 7, p. 278.

52. Ibid., pp. 213–16. For a discussion of the difference between re-experiencing and empathy, see Makkreel, *Dilthey: Philosopher of the Human Sciences,* pp. 252–53. Makkreel questions Rickman's translation in *Pattern and Meaning* of *nacherleben* as "empathy," because the latter suggests projecting contemporary feelings into past actors rather than imaginatively interpreting them.

53. Dilthey, *Gesammelte Schriften,* vol. 1, p. 254.

54. Owensby, *Dilthey and the Narrative of History,* p. 155.

55. Hayden White, *Metahistory: The Historical Imagination in Nineteenth-Century Europe* (Baltimore, 1973). Dilthey is virtually ignored in White's account, surfacing only as a "neo-Hegelian" surpassed by Croce (p. 381).

In addition to its epistemological pay-off—helping us to understand the past—re-experiencing also has a salutary impact on historians in the present, enriching their lives by showing them an expanded range of human possibility. Through a kind of appropriation of past experience, taking a detour through the narratives of others, we enlarge our own lives and emerge transformed, moving beyond mere introspection, which confirms what we already are. "The obscurity of experience is illuminated, the mistakes which arise from the narrower comprehension of the subject are corrected, experience itself is widened and completed, in the process of understanding other people—just as other people are understood through our own experience."[56] Because of the beneficial effects of vicarious experience, Dilthey maintained that a purely contemplative attitude toward the past, one in which our values and purposes were entirely suspended, was not only impossible, but also unhealthy. For it is only through history that man comes to know himself. Thus, although never going as far as Oakeshott was to go in collapsing past and present experience, Dilthey saw them as mutually entangled and meaningfully intertwined. To be fully human was to immerse oneself in the flow of historical becoming, compensating for the one-sided and partial character of our own personal experience through opening ourselves to that of others. The hermeneutic circle involves a constant move back and forth from text to interpretation, past to present, the life of the historian to the lives of those he or she studies. At its best, it can even lead to an expanded understanding that can genuinely claim to be objective knowledge, transcending the relativist implications of historicist thought.

The optimism expressed in such a claim was not, however, easy to sustain, and Dilthey's project to write a critique of historical knowledge comparable to those of Kant has generally been accounted a productive failure.[57] Epistemological objectivity and hermeneutic interpretation were harder to reconcile than he had thought. The passage from initial lived experience through worldview and expression leading to historical re-experiencing proved much rougher and more discontinuous than he expected. As in the case of Vico, the inevitable question demanded to be asked: who is the "we" who "makes" history and therefore can know it (or rather, who experiences history and can

56. Dilthey, *Pattern and Meaning in History,* p. 122. For a discussion of Dilthey's repudiation of his earlier faith in introspection, see Plantinga, *Historical Understanding in the Thought of Wilhelm Dilthey,* pp. 47–48.

57. For a still valuable assessment of Dilthey in the general context of other efforts to deal with the questions he raised, see Hughes, *Consciousness and Society,* chapter 6.

re-experience it)? Can we assume that the sum of individual actions produces a collective historical subject or that representative individuals really are typical of the groups who actively produce their world? Indeed, are "making" and "experiencing" simple synonyms? Is *homo faber* the only model of the human condition?[58]

Not only does the *verum-factum* principle problematically imply that history can be largely understood as the product of human intentionality rather than the outcome of impersonal forces, structures, circumstances, and sheer contingency, in addition to acts of human will. It also assumes an essential continuity between those who make the past and those who recognize it, a continuity that implicitly posits an enduring, transcendental, tacitly stable human subject, whose historical specificity is less critical than his generic uniformity. It takes for granted as well the existence of a grand narrative called History as a universal story made by that subject, a narrative whose assumed existence, it has since been shown, was itself a product of the epochal shift that marked the onset of modernity.[59] Thus, the very historicity Dilthey was so anxious to sustain against anti-historical thinkers like Nietzsche made the task of re-experiencing the past more difficult than he might have appreciated.[60] The ghost of Hegel's notion of history as the *Bildung* of the World Spirit surreptitiously returned, despite Dilthey's best efforts to exorcise it.[61] Biography and autobiography, Dilthey's critics warned, could only be the privileged models for historical re-experiencing if that *Bildung* were understood along the lines of an individual life, whose story could be recollected at the end of the narrative, almost like the collective memory of mankind.[62] As Michael Pickering points out, "there is insufficient recognition of lives running experientially in conflict with each other, of discord between experiences, and of the struggle to assert and place the meanings of certain experiences over those of others, which are then marginalized or made insignificant. Experience cannot be divorced from the clashes of interests, struc-

58. This question is insightfully addressed in Hannah Arendt, *The Human Condition* (Chicago, 1958).

59. Reinhart Koselleck, *Futures Past: On the Semantics of Historical Time,* trans. Keith Tribe (Cambridge, Mass., 1985), pp. 92–104.

60. To be fair to Dilthey, he did recognize the practical obstacles in specific cases, for example his own attempt to make sense of the religious sects of the Reformation, which he called "totally incomprehensible to me." See his remarks in *Der junge Dilthey,* p. 152.

61. Not all of his commentators, to be sure, accept this conclusion; see, for example, Hodges, *The Philosophy of Wilhelm Dilthey,* p. 319.

62. On the idea of history as "mankind's memory," see Bulhof, *Wilhelm Dilthey,* chapter 3. Stressing biography, moreover, sometimes allowed Dilthey to assume that great men somehow represented their *Zeitgeist.*

tural denials of opportunity and achievement, and relations of power which are implicated in these actualities of living."[63]

It was, in fact, one of the paradoxical implications of the heightened historical consciousness of Dilthey's own day that the gap between present and past was yawning wider, which in fact accounted for the increased methodological self-scrutiny evident in Dilthey himself. According to Rudolf Makkreel, Dilthey ultimately came to acknowledge that "while reflection on our experience may remain a *point of departure* for understanding others, such reflection is . . . indeterminate and cannot serve as the *foundation* for interpretation."[64] In fact, even for the cultural creator, the fit between experience and expression—or at least its historical meaning—may have been growing ever more attenuated. What Simmel was to dub in a famous essay of 1911 the "tragedy of culture" meant that subjective expressions and their objective cultural counterparts were increasingly at odds in a complex society, producing a tragic dissociation that resisted reconciliation.[65] No longer firmly grounded in the continuity of something called "tradition," historians had to struggle to familiarize the unfamiliar and redescribe it in terms that would make sense to themselves. As Gadamer was later to note,

> Just as the remoteness from experience and the hunger for experience, which come from the distress caused by the complicated workings of civilization transformed by the industrial revolution, brought the word *Erlebnis* into general usage, so the new distanced attitude that historical consciousness takes to tradition, gives to the concept of *Erlebnis* its epistemological function.[66]

But as an epistemological tool, *Erlebnis* could only go so far, at least in the direction of the objective knowledge that Dilthey stubbornly hoped could

---

63. Michael Pickering, *History, Experience and Cultural Studies* (New York, 1997), p. 128.

64. Rudolf Makkreel, introduction to Dilthey, *Descriptive Psychology and Historical Understanding*, p. 20 (emphasis in original).

65. Georg Simmel, "On the Concept and Tragedy of Culture," in John Rundell and Stephen Mennell, eds., *Classical Readings in Culture and Civilization* (London, 1998). For discussions of Simmel's general approach to the question of *Erlebnis*, see Rudolph H. Weingartner, *Experience and Culture: The Philosophy of Georg Simmel* (Middletown, Conn., 1962); and Sauerland, *Diltheys Erlebnisbegriff*, pp. 151–54. For a similar pessimism about the reconciliation of lived experience and cultural expression, see the essays written around the same time by Georg Lukács and collected as *Soul and Form*, trans. Anna Bostock (Cambridge, Mass., 1971).

66. Gadamer, *Truth and Method*, p. 58. Whether or not earlier historians were right to think they could assume a commonality of experience with past generations—did Gibbon really inhabit the same universe as Tacitus?—they tended not to agonize over the disparity.

be attained. In fact, he came in his last works to acknowledge its provisional status.[67] Although the debate continues to rage over how relativist his ultimate position actually was,[68] few commentators feel he attained his goal. Neo-Kantian social scientists like Max Weber attempted to concoct more methodologically plausible approaches than imaginative re-experiencing, while hermeneutic phenomenologists like Heidegger and Gadamer sought to redirect attention from epistemological to ontological questions.[69] By the 1920s, Dilthey's project to provide a rigorous tool of historical analysis had degenerated into little more than a vague and imprecise slogan in the struggle against the residues of "positivism." As Fritz Ringer has noted, "the rhetoric of *Erleben* was used to suggest intuitive *identification* just as 'phenomenological' methods were taken to authorize direct 'viewing' of 'essential' meanings *(Wesenschau)*."[70] Even those who still invoked its power decried what they saw as the residue of objectivism in Dilthey's vain attempt to produce a critique of historical reason.

COLLINGWOOD AND THE RE-ENACTMENT
OF PAST THOUGHT

Typical of this reaction was the critique of Dilthey's psychology made by the Oxford philosopher and historian R. G. (Robin George) Collingwood in his celebrated study *The Idea of History,* which was based on lectures delivered in 1936 and posthumously published a decade later with the editorial help of T. M. Knox.[71] For Collingwood, any attempt to ground history in psychology was a capitulation to the positivism and naturalism that Dilthey purported to be

---

67. See, for example, Dilthey, *Gesammelte Schriften,* vol. 7, p. 106.

68. For a summary of the different arguments, see Bambach, *Heidegger, Dilthey, and the Crisis of Historicism,* pp. 169–76.

69. See Fritz K. Ringer, *Max Weber's Methodology: The Unification of the Cultural and Social Sciences* (Cambridge, Mass, 1997); Bambach, *Heidegger, Dilthey and the Crisis of Historicism*; and Georgia Warnke, *Gadamer: Hermeneutics, Tradition and Reason* (Stanford, 1987), chapter 1. There were, to be sure, some literary critics who continued to employ Dilthey's *Erlebnis* concept in their work, for example Oskar Walzel and Josef Körner. See the discussion of their work in Sauerland, *Diltheys Erlebnisbegriff,* pp. 154–62.

70. Fritz Ringer, *Fields of Knowledge: French Academic Culture in Comparative Perspective, 1890–1920* (Cambridge, 1992), p. 206.

71. R. G. Collingwood, *The Idea of History* (New York, 1956), pp. 171–76. A somewhat revised edition appeared in 1993 edited by Jan van der Dussen. It is based on recently discovered manuscripts, whose implications van der Dussen discusses in "Collingwood's 'Lost' Manuscript of *The Principles of History,*" *History and Theory* vol. 36, no. 1 (1997). All references are to the earlier edition, which influenced generations of Collingwood's readers. Since that time, many unpublished manuscripts have become available; see Donald S. Taylor, *R. G. Collingwood: A Bibliography* (New York, 1988).

combating. Although misinterpreting the intent of Dilthey's "descriptive and analytical psychology," which sought to avoid causal, atomistic explanation in favor of a holistic understanding of the "real contents" of the mind, Collingwood was right in noting that Dilthey himself had considered his own attempts at producing a viable psychological foundation for historical re-experiencing ultimately a failure. Even as ardent a defender of those attempts against Collingwood's charge as Hajo Holborn had to acknowledge that psychology had given way to hermeneutics in his later work for a reason.[72]

Collingwood, however, continued to ponder the same questions that Dilthey had posed, hoping to effect what he called "a *rapprochement* between philosophy and history,"[73] and in so doing he provided yet another influential attempt to clarify the role of experience in historical inquiry, which had special resonance in the English-speaking world.[74] Although learning much from Oakeshott as well, he rejected the claim that history was merely an arrest in real experience, somehow deficient in the philosophical reflection marking absolute experience. As a practicing historian, most notably of Roman Britain, and the son of a distinguished archaeologist, Collingwood appreciated history from the inside.[75] History, he argued, "should be a living past, a past which, because it was thought and not mere natural event, can be re-enacted in the present and in that re-enactment known as past. . . . history is not based on a philosophical error [as Oakeshott claimed] and is therefore not in his sense a mode of experience, but an integral part of experience itself."[76]

Collingwood, however, shared many of Oakeshott's idealist inclinations, inviting the claim that he was a Hegelian at heart.[77] Insofar as his early work,

72. Holborn, "Wilhelm Dilthey and the Critique of Historical Reason," *European Intellectual History since Darwin and Marx*, ed. W. Warren Wager (New York, 1966), pp. 78–80.

73. R. G. Collingwood, *An Autobiography* (Oxford, 1939), p. 76.

74. For a comparison of their two positions, see Hodges, *The Philosophy of Wilhelm Dilthey*, chapter 10. For general appreciations of his work, see Louis O. Mink, *Mind, History and Dialectic: The Philosophy of R. G. Collingwood* (Bloomington, Ind., 1969); Michael Drausz, ed., *Critical Essays on the Philosophy of R. G. Collingwood* (Oxford, 1972); W. J. van der Dussen, *History as a Science: The Philosophy of R. G. Collingwood* (The Hague, 1981); David Boucher, James Connelly, and Tariq Modood, eds., *Philosophy, History and Civilization: Interdisciplinary Perspectives on R. G. Collingwood* (Cardiff, 1995); William H. Dray, *History as Re-enactment: R. G. Collingwood's Idea of History* (Oxford, 1995); and the special issue of *History and Theory* 29 (1990) devoted to "Reassessing Collingwood."

75. For a bibliography of Collingwood's work as a historian and archaeologist, see I. M. Richmond, *Proceedings of the British Academy* 29 (1943), pp. 481–485.

76. Collingwood, *The Idea of History*, p. 158.

77. According to Louis O. Mink, "In fact, if Collingwood can be associated with any single figure in the history of philosophy that one would be Hegel, although even then only by virtue of Collingwood's

most notably *Speculum Mentis* of 1924, sought to systematize knowledge and explore a totalistic dialectic of experience—including art, religion, science, and history—he revealed his debts to the legacy of F. H. Bradley and other late nineteenth-century British idealists.[78] According to one of his most distinguished interpreters, Louis O. Mink, "experience" was "not used by Collingwood as a term with systematic meaning except as roughly synonymous with *consciousness.*' It usually suggests any activity of consciousness insofar as it is an object for higher-level consciousness."[79]

Rather than attempting to spell out all of the varieties of experience *qua* consciousness for Collingwood, we can focus only on its crucial place in his understanding of that mode called history. For in answering the question "of what can there be historical knowledge?" in *The Idea of History,* he explicitly replied "of that which can be re-enacted in the historian's mind. In the first place, this must be experience. Of that which is not experience but the mere object of experience, there can be no history."[80] Like Dilthey, Collingwood understood historical experience to be more than the unmediated sense data of the naive empiricist. "In so far as it is merely immediate experience," he wrote, "a mere flow of consciousness consisting of sensations, feelings and the like, its process is not an historical process."[81] Although he misunderstood Dilthey to be saying that life "means immediate experience, as distinct from reflection or knowledge. . . . history by itself is mere life, immediate experience, and therefore the historian as such merely experiences a life which the psychologist as such and he alone understands,"[82] he shared with his German predecessor a belief that some sort of re-experiencing of the past was essential to historical knowledge.

In at least two major ways, however, Collingwood distanced himself from Dilthey. First, he argued for "re-enactment" rather than "re-experiencing," a

---

brief but illuminating reinterpretation of Hegel in *The Idea of History." Mind, History and Dialectic,* p. 5. Collingwood himself disliked the identification. He wrote to Gilbert Ryle in 1935 "I am afraid I resent both the label and the irresponsible manner of attaching it." Quoted in David Boucher, "The Life, Times and Legacy of R. G. Collingwood," in Boucher, Connelly, and Modood, eds., *Philosophy, History and Civilisation,* p. 27.

78. Collingwood, *Speculum Mentis* (Oxford, 1924). Collingwood's analysis is perhaps more Hegelian than Oakeshott's in *Experience and Its Modes* because it tries to arrange the modalities of experience in a hierarchy of increasing concreteness, each level surmounting the contradictions of its predecessor.

79. Mink, *Mind, History and Dialectic,* p. 271.

80. Collingwood, *The Idea of History,* p. 302.

81. Ibid.

82. Ibid., pp. 172–73.

distinction that emphasized the importance of actions in the past as the target of historical inquiry. "Geology presents us with a series of *events*," he argued, "but history is not history unless it presents us with a series of *acts*."[83] These were both external manifestations and internal motivations, the inside and outside of events. By stressing the importance of purposive individual actions, of *res gestae*, Collingwood was repudiating those historians who claimed that structures, institutions, discourses, or behavioral patterns were the proper subject of the historian's craft, a repudiation that brought him close to the humanistic Dilthey (even if Collingwood read him as a psychologistic generalizer). But what the stress on action also did was to marginalize all of those elements in experience that entailed a certain passivity or openness to encounters with the unexpected, betokened a willingness to submit to what occurred rather than willing it to occur, and drew on appetites and beliefs that subtended the conscious decision to act. Here that religious moment that we have seen in the Dilthey who learned so much from Schleiermacher, that moment of quasi-pantheistic surrender to the world, was absent. Religion in Collingwood's dialectic of mind in *Speculum Mentis* was tellingly subsumed under Science, and history was itself "a science of a special kind,"[84] inferential rather than directly observational.

Re-enactment for Collingwood also meant a bias for the rational motivations of action itself and the conscious reflexivity of thinking. "All history," he boldly proclaimed in one of his most controversial aphorisms, "is the history of thought."[85] Responding to the charge that experiences are so ineffable, personal, and unrepeatable that they cannot be re-enacted by later historians, he replied:

So far as experience consists of mere consciousness, of sensations, and feelings pure and simple, it is true. But an act of thought is not a mere sensation or feeling. It is knowledge, and knowledge is something more than immediate consciousness. The process of knowledge is therefore not a mere succession of states. . . . Thought itself is not involved in the flow of immediate consciousness; in some sense, it stands outside that flow. . . . [The] one and the same act of thought may endure through a lapse of time and revive after a time when it has been in abeyance.[86]

83. Ibid., p. 115.
84. Ibid., p. 251.
85. Ibid., p. 215.
86. Ibid., p. 286.

Because of the objective quality of thought, Collingwood contended, it was wrong to reduce re-enactment to a subjective process entirely in the present. It was no less mistaken to see what it re-enacted as carried away in the ongoing flux of consciousness. Arguing explicitly against Oakeshott's notion of historical experience as the present seeing the past *sub specie praeteritorum* and Croce's claim that all history is contemporary history, Collingwood insisted that re-enacting the thought of the past kept both poles of the equation in creative tension.[87] Historical thought was thus both subjective and objective at once. What Collingwood called the "a priori imagination" of the historian allowed him or her to turn the documents left by the past into re-enactments of the acts that originally produced them, a far more active intervention than the "scissors-and-paste" historian's collation of sources, a far more creative task than mere imitation. That imaginative re-enactment, he conceded, was premised on at least some minimal commonality of human experience, for to understand the texts of a past figure, "we must come to the reading of them prepared with an experience sufficiently like his own to make those thoughts organic to it."[88] But re-enactment also involved a critical dimension that extended beyond simple empathy with past experiences and entailed a willingness to take seriously the truth claims of prior thoughts understood as viable answers to real questions, questions that changed over time.[89]

Even when the history was based on one's own personal experience, it

87. Sometimes Collingwood is assimilated to Croce, for example by Siegfried Kracauer in *History: The Last Things before the Last* (New York, 1969), chapter 3, but he sought to avoid an overly presentist position. Kracauer, to be sure, was right to question the ease with which Collingwood moved from the present to the past on the basis of putative affinities between the two.

88. Collingwood, *The Idea of History*, p. 300. Elsewhere in his work, however, Collingwood struck a more relativist note, for example in his *Autobiography,* where he argued against the philosophical "realists'" assumption of perennial problems: "the history of political theory is not the history of different answers given to one and the same question, but the history of a problem more or less constantly changing, whose solution was changing with it" (p. 62). What allowed continuity between past and present, however, was his further assumption that history is concerned with endless processes, not discrete events, which implied that the past and the present were not radically incommensurable (p. 97).

89. According to Ermarth, Dilthey's *Verstehen* also involved the immanent critique of past ideas. See *Wilhelm Dilthey,* pp. 316–17, for a comparison with Collingwood on this point. For a summary of Collingwood's general defense of the logic of questions-and-answers as opposed to the logic of propositions, see *An Autobiography,* chapter 5. For a discussion of its influence on the work of Quentin Skinner and his school, see James Tully, ed., *Meaning and Context: Quentin Skinner and His Critics* (Oxford, 1988). Collingwood was acknowledged by Hans-Georg Gadamer as important for his own development as well. See his *Reason in the Age of Science,* trans. Frederick G. Lawrence (Cambridge, Mass., 1983), pp. 45–46; and *Truth and Method,* pp. 333–41. He also wrote the introduction to the German edition of Collingwood's *Autobiography.* Gadamer, however, always insisted that the questions asked by the historian are not simply re-enactments of those asked by historical actors. Collingwood, contrary to Gadamer's reproach, did seem to acknowledge this distinction in his *Autobiography,* when he wrote: "historical problems arise out

differed from memory precisely insofar as it went beyond passive spectacle to active re-enactment in present thought. "Memory," Collingwood argued, "as such is only the present thought of past experience as such, be that experience what it may; historical knowledge is that special case of memory where the object of present thought is past thought, the gap between present and past being bridged not only by the power of present thought to think of the past, but also by the power of past thought to reawaken itself in the present."[90] In the case of seemingly impersonal processes such as wars or economic trends, which were never directly experienced by the historian, re-enactment was made possible, Collingwood insisted, by focusing on the intentions of those who command in war or who make economic decisions.

With these premises, it is not surprising that Collingwood's theory of history has often been charged, to quote one of his most eminent commentators, "with being too intellectualistic, too rationalistic, too action-oriented, too mentalistic, and too individualistic."[91] Even friendly readers like Gadamer would complain that "a theory of planning or of action can never do justice to the experience of history in which our plans tend to shatter and our actions and omissions tend to lead to unexpected consequences."[92] Although conceding the existence of acting out of irrational motives, Collingwood did think it heuristically important to assume rationality first.[93] But the difficulty came in assuming a link between rational intentions and rational outcomes. Nor was it easy to understand how we might judge different historians' re-enactments in relation to the original acts that they did not mimetically reproduce but imaginatively reconstructed; for what criterion, after all, could guide such an assessment if the past could be accessed only through the re-enactments themselves? Was comparative coherence a sufficient criterion to

of practical problems. We study history in order to see more clearly into the situation in which we are called upon to act. Hence the plane on which, ultimately, all problems arise is the plane of 'real' life: that to which they are referred for their solution is history" (p. 114).

90. Collingwood, *The Idea of History*, p. 294.

91. Dray, *History as Re-enactment*, p. 109. Dray tries to provide nuanced defenses of Collingwood against many of these charges, often demonstrating ambiguities and adducing counter-examples in the larger corpus, unpublished as well as published, of Collingwood's work.

92. Gadamer, *Reason in the Age of Science*, p. 46

93. For discussions of this point, see Dray, *History as Re-enactment*, p. 118, and van der Dussen, "Collingwood's 'Lost' Manuscript of *The Principles of History*," p. 44. Here, although he would never have acknowledged the connection, Collingwood was following Max Weber's precept: "For the purposes of a typological scientific analysis it is convenient to treat all irrational, affectually determined elements of behavior as factors of deviation from a conceptually pure type of rational action." *The Theory of Social and Economic Organization*, ed. Talcott Parsons, trans. A. M. Henderson and Talcott Parsons (New York, 1947), p. 92.

distinguish among competing re-enactments? And finally, was it plausible to adopt the traditional argument against psychologism—that such mental acts as following the proofs of syllogistic logic revealed objective truths transcending their individual moments of enactment—to the semantically variable and culturally filtered thoughts of people in different times and places? The Law of the Excluded Middle may hold for Plato as well as for us, but was the Greek philosopher's understanding of justice really perfectly equivalent to ours and thus available for rational re-enactment?

Although some of the problem may have come from Collingwood's notoriously fuzzy use of concepts and the incompletion of his projected work, *The Principles of History*, at his death, as well as general ignorance of his other works beyond *The Idea of History* and parts of his *Autobiography*, it is nonetheless hard to deny the movement in his thought away from Dilthey's more inclusive notion of *Erlebnis*.[94] In Collingwood, we might fairly say, the blood of Dilthey's fully rounded subject of lived experience began to thin once again to that "diluted juice of reason" running through the veins of Locke, Hume, and Kant—or perhaps more appropriately, Hegel.[95] In his hostility to the psychologistic moment in Dilthey's work, which he saw as a residue of positivist naturalism, Collingwood too radically separated the content of thought, which could be re-enacted because it transcended the time of its being originally thought, from its various contexts of origin, transmission, and reception.[96] Dilthey's vitalistic notion of *Erlebnis* had to be spurned, after all, by someone who could write "of everything other than thought, there can be no history. Thus a biography, for example, however much history it contains, is constructed

94. For a consideration of the claim that Collingwood's manuscripts suggest a more expansive notion of human thought, see Parker, *The English Idea of History from Coleridge to Collingwood*. Parker concludes that "if Collingwood did, however, intend to make the re-enactment of emotion an important element in his philosophy of history, it represented the abandonment of a position in which he had surely invested a lot of intellectual capital. Either way the historical 'Collingwood' we have known since the publication of *The Idea of History* in 1946 appeared to be essentially rationalist in this respect, and his new position, if new it was, appears not to have been entirely thought through" (pp. 207–8).

95. As Gadamer notes, focusing on the rational intentions of individuals "is a legitimate undertaking only if Hegel's conditions hold good, i.e., that the philosophy of history is made party to the plans of the world spirit and on the basis of this esoteric knowledge is able to mark out certain individuals as of world-historical importance, there being a real co-ordination between their particular ideas and the world-historical meaning of events." *Truth and Method*, p. 334.

96. Oddly, Karl Popper took Collingwood to task precisely for the psychologism he was trying so hard to avoid. See *Objective Knowledge: An Evolutionary Approach* (Oxford, 1972), p. 187. For a thorough critique of Popper's misreading, see Peter Skagestad, *Making Sense of History: The Philosophies of Popper and Collingwood* (Oslo, 1975). Collingwood's general hostility to psychology is captured in his intemperate denunciation of it as a science of the mind in his *Autobiography*, where he compares it to astrology, alchemy, and phrenology: "the fashionable scientific fraud of the age" (p. 95).

on principles that are not only non-historical but anti-historical. Its limits are biological events, birth and death of a human organism: its framework is thus a framework not of thought but of natural science."[97] Once biological limits were avoided, the way was open for the covertly transcendental spiritualism that allowed Collingwood to assume the identity of thought over time.[98]

The phenomenological stress on a prereflective lifeworld so often discerned in Dilthey is only faintly evident in Collingwood, although he shared with Husserl and Heidegger a critique of psychologism in its naturalist guise. Perhaps only in his approach to the history of art did intuitive, non-rational re-enactment find a place.[99] Elsewhere, he seemed almost like an unwitting fore-runner of the rational-choice theory that was to dominate so much social science—although significantly not the discipline of history—in the years to come.[100] And rarely, if ever, did Collingwood, like Dilthey before him, consider the collective nature of experience, which so exercised historians interested in generational, class, ethnic, or gender identities. As a result, he could be faulted, in addition to all the other objections to his theory, for smuggling liberal ideological assumptions into his version of the past, as well as for having a frankly Eurocentric notion of mind.[101]

HISTORY AND EVERYDAY LIFE:
THE RECOVERY OF "ORDINARY" EXPERIENCE

Very different motivations underlay the call to recover historical experience made a generation or so later by those advocating E. P. Thompson's "history

---

97. Collingwood, *The Idea of History*, p. 304.

98. For a powerful analysis of its importance, see David Bates, "Rediscovering Collingwood's Spiritual History (In and Out of Context)," *History and Theory* 35, no. 1 (1996).

99. For a discussion, see Dray, *History as Re-enactment*, p. 139. See also Makkreel, *Dilthey: Philosopher of the Human Sciences*, pp. 409–10. He argues that by seeing artistic experience as fully unreflective and thoughtless, Collingwood makes it impossible to have a re-enactment in art history based on anything beyond faith in the testimony of the artist about his emotions. Lacking an interest in the historical development of styles, Collingwood risks making the opposite mistake from that of Heinrich Wölfflin, that is, rather than "history of art without names," "art names without history."

100. See S. M. Amadae, *Rationalizing Capitalist Democracy: The Cold War Origins of Rational Choice Liberalism* (Chicago, 2003).

101. For the first accusation, see Keith Jenkins, *Re-Thinking History* (London, 1991), p. 44. In *An Autobiography*, Collingwood acknowledged that "my attitude towards politics had always been what in England is called democratic and on the Continent liberal" (p. 153), and describes his fervent support for the anti-Fascist side in the Spanish Civil War. For the second, see William Debbins's introduction to Collingwood, *Essays in the Philosophy of History* (New York, 1996), p. xxxi.

from below."[102] Rather than seeking to re-enact the rational thought of the leading actors of the past, its champions turned their attention to the forgotten masses of men and women whose everyday life, however mundane, was taken to be a worthy subject of historical inquiry. Against Collingwood's attribution of active agency and rational reflection to all the actors whose experiences might be imaginatively re-enacted, they acknowledged the limits to agency and reflection produced by the social conditions constraining those whose experience inevitably registered the power of these constraints even as they may have struggled to overcome them.

What has been dubbed the "turn to ordinariness"[103] in history matched the "transfiguration of the commonplace" in artistic practice and echoed the valorization of simple piety, as opposed to esoteric dogmatics, fueling the earlier celebration of religious experience. Inspired by a populist and egalitarian desire to include those whose history had previously been ignored by scholars focusing exclusively on intellectual, social, or political elites, historians in many different countries during the late 1960s and 1970s began to seek ways to allow those whom Antonio Gramsci had called the "subaltern" to speak (sometimes even literally in the new emphasis on the usefulness of oral history). The "critique of everyday life," which had begun in isolation in the 1930s with the first halting efforts of Marxists such as Henri Lefebvre, became a preoccupation of many non-Marxists as well, such as Michel de Certeau.[104] In ancillary disciplines like geography, a humanist stress on lived experience and the everyday was also apparent in the work of influential figures such as Yi-Fu Tuan.[105]

102. For a general assessment, see Jim Sharpe, "History from Below," *New Perspectives on Historical Writing*, ed. Peter Burke (University Park, Pa., 1992). The term comes from an essay by Thompson in the *Times Literary Supplement*, April 7, 1966.

103. Pickering, *History, Experience and Cultural Studies*, chapter 3.

104. Henri Lefebvre and Norbert Guterman, "La mystification: Notes pour une critique de la vie quotidienne," *Avant-Poste* 2 (August 1933). Their work is discussed in Bud Burkhard, *French Marxism Between the Wars: Henri Lefebvre and the "Philosophies"* (Amherst, N.Y., 2000), chapter 7. It culminated in Lefebvre's multivolume *Critique de la vie quotidienne* (Paris, 1947–62), the first volume translated as *Everyday Life in the Modern World*, trans. S. Rabinovich (New York, 1971); subsequently translated as *Critique of Everyday Life*, vols. 1–2 trans. John Moore and vol. 3 trans. Gregory Elliott (London, 1994, 2002, 2004). Michel de Certeau wrote his two-volume *L'invention du quotidien* in 1980; the first volume was translated as *The Practice of Everyday Life*, trans. Steven Rendall (Berkeley, 1984). For a critical analysis of the role of the everyday in cultural studies, see Laurie Langbauer, "Cultural Studies and the Politics of the Everyday," *Diacritics* 22, no. 1 (Spring 1992). For a philosophical consideration of the same theme, see Agnes Heller, *Everyday Life*, trans. G. L. Campbell (London, 1984). For an overview of its importance, see Ben Highmore, *Everyday Life and Cultural Theory: An Introduction* (London, 2002).

105. Yi-Fu Tuan, *Space and Place: The Perspective of Experience* (Minneapolis, 1977). See also the essays devoted to him in Paul C. Adams, Steven Hoelscher, and Karen E. Till, eds., *Textures of Place: Exploring Humanist Geographies* (Minneapolis, 2001).

When "the new cultural history" began to push aside the social history that had come of age in the 1960s, mainstream historians began to deepen still further their appreciation of the importance of the quotidian sphere.[106] Here the "thick descriptions" advocated by cultural anthropologists like Clifford Geertz and Victor Turner served as a vital inspiration. Either as a site of mystification or a locus of resistance (or both at once), the "everyday" became a privileged arena for cultural historians with a critical bent and a distaste for rarified discourses and exclusive institutions. What became known in Germany as *Alltagsgeschichte* gained special attention in the 1980s when its target was everyday life during the Nazi era, where the issue of complicity, neutrality, or resistance to the regime by "ordinary Germans" was highly charged.[107] Although gaining access to the putative experience of those on the bottom of the social order was easiest in the modern period, when documents were more readily available, ingenious researchers like Emmanuel La Roy Ladurie, Carlo Ginzburg, Roger Chartier, Natalie Zemon Davis, Robert Darnton, Hans Medick, and Peter Burke developed methods to probe quotidian existence in the medieval and early modern eras as well. Here the monumental researches of the *Annales* School led by Fernand Braudel and Lucien Febvre were key inspirations, bringing to the fore a concern for the shared "mentalities" of cultural groups rather than the explicit ideas of intellectual elites. And in their quest for access to this region of past cultures, these scholars often opened the door to more self-conscious reflexivity about the historian's own experience, which was no longer so easily hidden behind a facade of authorial impersonality.[108]

The sources of the new international fascination with the broad experiences of the hitherto neglected were, in fact, multifarious. Explaining the ad-

106. See the essays in Lynn Hunt, ed., *The New Cultural History* (Berkeley, 1989).

107. See, for example, Alf Lüdtke, ed., *Alltagsgeschichte: Zur Rekonstruktion historischer Erfahrungen und Lebensweisen* (Frankfurt, 1989). For analyses, see David F. Crew, "*Alltagsgeschichte:* A New Social History 'From Below'," *Central European History* 22, nos. 3–4 (1989), and my "Songs of Experience: Reflections on the Debate over *Alltagsgeschichte*," *Cultural Semantics: Keywords of Our Time* (Amherst, Mass., 1998).

108. For an analysis of this tendency in the *Annales* school, see Philippe Carrard, "Theory of a Practice: Historical Enunciation and the *Annales* School," in Frank Ankersmit and Hans Kellner, eds., *A New Philosophy of History* (Chicago, 1995). Although historians were generally more restrained than literary critics, many of whom turned to confessional "*moi* criticism" rather than the traditional interpretation of texts, one can find a number of examples of greater willingness to incorporate the experiences of the historians into their narratives in the last two decades of the twentieth century. Perhaps the most bizarre case was Edmund Morris's *Dutch: A Memoir of Ronald Reagan* (New York, 1999), in which the author interjected fantasized accounts of his own meetings with the president in his supposedly nonfictional rendering of Reagan's life.

vent of "history from below" in Britain, one of its leading practitioners, Raphael Samuel of the History Workshop group recalled:

> The central place which History Workshop has often given to "real life experience," both as a subject for historical inquiry, and as a litmus-paper to test the abstract against the particular, may conjecturally be ascribed to a succession of different influences. In part it comes from our original constituency of mainly worker-writers, and the high claims we were making for historical work to which the writer was bringing the fruits not only of research, but also of personal life history. Then, from a very different source, there was the then-radicalizing influence of micro-sociology popularized in the middle 1960's by the early "deviancy" theorists, with their emphasis on informal modes of resistance in such captive institutions as prisons. A more substantial—if finally limiting—influence at this time, was that of social and cultural anthropology, with its method of participant observation, its local and familiar focus, and its attempt to give a theoretical and cultural dimension to the transactions of everyday life.[109]

Added to all of these stimuli was the powerful impetus of the new fascination with women's history, which was closely linked to the emergence of the political and social movement for women's liberation throughout the Western world and beyond.[110] The frequent valorization of experience in the struggle for women's rights has been often remarked, although no less striking is the vigorous debate over its implications, which continues to this day. Women's history encouraged a focus on the experience of everyday life in several salient ways. An insistence that "the personal was the political" directed attention to regions of private life, notably the family, mothering, leisure activity, and the sphere of domesticity, as well as women's work outside the home, which had been relatively neglected by historians focusing only on great deeds in the public sphere. Noting that the primacy of reason was often gendered male in Western thought, feminist historians subtly challenged Collingwood's assumption that experience to be retrievable by the historian had to be a rational activity capable of being re-enacted in

---

109. Raphael Samuel, "On the Methods of History Workshop: A Reply," *History Workshop* 9 (Spring 1980), pp. 165–66.

110. For a short account of the rise of women's history, see Joan Scott, "Women's History," in *New Perspectives in Historical Writing*. For an account of its emergence in the context of British "history from below," see Dennis Dworkin, *Cultural Marxism in Postwar Britain* (Durham, N.C., 1997), chapter 5; and Carolyn Steedman, "The Price of Experience: Women and the Making of the English Working Class," *Radical History Review* 59 (Spring 1994).

the present.[111] Stressing the value of shared story-telling, which had earned a privileged place in the "consciousness-raising" groups of the 1970s, led to a concern for collecting and reflecting on the narratives of women in the past, which related their seemingly banal experience in revealing ways. Often such experiences could serve as exemplary instances of resistance by victims to their oppression in ways that could easily be turned to political advantage in the present.

But even as women's experience began to cry out for historical rediscovery, voices were raised within the feminist community, as elsewhere, concerned about its potentially ideological implications. Not surprisingly, many of the same theoretically charged arguments directed at the work of E. P. Thompson and Raymond Williams by critics like Terry Eagleton and Perry Anderson, which we encountered in the previous chapter, found their way into the debates about the dangers inherent in a naively straightforward notion of women's experience. In Britain, one of the earliest salvos was fired by Juliet Mitchell, a member of the *New Left Review* circle and an ardent defender of Sigmund Freud against his detractors in the women's movement. In her influential *Psychoanalysis and Feminism* of 1974, she critically examined the existentialist evocation of experience in the work of R. D. Laing. Quoting such remarks from *The Politics of Experience* as "experience is man's invisibility to man. Experience used to be called The Soul. Experience as invisibility of man to man is at the same time more evident than anything. *Only* experience is evident. Experience is the *only* evidence. Psychology is the logos of experience,"[112] Mitchell noted that they were motivated by a "*mysticoreligious* pursuit of transcendental experience."[113] From a scientific point of view—and Mitchell was working with a definition of science that owed much to the Lacanian and Althusserian versions of scientificity—Laing was still operating with an empirical notion of the self, however dressed up it might be in phenomenological or existentialist terminology. His hostility to the alienation and objectification of the subject in modern capitalism had led him to posit a naively humanist subject that could not be the object of a true science of psychology, which worked instead, she argued, with a structural notion of the unconscious that called into question the self-evidence of experience. "Rather than use what to him is a contradictory term 'unconscious

111. Typical of this critique of the gendered nature of reason was Genevieve Lloyd, *The Man of Reason: "Male" and "Female" in Western Philosophy* (Minneapolis, 1984).

112. R. D. Laing, *The Politics of Experience and the Bird of Paradise* (London, 1967), p. 16, quoted in Juliet Mitchell, *Psychoanalysis and Feminism* (London, 1974), p. 236.

113. Mitchell, *Psychoanalysis and Feminism*, p. 240 (emphasis in original).

experience'," Mitchell complained, "Laing prefers to state that there are different *modes* of experience—imagination, memory, perception, dreaming, etc.
When one is *not aware* of what one is imagining (for instance) one is not in
good communication with either oneself or the other. . . . In other words,
the unconscious can be understood (rendered intelligible) in *exactly* the same
way as consciousness." [114]

Juliet Mitchell's critique was not directed specifically at the historical recovery of women's forgotten experience, but her skepticism about experiential self-evidence and her insistence on its mediation by more theoretical models of explanation, whether Freudian or not, soon found an echo among
feminist historians. [115] They may not have shared her hope for a scientific explanation of historical events comparable to the psychoanalytic theory she
struggled to rescue from its feminist detractors, but they found sympathetic
her wariness about the authority of subjective experience, either in the present
or past. Reinforcing this skepticism was a growing realization that the cultural anthropological exhortation to recover and record lived experience was
losing ground among anthropologists themselves. [116] What a panel at the
American Anthropology Association meetings in 1980 organized by Victor
Turner, Barbara Myerhoff, and Edward Bruner had hopefully dubbed "the
anthropology of experience" was already under fire when the conference proceedings were published under that title six years later. [117] Dilthey's transi-

114. Ibid., p. 255 (emphasis in original).

115. It should be noted, however, as Jane Gallop has observed, "the word 'history' is rampant in
Mitchell's discussions of psychoanalysis. . . . Mitchell has an idiosyncratic reading of Lacan which con-
strues Lacan as reinforcing the historical side of psychoanalysis." Gallop, "Moving Backwards or Forwards," in Teresa Brennan, ed., *Between Feminism and Psychoanalysis* (London, 1989), p. 34. Mitchell was
also involved in historical projects like *The Rights and Wrongs of Women* (Harmondsworth, 1976), which
she co-edited with Ann Oakley.

116. See, for example, Aletta Biersack, "Local Knowledge, Local History: Geertz and Beyond," in Hunt,
The New Cultural History. For two analyses of the key role played by Clifford Geertz in stimulating the
vogue of anthropology among historians, see Ronald Walters, "Signs of the Times: Clifford Geertz and
the Historians," *Social Research* 47, no. 3 (1980); and William H. Sewell Jr., "Geertz, Cultural Systems,
and History: From Synchrony to Transformation," *Representations* 59 (Summer 1997). On the general
impact of anthropology on "history from below," see Renato Rosaldo, "Celebrating Thompson's Heroes:
Social Analysis in History and Anthropology," in Harvey J. Kaye and Keith McClelland, eds., *E. P. Thompson: Critical Perspectives* (Oxford, 1990).

117. Victor W. Turner and Edward M. Bruner, eds., *The Anthropology of Experience* (Urbana, Ill., 1986).
In his epilogue to the volume, Clifford Geertz calls experience "the elusive master concept of this collection, one that none of the authors seems altogether happy with and none feels able really to do without"
and adds that the term's current vicissitudes "make the prospects for honest use of the word seem remote.
But it is equally true that without it, or something like it, cultural analyses seem to float several feet above
their human ground" (p. 374). .

tion from *Erlebnis* to *Ausdruck,* its contributors recognized, was far from smooth, and the linguistic codes and performative protocols that intervene between them confound any attempt to re-experience an original moment in its pure state.

Emblematic of the crisis of confidence among anthropologists was the powerful impact produced by an American intellectual historian, James Clifford, whose *Predicament of Culture* of 1988 questioned the cult of experience underpinning the fetish of fieldwork by participant-observers. Recognizing the cult's debt to Dilthey's evocation of *Erlebnis,* Clifford warned against the authority of experience:

> Like "intuition," it is something that one does or does not have, and its invocation often smacks of mystification. Nevertheless, one should resist the temptation to translate all meaningful experience into interpretation. If the two are reciprocally related, they are not identical. It makes sense to hold them apart, if only because appeals to experience often act as validations for ethnographic authority.[118]

Whether signifying "a participatory presence, sensitive contact with the world to be understood, a rapport with its people, a concreteness of perception," or "a cumulative deepening knowledge,"[119] experience elevated the subjective role of the anthropologist over intersubjective interaction with those he or she studied. It also short-circuited the textual and discursive production of the representations of that primal experience, which followed protocols irreducible to the fieldworker's unmediated experience, however that term might be understood.

Clifford's debunking of the assumed authority of the ethnographic experience, like that of Mitchell's Lacanian critique of Laing, derived in large measure from an embrace of what came to be known as the "linguistic turn," first in philosophy and then in the humanities as a whole. Serving as what one observer called "a catch-all phrase for divergent critiques of established historical paradigms, narratives, and chronologies, encompassing not only poststructuralist linguistic criticism, linguistic theory, and philosophy but also cultural and symbolic anthropology, new historicism and gender history,"[120]

118. James Clifford, *The Predicament of Culture: Twentieth-Century Ethnography, Literature, and Art* (Cambridge, Mass., 1988), p. 35.

119. Ibid., p. 37.

120. Kathleen Canning, "Feminist History after the Linguistic Turn: Historicising Discourse and Experience," *Signs* 19, no. 2 (1994), p. 417.

"the linguistic turn" soon became a rallying cry for critics of experience as the *ur*-object of historical inquiry. Abstruse attempts to pit language against experience, such as the Italian philosopher Giorgio Agamben's *Infancy and History* of 1978, began to find an echo in the work of practicing historians.[121] As the British historian Patrick Joyce put it in 1991, "The seemingly simple recognition that the category of 'experience' (out of which historians such as E. P. Thompson argue comes class consciousness) is in fact not prior to and constitutive of language but is actively constituted by language, has increasingly been recognized as having far-reaching implications."[122] What precisely were those implications was then, and remains today, a source of vigorous debate,[123] largely because there has been no consensus about which model of language is understood to motivate the turn. Suffice it to say that the rise of attention in the human sciences to language in whatever guise was accompanied by increased skepticism about the tradition we have identified with Dilthey, Oakeshott, and Collingwood that was subsequently democratized through "history from below," in which the fundamental object of historical inquiry was understood to be the experience of actors in the past.

In fact, by 1987 the pendulum had begun to shift so much in the new direction that defenders of that tradition, such as the American intellectual historian John Toews, could react with alarm at what he castigated as "a new form of reductionism . . . the reduction of experience to the meanings that shape it," which betrayed "the hubris of wordmakers who claim to be makers of reality." Arguing for the irreducibility of lived experience, he warned: "it is essential for our self-understanding, and thus also for fulfilling the historian's task of connecting memory with hope, that we recognize and examine the recent turn away from experience as a specific response to particular events and developments in the history of experience."[124]

---

121. Agamben, *Infancy and History: Essays on the Destruction of Experience*, trans. Liz Heron (London, 1993). I am not suggesting any direct influence of this book on historical practice, just that its radical differentiation of experience (understood as a prelinguistic state of bliss associated with infancy) from language and historical occurrence anticipated some of the same attitudes expressed by historians critical of the recovery of experience as a methodological principle.

122. Patrick Joyce, *Visions of the People: Industrial England and the Question of Class, 1848–1914* (Cambridge, 1991), p. 9.

123. For my own attempt to sort them out for intellectual history, see "Should Intellectual History Take a Linguistic Turn? Reflections on the Habermas-Gadamer Debate," in *Fin-de-Siècle Socialism* (New York, 1988); and "The Textual Approach to Intellectual History," in *Force Fields: Between Intellectual History and Cultural Critique* (New York, 1993).

124. John E. Toews, "Intellectual History after the Linguistic Turn: The Autonomy of Meaning and the Irreducibility of Experience," *American Historical Review* 92, no. 4 (1987), pp. 906–7.

Toews's challenge was soon answered by the distinguished social historian Joan Wallach Scott, who had been a pioneer in the history of the European working class.[125] Already in the mid-1980s, she had directly challenged E. P. Thompson's reliance on the bedrock of experience, suggesting that historians should "ask how and in what ways conceptions of class organized (perceptions of) social experience. Rather than assuming an exact fit between material life and political thought, between experience and consciousness, this approach disrupts that fit, refuses the opposition between them."[126]

Gender and the Politics of History, the 1988 collection that reprinted this essay, has been called "something of a watershed in the self-understanding of practicing historians"[127] for its introduction of a poststructuralist or deconstructionist approach to the past. By stressing gender as a relational category rather than rehearsing the discretely feminine or masculine stories told by "women's history," Scott opened up important questions about the ability of historians to reconstruct typical experiences according to sexual identity. Whether every poststructuralist was as suspicious as she of the category of experience with all of its various acceptations is an issue we will address in chapter 9. But this was the message that she forcefully promoted in the widely remarked essay first published in 1991 called "The Evidence of Experience."[128] Mobilizing the deconstructionist rhetoric of difference and expressing a typically poststructuralist distrust of transcendental foundations, Scott directly challenged the celebration of experience by historians who wanted to expand the scope of their research to include the previously ignored (here her initial example was homosexuals, illustrated by Samuel Delany's autobiographical The Motion of Light in Water, but it could just as easily have been women or ethnic minorities):

It is precisely this kind of appeal to experience as uncontestable evidence—as a foundation on which analysis is based—that weakens the critical thrust of

---

125. Joan Wallach Scott, The Glassworkers of Carmaux: French Craftsmen and Political Action in a Nineteenth-Century City (Cambridge, Mass., 1974); and, with Louise Tilly, Women, Work and the Family (New York, 1978).

126. Scott, "Women in The Making of the English Working Class," in Gender and the Politics of History (New York, 1988), p. 89.

127. Roberts, Nothing but History, p. 263.

128. Scott, "The Evidence of Experience," Critical Inquiry 17, no. 4 (Summer 1991), reprinted in James K. Chandler, Arnold I. Davidson, and Harry Harootunian, eds., Questions of Evidence (Chicago, 1994). See also Dominick LaCapra, History and Reading: Tocqueville, Foucault, French Studies (Toronto, 2000), which draws on and expands Scott's response to Toews.

historians of difference. By remaining within the epistemological frame of orthodox history, these studies lose the possibility of examining those assumptions and practices that excluded considerations of difference in the first place.[129]

Rather than a lived reality in the past that could be re-experienced in the present by the empathetic historian, "experience," Scott insisted, was itself always a constructed category that contained within it the ideological residues of the discursive context out of which it emerged. Although seeking to get beyond the fetish of "facts" favored by a discredited positivism, those scholars who privileged experience were no less naive in their search for an authentic bedrock of objective truth, which they located in individual *Erlebnis*. Even focusing on collective subjects did not help, for merely exposing putative past experience to the historian's gaze did little to illuminate the structural conditions that made it possible:

> Making visible the experience of a different group exposes the existence of repressive mechanisms, but not their inner workings or logics; we know that difference exists, but we don't understand it as relationally constituted. For that we need to attend to the historical processes that, through discourse, position subjects and produce their experiences. It is not individuals who have experience, but subjects who are constituted through experience.[130]

Ignoring this reversal meant underestimating the political underpinnings of the most seemingly personal of experiences. Even when politically progressive historians like Thompson attempted to situate experience in the relational contexts of class conflict and the mode of production, they ignored the ways in which subject-positions were constituted by overlapping relational networks, such as those constituting gender identities.

Others like Collingwood, whose *Idea of History* had "been required reading in historiography courses for several generations,"[131] had erred in assuming the self-evident existence not only of past subjects' experience, but also that of the historian in the present. Collingwood had also assumed too uncritically that historians were disinterested judges of the past, failing as a result to acknowledge his own concrete historical situatedness. What the intellectual historian Dominick LaCapra had called the "transferential" dimension of the historical reconstruction of the past meant that no simple re-experience

129. Scott, "The Evidence of Experience," *Critical Inquiry* 17, no. 4 (Summer, 1991), p. 777.
130. Ibid., p. 779.
131. Ibid., p. 783.

could occur without the mediation of the emotional investments of the historian, which could not be suppressed in the name of an unobstructed passage between past and present. The same misunderstanding, Scott contended, dogged the more recent attempt by John Toews to appeal to experience against the linguistic turn. His injunction to separate meaning from experience, a term he never tried to define even as he invoked it in a foundational way, ignored the fact that the community of historians in the present cannot itself assume an experiential commonality, which is belied by the fractures and conflicts in the present world. "Whatever diversity and conflict may exist among them," Scott argued, "Toews' community of historians is rendered homogeneous by its shared object (experience). . . . In Toews' article no disagreement about the term *experience* can be entertained, since experience itself somehow lies outside its signification."[132]

In short, experience as both the object of historical inquiry and something possessed by the contemporary historian seeking to re-experience or re-enact the past was inevitably mediated by precisely those linguistic and structural relations its celebrants sought to bracket. Only a radical resistance to any essentializing of categories like experience, which had to be understood as a contested rather than given discursive term, could restore a political dimension to historical inquiry. Only a genealogy of foundational concepts like experience—and here Scott appealed directly to Michel Foucault's recent appropriation of that Nietzschean method—could expose the ideological residues in their innocent use.

At the end of her essay, Scott had to concede that "*experience* is not a word we can do without, although, given its usage to essentialize identity and reify the subject, it is tempting to abandon it altogether. But *experience* is so much a part of everyday language, so imbricated in our narratives that it seems futile to argue for its expulsion."[133] She urged historians nonetheless to avoid assuming the originary existence of experience as a self-evident foundational concept, a misapprehension that will be overcome only "when historians take as their project *not* the reproduction and transmission of knowledge said to be arrived at through experience, but the analysis of the production of knowledge itself."[134] The beneficial result would not be the abolition of the subject, as some critics of the linguistic turn fear, but rather an understanding of how it comes into being in the first place.

132. Ibid., p. 790.
133. Ibid., p. 797.
134. Ibid.

As might be expected, Scott's sharp critique of the experiential turn in the feminist "history from below" engendered a no less vigorous response from those unconvinced by her assurances that agency and subjectivity would survive their deconstruction. Some rehearsed the typical anti-deconstructionist complaints that she had put texts before contexts, lacked an adequate explanation of historical change, and went too far in undermining the communicative function of language.[135] Others were troubled by Scott's candidly presentist bias with its explicitly political agenda, or charged that her evocation of politics was a rhetorical gesture with no real content.[136] Despite her disclaimers, charges of "linguistic idealism" or "pan-textualism" were leveled by those who worried that "rape or domestic male violence . . . are not phenomena which can be characterized as concerned solely with a struggle of discourses."[137] Still others were made anxious by her apparent reintroduction of precisely those impersonal forces of history that the feminist recovery of forgotten subjects had sought to challenge.[138] And while some accepted Scott's critique of naive notions of history as the recovery of past experience, they wondered about her wholesale and undialectical reduction of experience to nothing but a function of discourse, leaving no room for counter-hegemonic discourses made possible, as one critic put it, by "an experience semi-autonomous from and/or contradictory to dominant discursive constructions."[139] Perhaps the general verdict was summed up by another critic who noted, "Scott offers a masterful deconstruction of the concept of experience but stops short of actually redefining or rewriting it. So even if we might agree with her about what experience is *not* (transparent, visceral), we are left unsure as to what it might be."[140]

135. Laura Lee Downs, "If 'woman' is just an empty category, then why am I afraid to walk alone at night? Identity Politics Meets the Postmodern Subject," *Comparative Studies in Society and History* 35 (1993). Scott replied in "The Tip of the Volcano," followed by Downs's "Reply to Joan Scott" in the same issue.

136. Gertrude Himmelfarb, "Some Reflections on the New History," *American Historical Review* 94, no. 3 (June 1989), followed by Joan Wallach Scott, "History in Crisis? The Others' Side of the Story." See also the discussion of their debate in Roberts, *Nothing but History*, chapter 10. For the second criticism, see John Zammito, "Reading 'Experience': The Debate in Intellectual History among Scott, Toews and LaCapra," in Paula M. L. Moya and Michael R. Hames-García, eds., *Reclaiming Identity: Realist Theory and the Predicament of Postmodernism* (Berkeley, 2000), pp. 302–3.

137. Pickering, *History, Experience and Cultural Studies*, p. 228.

138. Louise Tilly, "Gender, Women's History and Social History," *Social Science History* 13, no. 4 (1989); and Eleni Varakis, "Gender, Experience and Subjectivity: The Tilly-Scott Disagreement," *New Left Review* 211 (May–June 1995).

139. Thomas Holt, "Experience and the Politics of Intellectual Inquiry," in Chandler, Davidson, and Harootunian, *Questions of Evidence*, p. 391.

140. Canning, "Feminist History after the Linguistic Turn," p. 424.

Scott herself, in replying to her critics, admitted that work was still to be done in clarifying a viable concept of experience. "In some circles," she wrote,

experience is the ground for an identity politics that understands differences among its constituents to be matters of false consciousness or opportunism. Experience is taken as an accurate description of closed systems of domination and oppression; knowledge is taken to be the simple reflection of objective experience. That's the version of experience I want to call into question, substituting for it a notion of experience as a theorized reading that is made possible, but not inevitably or singularly, by one's relationship to dominant institutions and discourses.[141]

Whether this notion of a theorized reading enabled by a relationship to dominant institutions and discourses still retained any of the various traditional meanings clinging to experience might well be questioned. Scott's reconstruction of the concept, in fact, remained more a promise than a realization. But she nonetheless had decisively undermined one of the reigning assumptions of the re-experiencing argument in its most recent form. Dilthey and Collingwood, it will be recalled, had spoken abstractly about the historian and his or her re-experiencing or re-enacting of past actors' experience, bracketing the question of the comparability of the historian's experience with that of those he or she studied. Whether it be life grasping life or rational re-enactment rehearsing rational action, the assumption was of a transcendental capacity shared by all historians and their subjects, a capacity that made past experience open to present reconstruction. In the climate of identity politics that followed from the feminist critique of "history from below," the contrary notion emerged that membership in a certain group in the present provided a privileged vantage point for knowledge about that group's predecessors. Thus, women could write best about women, minorities about minorities, workers about workers, and so on.

Scott's deconstruction of the essentialist categories assumed by such a claim was one source of its coming undone.[142] But even for those unconvinced by

141. Scott, "A Rejoinder to Thomas Holt," in Chandler, Davidson and Harootunian, *Questions of Evidence*, p. 399.

142. There were, to be sure, other less intransigently poststructuralist arguments that also went beyond simple identity politics representationalism. See, for example, the arguments for what became known as "post-positivist realism" in the work of Satya P. Mohanty and his followers, whose work is collected in Moya and Hames-García, *Reclaiming Identity*. Scott's position is criticized not only in Zammito's "Reading 'Experience'," but also in William S. Wilkerson, "Is there something you need to tell me? Coming

the linguistic turn, there was an important cautionary example in the histo-riography of the recent past that also powerfully supported her case. In the presidential address he had given to the American Historical Association in 1963, entitled "The Great Mutation," Carl Bridenbaugh, then a professor of American history at the University of California, Berkeley, had lamented the putative loss of a shared culture in the profession. With the entry of "young practitioners" who are "products of lower middle class or foreign origins," he warned "their emotions not infrequently get in the way of historical recon-structions. They find themselves in a very real sense outsiders on our past and feel themselves shut out. This is not their fault, but it is true. They have no experience to assist them, and the chasm between them and the Remote Past widens every hour."[143] In short, only native-born, white Anglo-Saxon Protestants from solidly middle-class families should write about colonial America. Here was an identity politics that revealed how dangerously re-strictive the appeal to experience might be.

In responding to Bridenbaugh's elitist twist on identity politics, Scott could not, however, revert back to a universalist model of the disinterested histo-rian able to re-experience anyone's past, something akin to Collingwood's spiritual transcendentalism. For she saw its pernicious presence in Briden-baugh's own tacit assumption that his group's view was untainted by parti-sanship. "Bridenbaugh," she noted, "does not suggest that [lower-class or foreign-born historians] have a *different* experience, or a *different* perspective on history; he cannot conceive that their experience constitutes history too, for that would undermine the supposed universality of his own view. Instead, he insists that there is one past ('our past') and only one way to recount it."[144] Giving up both the universalist and identity-politics reliance on re-experi-encing was necessary, she concluded, because the recovery of experience it-self could not suffice as the grounds for historical reconstruction, no matter whose past was at stake.

In so arguing, Scott the feminist pioneer ironically approached one of the positions we have noted earlier in the decidedly non-feminist Michael

Out and the Ambiguity of Experience," which focuses on gay identity and Scott's use of Samuel Delany in "The Evidence of Experience."

143. Carl Bridenbaugh, "The Great Mutation," *American Historical Review* 68, no. 1 (January 1963), p. 328. Scott was not the first to be offended by this argument. Lawrence W. Levine remembered that "Bridenbaugh's jeremiad was met with embarrassed silence and treated, when it was treated at all, as some sort of idiosyncratic aberration." "The Unpredictable Past: Reflections on Recent American Historiog-raphy," *American Historical Review* 94, no. 3 (1989), p. 675.

144. Scott, "History in Crisis?" p. 685.

Oakeshott in *Experience and Its Modes*. For Oakeshott, it bears repeating, also distrusted all models of re-experiencing, stressing instead the inevitability of the historian's active making of the past he or she studied. "For the 'historian' for whom the past is dead and irreproachable, the past is feminine," he had written. "He loves it as a mistress of whom he never tires and whom he never expects to talk sense."[145] Scott was neither an advocate of Oakeshott's neo-idealist celebration of Absolute Experience nor as hostile as he to the practical implications of historical research, and she certainly would not have countenanced his blatantly sexist rhetoric. But in questioning the authority of historical experience, even that of the women whose lives feminist historians hoped to recover, she echoed his skepticism about the past talking sense by itself. Whether history is a "world of ideas" produced by the historian, as Oakeshott claimed, or the reconstruction of "discursive events" that Scott saw as "necessarily tied to the historian's recognition of his or her stake in the production of knowledge,"[146] foundational primacy could never be given to past *Erlebnis* in itself.

F. R. ANKERSMIT AND THE EXPERIENTIAL SUBLIME

But was there perhaps still something left to the idea of historical experience in the present, something that set apart even the most linguistically aware historian from the literary *cum* philosophical deconstructer of texts? If past *Erlebnis* forever eluded re-experiencing, might there still be something else that could be considered as distinguishing historical experience in the present from other modes of experience? Oakeshott, as we have seen, answered the question by stressing the modal abstraction from Absolute Experience produced by organizing the world *sub specie praeteritorum*. But this formulation still emphasized the present construction of the sense of pastness. Might there still be some way in which historical experience happened without that constructive making, thus getting in touch with the passive moment that we have seen was so often understood to be a central component of experience in most of its guises? Might there be some way that the distinction between subjective experience and its object could be preserved without falling back on a naive notion of past *Erlebnis* as that object?

One suggestive attempt to answer these questions has been made by a con-

145. Oakeshott, "The Activity of Being an Historian," p. 166.
146. Scott, "The Evidence of Experience," p. 797.

temporary theorist himself very much influenced by poststructuralist and postmodernist ideas, the Dutch philosopher of history Franklin R. Ankersmit. Although Ankersmit is best known as a follower of Hayden White's narrativist and tropological critique of descriptive or explanatory historiography,[147] and thus initially no less of an enthusiast of "the linguistic turn" than Joan Scott, he has recently approached the issue of experience from a fresh perspective. We will end this chapter with a quick glance at his argument.[148] In a series of essays written during the 1990s, Ankersmit attempted to write what he called a "phenomenology of historical experience."[149] Explicitly rejecting the Diltheyan attempt to re-experience past experience—he dismissively calls it the "*copying* of experience rather than experience (of the past) *itself*"[150]—and unhappy with the radical constructivism he attributes to Oakeshott or the linguistic transcendentalism lurking behind Scott's use of deconstruction, Ankersmit argues for a sudden encounter with pastness that goes beyond mere acquaintance with documents in archives. Typical examples include the reactions of poets like Goethe or Byron on their first trips to the ruins of classical Rome or to Renaissance Venice, which act like Proustian madeleines for the remembrance of someone else's things past. Drawing on the great Dutch historian Johann Huizinga's notion of an "historical sensation," an "intellectual ebrity" (from the Latin for "drunken") that registers a more intimate contact with reality than observations or impressions, Ankersmit calls such an experience "a gift of the moment, [which] comes unannounced and unexpectedly and cannot be repeated at will."[151] These moments, rare as they may be, cannot be entirely subsumed under the mediating discursive categories stressed by Scott or under Oakeshott's general rubric of *sub specie praeteritorum:*

Essential to the notion of historical experience is that it provides us with a *direct* and *immediate* contact with the past; a contact that is *not* mediated by

147. See his *Narrative Logic: A Semantic Analysis of the Historian's Language* (The Hague, 1983).

148. My understanding of his position has been enormously enhanced by the chance to read in manuscript his forthcoming book *Historical Experience: The Embrace of Romeo and Juliet,* to be published by Stanford University Press.

149. F. R. Ankersmit, *History and Tropology: The Rise and Fall of Metaphor* (Berkeley, 1994), chapter 7; "Can We Experience the Past?," in Rolf Torstendahl and Irmline Veit-Brause, eds., *History-Making: The Intellectual and Social Formation of a Discipline* (Stockholm, 1996); and "Historicism: An Attempt at a Synthesis," *History and Theory* 34, no. 1 (1995). For a general overview and critique of Ankersmit's work, see John H. Zammito, "Ankersmit's Postmodernist Historiography: The Hyperbole of 'Opacity'," *History and Theory* 37, no. 3 (1998).

150. Ankersmit, *History and Tropology,* p. 20.

151. Ankersmit, "Can We Experience the Past?" p. 51.

historiographical tradition, by language or aspects of language (like tropology), by theory, narrative, ethical or ideological prejudice, etc. For if any of these factors would co-determine the content of historical experience, this would destroy the directness and immediacy that is claimed for historical experience.[152]

At times, such contact manifests itself as intense nostalgia, which Ankersmit describes as "the momentary dizzying experience of sudden obliteration of the rift between present and past, an experience in which the past for a fractional moment reveals itself 'as it is, or was.'" But then he adds, "this *as it is* is not the historist's *wie es eigentlich gewesen*, but the past invested with *difference.*"[153] In fact, the overpowering experience that summons up the past is like that foregrounded in the aesthetics of the sublime, for "in the sublime, we have an access to reality that is not mediated by the categories of the understanding and, *mutatis mutandis,* much the same can be said of historical experience."[154] The opacity of the sublime, its resistance to straightforward representation, gets us in touch with—Ankersmit specifically favors tactile metaphors against visual ones—a reality deeper than our own, giving us a hint of what is beyond our current consciousness or our capacity to make it up out of whole cloth.

In fact, because they undermine the attempt to make sense of events by seamlessly contextualizing them in large-scale diachronic narratives, such historical epiphanies make possible a more immediate participation in the life of the past, helping us to understand "what it was like" to live in that period. Comparing them to the gain in intensity and immediacy unexpectedly produced by the breakdown of language expressed in Hugo von Hofmannsthal's *Letter of Lord Chandos,* Ankersmit argued that "they do not primarily want to convey a (coherent) knowledge of the past that can only estrange us from experience, but rather to impart to the reader an 'experience' of the past that is as direct and immediate as the historian's language may permit."[155]

Struggling to cash out the value of such a notion of historical experience,

152. Ibid., p. 56.
153. Ankersmit, *History and Tropology,* p. 200 (emphasis in original). For a different understanding of nostalgia, see Angelika Rauch's discussion quoted in chapter 8, note 96.
154. Ankersmit, "Can We Experience the Past?" p. 56. Precisely what this might mean is difficult to say, but one experience I had before reading Ankersmit seems to anticipate his argument. See "The Manacles of Gavrilo Princip," in *Cultural Semantics.*
155. Ankersmit, "Historicism: An Attempt at Synthesis," p. 161.

equivalent neither to direct epistemological acquaintance with existing objects nor to present-day discursive constructions of an entirely imagined past, Ankersmit turned for help to Gadamer's claim that historical experience is a variant of its aesthetic counterpart, without, to be sure, accepting the latter's linguistic transcendentalism. For if there is a parallel between historical experience and the sublime, theories of aesthetic experience may be revealing about both. Noting that art objects were often the source of historical experiences—the Venetian architecture inspiring Byron or the Roman statues exciting Goethe—Ankersmit explored the heightened moment common to both, a moment in which "one passively 'undergoes' the picture" prior to the reflective act of "erudite scrutiny."[156]

Such a moment, he argued, had been central to the pragmatist aesthetics developed by John Dewey and more recently revived by Richard Shusterman. In *Art as Experience*, the art object was not allowed to be swallowed up entirely by the experiencing subject, but was granted its own space in a constellation of relationships. For Ankersmit, the moment of radical difference preserved in nostalgia captured some of the same irreducibility that Dewey had attributed to aesthetic experience, which is always an experience *of something not itself*. Although Ankersmit taxed Dewey for seeking to embed aesthetic experience too deeply in its various contexts (radical contextualism being merely the reverse side of transcendentalism), he admired the pragmatist's resistance to the dissolution of the art object entirely into its reception or interpretation.

Such objects, Ankersmit continued, "come close to the 'Hauch' or aura of objects that provide a historical experience,"[157] thus introducing a term primarily associated with Walter Benjamin, who defined it in terms of an unbridgeable distance between object and beholder. And, he concluded, "if we relate this insight into the nature of PAE [pragmatist aesthetic experience] to Heidegger's speculations about the Greek word for truth—'alētheia'—or 'Unverborgenheit', one might be justified in saying that the ultimate truth we can have of the world, is a truth in which the world 'exposes' itself to us free from context. And that truth is, paradigmatically, an aesthetic truth as we find it in PAE and in historical experience."[158] Such an elevation of the stakes of historical experience—which Ankersmit ac-

156. Ibid., p. 67.
157. Ibid., p. 68.
158. Ibid., p. 71.

knowledged "will remain by its very nature a rare and exceptional phenomenon in historical practice"[159]—was not likely to win-over more traditional historians.[160]

But it did resonate with the work of those scholars in literature and history who were developing at the same time what became known as "the new historicism," which drew on Foucault's evocation of the historical sublime.[161] And it also could give sustenance to those psychoanalytically inclined critics who were attempting to think-through the importance of individual or collective trauma in history, which produced what one called "unclaimed experiences" in those who could not fully absorb, assimilate, and make sense of the horrors they suffered.[162] For them, we might say an unbridgeable gap between experience and re-experiencing was paradoxically already evident in the initial traumatic experience itself, which has belatedness and unrepresentability as part of its basic structure. Unclaimed and perhaps perpetually unclaimable, such experiences defeated the possibility of the subjective *Bildung* so often seen as the fruit of experiential learning, as well as the process of contextual normalization.

But could they then be vicariously claimed by subsequent historians through their own contact with the sublime, producing a kind of empathetic community of shared trauma? Or were they even more hidden from later view than experiences of less traumatic variety? And if the transcendental

159. Ibid., p. 73.

160. In "Ankersmit's Postmodernist Historiography," Zammito notes dryly that "Ankersmit suspects that what he describes is likely to possess for a conventional historian 'an air of mystique and almost religious revelation.' He is not wrong" (p. 345).

161. See Catherine Gallagher and Stephen Greenblatt, *Practicing New Historicism* (Chicago, 2000), for the importance of Foucault's injunction to be open to the impact of experiencing material residues of the past as a rupture in the smooth workings of normal historicist narratives. Gallagher and Greenblatt quote a passage in which Foucault talks about coming across documents of singular lives, whose intensity he wanted to preserve undigested in his own work, asking "wasn't it best to leave them in the same form which had made me experience them?" (p. 67). The characteristic "new historicist" use of anecdote was designed to evoke a similar effect of the strangeness of past that normalizing narratives—or contextualizing in Ankersmit's terms—had integrated too effortlessly.

162. Cathy Caruth, *Unclaimed Experience: Trauma, Narrative, and History* (Baltimore, 1996). Caruth claims that "the experience of trauma, the fact of latency, would thus seem to consist, not in the forgetting of a reality that can hence never be fully known, but in an inherent latency in the experience itself. The historical power of the trauma is not just that the experience is repeated after its forgetting, but that it is only in and through its inherent forgetting that it is first experienced at all" (p. 17). The historian who has done the most to focus on trauma is Dominick LaCapra, but he prefers to see it as obscuring experience rather than producing a version of it (or at best, producing only a virtual simulacrum of it on the part of later historians). See his discussion in *History and Reading*, pp. 62–63.

universalism of the Dilthey/Collingwood historian, who re-experienced or re-enacted the past, and the culturally marked particularism of the historian whose identity matched that of the subjects he or she studied were both untenable assumptions, what in the historian's own present experience allowed privileged moments of access to the past? Ankersmit has given little guidance in resolving these questions. Nor does his evocation of the historical sublime and his call for openness to the experience of the past help much in deciding which experience of the past might win intersubjective validation in the present community of historians. The epistemological issues that had so vexed Oakeshott, Dilthey, and Collingwood, in fact, no longer seemed very much on his mind. Nor did the desire to rescue the lost experience of common people, which had motivated the historians from below.

Ankersmit, we might say, gave up the quest for a standard for historical truth as correspondence between past and present experience, preferring instead a frankly aesthetic alternative. In invoking Dewey, Benjamin, Heidegger, and a postmodernism that resisted linguistic transcendentalism, he demonstrated how much he had absorbed from the most provocative twentieth-century attempts to rethink the category of experience in a post-epistemological way. Those efforts were, in fact, often directed at an undoing of the radical modalization of experience—epistemological, religious, aesthetic, political, historical—which we have seen was a legacy of the early modern disaggregation of the unified notion last discerned in Michel de Montaigne. They also registered the crisis of the relatively strong notion of the subject of experience in late modernity, but without being willing to reduce it to nothing but a function of exterior structures or impersonal forces. The paradoxical search for experience without that centered subject, a subject whose individual *Bildung* was long assumed to be its telos, led, we might say, to songs of experience composed in a new and different key. Our task in the second half of this book will be to see whether we can catch their often strange and unexpected melodies.

SEVEN

The Cult of Experience
in American Pragmatism

James, Dewey, and Rorty

THE MODALIZATION OF EXPERIENCE, its fracturing into the discrete sub-categories we have designated as epistemological, religious, aesthetic, political, and historical, produced certain palpable benefits. By allowing the inherent logic of each variant to be isolated and developed in its own immanent terms, it helped clarify the complexity of the stakes involved in the general appeal to experience against its various contrasting terms: theory, reason, dogma, innocence, discourse, and so on. By segregating one discursive subcontext from another, it also permitted the issues raised in each to emerge with a precision that would have been much harder to attain if the boundaries were blurred.

Thus, for example, the debates between empiricist and idealist epistemologists about the reliability of sense experience as measured against an objective, external world would have been even muddier than they actually were if, say, religious or historical experience were accepted as dimensions of the same "experience." Assuming the split between knowing subject and known object allowed the natural world to be understood as composed of entities or processes that might be experienced solely in cognitive terms and ripe for instrumental manipulation, thus enabling the development of that experimental potential in experience so critical to the scientific method. Likewise, the claim that sensual disinterestedness was the primary criterion of aesthetic experience—viewing potentially lust-arousing naked bodies as chastely beautiful nudes—made possible the focus on formal properties that contributed so much to the discourse of the aesthetic. Searching for a specifically religious mode of experience was equally valuable in foregrounding those dimensions of pious behavior that were not subsumable under moral or cognitive systems of belief or subject to the same criteria of reliability as empirical sensation.

More than merely discursive distinctions, these differentiated notions of experience also operated as normative guides for practices sanctioned by the distinct social and cultural institutions that emerged to propagate and regulate them. What came to count as a legitimate scientific experiment was clearly not the same as the mystic's attempt to merge with divinity by deliberately disorienting his sensorium, even if both could justifiably be called experiences. When aesthetic experience spilled over the boundaries of the institution of art, it could be reproached by some for the inappropriate, even dangerous aestheticization of immoral or politically objectionable behavior. And believers in religious experience could dismiss as irrelevant attempts by skeptics to apply the critical methods of scientific experimentation to their deeply felt, personal states of mind, which they could also pointedly call "anaesthetic revelations."[1]

Modalization provided valuable post facto guidance as well for later commentators in differentiating among the manifold denotations and connotations, sometimes in tension or even outright contradiction, that accrued to the word over time. Someone who could claim, say, to have had a religious experience could be seen to have drawn on a welter of associations that were not the equivalent of those surrounding the experiences valued by their cognitive or aesthetic counterparts. Although some overlap necessarily occurred, as we have seen, for example, in the political evocation of experience by historians like E. P. Thompson or the aesthetic moment in religious experience evident in Friedrich Schleiermacher and historical experience in Franklin Ankersmit, far more striking is the extent to which meaningful distinctions can be discerned between those "modes" or "arrests" decried by Michael Oakeshott in experience.

Invoking Oakeshott, however, immediately alerts us to a very different reaction to modalization by a variety of critics who lamented the specialization of function endemic to modernity. Although the neo-Hegelian notion of "absolute experience" posited in *Experience and Its Modes* did not win many adherents, the chagrin Oakeshott registered over the dangers of compart-

1. This term comes from a pamphlet by Benjamin Paul Blood in 1874 called "The Anaesthetic Revelation and the Gist of Philosophy," which William James reviewed enthusiastically. The review is reprinted in James's *Essays, Comments, and Reviews*, vol. 17 of *The Works of William James* (Cambridge, Mass., 1987). For a discussion of Blood's importance for James, see G. William Barnard, *Exploring Unseen Worlds: William James and the Philosophy of Mysticism* (Albany, N.Y., 1997), pp. 29–34.

mentalizing experience can already be sighted as early as the Romantics and is evident in idealists like Hegel. It was perhaps only in the twentieth century that the chorus grew to encompass thinkers from many, often very different, traditions—philosophical as well as political. Hoping to recapture a more robust, intense, and all-encompassing notion of experience—whether it be called "authentic" or "essential" or "pure" or "inner"—they sought to reverse the process of differentiation. Often betraying a sense of nostalgia for what had purportedly been lost by modalization, they hoped to make whole what had been torn asunder, reinvigorating a common lifeworld that had relinquished its coherent meaning with the development of subcultures of expertise. Although an important difference separated those who thought the problem was inherently conceptual or philosophical—all that was needed, they contended, was a better grasp of what experience always already is— from those who insisted the real cause of the loss was a crisis in the larger social or cultural world as a whole, both decried differentiation as a process to be reversed. And they did so in that rhapsodic tone so often accompanying evocations of the word "experience," a tone allowing us to borrow William Blake's title for our own.

Not only did this deeply felt yearning manifest itself in a desire to overcome modalization; it also appeared in frequent calls to bridge the gap between the subject and object of experience, however they might be defined.[2] From the time of René Descartes and Francis Bacon, the agenda of Western philosophy, as is often remarked, was primarily set by epistemological rather than ontological or metaphysical questions: in the broadest of terms, who is the subject of knowledge, and how does he or she come to have reliable knowledge of external objects (or an objectified knowledge of subjective states of consciousness)? Modernity began, it might be argued, when the world could no longer be construed as a meaningful and legible text written by God—a result, *inter alia,* of the nominalist critique of real universals in late medieval theology, the hermeneutic challenge to singular textual authority presented by the Reformation, and the bewildering encounter with new lands during the Age of Discovery. "Real presence" faded from the world, save for special

---

2. The plea to get beyond this dualism became in fact almost a mantra of twentieth-century thought. Thus, to take a typical example, we find in 1969 the phenomenologist Calvin O. Schrag telling us yet again that "the basic error of both idealism and naturalism is that their peculiar inquiry standpoint is defined through the use of a bogus dichotomy. What is required is the elucidation of a commerce with the experienced world which is older than the subjectivistic and objectivistic categories, which precedes the thematic constitution of both, and which undercuts the dilemma as it is traditionally formulated." *Experience and Being* (Evanston, Ill., 1969), p. 6.

enclaves like the Catholic Mass. As God increasingly became a mysterious *Deus absconditus,* whose capricious and opaque will was more important than His rationality, it was increasingly difficult to assume that the world we happen to inhabit is the best of all possible worlds.

The nascent modern subject, withdrawn from a no longer transparently meaningful cosmos, came to rely on the fragile reed of experience, however defined, as the only bridge from interior to exterior reality. Even as the horizon of expectation began to move rapidly away from past experience—recall Reinhart Koselleck's argument about the temporalization of their relation in the *Neuzeit*—encounters with the new were still conceptualized in terms of experiments in living. Even when attempts were made to restore a more pantheistic worldview, elements of which we have seen in Schleiermacher, it was experience that was supposed to provide the locus for the revelation of the infinite in the finite.

Experience in this guise was always that of and for a subject, whether that subject was characterized as transcendental or immanent, universal or particular, collective or singular, punctual or temporally extended. Subjects were understood to be the ones who had the empirical sensations, underwent the formative learning processes, had the disinterested aesthetic pleasures, or were in the presence of the holy. *Erlebnis* and *Erfahrung* alike were dependent, it was usually assumed, on a subject able to undergo and register the intensities of immediate prereflective experience or the narrative coherence of a meaningful journey over time. At times the balance between subject and object in various discourses of experience threatened to tip entirely over to the subjective side, so that some critics of experience could accuse it of being solipsistically projective. At other times, the importance of the object's irreducible otherness was reasserted by those who stressed the value of experience as a way to get beyond the subject's point of departure, a way to learn from new encounters with obstacles from the outside. But in virtually all of these instances, it was assumed that experience involved an integrated, coherent, and more or less autonomous subject, possessed of consciousness and the ability to act in the world, who was its bearer and beneficiary.[3]

The persistence of this assumption to this day cannot be denied, as evidenced by contemporary identity politics in which group subjects replaced

---

3. The qualifier "more or less" has to be affixed to "autonomous" if we recall the critique of radical humanist autonomy made by defenders of religious experience like Schleiermacher, who stressed the feelings of dependence on God in the pious believer. But even he did not deny that individuals had to develop their God-given potential rather than assume it was absolutely predetermined.

individual ones. But it was also powerfully challenged by those who wanted to find a way to get beyond or restore a position preceding the fatal split between subject and object. What resulted may seem paradoxical: a still impassioned defense of experience without a strong notion of the subject who is its purported bearer. Intimations of an alternative can be discerned in the nineteenth-century aesthetes' attempts to turn their lives into a work of art, thus overcoming the distinction between aesthetic experience and the discrete object that occasioned it. But their efforts were often conducted within the still differentiated realm of the aesthetic, which they tended to accept rather than challenge. And frequently, the outcome was a reinforcement of the power of subjective sensibility and temperament over the external world.[4] It was left to twentieth-century thinkers such as Walter Benjamin, Martin Heidegger, Theodor Adorno, Georges Bataille, Michel Foucault, and Roland Barthes to work out the implications of the paradoxical ideal of experience without a subject in relation to the dedifferentiation of value spheres. Perhaps the first major philosophical expression of this quest, however, appeared not in twentieth-century Europe, but rather in late nineteenth-century and early twentieth-century America in the loose movement that came to be called pragmatism.[5] We have already encountered dimensions of it in our discussions of William James on religion and John Dewey on art, but it is now time to look more closely at the larger contribution they and the tradition they helped spawn made to the discourse of experience in a new, postsubjective key.

THE AMERICAN CULTURE OF EXPERIENCE

Even prior to the founding of the Republic, as we noted in chapter 5, Americans frequently drew on the rhetoric of experience as a source of legitima-

4. See, for example, Pater's claim in *The Renaissance* (New York, 1919) that "at first sight, experience seems to bury us under a flood of external objects, pressing upon us with a sharp and importunate reality, calling us out of ourselves in a thousand forms of action. But when reflexion begins to act upon these objects they are dissipated under its influence. . . . Experience, already reduced to a swarm of impressions, is ringed round for each one of us by that thick wall of personality through which no real voice has ever pierced on its way to us, or from us to that which we can only conjecture to be without. Every one of these impressions is the impression of the individual in his isolation, each mind keeping as a solitary prisoner its own dream of the world" (pp. 247–48).

5. The literature on pragmatism, including individual studies of its major figures, such as Peirce, James, Dewey, George Herbert Mead, Oliver Wendell Holmes, and Chauncy Wright, is too voluminous to cite. For recent selected bibliographies, see Louis Menand, ed., *Pragmatism: A Reader* (New York, 1997); and Morris Dickstein, ed., *The Revival of Pragmatism: New Essays on Social Thought, Law, and Culture* (Durham, N.C., 1998).

tion against rational abstraction or the deadweight of unexamined authority. Experience meant here both novel experimentation and learning valuable lessons from the past to be imaginatively applied to the future. It meant profiting from bodily encounters with a new and often harsh environment and drawing on the lessons they produced in the ordinary, everyday lives of common men and women. It meant improvising new ways of living together, worshiping God, and mastering nature. It meant applying to politics Patrick Henry's "lamp of experience," rather than the shadowy precepts of outworn textual authorities or the untested fantasies of utopian rationalists.

The result has been a widespread, often self-congratulatory tradition of identifying America *tout court* with what one typical enthusiast, the philosopher John J. McDermott, has called a "culture of experience." "From the Puritans to Dewey," McDermott writes, "one is offered a series of efforts, alternating in stresses and varying in success, to account for man's most profound difficulties and concerns within the context of ordinary experience. In that tradition, all-embracing systematic truth, whether it be theological, philosophical, or political, was consistently submitted to the broadly based canons of a constantly shifting collective experience."[6] According to another typical observer, John J. Stuhr, "what is American in philosophy is the use of the method of experience, not the endless cataloging of it independent of the context of its use, not the tedious formalization of its results into sacred categories. What is American is the emphasis on the continuity of belief and action *in experience,* not the mere assertion of this unity and continuity in theory alone."[7] Still a third celebrant, John E. Smith, identifies "America's philosophical vision" with "an account of experiencing that is far more in accord with what actually happens in our encounter with the world. Experience, among other things, was shown to be intimately connected with 'knowing how' to respond to situations and indeed with the entire range of habits formed in the interaction between self and world."[8] An even more sweeping claim about the "primal roots of American philosophy" has been promoted by Bruce Wilshire, who locates them in Native American organismic traditions of experiential oneness with nature, exemplified by the Oglala Lakota holy man Black Elk.[9]

6. John J. McDermott, *The Culture of Experience: Philosophical Essays in the American Grain* (New York, 1976), p. 15.

7. John J. Stuhr, *Genealogical Pragmatism: Philosophy, Experience, and Community* (Albany, N.Y., 1997), p. 32.

8. John E. Smith, *America's Philosophical Vision* (Chicago, 1992), p. 4.

9. Bruce Wilshire, *The Primal Roots of American Philosophy: Pragmatism, Phenomenology, and Native American Thought* (University Park, Pa., 2000).

Other commentators like Daniel Boorstin would extend the claim beyond a tradition of philosophy, detecting the very "genius of American politics" in its allegiance to the "givenness" of experience against the dogmatism of European political theories like Fascism and Communism.[10] The founding fathers, it has often been argued, bequeathed to us, despite their popular name, an anti-foundationalist bias against theory in favor of experience.[11] American jurisprudence, or at least the powerful tradition that came to called "legal realism," could be interpreted in similar terms, as evidenced by Oliver Wendell Holmes's celebrated claim in *The Common Law* of 1881 that "the life of the law has not been logic; it has been experience."[12] Likewise, although with a more skeptical evaluation, Philip Rahv, the editor of *Partisan Review,* discerned a "cult of experience in American writing" from Walt Whitman to Ernest Hemingway and Thomas Wolfe.[13] And Paul Tillich noted the "emphasis on religious experience in the movements of evangelical radicalism which have largely formed the American mind and have made of experience a central concept in all spheres of man's intellectual life."[14] In short, Charles Sanders Peirce seemed to speak for America as a whole—or so these commentators might lead us to believe—when he famously exclaimed: "Experience is our only teacher."[15]

It should be acknowledged, however, that Americans were not universally bedazzled by the lessons that experience putatively provided. As we noted in our discussion of the founding fathers in chapter 5, a number were more impressed by claims of universal human rights legitimated by deduction than by practical experience alone. Much later, the philosopher George Santayana would wryly remark that "experience abounds, and teaches nothing."[16] And Henry Adams would bleakly conclude in his autobiography that "experience

10. Daniel J. Boorstin, *The Genius of American Politics* (Chicago, 1953).

11. John Patrick Diggins, "Theory and the American Founding," in Leslie Berlowitz, Denis Donoghue, and Louis Menand, eds., *Theory in America* (New York, 1988).

12. Oliver Wendell Holmes, *The Common Law,* excerpted in Menand, ed., *Pragmatism,* p. 137.

13. Philip Rahv, "The Cult of Experience in American Writing," in *Literature and the Sixth Sense* (New York, 1969). Rahv did not, however, claim that the cult existed during an earlier period, when sacred rather than profane preoccupations dominated and experientially rich genres like the novel and drama were less important than romances and poetry.

14. Paul Tillich, "The Conquest of Intellectual Provincialism: Europe and America," in *Theology of Culture* (New York, 1959), p. 164.

15. Charles Sanders Peirce, *Collected Papers,* ed. Charles Hartshorne and Paul Weiss, vol. 5 (Cambridge, 1934), p. 37

16. George Santayana, "Apologia Pro Mente Sua," in Paul Arthur Schilpp, ed., *The Philosophy of George Santayana* (LaSalle, Ill., 1940), p. 540.

ceases to educate."[17] In fact, as the intellectual historian Bruce Kuklick has recently reminded us, it may be a mistake to homogenize American thought, especially philosophy, into a single mold based on trust in experience or anything else for that matter.[18]

Moreover, what experience supposedly taught could vary with the meaning given to the word. Wilshire, for example, argues that it signifies a holistic oneness with nature, which he sees expressed in the wisdom of indigenous people. In contrast, McDermott identifies its "historical roots in an anthropomorphic view of nature and a sense of frontier as human imaginative horizon,"[19] thus betraying his own tacit adherence to a subject-centered version of experience in which the natural world was there to be known, objectified, and mastered. The importance of Lockean sensationalism for the early American mind—even its theological component, as we remarked in the case of Jonathan Edwards during the first Great Awakening—reinforced this inclination towards subjectively registered, useful knowledge gained from a posteriori induction rather than a priori deduction.[20] But the impact of Locke came to wane over time in ways that we will explore shortly. The word could also vary according to its preferred antonyms. Thus, for example, if "innocence" were taken to be the favored contrasting term, it was possible to see Europe as the embodiment of a worldly experience and America as its innocent opposite, a polarity most subtly explored in the novels of Henry James. But if "theory" or "doctrine" were the antonyms of choice, then experience could be located on the American side.

If, then, it is an exaggeration to claim that America has always had a culture fundamentally based on the valorization of experience, it is far more plausible to argue that at least one of its most powerful intellectual movements did indeed give it pride of place: that small, but increasingly influential group of thinkers who became known as pragmatists after William James popularized the term—first coined by Peirce in the 1870s while discussing pragmatic belief in Kant's Second Critique—in a lecture at Berke-

17. Henry Adams, *The Education of Henry Adams* (New York, 1934), p. 294.

18. Bruce Kuklick, "Does American Philosophy Rest on a Mistake?" in Marcus G. Singer, ed., *American Philosophy* (Cambridge, 1985). James Kloppenberg also notes in a personal communication (letter of December 16, 2002) that he has always found the putative link between the Puritans and the pragmatists strained.

19. McDermott, *The Culture of Experience*, p. 17.

20. The one important residue of deductive truth in Locke was his belief in moral intuition, which also had an impact on American philosophy. I owe this observation to Morton White, who has traced it as far back as Henry Sidgwick.

ley in 1898.[21] And in doing so, they also redirected its meaning away from most of its earlier versions in imaginative ways, whose implications this chapter explores.

The sources of the pragmatist movement, as well as its range and influence, have been variously posited in the vast literature on the subject, with consensus still an elusive goal. In an influential account published in 1949, Morton White identified what he called "the revolt against formalism" in American social thought beginning in the 1880s, by which he meant the attack on deductive logic and abstract theory in pragmatism, legal realism, behaviorism, and economic institutionalism. "All of them," he claimed, "insist upon coming to grips with life, experience, process, growth, context, function."[22] Their turn toward a historicist and culturally organicist worldview was stimulated, White explained, by "the growth of science and capitalism, the spread of Darwinism, socialism, industrialization, and monopoly."[23]

More recent accounts have tried to flesh out this argument. Jeffrey Isaac, for example, has contended that pragmatism's

experimentalism and anti-essentialism gave expression to, and helped rationalize, the revision of foundational political and economic beliefs that had ceased adequately to explain American society to itself. In an age of emergent corporate capitalism the early liberal ideology of Lockean individual property rights

21. William James, "Philosophical Conceptions and Practical Results," in *Pragmatism* (Cambridge, Mass., 1975). Peirce disliked the attempt to lump his thought together with James's and began calling his own thought "pragmaticism," an ugly neologism he knew would not be easily appropriated by others. The loosely defined family of thinkers traditionally included in the original pragmatist camp extends beyond the major philosophers to include Oliver Wendell Holmes, Jane Addams, George Herbert Mead, and Randolph Bourne. The African-American intellectuals W. E. B. Dubois and Alain Locke have recently been added to their number. See Cornel West, *The American Evasion of Philosophy* (Madison, Wis., 1989); and Nancy Fraser, "Another Pragmatism: Alain Locke, Critical 'Race' Theory, and the Politics of Culture," in Dickstein, *The Revival of Pragmatism*. Their European allies would include Theodore Flournoy in France, Giovanni Papini, Giulio Cesare Ferrari, and Giovanni Vailati in Italy, and F. C. S. Schiller and William McDougall in Britain.

22. Morton White, *Social Thought in America: The Revolt against Formalism* (New York, 1976), p. 13. White included James in his later account of the historicist and organicist critique of formalism (*Pragmatism and the Politics of Epistemology* [Kyoto, 1986]), and he came to see the critique as a delayed reaction to the residual rationalism in the founding fathers.

23. White, *Social Thought in America.*, p. 6. White focused his attention on Thorstein Veblen, Charles Beard, and James Harvey Robinson, as well as Dewey and Holmes. He identified historicism with "the attempt to explain facts by earlier facts" and cultural organicism as "the attempt to find explanations and relevant material in social sciences other than the one which is primarily under investigation" (p. 12). For White's recollection of the book's mixed reception, see his *Philosopher's Story* (University Park, Pa., 1999), chapter 8.

and laissez-faire economics was increasingly seen as anachronistic, and in need of a more organic, holistic, *corporate* liberalism.[24]

A very different explanation has been offered by Jackson Lears, who sees a virulent anti-modernism rampant among patrician intellectuals after 1880, producing a desire for authentic and immediate experience as an antidote to the new vulgarities of the capitalist market and the pressures of professionalization.[25] Pragmatism shared their vitalist distrust of positivist science and abstract individualism, although, for the most part, not their anti-democratic elitism and intolerance of change. Louis Menand, in his widely admired collective biography *The Metaphysical Club*, goes further back in time to see the seeds of pragmatism in the trauma of the Civil War, "which tore a hole in their lives. To some of them the war seemed not just a failure of democracy, but a failure of culture, a failure of ideas. . . . The Civil War swept away the slave civilization of the south, but it swept away almost the whole intellectual culture of the north along with it."[26] Lockean notions of individual property rights were not the sole casualties; so too were the Lockean premises of earlier notions of subjective experience.

For those observers less inclined to isolate pragmatism as an essentially American phenomenon, the movement was part of a broader crisis of modern subjectivity, which was manifested in the modernist aesthetics and vitalist philosophies of the late nineteenth century. In 1911 the French Cartesian philosopher René Berthelot noted common traits linking William James with European thinkers like Friedrich Nietzsche and Henri Bergson, as well as certain Catholic modernists. They all were variants of an unstable amalgam he called utilitarian romanticism, which he deplored as irrationalist.[27] Although

24. Jeffrey C. Isaac, "Is the Revival of Pragmatism Practical?; or, What Are the Consequences of Pragmatism?" *Constellations* 6, no. 4 (1999), p. 564.

25. Jackson Lears, *No Place of Grace* (New York, 1981).

26. Louis Menand, *The Metaphysical Club: A Story of Ideas in America* (New York, 2001), p. x. The book's title refers to the informal group around Peirce, James, Holmes, and Wright that met in Cambridge, Massachusetts, after 1872. Menand acknowledges that "the year James introduced pragmatism was also the year the American economy began to move away from an individualist ideal of unrestrained competition and toward a bureaucratic ideal of management and regulation" (p. 371). Despite the generally positive reception of *The Metaphysical Club*, some students of American intellectual history have contested aspects of its argument. See the symposium in *Intellectual History Newsletter* no. 24 (2002), with contributions by Bruce Kuklick, James Kloppenberg, Giles Gunn, Karen Hanson, and Thomas Haskell, followed by Menand's reply.

27. René Berthelot, *Un romantisme utilitaire: Étude sur le mouvement pragmatiste*, vol. 1 (Paris, 1911), discussed in Richard Rorty, "Pragmatism as Romantic Polytheism," in Dickstein, *The Revival of Pragmatism*, p. 21.

Emile Durkheim resisted Berthelot's comparison with Nietzsche in the critical lectures he gave on pragmatism on the eve of the First World War, he too acknowledged the similarities between Bergson and James in their common hostility to conceptual thought.[28] Significantly, while skeptical of many aspects of pragmatism, when it came to the question of experience Durkheim shared the view that it was not "subjective, the inner experience of the individual (which in the last analysis would open the way to a flood of arbitrary and gratuitous interpretations which would negate all objective values). It is collective experience, the experience of man *in society*."[29]

More recently, and with a far more positive evaluation, the American intellectual historian James Kloppenberg situated pragmatism in the transAtlantic context of a search for a *via media* between natural science and moral/ religious thought, which involved going beyond both atomistic empiricism and rationalist metaphysics. Included in his account are philosophers like Dilthey, Nietzsche, Bergson, and Alfred Fouillée, as well as political activists like the German Social Democrat Eduard Bernstein, the French socialist Jean Jaurès, and the American progressive Herbert Croly. Along with James and Dewey, he argues, they all believed that "meaning must be interpreted on the basis of lived experience and informed with an understanding of the reflected experience of life."[30] What set them apart from earlier empiricist defenders of experience, as well as from their rationalist opponents, Kloppenberg shows, was a willingness to accept the uncertainties of modern life and the inevitable limitations of our ability to know the truth about it. In political terms, this usually meant refusing the determinist premises of orthodox Marxism, as well as the liberal individualist view of economic man, in favor of a more openended democratic pluralism.

These accounts may not do justice to the complexity of this period and the emergence of pragmatism: was this, for example, really the first time that the false idol of certainty was questioned by modern thinkers? What of the probability theory that emerged in the seventeenth century? Were its political inclinations likely to be democratic and progressive? If so, what was the

28. Emile Durkheim, *Pragmatism and Sociology*, trans. J. C. Whitehouse (Cambridge, 1983). In their prefaces, Armand Cuvillier and John B. Allcock provide helpful summaries of the French reception of pragmatism, which was more extensive in the case of James than that of Dewey. For a recent critique of Durkheim's reading of pragmatism, see Hans Joas, *Pragmatism and Social Theory* (Chicago, 1993), chapter 2.

29. Cuvillier, preface to the French edition of 1955, p. xviii. He then adds: "in addition—and this should be particularly noted—that collective experience should be the *object of rational thought*," a position not shared by the pragmatists.

30. James T. Kloppenberg, *Uncertain Victory: Social Democracy and Progressivism in European and American Thought, 1870–1920* (Oxford, 1986), p. 101.

source of its attraction for proto-fascists like the Florentine Giovanni Papini?[31] But they all concur that something radical happened to undermine the solidity of traditional notions of subjectivity, while the concept of experience was given a new lease on life. For what the literary critic Judith Ryan called "the vanishing subject" in both modernist art and the psychology of the late nineteenth century meant that to survive as a meaningful concept, experience needed to turn elsewhere.[32]

JAMES AND THE QUEST FOR PURE EXPERIENCE

Trying to find that somewhere else was the life's work of William James, of whom it has been rightly said, "experience was his salvation, his religion."[33] More than a hyperbolic metaphor, this description, in fact, captures a key di-

31. As noted in chapter 2, from Locke and Hume on, the empiricists were often more comfortable with probable knowledge than with certain knowledge. And before them, of course, Michel de Montaigne had understood, to put it in the words of Giorgio Agamben, that "experience is incompatible with certainty, and once an experience has become measurable and certain, it immediately loses its authority." *Infancy and History: Essays on the Destruction of Experience*, trans. Liz Heron (London, 1993), p. 18. As the work of Ian Hacking, Barbara Schapiro, David Bates, and other commentators discussed in chapter 2 has shown, Dewey's characterization of Western thought as a dogged "quest for certainty," which is also the premise of Kloppenberg's argument, is based to a significant measure on a straw man. Still, to the extent that the pragmatists explicitly jettisoned such a quest, they registered their movement away from subjectivism, for certainty is, after all, a personal state of mind or belief, not a characteristic of the world itself or of truthful knowledge of it.

For a discussion of the relations between Italian proto-fascism and pragmatism, see Anthony Marasco, "Papini's Corridor: Pragmatism, Democracy and the Lure of the Irrational in the Later Work of William James" (Ph.D. diss., University of California, Berkeley, 2003). It is also worth noting that during the Third Reich, German intellectuals like Arnold Gehlen and Eduard Baumgarten attempted to harness pragmatism for Nazi purposes, and for what it is worth, Mussolini also acknowledged its importance for his own worldview. According to Hans Joas, "Baumgarten associates his experience at the front during the First World War with the Americans' experience of the frontier and sees Hitler's seizure of power in 1933 as the start of a new pioneer age." *Pragmatism and Social Theory*, p. 110.

32. Judith Ryan, *The Vanishing Subject: Early Psychology and Literary Modernism* (Chicago, 1991). For a characteristic description of the modernist quest for experience beyond the subject, see Giorgio Agamben's gloss on Marcel Proust, in whom "there is no longer really any subject, but only—with singular materialism—an infinite drifting and a casual colliding of objects and sensations. Here the expropriated subject of experience emerges to validate what, from the point of view of science, can appear only as the most radical negation of experience: an experience with neither subject nor object, absolute." *Infancy and History*, p. 42.

33. Linda Simon, *Genuine Reality: A Life of William James* (New York, 1998), p. xxii. For other major biographies of James, see Gerald E. Myers, *William James: His Life and Thought* (New Haven, 1986), and the still indispensable Ralph Barton Perry, *The Thought and Character of William James*, 2 vols. (Boston, 1935). For an overview of the reception of his ideas and attempts to write his life (up until 1987), see the bibliographical essay in Daniel W. Bjork, *William James: The Center of His Vision* (New York, 1988).

mension of his intense fascination with experience. We have already encountered James as a fellow-traveling diagnostician of religious experience,
struggling throughout his life to find a way to overcome the gap between science and spirituality, naturalist explanation and the lure of the supernatural,
individual psychology and the larger world of impersonal consciousness. The
Swedenborgian overcoming of selfhood embraced by his father, Henry James
Sr., was a model of mystical monism he could never fully endorse, but he
understood from the inside the painful depressions—in Swedenborg's terms,
the "vastations" in which the self loses all sense of its own worth—that had
led his father to that conversion. His vivid and haunting description of the
"sick soul" in *The Varieties of Religious Experience,* it has been suggested, was
based on personal experience.[34]

James also knew and respected his family's friend, the great transcendentalist sage Ralph Waldo Emerson, whose celebrated paean to the overcoming of "mean egotism" in favor of becoming a "transparent eyeball . . . part
and parcel of God" was accompanied by an equally fervent defense of the
heroic individualism and authentic non-conformity of "self-reliance."[35] For
all his vaunted optimism about reconciling man and nature, Emerson seems
to have become increasingly aware of the limits of the individual self in accomplishing this goal.[36] As many commentators have noted, William James
himself oscillated between these two poles, at times veering towards self-ab-
negation and at others self-assertion.[37] Emerson, who is often seen as a proto-
pragmatist, also shared with James a dual suspicion of empiricist sensationalism and abstract intellectualism, and preferred emotional intensity and

34. See Kim Townsend, *Manhood at Harvard: William James and Others* (New York, 1996), p. 52.

35. Ralph Waldo Emerson, *The Complete Works of Ralph Waldo Emerson,* ed. Edward Waldo Emerson, 12 vols. (Boston, 1903–4), vol. 1, p. 10. Emerson, "Self-Reliance," in *Complete Works,* vol. 2. If there
seems a contradiction here, remember that it was Emerson who famously dismissed "a foolish consistency" as "the hobgoblin of little minds."

36. Even Emerson's great essay "Nature" displays a remarkable change of tone from its initial exhilaration about the poet's oneness with nature to its mournful recognition of the alienation between the
two. For an insightful reading of this abrupt transition, see R. Jackson Wilson, "Emerson's *Nature:* A Materialist Reading," in David Simpson, ed., *Subject to History: Ideology, Class, Gender* (Ithaca, N.Y., 1991).

37. See, for example, the account in Ross Posnock, *The Trial of Curiosity: Henry James, William James,
and the Challenge of Modernity* (New York, 1991), p. 18. James's mature appreciation of Emerson can be
found in his "Address at the Emerson Centenary in Concord," in Milton R. Konvitz and Stephen E.
Whicher, eds., *Emerson: A Collection of Critical Essays* (Westport, Conn., 1978). Dewey also wrote positively about him in "Ralph Waldo Emerson," in Joseph Ratner, ed., *Characters and Events: Popular Essays
in Social and Political Philosophy* (New York, 1929), vol. 2. Emerson's affirmative optimism and James's
more realistic understanding of the obstacles to human realization are often contrasted. See, for example, Arthur O. Lovejoy, *The Thirteen Pragmatisms and Other Essays* (Baltimore, 1963), p. 103.

hands-on practice to systematic philosophizing.[38] He fiercely rejected the Lockean trust in sense data, which he equated with Kant's Understanding (as he came to know it through Samuel Taylor Coleridge) and identified with the modern city, in favor of a deeper intuitive Reason best preserved in the countryside. And he was among the first to give Americans permission to believe that they were distinct from their metaphysically inclined European forebears when he famously insisted that "every ingenious and aspiring soul leaves the doctrine behind him in his own experience."[39]

Emerson, so the story is told, visited the James family in 1842 in New York, where he gave his blessing to the infant William, born earlier that year. As it happened, he was in mourning at that time for his own son, Waldo, who had only recently died of scarlet fever at the age of five. To deal with his grief, he composed one of his most powerful essays, simply entitled "Experience."[40] There is much that can be said about this moving and elusive text, but what needs to be stressed now is the aura of longing and mournfulness with which Emerson imbued the concept of experience itself. The loss of his son, he explained ruefully, has not allowed him to reach a deeper understanding of the universe: "I grieve that grief can teach me nothing," he soberly reported, "nor carry me one step into real nature . . . the dearest events are summer-rain, and we the Para coats that shed every drop. Nothing is left us now but death. We look to that with a grim satisfaction, saying, there at least is a reality that will not dodge us."[41] And then he generalized to the human condition itself: "I take this evanescence and lubricity of all objects, which lets them slip through our fingers then when we clutch hardest, to be the most unhandsome part of our condition."[42]

---

38. For a consideration of Emerson as a forerunner of the pragmatist tradition, see Stanley Cavell, "What's the Use of Calling Emerson a Pragmatist?" in Dickstein, *The Revival of Pragmatism;* for a comparison of their role in the tradition of anti-intellectualism in America, see Morton White, *Pragmatism and the American Mind: Essays and Reviews in Philosophy and Intellectual History* (New York, 1973), chapter 6. White also writes perceptively on Emerson and his reception in *Science and Sentiment in America: Philosophical Thought from Jonathan Edwards to John Dewey* (New York, 1972), chapter 5. See also Richard Poirier, *Poetry and Pragmatism* (Cambridge, Mass., 1992), for a discussion of Emerson, pragmatism, and American literature and criticism. A more cautious account of the parallels between Emerson and the pragmatists can be found in David Van Leer, *Emerson's Epistemology: The Argument of the Essays* (Cambridge, Mass., 1986), pp. 47–48.

39. *The Complete Works of Ralph Waldo Emerson,* vol. 2, p. 95. Emerson was among the first to argue for a unique American tradition based on our experiences in his 1837 Phi Beta Kappa address at Harvard, "The American Scholar."

40. Emerson, "Experience," *Essays and Lectures* (Cambridge, 1983).

41. Ibid., p. 473.

42. Ibid.

As Sharon Cameron remarks in perhaps the shrewdest analysis we have of "Experience," Emerson grieves not only for his lost son, but also for the deficiency of his ability to feel that grief, the unbridgeable gap between expectation and realization. As a result, she writes, "grief becomes a trope for experience because the self's relation to experience, like its relation to grief, is oblique, angled, contingent, dissociated. . . . Once the self understands its relation to experience, what it understands is something has been removed. Death is the source of that understanding, teaching us our relation to every other event."[43] As in Montaigne, one of Emerson's avowed idols, death becomes the limit of experience, although here it is not only one's own death, but that of a loved one as well. If there is any work of mourning in Emerson's essay, it is not of the type postulated by Freud as a successful working through and reintegration of the lost object, but something more brittle and fragile, perhaps more akin to melancholic repetition than completed mourning. For there is really no end to grief, no way to complete the mourning process.

Yet despite everything, Emerson finds in what he calls *"the universal impulse to believe"* a reason to keep going: "no man ever came to an experience which was satiating, but his good is tidings of a better. Onward and onward!"[44] Without engaging in instrumental action designed to produce specific effects—"many eager persons successively make an experiment in this way, and make themselves ridiculous"—we can still patiently wait in the belief that "there is victory yet for justice; and the true romance which the world exists to realize, will be the transformation of genius into practical power."[45] For all of its yea-saying, there is a nagging residue in "Experience" of the traumatic event that inspired it, a realization that perhaps all experience, as Stuart Hampshire would later phrase it, involves "the disappointment of natural hope."[46]

Without claiming that James in any way derived his own animadversions on this theme from reading this essay, it is striking that in his usage, the term "experience" often betrays a yearning for something lost or suppressed in the

43. Sharon Cameron, "Representing Grief: Emerson's 'Experience'," *Representations* 15 (Summer 1986), p. 29. See also the sustained analysis of the essay in Van Leer, *Emerson's Epistemology,* chapter 5. Van Leer sees "Experience" expressing Emerson's abandonment of the essentially Kantian epistemological project of his earlier work and with it a faith in human autonomy. What is left is an acceptance of contingency and a recognition of the unbridgeable gap between empirical and transcendental selves. For a more general consideration of the theme of mourning in Emerson, which explores his ambivalences about the course of American history during the antebellum era, see Eduardo Cadava, *Emerson and the Climates of History* (Stanford, 1997).

44. Emerson, "Experience," p. 486 (emphasis in original).

45. Ibid, p. 492.

46. Stuart Hampshire, *Innocence and Experience* (Cambridge, Mass., 1989), p. 150.

modern world, something occluded by conventional ways of grasping and ordering reality. Biographers of James, in fact, routinely note his frequent psychological crises, sometimes almost suicidal in intensity, and early flirtation with nihilism. They catalogue his persistent disappointments: at not fighting with his generation in the Civil War, at abandoning his early intention to become an artist, at never fulfilling his religious yearnings, at taking so long to find his proper calling as a philosopher, at failing to reconcile himself entirely to the legacy of his difficult and demanding father, at being let down by his protégés at Harvard (among them, Hugo Munsterberg), and at overcoming his frequent physical ailments, to mention only a few. In fact, at the height of his fame in 1899–1902, James had a second major crisis, rivaling in severity the one he suffered as a young man in the late 1860s. It sent him into a psychological, physical, spiritual, even professional tailspin from which he perhaps never fully recovered before his death in 1910.[47] Without the comforts of that intuitive knowledge of the Absolute that had sustained Emerson's optimism or faith in the Swedenborgian beliefs embraced by his father, he could only search for some sort of consolation elsewhere.[48] Experience was the paradoxically foundationless foundation that provided an answer, or at least sparked the persistent questioning that drove his work for much of his career.

Translated into his personal life, this quest meant a willingness to open himself up to practices that more cautious scientists would have found anathema—experiments with the occult and the paranormal, dubious mind cures, hallucinogenic drugs, and the like. Although he was not a reckless celebrant of action for its own sake, as shown by his critique of his former student Theodore Roosevelt's cult of bellicose virility,[49] James came close to the

47. Bjork, *William James*, p. 240. The psychodynamics of James's extraordinary family have been a major source of scholarly interest and speculation. Although perhaps the most spectacular casualty was his sister Alice, whose tragic life has been well recounted in Jean Strouse's *Alice James* (Boston, 1980), all of his siblings were plagued with one form or another of the "vastations" suffered by their father.

48. James's doubts about the Absolute are perhaps no more clearly spelled out than in the letter he sent to his friend Elisabeth Glendower Evans on December 11, 1906, which ends: "The Absolute has become only an abstract name, like 'Nature,' for the indefinitely prolonged content of experience, and we are all pragmatists again together. There may *be* an Absolute, of course: and its pragmatic use to us is to make us more optimistic. But it isn't forced on us by logic, as Royce and Bradley think, and its cash equivalent is the *atoning experience believed in*." Quoted in Elizabeth Glendower Evans, "William James and His Wife," in Linda Simon, ed., *William James Remembered* (Lincoln, Neb., 1996), p. 65 (emphasis in original).

49. James, "Governor Roosevelt's Oration" (1899), in *Essays, Comments, and Reviews*, vol. 17 of *Complete Works* (Cambridge, Mass., 1987). The issue was imperialism and the maltreatment of the Philippines. James did share, however, in the culture of virile masculinity and the strenuous life that was so much a part of post–Civil War America. For a discussion, see Townsend, *Manhood at Harvard*.

"redskin" type in American culture contrasted by Philip Rahv in 1939 to its "paleface" alternative, represented by the so-called genteel tradition and often identified with his novelist brother Henry.[50] Always more than a mere professional, academic philosopher, he risked entering the public realm to espouse unpopular political opinions and promote causes like mind-care reform.[51] As we saw in chapter 3, James courageously sought to heal the widening rift between science and religion. Always more than an armchair theorist, he went on a scientific expedition to Brazil, camped in the Adirondacks, restlessly traveled throughout Europe, and survived the San Francisco earthquake. In the words of his most recent biographer, Linda Simon, "eager to plumb the depths of his identity, he believed that one essential route was through the multiplicity of experiences. . . . More experiences—varied, novel, risky—had the potential to yield a portrait of himself as knower, perceiver, interpreter, actor. He championed the new, he hungered for astonishment."[52]

In philosophical terms, James's quest ultimately translated into the exploration of what he came to call "pure experience" through the method of "radical empiricism," terms that may have made some of his pragmatist colleagues such as Peirce uneasy, but that served as the vague rubric under which he subsumed his restless search for a language that would do justice to what it purported to describe. "Vague," it should be understood, is not meant here pejoratively, for as William Joseph Gavin has pointed out, James deliberately turned vagueness into a virtue.[53] For all his interest in the utilitarian functionality and "cash-value" of ideas, which has allowed some critics to reduce pragmatism to little more than an instrumentalist tool of accommodation to the status quo, James reveled in the messiness, ambiguity, and uncertainty of the experience whose vitality he hoped to recover beneath the crust of convention and the

50. Rahv, "Paleface and Redskin," in *Literature and the Sixth Sense*. For Rahv, the distinction—in reverse order to his title—was between "experience and consciousness—a dissociation between energy and sensibility, between conduct and theories of conduct, between life conceived as an opportunity and life conceived as a discipline" (p. 1). Walt Whitman was the quintessential "redskin," while his "paleface" counterpart according to Rahv was Henry James. For a persuasive refutation of this latter identification, see Posnock, *The Trial of Curiosity*. Santayana drew a similar opposition between William James and Josiah Royce in his seminal 1913 essay "The Genteel Tradition in American Philosophy," in David A. Hollinger and Charles Capper, eds., *The American Intellectual Tradition*, vol. 2 (New York, 2001). Santayana maintains that both James brothers were critics of the tradition, Henry by analyzing it from the outside, while William burst it from within through his vitalism.

51. For James's role in the public sphere, see George Cotkin, *William James: Public Philosopher* (Baltimore, 1990). Like many before him, Cotkin acknowledges the extent to which James's exhortation to heroic action was a compensation for his own feelings of indecisiveness and uncertainty (pp. 100–101).

52. Simon, *Genuine Reality*, p. xxii.

53. William Joseph Gavin, *William James and the Reinstatement of the Vague* (Philadelphia, 1992).

rigidities of conceptual thought. As early as his path-breaking analysis of mental life as a "stream of consciousness" in his first great work, *The Principles of Psychology* of 1890, and as late as the short pieces published by Ralph Barton Perry as *Essays in Radical Empiricism* after James's death in 1910, he sought to dive into the flux rather than observe from afar the world outside him.

There have been many attempts to periodize James's career, but perhaps one area of agreement is the increasing centrality of experience as the master term of his discourse. One commentator has even gone so far as to claim that "it is a large mistake to make pragmatism the irreducible core of James' philosophy. That much-publicized facet of Jamesian thinking was merely a way of dealing with the world of pure experience."[54] In *The Principles of Psychology* he could still investigate consciousness with a positivist's belief in the dualism of mind and body, although his description of the former stressed its ephemeral and fluid indeterminacy (a "big blooming buzzing confusion" in his memorable phrase). By the turn of the century, he was seeking a way beyond the dualism of the mental and physical world, which would allow him to overcome representationalist epistemology in the name of a "natural realism."

Among James's mentors in this regard was the now forgotten British philosopher Shadworth Hollway Hodgson (1832–1912), whom he first met in 1880.[55] Hodgson was a critic of Humean empiricism for its atomistic disarticulation of consciousness into discrete sensations, preferring instead to see it as a fluid stream. He also questioned the independent existence of substances and subjects in favor of the relations that subtended them. In his 1885 lecture to the British Aristotelian Society, which he headed for some thirteen years, entitled *Philosophy and Experience,* he called his position "experientialism" to distinguish it from the empiricism he disliked in Locke and Hume and the positivism then in fashion.[56] "There is no larger word," he wrote, "than *Experience.* It is the equivalent of *Consciousness.*" The world outside of consciousness was, moreover, included in it, for "we cannot go beyond experience, and assign a larger term, under which Being can be subsumed, and so explained."[57] Corresponding with James while the lecture was in preparation, he acknowledged that he had abandoned the idea of Mind as agent, or rather "it was got rid of before I came into the field at all; I found it *gone,*

54. Bjork, *William James,* p. 219.

55. For an account of his friendship with James, see Perry, *The Thought and Character of William James,* vol. 1, chapters 38–40.

56. Shadworth H. Hodgson, *Philosophy and Experience: An Address Delivered before the Aristotelian Society, October 26, 1885* (Edinburgh, 1885).

57. Ibid., pp. 6 and 16.

broken up by its inherent contradictions; and generating nothing but skepticism by its putrefaction. This being so, I resolved to base philosophy (no longer on an assumption but) on *experience. That* is the history and reason of my method. My aim is not to get rid of mind as agent, but to replace it; to have a philosophy based, not on it, but on experience."[58]

Hodgson called his approach the Metaphysical Method or the Method of Subjective Analysis, terms that never gained wide acceptance. James, for his part, was impressed more by the details of his friend's philosophizing than by the larger monistic and determinist implications Hodgson drew from it.[59] By the time Hodgson produced his multivolume *Metaphysic of Experience* in 1898, James could only diplomatically reply:

> If ever I hitch ahead positively at all in my own effort, it will now be thanks to the terms in which you have written your solution. The problem I take to be this: Assuming no duality of material and mental substance, but starting with bits of "pure experience," syncretically taken, to show how this comes to figure in two ways in conception, once as streams of individual thinking, once as physical permanents, without the *immediately real* ever having been either of these diremped things, or less than the full concrete experience or phenomenon with its two aspects.[60]

Now it was the dualism he complained about in Hodgson's metaphysics, preferring instead the pluralism that he was in the process of formulating.[61] By then, James was well on his way toward developing his own alternative,

---

58. Shadworth H. Hodgson to James, February 14, 1884, in *The Correspondence of William James*, 13 vols., ed. Ignas K. Skrupskelis and Elizabeth M. Berkeley, vol. 5 (Charlottesville, Va., 1997), p. 489.

59. See his letter to Charles Renouvier of May 8, 1882, in *The Correspondence of William James*, vol. 5, p. 208. Renouvier, the French liberal neo-Kantian, gave James a powerful belief in the existence of free will, which seems to have helped him to emerge from his first major depression in 1870. In his correspondence with Hodgson, liberally quoted in the chapters on their friendship in Perry, *The Thought and Character of William James*, vol. 1, James voiced the same reservations directly. It is worth noting, however, that at the end of his 1885 lecture, Hodgson endorsed the experiential approach even in matters like religion, as well as common sense, science, and philosophy, thus anticipating James's own expansion of the term's purview.

60. James to Hodgson, June 10, 1900, quoted in Perry, *The Thought and Character of Williams James*, vol. 1, p. 647 (emphasis in original)

61. James to Hodgson, October 7, 1900, in ibid. See also Hodgson's reply in his letter of October 18, 1900, where he writes "mine is not the dualism between mind and matter, but a dualism of *method*, a dualism imposed by the distinction in thought and made necessary by experience,—the distinction between οὐσία and γένεσις [essence and genesis]." Ibid., p. 649. James does not appear to have been convinced, although he acknowledged Hodgson's insistence that "realities are only what they are 'known-as'" as a forerunner of his own position in *Pragmatism* (1907), *Works*, vol. 1 (Cambridge, Mass., 1975), p. 30.

which he had begun to sketch out in notebooks dating from 1895, and seems to have been anxious to stress the differences between them rather than the similarities.[62]

Never fully satisfied with his formulations, a reflection of James's acknowledgment of the ultimate inadequacy of language to capture the reality he sought to understand, he struggled to express metaphorically his sense of an experience that was "pure."[63] Identifying it with the "one primal stuff or material in the world, a stuff of which everything is composed," he called it "the instant field of the present," which was only potentially divisible into subject and object or facts and values.[64] Despite the materialist overtones of this description, James insisted that pure experience was not to be understood as some sort of substance or entity, nothing like a deep structure or eternal form beneath the flux of appearances.[65] It was, however, in some sense prior to the subjective consciousness, streaming or otherwise, that he had investigated in his *Principles of Psychology,* when he still operated with a dualistic assumption about the separate reality of the external world. Consciousness, James now contended, is not an entity, but a function within experience, the function of knowing, which is added to it rather than a precondition of it. The "double-barreled" meaning of experience, at once subjective and objective, is an expression of its originally holistic and relational character.

Conceptual knowing or "knowledge about" is one step removed from the more basic perceptual knowing or "knowledge by acquaintance," in which there is no reflective separation of subjective knower and object of knowledge. For, as Hodgson had made clear, pure experience is a "that" before it is a "what," an existence before it can pretend to have an essence.[66] It is, James argued, sounding as if he were citing Dilthey on *Erlebnis,* "the immediate

62. For a discussion, see Bjork, *William James,* pp. 215–27.

63. As David C. Lamberth has shown in *William James and the Metaphysics of Experience* (Cambridge, 1999), pp. 83–87, the term was borrowed from the German philosopher of empiriocriticism Richard Avenarius, whose *Kritik der reinen Erfahrung* of 1888–90 James knew well.

64. James, *Essays in Radical Empiricism* (Lincoln, Neb., 1996), pp. 4 and 23.

65. There are, to be sure, places in his work where he professed agnosticism about such ultimate realities. For example, in his reply to the criticism of Walter Pitkin in 1906, he conceded "I am perfectly willing to admit any number of noumenal beings or events into philosophy if only their pragmatic value can be shown." "Discussion: Mr. Pitkin's Refutation of 'Radical Empiricism'," in Eugene Taylor and Robert H. Wozniak, eds., *Pure Experience: The Response to William James* (Bristol, 1996), p. 122.

66. James quotes Hodgson's *Metaphysic of Experience* appreciatively on this point in *Essays in Radical Empiricism,* p. 27.

flux of life which furnishes the material to our later reflection with its conceptual categories."[67] Moreover, as Bergson had understood in his philosophy of *élan vital*—James explicitly acknowledged the similarities[68]—experience is a dynamic, relational field rather than something that happens to an individual subject produced by a discrete object. In that field, *"the relations that connect experiences must themselves be experienced relations, and any kind of relation experienced must be accounted as 'real' as anything else in the system."*[69] That is, the transitions expressed linguistically by often neglected words like "of," "in," "and," and the like had as much ontological weight as the substantives they joined (a lesson often said to be well learned by one of James's most gifted students, the poet Gertrude Stein). Traditional empiricism had neglected these dimensions of experience, as it had those subliminal elements subtending religious experience, and therefore had to be "radicalized" to include all that was in the relational field. "To be radical," James explained, "an empiricism must neither admit into its constructions any element that is not directly experienced, nor exclude from them any element that is directly experienced."[70]

The field of experience was not, however, as completely unified and ultimately rational as assumed by latter-day Hegelians like F. H. Bradley or Josiah Royce (anticipating the position we have seen revived in the work of Oakeshott a generation later). Instead, James opined, "our experiences, all taken together [are] a quasi-chaos."[71] The cosmological implications of all

67. James, *Essays in Radical Empiricism,* p. 23. James and Dilthey knew and respected each other's work and had actually met in 1867. See Kloppenberg, *Uncertain Victory,* p. 29. Kloppenberg argues that in the 1890s both James and Dewey moved closer to Dilthey's notion of *Erlebnis* (p. 70).

68. In a letter of February 25, 1903, to Bergson, he called his friend's work "a philosophy of *pure experience.*" Bergson was also generously praised in *A Pluralistic Universe* (New York, 1909) for having shown the inadequacy of logic to express the fluidity of life. Shortly thereafter, Horace Kallen, one of James's most fervent disciples, wrote a sustained comparison, *William James and Henri Bergson* (Chicago, 1914), in which he contrasted the humanist pluralism of James to Bergson's faith in the *élan vital.* James himself, however, may have thought otherwise. In a letter to F. C. S. Schiller on June 13, 1907, he gushed about the publication of *Creative Evolution:* "It seems to me that nothing is important in comparison with that divine apparition. All *our* positions, real time, a growing world, asserted magisterially, and the beast intellectualism killed absolutely *dead!*" *William James: Selected Unpublished Correspondence, 1885–1910,* ed. Frederick J. Down Scott (Columbus, Ohio, 1986), p. 442.

69. James, *Essays in Radical Empiricism,* p. 42 (emphasis in original).

70. Ibid. Here we see the rationale for his generous inclusion of religious experience in *The Varieties of Religious Experience.*

71. James, *Essays in Radical Empiricism,* p. 65. For a discussion of his long debate with Royce, see James Conant, "The James/Royce Dispute and the Development of James's 'Solution'," in Ruth Anna Putnam, ed., *The Cambridge Companion to William James* (Cambridge, 1997).

this were therefore neither monistic nor dualistic, for "it is just because so many of the conjunctions of experience seem so external that a philosophy of pure experience must tend to pluralism in its ontology."[72] Groping for the right metaphor, James called his position a "mosaic philosophy" appropriate to a world in which the pieces hold together without a firm bedding beneath, and achieve expansion by accretion around the edges. Indeed, if there is a God above this world, James now admitted, even He is "no absolute all-experiencer, but simply the experiencer of widest actual conscious span."[73] In fact, rather than postulating a fully transcendent God, James preferred a kind of panpsychic immanence—one commentator has called it a "panexperientialism"[74]—in which spirit was inextricably intertwined with the material world.[75]

In addition to these metaphysical speculations about experience, James also employed it as the key term in his ruminations on epistemological questions. "The principle of pure experience," he wrote, "is also a methodical postulate. Nothing shall be admitted as fact, it says, except what can be experienced at some definite time by some experient; and for every feature of fact ever so experienced, a definite place must be found somewhere in the final system of reality. In other words: Everything real must be experienceable somewhere, and every kind of thing experienced must somewhere be real."[76] The pragmatist criterion of truth, he explained in *Pragmatism,* is based on the question, "what experiences will be different from those which would obtain if the belief were false? What in short, is the truth's cash-value in experiential terms?"[77] Fortunately, "experience is all shot through with regularities," so that the past is a guide to the future, but conversely, "experience, as we know, has ways of *boiling over,* and making us correct our present formulas."[78] There is thus a rough continuity between past, present, and future experience, leading us toward increased understanding, even if we can never achieve absolute knowledge:

> Men's beliefs at any time are so much experience *funded.* But the beliefs are themselves parts of the sum total of the world's experience, and become matter,

72. James, *Essays in Radical Empiricism,* p. 110.
73. Ibid., p. 194.
74. T. L. S. Sprigge, *James and Bradley: American Truth and British Reality* (Chicago, 1993), p. 45.
75. For a sustained and sympathetic consideration of James's pan-psychic pluralism, see Lamberth, *William James and the Metaphysics of Experience,* pp. 185–96.
76. James, *Essays in Radical Empiricism,* p. 160.
77. James, *Pragmatism,* p. 97.
78. Ibid., pp. 99 and 106 (emphasis in original).

therefore, for the next day's funding operations. So far as reality means experienceable reality, both it and the truths men gain about it are everlastingly in process of mutation—mutation towards a definite goal, it may be—but still mutation.[79]

Because sensation and belief were thus so inextricably intertwined, as James had endeavored to show in his defense of religious experience, even the purest of empiricisms could not be purified of its cultural and historical content.[80]

Unlike Peirce, who held on to the "cheerful hope"[81] that a rigorous scientific method would ultimately produce an intersubjective consensus about truth, James rested content with experience as endless experimentation. Precisely because experience was always richer and more complex than our feeble attempts to capture it in language or concepts, it generates an evolutionary dialectic—here James the enthusiastic Darwinian was speaking—without a teleological end point. Against the alienation of experience into the seemingly objective instruments of measurement that had characterized the scientific revolution—privileging the "testimony of nonhumans," to quote once again Bruno Latour's felicitous phrase—James wanted to reassert the primacy of the perceptual, embodied world, a position that has earned him a place in the genealogy of phenomenology as well as pragmatism.[82]

And yet James, like Emerson in his essay "Experience," revealed a certain disappointment at the impossibility of restoring pure experience to a language-speaking, logic-chopping, intellectualizing species like our own. "Only new-born babes, or men in semi-coma from sleep, drugs, illnesses, or blows may be assumed to have an experience pure in the literal sense of a *that* which

79. Ibid., p. 107.
80. For a helpful discussion of this aspect of his position, see David A. Hollinger, "William James and the Culture of Inquiry," *In the American Province: Studies in the History and Historiography of Ideas* (Bloomington, Ind., 1985).
81. The phrase is quoted in Gavin, *William James and the Reinstatement of the Vague*, p. 103. Chapter 5 of this book provides a helpful comparison of Peirce and James on this and other issues. Gavin claims that Dewey returned to Peirce's faith in the possibility of ultimate consensus. For another discussion, see Christopher Hookway, "Logical Principles and Philosophical Attitudes: Peirce's Response to James's Pragmatism," in Putnam, *The Cambridge Companion to William James*. Hookway argues that the crucial difference between them is that "where James simply looks for the experiences that would result if the proposition were true or the conduct one should carry out in those circumstances, Peirce looks for patterns in experience and lawlike interrelations of action and experience" (p. 152).
82. James first learned of Husserl through his Harvard colleague William Ernest Hocking in 1904. For a discussion of Hocking, who was among other things the author of a book called *The Meaning of God in Human Experience* (1912), see Wilshire, *The Primal Roots of American Philosophy*, chapter 8.

is not yet any *what,* tho' ready to be all sorts of whats; full both of oneness and of manyness, but in respects that don't appear; changing throughout, yet so confusedly that its phases interpenetrate and no points, either of distinction or of identity can be caught," he admitted in *Essays in Radical Empiricism.*[83] Although he clearly hoped that heightened moments of purity were worth striving for, it is not clear that he ever really felt content that they could be widely or enduringly achieved. It is often said that James's advocacy of the "will to believe" is too self-consciously candid about its own instrumental efficacy—you should believe because it will produce a good effect on you to do so—to be fully convincing. Something similar might be argued about his faith in the purity of experience prior to its diremptions.

Indeed, as one of his more sympathetic interpreters has admitted, pure experience is "vague in the sense that even James's own description of it is a hypothesis, one in which he has ultimate faith, to be sure, but a hypothesis nonetheless."[84] Less generous commentators—and there have been many ever since the day James began presenting his ideas—have been even more troubled by the tensions or even outright contradictions in the various formulations James introduced over his career to evoke what language was never able to express perfectly. Thus, for example, in 1906 Herbert Nicholls could survey the various uses of the word in James's oeuvre and come up with the following bewildering variety:

> From his "Psychology" we get this: "as universally understood . . . experience means experience of something foreign supposed to impress us." Plainly *"something foreign"* is not solipsistic. But from this JOURNAL *[Journal of Philosophy, Psychology and Scientific Methods]* we get these: "The *instant field of the present* is at all times what I call the pure experience." Again: "The instant field of the present is always experience in its 'pure' state." The context seems to make this "experience" *not* solipsistic; but in any case, since by "continuous transition" one's whole field of mind *always* is "the instant field of the present," how then "is the instant field of the present *always* experience in its *'pure'* state?" For, again: "'Pure experience' is the name I give to the *original* flux of life before reflexion has categorized it. *Only new born babes,* etc. have the experience pure in the literal sense." Again: "A pure experience can be postulated of any amount whatever of span or field." And again: "I called our experiences, taken together, a *quasi-chaos.*" And again: "Experience is only a collective name for

83. James, *Essays in Radical Empiricism,* pp. 93–94.
84. Gavin, *William James and the Reinstatement of the Vague,* p. 93.

all these sensible natures"; that is for "all the primal stuffs" with which Professor James "*starts* his thesis." While finally "Experience," with a capital "E" is the name he gives to the entire completed "Weltanschauung" or rational world, whose cognitive function *between* minds his philosophical writings are supposed to explain.[85]

Perhaps the main difficulty for critics like Nicholls was the uneasy juxtaposition of two different, perhaps even incommensurable, uses of the term. One continued James's earlier psychological investigations and identified experience with prereflective immersion in the flux of life; this was experience as *Erlebnis,* which was increasingly marginalized by or submerged under the linguistic and conceptual operations that inevitably came with our fall into culture (a fall that has not yet happened to newborns and that is temporarily overcome by stupors induced by drugs, blows to the head, and the like). Here the restless longing for what is lost, which, as we have seen, James shared with the Emerson of "Experience," is paramount. Here the motor for James's own cult of experiential variety and intensity finds its fuel.

The second meaning was the all-embracing metaphysical concept of experience, developed in his later works, as equivalent to the "primal stuff" prior to the dualistic division into self and other, consciousness and physical reality, facts and values. Here experience means the fundamental "thatness" of everything that is, a claim that sounds almost proto-Heideggerian in its sweep. It was this acceptation that has allowed some commentators to dub James a heterodox realist, even if he rejected the existence of an independently verifiable world.[86] But why then call it "experience"?

85. Herbert Nicholls, "Discussion: Professor James's Hole," in Taylor and Wozniak, *Pure Experience,* pp. 147–48. This volume conveniently collects many of the most crucial texts of the immediate reception of radical empiricism. It should be noted that complaints about irreconcilable interpretations of experience in James continue to this day. See, for example, Jonathan Crary's discussion of James in the context of the late nineteenth-century psychology of attention, where he concludes that "For James, individual attentiveness to the fringes, transitions, pulses of one's own particular 'pure experience' was never effectively reconciled with 'experience' as immersion in the tangled density of a shared, mutually inhabited world." *Suspensions of Perception: Attention, Spectacle, and Modern Culture* (Cambridge, Mass., 1999), p. 352.

86. See, for example, Hilary Putnam, "Pragmatism and Realism," in Dickstein, *The Revival of Pragmatism.* For a slightly different approach, see Charlene Haddock Seigfried, "William James's Concrete Analysis of Experience," *The Monist* 75, no. 4 (October 1992), where she writes: "pragmatist realism is not realism in its most recognizable sense of the assertion of an independently existing world, the essential structures of which can be abstracted without distortion. . . . James's claim to set metaphysics on a

This question was asked most insistently by contemporaries, untouched by the nascent phenomenological movement, who were still anxious to maintain the subject/object opposition. As Bertrand Russell protested, "to be 'given,' to be 'experienced,' is not the same thing as to 'be.' To be 'given' or 'experienced' seems to imply a subject, to be constituted in fact by a relation to a cognizing act."[87] Focusing only on the subjective moment in the whole, Arthur Lovejoy would challenge James's improper extension of the word to include what was normally outside of awareness—the processes of, say, metabolism and breathing—alongside the data available for reflection, insisting that James had therefore not really succeeded in reducing consciousness to a derivative of experience.[88] Even Peirce would exclaim with exasperation, "what you call 'pure experience' is not experience at all and certainly ought to have a name. It is downright bad morals so to misuse words, for it prevents philosophy from becoming a science."[89] For, as Charles Morris would later write, "If everything in and of itself is an 'experience' then the term 'experience' has lost its 'intellectual' or 'cognitive' purport (however appealing this usage may be on other grounds). To say that X is an item of experience is no longer to say anything whatsoever about it."[90]

---

firm foundation in the facts of experience can thus be reinterpreted as an appeal to the *full* facts of experience. . . . his metaphysics is better understood as a pragmatist hermeneutics and his natural scientific psychology as a pragmatic phenomenology of being human. Both together comprise his concrete analysis of experience" (pp. 547–48).

87. Bertrand Russell, "A Review of 'Essays in Radical Empiricism' by William James," in Taylor and Wozniak, *Pure Experience*, pp. 216–17.

88. Arthur O. Lovejoy, "James's *Does Consciousness Exist?*" in *The Thirteen Pragmatisms and Other Essays* (Baltimore, 1963).

89. See Peirce's letter of October 3, 1904, in *The Collected Papers of Charles Sanders Peirce*, 8 vols., ed. Charles Hartshorne and Paul Weiss (vols. 1–6) and Arthur W. Burks (vols. 7–8) (Cambridge, Mass., 1931–58), vol. 8, p. 206, para. 301. In the same letter, Peirce asserted that "*experience*, from the very essence of the word, consists of our belief about a universe—'the truth'—over against our opinions and beliefs, which are thought of as fallible and ignorant " (p. 204, para. 294). No better expression of Peirce's distance from James can be found than in this characterization, which shows his faith in the ultimate consensus about the truth sought by public, intersubjective scientific inquiry. For a short comparison of their two positions, see John Patrick Diggins, *The Promise of Pragmatism: Modernism and the Crisis of Knowledge and Authority* (Chicago, 1994), pp. 164–70.

90. Charles Morris, *The Pragmatic Movement in American Philosophy* (New York, 1970), p. 114. Even sympathetic readers of James like Hilary Putnam would remain troubled by this problem. See his "Pragmatism and Realism," in Dickstein, *The Revival of Pragmatism:* "The world, for James is the *experienceable* world, and since James has a praiseworthy reluctance to rule out any kind of talk that does real work in our lives, he is forced to talk of unobservables in physics, talk of counterfactual connections, mathematical talk, and so on in ways that are unconvincing and ultimately unsuccessful" (p. 48).

James, to be sure, was not without his loyal defenders.[91] Prominent among them was John Dewey, seventeen years his junior but already the center of a thriving pragmatist community of scholars at the University of Chicago and then, after 1904, at Columbia.[92] Like James, Dewey demonstrated an early impatience with the impoverished reduction of experience to sense data, which had rendered British empiricism philosophically inadequate. But his initial point of departure was neo-Hegelianism, absorbed during his graduate school days under the tutelage of George Sylvester Morris (himself a student of the British idealist T. H. Green), a philosophy that had never tempted James.[93] When the young Dewey bravely tried to marry the new psychology promulgated by James and the evolutionary theory of Darwin with the organic idealism of Hegel, he was in fact roundly criticized by Shadworth Hodgson, whose critique stimulated James to remark: "poor Dewey."[94]

The chastening seems to have worked, however, as Dewey began to shed the metaphysical certainties and logical scaffolding of absolute idealism by the early 1890s.[95] Unlike Oakeshott (and, as we will see, Walter Benjamin,

91. The abiding power of his personality and ideas is in evidence in the tributes collected by Linda Simon as *William James Remembered*. For a general appreciation of James's importance for later thinkers, see Ross Posnock, "The Influence of William James on American Culture," in Putnam, *The Cambridge Companion to William James*.

92. The best recent biographies of Dewey are Robert B. Westbrook, *John Dewey and American Democracy* (Ithaca, N.Y., 1991); Steven C. Rockefeller, *John Dewey: Religious Faith and Democratic Humanism* (New York, 1991); and Alan Ryan, *John Dewey and the Hightide of American Liberalism* (New York, 1995). For a full bibliography of commentaries on his work, see Barbara Levine, ed., *Works about Dewey, 1886–1995* (Carbondale, Ill., 1996). The CD-ROM edition contains a supplement of more recent works. Perhaps the most extensive study of his notion of experience is Gérard Deledalle, *L'idée d'expérience dans la philosophie de John Dewey* (Paris, 1967).

93. For James's attack on neo-Hegelianism, see his 1882 essay "On Some Hegelisms," in *The Will to Believe* (Cambridge, 1979). James did, however, come to appreciate the dialectical and dynamic moments in Hegel's thought, as well as his emphasis on internal relations. See Lamberth, *William James and the Metaphysics of Experience* (pp. 172–74), for an account of his nuanced reaction to Hegel. Dewey, on the other hand, had been an impressionable undergraduate at the University of Vermont, where German idealism had been enthusiastically taught (the transcendentalist James Marsh was the university's president). Dewey had studied Kant under Joseph Torrey, Marsh's successor in the chair of philosophy, and was also exposed to his successors in the idealist tradition. Still valuable as an account of the early Dewey is Morton White, *The Origin of Dewey's Instrumentalism* (New York, 1943).

94. John Dewey, "The New Psychology," "The Psychological Standpoint," and "Psychology as Philosophic Method," in *The Early Works of John Dewey, 1882–1898*, 5 vols. (Carbondale, Ill., 1967–72), vol. 1; Shadworth Hodgson, "Illusory Psychology," *Mind* 9 (1886); James to Hodgson, March 1887, quoted in Perry, *The Thought and Character of William James*, vol. 1, p. 641.

95. By 1906, Dewey had achieved a complete understanding of the limits of idealism, which he spelled out in "Experience and Objective Idealism," in *The Influence of Darwin on Philosophy and Other Essays*

although from non-idealist premises), he came to spurn the concept of "Absolute Experience, as if any experience could be more absolutely experience than that which marks the life of humanity."[96] But while rejecting the consoling function of rationalist theodicy implicit in Hegelianism, he never abandoned Hegel's emphasis on the social, intersubjective, historical dimension of philosophy or his unifying ambition to project his ideas into virtually all fields of human endeavor. He also retained the activist, transformational moment in neo-idealism, which he had inherited via Morris from British thinkers like Green; his naturalism was never determinist in character. Nor did Dewey relent on the question of the inadequacy of a purely epistemologically rendered notion of experience, always insisting that it was far more basic to existence than a mere method of cognition, including, as it did, moral, aesthetic, even metaphysical dimensions. Perhaps even more vigorously than James, he attacked the dualistic underpinnings of any theory that set knowing subjects apart from the objects that confronted them.[97] Adopting James's formula, he insisted that experience was a "double-barreled" word "in that it recognizes in its primary integrity no division between act and material, subject and object, but contains them both in an unanalyzed totality."[98] Against any philosophy that sought to identify the fundamental stuff of the universe, whether understood in material or spiritual terms or conceptualized as eternal substance or permanent flux, Dewey remained resolutely agnostic; against any philosophy that wanted to find the simplest building blocks of reality, whether discrete sense impressions, isolated events, or the smallest atoms, he emphasized the value of holistic complexity; against any philosophy that posited transcendental a priori principles, he claimed that even logic and mathematics must be situated in a context of discovery. Although he relinquished the Hegelian "quest for certainty," he never lost its no less powerful "quest for unity."[99]

Throughout the 1890s, Dewey defended these values on the terrain of psychology, following the lead of James's *Principles* and perhaps even outdoing

(Bloomington, Ind., 1910). His hostility to German idealism was given an added intensity during the First World War, when he published one of his least impressive works, *German Philosophy and Politics* (New York, 1915), which implausibly blamed Kant for German authoritarian militarism.

96. Dewey, *Experience and Nature* (La Salle, Ill., 1987), p. 52.

97. For a helpful account of this impulse in his thought, see Morton White, "John Dewey: Rebel Against Dualism," in *Science and Sentiment in America: Philosophical Thought from Jonathan Edwards to John Dewey* (New York, 1972).

98. Dewey, *Experience and Nature*, p. 10.

99. For a thorough exploration of the sources and implications of this quest, see Rockefeller, *John Dewey*, chapter 1.

him in naturalizing consciousness within an organic world.[100] In a seminal essay of 1896, he argued that on the level of conscious experience there was no real distinction between stimulus and response, except in rare cases of uncertainty about how to respond effectively. Experience was thus more of a circuit than an arc, and all psychic processes and operations, not only intellectual ones, were functional in addressing problems encountered by the individual interacting with his environment.[101] Both intellectualists and sensationalists failed to understand this circular unity and functional imperative, thus duplicating the mistakes made in epistemological terms by rationalists and empiricists. Thought and consciousness were not prior to experience, but rather a fold within it, allowing a kind of division of labor that had instrumental efficacy. Dewey would remain a confirmed holist, contextualist, naturalist, and, in Morton White's phrase, anti-formalist throughout his long career, continuing to elaborate—critics would say belabor—his fundamental arguments at every opportunity. Everything understood to be transcendental or a priori, he repeatedly insisted, was ultimately a reflection of an erroneous substantialization of functions and the deluded erection of thought into an independent entity above its manifestations in the actions of real people in real situations.[102] The Humean and Kantian distinction between analytic and synthetic judgments was equally deluded, as both are aspects of a single whole. Even the methods of science should be understood in behavioral terms based on what he called "instrumentalist" protocols of inquiry, which produce and test the logical forms that previous thinkers claimed were eternally true.[103] The "spectatorial" attitude of traditional scientific under-

100. On the extent of Dewey's debts to and departure from James, see Westbrook, *John Dewey and American Democracy,* pp. 66–67; and Richard M. Gale, "John Dewey's Naturalization of William James," in Putnam, *The Cambridge Companion to William James.* Gale argues that despite his frequent defense of James, Dewey's essays "gave a blatantly distorted, self-serving account of James's philosophy, the basic aims of which were to despookify and depersonalize it so that it would agree with Dewey's naturalism and socialization of all things distinctly human" (p. 49).

101. "The Reflex Arc Concept in Psychology," in his *Early Works,* vol. 5. This essay struck a powerful blow against the "introspectionist" school of psychology and helped to launch its functionalist successor. For a summary of Dewey's debts to James and the debate over how unequivocal they were, see Westbrook, *John Dewey and American Democracy,* chapter 3.

102. Whether Dewey was fully successful in exorcising a priori and transcendental moments from his own thought is unclear. For a skeptical consideration of this question, see Morton White, "Experiment and Necessity in Dewey's Philosophy," in *Pragmatism and the American Mind: Essays and Reviews in Philosophy and Intellectual History* (New York, 1973).

103. See the collaborative study published in 1903 as *Studies in Logical Theory,* Dewey, *The Middle Works, 1899–1904,* vol. 2, ed. Jo Ann Boydston (Carbondale, Ill., 1976). The best discussion of Dewey's "logic of experience" can be found in R. W. Sleeper, *The Necessity of Pragmatism: John Dewey's Conception*

standing, as well as much metaphysics ever since the Greeks,[104] had to be abandoned in favor of an active and participatory intervention in the world. Objects of knowledge are constituted by that participation, rather than being antecedent to it, although this does not make them any less "real." Indeed, at one point in his writings, Dewey would go so far as to argue that the experimental method *"substitutes data for objects,"* while defining the former as "subject matter for *further* interpretation" and the latter as completed "finalities."[105]

Experience thus grows out of experimentation, which moves us into the future rather than tying us down to the past. Although experience as memory of previous lessons is vital, it cannot be identified entirely with those lessons, for

> Dis-membering is a positively necessary part of re-membering. But the resulting *disjecta membra* are in no sense experience as it was or is; they are simply elements held apart, and yet tentatively implicated together, in present experience for the sake of its most favorable evolution; evolution in the direction of the most excellent meaning or value conceived.[106]

Unlike Dilthey or Collingwood, Dewey implied that re-experiencing or re-enactment could never recapture an earlier experienced whole, because of the priority of the needs of the present over the past, a priority that meant experience itself was forever in flux, always anticipating a future different from the past. Here he differed as well from other philosophers, such as F. H. Bradley or Alfred North Whitehead, whose appeal to immediate experience against abstraction was based on its recovery rather than constitution.[107]

There was nonetheless for Dewey a circuit between the experiments in living of daily life and those conducted in the scientist's laboratory, a continuity between the world of common sense and that of the most abstract scientific conclusions. In fact, even mathematics, Dewey came to argue, was ultimately grounded in the world of experience rather than hovering above

---

of Philosophy (Urbana, Ill., 2001). Sleeper challenges White's critique of the transcendental residues in Dewey.

104. We have already encountered Dewey's critique of Greek anti-experientialism and its limits in chapter 1. He did, however, warm to the Aristotelian view of inquiry as an instrumental organon of discovery, while jettisoning the Greek philosopher's belief that essences were the ultimate object of inquiry.

105. Dewey, *The Quest for Certainty* (New York, 1929), p. 99 (emphasis in original).

106. Dewey, "Experience and Objective Idealism," pp. 220–21.

107. For comparisons, see Robert D. Mack, *The Appeal to Immediate Experience: Philosophic Method in Bradley, Whitehead and Dewey* (New York, 1945); and Sprigge, *James and Bradley*.

it in an ideal realm of eternal essences.[108] He thus dismissed the fears of transcendentalists like Gottlob Frege and Edmund Husserl, who claimed that failing to acknowledge such a realm led to a debilitating "psychologistic" relativism, which undermined the validity of mathematics and logic. Turning the tables on his critics, Dewey argued that they were in fact the real psychologizers: "It is interesting to note that the transcendentalist almost invariably falls into the psychological fallacy; and then having himself taken the psychologist's attitude (the attitude which is interested in meanings as themselves self-inclosed [*sic*] 'ideas') accuses the empiricist whom he criticizes of having confused mere psychological existence with logical validity."[109]

Truth was not based on an accurate correspondence with an external world of objects or eternal ideas, but was a result of a successful resolution of a problem.[110] Verification was not a function of subjective experience being confirmed by an independent test of objective validity, but rather entailed the "cor-respondence," the mutual readjustment between purposeful plan and environmental response; in this sense, experience was a transactional concept.[111] Ultimately, this give-and-take can lead to a "satisfactory" outcome (the same standard, it will be recalled, invoked by Oakeshott in *Experience and Its Modes*). As Dewey explained in *The Quest for Certainty*,

> to say that something satisfies is to report something as an isolated finality. To assert that it is satis*factory* is to define it in its connections and interactions. . . . To declare something satis*factory* is to assert that it meets specifiable conditions. It is, in effect, a judgment that the thing "will do." It involves a prediction; it contemplates a future in which the thing will continue to serve; it *will*

---

108. Dewey, *Reconstruction in Philosophy* (New York, 1920). For a consideration of the difficulties of this position, see White, *Science and Sentiment*, pp. 280–85.

109. Dewey, "The Experimental Theory," in *The Influence of Darwin on Philosophy* (Bloomington, Ind., 1910), p. 103. Dewey, however, concurred with the later Husserl's contention that scientific knowledge grew out of the *Lebenswelt* of practices in everyday life. For an appreciative account of his attempt to overcome Peirce's formalism and James's psychologism, see Sleeper, *The Necessity of Pragmatism*, chapter 3.

110. For representative attempts by Dewey to grapple with this issue, see "A Short Catechism Concerning Truth" (1909) and "The Problem of Truth" (1911), in *Middle Works*, vol. 6.

111. Dewey would define "trans-action" in the following way: "where systems of description and naming are employed to deal with aspects and phases of action, without final attribution to 'elements' or other presumptively detachable or independent 'entities,' 'essences,' or 'realities,' and without isolation of presumptively detachable 'relations' from such detachable 'elements'." Dewey and Arthur F. Bentley, *Knowing and the Known* (1949), in *The Later Works, 1925-1953*, ed. Jo Ann Boydston (Carbondale, Ill., 1981–89), vol. 16, pp. 101–2.

do. It asserts a consequence the thing will actively institute; it will *do*. That it is satisfactory is a judgment, an estimate, an appraisal. It denotes an attitude *to be* taken, that of striving to perpetuate and to make secure.[112]

Rather than certainty purged entirely of contingent belief, the goal is increased probability, which involves a perpetual risk of being disproved in the future. Implicitly drawing attention to the "peril" embedded in the etymology of experience, Dewey would argue that "the distinctive characteristic of practical activity, one which is so inherent that it cannot be eliminated, is the uncertainty that attends it. Of it we are compelled to say: Act, but act at your peril. Judgment and belief regarding actions to be performed can never attain more than a precarious probability."[113]

Although Dewey may have relied on experience as the solvent of virtually all philosophical problems, he sought to avoid the dubious equation of it with existence or primal substance *tout court*, which had so troubled James's critics like Peirce and Morris. As we noted in chapter 4, he argued against the complete dissolution of the art object in the solvent of aesthetic experience. Likewise, in *Experience and Nature*, where he struggled to come up with a naturalist metaphysics, he was careful to note that "no one with an honest respect for scientific conclusions can deny that experience as an existence is something that occurs only under highly specialized conditions, such as are found in a highly organized creature which in turn requires a specialized environment. There is no evidence that experience occurs everywhere and everywhen."[114] There was nonetheless a basic "continuity" between experience and nature that was fundamental to any cognitive enterprise.[115] And so it was possible to go through experience—say the geologist's in the presence of rocks

112. Dewey, *The Quest for Certainty*, p. 260 (emphasis in original).

113. Ibid., p. 6.

114. Dewey, *Experience and Nature*, p. 3. The first chapter of *The Quest for Certainty* identifies "escape from peril" as the desire that led to the problematic quest for absolute and certain knowledge. For a critique of the claim that Dewey defended a "metaphysics of experience," advanced by commentators like Richard Bernstein, see Sleeper, *The Necessity of Pragmatism*. Sleeper argues instead that Dewey preferred a "metaphysics of existence," in which experience is a medium through which the world appears, rather than equivalent to that world. And what it discovers is never so lofty as the Being that purportedly underlies ephemeral and contingent existence.

115. Precisely what Dewey meant by that continuity—a continuum more than an identity, a possibility of growth from one to the other—is not easy to discern. For a thoughtful consideration of its ambiguities, see David Fott, *John Dewey: America's Philosopher of Democracy* (Lanham, Md., 1998), pp. 68–72. Earlier critics worried about the priority of experience itself as a basis for a robust naturalism, what George Santayana called a "foregrounding" of the human over the natural. See his "Dewey's Naturalistic Metaphysics," *Journal of Philosophy* 22, no. 25 (1925).

formed millions of years ago—to the natural world beyond it. Indeed, only through such experience did nature reveal itself.

But for such an outcome, further reflection was absolutely essential in order to move beyond the deficient understanding of common sense. Experience meant more than the immediacy of our encounter with the world—or rather, for that formula was still too beholden to subject/object dualism, more than the primordial holism prior to that split. "Our primary experience as it comes," Dewey cautioned, "is of little value for purposes of analysis and control. The very existence of reflection is proof of its deficiencies."[116] Dewey, the champion of instrumentalist experimentation, was no friend of the prejudicial wisdom defended by conservatives like Edmund Burke in their paean to accumulated experience, even if he warned against the wholesale rationalist repudiation of its lessons. In experience, as he understood it, was a normative striving for completion, fullness, and consummation. Although there were no guarantees provided by an inherent telos in nature, Dewey maintained faith in the potential to realize that outcome, at least if the tendencies he discerned in the world around him were continued.

Dewey, in fact, seems to have lacked the Emersonian pathos of unresolvable trauma that haunted James's striving for meaningful experience. Although by a bitter coincidence, he also endured the premature death of a beloved child—in fact, two sons, Morris and Gordon, died at early ages—Dewey did not allow their loss to darken his philosophy, which was notable for its lack of attention to the limit-experience presented by death.[117] As a result, he was able to paint a cautiously optimistic picture of how the goal of experiential consummation was being realized, on the communal as well as personal level.[118] On occasion, he extolled the "change that has taken place in the ac-

116. Dewey, *Experience and Nature*, p. 31. By stressing the necessity of reflection over immediate experience, however, Dewey may have introduced precisely the epistemological issues he was always at pains to avoid. How, after all, can we judge the superiority of one reflection over another, if the immediacy of experiential continuity with the world is an insufficient yardstick? For a trenchant criticism of the dilemmas into which he fell, see Lovejoy, *The Thirteen Pragmatisms*, chapter 6.

117. For a discussion of Dewey's avoidance of the issue of death, see Richard Shusterman, *Practicing Philosophy: Pragmatism and the Philosophical Life* (New York, 1997), p. 48. Shusterman contrasts his attitude with those of Wittgenstein and Foucault, both of whom confronted the implications of mortality more squarely.

118. According to Thelma Z. Lavine, "In the rhetoric of Emerson and Dewey there flows the same poetic symbolism of a sanctified unification of the self with a larger self, with nature, with community, with some source of divinity. The goal is *redemption through the process and experience of unification, through a sense of wholeness that overcomes self-interest and 'gaps, gulfs, and divisions' between self and other*." "The Contemporary Significance of the American Philosophical Tradition: Lockean and Redemptive," in Larry A. Hickman, ed., *Reading Dewey: Interpretations for a Postmodern Generation* (Bloomington, Ind., 1998),

tual nature of experience, its contents and methods, as it is actually lived," by which he meant the transition from empirical to experimental relations to the world, allowing "old experience . . . to suggest aims and methods for developing a new and improved experience."[119] But at other times, he acknowledged that the scientific revolution alone would not suffice. A diffuse religious piety toward nature, a belief that survived his personal abandonment of the sin-obsessed Congregationalist Christianity into which he had been born, was also necessary.[120] Although unlike Rudolf Otto, Dewey scorned the idea of the holy as the source of a dualism that divided the integrated world of experience and had no use for an "entirely other" deity, he approved of religious experience, freed from any doctrinal straightjacket, as an imaginative quest for harmonizing self and universe.[121] Having once had what he called a "mystic experience" while reading William Wordsworth's nature poetry, he seems to have felt that bliss, albeit fleeting and unstable, was within the realm of human experience.[122]

Perhaps even more important was the communitarian project of democratic practice, embodied in the egalitarian religious and political behavior he had witnessed during his Vermont childhood, which Dewey saw as es-

---

pp. 222–23. Although generally persuasive, this interpretation underplays that moment of despair and unresolved trauma that we have seen in Emerson's "Experience," which was much less evident in Dewey than in James. For a typical critique of Dewey's excessive optimism, see Diggins, *The Promise of Pragmatism*, where he juxtaposes Henry Adams to Dewey and remarks that "even if one grants, that after Darwinism, truth can no longer be regarded as an inherent quality of thought, one can only wonder, with Adams, what one is to learn from experience. Can experience itself illuminate the nature of moral and political authority, explaining not only how authority functions and why people obey but the more difficult question—why should they obey?" (p. 220).

119. Dewey, *Reconstruction in Philosophy*, pp. 83 and 94. The timing of this change, as Dewey presents it, is very fuzzy, supposedly coming after the empiricism of Locke and Hume, which was developed well after the scientific revolution.

120. His mother's oppressive piety had to be overcome before Dewey could embrace the more diffuse and almost naturalist belief he expounded in *A Common Faith* (1934), in *Later Works*, vol. 9, pp. 3–4. For discussions of his religious sentiments, see Rockefeller, *John Dewey*; Rockefeller's summary essay "Dewey's Philosophy of Religious Experience," in Hickman, *Reading Dewey*; and Westbrook, *John Dewey and American Democracy*, pp. 418–28.

121. See his remarks on the holy/profane distinction in *The Quest for Certainty*, pp. 10–14. Rockefeller notes his distance from Otto in *John Dewey*, p. 492, as well as his even greater repudiation of the crisis theology of Karl Barth (pp. 452–53). Although closer to Schleiermacher, Dewey never stressed the feeling of absolute dependence as the most fundamental aspect of religious experience or thought Kantian practical reason and emotionally infused piety were incompatible.

122. This unique moment occurred when he was in Oil City, Pennsylvania, from 1879 to 1881, and was reported much later to Max Eastman. See Rockefeller, *John Dewey*, p. 67. Whatever may have happened, it seems not to have led to any real sympathy in Dewey for supernatural realities.

sential to the realization of the fullest possible kind of experience.[123] "Shared experience," he enthused, "is the greatest of human goods."[124] In fact, his religious investment has sometimes been seen as leading to a civic faith that went beyond the procedures of liberal democratic government to a post-individualist overcoming of self-interest or, rather the realization of a higher individualism through intersubjective interaction and moral unity instead of atomistic competition.[125] Dewey's belief in participatory democracy may be compared with that exaltation of political experience for its own sake we have seen in Hannah Arendt, but because of his faith in enlightened communicative interaction, indeed in the critical scientific method broadly understood, it never descended into the dubious celebration of ecstatic self-immolation exemplified by Ernst Jünger with his aestheticized politics of the sublime (the sublime in fact played no meaningful role in Dewey's understanding of art at all). There was, moreover, in Dewey a belief that the fruits of experience were in the future rather than the present. To the question, "growth toward what end?" Dewey would have answered: "toward more growth." Such an open-ended telos could encourage skeptical responses, such as John Patrick Diggins's complaint that "with pragmatism in particular, the use of experience only prepares us for further experience, without experience itself being immediately self-illuminating or self-rewarding."[126] But others would see it as a wise acknowledgment that fulfilled democracy is always a project to be realized, always a condition still to come (an argument that has recently been repeated in that seemingly most un-Deweyan world of Derridian political thought).[127] As Kloppenberg has noted, "democracy provides a flexible mode of ethical life rather than an

123. This aspect of his work has generated a substantial commentary. See, for example, James Campbell, "Dewey's Conception of Community," and John J. Stuhr, "Dewey's Social and Political Philosophy," in Hickman, *Reading Dewey;* and Fott, *John Dewey.*

124. Dewey, *Experience and Nature,* p. 167.

125. Dewey, *Individualism: Old and New,* in *Later Works,* vol. 5. Westbrook, *John Dewey and American Democracy,* makes the point about civic religion (p. 427). The dangers in subsuming individualism and private life too completely under the communal and public are addressed by Ryan, *John Dewey and the High Tide of American Liberalism,* pp. 219–20 and 368.

126. Diggins, *The Promise of Pragmatism,* p. 20.

127. See, for example, Hent de Vries, *Philosophy and the Turn to Religion* (Baltimore, 1999), noting that for Derrida "the idea of democracy is seen as that which at every instant and in each single instance remains an always yet 'to-come' *(à venir).* As that which at every given point in time is always yet another step ahead can never be anticipated as such, it never reaches full plenitude or presence (to itself) but attains instead the elusive yet no less urgent quality of infinite, albeit also infinitely finite, future *(avenir)"* (p. 322).

explicit ethical norm, and it thus satisfies Dewey's maxim that growth is the only end."[128]

Beyond a mere political arrangement, democracy also has social and moral dimensions, and thus overcomes the conventional distinction between public and private spheres. To further this cause, Dewey argued, education for democracy was an absolute necessity. Such education must be based on experiential rather than book learning, creative investigation rather than rote memory, and a transactional relationship between child and environment rather than a passive, spectatorial one. His own thought, he always insisted, had come more from personal contacts and situations than from books. Indeed, his remarkable life as a philosopher proudly devoted to action in the public sphere—he was involved in virtually every liberal cause of his time, from founding the American Civil Liberties Union and the National Association for the Advancement of Colored People to the Commission of Inquiry into the Charges Made against Leon Trotsky in the Moscow Trials and the Committee for Cultural Freedom—could serve as model of the type of outcome his educational policy desired.

One of education's primary goals was also the nurturing of the child's artistic potential for all of the reasons we examined in chapter 4. As Dewey put it in *Experience and Nature*, "art—the mode of activity that is charged with meanings capable of immediately enjoyed possession—is the complete culmination of nature, and . . . 'science' is properly a handmaiden that conducts natural events to this happy issue."[129] It meant training the body of the child as well as the mind, as somatic therapists like F. Matthias Alexander, much admired by Dewey, had shown.[130] Artistic self-realization thus implied more than the creation of beautiful objects; it meant living a beautiful life, a life of harmonic variation, balanced growth, and the highest cultivation of the senses.

But such a goal did not mean retreating into a life of narcissistic self-absorption. Education for democracy, Dewey argued, must also involve the development of communicative, collaborative, and deliberative skills, which are the preconditions of any genuinely democratic culture. In the famous Laboratory School he helped found at the University of Chicago, in the pages of journals like the *New Republic*, and in such works as *Democracy and Education* and *Experience and Education*, he tirelessly worked to inspire what

128. Kloppenberg, *Uncertain Victory*, p. 140.
129. Dewey, *Experience and Nature*, p. 290.
130. Dewey's appreciation of the "Alexander Technique" is discussed in Rockefeller, *John Dewey*, pp. 333–44, and Shusterman, *Practicing Philosophy*, pp. 167–77.

became known as the "progressive movement" in American education.[131] The now familiar notions of educating the whole child, providing the tools for continued intellectual and moral growth, nurturing curiosity about the world, and instilling critical intelligence through experimentation are all implications of Dewey's influential educational philosophy. Although he vigorously sought to deflect the charge, he was often taxed with putting process over content, being student-centered rather than curriculum-centered, and privileging method (how to teach) over substance (what to teach).[132] Whatever the merits of these accusations—and they continue to arouse deep passions on both sides to this day—it might fairly be argued that the pragmatist focus on experience enjoyed its greatest practical impact in the area of educational policy in America.

The uneven quality of that impact, and indeed of Dewey's exaltation of experience in general, is shown by the ease with which he has been interpreted in ways that seem to betray his intentions. Thus, for example, the scientific and instrumental impulse in his philosophy allowed many critics to dismiss him as an advocate of the technological and utilitarian ethos of American life at its shallowest, a prophet of accommodation and adaptation rather than fundamental critique.[133] Was his contentless search for religious experience shorn of any doctrinal fiber, others would complain, really more than a reflection of the watered-down liberal Protestantism of his own day?[134]

131. Dewey, *Democracy and Education* (1916), *Middle Works*, vol. 9; *Experience and Education* (1938), *Later Works*, vol. 13.

132. For a good summary of the debates over Dewey's educational legacy, see Westbrook, *John Dewey and American Democracy*, chapter 6. The critique began as early as Robert M. Hutchins, *The Higher Learning in America* (New Haven, 1936), which urged a return to the canonical tradition of great books in the West.

133. This charge was perhaps first leveled by Dewey's estranged friend Randolph Bourne in the aftermath of Dewey's unexpected support for the American war effort in 1917. See Bourne's "The Twilight of the Idols," in Olaf Hansen, ed., *The Radical Will: Selected Writings* (New York, 1977). It was repeated by George Santayana in his "Dewey's Naturalistic Metaphysics," and came back again a generation later in Max Horkheimer, *Eclipse of Reason* (New York, 1947). For a critique of the Frankfurt School's appreciation of pragmatism, see Joas, "An Underestimated Alternative: America and the Limits of 'Critical Theory'," in *Pragmatism and Social Theory*. It was not until Habermas's incorporation of the work of George Herbert Mead and Charles Sanders Peirce that the second generation of Critical Theorists really drew from the pragmatist tradition. For an account of his similarities with Dewey, see Ryan, *John Dewey*, p. 357, which are confirmed in the generous review Habermas wrote of the German translation of *The Quest for Certainty* in 1998, reprinted in his *Zeit der Übergänge: Kleine politische Schriften* 9 (Frankfurt, 2001).

134. See, for example, John Herman Randall Jr., "The Religion of Shared Experience," in Sidney Ratner, ed., *The Philosopher of the Common Man: Essays in Honor of John Dewey to Celebrate His Eightieth Birthday* (New York, 1940), pp. 37–38.

Echoing Karl Barth's critique of Schleiermacher, neo-orthodox theologians railed against Dewey's humanocentric version of religion, in which God was turned into the predicate rather than the subject.[135] Still other critics wondered how Dewey could claim that artistic experience, with its capacity to provide intense moments of consummated meaning, was the model for experience at its best, when elsewhere, he seemed to turn experience into a future-oriented instrument in the name of a goal that could never be fully attained. Was he perhaps too quick, others wanted to know, to dismiss the lessons of the past taught by experience understood in the Burkean sense of the word?[136]

Was it ever really possible, other critics asked, to suppress the subjective connotation of the very word "experience," as both James and Dewey insisted was necessary, and allow it to stand for something deeper than the subject/object split?[137] Could experience, moreover, serve as a foundationless alternative to traditional grounding concepts in philosophy, one based on accepting uncertainty rather than seeking to overcome it, or was it merely another variation of the same fruitless quest? Was it, in the final analysis, really anything more than what one critic damned as "a vague, incantatory expression of Dewey's,"[138] which served less to answer hard questions than postpone them?

That Dewey himself came to realize he was fighting an uphill battle is evident in a frequently quoted admission he made in a revised edition of *Experience and Nature*, where he wrote in frustration: "I would abandon the term 'experience' because of my growing realization that the historical obstacles which prevented understanding of my use of 'experience' are, for all practical purposes, insurmountable."[139] In its place, he mused, he would now want

135. For an account of the neo-orthodox reaction to Dewey and his theological followers—among them, Reinhold Niebuhr—see Bruce Kuklick, *Churchmen and Philosophers: From Jonathan Edwards to John Dewey* (New Haven, 1985).

136. John Patrick Diggins, "Pragmatism and Its Limits," in Dickstein, *The Revival of Pragmatism*, p. 217. Diggins further claims that appeals to experience can have a welter of different political outcomes, not merely the democratic radicalism attributed to it by many pragmatists.

137. Occasionally, however, this reproach has been turned around and become a reason for praise. See, for example Phil Oliver, *William James's "Springs of Delight": The Return to Life* (Nashville, Tenn., 2001), which goes against conventional wisdom to claim that James was "an advocate for a type of *personal* transcendence owing at least as much to subjectivity as to pure experience" (p. 9).

138. Diggins, *The Promise of Pragmatism*, p. 220.

139. Dewey, *Later Works*, vol. 1, p. 361. Yet later in an appendix to the new edition, he would doggedly defend its necessity: "as long as men prefer in philosophy, (as they long preferred in science) to define and envisage 'reality' according to esthetic, moral or logical canons, we need the notion of experience to remind us that 'reality' includes whatever is denotatively found. . . . we need a cautionary and directive

to put the word "culture," thus duplicating virtually the same move made by Raymond Williams a generation later (and which would have surely led into the same swamps of meaning that almost drowned his British counterpart).[140] In his final work, jointly written with Arthur Bentley, *Knowing and the Known*, Dewey ruefully acknowledged that "experience" would no longer do the work he had thought it might, preferring "trans-action" instead, even if the basic premises of his thought had not really changed.[141]

RORTY'S LINGUISTIC TRANSCENDENTALISM

Although the pragmatist exaltation of experience did not entirely end with Dewey's death in 1952—it continued to serve as a master concept for many of his students and popularizers such as John E. Smith, Sidney Hook, and John J. McDermott[142]—the movement itself soon went into relative eclipse. "By the middle of the twentieth century," Morris Dickstein has explained, "pragmatism was widely considered a naively optimistic residue of an earlier liberalism, discredited by the Depression and the horrors of the war, and virtually driven from philosophy departments by the reigning school of analytic philosophy."[143] During the Cold War, Louis Menand has added, the pragmatists' belief in compromise over confrontation, tolerance over intransigence, and practical solutions over abstract principles was out of fash-

---

word, like experience, to remind us that the world which is lived, suffered and enjoyed, as well as logically thought of, has the last word in all human inquiries and surmises" (p. 372).

140. According to Menand, *The Metaphysical Club*, p. 437, Oliver Wendell Holmes had also considered "culture" and "experience" synonyms in *The Common Law* back in 1881. For a consideration of Dewey's tentative turn from experience to culture, which argues that it was a mistake, see Sleeper, *The Necessity of Pragmatism*, chapter 5.

141. Dewey and Arthur Bentley, *Knowing and the Known*, in *Later Works*, vol. 16. It was Bentley who encouraged the change of terminology. In a letter of May 12, 1944, Dewey wrote to him "I agree with what you say about dropping 'experience' as not needed. I should like the mode of treatment a little more sympathetic—probably because of my own past struggles." Quoted in T. Z. Lavine's introduction, p. xxxvi.

142. John E. Smith, *Experience and God* (New York, 1968); Sidney Hook, *Pragmatism and the Tragic Sense of Life* (New York, 1974); and McDermott, *The Culture of Experience*. There are even clear influences in the work of neo-Aristotelians like the University of Chicago philosopher Richard McKeon. See his "Experience and Metaphysics" (1953), in *The Selected Writings of Richard McKeon*, ed. Zahava K. McKeon and William G. Swenson, vol. 1 (Chicago, 1998).

143. Morris Dickstein, "Introduction: Pragmatism Then and Now," in *The Revival of Pragmatism*, p. 1. It might, of course, be argued that the scientist impulse in pragmatism prepared the way for analytic philosophy's triumph. See Timothy V. Kaufman-Osborn, *Politics/Sense/Experience: A Pragmatic Inquiry into the Promise of Democracy* (Ithaca, N.Y., 1991), pp. 13–14.

ion.[144] Conversely, in the climate of political radicalization and heightened theoretical reflexivity of the 1960s and 1970s, pragmatism was often judged insufficiently critical of the givens of American society and lacking the tools to tackle fundamental social and political problems.[145] Instrumentalist adaptation seemed the best the pragmatists might offer, and this smacked for many of the technological ethos that was deemed responsible for many of the problems of modernization. Echoing the critique of pragmatism made by Max Horkheimer in *Eclipse of Reason* two decades earlier, Herbert Marcuse could claim that Dewey was an example of the "one-dimensional thought" that plagued America.[146] Summing it all up in a formula he would later repudiate, the American intellectual historian David Hollinger could write in 1980 that "'pragmatism' is a concept most American historians have proved they can get along without."[147]

But when the tide turned back toward a more moderate politics in the 1980s and 1990s, and European-inflected theory lost some of its luster, an unexpected resurgence of interest once again elevated pragmatism to center stage. Now, however, it was in the context of the so-called linguistic turn, whose impact we have noted in the debates around history and experience. Because of its anti-foundationalist impulse and suspicion of universalist certainties, pragmatism could be refigured as the American contribution to postmodernist thought, just as it could be situated a century before in the context of European vitalism.[148] Although some commentators hoped to sustain or even broaden the radical democratizing impulse in Dewey's work—Cornel West, for example, tried to revive it through the prophetic message he de-

144. Menand, *The Metaphysical Club,* p. 441. Critics have responded that Menand has seriously underestimated the importance of continuing pragmatist influence on such philosophers as W. V. O. Quine and Morton White, historians of science like Thomas Kuhn, and Cold War liberal scholars like Arthur Schlesinger Jr., Louis Hartz, Merle Curti, Henry Steele Commager, and Daniel Boorstin.

145. This dismissal continues to generate controversy. In a personal communication, James Kloppenberg has noted that "the line running from Dewey's *Liberalism and Social Action* to the Port Huron Statement [which founded the Students for a Democratic Society] was clear to Tom Hayden even if it wasn't clear to most PLP [Progressive Labor Party] rabble-rousers." Letter of December 16, 2002.

146. Herbert Marcuse, *One-Dimensional Man* (Boston, 1964), p. 167. In his earlier, more extensive discussion of Dewey in *Soviet Marxism: A Critical Analysis* (New York, 1958), Marcuse summarized Soviet criticisms of pragmatism without distancing himself from them (pp. 210–14).

147. Hollinger, "The Problem of Pragmatism in American History," *In the American Province,* p. 25. By the time this essay of 1980 was republished in this collection, Hollinger was already acknowledging the prematurity of this claim.

148. See, for example, the essays in Hickman, *Dewey: Interpretations for a Postmodern Generation.* For an overview of pragmatism's return, see Richard J. Bernstein, "The Resurgence of Pragmatism," *Social Research* 59 (Winter 1992).

rived from W. E. B. Dubois, Antonio Gramsci, and Reinhold Niebuhr[149]—postmodernism was rarely congenial to redemptive politics.

The most notable advocate of a resurgent pragmatism, which would take into account the lessons learned from continental thinkers like Martin Heidegger, Hans-Georg Gadamer, Michel Foucault, and Jacques Derrida, was the philosopher—or perhaps, better put, post-philosopher—Richard Rorty, who had been stealthily laying the groundwork in the 1970s while shedding his earlier identity as a conventional analytic philosopher.[150] His *Philosophy and the Mirror of Nature* of 1979 radically altered the reception of Peirce, James, and Dewey, whose legacy he sought to marshal for a project that could just as easily be called post-philosophical as the reconstruction of philosophy.[151] Rorty, who moved from the Princeton philosophy department to the humanities and comparative literature departments at Virginia and Stanford, redirected pragmatism away from the epistemological and metaphysical issues that had still so troubled the founding fathers, and jettisoned virtually all residues of the earlier pragmatists' faith in the scientific method in favor of a frank erasure of the boundary between science and literature. "I think Dewey was at his best," he opined, "when he emphasized the similarities between philosophy and poetry, rather than when he emphasized those between philosophy and engineering."[152] It should, moreover, be a poetry akin to the literary modernism that understood the priority of text to world, for both philosophy and poetry were kinds of writing rather than generically distinct. As a result, the confidently activist streak in earlier pragmatism was replaced by a more ironic awareness of the contingency of our efforts to affect reality.[153] "An ironist," Rorty would explain, "is a nominalist and historicist who strives to retain a sense that the vocabulary of moral deliberation she uses is a product of history and chance . . . someone devoted to social justice who nevertheless takes her own devotion to this cause

149. West, *The American Evasion of Philosophy.*

150. For an insightful analysis of the development of Rorty's career, see Neil Gross, "Richard Rorty's Pragmatism: A Case Study in the Sociology of Ideas," *Theory and Society* 32, no. 1 (February 2003). Gross shows that rather than experiencing a radical break with his earlier position, Rorty was involved with pragmatism from the start of his career. Moreover, the lessons Rorty learned from within the analytic tradition, most notably from Donald Davidson, W. V. O. Quine, and Wilfred Sellars, as well as those imparted by Wittgenstein and Kuhn, prepared him for what seemed the bold apostasy of the late 1970s and 1980s.

151. Richard Rorty, *Philosophy and the Mirror of Nature* (Princeton, 1979). As the title indicates, Rorty was anxious to show that the anti-spectatorial inclinations of pragmatism were compatible with the hostility to ocularcentrism in Heidegger and the poststructuralists.

152. Richard Rorty, *Consequences of Pragmatism* (Minneapolis, 1982), p. 56.

153. Richard Rorty, *Contingency, Irony, Solidarity* (Cambridge, 1989).

as merely contingent."[154] That devotion, moreover, need not be taken as the measure of a meaningful life. In place of the earnest, world-reforming intentions of his predecessors, Rorty substituted the virtues of private pleasures and the frankly bourgeois liberal ideal of negative freedom.[155] Gradual edification—the term recalls the German idea of *Bildung*—through an open-ended and increasingly inclusive conversation replaced the vain search for ultimate answers or permanent solutions to problems.

One of the most hotly contested issues in the revival of pragmatism, as it turned out, was the centrality of "experience" to the tradition. For Rorty was bluntly outspoken in denying its importance. Seeking to dismiss the eternal philosophical questions that the earlier pragmatists had still tried to answer— What is truth? How can truth claims (or warranted assertions) be validated? Do reason and logic transcend context? How do subjects know objects?— as not only unanswerable but also no longer meaningful, he argued against the way in which experience had functioned as a pseudo-solution, a kind of crypto-foundationalism for thinkers who lacked the courage to live without one. Changing the tune, Rorty implied, would not be enough to salvage the song of experience, which, he insisted, should be dropped from the repertory altogether.

In an essay first written in 1975 and republished in his 1982 collection *Consequences of Pragmatism,* Rorty set out to save Dewey from his metaphysical ambitions. "Dewey's Metaphysics" begins with a rehearsing of the anecdote about Dewey's belated desire to replace "experience" with "culture" in the revised edition of *Experience and Nature,* and goes on to say that, despite its author's intentions, "it is unlikely that we shall find [in the book] . . . anything which can be called a 'metaphysics of experience' as opposed to a therapeutic treatment of the tradition."[156] Lamenting the fact that Dewey was a quintessential hedgehog rather than a fox, whose one obsessive grand idea continued throughout his career, Rorty then went back to Dewey's initial attempts to combine psychology and neo-Hegelian philosophy on the basis of the claim that they both deal with experience as an undivided totality. This

154. Richard Rorty, *Truth and Progress: Philosophical Papers,* vol. 3 (Cambridge, 1998), p. 307.

155. Although this is not the place to do justice to the full range and richness of Rorty's career, it should be noted that his apparent retreat from the public sphere was given the lie by his *Achieving Our Country* (Cambridge, Mass., 1998), in which he advocated a return to the political and economic questions left behind by cultural radicalism in the academy.

156. Rorty, "Dewey's Metaphysics," in *Consequences of Pragmatism,* p. 77. The notion of therapy is one Rorty owed to Wittgenstein, whose desire to rid us of philosophical confusions through linguistic clarification he eagerly embraced.

claim, Rorty recalled, had been ridiculed by Shadworth Hodgson back in 1886, and his criticism was "entirely justified. It parallels Santayana's criticism of the possibility of a 'naturalistic metaphysic' and neatly singles out a recurrent flaw in Dewey's work: his habit of announcing a bold new positive program, when all he offers, and all he needs to offer, is criticism of the tradition."[157] Although Dewey may have abandoned his early attempt to combine neo-idealism with psychology, he unfortunately never weaned himself of the mistaken belief that "what he himself said about experience described what experience itself looked like, whereas what others said was a confusion between the data and the products of their analyses."[158]

Moreover, Rorty charged, despite all his best efforts, Dewey never succeeded in presenting a coherent or persuasive notion of a non-dualistic experience that would allow him to combine Hegel's historicism with Locke's or Darwin's naturalism. Works like *Experience and Nature* foolishly tried to construct a metaphysical system that would embrace both, overcoming the apparent distinction between subjective encounters with natural phenomena and scientific descriptions of their hidden essence, getting us past the mind/body problem that has so long vexed philosophers. But in so doing he "blew up notions like 'transaction' and 'situation' until they sounded as mysterious as 'prime matter' or 'thing-in-itself'."[159] Instead, he should have remained at the level of contingent cultural criticism, understanding different philosophical positions as temporary moments in the ongoing conversation of humankind, without straining to trump them with a new metaphysics of his own. James too could betray his own best instincts, Rorty would later charge, when, for example, he claimed to spy "literal and objective truth" in religious experience, an assertion that was "unpragmatic, hollow and superfluous."[160]

Rorty returned to the question of Dewey and experience in 1991 in a paper that responded to the work done in the interim by intellectual historians like James Kloppenberg and David Hollinger on the importance of the concept for the founding fathers of pragmatism.[161] Now he focused on the assumption that "experience" could bridge the gap between us and the natural world, which was based on a problematic panpsychism, a blurring of the

157. Ibid., p. 78.
158. Ibid., p. 80.
159. Ibid., p. 84.
160. Rorty, "Pragmatism as Romantic Polytheism" in Dickstein, *The Revival of Pragmatism,* p. 30.
161. Rorty, "Dewey between Hegel and Darwin," in *Truth and Progress;* Kloppenberg, *Uncertain Victory;* and Hollinger, *In the American Province.*

noetic and non-noetic worlds. "But when we invoke panpsychism in order to bridge the gap between experience and nature," Rorty warned, "we begin to feel that something has gone wrong. For notions like 'experience,' 'consciousness,' and 'thought' were originally invoked to *contrast* something that varied independently of nature with nature itself."[162] James and Dewey would have been better off "if they had not tried to make 'true' a predicate of experiences and had instead let it be a predicate of sentences."[163] They would have then given up their vain quest for a surrogate for verification in the "agreeable leading" from one experience to another, and rested content with an acknowledgement of the culture-dependency of all knowledge and understanding of language as itself growing out of natural needs understood in a Darwinian sense. The yearning for a lost possibility of fulfilled experience expressed by Emerson, James, and Dewey was thus explicitly spurned by the resolutely anti-redemptive, anti-utopian Rorty.[164]

Rorty's provocation to the philosophical establishment was enormous, and critics from virtually all camps responded with gusto to every one of his challenges.[165] Among fellow pragmatists, however, it was his repudiation of the celebration of experience that seemed to touch the most sensitive nerve. Intellectual historians in particular were disturbed by his selective appropriation of the legacy of James and Dewey. Robert Westbrook, for example, fulminated against Rorty's "liberal, bourgeois, postmodern" misreading of the social democratic legacy of Dewey, complaining that "there is little in his social and political vision of the communitarian side of Dewey's thinking, nothing of Dewey's veneration of *shared* experience."[166] James Kloppenberg, endorsing the position we have seen defended by Dilthey, Collingwood, Thompson, and Toews, insisted that "connecting with experience is precisely what we historians do."[167] Beyond his resistance to Rorty's seeming dispar-

162. Rorty, "Dewey between Hegel and Darwin," p. 296.

163. Ibid., p. 298.

164. For an example of this attitude, see Rorty, "The End of Leninism, Havel, and Social Hope" (1991), in *Truth and Progress.*

165. See, for example, Alan Malachowski, ed., *Reading Rorty: Critical Responses to Philosophy and the Mirror of Nature* (Cambridge, 1990); Herman J. Saatkamp, ed., *Rorty and Pragmatism* (Nashville, Tenn., 1995); and John Pettegrew, ed., *A Pragmatist's Progress? Richard Rorty and American Intellectual History* (Lanham, Md., 2000).

166. Westbrook, *John Dewey and American Democracy,* pp. 541–42.

167. James Kloppenberg, "Pragmatism: An Old Name for Some New Ways of Thinking," in Dickstein, *The Revival of Pragmatism,* p. 84. Reading Joan Scott in a more charitable—and perhaps not fully accurate—way, Kloppenberg argues that "instead of dismissing the concept as Rorty does, Scott recommends examining how experience is said to yield unassailable knowledge, a strategy resembling that of James and Dewey" (p. 108).

agement of the historian's craft, which ironically contradicted Rorty's own frequent reduction of philosophy to little more than intellectual history, Kloppenberg also argued that a non-introspective concept of experience, one that was not rigidly or dogmatically opposed to language, still had important theoretical work to do, especially in breaking down the barriers between knowledge, ethics, aesthetics, and politics. Rorty, he concluded, had illegitimately hijacked the pragmatist tradition, which is better preserved in the recent work of other American philosophers like Richard Bernstein and Hilary Putnam.[168]

Other contemporary philosophers identifying themselves with that tradition also faulted Rorty's categorical rejection of experience. David Lamberth, for example, questioned his version of James as an anti-realist, an interpretation that reduced the latter's standards of expediency and satisfaction to mere effects of intersubjective agreement. Rorty, Lamberth charged, thus ignored the "thorough-going *pluralism* of James' radical empiricism, whose ambidextrous notion of pure experience refuses to grant primacy to either thought or thing—language or non-linguistic reality—and whose dynamic, two-fold account of knowing forwards this pluralism into epistemology."[169] Joseph Margolis derided Rorty's attempt to find common ground between Dewey and Heidegger, arguing that the phenomenologist to whom Rorty should have been turning for support was Maurice Merleau-Ponty, who grasped "the indissolubility of experience, knowledge, reason and whatever of reality such resource claims to address."[170] Contrary to Rorty's charge of panpsychism, Dewey was more of an evolutionary biologist, who shared Merleau-Ponty's stress on the body in the flesh of the world. R. W. Sleeper faulted Rorty for believing that Dewey held a dubious metaphysics of experience, when in fact, he had favored a metaphysics of existence, in which experience was crucial, but not equivalent to the whole of reality.[171]

Richard Shusterman, while applauding Rorty's stress on the aesthetic im-

168. Richard J. Bernstein, *Beyond Objectivism and Relativism: Science, Hermeneutics, and Praxis* (Philadelphia, 1983); *The New Constellation: The Ethical-Political Horizons of Modernity/Postmodernity* (Cambridge, Mass., 1992); Hilary Putnam, *Renewing Philosophy* (Cambridge, 1992), *Pragmatism: An Open Question* (Cambridge, Mass., 1995), and *Realism with a Human Face* (Cambridge, 1999).

169. Lamberth, *William James and the Metaphysics of Experience*, p. 213. That Rorty's response to James may be less critical than Lamberth avers is shown by his "Religious Faith, Intellectual Responsibility and Romance," in Putnam, *The Cambridge Companion to William James.*

170. Joseph Margolis, "Dewey in Dialogue with Continental Philosophy," in Hickman, *Reading Dewey,* p. 249.

171. Sleeper, *The Necessity of Pragmatism,* pp. 107–9.

pulse in pragmatism,[172] likewise insisted on the value of nondiscursive experience, even if Dewey had been wrong to use it for traditional epistemological purposes.[173] Disputing the conclusion that Dewey was consistently foundationalist in inclination and pointing to places in his work in which he seemed to be accepting the inevitable mediation of language, Shusterman nonetheless argued that his real goal was "to celebrate the importance of nondiscursive immediacy. Its importance was first of all aesthetic, central to the realm of experienced value. He always insisted that our most intense and vivid values are those of on-the-pulse experienced quality and affect, not the abstractions of discursive truth."[174] Dewey furthermore understood, as Rorty seems not to, that somatic experience is important for both cognition and action, as shown by his interest in the body therapy of F. Matthias Alexander. If Dewey made a major mistake, Shusterman concluded, it was "not in emphasizing the unifying quality of experience, but only in positing it as an antecedent foundational fact rather than regarding it as an end and means of reconstruction."[175] Dewey's main goal, in fact, was not metaphysical or epistemological, but rather practical: "improving experience by making it the focus of our inquiry, by affirming and enhancing the continuity between soma and psyche, between nondiscursive experience and conscious thought."[176] Here perhaps Michel Foucault's somatically informed "care of the self" might be a model for philosophy as an embodied way of life rather than a one-sided intellectual discourse or linguistic game.[177]

Perhaps the most sustained assault on Rorty's abolition of experience in favor of language was made by F. R. Ankersmit, whose vigorous defense of

172. Richard Shusterman, *Pragmatist Aesthetics: Living Beauty, Rethinking Art* (Cambridge, Mass., 1992), pp. 246–50. Shusterman did, however, detect a conflict between Rorty's ironist stress on unending curiosity and experimentation and his belief in the strong poet as someone who can force a self-unity through aesthetic means.

173. Richard Shusterman, "Dewey on Experience: Foundation or Reconstruction," *Philosophical Forum* 26, no. 2 (Winter 1994).

174. Ibid., p. 135.

175. Ibid., p. 138.

176. Ibid., p. 139.

177. Shusterman's own version of this project, which he called "somaesthetics," was developed in a number of subsequent publications, most notably *Performing Live: Aesthetic Alternatives for the Ends of Art* (Ithaca, N.Y., 2000); and *Surface and Depth: Dialectics of Criticism and Culture* (Ithaca, N.Y., 2002). See the symposium dedicated to his work in the *Journal of Aesthetic Education* 36, no. 4 (Winter 2002), which contains my own essay "Somaesthetics and Democracy: Dewey and Contemporary Body Art."

a certain postmodernist notion of experience akin to the aesthetics of the sublime we encountered in our previous chapter.[178] "Never has a philosophical position been defended," he complained, "that is more inimical to experience than Rorty's pragmatist interaction model. For the more language and reality are integrated—and surely the interaction model is the *ne plus ultra* of this strategy—the more experience will be squeezed out of existence."[179] In a sustained analysis of the roots of what he calls Rorty's "lingualism" or "linguistic transcendentalism," including subtle readings of Rorty's transformation of Donald Davidson's theory of metaphor into a spur to ironic skepticism and his attempted refutation of Thomas Nagel's objective phenomenology of prelinguistic experience, Ankersmit pitted against it Rorty's no less fervent embrace of historicism, whose guiding light was Gadamerian hermeneutics. Ultimately, Ankersmit averred, the two do not come together. For a consistent historicism must recognize the distinctiveness of different historical eras, which cannot be subsumed under a single model of language, an insight that Ankersmit attributed to Foucault with his notion of different epistemes. It must attempt instead to "describe how the world was experienced by the people from the past."[180] Thus the present historian has to resist assimilating the past too radically to contemporary concerns and idioms, which Rorty, with his stress on language all the way down, cannot avoid doing. He or she should register instead the strangeness of the residues of a past that is "other" to the present. Rorty betrays his overly comfortable identification with the tradition of American bourgeois liberalism not only in his avowed politics, but also in his refusal to open himself up to a past that is not continuous with our own present.

In the writings discussed in the previous chapter, Ankersmit turned to aesthetic experience and in particular that of the sublime to suggest a way out of the presentist linguistic transcendentalism he attributed to Rorty. Although works of art are not representations of an objective world prior to subjective experience, not based on a *tertium quid* that subtends representation and object, they nonetheless reveal something that goes beyond the language in which they are manifested. In historical writing as well, "the representation of reality is a verbalization of an (aesthetic) experience of reality."[181] In the

178. F. R. Ankersmit, "Between Language and History: Rorty's Promised Land," *Common Knowledge* 6, no. 1 (Spring 1997).
179. Ibid., p. 68.
180. Ibid., p. 65.
181. Ibid., p. 75.

work of the great artist as opposed to the poor one, something is revealed about the world rather than just the psychological interior of the artist. The same might be said of critics like Roland Barthes, "because he had an unequalled capacity for *experiencing* those texts [of Balzac, Flaubert, or Michelet] in a new and unprecedented way. And only after, and on the basis of this experience, was he able to develop a new semiotic or hermeneutic theory."[182] Only by submitting to those rare but vitally important experiences of the past that Johann Huizinga had singled out as so crucial to historical knowledge, can we get past the idea of experience as something that "smugly fits the historian's own memories, expectations and practical certainties" and "encounter the past itself in its uncompromising strangeness, or 'sublimity,' to use Hayden White's most appropriate terminology."[183]

True to his investment in a conversational rather than monologic model of philosophizing, Rorty was generous in responding to his critics. But he gave little ground, if any, on the question of experience. "The point of language," he continued to insist in 2000, "is not to represent either reality or 'experience' accurately, but, once again, to forge more useful tools. . . . The idea that experience is whatever the experiencer reports it as, and that there is no such thing as a language being more or less faithful to the way experience *really* is, has steadily gathered force among both 'analytic' and 'Continental' philosophers. Cutting out the intermediary—experience—between the causal impact of the environment and our linguistic response to the environment is an idea whose time has come."[184] Toward the contention that textualism or lingualism is a kind of anti-realist idealism, Rorty was no less incredulous: "the suggestions that language is something other than one more piece of reality, and that linguistic behavior is somehow less 'hard' than what is 'given in experience' need only to be stated to be dismissed."[185] Moreover, "none of us antirepresentationalists have ever doubted that most things in the universe are causally independent of us. What we question is whether they are representationally independent of us."[186] That is, everything is mediated by language, and we have no standpoint exterior to it by which to judge different descriptions, including those of our own experience.

182. Ibid., p. 77.
183. Ibid., p. 78.
184. Rorty, "Afterword: Intellectual Historians and Pragmatism," in Pettegrew, *A Pragmatist's Progress*, p. 209.
185. Ibid., p. 210.
186. Rorty, "Charles Taylor on Truth," in *Truth and Progress*, p. 86.

As for the charge of ignoring the "other" of language—say, the knowledge by direct acquaintance produced by eating an onion—Rorty countered, "we back up our refusal to be impressed by the taste of onions by interpreting the Gadamerian claim that '[b]eing that can be understood by language' in a Sellarsian way—redescribing knowledge by acquaintance as the ability to make noninferential linguistic responses to features of the passing scene (including states of our brains)—thereby claiming that (in Ayer's words) 'there is no "raw material of sensations".'"[187] What this uncharacteristically convoluted sentence seems to mean is that anything outside of linguistic mediation, even the seemingly direct physical acquaintance with the taste of an onion, must be rejected as an obsolete and unnecessary assumption like Kant's things-in-themselves.

The controversy stimulated by Rorty's provocative appropriation of the pragmatist legacy continues to reverberate, but on the question of language and experience, one or two things seem clear. First, his skepticism about the capacity to suffer "experience" in an unmediated way, whether it be the subjective experience of the subject or the equiprimordial experience that James and Dewey thought came before the subject/object distinction, has raised important doubts that cannot be simply brushed aside. Indeed, the entire enterprise of the book you are now reading is based on the premise that there are discourses of experience that inflect the ways in which the term has functioned in different contexts, even if there are enough family resemblances among them to permit a more general account.

Whether "to inflect" means to constitute out of whole cloth is perhaps another question. For if there are, in the phrase of Wilfred Sellars borrowed by Rorty to dismiss direct acquaintance, "non-inferential linguistic responses" to the exigencies of a world with sharp-tasting onions, why not admit that there are also responses that are non-linguistic as well? Indeed, to take seriously a naturalistic and Darwinian view of our species, which links us to the animal world, what of humans prior to our acquisition of language? Indeed, Giorgio Agamben has gone so far as to argue that "a primary experience, far from being subjective, could then only be what in human beings comes before the subject—that is, before language, a 'wordless' experience in the literal sense of the term, a human *infancy* [*in-fancy*], whose boundary would be marked by language."[188] Perhaps this is what James

187. Rorty, "The Contingency of Philosophical Problems: Michael Ayers on Locke," in *Truth and Progress*, p. 282.
188. Agamben, *Infancy and History*, p. 47.

meant when he said that "only new-born babes" had had pure experiences. Such experiences may be hard, if not impossible, to duplicate once we enter language, which is why Agamben claims that authentic experience is an unattainable quest, but it would be just as plausible to argue that adults carry with them the residue of their earliest years in ways it doesn't take a psychoanalyst to discern.

Another question that must be posed concerns the assumed opposition between experience and language in Rorty's scheme of things. There are, after all, other models of the linguistic turn besides the one he privileged. Among the pragmatist founders, it was Peirce who had most extensively occupied himself with linguistic questions, developing a general semiotics that some have seen as anticipating the linguistic turn. Although the revival of pragmatism in certain quarters—for example, Jürgen Habermas's reworked version of Frankfurt School Critical Theory—took him as an inspiration, Rorty emphatically did not. "Peirce," he charged, "never made up his mind what he wanted a general theory of signs *for*, nor what it might look like, nor what its relation to either logic or epistemology was supposed to be. His contribution to pragmatism was merely to have given it a name, and to have stimulated James."[189] In the last analysis, he was just another Kantian transcendentalist, looking for a way to get beyond historicist relativism. For his part, Rorty preferred a philosophy of language that was more deconstructionist than reconstructionist, more contextualist than systematic, more narrativist than explanatory, and more nominalist than representationalist.

But there were alternative ways to think about language and its relation to experience. Foucault, as we will see in chapter 9, was not only the critic of the subject and defender of discursively constituted epistemes, but also the champion of a powerful notion of "limit experiences" that pushed beyond the boundaries both of the subject and of discourse. Roland Barthes, as Ankersmit observed, also bore witness to the potential of reconciling a certain version of language with a craving for a certain kind of experience. And in the remarkable ruminations on language and experience in the work of Walter Benjamin, we can find an even bolder attempt to combine the narrativist mode with a version of redemptive nominalism that moved far beyond—or if you dislike it, regressed far behind—Rorty's relativist and ironic skepticism. Paradoxically, it combined an explicit yearning for absolute experience, which exceeded anything in James or Dewey, with an even more

189. Rorty, "Pragmatism, Relativism, and Irrationalism," in *Consequences of Pragmatism*, p. 161.

acute awareness of the obstacles to that utopian goal in the modern era than that revealed by Emerson in his great essay "Experience." Elaborated still further by Benjamin's friend Theodor Adorno, another song of experience without a subject was generated, but in a very different key from that of James and Dewey. It is to the Frankfurt School's lament about the destruction of experience in the modern world that we now must turn.

EIGHT

Lamenting the Crisis of Experience

Benjamin and Adorno

WRITING ON MAY 7, 1940, from his precarious exile in Paris, Walter Benjamin (1892–1940) expressed to his friend, Theodor W. Adorno (1903–1969), himself only recently uprooted to New York, his anguish at "the methodical destruction of experience."[1] From Benjamin, who had been writing about the theme of experience since 1913, Adorno had already absorbed the lesson that the parlous state of genuine experience—understood in ways to be explained shortly—was one of the most telling indicators of the modern era's decline into barbarism. The Frankfurt School's Critical Theory, still in the process of moving fitfully away from its Hegelian Marxist roots, found in the putative crisis of experience a human disaster comparable to the "reification" that Georg Lukács had argued in *History and Class Consciousness* in 1923 was

---

1. Walter Benjamin to Theodor Adorno, Paris, May 7, 1940, in Theodor W. Adorno and Walter Benjamin, *The Complete Correspondence 1928–1940*, ed. Henri Lonitz and Nicholas Walker (Cambridge, Mass., 1999), p. 326. Benjamin's concept of experience is discussed in virtually all of the extensive literature on him. For four recent essays that focus on it, see Marino Pulliero, "Erfahrung: Genèse d'une problématique de l'expérience dans la pensée de Walter Benjamin," *Internationale Zeitschrift für Philosophie* 1 (1993); Linda Simonis, "Walter Benjamins Theorie der Erfahrung," *Études Germaniques* 51, no. 1 (Jan.–Mar. 1996); Thomas Weber, "Erfahrung," in *Benjamins Begriffe*, ed. Michael Opitz and Erdmut Wizisla (Frankfurt, 2000); and Kai Lindroos, "Scattering Community: Benjamin on Experience, Narrative and History," *Philosophy and Social Criticism* 27, no. 6 (2001). For books that contain extended discussions, see Marleen Stoessel, *Aura: Das vergessene Menschliche* (Munich, 1983); Torsten Meiffert, *Die enteignete Erfahrung: Zu Walter Benjamins Konzept einer "Dialektik im Stillstand"* (Bielefeld, 1986); Michael Jennings, *Dialectical Images: Walter Benjamin's Theory of Literary Criticism* (Ithaca, N.Y., 1987); Michael Makropolous, *Modernität als ontologischer Zustand? Walter Benjamins Theorie der Moderne* (Munich, 1989); and Richard Wolin, *Walter Benjamin: An Aesthetic of Redemption* (Berkeley, 1994). Still very valuable is Miriam Hansen, "Benjamin, Cinema and Experience: 'The Blue Flower in the Land of Technology'," *New German Critique* 40 (Winter 1987).

the essence of capitalist exploitation and the "alienation" that was to come to the fore after the discovery a few years later of Karl Marx's 1844 Paris Manuscripts. As Detlev Claussen has put it, "the experience of the loss of experience is one of the oldest motifs of Critical Theory, which even outsiders from the circle around Max Horkheimer like Kracauer and Benjamin had already expressed in the 1920's."[2] But whereas reification and alienation, for all their subjective pathos, were philosophically generated terms, derived in large measure from a materialist reading of the legacy of German idealism, the origins of the idea of a crisis of experience lay elsewhere.

"There is no reason to conceal from you," Benjamin confessed to Adorno in his letter,

> the fact that the roots of my 'theory of experience' can be traced back to a childhood memory. My parents would go on walks with us, as a matter of course, wherever we spent the summer months. There would always be two or three of us children together. But it is my brother I am thinking of here. After we had visited one or other of the obligatory places around Freudenstadt, Wengen or Schreiberhau, my brother used to say, 'Now we can say we've been there.' This remark imprinted itself unforgettably on my mind.[3]

Many elements of Benjamin's remarkable and much discussed theory of experience, which Adorno himself would adapt and modify for his own purposes, are indeed contained in this anecdote: an insistence on the importance of seemingly trivial details, the cherishing of childhood moments of pleasure, a fascination with the auratic resonance of place names, some with the magical meaning of a Freudenstadt (city of joy),[4] and an appreciation of the collector's mentality. So too, is the importance of the entanglement of memory and experience—especially of childhood memories imprinting themselves "unforgettably" on Benjamin's mind—made explicitly clear. But no less ev-

2. Detlev Claussen, *Theodor W. Adorno: Ein letztes Genie* (Frankfurt, 2003), p. 20.

3. Benjamin to Adorno, May 7, 1940, in *The Complete Correspondence 1928–1940*, p. 326. The brother in question was Georg Benjamin (1895–1942), who became a Communist and died in a Nazi concentration camp.

4. It should be noted that not only are the individual names crucial, but also the valorization of qualitatively distinct "place" in itself as opposed to abstract, homogenous space. For an analysis of the recovery of place in the twentieth century, which includes in passing Benjamin's contribution, see Edward S. Casey, *The Fate of Place: A Philosophical History* (Berkeley, 1998). Casey points out the importance of lived corporeal experience for the valorization of place over space, for example the kinaesthetic experience of the walker discussed by Edmund Husserl in his 1931 fragment "The World of the Living Present and the Constitution of the Surrounding World External to the Organism." Benjamin's later fascination for the *flâneur* expresses a similar understanding.

ident in his retelling of the story is his chagrin at the threat to that experience produced by his brother's deflationary remark.

From these humble origins in what he took to be his own earliest experiences, rather than from any systematic philosophical inquiry into the meaning of the term, grew what might well be called the most complex and lyrical song of experience in the long history we have been following in this book. Alternating between utopian hope and elegiac despair, combining theological impulses with materialist analysis, Benjamin's ruminations on the crisis of experience went beyond anything we have encountered in our previous discussions. Sharing with the American pragmatists, whose work he never seems to have directly known, a desire to overcome the modalization of experience into its component parts and heal the split between subject and object, Benjamin infused that desire with a messianic intensity that was absent from William James and John Dewey. And knowing first-hand the rupture of cultural continuity produced by the First World War, exile, and the threat of Fascist victory, he registered the crisis of experience in the modern world with a saturnine bleakness spared his sunnier American counterparts. James's personal "vastations" may have allowed him to understand the dark side of Ralph Waldo Emerson's great essay on experience and grief, but whereas James only occasionally contemplated suicide, it was the sad case that Benjamin actually took his own life fleeing occupied France in 1940.

The auguries for so tragic an outcome were not very clear in the protected childhood of a privileged first-born son of an assimilated Jewish family from the upper middle class. Benjamin's father was an art merchant, his mother a distant relation of Heinrich Heine. Reminiscences of his Berlin childhood around 1900 spent in the elite west end of the city suggest an extraordinarily sensitive and observant boy growing increasingly alert to the ways in which the world of his parents would fail to fulfill his childhood fantasies, but with the determination to take them seriously nonetheless.[5] By the time Benjamin first addressed the theme of experience, he was already a restless and rebellious son, fiercely resisting assimilation into the world of philistine respectability. Rising to a leadership position in the Berlin branch of the Ger-

5. Benjamin, "A Berlin Chronicle" (1932), in *Selected Writings,* vol. 2, *1927–1934,* ed. Michael W. Jennings, Howard Eiland, and Gary Smith, trans. Rodney Livingstone and others (Cambridge, Mass., 1999). Benjamin's scattered autobiographical writings, with their complex invocation of a fragmented body rather than unified self, are the subject of an insightful analysis in Gerhard Richter, *Walter Benjamin and the Corpus of Autobiography* (Detroit, 2000). Benjamin's oblique reminiscences of his own experiences deliberately undermined the confessional mode of self-expression introduced by figures like Jean-Jacques Rousseau.

man Youth Movement led by Gustav Wyneken, the *Freie Studentenschaft,* Benjamin absorbed the utopian spiritualism of the movement, which he expressed in the essay he wrote for its journal *Die Anfang (The Beginning)* in 1913, simply entitled *"Erfahrung."*

Although the twenty-one-year-old Benjamin had not yet developed his mature theory—in fact, the concept seems to be treated more pejoratively than honorifically in this early essay—the attitude that would inform it is already here in embryonic form. Benjamin begins by naming what he denounces as the masked opponent of the youth movement: "the mask of the adult is called 'experience.' It is expressionless, impenetrable, and ever the same. The adult has already experienced *(erlebt)* everything: youth, ideals, hopes, woman. It was all an illusion."[6] Hoping to dampen the enthusiasm of the young—who are defined precisely by their expressive vitality, transparent openness, and defiance of the status quo—the adult wearily insists that rapturous youth will be followed by "grand 'experience,' the years of compromise, impoverishment of ideas, and lack of energy."[7] But such an adult, the young Benjamin insists, is only a philistine who "has taken experience as his gospel . . . he has never grasped that there exists something other than experience, that there are values—inexperienceable—which we serve."[8]

Indeed, to experience without spirit, Benjamin warns, leads nowhere. There is, however, a better concept of experience that refuses the defeatist cynicism of the philistine adult. It acknowledges the value of the mistakes made by youth, for as Benedict Spinoza understood, error is part of the search for truth. "To the one who strives, experience may be painful, but it will scarcely lead him to despair. . . . he will never allow himself to be anaesthetized by the rhythm of the philistine. . . . we know a different experience. It can be hostile to spirit and destructive to many blossoming dreams. Nevertheless, it is the most beautiful, most untouchable, most immediate because it can never be without spirit while we remain young. As Zarathustra says, the individual can experience himself only at the end of his wanderings."[9]

The gesture toward Nietzsche, the stress on expressivity, and the apotheosis of *Geist* (here understood more as "spirit" than "mind") all mark Benjamin as a creature of his time, when Expressionism was cresting as an aes-

6. Walter Benjamin, "Experience" (1913), in *Selected Writings,* vol. 1. *1913–1926,* ed. Marcus Bullock and Michael W. Jennings (Cambridge, Mass., 1996), p. 3.

7. Ibid.

8. Ibid., p. 4.

9. Ibid., pp. 4–5.

thetic movement and generational revolt was in the air.[10] In terms of the various discourses of experience we have already encountered, it is clear that he had little use for the conservative reading in, say, an Edmund Burke, with his trust in the wisdom of the past, but was no less hostile to the scientific disdain for the mistakes that have occurred in that past as mere illusions irrelevant to experience in the dialectical sense of the term. Although his positive concept of experience was still inchoate, Benjamin already revealed sympathy for the meanderings of experience that we noted in Michel de Montaigne, as well as a valorization of the experimental moment in the concept (anticipating among other things his later testing of the effects of hashish and other drugs). With Friedrich Schleiermacher and Rudolf Otto, he took seriously the religious—or more precisely theological—appeal to experience, which resisted the Kantian attempt to privilege morality over illumination.[11] Although never emulating their direct religious commitment, Benjamin shared their desire to grasp the ways the infinite could penetrate the world of human finitude. And like James and Dewey, he wanted to revive the integrated totality of experience denied by the modern world. While going beyond them in believing it was justified to call such an experience "absolute," Benjamin shared the openness—especially evident in James—to exploring its manifestations in the most unexpected and scientifically disreputable places.

Despite the onset of the First World War and his disillusionment with the Youth Movement, which lost its bearings by embracing German nationalism and the war effort, Benjamin refused to abandon his insistence that a different notion of experience was still worth fighting for.[12] He sought to honor the memory of his close friend Fritz Heinle, who had committed suicide to protest the outbreak of the war, by redoubling his efforts to invest ex-

10. For an ambitious attempt to situate Benjamin in his entire intellectual and cultural "field" (Pierre Bourdieu's concept), see John McCole, *Walter Benjamin and the Antinomies of Tradition* (Ithaca, N.Y., 1993).

11. There is no evidence of a direct influence on him of these thinkers, however. Benjamin wrote an essay on Schleiermacher's psychology for a class he took with the psychologist Paul Häberlin in 1918 in Bern, but told his friend Ernst Schoen that the only "negatively interesting thing in it is his theory of language." Benjamin to Schoen, January 13, 1918, in *The Correspondence of Walter Benjamin, 1910–1940,* ed. Gershom Scholem and Theodor W. Adorno, trans. Manfred R. Jacobson and Evelyn M. Jacobson (Chicago, 1994), p. 109. Otto is, as far as I can tell, not mentioned in Benjamin's correspondence or work, and he also seems not to have followed Karl Barth's critique of historicist theology. See his admission of ignorance to Karl Thieme in a letter of June 8, 1939, in ibid., p. 606.

12. In an emotional letter to Gustave Wyneken written on March 9, 1915, he poured out his bitterness at the betrayal of their common ideals but still stressed the importance of "having experienced that there is a pure spirituality among people." *The Correspondence of Walter Benjamin,* p. 76.

perience with a redemptive potential.[13] "To have admitted their yearning for a beautiful childhood and worthy youth is the precondition of creativity," Benjamin insisted in an essay of 1915 entitled "The Life of Students." "Without that admission, without the regret for a greatness missed, no renewal of their lives is possible."[14]

If keeping that flame from going out required transcending the bounds of "bourgeois" thought, as well as bourgeois respectability, Benjamin was eager to try, opening himself up to the nihilistic and apocalyptic temptations that were so powerful an intellectual aphrodisiac to German Jews of his generation.[15] But it also meant a deep suspicion of the way *Lebensphilosophie* had used the concept of experience as *Erlebnis* to glorify the war effort, as we have noted in chapter 3 in his indignant response to what he took to be Martin Buber's shameful bellicosity. Benjamin's fears were confirmed in 1930 when he reviewed Ernst Jünger's essay collection *War and Warriors* under the title "Theories of German Fascism" and urged that "all the light that language and reason still afford should be focused upon that 'primal experience' from whose barren gloom this mysticism of death of the war crawls forth on its thousand unsightly conceptual feet."[16]

Perhaps Benjamin's first halting attempts to fashion an alternative redemptive notion of experience, as Howard Caygill has recently shown, came in unpublished fragments he wrote just after the war began, on color.[17] Cryp-

13. For an attempt to make sense of Benjamin's response to the suicide, see my essay "Against Consolation: Walter Benjamin and the Refusal to Mourn," in *Refractions of Violence* (New York, 2003).

14. Benjamin, "The Life of Students" (1915), in *Selected Writings*, vol. 1, p. 46.

15. For discussions of these trends, see Michael Löwy, *Redemption and Utopia: Jewish Libertarian Thought in Central Europe*, trans. Hope Heany (Stanford, 1992); Anson Rabinbach, *In the Shadow of Catastrophe: German Intellectuals between Apocalypse and Enlightenment* (Berkeley, 1997); and Noah Isenberg, *Between Redemption and Doom: The Strains of German-Jewish Modernism* (Lincoln, Neb., 1999).

16. Benjamin, "Theories of German Fascism" (1930), in *Selected Writing*, vol. 2, p. 320. It should be noted that Gershom Scholem also reacted violently against the cult of *Erlebnis* in Buber. See the August 1916 diary entry in his *Tagebücher nebst Aufsätzen und Entwürfen bis 1923*, vol. 1, *Halbband 1913–1917*, ed. Karlfried Gründer and Friedrich Niewöhner, with Herbert Kopp-Oberstebrink (Frankfurt, 1995), p. 386. Benjamin wrote to Scholem approvingly about his attack on Buber and *Erlebnis* in his letter of March 30, 1918, in *The Correspondence of Walter Benjamin*, p. 122.

17. Benjamin, "Aphorisms on Imagination and Color" (1914–15) and "A Child's View of Color" (1914–1915), in *Selected Writings*, vol. 1. "Die Reflexion in der Kunst und in der Farbe" (1915), in *Gesammelte Schriften*, vols. 1–8, ed. Rolf Tiedemann and Herman Schweppenhaüser (Frankfurt, 1972), vol. 6; "Der Regenbogen," (1919), and "Der Regenbogen: Ein Gespräch über die Phantasie," in *Gesammelte Schriften*, vol. 9; Howard Caygill, *Walter Benjamin: The Colour of Experience* (London, 1998). Caygill may overestimate the importance of these early fragments, which he uses to say Benjamin is "above all a thinker of the visual" (p. xiv), but he does draw attention to a dimension of his work that has hitherto been marginalized.

tic and underdeveloped, these suggestive texts posit a utopian potential in the child's ability to see colors that anticipates similar arguments Benjamin made in different registers—linguistic, aesthetic, historical—in his later work. Whereas adults reflectively abstract colors from the objects that exist in time and space, Benjamin speculated that children have the ability to see them as prior to forms, which are merely expressions of the law rather than pure spirit. Their drawings saturate the page with color, which allows them to create an interrelated world without fixed and rigid boundaries. "Because children see with pure eyes," he wrote,

> without allowing themselves to be emotionally disconcerted, it is something spiritual: the rainbow refers not to a chaste abstraction but to a life in art. The order of art is paradisiacal because there is no thought of the dissolution of boundaries—from excitement—in the object of experience. Instead the world is full of color in a state of identity, innocence, and harmony. Children are not ashamed, since they do not reflect but only see.[18]

The rainbow serves as a figure of life because the gradations shifting from one hue to another are infinitesimally small and defy the attempt to impose a categorical structure with clear borders on them. Colors are relationally entangled, defining themselves by what they are not, rather than discrete and self-sufficient. The child is intuitively immersed in this chromatic world rather than standing apart from it and judging it reflectively; no subject yet sets itself as opposed to an object, no form is yet traced on a flat or even curved surface. We are still in a world of infinite and immanent intensity, a world of absolute experience.

That world comes as close as humanly possible to the Platonic ideal of anamnesis of a lost utopia. Writing of children's books in an unpublished fragment on the nineteenth-century illustrator Johann Peter Lyser, Benjamin argued that "by remembering they learn; what you put into their hands should have, insofar as human hand can impart it to paper, the color of paradise, just as butterfly wings have their patina. Children learn in the memory of their first intuition. And they learn from bright colors, because the fantastic play of color is the home of memory without yearning, and it can be free of yearning because it is unalloyed."[19] The art of adults preserves some of this

18. Benjamin, "A Child's View of Color," p. 51.
19. Benjamin, "Notes for a Study of the Beauty of Colored Illustrations in Children's Books" (1918–1921), in *Selected Writings*, vol. 1, p. 264.

feeling, but it is suffused with more of the yearning for something lost, a fulfillment that would come only when yearning itself ended.

This celebration of an innocent child's eye, inviting the obvious comparison with William Wordsworth at his most lyrical, is implicitly pitted
against Immanuel Kant's claim that experience involves the imposition of
categories and forms by the transcendental mind on the multiplicity of sensations. It challenges the assumption that subjects of experience are distinct
from their noumenal objects, an assumption which it tacitly identifies with
an adult corruption of the child's eye. Even more boldly, it rejects the limiting of experience to what can be known by synthetic a priori judgments,
which bracket metaphysical truths as unknowable and insists instead that
speculative knowledge of the absolute is possible. "In this experience," Caygill notes, "two components of Kant's account of experience—sensibility
and the understanding—collapse into each other, and the experiencing subject which would contain them dissolves into experience. The opposition
between gaze and the gazed upon collapses, both threatening a nihilistic dissolution into a pure featureless identity beyond subject and object but also
promising a new articulation of experience."[20]

That new articulation, Benjamin soon came to realize, might be present
in language as well. His linguistic turn was therefore very different from those
later versions we have seen in Joan Wallach Scott and Richard Rorty, which
pitted the mediation of language against raw experience. In several unpublished essays, most notably "On Language as Such and on the Language of
Man" of 1916 and "On Perception" of 1917, Benjamin expanded his critique
of Kant and neo-Kantians like Hermann Cohen, whose scientific reading of
the critical tradition he found particularly impoverished, to focus on their
inability to recover a robust notion of experience prior to its modalization.[21]
Their mistake was to focus on "the knowledge of experience" rather than "ex-

20. Caygill, *Walter Benjamin: The Colour of Experience*, p. 12.

21. At times, Benjamin attacked the neo-Kantians for having lost those impulses in Kant's own work
that suggested ways beyond the purely epistemological, mathematical, mechanical, and subject-oriented
notion of experience that dominated his legacy. At other times, Kant himself seems to have been his
villain. Although he was a student of the neo-Kantian Heinrich Rickert, from whose critique of *Lebensphilosophie*'s celebration of "mere life" he learned a great deal, Benjamin was far less sympathetic towards
the Marburg branch of the movement. He took a class devoted to Hermann Cohen's *Kants Begriff der
Erfahrung* and reported his deep disappointment to Scholem. See Gershom Scholem, *Walter Benjamin:
The Story of a Friendship*, trans. Harry Zohn (New York, 1981), p. 61. For a more extensive treatment of
this issue, see Astrid Deuber-Mankowsky, *Der frühe Walter Benjamin und Hermann Cohen: Jüdische Werte,
kritische Philosophie, vergängliche Erfahrung* (Berlin, 2000).

perience itself," which meant that: "the concept of experience that Kant relates to knowledge, without ever postulating continuity, has nothing like the same scope as that of earlier thinkers. What counts for him is the concept of scientific experience. Even this he strove in part to separate as far as possible from the ordinary meaning of the word."[22] Before Kant, however, "the symbol of the unity of knowledge that we know as 'experience' had been an exalted one; it had, even though to varying degrees, been close to God and the divine. During the Enlightenment, however, it was increasingly stripped of its proximity to God."[23]

Following Johann Hamann's religiously informed critique of Kant's belief that thoughts of transcendent ideas exist prior to their linguistic expression, Benjamin claimed that contact with the divine came in language. Or rather it appeared in a more fundamental "language as such," which was deeper than the instrumental and conventional "bourgeois conception of language." The latter "holds that the means of communication is the word, its object factual, and its addressee a human being. The other conception of language, in contrast, knows no means, no object, and no addressee of communication. It means: *in the name, the mental being of man communicates itself to God.*"[24] In the divine "language as such," there was an absolute relation between name and thing, in which the Creator made known His creation through giving it proper names, which are not accidental or contingent signs. Here language did not function as a medium to communicate something else, but communicated only itself. Here the speaker was dissolved into the language that spoke him. Here the frankly "magical" side of language, which theorists like Wilhelm von Humboldt had overlooked, was manifest.[25]

Man's language, after the Fall and the withdrawal of Adam's ability to name things in the Garden of Eden, lost this connection with the essence of things, a decline further exacerbated by the cacophony of separate languages that came with the Tower of Babel, which led to what Benjamin called "overnaming." No longer an unmediated expression of truth, language could now be used to lie as well, which required the faculty of judgment to decide between the two, the faculty that was privileged in Kantian critical philosophy. Not only were determinant judgments based on subsumption under laws a result of the Fall; so too were the reflective judgments Kant had applied to

22. Benjamin, "On Perception," p. 94.
23. Ibid., p. 95.
24. Benjamin, "On Language as Such and the Language of Man" (1916), in *Selected Writings*, vol. 1, p. 65.
25. Benjamin, "Reflections on Humboldt" (1925), in *Selected Writings*, vol. 1, p. 424.

aesthetic objects, which involved arguing from exemplars rather than rules. Both modes of judgment, Benjamin implied, were too dependent on privileging the subject over the object.

There were, however, traces of the original language still visible in its fallen counterparts, providing hints of ways to transcend the melancholy that followed the loss of the Adamic unity between name and thing and the muteness of a nature no longer able to speak. Of special importance was the possibility of translation from one language to another, a theme that Benjamin was later to explore in greater depth in "The Task of the Translator," written as the preface for his own translation of Charles Baudelaire's *Tableaux parisiens* in 1923.[26] The ability to translate from one human language to another was a cipher of possible redemption because like the colors of the rainbow, it involved a continuum of imperceptible transitions: "Translation passes through continua of transformation, not abstract areas of identity and similarity."[27] Individual languages do not copy what others can say, but rather supplement each other, each potentially possessing the others, as it were, between the lines.

There is also a residue of the initial language of nature, Benjamin contended, which can still be discerned in a non-scientific relationship to natural objects. "The uninterrupted flow of this communication runs through the whole of nature, from lowest forms of existence to man and from man to God. . . . The language of nature is comparable to a secret password that each sentry passes to the next in his own language, but the meaning of the password is the sentry's language itself. All higher language is a translation of lower ones, until in ultimate clarity the word of God unfolds, which is the unity of this movement made up of language."[28] Benjamin's memory of childhood walks in a nature whose deeper meaning he yearned to decode had clearly left its trace on his mature ruminations on the redemption of a fallen nature from its enforced muteness.

Another way in which absolute experience might be restored involved the realization of what Benjamin proclaimed with a certain bravado "the coming philosophy" in an unpublished essay of 1918.[29] At the end of "On Perception," he had cryptically written: "Philosophy is absolute experience deduced in a systematic, symbolic framework as language."[30] Perception, such

26. Benjamin, "The Task of the Translator" (1923), in *Selected Writings*, vol. 1.
27. Benjamin, "On Language as Such and the Language of Man," p. 70.
28. Ibid., p. 74.
29. Benjamin, "On the Program of the Coming Philosophy" (1918), in *Selected Writings*, vol. 1.
30. Benjamin, "On Perception," p. 96.

as a child's of color, was itself one of the languages of absolute experience, but taken as a whole, philosophy consisted of what he called *Lehre,* which can be translated as "doctrines" or "teachings." Combining religious with pre-critical philosophical insights, *Lehre* posited what Benjamin's friend Gershom Scholem called "the transcausal connectedness of things and their constitution in God."[31] Such a connectedness would reveal the hierarchy of orders of being, which had been occluded with the rise of modern, atomizing science.

The "coming philosophy," Benjamin contended, must restore a higher notion of experience than the one postulated by Kant and the neo-Kantians. It must get beyond the shallow Enlightenment's restriction of experience to scientific certainty and realize the future metaphysics to which Kant had intended his own critical philosophy to be a prolegomenon. Kant himself had not, in fact, really wanted to reduce all experience to its scientific variant, despite the historical impact of his thought. The neo-Kantians, however, had only emphasized "the mechanical aspect of the relatively empty Enlightenment concept of experience."[32] They had reduced experience to an object of knowledge, which was fit for psychology, rather than making it the medium of a higher, frankly metaphysical knowledge. This experience "includes religion, as the true experience, in which neither god nor man is object or subject of knowledge but in which this experience depends on pure knowledge as the quintessence of which philosophy alone can and must think god."[33]

Such a concept of experience, Benjamin contended in terms that would have been familiar to Schleiermacher, means that "the distinction between the realms of nature and freedom would be abolished,"[34] although it would be a mistake to collapse them entirely into each other. It would also involve a shift from the realm of epistemology based on the dualism of knowing subject and known object to the linguistic medium in which both were immersed: "The great transformation and correction which must be performed upon the concept of experience, oriented so one-sidedly along mathematical-mechanical lines, can be attained only by relating knowledge to language, as

---

31. Scholem, *Walter Benjamin: The Story of a Friendship,* p. 73. For recent discussions of the theological dimension of Benjamin's work, see David Kaufmann, "Beyond Use, Within Reason: Adorno, Benjamin and the Question of Theology," *New German Critique* 83 (Spring–Summer 2001); and Lieven de Cauter, *The Dwarf in the Chess Machine: Benjamin's Hidden Doctrine* (forthcoming).

32. Benjamin, "On the Program of the Coming Philosophy," p. 105.

33. Ibid., p. 104.

34. Ibid., p. 106.

was attempted by Hamann during Kant's lifetime."[35] Only then will the continuities between the phenomenal and noumenal realms, finitude and infinity, human existence and the absolute, and religion and philosophy be restored. This philosophy of the future must therefore "create on the basis of the Kantian system a concept of knowledge to which a concept of experience corresponds, of which the knowledge is the teachings [*Lehre*]." And with cryptic, almost oxymoronic, concision, he added: "Experience is the uniform and continuous multiplicity of knowledge."[36] As Giorgio Agamben has pointed out, the last time such a unity of knowledge and experience based on the valorization of multiplicity rather than universality had been so avidly defended was prior to the scientific revolution's quest for certainty in Montaigne's *Essays*.[37]

In the present fallen condition, Benjamin thought, there were still ciphers of what has been lost. With considerable effort, it would still be possible to "read" the world as if it were a legible text.[38] Paracelsus's doctrine of signatures, banished from the world by modern science, had to be revived. "We know of primitive peoples of the so-called preanimistic stage who identify themselves with sacred animals and plants and name themselves after them; we know of insane people who likewise identify themselves in part with objects of their perception, which are thus no longer *objecta*, 'placed before' them; we know of sick people who relate the sensations of their bodies not to themselves but rather to other creatures, and of clairvoyants who at least claim to be able to feel the sensations of others as their own."[39] The German Romantics, to whose concept of criticism Benjamin devoted his doctoral dissertation in 1919 at the University of Bern, had developed a method of relating to the natural world that promised to restore some of what had been suppressed by modern science. For them, "experiment consists in the

35. Ibid., pp. 107–8.

36. Ibid., p. 108. According to Lieven de Cauter, these goals betray a subtle affinity for the transcendental phenomenology of Husserl, whose critique of subjectivism and psychologism Benjamin clearly shared. Later he would come out firmly against the ahistorical quality of phenomenology's notion of experience.

37. Giorgio Agamben, *Infancy and History: Essays on the Destruction of Experience,* trans. Liz Heron (London, 1993), p. 18. Rather than certainty, which puts the emphasis on knowledge claims, the prior tradition that Benjamin wanted to rescue depended more on authority, which involves the power of objects to demand respect.

38. On the importance of the experience of reading in Benjamin, see Karlheinz Stierle, "Walter Benjamin und die Erfahrung des Lesens," *Poetica* 12, no. 1 (1980). Significantly, Stierle begins by comparing Benjamin with Montaigne as an avid reader of the world, who understood that the reading of texts helped gain access to it.

39. Benjamin, "On the Program of the Coming Philosophy," p. 103.

evocation of self-consciousness and self-knowledge in the things observed. To observe a thing means only to arouse it to self-recognition. Whether an experiment succeeds depends on the extent to which the experimenter is capable, through the heightening of his own consciousness, through magical observation, one might say, of getting nearer to the object and of finally drawing it into himself."[40]

Here the Romantics were very close to Goethe's concept of a "tender empiria" *(zarte Empirie),* which "conforms intimately to its object and that, through identification with it, becomes its true and proper theory."[41] Their criticism was not dependent on intersubjectively validated reflective judgments of taste, as in Kant, but rather on allowing the art object to reflect on itself: "The subject of reflection is, at bottom, the artistic entity itself, and the experiment consists not in any reflecting *on* an entity, which could not essentially alter it as Romantic criticism intends, but in the unfolding of reflection—that is, for the Romantics, the unfolding of spirit—*in* an entity."[42]

Benjamin's affinities with the Romantics whose mode of criticism he discussed in his doctoral dissertation are manifest. In notes written in 1932, he reminded himself "that experience and observation are identical has to be shown. See the concept of 'romantic observation' in my dissertation.— Observation is based on self-immersion."[43] His sympathy for the Romantics and their frankly "mystical terminology" helped forestall his acceptance of the post-Kantian narrative that culminated in Hegel's idealist system, which Benjamin always distrusted as overly rational and coercively totalizing, a position not shared, as we will see, by Adorno. If, as he argued, experience "is the uniform and continuous multiplicity of knowledge,"[44] it would involve an infinity of overlapping, continuous and supplementary variations rather than a closed, dialectically sublated system. As Benjamin wrote to Scholem with regard to the Hegelian Marxism of Georg Lukács, he "would be surprised if the foundations of my nihilism were not to manifest themselves against communism in an antagonistic confrontation with the concepts and assertions of Hegelian dialectic."[45]

40. Benjamin, "The Concept of Criticism in German Romanticism" (1920), in *Selected Writings,* vol. 1, p. 148.

41. Benjamin quotes these remarks from Goethe in a footnote to "The Concept of Criticism in the German Romanticism," p. 192.

42. Ibid., p. 151. For discussions of Benjamin's debts to Romanticism, see Beatrice Hanssen and Andrew Benjamin, eds., *Walter Benjamin and Romanticism* (New York, 2002).

43. Benjamin, "Experience" (1932), in *Selected Writings,* vol. 2, p. 553.

44. Benjamin, "The Program of the Coming Philosophy," p. 108.

45. Benjamin to Scholem, September 16, 1924, *The Correspondence of Walter Benjamin,* p. 248.

Looking elsewhere for guidance, Benjamin found inspiration in writers like Ludwig Klages, whose acquaintance he first made in 1914. Klages's frankly counter-Enlightenment defense of pseudo-sciences like graphology he found suggestive, as he did Klages's belief in the survival of the archaic in the modern developed in such works as *Von kosmogonischen Eros (On Cosmogenical Eros)* of 1922 and *Geist als Widersacher der Seele (Spirit as the Antithesis of Soul)* of 1929–33.[46] Although resisting many of the more reactionary dimensions of Klages's work, such as his wholesale repudiation of modern technology, celebration of irrational "soul" *(Seele)* over "spirit" *(Geist),* and frank anti-Semitism, Benjamin found in his "metaphysical psychology," with its belief in expressive gestures, an ally in the struggle to realize a redemptive notion of experience.

A similar willingness to risk entering territory that was potentially dangerous allowed Benjamin to find in astrology another cipher of an alternative notion of experience. As in the case of graphology, what astrological doctrine suggested was the survival of a way of experiencing the world that had been all but lost in modernity. In an unpublished essay probably composed in 1932, he claimed that "we have to reckon with the possibility that manifest configurations, mimetic resemblances, may once have existed where today we are no longer in a position even to guess at them. For example, in the constellations of the stars. The horoscope must above all be understood as an originary totality that astrological interpretation merely subjects to analysis."[47] If what he called "the mimetic genius" of the ancient world, "the most consummate expression of cosmic meaning," can be found today, Benjamin speculated, it would likely be in the acquisition of language by children.

Benjamin's exploration of the residues of what he called "the mimetic faculty"[48] and its various expressions—not only astrology and graphology, but also the play of children, dance, and the "semblance" *(Schein)* in beauty—focused on the similarities and elective affinities in phenomena that go be-

46. For a discussion of Benjamin's complicated debt to Klages, see McCole, *Walter Benjamin and The Antinomies of Tradition,* pp. 178–80 and 236–40. See Benjamin's mixed references to Klages in his 1926 review of Carl Albrecht Bernouilli's book on Johann Jacob Bachofen, in *Selected Writings,* vol. 1, and his more enthusiastic discussion in his 1928 review of Anja and Georg Mendelssohn's *Der Mensch in der Handschrift* and his 1930 essay "Graphology: Old and New," in *Selected Writings,* vol. 2.

47. Benjamin, "On Astrology" (1932 [?]), in *Selected Writings,* vol. 2, p. 685.

48. Benjamin, "On the Mimetic Faculty" (1933), in *Selected Writings,* vol. 2. For other works, most of them unpublished fragments, that address this issue, see "Analogy and Relationship" (1919), "On Semblance" (1919–20), "Beauty and Semblance" (1920–21), and "Goethe's Elective Affinities" (1919–22), in *Selected Writings,* vol. 1, and "Doctrine of the Similar" (1933) and "The Lamp" (1933), in *Selected Writings,* vol. 2.

yond mere analogous relationships. Here he drew on the legacy of nineteenth-century anthropological accounts of sympathetic magic, developed by Herbert Spencer, Edward Tylor, and James Frazer.[49] One way in which modern man might get in touch with the "pale shadow" of previous mimetic experience is "when he looks through a mask, or when, on southern moonlit nights, he feels mimetic forces alive in himself that he had thought long since dead, while nature, which possesses them all, transforms itself to resemble the moon. But he is transported into this very force field by his memories of childhood."[50]

But it was language that harbored the greatest potential for its recovery. Not only were similarities evident in the onomatopoeic ability of sounds to imitate their referents, but also in what Benjamin called "nonsensuous similarities." In addition to handwritten script revealing intentions unknown to the writer, which graphology might reveal, these were also manifest in the fact that words in different languages refer to the same thing. The redemptive task of translation was to allow these similarities, whose bearer or vehicle is semiotic meaning, to emerge in their own right. "In this way," Benjamin enthused, "language may be seen as the highest level of mimetic behavior and the most complete archive of nonsensuous similarity: a medium into which the earlier powers of mimetic production and comprehension have passed without residue, to the point where they have liquidated those of magic."[51] Naming the right name, we might say, is thus a kind of perception of God's original hand, which had formed the objects that existed in a prelapsarian state of grace.

There were, however, still other manifestations of mimetic experience, even in the seemingly disenchanted modern world, to which Benjamin was alerted by the French surrealists, whose "writings are concerned literally with experiences, not with theories, and still less with phantasms."[52] As early as 1927,

49. For an account of Benjamin's debts to these thinkers, as well as the similarities between his appropriation of the idea of mimesis and that of Aby Warburg, see Matthew Rampley, "Mimesis and Allegory: On Aby Warburg and Walter Benjamin," in Richard Woodfield, ed., *Art History as Cultural History: Warburg's Projects* (Amsterdam, 2001). For an attempt to situate Benjamin's and Adorno's use of the concept in its longer history, see Gunter Gebauer and Christoph Wulf, *Mimesis: Culture—Art—Society*, trans. Don Reneau (Berkeley, 1992).

50. Benjamin, "The Lamp," p. 692.

51. Benjamin, "On the Mimetic Faculty," p. 722.

52. Benjamin, "Surrealism" (1929), in *Selected Writings*, vol. 2., p. 208. For helpful discussions of Benjamin's debts to surrealism, see Margaret Cohen, *Profane Illumination: Walter Benjamin and the Paris of Surrealist Revolutions* (Berkeley, 1993); and Beatrice Hanssen, *Walter Benjamin's Other History: Of Stones, Animals, Human Beings, and Angels* (Berkeley, 1998).

he had been intrigued by Louis Aragon's attempt in his *Vague de rêves (Wave of Dreams)* to rescue the dreams not of psychological subjects, but of the object world of the modern city. Those dreams were still present in the banality of kitsch. Treating dream kitsch as the repository of ancient magical impulses, the surrealists had recovered something from the lost world of childhood as well: "The repetition of childhood experience gives us pause: when we were little, there was as yet no agonized protest against the world of our parents. As children in the midst of that world, we showed ourselves as superior. When we reach for the banal, we take hold of the good along with it—that good that is there (open your eyes) right before you."[53]

Benjamin, as he revealed in a letter to Scholem, came to think of himself as the "philosophical Fortinbras" of surrealism, inheriting its legacy and turning it to new purposes.[54] Translating parts of Aragon's novel of the miraculous side of urban life, *Le paysan de Paris (The Peasant of Paris)*, in the late 1920s proved a heady experience—just reading two or three pages of the book, he later told Adorno, left him dizzy with excitement[55]—and inspired him to begin the ambitious and ultimately unfinished project known to posterity as the *Passagenwerk*, or *The Arcades Project*, which would intermittently occupy him during the desperate decade before his suicide in 1940.[56] Reinforcing the lessons he had learned from his friendship with Franz Hessel, whose wanderings through "unknown Berlin" he lavishly praised,[57] Benjamin's immersion in surrealist writings about the perseverance of the magical in the modern gave him an idiom in which to combine, however fitfully, the theological impulses of his earliest work with the materialist ones he absorbed after his embrace of heterodox Marxism in the mid-1920s.[58] It encouraged him to read the "passages" of the nineteenth-century arcades as if they were passages in a layered text revealing the residues of the archaic in the modern cityscape or constellations of meaning like the fractured allegories whose critical value he had championed in his *Habilitationsschrift* entitled *The Origin*

53. Benjamin, "Dream Kitsch" (1927), in *Selected Writings*, vol. 2, p. 4.

54. Benjamin to Scholem, October 30, 1928, in *The Correspondence of Walter Benjamin*, p. 342.

55. Benjamin to Adorno, Paris, May 31, 1935, in Adorno and Benjamin, *The Complete Correspondence*, p. 88.

56. Benjamin, *The Arcades Project*, trans. Howard Eiland and Kevin McLaughlin (Cambridge, Mass., 2002).

57. Benjamin, "Review of Hessel's *Heimliches Berlin*" (1927), in *Selected Writings*, vol. 2.

58. Benjamin's turn to Marxism is often tied to his love affair with the Latvian actress Asja Lacis, which began on the isle of Capri in 1924. For an insightful account of his political development from nihilistic anarchism to heterodox Marxism with strong anarchist residues, see Uwe Steiner, "The True Politician: Walter Benjamin's Concept of the Political," *New German Critique* 83 (Spring–Summer 2001).

of German Tragic Drama. It moved him to consider the absolute still immanent even in the fallen world of modernity, an argument that extended the
Romantic notion of the artwork as the locus in which the infinite penetrated
the finite to include more general cultural phenomena.[59]

What Benjamin came to call a surrealist "profane illumination" was not
merely a dream or drug experience, but "a materialistic, anthropological inspiration, to which hashish, opium, or whatever else can give an introduc-
tory lesson."[60] Because their telos was earthly happiness rather than the messianic Kingdom of God, such illuminations produced by the montagelike
juxtaposition of linear elements deserved to be called profane. Although when
writing his most extensive appreciation of surrealism in 1929 he had come to
believe that its most heroic phase had passed and its concept of revolutionary "intoxication" was undialectical, Benjamin nonetheless praised its non-
bourgeois-humanist notion of freedom as a necessary complement to "the
other revolutionary experience, which we must acknowledge because it has
been ours—the constructive, dictatorial side of revolution."[61]

Whether Benjamin himself ever really experienced revolution in a direct
way is, to be sure, debatable. Despite his growing attachment to Marxism,
he always remained at a considerable distance from any concrete political
movement. In fact, rather than extolling the virtues of revolutionary experience, his work increasingly came to register the impossibility—or at least,
extreme difficulty—of achieving authentic experience in the modern world.
Using words like "atrophy" *(Verkümmerung)* and "poverty" *(Armut)* to describe what was in danger of disappearing entirely, he lamented the degradation of experience he saw around him—or at least did so when he was not
forcing himself to think dialectically about its positive implications. Benjamin
was, to be sure, not alone in bemoaning the crisis of experience, a note we
have seen already sounded by figures as disparate as Michael Oakeshott and
the American pragmatists. It can also be detected in novelists like the Austrian Robert Musil, whose great unfinished masterpiece, *The Man without
Qualities,* set in 1913 Vienna, includes the lament:

> Have we not noticed that experiences have made themselves independent of
> people?. . . . A world of qualities without a man has arisen, of experiences with-
> out the person who experiences them, and it almost looks as though ideally

59. See Caygill, *Walter Benjamin: The Colour of Experience,* chapter 2, for an analysis of the relationship between experience and immanent critique.
60. Benjamin, "Surrealism," p. 209.
61. Ibid., p. 215.

private experience is a thing of the past, and that the friendly burden of personal responsibility is to dissolve into a system of formulas for possible means. Probably the dissolution of the anthropocentric point of view, which for such a long time considered man to be the center of the universe but which has been fading away for centuries, has finally arrived at the "I" itself, for the belief that the most important things about experience is the experiencing, or of action in the doing, is beginning to strike most people as naïve.[62]

But no one became so acute and persistent a diagnostician of the crisis as Walter Benjamin. In the decade or so before his death, Benjamin extended his analysis of that impoverishment well beyond that neo-Kantian reduction of experience to its scientific, mechanical variant against which he had railed in "On the Program of the Coming Philosophy." By focusing on what was lost, Benjamin was able to enrich his concept of experience beyond the realm of mimetic similarities and religious doctrine to include complicated explorations of temporality, narrative, memory, tradition, destruction, technology, mass culture, and the categorical distinction between two versions of experience, *Erlebnis* and *Erfahrung*. As a result, his ruminations gained a political and historical texture largely absent from his earlier efforts. Whether all of his analyses, theological and materialist, historical and ontological, linguistic and social, fit perfectly together is, however, an open question. One commentator has gone so far as to see a "notable fracture" between Benjamin's early and late musings on experience.[63] Whether they are completely convincing is another, which, as we will see momentarily, was even addressed with some skepticism by Adorno, whose debt was nonetheless overwhelming.

The turn toward a more historical and political emphasis became apparent in Benjamin's 1933 essay "Experience and Poverty," published in the first year of his exile. Beginning with an anecdote about childhood anthologies that included a fable of an old man who passed on a valuable lesson to his sons at his deathbed, Benjamin explained:

Everyone knew precisely what experience was: older people had always passed it on to younger sons. It was handed down in short form to sons and grandsons, with the authority of age, in proverbs; with an often long-winded eloquence, as tales; sometimes as stories from foreign lands, at the fireside.—Where has it all gone? Who still meets people who really know how to tell a story? . . .

62. Robert Musil, *The Man without Qualities*, vol. 1, trans. Sophie Wilkins (New York, 1996), pp. 158–59. Volume 1 was first published in 1930.
63. Lindroos, "Scattering Community," p. 19.

who will even attempt to deal with young people by giving them the benefit of their experience?[64]

Like Montaigne four centuries before, Benjamin understood the importance of transmitting the wisdom of the past through proverbs, tales, and oral histories. In an unpublished fragment written the previous year, he had postulated a link between his doctrine of mimesis and experience as something lived over time: "There is no greater error than to construe experience—in the sense of life experience—according to the model on which the natural sciences are based. What is decisive here is not the causal connections established over the course of time, but the similarities that have been lived."[65] The similarities were understood here less in terms of cosmic affinities than as the residues of past learning that could still be communicated and might be functional in the future. The proverb, Benjamin wrote in another unpublished fragment the same year, "speaks a *noli me tangere* of experience. With this, it proclaims its ability to transform experience into tradition. . . . It turns the lesson that has been experienced into a wave in the living chain of innumerable lessons that flow down from eternity."[66]

But with the horrors of the First World War, Benjamin charged, the generational link, which was already growing tenuous, had snapped, with the result that "experience has fallen in value." Returning from the front stunned and silent, the survivors were "poorer in communicable experience," and the reasons were obvious:

> For never has experience been contradicted more thoroughly: strategic experience has been contravened by positional warfare; economic experience, by the inflation; physical experience, by hunger; moral experiences, by the ruling powers. A generation that had gone to school in horse-drawn streetcars now stood in the open air, amid a landscape in which nothing was the same except the clouds and, at its center, in a force field of destructive torrents and explosions, the tiny fragile human body.[67]

The resulting poverty of experience, Benjamin warned, meant a new variety of barbarism, which involves much more than the individual; it suggests as well the exhaustion of culture itself.

64. Benjamin, "Experience and Poverty" (1933), in *Selected Writings* vol. 2, p. 730.
65. Benjamin, "Experience" (1932), in *Selected Writings*, vol. 2, p. 553.
66. Benjamin, "On Proverbs" (1932), in *Selected Writings*, vol. 2, p. 582.
67. Benjamin, "Experience and Poverty," p. 732.

But where there is such a collapse, Benjamin defiantly if somewhat desperately asserted, there is also a new opportunity. "For what does poverty of experience do for the barbarian? It forces him to start from scratch; to make a new start; to make a little go a long way; to begin with a little and build up further, looking neither left nor right."[68] The signs of the *tabula rasa* were everywhere: in Albert Einstein's physics, the art of the cubists and Paul Klee, the architecture of Adolf Loos and Le Corbusier, even Mickey Mouse cartoons.[69] As the novelist Paul Scheerbart had observed in the work he coauthored with Bruno Taut on glass architecture, the cold and transparent new buildings of the modern city had dispensed with the "aura" of old buildings, as well as a culture of secrecy and deceit. Even the decline of "communicable experience" might not be so bad, if it allows those non-communicative potentials in language that Benjamin had extolled in his earlier work to come to the fore. Thus the idea of "poverty of experience," he concluded, "should not be understood to mean that people are yearning for new experience. No, they long to free themselves from experience; they long for a world in which they can make such pure and decided use of their poverty—that it will lead to something respectable."[70] But that "something new" may well involve outliving culture as it is now understood.

Benjamin's unexpected valorization of the crisis of experience in this essay, mixing echoes of Rosa Luxemburg's warning that the only choice was between socialism and barbarism with apocalyptic religious fantasies of redemption through destruction, was not merely an expression of what he had often called the "nihilistic" impulse in his thought. It was also symptomatic of a new, more hopeful strain nurtured by his growing friendship with Bertolt Brecht. "Brecht's subject," he had written in 1930, "is poverty . . . the physiological and economic poverty of man in the machine age."[71] One of his characters, Herr Keuner, understood poverty as "a form of mimicry that allows you to come closer to reality than any rich man can."[72] If experience is relevant to Brecht, it is only in its acceptation as "experiment" developed in his notion of "epic theater." As Benjamin was to write in his 1934 essay "The

68. Ibid.

69. In a fragment written in 1931, Benjamin called Mickey Mouse cartoons instruments that help mankind to prepare for the survival of civilization's collapse, adding that "these films disavow experience more radically than ever before. In such a world, it is not worthwhile to have experiences." *Selected Writings,* vol. 2, p. 545.

70. Benjamin, "Experience and Poverty," p. 734.

71. Benjamin, "Bert Brecht" (1930), in *Selected Writings,* vol. 2, p. 370.

72. Ibid.

Author as Producer," "To the total dramatic artwork, [Brecht] opposes the dramatic laboratory. He makes use in a new way of the great, ancient opportunity of the theater: to expose what is present. At the center of his experiment stands the human being. Present-day man; a reduced man, therefore, chilled in a chilly environment. But since this is the only one we have, it is in our interest to know him."[73]

But the Brechtian strain in Benjamin's work, his cold diagnostician's embrace of modernist experimentation in theater as well as architecture, did not really succeed in extinguishing the emotional intensity of his mourning—or perhaps better put, the melancholic rehearsal of his lament—for lost experience. The saturnine impulse in his character, reinforced as external events went from bad to worse in the last decade of his life, often overwhelmed his willful efforts to overcome what he called "left-wing melancholy" and embrace the ground-clearing efforts of "the destructive character."[74] For all his avowed celebration of the end of the cultic "aura" surrounding works of art in modern technologies like the cinema and photography, expressed in perhaps his most famous essay, "The Work of Art in the Age of Mechanical Reproduction," Benjamin never overcame his deep ambivalence at the cost.

The most explicit expression of Benjamin's apparent nostalgia for past experience came in his 1936 essay "The Storyteller."[75] Reflecting on the work of the nineteenth-century Russian writer Nicolai Leskov, he expanded on an argument he had already begun four years earlier in an essay called "The Handkerchief." There he had answered the question "why is storytelling on the decline?" by noting several possible causes:

> people who are not bored cannot tell stories. But there is no longer any place for boredom in our lives. The activities that were covertly and inwardly bound up with it are dying out. A second reason, then, for the decline in storytelling is that people have ceased to weave and spin, tinker and scrape, while listening to stories. In short, if stories are to thrive, there must be work, order and

73. Benjamin, "The Author as Producer" (1934), in *Selected Writings*, vol. 2, p. 779.

74. "Left-Wing Melancholy" is the title of his 1931 critique of unaffiliated Weimar leftists like Erich Kästner; "The Destructive Character" is the title of an article written the following year. Both are in *Selected Writings*, vol. 2. For essays that deal with the link between destruction and experience, see Andrew Benjamin and Peter Osborne, eds., *Walter Benjamin's Philosophy: Destruction and Experience* (London, 1984), in particular Irving Wohlfarth, "No-man's-land: On Walter Benjamin's 'Destructive Character'."

75. Benjamin, "The Storyteller," in *Illuminations*, ed. Hannah Arendt, trans. Harry Zohn (New York, 1968).

subordination. . . . another reason no proper stories can be heard today is that things no longer last the way they should.[76]

In his essay on Leskov, Benjamin also blamed the rise of the novel and the replacement of narrative by information in the modern world, repeating almost verbatim his paragraph from "Experience and Poverty" about the effects of the war.[77] With the decline of the capacity to hand down stories from generation to generation, what he called the "haggadic" nature of truth—epitomized by the story of Exodus retold at every Passover seder—was put in jeopardy. So too was the "epic side of truth, wisdom,"[78] which was derived from the storyteller's rootedness in the people, especially when they were a community of craftsmen. As he acknowledged in a letter to Adorno, the crisis of storytelling was related to the general decline of the aura in other arts as well.[79] The atrophy of authentic experience, based as it was on the cultic residues of magical similarities, was expressed in the loss—or more precisely, decline or dwindling—of "aura," which he defined with reference to natural objects as "a strange weave of space and time: the unique appearance or semblance of distance, no matter close it may be."[80] Such a distance was as much temporal as spatial because it involved the experience of a distinction between past and present, which was in danger of collapsing in the modern world. Without that distance, the ability of the object to return our gaze that Benjamin saw as fundamental to thwarting the domination of the subject over the object would be jeopardized.

In certain of his moods Benjamin defiantly celebrated the decay of the aura as producing positive political effects by liberating us from cultic dependence. Technologically reproduced art, he declared in "The Work of Art in the Age of Mechanical Reproduction," has an "exhibition value" that opens art to mass appropriation, photographs bring things closer and diminish auratic distance, and even the incoherence of information in newspapers, he insisted in 1934, may be preparing the way for salvation.[81] But at other times,

76. Benjamin, "The Handkerchief" (1932), in *Selected Writings*, vol. 2, p. 658.

77. Benjamin, "The Storyteller," pp. 83–84. But in this essay, there is none of the forced glee at this outcome evident in the earlier essay.

78. Ibid., p. 87.

79. Benjamin to Adorno, June 6, 1936, in *The Complete Correspondence*, p. 140.

80. Benjamin, "Little History of Photography" (1931), in *Selected Writings*, vol. 2, p. 518. There is an extensive literature on the vexed concept of "aura" in his work. Perhaps the best account is still Marleen Stoessel, *Aura: Das vergessene Menschliche* (Munich, 1983).

81. Benjamin, "The Work of Art in the Age of Mechanical Reproduction," *Illuminations*; and "The Newspaper" (1934), in *Selected Writings*, vol. 2.

he acknowledged its abiding critical potential and worried about its complete extirpation. Thus, in 1939, he argued that "the replacement of the older narration by information, of information by sensation, reflects the increasing atrophy of experience. In turn, there is a contrast between all these forms and the story, which is one of the oldest forms of communication. It is not the object of the story to convey a happening *per se,* which is the purpose of information; rather it embeds it in the life of the storyteller in order to pass it on as experience to those listening."[82] Because it preserved the temporal distance between subject and object, while nonetheless linking the two, it resisted the collapse of experience into a momentary intensity without any narrative resonance. It was the latter that Benjamin identified with *Erlebnis* and whose pernicious effects he had seen in the *Lebensphilosophen* and Buber.

One of the earliest programmatic distinctions between two types of experience came in his 1929 essay on Hessel entitled "The Return of the *Flâneur,*" in which he wrote: "there is a kind of experience [*Erlebnis*] that craves the unique, the sensational, and another kind [*Erfahrung*] that seeks out eternal sameness."[83] Whereas the former were singular occurrences, unable to generate meaningful repetitions over time, the latter had durability. Understood in this sense, *Erfahrungen* were a far cry from the scientific or sensory experiences identified with that word—whether for praise or condemnation— by writers like Dilthey, Buber, and Cohen. Although not equivalent to dialectical experiences in the sense extolled by Hegel or Gadamer, which smacked too much of the ideology of *Bildung* Benjamin despised, they nonetheless had a narrative dimension. Walkers through the city resist the hectic impressionism of most travel writers, Benjamin explained; instead, like Hessel, they narrate rather than merely describe, repeating the stories they have been told since they were children, recalling memories that are not only their own. Hessel's *Spazieren in Berlin* is thus "an epic book through and through, a process of memorizing while strolling around, a book for which memory has not acted as the source but as the Muse. It goes along the streets in front of him, and each street is a vertiginous experience [*Erfahrung*]."[84]

By "epic book" Benjamin meant the kind of narrative that he identified with the storyteller and not the novelist. As he had explained in his 1930 review of Alfred Döblin's *Berlin Alexanderplatz*—an experimental work that he saw as the antithesis of the conventional novel—the novelist is a like a

82. Benjamin, "On Some Motifs in Baudelaire," *Illuminations,* p. 161.
83. Benjamin, "The Return of the *Flâneur,*" p. 266.
84. Ibid., p. 262.

solitary voyager on the sea, an isolated individual who "can no longer speak of his concerns in exemplary fashion, who himself lacks counsel and can give none. To write a novel is to take that which is incommensurable in the representation of human existence to the extreme."[85] In contrast, "in epics, people rest after their day's work; they listen, dream and collect."[86] Whereas novels draw on the interiority of their characters and author, epics narrate in paratactic form the exteriority of communal experience, preserving a sense of duration in their readers or listeners.[87] Only the dense texture of Döblin's montage, in which the author's idiosyncratic voice is replaced by the juxtaposition of the detritus of the modern city, can approximate the epic narration that traditional novels—the occasional exception like Gottfried Keller aside—had abandoned.[88]

By "memory . . . not as the source but as the Muse," Benjamin seems to have meant a mode of relating to the past that did not claim the ability to recapture retrospectively the entirety of what had preceded the present as if it were a single coherent plot. Memory in the sense of *Erinnerung,* or anamnestic reinteriorization of what had been alienated or reified, was too close to the Hegelian dialectics Benjamin always distrusted.[89] It was predicated on the existence of a collective subject of history, which recognizes itself in its objectifications over time, a premise he consistently rejected as too idealist. The experience that a Hessel or a Döblin is able to evoke is thus narrative, but not in the sense of an exfoliation of an idea from the author's subjective

85. Benjamin, "The Crisis of the Novel" (1930), in *Selected Works,* vol. 2, p. 299. Not even Marcel Proust, whose work he translated and clearly found stimulating, escaped this reproach. In his 1929 essay "On the Image of Proust," Benjamin would claim that "Proust's writing, too, has as its center a solitude which pulls the world down into its vortex with the force of a maelstrom. And the overload and inconceivably hollow chatter which comes roaring out of Proust's novels is the sound of society plunging into the abyss of this solitude." *Selected Works,* vol. 2, p. 245. In so radically distinguishing the epic (and its prose descendents, the story, the saga, proverb, and comic tale) from the novel, Benjamin implicitly criticizing Georg Lukács' famous definition of the novel as the "bourgeois epic" in *The Theory of the Novel.* For an attempt to salvage a dimension of the traditional novel that Benjamin ignored, which may nonetheless express something of what he thought was the *Erfahrung* in the epic, see my essay "Experience without a Subject: Walter Benjamin and the Novel," in *Cultural Semantics: Keywords of Our Time* (Amherst, Mass., 1998).

86. Benjamin, "The Crisis of the Novel," p. 299.

87. Although the stress on duration might seem to evoke Bergson's notion of *durée,* Benjamin objected to its presentist implications and smoothing over the historical gaps between past and present.

88. For Benjamin's appreciation of Keller, see his "Gottfried Keller" (1927), in *Selected Works,* vol. 2.

89. As a result Benjamin's version of memory was very different from that of another figure associated with the Frankfurt Institute, Herbert Marcuse. For an account of his belief in anamnestic totalization, see my *Marxism and Totality: The Adventures of a Concept from Lukács to Habermas* (Berkeley, 1984), chapter 7.

imagination, a hypotactic plot like that found in Hegel's dialectical history. It is instead an experience like that of the collector, who juxtaposes elements from the past, bringing together what has been scattered in new constellations. And if there were any doubt that such experiences are dependent on at least some residue of the aura, Benjamin quoted a passage from Hessel's work: "We see only what looks at us. We can do only . . . what we cannot help doing"; and added "the philosophy of the *flâneur* has never been more profoundly grasped than in these words of Hessel's."[90]

It was, of course, Baudelaire, who was the first to recognize the importance of the *flâneur* in the city Benjamin came to call "the capital of the nineteenth century": Paris. In "On Some Motifs in Baudelaire," contributed in 1939 to the Institut für Sozialforschung's journal *Zeitschrift für Sozialforschung,* he mined his ongoing Arcades Project to produce a pilot study for the book that was never finished. Benjamin's struggle to present his enormously complex and fluidly developing ideas in coherent form was not an easy one, as his now famous correspondence with Adorno over the project amply testifies.[91] It is therefore impossible to render his definitive position with complete confidence, but there can be no doubt that the question of experience was at its center.

Indeed, Benjamin was able to invoke *Erfahrung* in a surprisingly direct way in responding to Adorno's most serious criticism of the first draft of the essay, which reflected the latter's greater adherence to Hegelian dialectics: "the theological motif of calling things by their names tends to switch into the wide-eyed presentation of mere facts. . . . your study is at the crossroads of magic and positivism. This spot is bewitched."[92] Lacking explicit theoretical mediation, Adorno warned, the mere juxtaposition of materials produces "a deceptively epic character." Benjamin's answer was that "the appearance of closed facticity which attaches to philological investigation and places the investigator under its spell dissolves precisely to the degree in which the object is construed from a historical perspective. The base lines of this construction converge in our own historical experience."[93]

90. Benjamin, "The Return of the *Flâneur*," p. 265.
91. See, in particular, the exchanges beginning with Adorno's critical letter of November 10, 1938, in Benjamin and Adorno, *The Complete Correspondence.*
92. Ibid., p. 283.
93. Benjamin to Adorno, September 1, 1938, in *The Complete Correspondence,* p. 292. It should be noted that Adorno, for all his own lament about the withering of experience, could continue to use the term in the same straightforward way, as in his letter of February 1, 1939, where he says that his 1938 essay "The Fetish Character of Music and the Regression of Hearing" must be seen "essentially as an expression of my experiences here in America" (p. 305).

The implication of this response was that for all its atrophy and decay, some *Erfahrung* was still possible in the modern world, and indeed could be the basis for a critical method. And that experience could justifiably be called historical. But it could no longer be equated with mimetically recovering the ciphers of the absolute that Benjamin's earliest and more metaphysical writings had sought in astrology, graphology, and the nonsensuous similarities of translation. Now a more complicated process was needed, which combined passive and active moments and would both acknowledge the traumatic shocks of modern life and find a way to salvage them for a future realization of experience at its most redemptive.

Baudelaire, Benjamin argued, had been among the first to recognize and attempt to fend off those shocks, which were produced by life in the modern city—and the reduction of the craftsman's work to assembly-line production—in which the capitalist exchange principle dissolved traditional relationships and reduced everything into phantasmagoric commodities.[94] Baudelaire's lyric poetry courageously attempted to turn such *Erlebnisse* into *Erfahrungen,* moving beyond mere nostalgia for the decayed aura into a new way of dealing with the temporal gap between then and now. Heroically, his poems juxtaposed the language of modern life with the forms left by older poetic traditions and in so doing avoided the shallow optimism of bourgeois champions of progress. Instead, he bore witness to the shattered dreams of the past, making his heroism like that of the protagonists of the German baroque *Trauerspiel,* who mourned what was lost and knew that only allegorical rather than symbolic prefigurations of redemption were now possible in the fallen world of the present. His search for *correspondences* between the ephemeral and the eternal records "a concept of experience which includes ritual elements. Only by appropriating these elements was Baudelaire able to fathom the full meaning of the breakdown which he, a modern man, was witnessing."[95]

More precisely, Baudelaire—and here Benjamin was speaking of himself as well—maintained a melancholic relationship to the valued objects that were gone, rather than working them through in a process of completed

94. For an insightful analysis of this aspect of Benjamin's argument, see Gyorgy Markus, "Walter Benjamin; or, The Commodity as Phantasmagoria," *New German Critique* 83 (Spring–Summer 2001).

95. Benjamin, "On Some Motifs in Baudelaire," *Illuminations,* p. 183. Lindroos claims that the *correspondences* refer to a third variety of experience beyond *Erlebnis* and *Erfahrung* because it is based on the new forms of narration in modernist fiction, film montage, and photomontage. "Scattering Community," p. 29. I think it is perhaps better to see them as variations of the analogical and mimetic notion of *Erfahrungen* in Benjamin's earlier work.

mourning or wallowing in a nostalgia that remains on the level of an imaginary return home.[96] Some of the same melancholy was also abetted by an invention that Baudelaire in fact had mistakenly disdained: photography. The "optical unconscious" revealed by the photograph, Benjamin had already argued in his 1931 "Little History of Photography," exposed residues of a past reality that no amount of aesthetic transfiguration could obscure. "No matter how artful the photographer, no matter how carefully posed his subject, the beholder feels an irresistible urge to search such a picture for the tiny spark of contingency, of the here and now, with which reality has (so to speak) seared the subject, to find the inconspicuous spot where in the immediacy of that long-forgotten moment the future nests so eloquently that we, looking back, may rediscover it."[97] In other words, photography resisted the completed mastery of the past by the present, allowing the latter to disrupt the smooth surface of present consciousness and create an experience of the past very much like that sudden incursion we have seen Frank Ankersmit defend as historical experiences at their most sublime.[98] Not surprisingly, Benjamin would once again invoke Goethe's concept of "tender empiricism," the nondominating relationship with objects that he had employed in his analysis of mimesis, to characterize the work of one of his favorite Weimar photogra-

96. The distinction is nicely made by Angelika Rauch in *The Hieroglyph of Tradition: Freud, Benjamin, Gadamer, Novalis, Kant* (Madison, N.J., 2000). Melancholy, she notes, "differs from nostalgia in that it does not aspire to go where the other was. It does not regress to an imaginary place libidinally invested as home or maternal ground. If nostalgia signifies the pain of such a longing for another place and another time, the distance and separation between self and other is nonetheless keenly observed. In contrast, melancholy actively transports this other into the present and relocates it in the symbolic status this object or place may have in the here and now. If the other becomes part of the self, nostalgia remains on the level of the imaginary. Melancholy performs a cognitive act with respect to the past; it exhumes the past's potential for a symbolic sense in the future and for the very concept of a future" (p. 210).

97. Benjamin, "Little History of Photography," p. 510. Benjamin's praise for the impersonal photography of Eugène Atget as emancipating objects from their aura is another instance of his desire to make a virtue out of the decay of auratic experience.

98. In a personal communication on March 20, 2002, Ankersmit has acknowledged certain similarities between his position and Benjamin's understanding of photography. Although Benjamin did not stress the sublime, it is significant that he disdained the contemporary attempt by the *neue Sachlichkeit* photographer Albert Renger-Patsch to show that "the world is beautiful" (the title of one of his photo albums). This effort "succeeded in transforming even abject poverty—by apprehending it in a fashionably perfected manner—into an object of enjoyment." "The Author as Producer," p. 775. The parallel to Benjamin's celebrated critique of the Fascist aestheticization of politics is obvious.

For another analysis of the photography/history nexus in Benjamin, see Eduardo Cadava, *Words of Light: Theses on the Photography of History* (Princeton, 1997). See also Lindroos, "Scattering Community," for a discussion of the way in which Benjamin's evocation of past moments in images or text-fragments is intended to disrupt the smooth notion of the past as a totality that can be understood holistically (p. 32).

phers: August Sander.[99] By preserving a moment of the past in this manner, the possibility of a different future was also protected.

What the photograph could produce by imposing a residue of the past on the viewer was comparable, if in a less subjective register, to what Marcel Proust had understood as *mémoire involontaire,* emblematized by the evocative power of the madeleine at the beginning of *A la recherche du temps perdu.* Unlike the anamnestic totalization of *Erinnerung,* which assumed a collective maker and recollector of history with the ability to remember it all, such memory was closer to what in German is called *Eingedenken,* which Benjamin claimed suggested a certain forgetting as well as remembering, a willingness to move beyond personal, subjective experience to something larger. As he put it in his 1929 essay "The Image of Proust":

> The important thing to the remembering author is not what he experienced, but the weaving of his memory, the Penelope work of recollection [*Eingedenken*]. Or should one call it, rather, a Penelope work of forgetting? Is not the involuntary memory, Proust's *mémoire involontaire,* much closer to what is normally called forgetting than what is usually called memory?[100]

In that essay, Benjamin attributed Proust's Penelope-like labors to what he called an "elegiac" notion of happiness: "the eternal repetition, the eternal restoration of the original, first happiness," and added that it was demonstrated in the French author's "impassioned cult of similarity."[101]

Benjamin called memory constituted by unconscious traces of the past, which were then belatedly recoverable, *Gedächtnis,* a concept like *Eingedenken* that could be opposed to *Erinnerung.*[102] *Erlebnisse,* Benjamin claimed, were

99. Benjamin, "Little History of Photography," p. 520. This citation is then followed by an approving nod to the novelist Döblin for having understood the "scientific" implications of such photography.

100. Benjamin, "The Image of Proust," p. 238. One of the most helpful glosses on this term is provided by Rebecca Comay in "Benjamin's Endgame," in Benjamin and Osborne, *Walter Benjamin's Philosophy:* it means "precisely the *opposite* of the unifying inwardness of a thought affirming its self-actualization as a culture returning to itself in the recollection of its own formation or *Bildung* (the opposite, in a word, of the Hegelian *Erinnerung* which it lexically recalls)—Benjamin's *Eingedenken* is no longer strictly one or inward *(Ein-)* and no longer strictly thought *(-Denken).* It announces, rather, a mindfulness or vigilance which refuses to take in (or be taken in by) a tradition authorizing itself as the continuity of an essential legacy, task or mission to be transmitted, developed or enacted. . . . *Eingedenken* inaugurates repetition as the return of that which strictly speaking never happened: it announces the redemption of a failed revolutionary opportunity at the moment of most pressing danger" (p. 266).

101. Benjamin, "On the Image of Proust," p. 239.

102. Whether Freud himself made the contrast is not clear; Benjamin himself notes that there is no such distinction in *Beyond the Pleasure Principle.* See his remarks in "On Some Motifs in Baudelaire," p. 162. For a helpful comparison of Freud and Benjamin, see Rauch, *The Hieroglyph of Tradition,* chapter 1.

precisely those experiences that failed to leave such an emotionally laden trace—whether of an original moment of bliss or not—and thus were unable to be recollected involuntarily. "Only that which has not explicitly and consciously been experienced *(erlebt)*, what has not happened to the subject as experience *(Erlebnis)* can become a component of the *mémoire involontaire.*"[103] *Erfahrung,* in contrast, involved the ability to translate the traces of past events into present memories but also to register the temporal distance between now and then, acknowledge the inevitable belatedness of memory rather than smooth it over, and preserve an allegorical rather than symbolic relationship between past and present (and thus between present and potential future).

Benjamin's suggestive but in many ways underdeveloped ruminations on the relationships between modes of experience, the aura, memory, tradition, and the modern city were still generating questions from Adorno after the publication of his essay in the *Zeitschrift.* In an extensive letter written in February 29, 1940, Adorno expressed his enthusiasm for the revised version but wondered about the entirely unconscious quality of involuntary memories, claiming that what might be needed was a more dialectical approach. "Is it not the case," he asked,

> that the real task here is to bring the entire opposition between sensory experience *(Erlebnis)* and experience proper *(Erfahrung)* into relation with a dialectical theory of forgetting? Or one could equally say, into relation with a theory of reification? For all reification is a forgetting: objects become thinglike the moment they are retained for us when something of them is forgotten. This raises the question of how far this forgetting is one that is capable of shaping experience, which I would call epic forgetting, and how far it is a reflex forgetting.[104]

Because of the surprisingly salutary dimension of epic forgetting, it would be meaningful, Adorno continued while tacitly criticizing the Hegelian Marxism of a Lukács, to distinguish between a good and a bad reification, both of which are linked with the objectification of human labor. The former, he then speculated, might be connected to the persistence of the aura, a concept he complained had not been completely thought out by Benjamin. "Is not the aura," he asked, "invariably a trace of a forgotten human moment in the thing, and it is not directly connected, precisely by virtue of this forget-

---

103. Benjamin, "On Some Motifs in Baudelaire," p. 163.
104. Adorno to Benjamin, February 29, 1940, in *The Complete Correspondence,* p. 321.

ting with what you call 'experience' *(Erfahrung)?* One might even go so far as to regard the experiential ground which underlies the speculations of idealist thought as an attempt to retain this trace—and to retain it precisely in those things that have now become alien."[105]

On May 2, 1940, in the last substantive letter Benjamin was able to write before being overwhelmed by the events that cost him his life, he attempted to clarify his position. After agreeing that Adorno's work on the regression of hearing had complemented his own investigations of the destruction of experience, he provided the childhood anecdote about the true origin of his theory quoted at the beginning of this chapter. He then agreed to think more about the distinction between epic and reflex forgetting but resisted Adorno's suggestion that the aura and reification might have something to do with human labor. "The tree and the shrub which offer themselves to us are not made by human hands. There must therefore be something human in the things themselves, something that is *not* originated by labor."[106] And as for original childhood experiences, like the first taste of the madeleine involuntarily recalled by Proust, he insisted they were indeed unconscious.

Benjamin's premature death at the age of forty-eight ended his quest to displace his originally metaphysical and theological concept of experience into an entirely materialist register, if indeed this was the fundamental task he set himself. Benjamin may have wanted to salvage the redemptive project by secularizing it, but how successful he really was remains very much in dispute. Benjamin's critique of the impoverishment of experience—both conceptually in the guise of neo-Kantian scientific *Erfahrung* or vitalist *Erlebnis* and historically in the form of bourgeois subjectivity—has been frequently admired, and his search for a way beyond the dualism of subject and object has often struck a respondent chord. But the ultimately theological premises of his alternative have rarely been scrutinized with any rigor.[107] Nor have the anthropological underpinnings of his theory of mimesis.[108] Frankly dogmatic and based on a doctrinal belief in the Absolute, which could somehow manifest itself in mundane experience, Benjamin's maximalist definition of gen-

---

105. Ibid., p. 322.

106. Benjamin to Adorno, May 7, 1940, in *The Complete Correspondence,* p. 327.

107. One exception is the attempt by Jeffrey Mehlman in *Walter Benjamin for Children: An Essay on His Radio Years* (Chicago, 1993) to detect in his work a sinister residue of the Sabbatian heresy that did so much damage to early modern Jewish culture.

108. The anthropology of Spencer, Tylor, and Frazer with its belief in a primitive mimetic mentality has been criticized by G. E. R. Lloyd, *Demystifying Mentalities* (Cambridge, 1990). See also Stanley Tabiah, *Magic, Science, Religion and the Scope of Rationality* (Cambridge, 1990).

uine experience could only be a utopian counter-factual to virtually everything that is normally understood by the term. Seeking residues of it in such dubious practices as astrology and graphology did little to reassure the skeptics among his readers. Nor did many feel comfortable with the uncompromisingly anti-subjectivist impulse in his thought. Even Adorno would later remark: "Before his Medusan glance, man turns into the stage on which an objective process unfolds. For this reason Benjamin's philosophy is no less a source of terror than a promise of happiness. . . . one will search his writings in vain for a concept like autonomy."[109]

Benjamin's attribution of a magical residue of that Absolute in childhood experiences of color and the like also drew on a version of infant bliss that cried out for critical examination. Even if it were a plausible account of what children really experience, there was no obvious warrant for the expectation that it might somehow be continued in adulthood, no matter how idyllic life might become "after the Revolution." This doubt was particularly compelling when applied to Benjamin's hope that an Adamic language of names might somehow be restored and the "overnaming" of Babel brought to an end. As one of his most sympathetic readers, Giorgio Agamben, has pointed out, Benjamin's belief that language might itself be the site of redemptive experience comes up against the difficulty of looking in language for precisely what can only precede it. *"In terms of human infancy,"* Agamben writes, *"experience is the simple difference between the human and the linguistic. The individual as not already speaking, as having been and still being an infant—this is experience."*[110] That is, the redemptive notion of experience harkens back to a time before the fall into language—*in-fans* means "without language"—and history only begins with that fall. "In this sense, to experience necessarily means to re-accede to infancy as history's transcendental place of origin. The enigma which infancy ushered in for man can be dissolved only in history, just as experience, being infancy and human place of origin, is something he is always in the act of falling from, into language and into speech."[111] Even if one resists Agamben's identification of experience with prelinguistic bliss—it sounds, after all, suspiciously like one of the term's traditional antonyms, innocence—his warning against seeking it in linguistic terms is worth heeding. For might it not be the case that Babel is itself a salutary check on the

109. Adorno, "A Portrait of Walter Benjamin," *Prisms,* trans. Samuel and Shierry Weber (London, 1967), pp. 235–36.

110. Agamben, *Infancy and History,* p. 50 (emphasis in original).

111. Ibid., p. 53.

desire for a single meta-language, which coercively reduces plurality to a universal core?[112]

No less problematic are the implications of Benjamin's ambivalence about the decay of experience itself or his vagueness in providing a chronology for its decline. At certain moments, as we have seen, he expressed a palpable regret that "experience has fallen in value," yet at others he reveled in the opportunities opened up by its imminent disappearance. With the passage of time, Benjamin's gamble on the redemptive power of destruction, his apocalyptic reliance on a messianic "divine violence" that may appear in the proletarian general strike, seems increasingly like a dangerous expedient with little appeal.[113] It is not hard to understand why Benjamin might have thought in his "Theses on the Philosophy of History," written in that most desperate year, 1940, that to fight Fascism "our task is to bring about a real state of emergency."[114] But blank checks for the destructive characters who will "clear the space" for an alternative future are harder to cash in a world in which redemptive politics has lost much of its allure, save for those apocalyptic fundamentalists whose embrace of violence we have come to know all too well.[115]

ADORNO'S RESTITUTION OF THE NON-IDENTICAL DIALECTIC OF SUBJECT/OBJECT

Did Adorno's appropriation of Benjamin's theory of experience avoid some of the same pitfalls?[116] The first point to make in addressing this question is

112. For a subtle analysis of this issue, which draws on Derrida's reflections on Benjamin, see Hent de Vries, *Religion and Violence: Philosophical Perspectives from Kant to Derrida* (Baltimore, 2002), chapter 3.

113. Benjamin, "Critique of Violence" (1921), in *Selected Writings*, vol. 1. This essay with its echoes of Sorel and Schmitt has generated a vigorous debate in recent years, much abetted by Jacques Derrida's cautious discussion of it in "Force of Law: The 'Mystical Foundation of Authority'," *Cardozo Law Review* 11 (1990).

114. Benjamin, "Theses on the Philosophy of History," *Illuminations*, p. 259. The phrase "state of emergency" came from Carl Schmitt, whose influence on Benjamin's politics can still be found at this late date.

115. For my own gloss on this situation, see "Fin-de-siècle Socialism," in *Fin-de-siècle Socialism and Other Essays* (New York, 1989); and "The Paradoxes of Religious Violence," in *Refractions of Violence* (New York, 2003).

116. There is a considerable discussion in German of Adorno's concept of experience. See, for example, Hans-Hartmut Kappner, *Die Bildungstheorie Adornos als Theorie der Erfahrung von Kultur und Kunst* (Frankfurt, 1984); Peter Kalkowski, *Adornos Erfahrung: Zur Kritik der Kritischen Theorie* (Frankfurt, 1988); and Anke Thyen, *Negative Dialektik und Erfahrung: Zur Rationalität des Nichtidentischen bei Adorno* (Frankfurt, 1989).

that Adorno never displayed the ambivalence that we have seen in Benjamin about the decay of experience; there was none of the wishful thinking about the opportunities opened up for radical renewal evident in such essays as "Experience and Poverty." Adorno never celebrated the liberating power of new technologies in themselves, nor sought to hasten the "emergency situation" to its apocalyptic end. Surviving the Second World War and the Holocaust reinforced his earlier caution when it came to radical political solutions of any kind. For him, the crisis of experience was only a source of lamentation.

The second point to acknowledge is that, despite these differences, virtually all of Adorno's animadversions on the putative decay of experience were directly borrowed from formulae we have already encountered in Benjamin. The latter's exaltation of the child's vision of color would, for example, reappear in Adorno's claim in *Negative Dialectics,* published in 1966, that "the resistance to the fungible world of barter is the resistance of the eye that does not want the colors of the world to fade."[117] He would likewise adopt Benjamin's fascination for the magic of place names for children in the following description of "metaphysical experience" also from *Negative Dialectics:*

> If we disdain projecting it upon allegedly primal religious experiences, we are most likely to visualize it as Proust did, in the happiness, for instance, that is promised by village names like Applebachsville, Wind Gap, or Lords Valley. One thinks that going there would bring fulfillment, as if there were such a thing. . . . To the child it is self-evident that what delights him in his favorite village is found only there, there alone and nowhere else. He is mistaken; but his mistake creates the model of experience, of a concept that will end up as the concept of the thing itself, not as a poor projection onto things.[118]

Adorno's normative notion of experience was clearly derived, if at a certain distance, from the theological premises of Benjamin's concept of "absolute experience." Whether understood as a "negative theology," a "theology in brackets," "a theology in pianissimo," a "figure of theology," or only a "cryptotheology," to cite a few of the many attempts to characterize it, Adorno's ultimate plea was, as he put it in one of the most frequently quoted passages in all of his work, to regard the world "from the standpoint of redemption."[119] And like Benjamin, he resisted the reduction of the theological notion of ex-

117. Adorno, *Negative Dialectics,* trans. E. B. Ashton (New York, 1973), p. 405.
118. Ibid., p. 373 (translation emended).
119. Adorno, *Minima Moralia: Reflections from Damaged Life,* trans. E. F. N. Jephcott (London, 1974), p. 247.

perience to the subjective version we have seen in Schleiermacher and others. In fact, in his critique of the American right-wing demagogue Martin Luther Thomas, written at the same time as he was involved in the preparation of *The Authoritarian Personality,* he would go so far as to say that "the basis for the fascist manipulation of religious subjectivism for political, ultimately anti-religious purposes is the stressing of personal experience as against any objectified doctrine. . . . the appeal to immediate, personal religious experience means a weakening of rational control, as represented by coherent religious doctrines."[120]

So too, Benjamin's pathos about the decline of experience in the modern world was repeated in many different places in his friend's work. In "The Position of the Narrator in the Contemporary Novel," included in his *Notes to Literature,* Adorno wrote: "The identity of experience in the form of a life that is articulated and possesses internal continuity—and that life was the only thing that made the narrator's stance possible—has disintegrated. One need only note how impossible it would be for someone who participated in the war to tell stories about it the way people used to tell stories about their adventures."[121] In *Minima Moralia,* his personal "reflections from damaged life," he would claim that the war is

> as totally divorced from experience as is the functioning of a machine from the movement of the body, which only begins to resemble it in pathological states. Just as the war lacks continuity, history, an "epic" element, but seems rather to start anew from the beginning in each phase, so it will leave behind no permanent, unconsciously preserved image in the memory. . . . Life has changed into a timeless succession of shocks, interspersed with empty, paralyzed intervals. . . . The total obliteration of the war by information, propaganda commentaries, with cameramen in the first tanks and war reporters dying heroic deaths, the mishmash of enlightened manipulation of public opinion and oblivious activity: all this is another expression for the withering of experience, the vacuum between men and their fate, in which their real fate lies.[122]

Here the war in question was the Second World War, not the First, but Adorno was simply rehearsing the points Benjamin had made about its predecessor.

120. Adorno, *The Psychological Technique of Martin Luther Thomas' Radio Addresses* (Stanford, 2000), pp. 89–90.

121. Adorno, "The Position of the Narrator in the Contemporary Novel," in *Notes to Literature,* vol. 2, trans. Shierry Weber Nicholsen (New York, 1992), p. 31.

122. Adorno, *Minima Moralia,* pp. 54–55.

Likewise, in his 1960 essay "Presuppositions," Adorno would claim that in the modernist writing of James Joyce and Proust one can see "the dying out of experience, something that ultimately goes back to the atemporal technified process of the production of material goods."[123] And in his essay of the previous year, "Theory of Pseudo-Culture," he would complain that experience, which he defined in almost Burkean terms as "the continuity of consciousness in which everything not present survives, in which practice and association establish tradition in the individual," has now been "replaced by the selective, disconnected, interchangeable and ephemeral state of being in-formed which, as one can already observe, will promptly be cancelled by other information."[124] Indeed, as late as his posthumously published final work, *Aesthetic Theory*, Adorno could still write, "The marrow of experience has been sucked out; there is none, not even that apparently set at a remove from commerce, that has not been gnawed away."[125]

Attempts to revive a robust variety of experience in the present, Adorno would moreover argue, are doomed to failure, especially when they seek to recover a purported *ur*-experience that is somehow deeper than the media-tions of culture and society. In *The Jargon of Authenticity*, he would mock efforts by latter-day adepts of *Lebensphilosophie* to re-enchant the world:

> The contrast between primal experiences and cultural experiences, which [Friedrich] Gundolf invented *ad hoc*, for [Stefan] George, was ideology in the midst of superstructure, devised for the purpose of obscuring the contrast be-tween infrastructure and ideology. . . . [Ernst] Bloch rightfully made fun of Gundolf for his belief in today's primal experiences. These primal experiences were a warmed-over piece of expressionism. They were later made into a per-manent institution by Heidegger. . . . In the universally mediated world everything experienced in primary terms is culturally preformed.[126]

Not only did Adorno scorn the vitalist reduction of experience to *Erleb-nis*, he also shared Benjamin's hostility to the scientistic alternatives in neo-Kantianism or positivism. As early as 1936, when he was at Merton College, Oxford, he could advise Max Horkheimer, who was writing an essay on the

123. Adorno, "Presuppositions: On the Occasion of a Reading by Hans G. Helms," in *Notes to Liter-ature*, vol. 2, p. 101.

124. Adorno, "Theory of Pseudo-Culture," *Telos* 95 (Spring 1993), p. 33.

125. Adorno, *Aesthetic Theory*, ed. Gretel Adorno and Rolf Tiedemann, trans. Robert Hullot-Kentor (Minneapolis, 1997), p. 31.

126. Adorno, *The Jargon of Authenticity*, trans. Knut Tarnowski and Frederic Will (London, 1973), p. 99.

current fad of neo-positivism, that: "one must analyze the experience concept of the new positivism. It will be especially important for you to pursue the ambivalence of the concept of experience from the very beginning of bourgeois thought. While in Bacon it was intended to be thoroughly progressive, by Hobbes, it already had the opposite orientation to the power of unalterable crude facts."[127] As such, it promoted skepticism towards both theory and an emphatic concept of truth, and thus abetted relativism and the acceptance of the status quo. Twenty-five years later, he would expand the reproach in his introduction to *The Positivist Dispute in German Sociology:*

> The regimented experience prescribed by positivism nullifies experience itself and, in its intention, eliminates the experiencing subject. The correlate of indifference towards the object is abolition of the subject, without whose spontaneous receptivity, however, nothing objective emerges. As a social phenomenon, positivism is geared to the human type that is devoid of experience and continuity, and it encourages the latter—like Babbitt—to see himself as the crown of creation.[128]

And against the attempt by phenomenologists to salvage a more essential and ontological notion of experience, Adorno would argue that in Husserl, "what is thought becomes essence through the isolation of individual 'acts' and 'lived experiences' *(Erlebnisse)* over against an experience *(Erfahrung)* which, as a whole has by this time practically disappeared from the field of vision of his philosophy. The decaying individual is just the content of lived experiences which are touted as surrogates of concrete experience, but no longer have control over such experience itself."[129] By abstracting an isolated moment from reified existence and giving it the dignity of the universal, Husserl had merely elevated the subjectivism he sought to replace into a transcendental notion of truth. Even the prereflective *Lebenswelt* in Husserl's later thought, which phenomenologists would often see as a powerful tool in exploring the world of experience because of its over-

127. Adorno to Horkheimer, November 28, 1936, in Horkheimer, *Gesammelte Schriften,* ed. Gunzelin Schmid Noerr, vol. 15 (Frankfurt, 1995), p. 759. Horkheimer was writing at the time the essay "Der neuste Angriff auf die Metaphysik," *Zeitschrift für Sozialforschung* 6 (1937).

128. Adorno, introduction to Adorno and others, *The Positivist Dispute in German Sociology,* trans. Glyn Adey and David Frisby (London, 1976), pp. 57–58.

129. Adorno, *Against Epistemology: A Metacritique,* trans. Willis Domingo (Cambridge, Mass., 1983), p. 91. Husserl had treated the question of experience most explicitly in his *Experience and Judgment: Investigations in a Genealogy of Logic,* ed. Ludwig Landgrebe, trans. James M. Churchill and Karl Ameriks (Evanston, Ill., 1973).

coming the Cartesian dualism of subject and object, was far too ahistorical for Adorno.[130]

In comparison with Benjamin, in fact, Adorno expressed greater caution about the ways in which ciphers of redemption manifested themselves in the modern world. Although he took seriously Benjamin's defense of mimesis—indeed it served as a fundamental assumption of his own philosophy[131]—Adorno never endorsed Benjamin's search for its presence through such methods as graphology or astrology. In his correspondence over the Arcades Project, he fretted over the danger of using Ludwig Klages in a mythical way, which he compared with the problematic psychology of Carl Gustav Jung.[132] And as demonstrated in the aphorism called "Theses against Occultism" in *Minima Moralia* and the extensive 1953 study, entitled "The Stars Down to Earth," that he devoted to the *Los Angeles Times* astrology column, Adorno resolutely scorned the ideological function of horoscopes and other magical thinking.[133]

Adorno also resisted the temptation, to which Benjamin sometimes succumbed, to turn radical politics into an effective vehicle for the recovery of genuine experience. Unlike those champions of political experience for its own sake, whose celebration of *politique pour la politique* we encountered in chapter 5, he preferred to think of theory as itself a form of praxis.[134] Although an endless source of controversy during his last years, this position reflected his deep pessimism about the crisis of experience, which he claimed had survived in displaced form only in critical theory and certain works of art.

Accordingly, Adorno moved away from Benjamin in showing a far greater sympathy for Hegel's conceptualization of experience, which demonstrated his links with the other Frankfurt School philosophers.[135] Perhaps the differ-

130. For a typical phenomenological account of the virtues of Husserl's later work for a theory of experience, see Calvin O. Schrag, *Experience and Being: Prolegomena to a Future Metaphysics* (Evanston, Ill., 1969), pp. 42–44.

131. For my own attempt to explore this issue, which has references to the extensive prior literature on it, see "Mimesis and Mimetology: Adorno and Lacoue-Labarthe," in *Cultural Semantics*.

132. Adorno to Benjamin, August 2–August 4, 1935, and September 22, 1937, in Benjamin and Adorno, *The Complete Correspondence*, pp. 107 and 212.

133. Adorno, "Theses against Occultism," *Minima Moralia*, and *The Stars Down to Earth and Other Essays on the Irrational in Culture*, ed. Stephen Crook (New York, 1994).

134. For two sympathetic attempts to sort out the political implications of his work, see Russell Berman, "Adorno's Politics," and Henry W. Pickford, "The Dialectic of Theory and Practice: On Late Adorno," in Nigel Gibson and Andrew Rubin, eds., *Adorno: A Critical Reader*, eds. (Oxford, 2002).

135. One commentator, Brian O'Connor, goes so far as to claim that "Adorno's concept of experience is largely indebted to the version offered by Hegel in the Introduction to the *Phenomenology of Spirit*." See the introduction to O'Connor, ed., *The Adorno Reader* (Oxford, 2000), p. 11. But he then adds that the key difference between them is that "whereas Hegel presents experience as an irrevocable process,

ence between their two positions is best shown in Adorno's defense of Hegel against the attack launched by Martin Heidegger in the latter's *Holzwege* of 1950.[136] Taking a brief tour through this territory will allow us to understand more fully the subtle distinction between Adorno and Benjamin's notions of experience, as well as give us an opportunity to consider, if only fleetingly, Heidegger's own contribution to the discussion of this vexed term.

It would, of course, be a mistake to conflate Benjamin and Heidegger, who were in many respects very different—for example, in their attitude toward the political implications of the decay of the aura (Benjamin ambivalently welcomed it, while Heidegger wanted the aura restored). But on the issue of experience they shared many similar inclinations.[137] Both were, for example, hostile to the privileging of immediate "lived experience," or *Erlebnis*, in *Lebensphilosophie;* both were against the reduction of experience to an epistemological category in the Kantian or empiricist sense; and both were anxious to transcend psychologistic subjectivism and restore a notion of experience prior to the split between subject and object. And finally, Heidegger, like Benjamin, was determined to return to more fundamental levels of truth, whether they be called the metaphysical absolute or the ontological real, than the tradition of disenchanted, secular humanism or idealist metaphysics had allowed.

In *Holzwege,* Heidegger juxtaposed passages from Hegel's *Phenomenology of Spirit* with extended commentaries on their significance. He highlighted the fact that Hegel had first called the work "Science of the Experience of Consciousness," and argued that his version of phenomenology was still

---

Adorno argues that it is absent from those who cannot perceive the contradiction which clearly shapes their lives" (p. 13).

136. The relevant section is translated as Martin Heidegger, *Hegel's Concept of Experience* (New York, 1970). For a suggestive commentary, see Robert Bernasconi, *The Question of Language in Heidegger's History of Being* (Atlantic Highlands, N.J., 1986), chapter 6.

137. All of Benjamin's recorded reactions to Heidegger were critical; Heidegger seems to have been unaware of Benjamin's work. Nonetheless, similarities between Heidegger and Benjamin were first stressed by Hannah Arendt in her controversial introduction to Benjamin, *Illuminations.* For more recent attempts to see parallels, as well as some distinctions, see Howard Caygill, "Benjamin, Heidegger and the Destruction of Tradition," and Andrew Benjamin, "Time and Task: Benjamin and Heidegger Showing the Present," in Andrew Benjamin and Peter Osborne, eds., *Walter Benjamin's Philosophy: Destruction and Experience* (London, 1994); and Willem van Reijin, *Der Schwarzwald und Paris: Heidegger and Benjamin* (Munich, 1998) and Christopher P. Long, "Art's Fateful Hour: Benjamin, Heidegger, Art and Politics," *New German Critique* 83 (Spring–Summer 2001). For discussions of the differences between the two, see Wolin, *Walter Benjamin: An Aesthetic of Redemption,* p. 102; and Hanssen, *Walter Benjamin's Other History,* p. 2.

deeply indebted to that project. Heidegger foregrounded Hegel's non-commonsensical definition of experience, which reads as follows: "this *dialectical* movement, which consciousness exercises on itself—on its knowledge as well as its object—is, *in so far as the new, true object emerges to consciousness* as the result of it, precisely that which is called *experience*."[138] Glossing this passage, Heidegger claimed that Hegel means by "experience" the "Being of beings. . . . Experience now is the word of Being, since Being is apprehended by way of beings *qua* beings."[139] Here he seemed to be assimilating Hegel's position to his own.

But then Heidegger added that for Hegel, "Experience designates the subject's subjectness. Experience expresses what *'being'* in the term 'being conscious' means—in such a way that only by this 'being' does it become clear and binding what the word 'conscious' leaves still to thought."[140] Thus, Hegel's notion of experience remains hostage to that fateful privileging of the subject that Heidegger found so distressing in modern metaphysics. This bias is revealed, Heidegger continued, because experience for Hegel involved the presentation of an appearance for a consciousness, a manifestation of being to a subject in the present. In fact, Hegel's dialectical method is itself grounded in a still subjective view of experience: "Hegel does not conceive of experience dialectically," Heidegger wrote, "he thinks of dialectic in terms of the nature of experience. Experience is the beingness of beings, whose determination, *qua subjectum,* is determined in terms of subjectness."[141] The ultimate subject for Hegel is, of course, the Absolute Spirit. Thus, Heidegger claimed that for Hegel, "experience is the subjectness of the absolute subject. Experience, the presentation of the absolute representation, is the *parousia* of the Absolute. Experience is the absoluteness of the Absolute, its appearance in absolving appearance to itself."[142]

Heidegger conceded that Hegel understood natural consciousness to lack this more exalted, metaphysical notion of experience, because it ignores the deeper question of Being. But the way in which the Hegelian Absolute exteriorizes itself and re-collects itself at a higher level produces the questionable claim that the experience of consciousness lends itself to a post facto scientific recapitulation. Significantly, Heidegger pointed out, "experience" occupies the middle position between "science" and "consciousness" in the

138. Heidegger, *Hegel's Concept of Experience,* p. 112 (emphasis in original).
139. Ibid., p. 114.
140. Ibid.
141. Ibid., p. 119.
142. Ibid., pp. 120–21.

title "Science of the Experience of Consciousness," which indicates that for Hegel, "experience, as the being of consciousness, is in itself the inversion by which consciousness presents itself in its appearance. That is to say: in making the presentation, experience is science."[143]

Heidegger concluded by speculating on the reasons Hegel dropped this original title shortly before the book was published and substituted "phenomenology of spirit" instead. Noting that for Kant, "experience" had merely meant "the only possible theoretical knowledge of what is," he hazarded the guess that Hegel had found it too daring to restore an earlier meaning: "a reaching out and attaining, and attaining as the mode of being present, of εἶναί, of Being."[144] Perhaps because of this failure of nerve, Hegel had not quite attained the level of insight into Being that Heidegger ascribed to his own thought. His sympathetic interpreter Robert Bernasconi summarizes the essential differences between the two thinkers in the following terms: "'Experience' in Heidegger does not have the sense of a progressive development as it has in Hegel. For Heidegger, experience almost always takes place in the face of a lack. . . . For the phenomenological thinking of Heidegger, a lack or default gives access to Being. . . . The difference between Hegel's concept of experience and Heidegger's is that the former is tied to the rule of presencing and the latter commemorates it. Phenomenology for Hegel is a *parousia*, whereas for Heidegger it is letting the nonapparent appear as nonapparent."[145]

Commemorating what has been lost—the oblivion of Being in Heidegger's case—rather than celebrating presence as the cumulative realization of a successful dialectical process, is reminiscent of Benjamin's critique of Hegelian memory as *Erinnerung*, a too harmonious re-membering in the present of what had been sundered in the past. A commonality between Heidegger and Benjamin might also be found in the recognition in both their work of the etymological link between *Erfahrung* and *Gefahr*, the danger that must be encountered in the perilous journey that is experience (which, it bears repeating, has the Latin *experiri* in its root, giving us as well the English word "peril"), a danger that in the modern period is perhaps best revealed in the context of technology with its destructive as well as emancipatory potential.

143. Ibid., p. 139.

144. Ibid., p. 143.

145. Bernasconi, *The Question of Language in Heidegger's History of Being*, pp. 83–85. For another analysis, see Walter Lammi, "Hegel, Heidegger, and Hermeneutical Experience," in Shaun Gallagher, ed., *Hegel, History, and Interpretation* (Albany, N.Y., 1997). Lammi argues that Gadamer salvages Hegel's notion of experience from Heidegger's misreadings.

And both thinkers were arguably at one in their dissatisfaction with Hegel's contention that knowledge or science *(Wissenschaft)* can be perfectly reconciled with experience, an assumption that rests, as Gadamer was to claim in *Truth and Method,* on the solipsistic nature of the Hegelian subject who ultimately absorbs into himself the object and never really has an encounter with what is truly different and alien to him.[146]

Such an encounter was, of course, also the earmark of Adorno's Negative Dialectics, which sought to avoid idealism's coercive sublation of difference and to preserve the non-identity of subject and object. We can now return to the question of Adorno's debts to Benjamin and subtle departures from him with a deeper appreciation of the stakes involved. Adorno's own interpretation of Hegel's notion of experience was designed to resist the ontological distortions of Heidegger's *Holzwege* and read Hegel against the grain, finding in him what both Heidegger and Benjamin had claimed he had denied. Adorno deliberately began the essay entitled "The Experiential Content of Hegel's Philosophy," first published in 1959 and included in the 1963 collection *Hegel: Three Studies,* by distancing himself from Heidegger's reading:

> The concept [of experience] is not intended to capture phenomenological 'ur-experience'; nor, like the interpretation of Hegel in Heidegger's *Holzwege,* is it intended to get at something ontological. . . . His thought would never have ratified Heidegger's claim that 'The new object that arises for consciousness in the course of its formation' is 'not just anything that is true, or any particular being, but is the truth of what is true, the Being of Beings, the appearance of appearance.' Hegel would have never called that experience; instead for Hegel, what experience is concerned with at any particular moment is the animating contradiction of such absolute truth.[147]

If experience for Hegel is more than the presubjective "event" or "appropriation" *(Ereignis* in Heidegger's special lexicon) of Being, it is also not the unmediated sense perception assumed by empiricists like Hume. Experience is not for Hegel something undergone by the isolated individual, but entails the interdependency of subjects with each other and with the world. Nor, and this is even more important, is it equivalent to the science of knowledge, the *Wissenschaft* that was its tombstone: "by no means does the experiential content of idealism simply coincide with its epistemological and metaphys-

146. Hans-Georg Gadamer, *Truth and Method* (New York, 1986), pp. 318–19.

147. Adorno, *Hegel: Three Studies,* trans. Shierry Weber Nicholsen (Cambridge, Mass., 1993), p. 53.

ical positions."[148] Tacitly respecting the limits on knowledge placed by Kant even as he ultimately hoped to overcome them, Hegel identified experience precisely with the obstacles to full transparency presented by the contradictions in reality, not merely in thought. According to Adorno, Nietzsche's claim that "there is nothing in reality that would correspond strictly with logic"[149] captures Hegel's notion of experience better than attempts, such as those of orthodox dialectical materialists, to impose dialectical reason onto the world without remainder.

Hegel, to be sure, had wrongly thought his philosophy could ultimately encompass the whole and reveal its truth. But, Adorno argued, "even where Hegel flies in the face of experience, including the experience that motivates his own philosophy, experience speaks from him. . . . the idea of a positivity that can master everything that opposes it through the superior power of a comprehending spirit is the mirror image of the experience of the superior coercive force inherent in everything that exists by virtue of its consolidation under domination. This is the truth in Hegel's untruth."[150] Another unintended truth, one with a very different implication, is revealed, Adorno continued in a later essay on Hegel's opaque style,[151] in the tension between his desire to work entirely with concepts adequate to their objects and the linguistic medium through which he necessarily expressed them. That is, "in Hegel the expressive element represents experience; that which actually wants to come out into the open, but cannot, if it wants to attain necessity, appear except in the medium of concepts, which is fundamentally its opposite. . . . The whole of Hegel's philosophy is an effort to translate intellectual experience into concepts."[152] But the medium of its expression inevitably interferes with this goal, for "thought, which necessarily moves away from the text, from what is said, has to return to it and become condensed within it. John Dewey, a contemporary thinker who for all his positivism is closer to Hegel than their two alleged standpoints are to one another, called his philosophy 'experimentalism.' Something of this stance is appropriate for the reader of Hegel."[153]

Adorno's surprising reference to Dewey, whose pragmatism the Frankfurt School often disparaged, suggests a certain countercurrent in Adorno's

148. Ibid., p. 61.
149. Ibid., p. 76.
150. Ibid., p. 87.
151. Adorno, "Skoteinos; or, How to Read Hegel," in *Hegel: Three Studies.*
152. Ibid., p. 138.
153. Ibid., p. 144.

thought to his own lament about the virtually complete withering of experience, for Dewey was cautiously optimistic about the possibilities of genuine experience at the present time. Adorno, to be sure, resisted Dewey's identification of "experiment" with its scientific variety, preferring instead the literary essay, which "invests experience with as much substance as traditional theory does mere categories."[154] But that substance, he claimed, involves an opening to what is new, rather than a ratification of what has been. "What Kant saw, in terms of content as the goal of reason, the creation of humankind, utopia, is hindered by the form of his thought, epistemology. It does not permit reason to go beyond the realm of experience which, in the mechanism of mere material and invariant categories, shrinks to what has always already existed. The essay's object, however, is the new in its newness, not as something that can be translated back into the old existing forms."[155]

If Adorno shared with Dewey a belief that some sort of experimentation pointing toward the renewal of experience was possible even in the totalizing system of domination that he saw as the sinister reversal of Hegel's dictum that the "whole was the true," he also agreed that aesthetic experience in particular was its privileged laboratory. In such works as *Art as Experience* of 1934, "the unique and truly free John Dewey," as Adorno once called him, had ruminated on the significance of aesthetic experience as a model for a more general mode of unalienated existence.[156] Although it has sometimes been argued, most notably by Hans Robert Jauss,[157] that Adorno's own understanding of aesthetic experience was too negatively ascetic and lacking an appreciation of the communicative function of art even in the present "administered world," it is clear that he shared with Dewey an appreciation of the utopian moment in that experience.

This is not the place to attempt a full-fledged analysis of what Adorno meant by aesthetic experience, but several points warrant emphasis.[158] First of all, it should be understood that contrary to the image of him as a man-

154. Adorno, "The Essay as Form," in *Notes to Literature*, vol. 1, p. 10. Adorno explicitly identifies his position with that of Montaigne against the fetish of method in early modern science.

155. Ibid., p. 21. In this passage Adorno seems to forget the redemptive notion of experience he inherited from Benjamin and uses the term instead to refer only to the epistemological synthetic a priori judgments of Kant's First Critique.

156. Adorno, *Aesthetic Theory*, p. 335; John Dewey, *Art as Experience* (New York, 1934).

157. Hans Robert Jauss, *Aesthetic Experience and Literary Hermeneutics*, trans. Michael Shaw (Minneapolis, 1982), pp. 13–22.

158. For helpful recent discussions, see Shierry Weber Nicholsen, *Exact Imagination, Late Work: On Adorno's Aesthetics* (Cambridge, Mass., 1997); and Thomas Huhn and Lambert Zuidervaart, eds., *The Semblance of Subjectivity: Essays on Adorno's Aesthetic Theory* (Cambridge, Mass., 1997).

darin elitist, Adorno never considered aesthetic experiences, even those engendered by the most advanced modernist art, as if they were an entirely protected sphere in which the horrors of modern life were somehow successfully kept at bay. As he once wrote in an essay on the great nineteenth-century realist novel *Lost Illusions,* "Balzac knows that artistic experience is not pure, official aesthetics to the contrary; that it can hardly be pure if it is to be experience."[159] Aesthetic experience, at least in this usage, which we might call descriptive rather than normative, is necessarily impure, because it is damaged by the changes outside art to which we have already alluded: modern warfare, the replacement of narrative by information, alienating technology, and capitalist industrialization. By itself, it cannot bring back the world of Benjamin's storyteller. Its truth content, Adorno always emphasized, thus had to be brought out by an accompanying philosophical *cum* social theoretical analysis that provided the critical discursive tools that art inevitably lacked.

But it is also the case that for Adorno, aesthetic experience, however maimed, can preserve a certain trace of what existed before, which somehow has not been completely obliterated. Here he employed "experience" in an explicitly normative sense. Proust, Adorno claimed, was able to provide an almost Hegelian model of that preservation, for in his work, "undamaged experience is produced only in memory, far beyond immediacy, and through memory aging and death seem to be overcome in the aesthetic image. But this happiness achieved through the rescue of experience, a happiness that will not let anything be taken from it, represents an unconditional renunciation of consolation."[160]

Genuine experience, experience worth rescuing from the damaged variety of modern life, is thus closely tied to the memory of happiness, whose faint promise to return is what art is able to offer, as Stendhal, Nietzsche, and Herbert Marcuse had argued. Against Kantian notions of contemplative disinterestedness and the elevation of taste or judgment above the objects that produce an experience, Adorno insisted on the precedence of the object and its promise to provide genuine gratification. Although necessarily a semblance of such a mimetic paradise and not the real thing—indeed precisely because it is such a semblance and knows itself as such—art gestures toward the hap-

159. Adorno, "On an Imaginary Feuilleton," in *Notes to Literature,* vol. 2, p. 33. In *Aesthetic Theory,* he makes a similar point: "no particular aesthetic experience occurs in isolation, independently of the continuity of experiencing consciousness. . . . The continuity of aesthetic experience is colored by all other experience and all knowledge, though, of course, it is only confirmed and corrected in the actual confrontation with the phenomenon" (pp. 268–69).

160. Adorno, "On Proust," in *Notes to Literature,* vol. 2, p. 317.

piness of genuine metaphysical experience, which the current world denies and the merely epistemological concept cannot even envisage. It does so paradoxically through its mimesis of the other, which resists reduction to subjective constitution and protects some of the enigmatic quality of objects that go beyond the intentionality of subjects. Experience, despite its often being understood in subjective terms alone, comes only with an encounter with otherness in which the self no longer remains the same. To be undamaged, that experience must treat the other in a non-dominating, non-subsumptive, non-homogenizing manner, as if it were a proper name referring only to itself and not serving as a token of something else. This was the role of mimesis, understood as more than that faithful reproduction of the world as it is, favored by realist or naturalist aesthetics.

For this reason, the preservation of the concrete, particular, autonomous art object is an absolutely crucial dimension of aesthetic experience rightly understood, which means that the lament about the vanishing of the object and the hypertrophy of the subject expressed by critics like Murray Krieger and Michael Fried, discussed in chapter 4, is based on a one-sided understanding of experience as only *Erlebnis*. Or rather, it reflects the reduction of experience in the modern world to mere *Erlebnis,* which has even infected the realm of art. Art should not be understood as an expression of the artist's personal *Erlebnis,* which is then able to provoke a comparable lived experience in the reader, beholder or listener. Instead, it should be understood to transcend the artist's emotional state and be able to arouse a feeling of concern *(Betroffenheit)* in the recipient, which follows from the shudder or tremor *(Erschütterung)* he or she feels from the work itself. "The experience of art as that of its truth or untruth is more than subjective experience. It is the irruption of objectivity into subjective consciousness. The experience is mediated through subjectivity precisely at the point where the subjective reaction is most intense," Adorno insisted.[161] Such an intense shudder registers the painful liquidation of the ego in modernity, but it is also a protest against it. Adorno's dialectical imagination, in short, prevented him from abandoning the hope that aesthetic encounters with art objects might also contain prefigurations of genuine *Erfahrung.*

Can such encounters, however, be with what Benjamin called "the absolute" in his earliest writings on colors? Certainly, some of the pathos of that claim clings to many of Adorno's statements about experience and its decay, which are written from what the last aphorism in *Minima Moralia* called "the stand-

161. Adorno, *Aesthetic Theory,* pp. 244–45.

point of redemption." We have already noted the claim in *Negative Dialectics* that resistance to the world of exchange "is the resistance of the eye that does not want the colors of the world to fade." As a result, some commentators have ignored Adorno's attempts to distance himself from "allegedly primal religious experiences," and decried what they see as the "mystical" underpinnings of his concept of experience.[162]

But what indicates the inadequacy of such a reading, and by extension suggests that Adorno was not entirely happy with Benjamin's formulation of the problem, is his unwillingness to go all the way toward what can be called "experience without a subject," that moment of equiprimordiality prior to the split between self and other. Agamben has noted in his essays on the destruction of experience, *Infancy and History,* that "in Proust there is no longer really any subject. . . . Here the expropriated subject of experience emerges to validate what, from the point of view of science, can appear only as the most radical negation of experience: an experience with neither subject nor object, absolute."[163] Adorno, as we have seen, may have approvingly invoked Proust's preservation of childhood happiness through memory, but he did not embrace the ideal of absolute experience in which neither subject nor object was preserved. As his disdain for Heidegger's appropriation of Hegel's "science of the experience of consciousness" for his own project of the recollection of Being illustrates, Adorno was loath to short-circuit a negative dialectic that preserved some distinction between the two. His resistance to what he called Benjamin's "Medusan glance" meant a sensitivity to the importance of retaining some notion of a subject, no matter how debased that concept had become in modern life. The unsublatable dialectic of art and philosophy, like those between mimesis and construction or concept and object, suggests that even the most metaphysical of experiences for Adorno could not be reduced to perfect reconciliation or the restoration of equiprimordiality. Despite his occasional mobilizing of the rhetoric of Adamic names, as in the passage quoted from *Negative Dialectics* above, Adorno never relied on mimesis alone to provide the model of realized utopia. Without rationality, mimesis would become little more than the mimicry of the natural world, especially its inanimate and ossified dimensions.

But such an acknowledgment still does not answer a crucial question: is there a crisis of experience that can be understood in genuinely historical

162. Kalkowski, *Adornos Erfahrung,* pp. 110–11.
163. Agamben, *Infancy and History,* p. 42.

terms, involving a loss of something that once actually existed? Or is it an example of what Dominick LaCapra has recently called transhistorical "absence" rather than real historical "loss?"[164] Nor does it fully counter the objection made by Agamben that experience understood as a prelinguistic unity involves nostalgia for a condition prior to the fall into history and thus a utopian impossibility beyond realization. Even as sympathetic a reader of the Frankfurt School tradition as Albrecht Wellmer could extend this skeptical conclusion beyond Benjamin, claiming that Adorno too, "like Schopenhauer, conceives aesthetic experience in ecstatic terms rather than as a real utopia; the happiness that it promises is not of this world."[165]

What may allow us to salvage a more plausible reading of Adorno's lament about the loss of experience is the recognition of his subtle movement away from the more intransigently absolutist position of Benjamin and the Heidegger of *Holzwege*. For Agamben's rebuke only draws blood if we understand his description of absolute experience, prior to the fall into language, anterior to the split between subject and object, as, in fact, converging with what is normally understood as experience's most charged antonym: total innocence. Although Adorno did have positive things to say about childhood and the memory of happiness, he showed little real nostalgia for any historical time of alleged prelapsarian grace. Witness the following passage from *Negative Dialectics:*

> The meaningful times for whose return the early Lukács yearned were as much due to reification, to inhuman institutions, which he would later attribute only to the bourgeois age. Contemporary representations of medieval towns usually look as if an execution were just taking place to cheer the populace. If any harmony of subject and object should have prevailed in those days, it was a harmony like the most recent one: pressure-born and brittle. The transfiguration of past conditions serves the purpose of a late, superfluous denial that is experienced as a no-exit situation; only as lost conditions do they become glam-

164. Dominick LaCapra, *Writing History, Writing Trauma* (Baltimore, 2001), chapter 2. For an analysis of Adorno in relation to LaCapra's categories, see Katja Garloff, "Essay, Exile, Efficacy: Adorno's Literary Criticism," *Monatshefte* 94, no. 1 (Spring 2002). Garloff concludes: "Adorno would generally support, I believe, LaCapra's view that the faculty of historical judgment and the ability to distinguish between different forms of trauma are indispensable for an adequate response to it. And yet he resists, in his own writing, the closure of the hermeneutic circle which LaCapra at least implicitly demands: Adorno leaves the traumatic ambiguity of the word *Wunde* [in his essay "Heine the Wound"] unresolved while countering its tendency to elide historical difference" (p. 91).

165. Albrecht Wellmer, *The Persistence of Modernity: Essays on Aesthetics, Ethics and Postmodernism*, trans. David Midgley (Cambridge, Mass., 1993), p. 12.

orous. Their cult of pre-subjective phases arose in horror in the age of individual disintegration and collective regression.[166]

In Adorno's studies of Hegel, it will be recalled, the experience he claims shines through the *Phenomenology* expresses both life's inability to be subsumed entirely under concepts and the extent of the present order's totalizing power to compel a social equivalent of precisely that outcome. It is the tension between these two insights, which Adorno called Hegel's depiction of the antagonistic totality, that idealism and *Lebensphilosophie* each forgets. However often he drew on Benjamin's rhetoric of the loss of absolute experience, Adorno understood, as he put it in *Negative Dialectics,* that "the concept of metaphysical experience is antinomical, not only as taught by Kantian transcendental dialectics, but in other ways. A metaphysics proclaimed without recourse to subjective experience, without the immediate presence of the subject, is helpless before the autonomous subject's refusal to have imposed upon it what it cannot understand. And yet, whatever is directly evident to the subject suffers from fallibility and relativity."[167]

In short, redeemed experience, undamaged experience, authentic experience, if indeed such a condition can ever be attained, would not mean a restoration of innocence before the fall into language or a harmonious reconciliation in a utopian future, but rather a non-dominating relationship between subject and object. It would paradoxically retain at least some of the distinctions felt as alienated diremptions by what Hegel had called "the unhappy consciousness," but now in such a way that they no longer frustrate the subject's desire to master the world through conceptual and practical activity. Instead, the experiential happiness that is promised by works of art restores one of the fundamental senses of "experience" itself: a passive suffering or undergoing through an encounter with the new and the other, which moves us beyond where we, as subjects, were before the experience began. It is for this reason, as J. M. Bernstein notes in his account of Adorno, that "the image of life without experience is finally the image of life without history, as if the meaning of life were in its eternal cessation: death. There cannot be historical life without experience; only lives articulated through experience can be fully and self-consciously historical."[168] Here precisely the opposite

166. Adorno, *Negative Dialectics,* p. 191 (translation emended).
167. Ibid., p. 374 (translation emended).
168. Bernstein, "Why Rescue Semblance? Metaphysical Experience and the Possibility of Ethics," in Huhn and Zuidervaart, *The Semblance of Subjectivity,* p. 203. See also the excellent account of Adorno's defense of the "complex concept" in J. M. Bernstein, *Adorno: Disenchantment and Ethics* (Cambridge,

conclusion is reached from Agamben, who identifies history with the fall out of the pure experience that is pre-linguistic infancy or post-linguistic death.

Adorno himself, we have to admit in conclusion, never fully sorted out the welter of denotations and connotations that cling to the numinous word "experience." At times he expressed nostalgia for a lost undamaged experience; at others, he mocked romanticizations of a purported state of prelapsarian bliss. While invoking the rhetoric of a progressive loss, he only vaguely hinted at the existence of an actual historical time before the decay. Accepting Benjamin's critique of empiricist or Kantian notions of experience, he nonetheless resisted accepting the maximalist notion of absolute experience that also infuses, as we have seen, Heidegger's reading of Hegel in *Holzwege*. Looking for traces or prefigurations of undamaged experience in aesthetic experience, he clearly knew that semblance is not reality and that a gap looms large between works of art and redeemed life, which may never be as close to the absolute as Benjamin in his more messianic moods had hoped. In short, the experience of reading Adorno on experience is itself one of non-identical refusals of easy consistencies, producing the realization that experience is an openness to the unexpected with its dangers and obstacles, not a safe haven from history, but a reminder of the encounters with otherness and the new that await those who, despite everything, are willing and able to embark on the voyage.

Among those who were anxious to climb on board are several French thinkers who are now loosely called poststructuralist or figure in the prehistory of the movement. Poststructuralism is often understood to reflect that turn toward language we have seen fueling the critiques of experience by Joan Scott and Richard Rorty, and is normally acknowledged as impatient with the recourse to "lived experience" in the phenomenology of Maurice Merleau-Ponty and Jean-Paul Sartre. But in the case of three thinkers in particular, Georges Bataille, Michel Foucault, and Roland Barthes, we will find a surprisingly emphatic celebration of a certain notion of experience. Our final chapter will be devoted to the exploration of "inner experience" or "limit experience" as a powerful component of their work, and perhaps their lives as well.

2001), which distinguishes it from the abstract or universalizing concept of the Enlightenment and argues for its compatibility with experience.

NINE

The Poststructuralist Reconstitution of Experience

Bataille, Barthes, and Foucault

"EXPERIENCE IS A MODERN FIGURE," Jean-François Lyotard explained dismissively in 1981.

> It needs a subject first of all, the instance of an "I", someone who speaks in the first person. It needs a temporal arrangement of the type: Augustine's *Confessions,* book XI (modern work if ever there was one), where the view of the past, the present and the future is always taken from the point of an ungraspable present consciousness. With these two axioms, one can already engender the essential form of experience: I am no longer what I am, and I am not yet what I am. Life signifies the death of what one is, and this death certifies that life has a meaning, that one is not a stone. A third axiom gives experience its full scope: the world is not an entity external to the subject, it is the common name for the objects in which the subject alienates himself (loses himself, dies to himself) in order to arrive at himself, to live.[1]

For Lyotard, experience understood in this way was derived from the Christian model of salvation, whose philosophical correlate is the dialectical sublation of antitheses and whose aesthetic correlate is the aura, which still informed the work of Marcel Proust as much as that of Jules Michelet. It also manifested itself in phenomenological thought, whether that of Hegel ("the word *experience* is the word of the *Phenomenology of Mind,* the 'science of

---

1. Jean-François Lyotard and Jacques Monory, *The Assassination of Experience by Painting—Monory,* trans. Rachel Bowlby (London, 1998), p. 85.

the experience of consciousness'"[2]) or of Husserl ("an experience can be described only by means of a phenomenological dialectic, as, for example, in the perceptive experience: this thing seen from this angle is white, seen from this other angle it is gray"[3]). Likewise, attempts such as that of Jürgen Habermas to derive from the reflective judgments of aesthetic experience a way of bridging the gap between cognitive, ethical, and political discourses betray a utopian goal, "the unity of experience,"[4] which seeks in vain to overcome the incommensurable "differends" dividing language games or phrases in dispute.

But now in our postmodern age, Lyotard claimed, experience in whatever guise is in a terminal crisis, undermined by capitalist techno-science, the mass life of the metropolis, and the loss of any sense of temporal dialectic culminating in retrospective meaning. Postmodern art, although experimental, is thus "poles apart from experience . . . in the sense of a passion of the spirit traversing perceptible forms of order to arrive at the total expression of self in the discourse of the philosopher."[5] The Holocaust is the most powerful expression of that passion's decline. The name "Auschwitz," Lyotard argued with a nod to Adorno, refers at best to a "para-experience."[6] It stands for the ultimate withering of experience in modern life, for an event even worse than normal death, which is utterly impossible to comprehend through experiential narratives of dialectical sublation.

In so arguing, Lyotard was expressing a now familiar judgment assumed to be shared by many French intellectuals of his postphenomenological generation, which has come to be identified variously with structuralist, poststructuralist, or postmodernist thought. Their ruthless dissolution of the integrated self and stress on the constitutive importance of language, so it has seemed, led them to go even beyond that quest for experience without a subject we have discerned in certain pragmatist and Frankfurt School writings. The appropriation of structuralist and poststructuralist theory in the Anglo-

2. Jean-François Lyotard, *The Differend: Phrases in Dispute,* trans. George Van Den Abbeele (Minneapolis, 1988), p. 153.

3. Ibid., p. 45. Significantly, Heidegger, whose impact on poststructuralist thought was profound, is exempted from the criticism that his version of phenomenology depended on a problematic notion of subjective experience. Heidegger did in fact often challenge the reduction of experience to subjectivity, for example, in his critique of Martin Buber's "I-Thou" relation. See his "A Dialogue on Language," in *On the Way to Language,* trans. Peter Hertz and Joan Stambaugh (New York, 1971), pp. 35–36.

4. Jean-François Lyotard, *The Postmodern Condition: A Report on Knowledge,* trans. Geoff Bennington and Brian Massumi (Minneapolis, 1984), p. 72.

5. Jean-François Lyotard, "Philosophy and Painting in the Age of Their Experimentation: Contribution to an Idea of Postmodernity," in Andrew Benjamin, ed., *The Lyotard Reader* (Cambridge, Mass., 1989), p. 191.

6. Lyotard, *The Differend,* p. 88.

American academy, as we saw in the case of Joan Wallach Scott's feminist historiography, was often accompanied by a deep suspicion of naive notions of "lived experience," which still informed the work of earlier feminists like Simone de Beauvoir.[7] To quote a typical account: "structuralism views experience not as the ground of culture but as its effect, the product of the ways in which individuals are transformed into thinking, feeling and perceiving subjects of different kinds in the context of different structured relations of symbolic exchange."[8]

And indeed, there is ample warrant for this generalization. As we have already noted in our discussion of debates about politics and experience, Louis Althusser identified "lived experience" with an ideological relationship to the real, which only his Marxist science could objectively investigate. In deconstruction a similar suspicion can be frequently discerned. In *Blindness and Insight*, Paul de Man put it in straightforward terms: "Instead of containing or reflecting experience, language constitutes it."[9] Likewise, in *Of Grammatology*, Jacques Derrida asserts that experience is an "unwieldy" concept that "belongs to the history of metaphysics and we can only use it under erasure (*sous rature*). 'Experience' has always designated the relationship with a presence, whether that relationship had the form of consciousness or not."[10] The phenomenological attempt to raise it to a transcendental level was deeply problematic, he continued, because it "is governed by the theme of presence, it participates in the movement of the reduction of the trace,"[11] and therefore fails to understand the temporal disunity of "difference." As Derrida explained in one of his interviews, phenomenology naively believes that "all experience is the experience of meaning."[12] And elsewhere in his essay on

---

7. The role of experience in de Beauvoir was, to be sure, itself complicated. As Toril Moi has noted, "For Beauvoir as for Sartre experience is never 'full': even in the most ecstatic moments of our life, we are always projecting ourselves into the future. The novel, for Beauvoir, is an attempt to *produce* the fullness of experience that always escapes us." *Simone de Beauvoir: The Making of an Intellectual Woman* (Oxford, 1994), p. 248.

8. Tony Bennett and others, eds., *Culture, Ideology, and Social Process: A Reader* (London, 1981), p. 12.

9. Paul de Man, *Blindness and Insight* (New York, 1971), p. 232.

10. Jacques Derrida, *Of Grammatology*, trans. Gayatri Chakravorty Spivak (Baltimore, 1976), p. 60.

11. Ibid., pp. 61–62. Derrida's critique of phenomenological notions of experience was likely reinforced by the connection between Husserl's notion of evidence and the privileging of sight, for example in *Cartesian Meditations*, trans. Dorion Cairns (The Hague, 1960), where he writes "Evidence is, in an extremely broad sense, an '*experiencing*' of something that is, and is thus; it is precisely a mental seeing of something itself" (p. 52, emphasis in original). For a discussion of Derrida's complicated response to ocularcentrism, see my *Downcast Eyes: The Denigration of Vision in Twentieth-Century French Thought* (Berkeley, 1993), chapter 9.

12. Jacques Derrida, *Positions*, trans. Alan Bass (Chicago, 1981), p. 30.

Emmanuel Levinas, he would add, "can one speak of an *experience* of the other or of difference? Has not the concept of experience always been determined by the metaphysics of presence? Is not experience always an encountering of irreducible presence, the perception of a phenomenality?"[13] Derrida was no less hostile to the hermeneutic appeal to dialogic experience, as demonstrated by his rebuke of Hans-Georg Gadamer in their painfully unproductive encounter of 1981: "Professor Gadamer has insistently referred to 'that experience [*Erfahrung*] that we all recognize,' to a description of experience that is not in itself to be taken metaphysically. But usually—and maybe even always—metaphysics presents itself as the description of experience as such, of presentation as such. Furthermore, I am not convinced that we ever really do have this experience that Professor Gadamer describes, of knowing in a dialogue that one has been perfectly understood or experience the success of confirmation."[14]

All of these examples would seem to confirm the conclusion that poststructuralism welcomed, even sought, what one observer has called "the demise of experience,"[15] which its adherents variously identified with dialectical rationality, the metaphysics of presence, too quick a confidence in the pervasiveness of meaning, and a strong notion of a centered subject whose meaningful life could be narrativized in a coherent way. Many of the criticisms of Hegel's use of the term in *The Phenomenology of the Spirit* made by Martin Heidegger in *Hegel's Concept of Experience,* which, as we saw, so aroused Theodor Adorno's ire, seem to have found their way into the discourse of his French readers.

---

13. Jacques Derrida, *Writing and Difference,* trans. Alan Bass (Chicago, 1978), p. 152. Not surprisingly, Derrida's position against the self-evidence of experience would earn him a comparison with Karl Barth, whose attack on Friedrich Schleiermacher's reliance on religious experience we have already encountered. See Graham Ward, *Barth, Derrida, and the Language of Theology* (Cambridge, 1995). For a defense of Levinas against the claim that his work valorizes experience, see Paul Davies, "The Face and the Caress: Levinas's Ethical Alterations of Sensibility," in David Michael Levin, ed., *Modernity and the Hegemony of Vision* (Berkeley, 1993): "The introduction of the face, the introduction of the phrase 'the face of the other' into a work of philosophy has the effect of altering the notion of 'experience.' Note that it is not a matter of expanding the notion of experience to accommodate the face, for if one were to approach the issue in this fashion one would have already admitted that the face is an object of experience" (p. 255).

14. Jacques Derrida, "Three Questions to Hans-Georg Gadamer," in Diane P. Michelfelder and Richard E. Palmer, eds., *Dialogue and Deconstruction: The Gadamer-Derrida Encounter* (Albany, N.Y., 1989), pp. 53–54.

15. Alice A. Jardine, *Gynesis: Configurations of Woman and Modernity* (Ithaca, N.Y., 1985), chapter 7. The same assessment can be found much later in Sonia Kruks, *Retrieving Experience: Subjectivity and Recognition in Feminist Politics* (Ithaca, N.Y., 2001), where she complains that "postmodern feminist theory, informed by the work of Derrida, Foucault, and others, insists that such selves and their experiences can never be other than discursive effects" (p. 132).

But as might be expected from a body of thinkers whose apparent unity is far more a function of external labeling than internal consensus, the story is considerably more complicated and its implications more interesting than this flat rejection narrative might suggest. The now canonical view to the contrary, the break with phenomenology and its concern with experience was less complete than is often assumed.[16] In what follows, I want to examine in particular three figures who loom large in any retelling of that story, one of whom was an honored predecessor of what has come to be called "poststructuralism" and the others exemplary instances: Georges Bataille (1897–1962), Roland Barthes (1915–1980), and Michel Foucault (1926–1984).[17] In each case, we will find a complex and often positively inclined attitude toward something that they explicitly called experience.

That such an attitude may, in fact, not have been theirs alone will be suggested if we pause before passing on to their work to acknowledge that it has been recently discerned as well in that of Derrida by several commentators, who discount the exemplarity of the criticisms quoted above. In *Feeling in Theory: Emotion after the "Death of the Subject,"* Rei Terada contends that as early as his 1964 essay on Descartes, "Cogito and the History of Madness," Derrida was scolding those who attend to the philosopher's "framework of the Cogito, rather than to the critical experience of it."[18] She argues that despite Derrida's overt hostility to experience, when it came to stressing the gap between emotional and rational identities, he could mobilize experience—in particular, the experience of self-differentiation produced by emotional instability—as a way to undermine the centered subject.[19] Here experience involves that moment of "pathos" that we have seen was one of the original Greek connotations of the term, a moment of self-surrender and passivity

---

16. For a recent critique of the conventional view, see Tilottama Rajan, *Deconstruction and the Remainders of Phenomenology: Sartre, Derrida, Foucault, Baudrillard* (Stanford, 2002).

17. Another possible candidate would be Jacques Lacan, who often used the term in a positive sense, often conflating it with experiment, either mental or practical, in his work. For an analysis, see François Regnault, "Lacan and Experience," in Alexandre Leupin, ed., *Lacan and the Human Sciences* (Lincoln, Neb., 1991). Still others might include Philippe Lacoue-Labarthe, the author of *Poetry as Experience*, trans. Andrea Tarnowski (Stanford, 1999); Jean-Luc Nancy, *The Experience of Freedom*, trans. Bridget McDonald (Stanford, 1993); and Philippe Sollers, *Writing and the Experience of Limits*, ed. David Hayman, trans. Philip Barnard and David Hayman (New York, 1983). All attempt to generate a plausible, non-phenomenological notion of experience.

18. Derrida, "Cogito and the History of Madness," *Writing and Difference*, p. 56, discussed in Rei Terada, *Feeling in Theory: Emotion after the "Death of the Subject"* (Cambridge, Mass., 2001), pp. 22–24.

19. In so arguing, Derrida is not really all that far from the William James who could also say that our experience "has ways of *boiling over*, and making us correct our present formulations." *Pragmatism and the Meaning of Truth* (Cambridge, Mass., 1978), p. xxiv (emphasis in original).

rather than self-productive activity. "Derrida's work," Terada writes, "extends the descriptive fineness of phenomenology but reformulates the meaning of such descriptions. It implies that self-difference—falsely resolved in the Cartesian tradition, rejected as nonsense in the realist tradition—is experience itself, nonsubjective experience."[20] Or to put it another way, against the solipsistic notion of "auto-affectivity," which Derrida saw in Husserl's reflexive notion of an integral subject, he favored what might be called "hetero-affectivity," in which emotion served to undermine the ideal of a completely self-sufficient subject. In this sense, experience is not the enemy or ideological inverse of textuality, with its dispersal of authorial power, but its correlate. The choice is not, *pace* Richard Rorty, between language and experience, for there is a potential compatibility between versions of both.

Even more recently, David Wood, stressing the influence of Heidegger's critique of the active subject, has claimed that Derrida should be read as a radical phenomenologist, who always mobilizes the openness of experience against the closure of conceptual reason. Although acknowledging that the word is misleading if it implies a unified subject resisting the abyssal loss of meaning, Wood insists that if we equate it with the trembling engendered by confronting that loss, experience is an honorific term in Derrida's vocabulary. In fact, the development of Derrida's writing, he concludes, is "nothing *other* than *experience regained.* Deconstruction is, if you like, the experience of experience."[21]

BATAILLE AND INNER EXPERIENCE

Although possibly a one-sided appraisal of Derrida's extensive and still developing corpus, these surprising defenses of a certain version of experience can be even more plausibly extended to the three figures whose careers are the focus of this chapter. Let us begin with Georges Bataille, whose remarkable ruminations on what he called "inner experience" helped differentiate the concept from the Hegelian version identified with it *tout court* by Lyotard and other critics of its purported complicity with a metaphysics

20. Terada, *Feeling in Theory,* p. 24. A similar conclusion is reached by Rudolf Bernet, who writes that "Derrida's positive contribution to the analysis of self-experience is above all the indication of the necessity of self-*representation* and its *differential* structure. There exists no interior self-consciousness without an exterior appearance of the subject in pronouncements, gestures, activities, and so on. The subject experiences his own self only by means of these expressions." "The Other in Myself," in Simon Critchley and Peter Dews, eds., *Deconstructive Subjectivities* (Albany, N.Y., 1996), p. 178.

21. David Wood, *Thinking after Heidegger* (Malden, Mass., 2002), p. 26 (emphasis in original).

of presence.[22] Derrida, it might be noted, seems to have been uncertain of whether such a differentiation was possible, at least in the important 1967 essay he devoted to Bataille called "From Restricted to General Economy: A Hegelianism without Reserve." "That which *indicates itself* as interior experience," Derrida wrote, "is not an experience, because it is related to no presence, to no plenitude, but only to the 'impossible' it 'undergoes' in torture. This experience above all is not interior, and if it seems to be such because it is related to nothing else, to no exterior (except in the modes of nonrelation, secrecy and rupture), it is also completely *exposed*—to torture— naked, open to the exterior, with no interior reserve or feelings, profoundly superficial."[23]

But, we have to ask, can there be experiences worthy of the name, experiences without the robust, integrated subject, which deny presence, plenitude, interior depth, and narrative completion? Can there be a non-phenomenological notion of an experience that isn't so much actively "lived" as suffered or endured? Must a plausible notion of experience mean refusing the insight that the object, thing, or other at least to some degree inhabits or haunts the subject, agent, or self? Can the ecstatic de-centering of the self produce an experience that resists location in an integral, coherent ego? These are the questions that Bataille, Foucault, and Barthes pose (and, if Terada and Wood are right, Derrida himself answered in the affirmative elsewhere in his work).

Bataille's most elaborate development of the idea of "inner experience" came only at the midpoint of his career, during the Second World War and the occupation of France, when he had abandoned unsuccessful collaborative efforts to restore a sacred foundation for a revivified community and thus re-enchant modern society. Uneasily tied to the surrealist movement, with whose leader, André Breton, he had a long and unsettled relationship,[24]

22. Georges Bataille, *Inner Experience*, trans. Leslie Anne Boldt (Albany, N.Y., 1988). For general discussions of Bataille, see Michele H. Richman, *Reading Georges Bataille: Beyond the Gift* (Baltimore, 1982); Allan Stoekl, *Politics, Writing, Mutilation: The Cases of Bataille, Blanchot, Roussel, Leiris, and Ponge* (Minneapolis, 1985); Francis Marmande, *Georges Bataille Politique* (Lyon, 1985); Denis Hollier, *Against Architecture: The Writings of Georges Bataille*, trans. Betsy Wing (Cambridge, Mass., 1989); Allan Stoekl, ed., *On Bataille*, Yale French Studies 78 (1990); Carolyn J. Dean, *The Self and Its Pleasures: Bataille, Lacan and the History of the Decentered Subject* (Ithaca, N.Y., 1992); Carolyn Bailey Gill, ed., *Bataille: Writing the Sacred* (London, 1995); Denis Hollier, ed., *Georges Bataille après tout* (Paris, 1995); and Michel Surya, *Georges Bataille: An Intellectual Biography*, trans. Krzysztof Fijalkowski and Michael Richardson (London, 2002).

23. Jacques Derrida, "From Restricted to General Economy: A Hegelianism without Reserve," *Writing and Difference*, p. 272.

24. Bataille's writings on surrealism are collected in *The Absence of Myth: Writings on Surrealism*, ed. and trans. Michael Richardson (London, 1994), which includes an introduction detailing his feuds and rapprochements with Breton.

Bataille had experimented with different collective ventures—an anti-Fascist political group called *Contre-Attaque*, the secret society and journal *Acéphale*, and, most important, the Collège de sociologie[25]—before coming to the conclusion that communal ecstasy and the restoration of mythic consciousness were not on the immediate agenda, certainly not during the dark days of the Nazi occupation of Paris. The results were evident in the first volume of his three-volume *Somme athéologique*, started in 1941 and published in 1943 as *Inner Experience*.[26] Although many of Bataille's perennial themes—sacrifice, auto-mutilation, expenditure *(dépense)*, sovereignty, formlessness *(informe)*, base materialism, heterogeneity, mad laughter, acephalism, abjection, horizontality, the denigration of vision—can be still indirectly detected, they were now sounded in a new key.[27]

Possibly because he came to understand that his own political adventures had come dangerously close to the Fascism he was at pains to combat or perhaps as a result of the severe health problems that followed from the return of tuberculosis in 1942, Bataille appears to have retreated into the solitude of the suffering individual. Having been abandoned by many of his friends from the 1930s, still mourning the death in 1938 of his lover Colette Peignot (or Laure, as she was known), Bataille seems to have lost his faith in a collective enterprise. One commentator has gone so far as to claim that in this new phase of his career, "the experience itself is *one individual's*, and is at least related to certain meditative practices."[28] What has been called by another the "virile activism" of the 1930s was replaced with a turn "inward" in which he no longer sought solutions to the crisis of modern life on the level of immediate political redemption.[29]

25. Denis Hollier, ed., *The College of Sociology, 1937–1939*, trans. Betsy Wing (Minneapolis, 1988).

26. The two other volumes, originally published in 1944 and 1945, were *Guilty*, trans. Bruce Boone (New York, 1988); and *On Nietzsche*, trans. Bruce Boone (New York, 1992).

27. There is ample discussion of these themes in the extensive literature on Bataille. For my own earlier efforts to explicate several of them, see "The Reassertion of Sovereignty in a Time of Crisis: Carl Schmitt and Georges Bataille," in *Force Fields: Between Intellectual History and Cultural Critique* (New York, 1993); and "The Disenchantment of the Eye: Bataille and the Surrealists," in *Downcast Eyes*. An earlier version of the argument of this chapter can be found in "The Limits of Limit-Experience: Bataille and Foucault," in *Cultural Semantics: Keywords of Our Time* (Amherst, Mass., 1998).

28. Allan Stoekl, *Agonies of the Intellectual: Commitment, Subjectivity, and the Performative in the Twentieth-Century French Tradition* (Lincoln, Neb., 1992), p. 268.

29. See Susan Rubin Suleiman, "Bataille in the Street: The Search for Virility in the 1930's," in Gill, *Bataille*. In contrast, Jean-Michel Besnier argues for less of a break in Bataille's career, claiming that *Inner Experience* "does not constitute a turning point, for Bataille did not come to deny himself. Privileging action obviously meant taking existence to its boiling point or, to put it another way, experiencing one's limits and feeling the fundamental continuity which fuses individuals together. In privileging the

But precisely what the alternative "level" of "inwardness" may have been is not easy to say. Bataille had absorbed well the lessons of Durkheimian sociology about the importance of collective effervescence, the role of sacrifice, and the power of the sacred (not the "right" sacred of religious or political leaders, but the "left" sacred of the debased and reviled).[30] Situated in a long line of sacrilegious Catholics stretching back to the nineteenth-century decadents, if not the Marquis de Sade, he understood the function of institutions and rituals as the defining context, at once limiting and crying out for transgression, in which experience might take place.[31] As a result, he never felt attracted to conventional notions of subjective individuality—largely Protestant in origin—or the integrity of the self as active agent. The Durkheimian school, in particular the work of Henri Hubert and Marcel Mauss, alerted him to the importance of sacred self-sacrifice in which the executioner and the victim were the same, an anthropological version of the grammatical mode of the intransitive "middle voice," neither fully active, nor fully passive.[32]

Accordingly, experience could not be located in a traditional notion of the self able to undergo a cumulative process of formation or cultivation *(Bildung)*. "Man achieves inner experience," he argued, "at the instant when bursting out of the chrysalis he feels that he is tearing himself, not tearing something outside that resists him."[33] Nor was a purely psychoanalytic understanding of unconscious interiority plausible, at least if the unconscious were taken to be prior to and more fundamental than the exterior world.[34] The flooding in of that exterior meant that no integral self based on what Bataille's friend Jacques Lacan would call the "mirror stage" of ego constitution could solidify; as Julia Kristeva later remarked, "inner experience is a crossing that is against the grain of specularization as the initial moment of

---

ascetic experience, the issue is the same, even if the quest is from now on a solitary one, sheltered from the solicitations of history." "Bataille, the Emotive Intellectual," in Gill, *Bataille*, p. 20. For still another critique of the purported shift to inwardness, see Alexander Irwin, *Saints of the Impossible: Bataille, Weil, and the Politics of the Sacred* (Minneapolis, 2002), chapter 1.

30. See Michele H. Richman, *Sacred Revolution and the College of Sociology* (Minneapolis, 2002). Bataille also learned from two of Emile Durkheim's disciples, Marcel Mauss and Henri Hubert, who deemphasized the utilitarian function of sacrifice in Durkheim's analysis and stressed instead its destructive uselessness.

31. For a discussion of his links with the tradition of decadent Catholicism, see Michael Weingrad, "Parisian Messianism: Catholicism, Decadence, and the Transgressions of Georges Bataille," *History and Memory* 13, no. 2 (Fall–Winter 2001).

32. See Irwin, *Saints of the Impossible*, p. 31.

33. Bataille, *Erotism: Death and Sensuality*, trans. Mary Dalwood (San Francisco, 1986), p. 39.

34. Bataille's complicated relationship to psychoanalysis, tied up with his friendship with Lacan, is sensitively discussed in Dean, *The Self and Its Pleasures*. It should be noted that Bataille was himself analyzed during the period 1925–1927 by Adrien Borel, with whom he was to form a life-long tie.

the constitution of the subject."[35] Even Jean-Paul Sartre's claim that the *pour-soi* was a non-essentialized locus of infinite possibility, utterly unconstrained in its ability to decide on the project that it would pursue, seemed deeply problematic to Bataille. Indeed, as we will see shortly, the two were to quarrel bitterly over the implications of inner experience.

As on many other issues, Bataille's interpretation of that term owed much to his sympathetic reading of Friedrich Nietzsche, who had often been celebrated by adepts of irrational *Erlebnis* in Germany and elsewhere.[36] Bataille, however, sought to distance himself from their simplistic understanding of his legacy, especially when it was turned into a justification for the *Kriegser-lebnis* of the First World War, and he was at pains to rescue Nietzsche's work from its identification with Fascism during the interwar years.[37] He was also anxious to resist the criticism of Nietzsche as a nihilist, which Albert Camus had extended to Bataille himself. In 1946, he would protest that "to the end I have sought the implications and significance of Nietzsche's experience. I have discovered there *only* the most open experience beginning from a collapse, in which I speak, as far as I am concerned, of repetition. . . . Some of Camus's words about Nietzsche are perhaps not directly reported, but they seem to me to imply the usual judgment about Nietzsche; his experience is from the outside."[38]

From the inside, Nietzsche's experience seems to have meant for Bataille a willingness to live life as a radical experiment, involving the body as well as the mind, risking danger in the quest for a certain version of redemption. It could also entail wandering aimlessly in the darkness of the labyrinth rather than seeking a God's-eye view of the world.[39] As Nietzsche had wondered in an aphorism in *The Dawn of Day* called "Experience and Invention," "should we perhaps say that nothing is contained in them? that experiences in them-

35. Julia Kristeva, "Bataille, l'expérience et la pratique," in Philippe Sollers, ed., *Bataille* (Paris, 1973), p. 290.

36. See Steven E. Aschheim, *The Nietzsche Legacy in Germany 1890–1990* (Berkeley, 1992), for examples of this reading by enthusiasts like Martin Buber and Ernst Jünger. Aschheim quotes Thomas Mann's remark of 1918 that one doesn't merely "read" Nietzsche, one "experiences" him (p. 10).

37. See his essays "Nietzsche and the Fascists" and "Nietzschean Chronicle," in Allan Stoekl, ed., *Visions of Excess: Selected Writings, 1927–1939* (Minneapolis, 1985), and *On Nietzsche*. For an interpretation of Nietzsche's importance for Bataille, see Stoekl, *Agonies of the Intellectual*, chapter 10. For a general assessment of the importance of Nietzsche for French poststructuralism, see Alan D. Schrift, *Nietzsche's French Legacy: A Genealogy of Poststructuralism* (New York, 1995).

38. Bataille, "The Problems of Surrealism," in *The Absence of Myth*, p. 101.

39. For a comparison of Nietzsche and Bataille on the labyrinth, see Hollier, *Against Architecture*, chapter 3.

selves are merely works of fancy?"[40] Motivating those inventions of fancy was a willingness to hazard, perhaps even court, ecstatic self-immolation, the sacrifice of the integral, armored self in the hope of recovering a lost Dionysian community.[41] The philosopher, Nietzsche argued in *Beyond Good and Evil*, can only affirm life through "the widest—perhaps most disturbing and shattering—experiences . . . [he] lives 'unphilosophically' and 'unwisely,' above all *imprudently*, and bears the burden and duty of a hundred attempts and temptations of life—he risks *himself* constantly, he plays *the* dangerous game."[42] "Self-overcoming," the endless challenge of the "superman" posited in *Thus Spake Zarathustra*, could mean overcoming a strong notion of the self. As Karl Jaspers put it, "experience is for [Nietzsche] no longer a substance certain of itself, and cognition is never a permanent and unchanging knowledge. Consequently he is not always sure of himself. He deliberately runs the risk of the possible, of the disintegrating experience of mere experimenting, and of the fusion of the genuine and the false; he exposes himself to this danger to an extent that to most people either remains unknown or proves fatal."[43] Or in Nietzsche's own words, unlike religious adepts of miraculous experiences, "we others who thirst after reason . . . are determined to scrutinize our experiences as severely as a scientific experiment—hour after hour, day after day. We ourselves wish to be our experiments and guinea pigs."[44]

Despite his celebrated declaration of God's demise, Nietzsche, as Bataille read him, was aware of the importance of the archaic sacred community and hoped for its resurrection through myth and violence. Nietzsche had, moreover, been keenly attuned to the impoverishment of such experiences in the modern world. In the preface to *On the Genealogy of Morals*, he had lamented: "Whatever else there is in life, so-called 'experiences'—which of us has sufficient earnestness for them? Or sufficient time? Present experience has, I am afraid, always found us 'absent-minded': we cannot give our hearts to it— not even our ears."[45] An important reason that modern man shut his ears

40. Friedrich Nietzsche, *The Dawn of Day*, trans. J. M. Kennedy (New York, 1964), p. 128.

41. On the importance of ecstatic experience in Nietzsche, see David B. Allison, "Musical Psychodramatics: Ecstasis in Nietzsche," in Alan D. Schrift, ed., *Why Nietzsche Still? Reflections on Drama, Culture and Politics* (Berkeley, 2000).

42. Friedrich Nietzsche, *Beyond Good and Evil*, trans. R. G. Hollingdale (London, 1972), p. 113 (emphasis in original).

43. Karl Jaspers, *Nietzsche: An Introduction to the Understanding of His Philosophical Activity*, trans. Charles F. Wallraff and Frederick J. Schmitz (Baltimore, 1997), pp. 389–90.

44. Friedrich Nietzsche, *The Gay Science*, ed. and trans. Walter Kaufmann (New York, 1974), p. 253.

45. Friedrich Nietzsche, *On the Genealogy of Morals*, ed. and trans. Walter Kaufmann (New York, 1969), p. 15.

was his fear of pain. As Nietzsche put it in *The Gay Science*, "we moderns may well be, all of us, in spite of our frailties and infirmities, tyros who rely on fantasies, for lack of any ample firsthand experience—compared to the age of fear, the longest of all ages, in which individuals had to protect themselves."[46] Because of our fear of pain, our inability to endure misery, we were morally deficient, at least in terms of the master morality of "good and bad" held by the Greeks. For "all experiences are moral experiences, even in the realm of sense perception."[47]

Not only did Bataille absorb Nietzsche's affirmation of the value of pain and self-immolation, but he also echoed in his own life the German philosopher's candid acknowledgement that he himself had not been able to live his credo with any consistency. Just as Nietzsche was not Zarathustra and knew it, Bataille the professional librarian and closet revolutionary was not able to sustain the ecstatic condition of "inner experience" in his own life. For all his experimentation with sexual debauchery—he was an inveterate visitor to brothels and a frequent adulterer—and participation in communal rituals of uncertain nature, Bataille kept at bay the total descent into madness and self-evisceration that beckoned.[48] There was no organic unity between life and work, no realization of the frankly impossible task he had mandated as a way beyond the constraining world of "homogeneity" and "the restricted economy" of modern life.[49] Michel Surya, his most important biographer, was thus right to subtitle his book "la mort à l'oeuvre,"[50] which indicates Bataille's resistance to self-fashioning his life as if it were a work of art (and also his fascination with death as the inevitable limit of life). Indeed, even his authorial persona was fractured, with many of his secret pseudonyms (mandated by the scandalously pornographic nature of much of his early writing) disclosed only after his death. If he had personally known "inner experiences," they were fleeting interruptions in a life that seemed no more or less mun-

46. Nietzsche, *The Gay Science*, p. 112.

47. Ibid., p. 174.

48. Surya's biography contains many examples of Bataille's dissolute and transgressive behavior but notes the impossibility of knowing for certain what went on in the secret societies, like Acéphale, that he created.

49. Among Bataille's most significant dichotomies are homogeneity/heterogeneity and general/restricted economy. Whereas homogeneity signifies the integration and consolidation of disparate elements into a unified whole, heterogeneity means the incommensurability of those elements, which always resist attempts to contain them. A "general" economy is one in which uncompensated loss, excessive waste, unredeemed sacrifice, and reckless consumption overflow the boundaries of an economy of scarcity, exchange and production, which is its "restricted" antithesis.

50. The English translation of Surya's biography cited above (note 22) adopted another subtitle.

dane than countless others, at least on the surface.[51] If he tried to live the life of a self-sacrificing saint, it was, as Alexander Irwin argues, a sainthood of "the impossible."[52] As in the case of Nietzsche, only gestures toward something not attained, explosive disruptions of existing models of selfhood and interiority, emerged from Bataille's struggle to render discursively what was beyond the means of discourse to express.[53] Like Michel de Montaigne, albeit without his great predecessor's personal equilibrium, Bataille knew full well that the limit of experience was met only in a death that was both impossible to incorporate into life and also its most intense, ecstatic, and profound moment.

Inner Experience itself resists paraphrastic redescription, lacking, as it does, a unified argument. Indeed, not only in terms of content, but also formally, it defies easy categorization. It is, as Denis Hollier points out,

> an autotransgressive book: it is not a book. It took too long to write for that. So long that one might say that time itself wrote it—is inscribed in it. Bataille wrote it with time, in defiance of planning. He put time into it, in the literal sense. Which precludes our reading this book in any way other than in the space of textual heterogeneity outside the book. The texts composing it are not contemporary: no simultaneity ever existed among them. Their juxtaposition makes us read the gap making them different from the project that gave birth to them.[54]

The temporality of "inner experience" also resists the ideal of cumulative wisdom over time, the development of a project of self-formation producing retrospective totalization. Bataille's deep aversion to—mixed with a certain fascination with—Hegelian dialectics, which he had encountered in the celebrated lectures of Alexander Kojève at the École des Hautes Études in the

51. One of his biographers, Pierre Prévost, *Rencontres avec Georges Bataille* (Paris, 1987), reports that shortly after the beginning of the war, Bataille was walking in Paris with his umbrella still open after the rain ceased: "At a certain moment, he began to laugh, an intense laugh, and let the umbrella drop. It covered his head. He immediately fell into a state of unique entrancement, like none he had ever known. . . . It was that night that he discovered what he called 'inner experience'" (p. 74). It can safely be assumed that Bataille could not walk around with an umbrella on his head all the time, however manic the laughter it produced.

52. Irwin, *Saints of the Impossible.*

53. For a helpful attempt to analyze the rhetorical means Bataille employed to convey the unconveyable and yet not sink entirely into silence or nonsense, see Leslie Ann Boldt-Irons, "Sacrifice and Violence in Bataille's Erotic Fiction: Reflections from/upon the *mise en abîme*," in Gill, *Bataille.*

54. Hollier, *Against Architecture*, p. 45.

1930s,[55] meant that he resisted any notion of Minerva's owl knowing and making sense of the whole only after it had been experienced. "Nietzsche is to Hegel," he once wrote, "what a bird breaking its shell is to a bird contentedly absorbing the substance within."[56]

Nor can one argue that another version of totalization, that implied by mystical experience understood as oneness with the universe or unity with God, was the goal of inner experience itself. As Surya has noted, "if *Inner Experience* has a motivation, it is not, as might be thought, to become *everything* but no longer to be it. . . . in other words [no longer] an absurd desire for *salvation*."[57] To be sure, Bataille had known the temptations of mysticism in his youth, when he went through a deeply religious phase before violently rejecting Christianity, and there are passages in his later work where they are positively acknowledged.[58] His ambivalence is apparent at the beginning of *Inner Experience:*

> By *inner experience* I understand that which one usually calls *mystical experience:* the states of ecstasy, rapture, at least of meditated emotion. But I am thinking less of *confessional* experience, to which one has had to adhere up to now, than of an experience laid bare, free of ties, even of an origin, of any confession whatever. This is why I don't like the word *mystical.*[59]

Mysticism is a problematic term not only when it conjures up conventional religion—what Bataille called "dogmatic servitude"—but also when it means a completed unity between self and God, a nostalgic return to a primal fusion prior to any fall into alienated differentiation.[60] Bataille's "atheological" insistence on heterogeneity, loss, and impossibility meant that any mystical quest in these terms was doomed to failure. "What characterizes such an experience, which does not proceed from a revelation—where nothing is revealed either, if not the unknown—is that it never announces anything re-

55. Bataille acknowledged the importance of Kojève's lectures in his 1946 essay "From the Stone Age to Jacques Prévert," *The Absence of Myth,* p. 153.

56. Bataille, "The Obelisk," in *Visions of Excess,* p. 219.

57. Surya, *Georges Bataille,* p. 398.

58. In 1922, Bataille spent time at a Benedictine abbey on the Isle of Wight, where he seems to have sought mystical experiences. In places in his work, for example, his discussion of Emily Brontë in *Literature and Evil,* trans. Alistair Hamilton (New York, 1973), pp. 14–15, he invokes mystical experience in a positive way.

59. Bataille, *Inner Experience,* p. 3.

60. There are, to be sure, moments in his work when Bataille's rhetoric does suggest this goal. Some of them are listed in Rebecca Comay, "Gifts without Presents: Economics of 'Experience' in Bataille and Heidegger," *Yale French Studies* 78 (1990), p. 78.

assuring."[61] One of the "maladies of inner experience" was precisely the mystic's "power to animate what pleases him; the intensity suffocates, eliminates doubt and one perceives what one was expecting."[62]

A second malady was making the acquisition of inner experience into a deliberate project, the goal of a plan of action, the reason to become an "engaged intellectual." In fact, "inner experience," Bataille insisted, "is the opposite of action. Nothing more. 'Action' is utterly dependent on project."[63] The problem with a project, Bataille explained, is that it is dependent on prior discursive intentions, which define it in advance. As such, it is too much a result of reflection, of the knowledge that Bataille, deliberately resisting Hegelian totalization, saw as the antithesis of inner experience.[64] It also came too close to the mundane world of productive work rather than the sacred world of ecstatic play or expenditure. The project was flawed as well because it put its temporal emphasis on an imagined future, rather than on the present, a present, to be sure, that was never itself a moment of plenitudinous meaning and self-sufficiency. And even if inner experience can be said in some sense still to be a project, despite everything, it is no longer "that, positive, of salvation, but that, negative, of abolishing the power of words, hence of project."[65]

Thus, despite its dangerous resemblance to the "inner experience" celebrated by Ernst Jünger in connection with the war, Bataille's alternative resisted the activist, virile heroism promoted by his German counterpart. *Krieg als innere Erlebnis* was translated, to be sure, into French in 1934 as *La guerre notre mère* and may have had some echo in Bataille's 1938 essay "The Structure and Function of the Army."[66] But while Jünger's sado-masochistic fetish

61. Bataille, *Inner Experience*, p. xxxii.

62. Ibid., p. 54.

63. Ibid., p. 46.

64. As he put it in *Erotism*, Hegel's system "assembles ideas, but at the same time, cuts those assembled ideas off from experience. That no doubt was his ambition, for in Hegel's mind, the immediate is bad, and Hegel would certainly have identified what I call experience with the immediate" (p. 255). In *Inner Experience*, he criticized the more recent phenomenology of Husserl for a similar privileging of knowledge over experience itself: "For some time now, the only philosophy which lives—that of the German school—tended to make the highest knowledge an extension of inner experience. But this *phenomenology* lends to knowledge the value of a goal which one attains through experience. This is an ill-assorted match: the measure given to experience is at once too much and not great enough" (p. 8). For an analysis of his relationship to phenomenology, see Brian Wall, "Written in the Sand: Bataille's Phenomenology of Transgression and the Transgression of Phenomenology," in Tilottama Rajan and Michael J. O'Driscoll, eds., *After Poststructuralism: Writing the Intellectual History of Theory* (Toronto, 2002).

65. Bataille, *Inner Experience*, p. 22.

66. Bataille, "The Structure and Function of the Army," in Hollier, *The College of Sociology*. Hollier discusses the possible impact of Jünger on p. 138, and then adds several quotations of antiwar sentiments

of pain and demand for a return to mythic consciousness resemble similar moments in Bataille's thought, his stress on will and ascetic self-mastery did not. Although admitting that asceticism might be conducive to a certain variant of experience by stilling the desire for objects, Bataille claimed it fell short because it made of experience itself a kind of object—or rather, a blissful state of being—to be desired. "My principle against ascesis," he explained, "is that the extreme limit is accessible through excess, not through want. . . . Ascesis asks for deliverance, salvation, the possession of the most desirable object. In ascesis, value is not that of experience alone, independent of pleasure or suffering; it is always a beatitude, a deliverance, which we strive to procure for ourselves."[67] Desire and emotion cannot, in fact, be entirely mastered; indeed, it is the inability to satisfy desire that takes the subject outside himself and undermines any claim to individual self-sufficiency.

Nor did Bataille ultimately accept Jünger's identification of experience with the intensity of *Erlebnis,* which, like his friend Walter Benjamin, he found problematic because of its stress on lived immediacy and the present moment.[68] His position may come a bit closer to what Benjamin had designated *Erfahrung,* at least at the moments when that term was not equated with narrative coherence and cumulative wisdom. When it meant instead registering the imaginary quality of a moment of primal plenitude and acknowledging the always vain nature of the quest for its restoration, *Erfahrung* approached Bataille's notion of "inner experience." In this sense, as Rebecca Comay notes, "*Erfahrung*—the *experience lost*—is nothing other than the *experience of loss.*"[69]

Loss without compensation, the evacuation of the individual self without fusion with God, neither active self-fashioning nor the project of salvation, inner experience could never be captured in a positive formula. Following the lead of his provocative definition of *informe* as more of a task than a simple word with a solid meaning, as "a term that serves to bring things down in the world,"[70] Bataille resisted turning "inner experience" into anything that might be captured in a straightforward statement. "The difference between inner ex-

---

in notes Bataille wrote in 1941. Two years earlier, in "The Practice of Joy Before Death," *Visions of Excess* (p. 239), Bataille had proclaimed "I MYSELF AM WAR," but this identification, which appeared in a section entitled "Heraclitean meditation," seems to have been a way to imagine his violent self-destruction rather than the thrill of killing others.

67. Bataille, *Inner Experience,* pp. 21–22.

68. Comay, "Gifts without Presents," p. 84. Irwin makes a persuasive case for Bataille's initial fascination with Jünger's position, but acknowledges that he came to question the German's redemption of war as a goal-directed activity. See *Saints of the Impossible,* chapter 4.

69. Comay, "Gifts without Presents," p. 85.

70. Bataille, "Formless," in *Visions of Excess,* p. 31.

perience and philosophy," he explained, "resides principally in this: that in experience, what is stated is nothing, if not a means and even, as much a means, an obstacle; what counts is no longer the statement of wind, but the wind."[71] Simultaneously a means and an obstacle, more of a force than a form, inner experience is thus a negation without the possibility of positive resolution. Or more precisely, "by virtue of the fact that it is negation of other values, other authorities, experience, having a positive existence, becomes itself positive value *and authority*."[72] That is, it is never beholden to another authority beyond itself. But then he added in a footnote: "the paradox in the authority of experience: based on challenge, it is the challenging of authority; positive challenge, man's authority defined as the challenging of himself."[73]

Such an authority is thus always pursuing the aim of what Bataille's close friend Maurice Blanchot, whose novel *Thomas the Obscure* is approvingly cited in *Inner Experience,* would call "contestation of itself and non-knowledge."[74] Such contestation meant that the boundaries of the self were always porous, its integrity always decentered and dispersed, so much so that "inner experience" inevitably invoked that larger sacred community Bataille so assiduously sought to recover. "In experience," he explained, "there is no longer a limited experience. There a man is not distinguished in any way from others: in him what is torrential is lost within others. The so simple commandment: 'Be that ocean,' linked to the *extreme limit,* at the same time makes of a man, a multitude, a desert. It is an expression which resumes and makes precise the sense of a community."[75]

Although as Jean-Luc Nancy was to note, for Bataille, "outside of community, there is no experience,"[76] what he meant by it was never easy to

71. Bataille, *Inner Experience,* p. 13.

72. Ibid., p. 7.

73. Ibid.

74. Ibid., p. 102. Many years later, in his 1983 *The Unavowable Community,* trans. Pierre Joris (Barrytown, N.Y., 1988), Blanchot would repeat this definition: "inner experience," he says, "is a movement of contestation that, coming from the subject, devastates it, but has as a deeper origin the relationship with the other which is community itself, a community that would be nothing if it did not open the one who exposes himself to it to the infiniteness of alterity, while at the same time deciding its inexorable finitude" (p. 17). The question of Bataille's friendship with Blanchot is sensitively addressed in Eleanor Kaufman, *The Delirium of Praise: Bataille, Blanchot, Deleuze, Foucault, Klossowski* (Baltmore, 2001). Kaufman compares it to Montaigne's friendship with Étienne de la Boétie, arguing that theirs was based more on harmony and accord, while that between Bataille and Blanchot included discontinuity and contradiction (pp. 42–43).

75. Bataille, *Inner Experience,* p. 27.

76. Jean-Luc Nancy, *The Inoperative Community,* ed. Peter Connor, trans. Peter Connor, Lisa Garbus, Michael Holland, and Simona Sawhney (Minneapolis, 1991), p. 21. For further elaborations of

grasp. As we have seen, community does not mean the overcoming of all boundaries and the fusion of its members into a collective whole. A similar skepticism motivated his disdain for the orgy as a comparable overcoming in the register of erotic experience.[77] Nor did community mean something like an organized church or order. When attempts are made to contain the heterogeneous effervescence of community in homogeneous forms like the modern state, the outcome, in fact, can be fascism.[78] Limits, especially the extreme limit that is the death of the individual, both forge a commonality and keep it riven with fault lines. In fact, Bataille always posited an unsublated dialectic of limits and their transgression, which can be seen in the continuing power he accorded to precisely those homogeneous systems he mocked and challenged: Christianity, Hegelian idealism, the state, surrealist sublimation, and any version of aesthetic transfiguration. They provided the limits against which transgression had to struggle in a never-ending battle to attain the impossible. It was for this reason that erotic and religious experience are so intimately intertwined: "The inner experience of eroticism demands from the subject a sensitiveness to the anguish at the heart of the taboo no less great than the desire which leads him to infringe it. This is religious sensibility, and it always links desire closely with terror, intense pleasure and anguish."[79] No limits meant no transgression, and so both were critical in any understanding of the community suggested by inner experiences

Among the most trenchant interpreters of Bataille's understanding of the relationship between inner experience and community were Jean-Luc Nancy and Blanchot. In *The Inoperative Community* of 1986 *(La communauté désoeuvrée* can also be translated as the "unworked" community), Nancy stressed the impossibility of perfect communion and absolute immanence in an ecstatic community based on a realization of finitude and mortality. "That is why the 'inner experience' of which Bataille speaks is in no way 'interior' or 'subjective,' but is indissociable from the experience of this relation to an incommensurable outside. . . . The crucial point of this experience was the exigency, reversing all nostalgia and all communal metaphysics, of a 'clear con-

---

Nancy's position, see the essays in *Community at Loose Ends,* ed. the Miami Theory Collective (Minneapolis, 1991).

77. For a discussion of Bataille's preference for a determinate relationship with a particular woman as opposed to an orgy, see Suzanne Guerlac, *Literary Polemics: Bataille, Sartre, Valéry, Breton* (Stanford, 1997), p. 23.

78. Bataille, "The Psychological Structure of Fascism," in *Visions of Excess.*

79. Bataille, *Erotism,* pp. 38–39.

sciousness' of separation . . . that immanence or intimacy cannot, nor are they ever to be, *regained*."[80] Nor was it the expression of a common essence or shared substance in the present. In fact, it never actually is in existence in fully positive form, but instead is always "to come."

Because such a community is not the deliberate work of a meta-subject or even an intersubjective contract, it always bespeaks a condition of heteronomy, of transcendence within immanence. It is thus not like a work of art, if the latter is understood as an organically formed totality, as an autotelically self-sufficient entity.[81] Indeed, work is not its essence, in the same way that expenditure and waste rather than production and exchange are the principles ruling the general economy as opposed to its restricted counterpart. The moment of passivity that we have often seen in experience, distinguishing it from praxis or action, is here given pride of place. As Blanchot was to note in his 1983 *The Unavowable Community,* referring to the one group led by Bataille that seems to have tried to realize "inner experience," submitting to sacrifice was the main activity of its members: "to link oneself with Acéphale is to abandon and to give oneself: *to give oneself wholly to limitless abandonment.* That is the sacrifice that founds the community by undoing it. . . ."[82]

What also distinguishes Bataille's notion of an unworked or unavowed community is its distance from the protocols of communication, at least when that term is understood as an attempt to reach an intersubjective consensus and linguistic transparency through symmetrical rational dialogue. Not surprisingly, he would be excoriated by defenders of that alternative, such as Jürgen Habermas in *The Philosophical Discourse of Modernity.*[83] Experience for Bataille was precisely that which transcended attempts of discourse to validate its claims. As Kristeva was to note, "the weakness of Christianity, according to Bataille, is its inability to disengage the non-discursive operations from discourse itself, its confusion of experience with discourse, and thus its reduction to the possibilities of discourse what largely exceeds it."[84]

What also set Bataille apart from Christianity was his rejection of the premise of a transcendent God who was the interlocutor in a dialogic no-

80. Nancy, *The Inoperative Community,* pp. 18–19.

81. Blanchot used the word "*désoeuvrée*" to indicate the lack of self-sufficient being in works of art, the lack of self-presence. See the translator's notes to Blanchot, *The Unavowable Community,* pp. xxviii–xxix.

82. Blanchot, *The Unavowable Community,* p. 15.

83. Trans. Frederick Lawrence (Cambridge, Mass., 1987), chapter 8.

84. Kristeva, "Bataille, l'expérience et la pratique," p. 272.

tion of religious experience. As a result, he might well seem especially vulnerable to the charge that we have seen previous critics of religious experience, such as Karl Barth, leveling against its tacit diminution or even elimination of the divine Other. For far more than Friedrich Schleiermacher or Rudolf Otto, he opposed the separate existence of *"das ganze Andere,"* the ineffable God encountered in religious experience itself. But what might perhaps save Bataille from the related conclusion that this opposition privileged the pious subject over his object of piety was his insistence that there was always a heterological difference contained in even the most seemingly homogeneous inner experience. Thus, when Blanchot later argued that "there is evidence—overpowering evidence—that ecstasy is without object, just as it is without a why, just as it challenges any certainty,"[85] it would be important to add that it also meant undermining the coherent subject of experience as well.

It was this very undermining, however, that troubled many of the first readers of the book when it appeared in 1943; some even went so far as to see it as tacitly colluding with the Occupation.[86] Although surrealists like Patrick Waldberg and Christians like Gabriel Marcel were among the book's critics, the most prominent was Jean-Paul Sartre, whose *Being and Nothingness* came out the same year. In three articles in the October, November, and December 1943 issues of *Le Sud,* subsequently collected in the first volume of *Situations,* Sartre claimed that Bataille, showing the residues of his debts to the objectivist sociology of Emile Durkheim, had taken an impossibly external point of view on the subject, as if he himself were a member of an alien species.[87] Because Bataille wrongly identified inner experience with singular moments of intensity and neglected the role of intentionality, he also misunderstood its futural temporal flow. Sarcastically mocking Bataille's embrace of martyrdom as a confessional indulgence and seeing more of Blaise Pascal than Nietzsche in his defense of mysticism, Sartre damned *Inner Experience* as an exercise in "bad faith," in which discursive explanation mingled inconsistently with the refusal of rationality and communicability. As for his impassioned call for sacrifice, Sartre wondered, "is it sincere? For after all, M. Bataille writes, he occupies a position at the Bibliothèque Nationale, he

---

85. Blanchot, *The Unavowable Community,* p. 19.

86. For an account of the negative reception of the book, see Surya, *Georges Bataille,* pp. 329–36. It was Boris Souvarine who later accused it of tacit acceptance of the German Occupation.

87. Jean-Paul Sartre, *Situations* 1 (Paris, 1947). For analyses of the dispute, mostly from Bataille's side, see Richman, *Reading Georges Bataille,* chapter 5, and Surya, *Georges Bataille,* pp. 331–36.

reads, he makes love, he eats."[88] Ultimately, such a book, he concluded, calls for a psychological explanation. What Sartre perhaps most disliked about *Inner Experience,* however, was its explicit rejection of the importance of the active project in defining human subjectivity and the meaningful experience of commitment it could produce. The result was the abandonment of human autonomy and the valorization of the inauthentic existence of what Heidegger had called *Das Man.*

Despite the aggressive quality of this critique, Bataille and Sartre continued to talk about the issues between them, leading to a debate at the home of a mutual friend in March 1944, sparked by a lecture by Bataille later published as "A Discussion about Sin."[89] Bataille defended the need to introduce both perspectives—the sociological one from "the outside" and the phenomenological one from "within"—rather than believing that experience was entirely an affair of the subject. "The *cogito,* for Sartre," he complained, "is the inviolable, atemporal, irreducible foundation. . . . For me, it exists only within a relation. . . . *it is a network of communications, existing in time* . . . Sartre reduces a book to the intentions of an author, the author. *If, as appears to me, a book is a communication, the author is only a link among different readings.*"[90]

Although relations between the two figures softened somewhat after this encounter, the mood in postwar France was clearly more hospitable to Sartre's defense of intellectual engagement and the project, soon understood in largely Marxist terms, than to Bataille's defense of an inner experience that seemed to have no obvious political implications. Action rather than intoxication, commitment rather than ecstasy, the possible rather than the impossible, seemed the order of the day. Although Bataille's new journal, *Critique,* was one of the most successful he had launched in his career, it could not compete with Sartre's *Les temps modernes* for influence over the postwar generation. For reasons of health as well as employment, Bataille lived outside of Paris after 1945, thus increasing his marginalization. Although continuing to write both fiction and treatises, such as *The Accursed Share* in 1949 and *Erotism* in 1957, he seems to have occupied himself more and more with the impending limit-experience that was his own death, which came in 1962.[91]

88. Sartre, "Un Nouveau Mystique," in *Situations* I, p. 175.

89. Bataille, "La discussion sur la péché," *Dieu vivant* 4 (1945), in *Oeuvres complètes,* ed. Henri Ronse and Jean-Michel Rey, vol. 6 (Paris, 1973).

90. Ibid., p. 408 (emphasis in original).

91. For an account of Bataille's last years, see Surya, *Georges Bataille,* pp. 474–92.

It was not perhaps until the post-existentialist generation of French thinkers, who came of age during what came to be called, somewhat imprecisely, the "age of structuralism," that Bataille gained a new audience. Around journals like *Tel Quel,* founded in 1960 as an antidote to the engaged philosophy of *Les temps modernes,* the exploration of "inner experience" became an inspiration for a poetics of transgression.[92] Its main figures, Philippe Sollers and Julia Kristeva, continued, in fact, to invoke Bataille's ideas throughout the next two decades of the journal's turbulent odyssey, which took it from apolitical avant-gardism through Althusserian Marxism and Maoism and finally to anti-Communist dissidence.

Among the earliest of their cohort to appreciate the implications of Bataille's defense of heterology and erotic excess was the literary critic and cultural analyst Roland Barthes, whose positive response to *The Story of the Eye* appeared the year of Bataille's death.[93] It was, in fact, one of the first attempts to take this previously ignored pornographic text seriously. Barthes, then at the height of his most "scientific" period, in which he hoped to make structuralist linguistics or semiology the foundation of a metalanguage of critical practice, concluded that "Bataille's erotic language is connoted by Georges Bataille's very being, it is a style; between the two, something is born, something which transforms every experience into a warped language and which is literature."[94]

Barthes' celebration of the literary as the transfigured endpoint of experience in this essay was very much of a piece with the early Telquelian fetish of language, poetics, and textuality. "How do you classify a writer like Georges Bataille?" he asked in 1971. "Novelist, poet, essayist, economist, philosopher, mystic? The answer is so difficult that the literary manuals generally prefer to forget about Bataille who, in fact, wrote texts, perhaps continually one text."[95] But Barthes soon abandoned his faith in the "euphoric dream of scientificity,"[96] which had informed his Marxist and structuralist phase, and came to appreciate the more direct bodily experiences of desire and pleasure

92. For an analysis of Bataille's importance for *Tel Quel,* see Danielle Marx-Scouras, *The Cultural Politics of Tel Quel: Literature in the Wake of Engagement* (University Park, Pa., 1996), pp. 87–91.

93. Roland Barthes, "La métaphore de l'oeil," *Critique* 195–96 (1962), in *Critical Essays,* trans. Richard Howard (Evanston, Ill., 1972), from which the following quotation is taken.

94. Ibid., p. 247. For a recent attempt to rescue the early structuralist moment in Barthes' career, see Jonathan Culler, "Barthes, Theorist," *Yale Journal of Criticism* 14, no. 2 (Fall 2001).

95. Roland Barthes, "From Work to Text," in *Image, Music, Text,* trans. Stephen Heath (New York, 1977), p. 157.

96. Roland Barthes, "Réponses," *Tel Quel* 47 (Autumn 1971), p. 97.

that somehow exceeded their textual expression. Although Bataille only sporadically reappeared in Barthes' subsequent oeuvre—most notably in the appreciative rumination composed in 1972 on the implications of Bataille's essay "The Big Toe"[97]—it is arguable that he had absorbed many of Bataille's attitudes toward inner experience. For not only could Bataille be understood as transgressing the boundaries separating different genres of texts; he also could be appreciated for undermining the self-sufficiency of the realm of textuality and language itself.

While never explicitly celebrating "inner experience," as did Sollers and Kristeva, Barthes was also never apologetic about positively using the word "experience" in his work, often in fact prefacing it with the first-person possessive pronoun. On numerous occasions, he explicitly acknowledged learning from his personal experience.[98] When asked to define his identity, for example, he replied, "What I do within myself is philosophize, reflect on my experience."[99] Even during his most militantly structuralist period in 1963, he would claim that "there exist certain writers, painters, musicians in whose eyes a certain exercise of structure (and no longer merely its thought) represents a distinctive experience, and that both analysts and creators must be placed under the common sign of what we might call *structural man,* defined not by his ideas or his languages, but by his imagination—in other words, by the way in which he mentally experiences structure."[100]

Barthes, to be sure, did not remain a rigorous structuralist for very long, and so it would be a mistake to identify his own experience in general with that of *homo structuralis.* What then was the alternative or alternatives he proposed or, better put, embodied? "Embody" is, of course, not an innocent verb here, and it helps us to begin an answer, for Barthes knew that experience was not merely a mental category, but involved the somatic dimension of human existence. Accordingly, such works as *The Pleasure of the Text* have earned a comparison with the seminal essay "Of Experience" by Montaigne, which so vividly incorporated its author's physiological and anatomical preoccupations.[101] More than the phenomenological body sit-

97. Roland Barthes, "Outcomes of the Text," *The Rustle of Language,* trans. Richard Howard (Berkeley, 1989).

98. See, for example, the 1973 interview "An Almost Obsessive Relation to Writing Instruments," in *The Grain of the Voice: Interviews 1962–1980,* trans. Linda Coverdale (New York, 1985), pp. 179 and 181.

99. Barthes, "On the Subject of Violence," in *The Grain of the Voice,* p. 307.

100. Barthes, "The Structuralist Activity," *Critical Essays,* trans. Richard Howard (Evanston, Ill., 1972), p. 214.

101. Steven Ungar, *Roland Barthes: The Professor of Desire* (Lincoln, Neb., 1983), p. 138.

uated in the flesh of the world, the body of, say, Maurice Merleau-Ponty, his was above all a desiring body hungry for sensual encounters with the world and with others.[102] There can in fact be few other writers who have shared with his readers the intensities of his pleasures and the depths of his frustrations, the variety of his lusts, and the range of his maladies as abundantly as did Barthes. In addition, his hypersensitivity to what he liked to call the "grain" of the other's body, which appeared not only in the singing voice, but also in performing limbs and writing hands, suggested an openness to the material significations that were there to be experienced by anyone able to apprehend them—apprehend them, that is, erotically.[103] But it was not, he carefully pointed out, the psychological subject in him who was erotically open to the distinguishing grain of the other, not the orthopsychic ego constituted by the specular doubling whose ideological implications he had learned from Lacan. It was rather something less organized and integrated, a dispersed self, resistant to coherent narrative reconstruction. When Barthes came to write of his movie-going habits, he noted that he allowed himself to be fascinated both by the image on the screen and by everything else in the theater, "as if I had two bodies at the same time: a narcissistic body which gazes, lost into the engulfing mirror, and a perverse body, ready to fetishize not the image but precisely what exceeds it: the texture of the sound, the hall, the darkness, the obscure mass of the other bodies, the rays of light, entering the theater, leaving the hall: in short, in order to distance, to 'take off,' I complicate a 'relation' by a 'situation'."[104] This was a form of experience that was, *pace* Lyotard, suffered or enjoyed without a strong, centered subject, but, so Barthes implicitly insisted, it was experience nonetheless.

As in the case of Bataille, the alternative could be understood by invoking the linguistic notion of the intransitive "middle voice," which Barthes argued was characteristic of writing in the modernist era. Significantly, when he came to define it, he turned to the example of sacrifice: "According to the classic example given by [Antoine] Meillet and [Emile] Benveniste, the verb *to sacrifice* (ritually) is active if the priest sacrifices the victim in my place and for me, and it is middle voice if, taking the knife from the priest's hands, I

102. According to Barthes, "classical phenomenology . . . had never, so far as I could remember, spoken of desire or of mourning." *Camera Lucida: Reflections on Photography,* trans. Richard Howard (New York, 1981).

103. Barthes, "The Grain of the Voice," in *The Responsibility of Forms,* trans. Richard Howard (New York, 1985).

104. Barthes, "Leaving the Movie Theater," in *The Rustle of Language,* p. 349.

make the sacrifice for my own sake; in the case of the active voice, the action is performed outside the subject, for although the priest makes the sacrifice, he is not affected by it; in the case of the middle voice, on the contrary, by acting, the subject affects himself, he always remains inside the action, even if that action involves an object."[105]

Another clue to the type of experience sought by Barthes can be found in the description he gave of gay cruising in the preface he wrote to the novel *Tricks* by Renaud Camus. Here the perverse body gains the upper hand over its narcissistic twin:

> The *Tricks* repeat themselves; the subject is on a treadmill. Repetition is an am-
> biguous form; sometimes it denotes failure, impotence; sometimes it can be
> read as an aspiration, the stubborn movement of a quest which is not to be
> discouraged; we might very well take the cruising narrative as the metaphor of
> a mystical experience.[106]

How are we to interpret this bold analogy, which dares to compare the repetitive hunting for forbidden sexual pleasure with the yearning to achieve oneness with God? Is Barthes really asking us to believe that cruising is akin to the experience of a religious mystic?

Mystical experience is, of course, itself not easy to define, as we have already remarked in discussing Bataille's own ambivalent evocation of it. But perhaps in one of its guises it can plausibly support Barthes' suggestive analogy. The quest for mystical experience, Michel de Certeau once pointed out, can involve the separation of utterances from the objective, formal order of theological statements, an order in which the act of uttering is subordinated to a system of formal meanings. Instead, it involves a more direct relation between the subjective act of uttering and the messages it utters. "The term 'experience'," de Certeau wrote, "connotes this relation. Contemporaneous to the act of creation, outside an unreadable history, 'utopian' space having provided a new faculty of reason a no-place in which to exercise its ability to create a world as text—a mystic space is constituted, outside the fields of knowledge. It is there that the labor of writing which is given birth through the animation of language by the desire of the other takes place."[107]

Although this reading of mystical experience stresses the *hic et nunc* of the

105. Barthes, "To Write: An Intransitive Verb?" in *The Rustle of Language*, p. 18.
106. Barthes, "Preface to Renaud Camus's *Tricks*," in *The Rustle of Language*, p. 294.
107. Michel de Certeau, "Mystic Speech," in *Heterologies: Discourse on the Other*, trans. Brian Massumi (Minneapolis, 1986), p. 89.

creative moment as opposed to the ambivalent repetition of cruising, at once aspiration and frustration, both can be said to challenge the notion that experience is equivalent to the dialectical narrative of progressive *Bildung* posited by Lyotard as its essential template. If it is therefore somehow religious, it is not that of an orthodox Christian soteriological narrative seen by Lyotard as the model for experience *tout court.* For the religious experience of the mystic is by no means the same as the redemptive story of the Fortunate Fall from innocence that subtends so much of Western culture.[108] Instead, it privileges those moments of intensity that resist incorporation into such a progressive narrative, in a manner not unlike that described in Renaud Camus's *Tricks.*

Both mystical experience and cruising, as Barthes understood it, also involve a textualization of the desire for the other, whether it be the sexual body of a mundane love object or the spiritual body of God. What de Certeau called the "labor of writing" in which the world is constituted as a text does not mean, it must be stressed, the reduction of experience to a kind of post facto secondary elaboration of its essential elements.[109] It is not an emplotted narrative with a culminating moment of closure. In his study of the founder of the Jesuit order, Ignatius Loyola, Barthes noted the characteristic hostility to images in mystical experience, which reveled instead in the dark, shadowy, unseeable "face of sublime nothingness."[110] He then went on to characterize Loyola's attempt to overcome mysticism in his *Exercises* by privileging images, but doing so, *nota bene,* by organizing them in what was tantamount to a rigid linguistic system. "To constitute the field of the image as a linguistic system is in fact to forearm oneself against the suspect marginal zones of the mystical experience: language is the guarantor of orthodox faith doubtless (among other reasons) because it authenticates the specificity of the Christian confession."[111]

The mystical utterance, on the other hand, steadfastly resists not only images, but also their transformation into a controlled order like a linguistic sys-

---

108. The classic account of its power is M. H. Abrams, *Natural Supernaturalism: Tradition and Revolution in Romantic Literature* (New York, 1971).

109. In his account of the language of the seventeenth-century mystic Joseph Surin, de Certeau would note its internal "dialectic between 'language' (*langue:* the system that defines the world and fills it with objects) and the 'word of God' (*le langage de Dieu:* spiritual experience that language 'cannot express' and that 'has no name')." "History and Mysticism," in Jacques Revel and Lynn Hunt, eds., *Histories: French Constructions of the Past,* trans. Arthur Goldhammer (New York, 1995), p. 439. De Certeau's point is not that mystical experience is utterly outside of language, as Ludwig Wittgenstein may have thought, but rather that it involves a split within language itself, a relation rather than a silence.

110. Barthes, *Sade, Fourier, Loyola,* trans. Richard Miller (New York, 1976), p. 66. The quoted phrase is from the fourteenth-century Belgian mystic Jan van Rusbroeck.

111. Ibid., p. 67.

tem. It has no truck with secondary elaborations, those post facto narratives posited by Sigmund Freud as the final operation of dream work. Instead, it produces a text that is in excess of such attempts to contain it, a text that undermines not only the systematicity of language but also the centered subjectivity of those who employ it instrumentally. If the mystical subject strives to lose his integral selfhood by merging with the divine, the cruising subject with his perverse rather than narcissistic body does the same through the characteristic suppression of his proper name, assuming the mantle of anonymity. As D. A. Miller has pointed out in his moving and provocative rumination on Barthes' own cruising journals, the signifying subject tied to the Name is understood by Barthes as "an instrument of domination and death," while "in contrast, the Letter is always a good object for Barthes."[112] Even the seemingly liberating act of embracing the designation of "homosexual" is one that he sought to avoid, echoing Sartre's celebrated critique of the well-meaning advocate of sincerity, who unwittingly reifies his friend's sexual acts into the fixed identity of a "pederast."[113] There is therefore no latent or occluded truth to confess in the manner of Loyola's guarantee of orthodox faith.

Significantly, however, Barthes did not share Sartre's hostility to the importance of the past in shaping present experience, even if he broke with conventional dialectical notions of the way in which the past could be successfully integrated into the present. His body, he argued, was not only capable of enjoying or suffering the moment, but also of registering the effects of what had gone before. As he noted in his reflections on "The Light of the Sud-Ouest," "I enter these regions of reality in my fashion, that is, with my body; and my body is my childhood, as history has made it. . . . 'to read' a country is first of all to perceive it in terms of the body and of memory, in terms of the body's memory. I believe it is to this vestibule of knowledge and analysis that the writer is assigned: more conscious than competent, conscious of the very interstices of competence."[114]

112. D. A. Miller, *Bringing Out Roland Barthes* (Berkeley, 1992), p. 18. In a later essay, "Foutre! Bougre! Écriture!" *Yale Journal of Criticism* 14, no. 2 (Fall 2001), Miller laments the costs of Barthes' reluctance to embrace a homosexual identity, which he charges is a tacit perpetuation of the tradition of closeted self-denial.

113. Jean-Paul Sartre, "Existentialism Is a Humanism," Walter Kaufmann, ed., *Existentialism from Dostoevsky to Sartre* (New York, 1963), pp. 261–62. For a more recent analysis of the complications of gay identity and the demand for recognition, see Alexander García Duttman, "The Culture of Polemic: We're queer, we're here, so get fuckin' used to it," in *Between Cultures: Tensions in the Struggle for Recognition*, trans. Kenneth B. Woodgate (London, 2000).

114. Barthes, "The Light of the Sud-Ouest," in *Incidents*, trans. Richard Howard (Berkeley, 1992), pp. 7–9.

In the interstices of competence, Barthes implied, lay the undigested residues of the past, and they are felt in the body, perhaps most clearly in that perverse body that denies the holistic unity of the narcissistic body. It is, moreover, through writing and the textualization of the body's memory as well as its desire that experience makes its halting appearance. In rescuing the dimension of experience that is equivalent to experimentation and carrying them out through what we might call the grain of his pen, Barthes was a stylist whose innovations have been long admired. Even in such autobiographical works as *Roland Barthes*, he provided experiments on himself through writing. To quote Miller once again, it was here that he traded the "self-appointed securities of the personal for the disorienting effects—of intermittence, plurality, violation, exhaustion—produced on the subject by the principle of aberration that Barthes terms the Text."[115] As in de Certeau's definition of mystical experience, the "labor of writing," the passage through the materiality of the letter, is part of the experience itself and not a delayed attempt to give it retrospective coherence.

Although one might well resist Barthes' ideal of mystical experience in its various secular forms, it at least helps us to appreciate the resilience of the term in the face of those who would write its premature epitaph. For what Barthes did by holding on to the possibility of experience without the strong notion of a centered subject was to alert us to the presence of the arbitrarily naturalized code that subtended critiques like that of Lyotard, a code that Barthes would have called proairetic. That is, experience understood as a secular version of a Christian story of salvation based on innocence, alienation, and redemption was itself hostage to an underlying concept of meaning as dependent on unidirectional, sequential, narrative development over time.[116] By too quickly reducing experience to that model of familiar emplotment, which we might call that of the classical *Bildungsroman,* its critics, Barthes implied, short-circuit the possibility of alternatives that were not debased or impoverished versions of that dominant norm. Accordingly, there was little in Barthes of that bitter lament about the purported withering, loss, or de-

115. Miller, *Bringing Out Roland Barthes*, p. 50.

116. As Lawrence D. Kritzman has noted with reference to Barthes' cruising journals: "The book's title, *Incidents,* from the Latin, *incidens* or *incidere,* signifies to fall into or to fall upon or, derivatively, that which happens by chance. Barthes's text depicts the fatalistic encounter of sexuality and death, both as biological entities and in terms of the deathliness of drives. Accordingly, the peripatetic movement of Barthes's cruising in *Incidents* recalls Ross Chambers's notion of 'loiterature' (an open-ended non-narrative form) for it is emblematic of the repetitive emptiness of these '*soirées vaines*' ('futile evenings') acted out in public spaces." "Barthes's Way: *Un Amour de Proust*," *Yale Journal of Criticism* 14, no. 2 (Fall 2001), p. 540.

cay of genuine experience that we have seen coursing through the writings of other twentieth-century cultural critics, like Raymond Williams in Britain and Theodor Adorno in Germany and America.

This resistance to nostalgia did not, to be sure, mean that Barthes held on to a utopian concept of experience comparable, say, to that paradoxical restoration of pre-linguistic innocence we have seen criticized by Giorgio Agamben. His sober reflections on the implications of mortality amply demonstrate this point. Barthes was, in fact, as preoccupied with the question of death and its place in human experience as Bataille had been. *Camera Lucida* is perhaps his most profound meditation on that impossible topic. This is not the place to rehearse its complicated argument or mull over the countless commentaries it has engendered. But it should be noted that he conceived of the experience of looking at photographs as precisely the opposite of Lyotard's notion of experience as a life lived progressively forward through the dialectical negation of what precedes each moment. Lyotard, it bears repeating, wrote that "life signifies the death of what one is, and this death certifies that life has a meaning, that one is not a stone." Barthes replied, "if dialectic is that thought which masters the corruptible and converts the negation of death into the power to work, then the photograph is undialectical: it is a denatured theater where death cannot 'be contemplated,' reflected and interiorized."[117] The photograph is therefore not in the service of memory or mourning, but rather of coming to grips with death undialectically and without the consolation of imputed meaning.

Here it was the celebrated encounter with the photo of his mother as a five-year-old child in a glassed-in conservatory called a Winter Garden that provided the crucial, eye-opening experience for Barthes himself. "Ultimately," Barthes wrote, "I experienced her strong as she had been, my inner law, as my feminine child. Which was my way of resolving Death." That resolution came because Barthes, who had no children of his own and therefore could not participate in the grand narrative of procreation that supposedly gives the individual's death a meaningful place in the story of our species, had somehow fantasized that he was his mother's parent. But when the child in the photograph herself died, Barthes realized, "I no longer had any reason to attune myself to the progress of the superior Life Force (the race, the species). . . . From now on I could no more than await my total, undialectical death."[118]

117. Barthes, *Camera Lucida*, p. 90.
118. Ibid., p. 72.

As in the vain, interminable quest of gay cruising, the repetitive search for mystical experience, and the privileging of the letter over the name, the manic and the melancholic mingle to produce experiential intensities that refuse to be contained in narratives of closure and completion. What Barthes famously called the *punctum,* the uncoded detail that eludes the unitary image he dubbed the photo's *studium,* could disrupt the totalizing potential in specularity and unleash an unending chain of metonymic displacements. Here was a visual practice that eluded the power of the mirror stage and narrative recuperation, a practice that abetted the dispersion of the perverse body rather than the integrity of its narcissistic counterpart. Such photographs, Barthes soberly concluded, make us confront the truth that totalized narratives are never really possible: "In front of the photograph of my mother as a child, I tell myself: she is going to die: I shudder, like Winnicott's psychotic patient, *over a catastrophe which has already occurred.* Whether or not the subject is already dead, every photograph is this catastrophe."[119]

Like that shock of sublime historical experience we have seen defended by Frank Ankersmit, the *punctum* of the photograph interrupts all attempts to contextualize it in a single meta-narrative. Like the traumatic experience that refuses to be claimed by post facto incorporation, it resists sublimation into a retrospective work of commemorative assimilation.[120] It need not therefore be equated with dialectical *Erfahrung,* unless it be of the negative kind defended by Adorno. Nor must it be understood in the terms of *Erlebnis,* when that word implies situating moments of extreme intensity in an evolutionary narrative of the life of the species. Experience, we might say, *pace* Lyotard, can thus teach us the hard truth that we are in some sense precisely the meaningless stones that the ideology of Life refuses to acknowledge.

FOUCAULT AND LIMIT EXPERIENCE

Still other alternatives to the conventional definitions of the term were elaborated in the work of another sympathetic reader of Bataille, who had himself come to question the ideology of Life as a nineteenth-century fiction:

119. Ibid., p. 96 (emphasis in original).

120. On the parallel between Barthes' *punctum* and trauma, see Anselm Haverkamp, "The Memory of Pictures: Roland Barthes and Augustine on Photography," *Comparative Literature* 45, no. 3 (Summer 1993), p. 265.

Michel Foucault.[121] Foucault's distrust of that ideology was of a piece with his growing suspicion of the idea of "lived experience" in phenomenology, a philosophy that he described in *The Order of Things* as resolving into "a description—empirical despite itself—of actual experience, and into an ontology of the unthought that automatically short-circuits the primacy of the 'I think.'"[122] Although Foucault was certainly not interested in restoring the "I think" of the Cartesian ego, he avoided privileging pre-reflective experience, close to the German idea of *Erlebnis* in most of its usages, as its antidote.

In his earlier, still phenomenologically inflected work, Foucault did, to be sure, permit himself some locutions that suggested otherwise. For example, in the preface to *Madness and Civilization*, published in 1961, he urged a return to "that zero point in the course of madness at which madness is an undifferentiated experience."[123] But by the time Foucault wrote his first methodological treatise, *The Archaeology of Knowledge*, in 1969, he was clearly backtracking: "Generally speaking, *Madness and Civilization* accorded far too great a place, and a very enigmatic one too, to what I called an 'experience,' thus showing to what extent one was still close to admitting an anonymous and general subject of history."[124]

From the philosophers of science Gaston Bachelard and Georges Canguilhem, Foucault took the lesson that the structural unconscious of science is not raw experience but discursive infrastructures and the technical instruments that are designed in accordance with their expectations. He thus resisted the reduction of science to concrete practices in the prereflective world, for which the later Husserl had argued.[125] In fact, Foucault's repudiation of this assumption allowed one commentator to go so far as to claim that "one is struck by the total disappearance of the concept 'experience'"[126] in his work after 1963, and another to argue that his major achievement was "the con-

121. On the issue of Life, see Michel Foucault, *The Order of Things: An Archaeology of the Human Sciences* (New York, 1973), chapter 8.

122. Ibid., p. 326.

123. Michel Foucault, *Madness and Civilization: A History of Insanity in the Age of Reason*, trans. Richard Howard (New York, 1965), p. ix.

124. Michel Foucault, *The Archaeology of Knowledge*, trans. A. M. Sheridan Smith (New York, 1972), p. 16. The translator renders *expérience* as "experiment," but the word's broader meaning was intended by Foucault.

125. Foucault, introduction to Georges Canguilhem, *On the Normal and the Pathological*, ed. Robert S. Cohen, trans. Carolyn R. Fawcett (Dordrecht, 1978); see also Dominque Lecourt, *Marxism and Epistemology: Bachelard, Canguilhem, Foucault*, trans. Ben Brewster (London, 1975).

126. Allan Megill, *Prophets of Extremity: Nietzsche, Heidegger, Foucault, Derrida* (Berkeley, 1985), p. 202.

version of phenomenology to epistemology. . . . Everything is knowledge, and this is the first reason why there is no 'savage experience': there is nothing beneath or prior to knowledge."[127]

There is some truth to these assessments, at least in relation to certain of his texts, and we will return to their implication shortly. But it is also important to recall that Foucault was at the same time one of Bataille's closest and most attentive readers, helping prepare and publish his *Oeuvres complètes*. He was also the author of a moving eulogy published in *Critique* in 1963, shortly after Bataille's death, entitled "Hommage à Georges Bataille" (in English as "A Preface to Transgression").[128] Anticipating the bold argument he was to make famous many years later in the first volume of his *History of Sexuality*, Foucault began his *hommage* by contesting the assumption that a liberated sexuality had been revealed in all of its essential truth as a fact of nature in the modern world. Instead, he claimed, it had been far more radically expressed in the world of Christian mystic spirituality, where it seemed an outpouring of the divine love that subtended it. Now, however, it was the site of an internal fissure, a self-disruptive frenzy, a limit-condition, which pointed to nothing outside itself. The change was due, as Nietzsche and, after him, Bataille had known, to the death of God, which replaced infinity with finitude:

> By denying us the limit of the Limitless, the death of God leads to an experience in which nothing may again announce the exteriority of being, and consequently to an experience which is *interior* and *sovereign*. But such an experience, for which the death of God is an explosive reality, discloses its own secret and clarification, its intrinsic finitude, the limitless reign of the Limit, and the emptiness of those excesses in which it spends itself and where it is found wanting. In this sense, the inner experience is throughout an experience of the *impossible* (the impossible being both that which we experience and that which constitutes experience).[129]

God's death, Foucault credited Bataille with realizing, meant that we live in a "world exposed by the experience of its limits, made and unmade by that excess which transfigures it."[130] As a result, transgression becomes the "sin-

127. Gilles Deleuze, *Foucault,* trans. Sean Hand (Minneapolis, 1986), p. 109.

128. Foucault, "A Preface to Transgression," in *Language, Counter-Memory, Practice,* ed. Donald F. Bouchard (Ithaca, N.Y., 1977).

129. Ibid., p. 32.

130. Ibid.

gular experience" that may one day supplant contradiction, the dialectical mode of thinking negation only in the context of totality, as "decisive for our culture."[131] Unlike dialectics, however, such a philosophy would be one of "non-positive affirmation," what Blanchot had called "contestation," "an affirmation that affirms nothing, a radical break of transitivity."[132]

Like Barthes at the same time, Foucault argued not for an opposition between language and experience, but rather for their interpenetration. But the language in which inner experiences might manifest themselves is decisively "nondiscursive," manifesting an erotics of disruption, which does away with the unified subject of traditional philosophy. "This experience forms the exact reversal of the movement which has sustained the wisdom of the West at least since the time of Socrates, that is, the wisdom to which philosophical language promised the serene unity of a subjectivity which would triumph in it, having been fully constituted by it and through it."[133] For Foucault, as for Barthes, Bataille's *Story of the Eye* was the locus of this non-discursive language in which inner experience finds its expression.

It was also a language in which subjectivity—the grammatical assumption of a first-person singular or plural prior to the predicate of a sentence, an integral self-consciousness entirely interior to itself—was fully undermined. In an essay written in 1966 celebrating Blanchot's "experience of the outside," Foucault made clear his adherence to what he called a tradition launched by the Marquis de Sade and Friedrich Hölderlin, which had shadowed the hegemonic dialectical tradition of alienation and interiorization. "The same experience," he claimed, "resurfaced in the second half of the nineteenth century at the very core of language, which had become—even though our culture was still seeking to mirror itself in it as if it held the secret of interiority—the sparkle of the outside."[134] In Friedrich Nietzsche, Stéphane Mallarmé, Antonin Artaud, Pierre Klossowski, Blanchot, and Bataille, "when thought ceases to be the discourse of contradiction or of the unconscious, becoming the discourse of the limit, of ruptured subjectivity, transgression,"[135] this experience found new life.

In his "Preface to Transgression," Foucault hewed closely to Bataille's elaboration of an "inner experience" that paradoxically opens to "the outside,"

131. Ibid., p. 33.
132. Ibid., p. 36.
133. Ibid., pp. 43–44.
134. Foucault, "Maurice Blanchot: The Thought from Outside," in *Foucault/Blanchot*, trans. Jeffrey Mehlman and Brian Massumi (New York, 1987), p. 19.
135. Ibid.

an experience that exceeds virtually all traditional acceptations of the word, moving it into a realm of ecstatic self-denial that culminates in sexual excess, madness, and the limit-experience that is death. Although perhaps ultimately more ambivalent about the positive virtues of transgression than Bataille,[136] Foucault in this essay put little distance between their two positions. He seemed, in fact, to endorse the untamed "other" of Cartesian reason that would allow Derrida to criticize him for too binary a distinction between rationality and irrationality.[137] In an interview in 1971, he went so far as to claim that "it is possible that the rough outline of a future society is supplied by the recent experiences with drugs, sex, communes, other forms of consciousness, and other forms of individuality. If scientific socialism emerged from the *Utopias* of the nineteenth century, it is possible that a real socialization will emerge, in the twentieth century, from *experiences.*"[138]

Elsewhere in his early work, however, Foucault did develop a more sober analysis, essentially epistemological in nature, of what he later called his perennial concern: "the relations between the subject, truth, and the constitution of experience."[139] Radicalizing the lessons of Canguilhem and Bachelard, he questioned not only how experience was constituted, but also how truth itself was a function of linguistic regimes of meaning that preceded it. Here he fell back on a notion of discursivity—perhaps even discursive determinism that could be known by the objective researcher—that his celebration of Bataille's inner experience seemed to rule out (although Bataille himself could be accused, and was by Habermas, of vacillating between the two).[140] As Béatrice Han has recently shown, this analysis took the form of a prolonged exploration of the ambivalence in Kant's legacy between his tran-

136. For a discussion of the differences, see Charles C. Lemert and Garth Gillan, *Michel Foucault: Social Theory as Transgression* (New York, 1982), pp. 65–68.

137. Derrida, "Cogito and the History of Madness." Foucault responded in an appendix to the second edition of *Histoire de la folie* called "Mon corps, ce papier, ce feu." For a discussion of their debate, see Peter Flaherty, "(Con)textual Contest: Derrida and Foucault on Madness and the Cartesian Subject," *Philosophy of the Social Sciences* 16 (1986).

138. Foucault, "Revolutionary Action: 'Until Now'," in *Language, Counter-Memory, Practice,* p. 231 (emphasis in original).

139. Foucault, "An Aesthetics of Existence," in *Politics, Philosophy, Culture: Interviews and Other Writings, 1977–1984,* ed. Lawrence D. Kritzman, trans. Alan Sheridan and others (New York, 1988), p. 48.

140. Habermas, *The Philosophical Discourse of Modernity:* "the knowing subject would—paradoxically—have to surrender his own identity and yet retrieve those experiences to which he was exposed in ecstasy—to catch them like fish from the decentered ocean of emotions. In spite of this paradox, Bataille stubbornly makes a claim to objectivity of knowledge and impersonality of method—even for this science 'from within,' for the grasp of 'inner experience'" (p. 238).

scendental and empirical notions of the subject, what might be called his critical and anthropological impulses.[141] In siding with the latter, she points out, Foucault

reverses both the direction of the critical process and the significance of experience: where Kant sought to *anticipate* the possibility of all knowledge by prescribing to it in advance its own laws, Foucault instead intends to begin from already constituted forms of knowledge to define *retrospectively* that which rendered them possible. The experience is, for Foucault, who here intends it in a precritical sense, a given whose conditions of possibility must be searched for elsewhere—in the historical *a priori*.[142]

Initially this search meant an "archaeological" attempt to discern the discursive regularities in different historical epochs and then a "genealogical" investigation of the apparatuses of power that subtended them, an attempt that would lead many commentators to conclude that Foucault had simply left behind the question of experience as naive, or at least reduced it entirely to question of its "conditions of possibility."

But in his final work, Foucault came to focus his attention on the constitution of the subject of knowledge in such a way that experience once again began to resist reduction to such conditions, whether understood in terms of epistemic discourses or apparatuses of power. In so doing, he returned to his earlier fascination for Bataille's notion of inner experience, while at the same time reproducing some of the unresolved tensions that critics like Habermas had discerned in Bataille's approach to the issue. Perhaps the best way to highlight these ambiguities is to focus on two late texts in which experience once again became an explicit theme: *The Use of Pleasure,* the second volume of *The History of Sexuality,* published in 1984, the year of his death, and the interviews Foucault gave the Italian journalist Duccio Trombadori, the editor of the Communist *L'Unità,* six years earlier.

To begin with the later work first, Foucault unself-consciously opened *The Use of Pleasure,* his history of Greek sexual codes and practices, by saying his goal was understanding how an "'experience' came to be constituted in modern Western societies, an experience that caused individuals to recognize them-

---

141. Béatrice Han, *Foucault's Critical Project: Between the Transcendental and the Historical,* trans. Edward Pile (Stanford, 2002). Han points out that Foucault went beyond Canguilhem in situating truth claims in a normative discourse of "being in the truth," rather than independent of them (p. 81).

142. Ibid., p. 43.

selves as subjects of a 'sexuality,' which was accessible to very diverse fields of knowledge and linked to a system of rules and constraints."[143] What exactly did he mean by "experience" in this context? Interestingly, Foucault's answer gave little hint of the influence of Bataille: "experience is understood as the correlation between fields of knowledge, types of normativity, and forms of subjectivity in a particular culture."[144] In other words, it is a multi-layered structure, general to a culture and based on a correlation of factors rather than their mutual contestation, which can be observed from the outside by the dispassionate historian as an object of inquiry. It is, moreover, a structure that is not a derivative effect of epistemic discourses or normative rules, but something that arises when they are correlated with different forms of subjectivity. Experience in this sense is thus understood to *cause* the discourse of sexuality in Western culture, not follow from it.

But because of the role of "forms of subjectivity" in producing experience understood in this objective way, another, more modest notion also seems to have tacitly crept into his analysis: the idea of the "experience" of the subject prior to its combination with fields of knowledge and normative power apparatuses. As Han has noted, this usage is evident in other passages of Foucault's writings, such as his characterization of the question he wanted to answer in an interview given in 1979: "In what way are those fundamental experiences of madness, suffering, death, crime, desire, individuality connected, even if we are not aware of it, with knowledge and power?"[145] Here experience is seen as different from both knowledge and power, and not yet the result of the larger cultural correlation between them and forms of subjectivity. It suggests a mode of self-formation that allows experience to be *of* sexuality or power rather than an effect of them. As a result, Han worries that "experience is thus defined at the same time as an overall structure and as one of the elements supposedly united by this structure, which brings back the unwelcome memory of the regressions characteristic of the empirico-transcendental doubles."[146]

If there is a way out, she suggests, it may seem to be in Foucault's discussion of subjectivation as a process of recognition, in which reflective experience is central to the process of self-constitution. The subject is not an a priori substance but the outcome of this process. After noting a possible

---

143. Michel Foucault, *The Use of Pleasure*, trans. Robert Hurley (New York, 1990), p. 4.
144. Ibid.
145. Foucault, "Politics and Reason," *Politics, Philosophy, Culture*, p. 71.
146. Han, *Foucault's Critical Project*, p. 155.

resemblance to what she calls a Hegelian notion of "*Erfahrung* through which consciousness determines itself in a series of apparently objective figures which it is each time led to recognize as its own,"[147] a parallel that would make Foucault open to Lyotard's charge of duplicating the dialectical trope of experience, she concludes that Foucault adopts instead "the Nietzschean perspective of the creation/destruction of the self. . . . [an] insistence on an alterity that defies any mediation."[148] But ultimately, Han concludes, this subjectivist version of experience as dynamic self-constitution is never fully integrated with his more objectivist version of experience as a correlation among epistemic discourses, normative power apparatuses and modes of subjectivation. In fact, the two versions of experience remain in unreconciled contradiction.

That Foucault himself may have understood the tensions in his various approaches to the question of experience, and perhaps even saw them as virtues, is suggested by the candid answers he gave in his 1979 interviews to Trombadori, which Han unfortunately neglects.[149] Here surprisingly the experience in question is explicitly his own, an acknowledgment of the personal dimension that in other contexts he had been at such pains to deny.[150] Now he admitted that "the books I write constitute an experience for me that I'd like to be as rich as possible. An experience is something you come out of changed. . . . In this sense, I consider myself more an experimenter than a theorist; I don't develop deductive systems to apply uniformly in different fields of research."[151] His inspiration, he explained, came from non-philosophers in the traditional sense, in particular from Nietzsche, Bataille, Blanchot, and Klossowski: "What struck me and fascinated me about them is the fact that they didn't have the problem of constructing systems, but of having direct, personal experiences."[152]

Pressed to specify the distinction between their version of experience and

147. Ibid., p. 163.

148. Ibid.

149. Han also ignores Foucault's earlier claim in "A Preface to Transgression" that inner experience is the experience of the impossible, "the impossible being both that which we experience and that which constitutes the experience" (p. 32).

150. The most celebrated expression of that denial came at the end of the introduction to *The Archaeology of Knowledge*, where Foucault protested: "I am no doubt not the only one who writes in order to have no face. Do not ask who I am and do not ask me to remain the same: leave it to our bureaucrats and our police to see that our papers are in order" (p. 17).

151. Foucault, "How an 'Experience-Book' Is Born," *Remarks on Marx: Conversations with Duccio Trombadori*, trans. R. James Goldstein and James Cascaito (New York, 1991), p. 27.

152. Ibid., p. 30.

that of the phenomenologists, Foucault replied by reaffirming the argument he had made in his 1963 essay on *The Story of the Eye:*

> The phenomenologist's experience is basically a way of organizing conscious perception *(regard réflexif)* of any aspect of daily, lived experience in its transitory form, in order to grasp its meaning. Nietzsche, Bataille, and Blanchot, on the contrary, try through experience to reach that point of life which lies as close as possible to the impossibility of living, which lies at the limit or the extreme. They attempt to gather the maximum amount of intensity and impossibility at the same time.[153]

Phenomenology, he continued, sought to find within daily experience an ultimately integrated, transcendental subject, whereas the figures he followed gave experience "the task of 'tearing' the subject from itself in such a way that it is no longer the subject as such, or that it is completely 'other' than itself so that it may arrive at its annihilation, its dissociation. It is this desubjectifying undertaking, the idea of a 'limit-experience' that tears the subject from itself, which is the fundamental lesson that I have learned from these authors."[154]

Tacitly anticipating the charge that his methods, whether archaeological or genealogical, provided an inadequate criterion of truth—betraying, as Han has charged, a crippling vacillation between a transcendental and historical notion of the subject of true knowledge—Foucault argued that his books "function as an experience, much more than as the demonstration of a historical truth. . . . what is essential is not found in a series of historical verifiable proofs; it lies rather in the experience which the book permits us to have."[155] The goal therefore is not to get the past right, not to play a truth game about historical reality, but rather to have a present experience.

Foucault then added a new wrinkle to his argument, which introduced two further dimensions to experience: its posthumous moment and its collective dimension: "Experience," he argued, "is neither true nor false: it is always a fiction, something constructed, which exists only after it has been made, not before; it isn't something that is 'true,' but it has been a reality."[156] That is, experience is paradoxically not only a proactive "tearing" of the subject from himself, but also a reactive, post facto reconstruction of that deed.

153. Ibid., p. 31.
154. Ibid., pp. 31–32.
155. Ibid., p. 36.
156. Ibid.

In this sense, experience could include at least a moment of that post facto "secondary elaboration" Barthes had tried to deny.

As for it being entirely personal, although conceding that his own experiences with madness, illness, and even death had played a key role in the choices of his topics, Foucault stressed that experience can be meaningful for others: "starting from experience, it is necessary to clear the way for a transformation, a metamorphosis which isn't simply individual but which has a character accessible to others: that is, this experience must be linkable, to a certain extent, to a collective practice and to a way of thinking."[157] As in the case of Bataille's inner experience, there is a communal dimension that cannot be ignored: "an experience is, of course, something one has alone; but it cannot have its full impact unless the individual manages to escape from pure subjectivity in such a way that others can—I won't say re-experience it exactly—but at least cross paths with it or retrace it."[158] Thus, without wanting to fall back on Wilhelm Dilthey's notion of *nacherleben* or re-enactment in R. G. Collingwood's sense, which were too harmonious in their implications, Foucault nonetheless argued that limit-experiences transcend their moments of origin and can become available for later appropriation.

Perhaps the most cogent characterization of Foucault's complicated project can be found in the following reflection from one of the Trombadori interviews:

> I have taken pains to understand how man had reduced some of his limit-experiences to objects of knowledge *(connaissance)*: madness, death, crime. Here, if you like, the themes of Georges Bataille may be recognized, reconsidered from the point of view *(optique)* of a collective history, that of the West and its knowledge *(savoir)*. The relationship between limit-experiences and the history of truth: I am more or less imprisoned or wrapped up in this tangle of problems.[159]

That is, in his role as an archaeologist or genealogist, indebted to the French philosophers of science, Foucault sought to uncover the historically variable reductions of limit-experiences to epistemological objects, to objects of "truth." But in his own life, he wanted to suffer those ecstatic limit-experiences themselves, experimenting on his own subjectivity, opening himself up to the heterogeneous impossibilities that Bataille had designated as the realm of *"non-savoir."*

157. Ibid., pp. 38–39.
158. Ibid., p. 40.
159. Ibid., p. 71.

The result was a frank "imprisonment" in the "tangle of problems" that resisted solution either on the level of life or of work. Attempts to smooth over those unresolved problems and read Foucault's work as an organic expression of his life's quest for limit-experiences fails to acknowledge the impossibility lurking at the heart of experience as he, following Bataille and in sympathy with Barthes, understood it.[160] That is, experience for these writers turns out not to be a dialectical narrative of meaningful development (*Bildung*) or the outcome of an organic notion of aesthetic self-fashioning. Nor do they see it as a derivative function of discursive or linguistic structures prior to subjective interiority or, what would be the opposite mistake, as something already present in prereflective, phenomenologically grasped "life" prior to those structures.

Instead, experience turns out to be a dynamic force-field of all these elements, neither wholly inside nor outside the self, a self that is never prior to experience anyway and refuses to be reduced either to its transcendental or empirical modes. Charged with the energy of desire, it resists domestication into conventional discourses of sexuality, heteronormative, procreative, and beholden to narratives of species propagation. Although refusing any one single temporal mode, it generally follows a logic of repetition and displacement rather than dialectical sublation. It involves language, yet exceeds it; it is available for objective observation, yet is a fiction produced after the fact; it actively seeks moments of ecstatic, perhaps even mystical intensity, yet acknowledges the power of passivity and openness to what may come without willing it. As such, it is part of Bataille's general rather than restricted economy, one in which loss is never entirely recuperated, the wounds of alienation never fully healed, and meaning never perfectly realized. Foucault, we might note in conclusion, was thus speaking for both Bataille and Barthes when he glossed his widely remarked announcement in *The Order of Things*, so scandalous to defenders of humanism, of the "death of man" in the following terms: "man is an animal of experience, he is involved *ad infinitum* within a process that, by defining a field of objects, at the same time changes him, deforms him, transforms him and transfigures him as a subject."[161]

160. For an attempt to read Foucault in this way, see James Miller, *The Passion of Michel Foucault* (New York, 1993), and his essay "Foucault's Politics in Biographical Perspective," *Salmagundi* 97 (Winter 1993), which is followed by critical responses by Lynn Hunt, Richard Rorty, Alasdair MacIntyre, and David M. Halperin. For my own critique of Miller's argument, see "The Limits of Limit-Experience: Bataille and Foucault," pp. 67–69.

161. Foucault, "Adorno, Horkheimer, and Marcuse: Who is a 'Negator of History?'" in *Remarks on Marx*, p. 124.

CONCLUSION

Well, it's all experience, though it's a pity
there had to be so much of it.

KINGSLEY AMIS

The readers of the foregoing account may be forgiven if they share Amis's sardonic sentiments, at least about the welter of competing, often discordant meanings that have accrued to this numinous word over time. Ending our song cycle with theorists who call "inner experience" the "experience of the outside" while claiming that it requires the dissolution of the very subject who has traditionally been seen as its bearer might, after all, seem ample warrant for wondering if the term means anything coherent at all. Because I have resisted the temptation to bestow the normative aura of "real" or "authentic" or "genuine" experience on any of the contenders, the effect may appear to be little more than adding still more noise to an already cacophonous chorus. The opponents of experience—those distrusting the unreliable senses, or valuing language over the immediacy of "life," or preferring critique to the authority of the past—may therefore seem vindicated if we cannot decide on how to define the word in the first place.

And yet, the map of different meanings this book has attempted to draw, to switch metaphors from the aural to the visual, may still provide some useful guidance for those who want to reflect on the work this polysemic word has done in the past and, despite all attempts to write its epitaph, continues to do today. Although Michel Foucault's claim that "man is an animal of experience" may be as inadequate as all other attempts to define the human condition—*zoon politikon, homo economicus, homo sapiens, homo faber, homo ludens*, and so on—it alerts us to the impossibility of thinking

The epigraph is from a remark by Kingsley Amis to Robert Conquest, quoted in Martin Amis, *Experience: A Memoir* (New York, 2000), 214.

of our curious role in the world without reference to at least some of its meanings.

In an interview given near the end of his long life, Hans-Georg Gadamer was asked about his concept of experience, which he had contrasted to scientific experimental method in *Truth and Method*. He responded that "being experienced does not mean that one now knows something once and for all and becomes rigid in this knowledge; rather, one becomes more open to new experiences. A person who is experienced is undogmatic. Experience has the effect of freeing one to be open to new experience. . . . In our experience we bring nothing to a close; we are constantly learning new things from our experience . . . this I call the interminability of all experience."[1] Although this book—both the experience of writing and reading it—must come to an end, it may be useful to honor the spirit of Gadamer's injunction by finishing with tentative suggestions rather than definitive answers to many of the questions it has raised.

Perhaps the first of these concerns the relationship between experience as an all-inclusive category and its modalization into specific various subcategories. The characteristic differentiation process of modernization has led, as we have seen, to the development of relatively autonomous discourses about cognitive, religious, and aesthetic experience, as well as attempts to isolate and analyze its importance in historical and political contexts. The exploration of what counts as an experience in each of these arenas has often enabled us to register the various, at times even contradictory possibilities lurking within the general category, which defy easy reduction to a common denominator.

As a countercurrent, however, we have recorded a number of efforts to restore a robust concept of experience that would heal the wounds supposedly produced by its modalization. Here the links between experience and the everyday life of the *Lebenswelt* are often emphasized, as is the importance of the "lived body" as the holistic site of experience in the most all-inclusive sense of the word. Whether construed as an always already state of affairs needing only recognition, as in the case of Michael Oakeshott, or a desideratum to be sought through changing the world, as the Frankfurt School and the American pragmatists in some of their moods contended, overcoming the impoverishment of experience has been a frequent goal.

But, as we have seen, efforts to produce that solvent of differences often

1. Hans-Georg Gadamer, *Gadamer in Conversation: Reflections and Commentary*, ed. and trans. Richard E. Palmer (New Haven, 2001), pp. 52–53. This interview was conducted by Carsten Dutt in 1993.

rest on a tacit privileging of one over others, which then imperialistically colonizes the alternative versions. Or it tacitly denigrates those alternatives as being diminished or wrong-headed versions of experience in its "genuine" form. Although the yearning for an all-inclusive concept of experience cannot be brushed aside as necessarily problematic, the jury is still out on the costs that even a successful overcoming of modalization might produce. The quest for the holy grail of "absolute experience" may ironically be little more than a vain desire for the purity of an innocence that can produce, as William Blake knew, a songbook all of its own.

The second question derives in a way from the first, although the terms are somewhat different. It addresses the vexed relationship between the experiencing subject and the object of experience. The desire for a more all-encompassing notion of experience often, to be sure, betrays impatience with the undialectical dualism of subject and object that has been so much a part of Western thought since René Descartes elevated epistemology over ontology. Experience, so phenomenologists, Critical Theorists, pragmatists, and poststructuralists alike insisted, cannot be reduced to what an isolated, contemplative, integrated subject has of an object that is entirely external to him or her. For these commentators, experience implies a state or condition prior to or deeper than the interior registering of or reflection on something that stands entirely without. Although disputing the precise way in which an equiprimordial alternative notion of experience might be sought—some preferring a *via media* overcoming binary oppositions, others endorsing an unsublatable dialectic of inside and outside, which permeates boundaries but does not entirely efface them—they all sought to undermine the simple notion that experience was an attribute entirely of a subject confronting an object.

But as in so many other attempts to find ways around the troublesome dualism of subject and object, here too one might wonder if it will return to haunt efforts in the case of experience as well, especially if it threatens to produce a monistic alternative. For if we take seriously the notion that experience in virtually all of its guises involves at least a potential learning process produced by an encounter with something new, an obstacle or a challenge that moves the subject beyond where it began, then the necessity of an outside to the interiority of the subject is hard to deny. As we have seen when discussing the anxiety about the loss of God in the debate over religious experience and the art object in aesthetic experience, it is precisely the tension between subject and object that makes experience possible. In epistemological terms, the same issue appears if we accept what philosophers since Franz

Brentano and Edmund Husserl have called the intentionality of consciousness, which is always of an object outside itself.

Another way to put this point involves that stubborn refusal to dissolve experience entirely in language we have seen motivating attempts like that of Frank Ankersmit to restore historical experience to its rightful place even after the "linguistic turn." A similar, if unexpected, distrust of the idea that it is language "all the way down" can be found, as we have seen, in the different vocabularies of the thinkers we have located in what is loosely called poststructuralism. Although they are fully aware that language cannot be brushed aside as if it were a transparent veil hiding "raw," "immediate," "felt" reality, they disdain the opposite impulse to make it all-determining. The same motivation fuels their suspicion of the claim that experience is necessarily narrative in form, following the model of progressive and cumulative *Bildung* or what Sigmund Freud would have called the retrospective secondary elaboration of dreams.

Such suspicion can, to be sure, lead to the no less problematic claim that only those moments of maximum transgression and intensity, defying all attempts to contain them within any contextual or narrative frame, should warrant the name experience. Curiously, such a position parallels that of the antitheoretical conservative and radical political thinkers who believe that something called "experience" is a foundational term, able to provide an incorruptible immediacy that somehow avoids the mystifications of ideology or representation. In both cases, the word is used as the opposite of anything that threatens to smother spontaneity and creativity, whether it comes in the form of a neatly emplotted narrative, the rules of language games, or the abstractions of theory.

Instead, it might be better to think of it as the site of a productive struggle between all of these contesting impulses or demands, the place in our lives in which neither binary dualisms nor reductive monisms rule out the experimental moment in living. The suggestive notion of the "middle voice," which we have seen Roland Barthes in particular bring to the fore, captures the oscillation that avoids the active/passive binary.[2] So too does William James's insistence that experience is a "double-barreled word" and Theodor Adorno's appropriation of Walter Benjamin's stress on the role of the mime-

---

2. If, however, the middle voice leads to a total obliteration of that binary, it may have its costs, especially in terms of distinguishing between agents and victims in history. For a critique of this potential, see Vincent Pecora, "Ethics, Politics and the Middle Voice," *Yale French Studies* 79 (1991). A similar concern has animated some critics of Cathy Caruth's work on trauma and language; see, for example, Amy Hungerford, *The Holocaust of Texts: Genocide, Literature, and Personification* (Chicago, 2003), pp. 110–19.

sis of otherness in *Erfahrung*. That is, the subject of experience, rather than being a sovereign, narcissistic ego, is always dependent to a significant degree on the other—both human and natural—beyond his or her interiority. Experience is never created entirely by intentional action, many of our commentators have realized, but instead involves a kind of surrender to or dependency on what it is not, a willingness to risk losing the safety of self-sufficiency and going on a perilous journey of discovery.

Another way to clarify why "experience" is so volatile a concept, sometimes gravitating towards its subjective pole and sometimes to its objective, can be understood if we see its ability to be employed in either a subjective or objective genitive case. That is, it can be understood as epistemological experience or the experience *of* real objects in the world, as aesthetic experience or the experience *of* art, as religious experience or the experience *of* God, and so on. The question then is what are the implications of its being either entirely construed as a subjective genitive—something undergone, possessed, or even generated by the subject—or as an objective genitive—entirely a function of the object, whose reality is prior to the experience of it? Will it be located in the interiority of the pious believer or closer to the God with whom he is in holy relation? Will it be the feelings, judgments, appreciation of the beholder of beauty or the objects and processes, either natural or man-made, which properly invite an aesthetic response? Will it be the narrative reconstruction of the historian or the powerful impact of the residues of the past, interrupting conventional wisdom, that makes for historical experience? Will it be the thrill of political activism or the objective results produced by intervening in the public sphere? Can one even go so far as to say that the experience is actually undergone by the object rather than the subject, a claim made by those theologians who want to make God the true Subject and humankind merely the predicate?[3]

Failing to remain oscillating within the tension generated by the alternative cases can produce potentially problematic outcomes. If the subjective case is pushed to an extreme, it can allow the inappropriate slippage that turns anything into, say, an aesthetic experience, no matter what its precipitating object might be. Although the capacity to experience natural and even artificial objects, events, and processes in aesthetic terms can be valuable—indeed, for thinkers like John Dewey in certain of his moods it defines experience at its most successful—the indiscriminate aestheticization of morally or polit-

---

3. Even in aesthetic terms, similar projections of subjectivity onto objects can happen. See, for example, W. J. T. Mitchell, "What Do Pictures Want?" *October* 77 (Summer 1996).

ically fraught phenomena can also have disastrous consequences, as Benjamin famously warned. The same might well happen with the promiscuous extension of religious experience, which we might call the sacralization of objects or persons other than the divine or the holy (assuming that one accepts their existence), for it can lead to the uncritical worshiping of what does not deserve reverential piety. Likewise, a politics of experience indifferent to the goals of political action that becomes an end in itself can result in a kind of narcissistic insouciance about the actual effects of that action on others in the world. When an Ernst Jünger celebrates war and struggle as the highest forms of "inner experience," violence can become an end rather than a means. Even when attempts are made to identify experience with something beyond the subject/object dualism, the question always needs to be asked: experience in the service of what end?

The opposite extreme, turning the subject into a totally passive receptacle of external influences—whether it be the a posteriori epistemology of the positivists or the notion of the pious believer mindlessly enraptured by divinity (or seduced by its demonic simulacrum)—short-circuits the constructive moment that allows experience to transcend mere sensual stimulation. It also can obliterate or at least suppress the role of memory and past experience on the present, abetting the reduction of experience to little more than momentary excitation, which Benjamin and Adorno found so problematic in *Erlebnis*. It also fails to register the ways in which experience may have a powerful future-orientation as well, thus complicating any belief in absolute presence or immediacy as the quintessence of "an experience."

Immanuel Kant's celebrated attempt to ground epistemological experience in synthetic a priori judgments has been widely criticized, but one might say that his instinct to seek the answer in a mixture of passivity and activity, of allowing the world to impinge, but on a mind that is not a blank recipient of stimuli from without, nicely captures the mixed nature of experience, at least in many of its most productive acceptations. Here experience is not the antithesis of language, reflection, and judgment, but includes dimensions of each, even if they may or may not produce a harmonious outcome. Similarly, Kant's solution to the antinomy of taste, at once a subjective judgment resisting subsumption under a rule and a claim to universal assent, may not satisfy all critics. But by alerting us to the delicate interplay between subjectivity and intersubjectivity, bodily sensations and the assent of all who share the same capacity for appreciating beauty, it forces us to acknowledge that experience is at once deeply personal and yet to a significant extent capable of being shared with others.

A final cluster of questions is raised by the theorists we have met who assert that experience, generally understood in honorific terms, is now itself on the endangered list. Benjamin and Adorno, the pragmatists in certain of their moods, Martin Heidegger and some of his poststructuralist progeny, anti-structuralists like the British Marxists, all lament the loss of authentic experience, however they may understand it. They may well be on to something, although it may be difficult to show that an earlier period really allowed for a more fully experienced life. The irony, of course, is that from another perspective, it has been argued that the domination of a less healthy version of experience is precisely what defines the contemporary era. Not only have we noted this claim in the debate over the evaporation of the aesthetic or religious object of experience, but we have seen it surface in the critique of mere *Erlebnis* made by the Frankfurt School Critical Theorists.

When our society is called an *Erlebnisgesellschaft* by sociologists who point to the commodification of experiences as one of the most prevalent tendencies of our age, ranging from extreme sports to packaged tourism, they are not celebrating that development. What one might, in fact, say is that the very notion of experience as a commodity for sale is precisely the opposite of what many of the theorists in our survey have argued an experience should be, that is, something which can never be fully possessed by its owner. Instead, because experiences involve encounters with otherness and open onto a future that is not fully contained in the past or present, they defy the very attempt to reduce them to moments of fulfilled intensity in the marketplace of sensations. In fact, one might argue that one of the distinguishing marks that separate art from mere entertainment is that the latter sells commodified experiences, whereas the former does not.

The unhappy outcome of packaging experience into a commodity to be bought and sold takes us to one last critical issue, the function of experiential legitimation in identity politics disputes. For it is precisely the claim to exclusive ownership of an experience, shared only with members of one's group, that defines the way it serves to cut short the possibility of including others in a conversation.[4] That is, it seeks to have its *past* experience recognized as an unimpeachable source of group identity in the *present*, refusing to risk leaving the comfort of safe harbors for a new journey. By forgetting

4. There have been, of course, sophisticated attempts to get beyond this impasse without entirely abandoning the importance of subject positions in epistemology. See, for example, Satya P. Mohanty, "The Epistemic Status of Cultural Identity: On *Beloved* and the Postcolonial Condition," in Paula M. L. Moya and Michael R. Hames-García, eds., *Reclaiming Identity: Realist Theory and the Predicament of Postmodernism* (Berkeley, 2000).

that experience involves an encounter with otherness, which leaves the subject or subjects no longer where they were before it occurred, it produces a fortress of sameness, which it then protects against further experimentation. The result is not only to solidify exclusive tribal identities, but also to taint the concept of experience with the stigma of conservative essentialism, which in so many other contexts it serves to undermine.

In fact, our tour of the different notions of experience demonstrates that if it means anything at all, it involves an openness to the world that leaves behind such exclusivist fortresses. In this sense, we might speak of the strong identity politics version of experience as the diametrical opposite of the unclaimed variety that has been so often linked with trauma. That is, it is a kind of overly claimed experience, which cuts short precisely that interminability we have seen Gadamer identify with one of the chief lessons of experience itself. Even before that search for a notion of experience without the subject, which we have traced in several twentieth-century theorists, experience involved a willingness to open the most seemingly integrated and self-contained subject to the outside, thus allowing the perilous, but potentially rewarding journey to begin.

William Blake himself seems to have known this when he composed *Songs of Experience* in the shadow of the still uncertain outcome of the French Revolution. It has long been recognized by students of his work that whereas in *Songs of Innocence,* text and images were fully in accord, in the second cycle they often had an ironic, oblique, even contradictory relationship.[5] Like Michel de Montaigne before him and Georges Bataille after, Blake performatively instantiated the ideas he was trying to convey. The experience of reading *Songs of Experience* is thus one in which the self-conscious reader feels the fallen quality of his own state, knowing that he has to struggle to make sense out of the challenges presented to him by the poet/artist, and may never in fact find a satisfactory resolution.

One implication of this insight was drawn by the contemporary English philosopher Stuart Hampshire when he wrote that "the idea of experience is the idea of guilty knowledge, of the expectation of unavoidable squalor and imperfection, of necessary disappointments and mixed results, of half success and half failure. A person of experience has come to expect that his usual choice will be the lesser of two or more evils."[6] A less sour interpretation,

---

5. See, for example, Ronald Paulsen, *Representations of Revolution (1789–1820)* (New Haven, 1983), p. 109.

6. Stuart Hampshire, *Innocence and Experience* (Cambridge, Mass., 1989), p. 170.

which is in accord with the stubborn utopian moment in Blake's outlook, might see the struggle itself as the reward, allowing those brave experiments in living that tie experience to the future as much as to the past.

The journey that began this experience-book about experience has now, however, itself finally come to an end, or at least a rest stop on the road to a still uncertain destination. In my introduction, written too many years ago to admit without embarrassment, I said that I expected that "the experience of writing *Songs of Experience* may lead me where I do not expect to go." This has indeed been the case, but the trip is still, I hope, not entirely over. Those of you who have been hearty enough to read this far— those of you, that is, who are the others making my own experience possible and whose experiences I hope will be enriched in return—are thanked for their endurance, and warmly invited to come along as the ride continues.

INDEX

American Civil War, 105n, 270, 276
American Constitution, 171–172
American Historical Association, 254
American jurisprudence, 267
    "legal realism," 267, 269
American Revolution, 171
Amis, Kingsley, 401
Amis, Martin, 401n
anamnesis, 19, 115, 118, 318, 335–336, 339
Anderson, Perry, 170, 198, 198n, 201–202,
    207–209, 245
    Arguments within English Marxism,
        207–209
Ankersmit, F. R., 217, 255–260, 262, 306–
    308, 310, 338, 338n, 390, 404
    the experiential sublime, 257
Anselm, Saint, 81
anthropology, 243, 246–247, 326, 341
Antiphon, 17
Apelt, Ernst Friedrich, 113n, 114n
Aragon, Louis, 327
Arendt, Hannah, 15n, 176–177, 214, 215n,
    232n, 295, 349n
    The Human Condition, 176
Aris, Daniel, 27n
Aristophanes, 15
Aristotle, 12, 13–14, 13n, 16, 17, 18, 55, 115n, 205
    Metaphysics, 12, 16
    Nicomachean Ethics, 12, 16
    Posterior Analytics, 13n, 16, 16n
    and scholasticism, 15, 36n
Arnauld, Antoine, 45
Arndt, Johann, 91
Arnold, Gottfried, 91
Arnold, Matthew, 193, 194
art, 130, 132, 133, 138, 144, 159, 162, 193–194,
    207, 228, 236, 258, 262, 272, 296,
    307, 318–319, 332, 348, 354, 355, 357,
    359, 360, 362, 372, 405, 407
    the artwork, 158–161, 166, 168, 328, 356,
        372
    autonomy of, 132, 134n, 145, 147, 155,
        157–158, 168
Artaud, Antonin, 393
Aschheim, Steven E., 370n
astrology, 325, 337, 342, 348
Atget, Eugène, 338n

Attridge, Derek, 10
Auerbach, Erich, 32n
Aufklärung, 67, 77, 87, 94, 95n, 113, 134n
Augustine, Saint, 19, 23, 81, 361
    Confessions, 23
Avenarius, Richard, 280n
Ayer, A. J., 45n, 65, 109n, 309

Bachelard, Gaston, 198, 391, 394
Bachofen, Johann Jacob, 325n
Backschieder, Paula R., 30n
Bacon, Francis, 5, 14, 28–39, 29n, 41, 45n, 46,
    47, 49, 55, 69, 184, 188, 205, 263, 347
    controlled experiment, 34
    on experience, 31
    idola, 36
    inductive method, 32–33, 41, 44
    Instauratio magna (Great Renewal), 29
    The New Atlantis, 34
    Novum Organum, 30n, 31n, 37n, 44–45
    reaction to Copernicus, 30–31
Bacon, Roger, 18
Baker, Houston, 3
Baker, Keith Michael, 47n
Bakunin, Mikhail, 174
Balzac, Honoré de, 308, 355
Bambach, Charles R., 223n, 224n, 234n
Barnard, G. William, 262n
Barnes, Albert, 162
Barnett, Anthony, 200–202
Barth, Karl, 93, 100–101, 101n, 102, 103n,
    108, 112, 116, 118, 128, 129n, 159,
    294n, 298, 316n, 364n, 380
Barthes, Roland, 265, 308, 310, 360, 365,
    367, 382–390, 393, 399–400, 404
    Camera Lucida, 389
    gay cruising, 385–387, 390
    on the photo, 389–390
    The Pleasure of the Text, 383
    Roland Barthes, 388
Bataille, Georges, 8n, 265, 360, 365, 366–
    381, 382–385, 389, 390, 392–394,
    395–396, 397–400, 408
    and Christianity, 378–380
    Erotism, 375n, 381
    Inner Experience, 8n, 366–370, 372–
        378, 380–381, 395, 399

Eastwood, Bruce S., 18n
Eckermann, Johann Peter, 25n
Eckhart, Meister, 125
Eco, Umberto, 131–132n
Edict of Nantes, 26
Edwards, Jonathan, 80, 80n, 109n, 268
Egan, Jim, 171
Einstein, Albert, 331
Eliade, Mircea, 121
Eliot, T. S., 193, 194, 205
Emerson, Ralph Waldo, 27, 273–276, 283,
    285, 293, 294n, 304, 311, 314
    "Experience," 274–275, 283, 285, 294n,
    311
empiricism, 43–45, 45n, 47, 48n, 54, 55, 56,
    58, 60, 62n, 65, 69, 71, 73, 76, 80,
    94, 96, 103, 110, 125, 137, 139, 152,
    178–179, 186, 199, 203, 207, 211–
    212, 214, 222n, 224, 236, 261, 271,
    272n, 278, 281, 283, 287, 289, 305,
    352
Enlightenment, 6, 26, 42, 58n, 82, 84, 93n,
    133, 137, 139, 146, 147, 153, 159, 161,
    320, 322, 325, 360
Epicurus, 49n, 52n
Erasmus, 82
Erfahrung, 10n, 11, 15, 20, 66, 74, 95, 96n,
    125, 129, 153, 159, 163, 172n, 184, 210,
    215, 222, 224n, 225, 227n, 264, 315,
    329, 334, 336–337, 340–341, 347, 351,
    356, 364, 376, 390, 397, 405
Erigena, Johannes Scotus, 141
Erlangen, University of, 111
Erlebnis, 11, 66, 81, 95, 96, 101, 112, 124,
    125–129, 149n, 153, 160n, 163, 182,
    210, 222, 224–229, 233–234, 240,
    247, 250, 255, 264, 280, 285, 317,
    317n, 329, 334, 337, 340–341, 347,
    356, 370, 376, 390, 391, 406
Ermarth, Michael, 223n, 225n, 238n
Euripides, 15
Evans, Elisabeth Glendower, 276n
experience. See also aesthetic experience;
    Erfahrung; Erlebnis; historical
    experience; religious experience
    American "culture of experience," 265–
    272
    authenticity of, 2, 7, 172, 176, 209, 213,

263, 270, 310, 328, 333, 359, 381, 401,
    407
    crisis of, 2–4, 166, 260, 312–314, 333–
    334, 344–348, 357–358, 362–364
    empeiria (Greek), 10, 16
    epistemology and, 5, 17, 38, 42–43, 45n,
    47, 61–62, 65, 70–76, 78–79, 96,
    104, 109, 130, 131, 137, 140, 174, 203,
    221, 261, 263, 282, 288–289, 322,
    354, 392, 402–404, 405–406
    esperienza (Italian), 10
    etymology of, 10–12, 38
    expérience (French), 10
    experience without a subject, 129, 156,
    260, 265, 311, 357, 362, 367, 384, 388,
    401, 408
    experientia (Latin), 10
    inner experience, 19, 263, 360, 366–
    370, 372–378, 380–381, 382–383,
    393–394, 395, 397n, 399, 401, 406
    "limit experience," 360, 378, 381, 398–
    400
    "lived experience," 192, 198–200, 209,
    224, 225, 228, 242, 248, 271, 347,
    360, 363, 391
    and otherness, 7, 111, 221, 264, 356,
    359–360, 398–400, 405, 407–409
    politics and, 5, 39, 61, 76, 150, 167, 170,
    172, 173, 174–177, 178, 188–190,
    191–193, 211–215, 221, 261–262, 266,
    295, 348, 363, 402, 405–406
    "pure experience," 4, 108, 109, 263
Expressionism, 315–316

Fackenheim, Emil, 97n
Falasca-Zamponi, Simonetta, 175n
Falck, Colin, 190n
Fascism, 175, 207, 267, 314, 317, 343, 368,
    370, 378
Febvre, Lucien, 243
Fechner, Gustav, 133n, 137n
Feigel, Friedrich Karl, 120
feminism, 3, 170, 177, 211, 215n, 244–246,
    252, 253, 255, 363, 364n
Fenves, Peter, 2n
Ferrari, Giulio Cesare, 269n
Feuerbach, Ludwig, 101, 101n, 124, 124n,
    129, 187

distrust of experience, 13–18
phronesis, 15, 16
and theater, 15
theoria, 13, 16
Green, Martin, 191n
Green, T. H., 287, 288
Greenblatt, Stephen, 196n, 259n
Greene, Jack P., 171n, 172n
Greenleaf, W. H., 183n
Greenlee, Douglas, 52n
Gross, Neil, 301n
Grosseteste, Robert, 18n
Guerlac, Suzanne, 378n
Gundolf, Friedrich, 160n
Gunn, Giles, 270n
Guyer, Paul, 67n, 69n

Ha'am, Ahad, 123
Häberlin, Paul, 316n
Habermas, Jürgen, 19, 20n, 104n, 135, 135n,
145, 297n, 310, 362, 379, 394–395,
394n
public sphere, 135, 135n
Hacking, Ian, 45, 46, 55n, 272n
Hahn, Robert, 69n
Halbfass, William, 5n
Hall, Stuart, 198n, 209, 215n
Halle, University of, 89
Halperin, David M., 400n
Hamann, Johann Georg, 87, 320
Hamilton, Alexander, 171
Hamilton, William, 47n, 75n, 138n
Hampshire, Stuart, 275, 408
Han, Béatrice, 394–395, 396–398, 397n
Hansen, Miriam, 172n, 312n
Hanslick, Eduard, 135
Hanson, Karen, 270
Hanssen, Beatrice, 159–160n, 324n, 326n,
349n
Hart, Heinrich, 125
Hart, Julius, 125
Hartley, David, 53n
Hartz, Louis, 300n
Hasidism, 82
Haskell, Thomas, 270n
Haverkamp, Anselm, 390n
Hayden, Tom, 300n

Hegel, Georg Wilhelm Friedrich, 42, 44,
45n, 65, 88, 90, 96n, 98n, 101n, 116,
123n, 133, 149n, 150n, 153, 158, 162,
166, 183n, 184–186, 187, 189, 221,
226, 229, 232, 235–236n, 240, 240n,
263, 287–288, 287n, 303, 324, 334,
348–349n, 348–353, 354, 357, 359–
360, 361–362, 364, 366, 374, 375n,
397
Hegelian dialectics, 336, 348–349, 350,
373–374
neo-Hegelianism, 183, 185, 188, 189, 194,
212–213, 214, 220–221, 235, 262,
281, 287–288, 287n, 302
Phenomenology of Spirit, 184–185,
349–352, 359, 361–362, 364
Sittlichkeit, 185n, 189, 194
Heidegger, Martin, 27, 68n, 129, 159, 159n,
184, 224, 224n, 234, 241, 258, 260,
265, 285, 301, 301n, 305, 349–352,
349n, 357–358, 360, 362n, 364, 366,
381, 407
on Hegel, 349–352, 364
Heine, Heinrich, 314
Heinle, Fritz, 316
Heller, Agnes, 242n
Hemingway, Ernest, 267
Henri IV, 26
Henrich, Dietrich, 68n
Henry, Patrick, 171, 266
Herder, Johann Gottfried von, 71n, 141n
Herf, Jeffrey, 170
Hermann, Wilhelm, 86n, 115
hermeneutics, 89, 97, 119, 121n, 224, 224n,
227, 235, 307, 308, 364
hermeneutic circle, 231
Hermogenes, 32
Herz, Henriette, 90
Herz, Markus, 90
Herzl, Theodor, 123
Hess, Jonathan M., 134n, 135n, 139n, 148n,
167
Hessel, Franz, 327, 334–336
Highmore, Ben, 242n
Hill, Christopher, 196n
Hilton, Rodney, 196n
Himmelfarb, Gertrude, 220n, 252n

Marxism, 70, 170, 172, 187, 194, 196–199, 209, 214, 242, 271, 312, 324, 327, 328, 340, 381, 382, 407
    British Marxist humanism, 190–197, 199–212, 214, 407
    Hegelian Marxism, 312, 324, 340
    structuralist Marxism, 198, 205–211, 215, 382
    Trotskyism, 199
    Western Marxism, 198–199, 200–201
Marx-Scouras, Danielle, 382n
Mason, George, 171
mathematics, 13, 17, 32n, 41, 46, 290–291
Maupassant, Guy de, 153n
Maurice, F. D., 81n
Mauss, Marcel, 369, 369n
McCann, Edwin, 52n
McClelland, Keith, 210n
McCole, John, 316n, 325n
McDermott, John J., 16n, 266, 268, 299
McDougall, William, 269n
McKeon, Richard, 299n
McManners, John, 40n
McPherson, C. B., 180n
McTaggart, J. M. E., 183
Mead, George Herbert, 265n, 269n, 297n
Medick, Hans, 243
Megill, Allan, 391n
Meiffert, Torsten, 312n
Meiland, Jack W., 219n
Meillet, Antoine, 384
memory, 3, 16, 19, 24n, 36, 61, 63, 64, 65, 70, 179–181, 219, 227, 232, 239, 246, 313, 318–319, 329, 335, 339–340, 355, 387, 389, 406
Menand, Louis, 265n, 270, 270n, 299–300, 299n, 300n
Mendelssohn, Anja, 325n
Mendelssohn, Georg, 325n
Mendelssohn, Moses, 68n
Mendes-Flohr, Paul, 2n, 125, 127n
Menke, Christophe, 147n
Merleau-Ponty, Maurice, 27, 198, 305, 360, 384
Methodism, 82, 91, 105, 105n, 205
Michelet, Jules, 308, 361
Mickey Mouse, 331, 331n
Mill, John Stuart, 193, 194, 224

Miller, D. A., 387–388, 387n
Miller, James, 400n
Mink, Louis O., 235–236n, 236
Mitchell, Juliet, 245–246, 246n, 247
Mitchell, W. J. T., 405n
modernism, 151, 157–158, 158n, 170, 270, 272, 301, 332, 346, 355, 384
modernity, 7, 19, 20, 36, 37n, 38, 41, 76, 123, 132, 145, 147–148, 162, 168, 176, 260, 263–264, 271, 314, 325, 327–328, 337, 356, 361–362, 368, 371–372, 402
    as differentiation of value spheres, 38–39, 261–265
    ocularcentric bias of, 37n
Modood, Tariq, 235n
Mohanty, Satya P., 253n, 407n
Moi, Toril, 363n
Montaigne, Michel de, 5, 22–32, 29n, 32n, 34, 35, 36, 38–39, 40, 40n, 42, 46, 49, 61, 70, 78, 260, 272n, 275, 316, 323, 323n, 330, 354n, 373, 377n, 383, 408
    on the Ancients, 24
    attitude toward the body, 27
    and confession, 23–24
    and death, 27–28
    debt to skepticism, 26
    debt to Socrates, 26–27
    Essays, 23, 29, 323
    "Of Experience," 23, 25, 33, 42n, 383
    on probability, 46
    on time, 24–25
Montesquieu, 136
Moore, G. E., 185n
Moore, W. G., 25n
More, Henry, 17, 47
Moriarty, Michael, 201n
Moritz, Karl Philipp, 134n, 139, 148n
Morley, John, 180n
Morris, Charles, 286
Morris, Edmund, 243n
Morris, George Sylvester, 162, 287, 288, 292
Morris, William, 157, 163, 207
Mortensen, Preben, 132n, 134n, 137n
Mosley, Oswald, 176
Mosse, George L., 2n, 127n, 175

Compositor:	Integrated Composition Systems
Text:	11/13.5 Adobe Garamond
Display:	Adobe Garamond, Perpetua
Printer and binder:	Maple-Vail Manufacturing Group